No.305
56 Leonard Street
p.108 Project
p.181 Plans
p.300 Images

No.312
Helsinki Dreispitz
p.130 Project
p.188 Plans
p.310 Images

No.317
Iglesia de la Natividad
p.138 Project
p.190 Plans

No.294
VitraHaus
p.78 Project
p.174 Plans
p.292 Images

No.306
Pérez Art Museum Miami
p.114 Project
p.184 Plans
p.304 Images

No.319
Naturbad Riehen
p.144 Project
p.191 Plans
p.314 Images

No.284
Actelion Business Center
p.62 Project
p.168 Plans
p.282 Images

No.282
Espacio Goya
p.54 Project
p.167 Plans

No.269
Beijing Film Academy Qingdao
p.20 Project

No.295
Burgos Bulevar
p.86 Project
p.176 Plans
p.296 Images

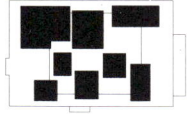

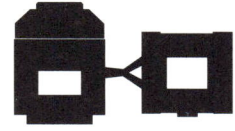

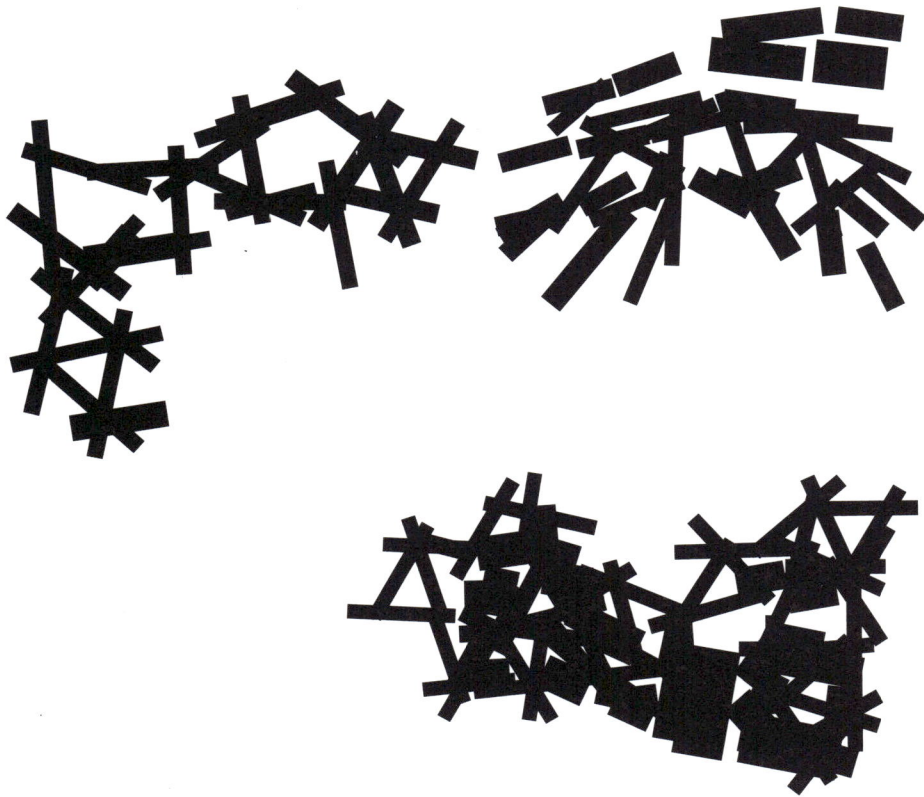

HERZOG & DE MEURON
2005–2007

Gerhard Mack

HERZOG & DE MEURON 2005–2007

**The Complete Works
Volume 6**

Birkhäuser

Basel

- Design and Typesetting Volume 6:
  Ludovic Balland Typography Cabinet, Basel
  With Chantal Durante, Pasqual Schillberg
- Concept and Redesign Volume 4:
  Ludovic Balland Typography Cabinet, Basel
- Redesign and Cover Colors Volume 3:
  Rémy Zaugg, Pfastatt, France,
  in cooperation with Katharina Erich, Basel
- Layout and Cover Design Volumes 1 and 2:
  Meissner & Mangold, Basel

- Project Team Volume 6:
  Herzog & de Meuron, *kitchen*
  Jacques Herzog, Pierre de Meuron
  Esther Zumsteg (Partner in Charge),
  Donald Mak (Associate)
  Petr Khraptovich, Stefanie Manthey, Martin Marker Larsen,
  Francisco Ramos Ordóñez

- Translation from German into English:
  Ishbel Flett, Edinburgh, and Fiona Elliott, Edinburgh (Gerhard Mack)
  Catherine Schelbert, Hertenstein/Weggis (Herzog & de Meuron)
- Copy Editing:
  Catherine Schelbert, Hertenstein/Weggis
  Louise Stein, London

- Project Management Birkhäuser:
  Petra Schmid, Katharina Kulke
- Production Birkhäuser:
  Katja Jaeger, Kathleen Bernsdorf
- Lithography and Printing:
  DZA Druckerei zu Altenburg GmbH, Altenburg
- Paper: 120g/m^2 UPM fine white, 135g/m^2 Multi Art Silk

- This publication is also available in a German language edition
  (ISBN 978-3-0356-1003-1).

- Library of Congress Cataloging-in-Publication data A CIP catalog
  record for this book has been applied for at the Library of Congress.

- Bibliographic information published by the German National Library
  The German National Library lists this publication in the Deutsche
  Nationalbibliografie; detailed bibliographic data are available on the
  Internet at http://dnb.dnb.de.

© 2018 Birkhäuser Verlag GmbH, Basel
P.O. Box 44, 4009 Basel, Switzerland
Part of Walter de Gruyter GmbH, Berlin/Boston

Printed on acid-free paper produced from chlorine-free pulp. TCF ∞

Printed in Germany

ISBN: 978-3-0356-1004-8

9 8 7 6 5 4 3 2 1

www.birkhauser.com

Foreword
Introduction
Buildings and Projects
2005–2007

Foreword   p.7
Introduction   p.9
Buildings and Projects   p.19

No. 269   p.20
Beijing Film Academy
Qingdao
Qingdao, China

No. 274   p.26
Tristan and Isolde,
Stage Design
Staatsoper Unter den Linden, Berlin, Germany

No. 320
Attila,
Stage Design
The Metropolitan Opera, New York, New York, USA

No. 276   p.34
House above a Lake
Germany

No. 279   p.40
1111 Lincoln Road
Miami Beach, Florida, USA

No. 280   p.48
Auditorium du Jura
Courgenay, Switzerland

No. 282   p.54
Espacio Goya
Zaragoza, Spain

No. 284   p.62
Actelion Business Center
Allschwil, Switzerland

No. 318
Actelion Research
and Laboratory Building
Allschwil, Switzerland

No. 293   p.70
Park Avenue Armory
New York, New York, USA

No. 294   p.78
VitraHaus
Weil am Rhein, Germany

No. 295   p.86
Burgos Bulevar
Burgos, Spain

No. 296   p.94
Tai Kwun, Centre for
Heritage & Art
Hong Kong, China

No. 300   p.102
Artist's Choice:
Herzog & de Meuron,
Perception Restrained
The Museum of Modern Art, New York, New York, USA

No. 305   p.108
56 Leonard Street
New York, New York, USA

No. 306   p.114
Pérez Art
Museum Miami
Miami, Florida, USA

No. 307   p.122
Triangle
Paris, France

No. 312   p.130
Helsinki Dreispitz
Münchenstein/Basel, Switzerland

No. 317   p.138
Iglesia de la Natividad
Culiacán, Mexico

No. 319   p.144
Naturbad Riehen
Riehen, Switzerland

No. 324   p.152
New Headquarters
for BBVA
Madrid, Spain

Plans
Texts Herzog & de Meuron
Work Chronology
Appendix
Images

Plans   p.161
Texts Herzog & de Meuron   p.197
Work Chronology   p.209
Appendix   p.253
Images   p.265

Nine years have passed since the publication of the previous volume of the *Complete Works* of Herzog & de Meuron. That so much time should elapse reflects both the growth of their practice and the conditions in the construction industry. Although Herzog & de Meuron were already active in different continents around the millennium—that last volume, no. 4, covered the period 1997–2001—they have since been increasingly in global demand. It is not only the complexity of the planning and execution of their megaprojects that makes their work ever more challenging: there are also the vagaries of diverse appeals, the ever more precise building regulations, and the clients' desire to leave certain matters open as long as possible, so that they can still have significant adjustments made at the last minute. Add to that the major impact on investors (both positive and negative) of volatile financial markets. The parking garage in Miami would no doubt never have been built if construction firms had not been prepared to take on more complex projects to make up for the dearth of simpler commissions due to the financial crisis. And the residential tower in New York had to wait until the client felt more bullish about the market.

The sequence of the Complete Works also reflects these complications. Herzog & de Meuron chronicle their projects according to the date the initial contract is signed. This volume, the sixth in the Complete Works, is being published before the fifth, which covers the period that includes the inception of the Elbphilharmonie in Hamburg. The Elbphilharmonie exemplifies the consequences of conflicting interests, of parties often unable to see any further than their own vested interests, who have lost sight of the common goal—the completion of a new cultural center—and insist on going to court to fight their legal battles. In 2012 Herzog & de Meuron told the whole story in a salutary presentation at the Architecture Biennale in Venice; following the recent, magnificent opening of the Elbphilharmonie, this whole sequence of events can now be studied in even greater detail. Yet this departure from the expected publication order is nothing new. Volume 2 in fact preceded volume 1, due to the amount of work needed on the archive. This is no more than par for the course when it comes to scholarly publications. The design of the present volume adopts, develops, and sometimes refines, the new design first seen in volume 4.

The present volume covers the years 2005 to 2007 and sixty projects in the lives of Herzog & de Meuron. Certain themes come to light, such as the use of smaller-scale private residences to pursue investigations into wider questions. Above all, however, this period is marked by the architects' active and fruitful engagement with the vocabulary of classical modernism and with aspects of their own earlier work. In so doing, they were reacting to the euphoria—before the global financial crisis of 2008—of the grand gestures, unique structures, and liberated forms made possible by a combination of new computer software and clients seeking status symbols. Herzog & de Meuron thus revealed a sensibility that enabled them not only to combine unlikely idioms but also to discover the unexpected by exploiting computer technology without succumbing to its dictates. In fact, while CATIA and other related programs reigned supreme in design offices all over the world and assisted in realizing a steady stream of deconstructivist projects, at Herzog & de Meuron drawing

utensils were coming back into their own. It had been a long time since Jacques Herzog did as many sketches as in those three years. The architects' designs now reflected their renewed interest in classical modernism, a *retour à l'ordre*, in buildings such as the Pérez Art Museum Miami, which also revels in aspects of subtropical modernism and the vibrant spirit of the 1960s: modernism goes pop. Having variously used stacking throughout their career, Herzog & de Meuron now deployed it in a variation on "fancy architecture." Following their part in the development of the "box" as a minimalist spatial component, they now found ways to stack it that more than met their clients' desire for prestigious architecture yet still had utter programmatic integrity. This process was taken a stage further in the VitraHaus, where the basic module is based on the classic image of a house with pitched roof—all without the slightest hint of ideology or technology for its own sake. Meanwhile other projects created new connections between moments in architectural history: the archive and apartment block in the Dreispitz district of Basel has echoes of both the Renaissance and Brutalism. Projects such as the Naturbad Riehen benefitted from a new appreciation of craft skills, in contrast to the increasing uniformity of technology-based architecture. It was at this point in their careers that the architects designed their first stage sets for major opera houses in Berlin and New York, which in effect allowed them to advance their earlier spatial investigations in a medium that was entirely new to them.

Even more than its predecessors, the present volume could not have come about without the active engagement of many individuals, whom it is my pleasure to thank here. First and foremost our thanks go to Jacques Herzog. Despite his many commitments, he found time to write new texts on the main projects described in this volume. In these texts he takes a fresh look at those designs and looks back at their genesis and main features. Pierre de Meuron was equally involved in the project and read the editor's texts with the greatest care, for which I am extremely grateful. I also owe a deep debt of gratitude to the senior partners at Herzog & de Meuron, the partners, numerous project leaders, and staff members for conversations, ideas, and their reading of the texts. I should like to make special mention of Christine Binswanger, Ascan Mergenthaler, Stefan Marbach, Michael Fischer, Andreas Fries, Robert Hösl, Vladimir Pajkic, and Esther Zumsteg. It was the latter, Esther Zumsteg, and her team who prepared and oversaw every aspect of this book with unstinting attention to detail. It gives me particular pleasure to single out one of her team members, Donald Mak, who led the project with such skill. Without him this volume would not exist, so I should like to express special thanks to him. My sincere gratitude also goes to Ludovic Balland, who again masterminded the design, and to Birkhäuser Verlag, who have again realized a complex project with great professionalism. Last, but not least, I should like to thank the translators, Catherine Schelbert, Fiona Elliott, and Ishbel Flett for their meticulous translations from German into English. It is my pleasure, however, to take ultimate responsibility for this collective production.

April 2017
Gerhard Mack

Complexity and Simplicity

On the Return of Classical Elements in the Architecture of Herzog & de Meuron

At the Venice Biennale of Architecture in 2006 Herzog & de Meuron presented the work of ETH Studio Basel, which they had cofounded. This presentation was the culmination of a four-year study of Switzerland as an urban settlement by Herzog & de Meuron, fellow architects Roger Diener and Marcel Meili, and geographer Christian Schmid.[1] The thousands of small photographs filling the room made it instantly obvious that big ideas had been at least temporarily sidelined, that the strategic issues raised by coherent planning should shape the spotlight on the individual object, which in certain areas—in Swiss architecture, for instance—was threatening to become a fetish of construction perfection. The theme of that 10th International Architecture Exhibition, chosen by director Richard Burdett, was "Cities: Architecture and Society." In some ways that sounded like a distant echo of the same event six years earlier at the dawning of the new millennium, when Massimiliano Fuksas's plea for "less aesthetics, more ethics" had largely fallen on deaf ears. Following the fall of the Berlin Wall in 1989 globalization had been gathering pace in architecture, too. China had awakened from its slumber and was luring star architects (of different magnitudes) with the bait of megastructures or even whole new urban districts. The sobering reality of the construction industry in the Middle Kingdom was not yet public knowledge. The 2008 Olympic Games in Beijing were still in the future. Western architecture, in the shape of the Olympic stadium by Herzog & de Meuron, would enjoy its most symbolic success at the Games. The "Bird's Nest" was the crowning architectural glory of what was proving to be an extremely heterogeneous construction boom in this flowering of Chinese growth. The shock of the Islamist attacks on the World Trade Center in New York on September 11, 2001, only gradually made itself felt in the global architecture scene. The Venice Biennale of Architecture is a reliable barometer in this respect: in 2002 Greg Lynn and Hani Rashid chalked up notable successes with their blob architecture; two years later the Zurich art historian Kurt W. Forster chose the theme "Metamorph" and filled the main exhibition with organic, crystalline architectural shells. The preferred projects at that time seemed to be museums, churches, and concert halls, which gave architects more or less free rein to explore their artistic leanings. Space, in particular urban and therefore social space, was not deemed worthy of special attention and Vitruvius's *utilitas* seemed to be a thing of the past. Computer programs were now calculating structures that would previously have been impossible to envision, let alone build. For a time architects, like excited children, seemed obliviously immersed in exploring the potential of their new toys. People who make up games can also make up their own rules, which—notably—need not be constrained by reality. There was an urge to discover the extremes of technical achievability, there was talk of surfaces and ornament, of new materials and the half-life of buildings, which cease to meet the investors' demands in just a few years and are torn down almost as quickly as they are put up. The most striking examples of this "overheating" were seen around the Persian Gulf, above all in Dubai and Qatar.

New Moves Afoot Worldwide

Herzog & de Meuron were main players in the architecture of these years: their buildings and projects shaped the debate more than most. They were already working on major projects, such as the Elbphilharmonie and the Olympic stadium, which might even be seen as symbolic of the prevailing sense of new beginnings and infinite possibilities in architecture. Their practice was also drawn into the global construction boom on a less symbolic level: they won various contracts for projects in China, most of which were, however, halted at some point. They worked on numerous projects for Spanish sites, with the master plan for Burgos being the most comprehensive, and they increasingly engaged with clients in Latin America. They developed plans for new towns in Russia. They had their fingers on the pulse of the frenzy of high-rise construction from St. Petersburg to Las Vegas. It was an architectural gold rush of international proportions. The ready availability of investment capital and new construction techniques fostered new developments in high-rise designs. In Paris Herzog & de Meuron proposed a pyramid, in Basel they envisaged a double helix for the headquarters of Roche—although this design saw the pharmaceuticals company take fright at its own audacity, setting in motion a process that led to a solution better suited to the company's ethos. The regularly stepped form of the west side of the new Building 1 at Roche's headquarters harmonizes with the rectangular geometry of the site as a whole.

Herzog & de Meuron embraced the freedom of that time and experimented with a whole range of new forms, some distinctly pictorial. They largely did without self-imposed limitations, as is seen in their designs for Las Vegas. Here different versions of the basic module (casino, shopping, restaurants, and hotel) are integrated into a vast, overarching composition inspired by the contrast between the glittering metropolis and the desert around it. Two planes propped up against each other look like the pages of an open book; a landscape of towers combines the rock formations of the desert with the artificial world of science fiction; huge canyons and arcs penetrate the buildings as if the latter were being reclaimed by the landscape. The architects devised a mountainscape skyline of structures for a new city district. At the same time the tradition of themed hotels still lives on in their designs, as does Robert Venturi's appreciation of the Strip. Only this imagery has now entered the third dimension. None of these projects made it beyond the presentation stage.

Hotel Casino, Las Vegas, 2005.

Yet even these projects, done in the years of seemingly boundless freedom, show how Herzog & de Meuron, however dazzling their ideas, were never swept into the mainstream of boom architecture. Their proposals for themed hotels in Las Vegas are never just architectural shells; they are informed by the architects' in-depth deliberations on the urban fabric of apartments, paths, and open spaces, as in all their other projects. The only difference is that urban aims have been translated here into the language of Las Vegas. Moreover, Herzog & de Meuron's technically demanding structures of that period do not rely on computer programs to evolve different kinds of blob architecture but are in fact carefully considered combinations of complexity and simplicity. This is perfectly exemplified in the headquarters of the biotech company Actelion, near Basel. The main points of the design brief were the client's specific spatial requirements and desire for a representative building that would also enhance internal communications between its staff members. The available plot was far too small to accommodate the required space in a mainly horizontal design. Moreover, simple upright blocks, even interlinked, would not have encouraged communications. In the end Herzog & de Meuron returned to the idea of simple horizontal modules arranged to create a highly complex form with an exceptionally large number of intersections. The resulting design facilitates vertical movement and is outwardly transparent. The individual modules are simple boxes that work like bridge girders. By means of an additive, building-kit process they are combined to create a highly complex structure; the required calculations and assembly push the boundaries of what is computationally and technically possible. The mostly single-story units, consisting of offices and corridor areas, are in fact suspended although their appearance creates the impression that they have been stacked like building blocks. The same principle is seen in the new VitraHaus not far from Basel, although in an even more complex form. The basic unit of the VitraHaus is based on standard pitched-roof dwellings. This form is then elongated and defamiliarized. The ensuing modules are not merely stacked but also variously interconnect creating highly complicated geometries, above

all inside the building. At the intersections of stairwells the crystalline language of the modules encounters biomorphous forms, such that an internal dialog between the two idioms creates a new scenery. Once again, the inspiration emerged from the client's requirements: Vitra wants visitors to see for themselves how readily and successfully very different design ideas can be combined.

A Actelion Business Center, Allschwil, 2010.
B VitraHaus, Weil am Rhein, 2009.

Both buildings, which were dreamt up on neighboring drawing boards, partly by the same teams, are indicative of the euphoria that coursed through architecture before the collapse of Lehman Brothers in New York in September 2008 plunged the global financial system into crisis. Investment in new buildings dried up so dramatically that in places such as Dubai even demolition projects were halted in their tracks, leaving broken pieces of reinforced concrete hanging in midair. But Herzog & de Meuron are the masters of their own fate and respond in their own way to unfolding events. If it is not taking a point too far, it is not so very different to Gerhard Richter in the 1980s, when he responded to the new boom in painting with his own ever-so-colorful squeegee paintings. While these may be astonishing to behold, the contemporary viewer can also not help but admire how Richter grasps hold of the latest trend and adds his own distinctive commentary.

Destabilizing Modernism

As Herzog & de Meuron found themselves in demand the world over for much larger projects, their particular, active combination of complexity and simplicity allowed them to increase the scope of their own language. It also allowed them to see their past projects in a more nuanced light. In a perfect example of the Swiss Box—the new gallery building for the Goetz Collection in Munich—the ambivalence of "simplicity" comes to light all the more clearly: What looks from outside like a simple box made from wood and glass, in fact contains labyrinthine internal complexities and challenges the visitor's sense of space and orientation. The glass ribbon that appears to be on the ground floor when seen from the outside in fact allows light into the lower ground floor. The rooms all have a certain similarity, making it impossible for visitors to tell which floor they are on. Yet the relatively modest dimensions of the museum ensure that visitors are not alarmed by their experience there. It is as though complexity, here, is built into a form which, in later projects, becomes just one of many similar modules in a larger whole.

Complex, large-scale projects such as the Actelion headquarters and the seemingly simple, basic form of the museum box for the Goetz Collection induce a similar emotional response: the visitor is unsettled. In the case of the early box the confusion is created by the chameleon-like nature of the materials and rooms. Who would imagine that the sections of beech wood, which seem to float above the glass ribbon, are in fact load-bearing components? At the Actelion headquarters the visitor is disconcerted by the seemingly random arrangement of segments, which seem to be stacked like pieces of kindling in a campfire. Here spaces close off and open up, changing

Goetz Collection, Munich, 1992.

their character so quickly that it is best just to allow oneself to be swept along through them, because questions as to their actual status are too hard to answer and in any case at odds with the pervading sense of lightness in this building. In retrospect it seems that from an early point in their shared history Herzog & de Meuron already had a preference for simple shapes and clear geometries, but were just not able to trust the calm and sense of security that these exude. It may even be that from time to time they go for the greatest possible simplicity precisely in order to discover where that elusive quality known as "clarity" actually can be found. Moreover, if one is as convinced as Herzog & de Meuron that the world is purely a matter of perception, then even the most reliable, solidly built, usable form is affected by that underlying relativity, which refuses to recognize givens, since it is entirely dependent on the viewer's knowledge and perceptions.

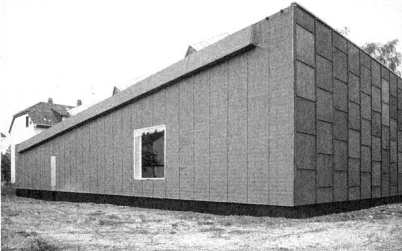

A House for a Veterinary Surgeon, 1984.
B Frei Photographic Studio, Weil am Rhein, 1982.

Herzog & de Meuron's designs thus became the signature of a particular epoch. In a sense every aspect of architecture, including its simplest concepts, is drawn into the insecurity of modernism, which states that nothing is necessarily as it appears, that every position has to stake its claim anew and can only refer to its forerunners and the past in an act of obliteration. The new is triumphant, but only at the cost of infinite losses. Failure is the price of progress. In this illusion-free, pragmatic view of modernism Herzog & de Meuron occupy a position close to that of philosopher Walter Benjamin. They have always been ready to adopt the pose of the angel of history,[2] albeit with one significant difference. The philosopher describes a figure that is being blown backward into the future by the force of historical developments and has no choice but to gaze at the debris left by the storm of history. It is blind to the future and at its mercy. Nor does it have access to the present, which is not a realm that it can linger in or help to shape. At most it can interpret the present, extrapolating it from the destruction left by the forward propulsion of history. The present does not exist for the angel. That would be an impossible position for the architects. They need the present; even if a design of theirs remains a virtual reality, it can only exist if it pertains to the Here and Now.[3] Significantly, this is not a matter of regret to Herzog & de Meuron. Unlike Benjamin, the pessimistic Romantic, they see the past as an opportunity. If we see the "debris" as "everything that is the case," as Ludwig Wittgenstein put it in his description of reality, in other words, as everything around us, then it is this that the Basel

architects draw on. From the start they have focused on what is to hand, literally, on what they see around them. When they founded their architectural practice in 1978 the Western world was in the grip of postmodernist ideas and architecture was one of the main arenas where these played out. The history of building came to be treated as a reservoir of forms that were then used in designs like pieces in a puzzle. This attitude was ideological in the extreme. Paul Feyerabend's catch phrase "anything goes" may have been taken by some as confirmation that outmoded conventions no longer applied, but instead of turning the spotlight on the world as it was, it introduced a whole new set of values.[4] Herzog & de Meuron were in fact the first to really see "everything that is" and to accept this as their point of departure. In a house for a veterinary surgeon in Switzerland they combined all possible window elements with thoroughly postmodernist enthusiasm, but when it came to a photography studio near Basel they used the cheapest of materials, such as bitumen sheets and plywood. Ever since then they have been frequent visitors to the depot for industrial building supplies. But in their use of beech wood in their iconic building for the Goetz Collection in Munich they also paid their respects to Alvar Aalto and his particular version of modernism. And they have published essays analyzing the architecture of the 1970s and the brown suits so beloved of the managers they used to see out and about.[5] What looks like debris to Benjamin's angel appears to them as the rich treasure trove of the real world on their own doorstep. The curious observer will discover in it a huge wealth of materials, forms, and attitudes. There is everything from advertising slogans and neon signs to carved stone, aggregate concrete with silicone joints, and the precision work of the master craftsman; there are countless standards for building materials and processes and tailored solutions for individual cases. How could anyone be so arrogant as to ignore all of that! Isn't it the architect's good fortune to be able to observe and assess and adapt all that there is, more than perhaps anyone else? To be able to create new perspectives by making small changes, introducing new spaces and generating a habitable environment where there was once isolation? Is it not much more productive to seize hold of all these things rather than dismiss them as decay and detritus? And is it not also more honest—because we can only work with the things we have to hand and because the world only becomes freer if we liberate it from preconceived notions of how it ought to be?

Probing the World's Potential

Herzog & de Meuron do nevertheless share Walter Benjamin's critique of the doctrine of progress as the main factor shaping modernism. As children of postmodernism they almost intuitively shelved the notion that historical change is linear, that what exists now is by definition inferior to what is yet to come and should therefore be destroyed. Attitudes of this kind had already wrought too much destruction in European cities—more than the air raids of the Second World War. And in any case, the notion of progress had already been taken to absurd extremes. Modernism existed in isolated, groundbreaking architectural designs, sometimes in ensembles, but in everyday life it was yet another rerun of precepts that had already proved unrealizable or even totalitarian: The separation of different realms according to function, the car-friendly city had led to developments that were now crying out to be rectified. Lucius Burckhardt was fighting for the cause in Basel and favored the "smallest possible intervention" rather than the prevailing, unquenchable thirst for the new.[6] The doctrine of modernism had failed and to this day the gap has not been filled by any substitute religion. So it seemed more promising to work with what was there and to leave

Artaria & Schmidt, Haus Schaeffer, Riehen, 1928.

the built residue of modernism in that contemporary panorama. The new way forward was dialog, not progress. And this was as true of existing built structures as it was of clients and the development of designs and proposals.

Surprisingly, this dialog, this exploratory approach to the world—weighing up, discarding, returning to things—this basic questioning, inquisitive attitude to architecture made it possible for Herzog & de Meuron to take a new look at modernism, to reassess its impulses and to incorporate these in their own reactions to the present. Although there were of course the amoeba-like undulations of the library building in Cottbus and the double helix of the first design for a new office tower for Roche in Basel, the architects specifically engaged with the crystalline geometries of modernism long before 2008, when the global financial crisis saw free experimentation and the frenzy to invest being stigmatized as the irresponsible squandering of resources and indifference to the needs of an increasingly urbanized world. Even as students at ETH Zurich in 1977 Jacques Herzog and Pierre de Meuron prepared a seminar paper on modernist housing in the Basel area.[7] In 1990 when Haus Schaeffer in Riehen, built by Hans Schmidt and Paul Artaria in 1928, came up for sale, Pierre de Meuron bought it. Having first freed it of all the many alterations it had endured, he then updated it with the greatest care. Its original, almost ephemeral air of fragility came fully to light once again.[8]

A 1111 Lincoln Road, Miami Beach, 2010.
B Private residence, Los Angeles, 2007.

The architects' intuitive handling of the language of modernism, combined with a determination to achieve a new simplicity and directness, is seen in a number of buildings that respond to the changed conditions of architecture by both reinvigorating and probing that same modernism. It is not by chance that this is exemplified in two projects, both for clients in Miami. The subtropical climate there is more forgiving than Europe north of the Alps. Presented with the opportunity to renovate a massive structure built in 1968 at the far end of the only pedestrian zone in Miami Beach and to add a parking garage, the architects came up with a bold riposte to the car-friendly American city. Their parking garage is not conceived merely as a place to leave cars—that function is fulfilled almost en passant. Its much more important role is that of a catalyst promoting the development of a largely neglected part of the city. Herzog & de Meuron have extended the pedestrian zone, which had previously just petered out, and have given it a striking end point in the parking structure. The addition of trees, seating, and a pavilion sculpture by Dan Graham creates a welcoming area fringed by new shops at ground level; a dramatic staircase takes visitors up into the parking garage and leads car drivers out into the city. One of the hallmarks of European cities—lively, public spaces where people can congregate—is thus combined with the American model of a car-based city. Visitors are encouraged by various attractions to leave their cars and continue on foot. At the same time, the design introduces various characteristics of European modernism, which allow other uses to be added to the building's prime function. Although the initially envisaged white finish was abandoned in favor of carefully treated

exposed concrete, the perimeter railings evoke designs by Le Corbusier and his picture of an ocean liner, which is entirely apposite for Miami Beach. The parking garage also doffs its cap to Frank Lloyd Wright's spiral in the Solomon R. Guggenheim Museum in New York: whereas Wright turned the idea of a parking garage ramp into a museum, Herzog & de Meuron reverse the procedure and transform a parking garage, with its spiraling access, into a multifunctional venue. With a showroom on an upper floor and different ceiling heights it is also a place for seeing and being seen, for looking out over the city and gazing in wonder at the coastline. As though that were not enough, the owner of the facility is provided with a 500-square-meter rooftop villa that cites the villas of classical modernism and is surrounded by sumptuous gardens. A project of this kind is no longer just a parking garage, it is a multifaceted instrument that can reshape a whole urban area. There is no certainty here that things are what they appear to be. On the contrary, users can help to define the structure and what they want to do there. This dilution of distinct functions is encouraged by the design of the open facade with its tapering floor slabs. It is all but impossible for the viewer to tell where the building starts and ends; there is a virtual building line, but in real terms this is at best perceived as a visible zigzag. This is clearly a classic modernist design, but it is as though it has been built without its skin. Could there be anything more vulnerable than a skinned body? In another situation the architects came up with a very different response to the role of the automobile in American life: tasked with designing a private residence in the hills high above Los Angeles, they dreamt up a picturesque access road—including a turning circle—that sweeps upward and becomes the roof of the house. The roadway covers and merges into the residence in an unprecedented marriage of a private home, the most intimate of spaces, and the public space of a road.

Reassessing Traditions

In Herzog & de Meuron's second project in Miami, when they again both reinvigorated modernism and gave it a new contemporary twist, there is a similar lack of any skin or distinct external boundary. The Pérez Art Museum Miami (PAMM) occupies one of the few public spaces directly on the waterfront. The architects lifted it up on stilts since it has to be above the storm surge level, but they did so in a manner that recalls a typology that goes right back to antiquity. The elongated, very flat structure is reminiscent of certain late modernist cultural venues, such as the Kennedy Center by the Potomac River in Washington, DC. It also recalls Mies van der Rohe's Neue Nationalgalerie in Berlin and has echoes of the Parthenon, which inspired Mies. But all these allusions play out on a purely visual level; this and the practical purpose of the museum help to ward off the potential pathos of references to architectural history. The PAMM—on a platform, like the Neue Nationalgalerie in Berlin—stands proud like an Acropolis. But it is not an acropolis hill nor does it have a solid ground floor of exhibition spaces. Instead the platform covers an open parking level. The platform itself is partly constructed from thin concrete slabs with gaps allowing daylight to penetrate to the lower level. The supports they stand on recall simple wood-stilt houses in Biscayne Bay, Florida.

However, besides these allusions to temple structures the PAMM has a certain affinity to the residential pavilion, albeit without anything of the privacy of that epitome of modern living. In fact a building could hardly be more public than the PAMM. The full-width stairway that leads up from the waterfront to the museum platform calls to mind the wide steps up to the Neue Nationalgalerie in Berlin, but the PAMM stairway also makes a major representative statement and actively connects the waterfront promenade and the museum. The visitor ascends the steps as though approaching a temple or a church, but—importantly—it is equally possible to linger there. The stairway provides an inviting meeting and resting place by the water that extends into the veranda-like space under the canopy and helps to alleviate the lack of public spaces in Miami. A tried and tested mark of architectural distinction that goes right back to antiquity is used here in the context of popular culture. The grandeur of classical design is not used here to represent institutional power, or a government, or a collector—not even the pseudo-religion of art: it signals a meeting place. And it enters into dialog with nature.

A Pérez Art Museum Miami, 2013.
B Leshaw House, Stiltsville, Florida, ca. 1950–1959.

This nuanced treatment of pictorial traditions, this fading in and out of forms and formulas is visibly reinforced by the layered exhibition spaces. Herzog & de Meuron stack different volumes like boxes but avoid enclosing them in a facade. In a sense the PAMM reveals its own innards. Functions, the museum's internal requirements, the need for particular spaces and their shapes are all in full view—and with no hint of embarrassment, perfectly naturally, as though the need to conceal the weak spots in a body were a thing of the past. The PAMM is like a house without a shell that gladly faces the outside world, inviting it in and using specific plants and vegetation to show what a symbiosis between inside and outside can look like. The museum is like a body that is just waiting to be overgrown, like the built structures in Peter Doig's series of paintings depicting glimpses of Le Corbusier's *Unité d'Habitation* as a last remnant of civilization in the depth of a forest. The numerous columns of the PAMM that rise up through the terraces to the roof accentuate this combination of vulnerability and openness.

A Donald Judd, Untitled (Bernstein 78–69), 1978.
B 56 Leonard Street, New York, 2017.

As a principle the layering of volumes is reminiscent of Donald Judd's stacks and plays a part in many of Herzog & de Meuron's projects. It obviates certain compositional questions and aesthetic deliberations, and affords the architects greater flexibility in their response to the client. The most striking example of this is seen in the residential tower on Leonard Street in New York. Located on a very restricted plot of land, the three-part high-rise twists upward to a height of 250 meters. Its shape is determined by the apartment units the investor has requested in view of the current demand for dwellings. However,

the structure of the building—with its supports and floor slabs—is extremely adaptable and during the planning phase numerous different ideas were tried out as the demand for apartments changed and evolved. It was even possible to incorporate the classic New York brownstone. The layout and size of individual apartments are matched to potential residents' needs; all but five of the 145 apartments are unique. Ultimately the architects congregate the differently sized functions in three distinct zones. The plinth segment contains general facilities such as the lobby, the pool, and the parking garage as well as two town houses and a number of smaller apartments; the central section contains medium-sized apartments; the slender top is occupied by ten penthouses. With its boldly expressive forms this tower is nevertheless again identifiably a stacked structure. The ziggurat, the iconic tip to a New York skyscraper, can only be recreated in the context of this kind of ambivalence. On a more detailed level this vertical community of villas in the sky echoes classics of modern living from Pierre Koenig's Case Study House to Mies van der Rohe's Farnsworth House, from the Schindler House to Frank Lloyd Wright's Fallingwater with its cantilevered terraces. The architects' engagement with a prototype of classical modernism, the villa, is relocated to a different terrain—the tower—and takes place in the air rather than on the ground. Herzog & de Meuron take the liberty to reinterpret the classic structure of the New York skyscraper, with its base, shaft, and capital, as a game with shapes that pushes the boundaries of structural viability. Ultimately the form is determined by individualistic apartments and almost dissipates in an accumulation of precarious balances. It would hardly be possible to more dramatically demonstrate the interplay of individuality and community that defines society today.

Pierre Koenig, Case Study House No. 22,
Los Angeles, 1960.

A Direct Language of Materials

The building is open, reassesses modernism, and revisits reduction, all features that go hand in hand with the immediacy of the materials, which could be seen as a nod to Brutalism and to some of the architects' early projects, such as the student housing in Dijon. Concrete is now left in full view and its weight and mass are made manifest, as though these buildings might otherwise evanesce or float away, if they really were as light as many of Herzog & de Meuron's designs appear. In Spain they masterminded a vast new headquarters for BBVA (Banco Bilbao Vizcaya Argentaria), the country's second-largest banking group. Like a monastery, the structure turns its back on the extremely heterogeneous buildings in the surrounding area that sprang up during the boom years in Spain. Inside the complex there is an openness that combines the traditions of southern European cities with northern European certainty. Eight unfinished buildings already occupied part of the site when the Basel architects won the contract to develop this site; part of their remit was to incorporate as much as possible of these existing buildings into their own design. They opted for a sculptural approach, pared the unfinished buildings back to their skeletons and cut these to fit the linear carpet of buildings that extends across the whole site. This solution has a roughness worthy of Gordon Matta-Clark and an elegance seen in the South American modernism of one such as Lina Bo Bardi. Ceilings and substructures are shorn so that, together with their supports, they call to mind the classical vocabulary of column and capital, just much more bulkily and without ornamentation. Recessed windows make this all the more apparent. The entire complex is animated by the interplay of solidity and lightness. Courtyards and pathways are cut into blocks, which themselves have been hollowed here and there to create light-filled spaces. And an upright oval disc—a landmark signaling the location of the bank's headquarters and clearly visible from afar—is stabilized by a vast plinth-like base, while its upper realms appear precariously balanced, as though the whole disc were constantly on the point of rolling away—provoking an intriguing, unsettling game of opposite effects, which alludes to *firmitas* by highlighting potential instability. A sense of security, the feeling of standing firmly on the ground, can now only be provided by images that openly question it. And this is all the more true when the same design includes what looks like a demonstration of archaic power, as in the case of BBVA.

A Gordon Matta-Clark, Conical Intersect, 1975.
B New Headquarters for BBVA, Madrid, 2015.

Elegance and precariousness also distinguish this emphasis on solid forms from Brutalism as it developed (until the late 1960s) after Alison and Peter Smithson's design for a new school in the English town of Hunstanton. Their use of exposed concrete was not provocative rebellion but rather an attempt to replace solidity and gravity with a feeling of buoyancy. This can sometimes be achieved by means of just a few accents. In Switzerland the client's requirements for a laboratory and office block on the Roche campus in Basel left Herzog & de Meuron little scope for inventive design. Nevertheless, by slightly rounding the concrete supports set back from the facades the architects managed to give the building a touch of elegance, which has all the more impact on the atmosphere simply because it is so unexpected in this context. Mention has already been made of the tapering concrete floors of the parking garage at 1111 Lincoln Road in Miami Beach. The archive and residential building on Helsinki-Strasse in the Dreispitz area of Basel is encased in a substantial concrete grid. However, slight deviations from strict alignments, the visible transfer of loads to seemingly minimal diagonal supports, allusions to timber-frame constructions, and the optical foreshortenings that arise from the fact that the base of the building is slightly curved give this very substantial building a different, filigree dimension, which sees the clear shape of the structure as a whole all but disappearing. In addition, the building also comments playfully on its situation at the end of a line of buildings. At one moment it can be read figuratively as a head, at the next it turns back

Helsinki Dreispitz, Münchenstein/
Basel, 2014.

into an abstract geometric form. This in itself distinguishes projects of this kind from Herzog & de Meuron's student housing in Dijon. The latter was designed using only simple rectangular forms; at the last minute extreme financial pressure halted the planned inclusion of fine, wood components. In their most recent projects they blend different geometries. The hybridization that is perfectly exemplified in the multifunctional parking garage in Miami Beach also informs the language of their designs, which are thus open to multiple readings.

Multilayered Images

A similarly complex pictoriality is taken to a new extreme in the architects' design for the Iglesia de la Natividad in Culiacán, Mexico. Rising up from what was once wasteland at the entrance to a gated community still under construction, it weaves together hints of fortified churches, chimney stacks, and bizarre rock formations. The symbolic place of transcendence is tied to its opposite: to this Earth and the underworld. Of course the architects only embarked on this project following detailed historical investigations into church construction since the classical basilica, and the finished design clearly incorporates the local tradition of church architecture. Rather than clinging to the grand traditions of the Hispano-Mexican Baroque it alludes to the local mission churches, which are poorer, more archaic, and with closer ties to the history of invasion and the Conquista in that particular region of the State of Sinaloa. But the proposal also references Le Corbusier's design for a church in Firminy, France, which was only completed in 2006 thanks to his student José Oubrerie. Although both sacred interiors echo the upward pull of a chimney, Herzog & de Meuron's design can almost be seen as a response to Le Corbusier's ideas some fifty years earlier.[9] The primal shape of a diagonally lopped pyramid poised on a series of plates can be seen as the civilizing declaration of a sacred space for a secular society. However, the models for the Iglesia de la Natividad depict a form that evolves from a mountain, that is even more at one with nature than the university library in Cottbus, which is conceived as a natural extrusion. The proposed use of adobe in Culiacán adds to the expressive impact of the church.

Iglesia de la Natividad, Culiacán, 2008.

The complexity of these images can be read as a way of adding architectural value to the design. But it can also be read as a question. Central American Catholicism is still a mainstay of Mexican society; even Mafia families build churches and pray to their favorite saints. This situation is visibly reflected in the rock-like form of this design: the Church likes to see itself as a mighty fortress. At the same time, the reference to the mission churches of the past recalls a time when this same religion was imposed on the indigenous population by the Spanish conquistadors. And, not least, the design questions the place and nature of religious belief in a globalized world. It is part of a widespread sense of destabilization, not necessarily an answer, and should perhaps be seen as evidence of anthropological need rather than as a declaration of belief.

Auditorium du Jura, Courgenay, 2006.

This connection to the landscape is, however, complicated by the seemingly textile aspect of the form, which almost appears to be pushing through a cloth laid over a hill and derives its shape from the ensuing tension. In that respect the project recalls another unrealized design, a concert hall and cultural center at Courgenay, Switzerland, which was first conceived together with the late Rémy Zaugg— artist and close friend of Herzog & de Meuron—who died in 2005. With its meticulous craftsmanship and references to agricultural barns in that region, it connects with a whole series of works by Herzog & de Meuron in a style that could be described as rural minimalism. In these designs the architects combine their renewed interest in classical modernism and their own history of reduced geometries with traditional agricultural structures, whose simple forms are a response to the functional requirements of the natural surroundings. Pride of place among these structures is taken by the barn, closely followed by the shed, which also calls to mind the top-light designs developed for factory buildings. These forms abound in the architects' second, realized design for the Parrish Art Museum on Long Island, New York, where a basic shape is doubled, extruded, and varied by recessing walls to create verandas. Simple forms combine regional materials with the fluid spatiality seen in the work of Donald Judd. As soon as it opened in 2012 the museum became an icon for architecture's departure from the flamboyance of the early-to-mid-2000s and for the growing interest in less showy designs more in keeping with the changed state of society following the global financial meltdown of 2008.[10] The incorporation of rural forms into cutting-edge designs is seen on a larger scale in the proposal for a project around a private residence by a lake in southern Germany. Not only is the complex internal structure of the main building covered by a simple pitched roof made from corrugated fiber cement (reminiscent of farm buildings), the building itself is conceived as part of a rural hamlet. And despite the different functions of the other buildings grouped around the central area—depot, print shop, and studio—they are all variants on the conventional barn.

Remembering Craft Skills

This expansion of a minimalist language of forms brings with it a new appreciation of craft skills, not as nostalgic echoes of a pre-industrial era, but as part of the architects' reassessment of their own earlier thinking. From the outset Herzog & de Meuron's projects have always united conceptual precision with meticulous execution. Structures such as the Plywood House in Bottmingen and the House for an Art Collector in Therwil could never have been realized without the architects' detailed understanding of construction techniques. The singular solutions they devised for their early interventions in the house of art collector and Ricola co-owner Alfred Richterich—from display case to bathroom—combined architectural inspiration with the skills of the cabinetmaker. Their series of signal boxes wrapped in copper, like electrical-wire spools, could never have been realized without the close collaboration of highly skilled metallurgists. Even as vast a project as the Schaulager for the collection of the Emanuel Hoffmann Foundation, completed in 2003, is realized with the same painstaking precision following detailed discussions with craftspeople and in-depth knowledge of production processes. Yet this is by no means at odds with the architects' response to American minimalism, which influenced the reduced geometries of their early designs. On the contrary, their reengagement with craft skills led to a closer reading of minimalism. The focus is usually on the minimalists' use of readily available industrial materials, which Judd, Andre, and others procured from buildings suppliers on Canal Street in SoHo. Often too little is made of the importance Judd attached to the precise execution of his works. It is not for nothing that some of his pieces were made in Swiss workshops.[11] The potential inherent in advanced craft skills is seen in the architects' design for a natural swimming pool in the municipality of Riehen on the outskirts of Basel. The wooden perimeter fence includes a canopy supported by spliced spars, which—together with the precise placement of the timbers—give this simple form an artistic presence of its own. On the inside the fence incorporates a deck and changing facilities, fronted by showers attached to upright concrete slabs, which initiate a dialog between different materials. The complex, as

a cultural entity, subtly sets itself apart from its surroundings: it remains part of the natural landscape yet also demonstrates that even on the periphery of urban life culture still means difference.

A Plywood House, Bottmingen, 1985.
B Naturbad Riehen, 2014.

As it happened the architects' reevaluation of their own history of reduced designs and the traditions of modernism coincided with their engagement with premodern architectures. Herzog & de Meuron took on two major restoration projects, one in New York and the other in Hong Kong. In both cases the aim was to revitalize neglected architectural monuments by introducing new cultural uses. The Park Avenue Armory in Upper Manhattan, New York, is an icon of the American Gilded Age. It was there, in the drill hall, that the sons of New York's elite were put through their paces; the young officers turned their reception rooms into a thriving social hub and put on spectacular balls that quickly caught the public's imagination. The interiors were styled in the latest fashions by the best designers in the land, from Louis Comfort Tiffany to Herter Brothers. However, social change and the Armory's subsequent use by military personnel saw its substance falling into neglect. The Armory has been listed as a National Historic Landmark and, thanks to a private initiative, Herzog & de Meuron have taken the lead role in its progressive revitalization and historic restoration. However, contrary to the customary practice in the USA, they are not simply remaking the original interior; they are retaining aspects of interventions throughout the Armory's history and integrating these into an overarching design derived from its most important phase. Each room has its own particular look and visitors are met with a deliberately overwhelming wealth of detail and design that tells of another era. Wherever new elements have to be incorporated—from lighting to elevators to furnishings—the architects highlight their introduction by means of special material finishes, preferably copper. Herzog & de Meuron thus avoid confrontation and competition between the old and the new. The building as a whole and the individual rooms within it are treated as an alternative to the modernist architecture that abounds in the metropolis. Moreover, by taking such a radically different approach, they have fueled the debate surrounding contemporary architecture and have created rooms for art and performance that have little to do with the reductionism of prevailing museum architecture. Herzog & de Meuron, who were instrumental in the evolution of the White Cube, have coined the term *Anchor Rooms* for spaces of this kind. The specially devised architecture and interiors of a museum's Anchor Rooms raise the profile of the institution as a whole. Perhaps the most striking example of these is seen in the Goya rooms in the architects' proposal for an Espacio Goya in Zaragoza, which reconstruct four historical interiors closely associated with Goya.

In the case of the restoration and expansion of the Central Police Station in the historical city center of Hong Kong the notion of connecting old and new spreads out into an entire district. Each of the eighteen existing buildings has its characteristic rooms and its own history and is differently tied into the profusion of squares and alleyways. At the upper edge of the sloping site two new buildings are constructed, matching the proportions of the existing family of structures and connected to them by means of bridges, steps, and courtyards. The aluminum elements in the new facades echo the brickwork of the old buildings while also introducing the present day into the site. For all the care that is taken restoring buildings, rooms, and materials, sight is never lost of contemporary methods or of the intended users. The architects' acute awareness of the historical significance of this former headquarters of the British colonial administration and long-standing prison in a city that is constantly evolving and building higher and higher on a highly restricted land mass, heightens their sensitivity to materials and methods and sees this new cultural quarter becoming a historical beacon in the urban development of the city. Conversely, knowledge of the groundswell of modernism and its global dynamics as well as the suppression and destruction it has wrought, heightens their awareness of the need to seek out detached positions from which to evolve new perspectives and more productive attitudes that will foster the renewal of architecture. For years, as they have worked on their many projects in China, Herzog & de Meuron have also been keenly aware of the tempo governing any such renewal.

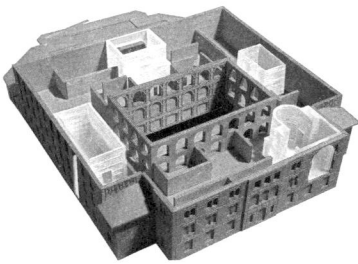

A   Park Avenue Armory, New York, 2011.
B   Espacio Goya, Zaragoza, 2007.

Thus, for all the brevity of this survey of the years leading up to the financial crisis of 2008, it shows how intensely Herzog & de Meuron used this time of expressive freedom and new technical possibilities to review their own relationship to modernism and to their own early work, when the relevant precepts were being declared obsolete in numerous contemporary projects. But precisely that combination of complexity and simplicity opened up new perspectives and inspired new, productive ways of reading and deploying ideas that had seemingly run dry. In his famous manifesto[12] Robert Venturi countered the claims of the champions of ideological modernism with the factual impact of complexity, architectural contradiction, and the resistance of the everyday and the banal. Jacques Herzog and Pierre de Meuron found that same modernism everywhere on their daily forays into Basel and saw it confirmed in writing—although they preferred Mies van der Rohe's "Less is more" to Venturi's "Less is a bore." And they always identified less with the theoretical positions of the avant-garde than with Walter Benjamin's angel: a positive figure looking backward at what advancing time has spit out for us to look at again. That debris of materials, buildings, projects, and

theories could be the greatest resource for a new architecture. In those years Herzog & de Meuron honed and fully developed their vocabulary and strategies, providing themselves with the tools to perceive and give expression to an era that is increasingly confused, insecure, and vulnerable. Without denying any of these developments, their profoundly complex buildings and glittering images counter the world's travails with beauty—as a sign of hope.

1   Roger Diener, Jacques Herzog, Pierre de Meuron, Marcel Meili, Christian Schmid, *Switzerland. An Urban Portrait*, ed. ETH Studio Basel Contemporary City Institute, 4 vols., Basel 2005.
2   "There is a picture by Klee called *Angelus Novus*. It shows an angel who seems about to move away from something he stares at. His eyes are wide, his mouth is open, his wings are spread. This is how the angel of history must look. His face is turned toward the past. Where a chain of events appears before *us, he* sees one single catastrophe, which keeps piling wreckage upon wreckage and hurls it at his feet. The angel would like to stay, awaken the dead, and make whole what has been smashed. But a storm is blowing from Paradise and has got caught in his wings; it is so strong that the angel can no longer close them. This storm drives him irresistibly into the future to which his back is turned, while the pile of debris before him grows toward the sky. What we call progress is *this* storm." Walter Benjamin, "On the Concept of History," 1940, no. IX, in Walter Benjamin, *Selected Writings*, vol. 4, 1938–1940, trans. Edmund Jephcott and others (Cambridge, MA: Belknap Press, 2003), 392.
3   Ludwig Wittgenstein opens his *Tractatus Logico-philosophicus* (finished in 1918) with the words "The world is everything that is the case," in idem, *Tractatus Logico-philosophicus*, trans. D. F. Pears and B. F. McGuiness (London: Routledge, 1961), 5.
4   Paul Feyerabend, "The only principle that does not inhibit progress is: *anything goes*," in idem, *Against Method*, 3rd ed. (London: Verso, 1993), 5.
5   In March 1981 Jacques Herzog gave a talk at Kunsthalle Basel called "The Specific Gravity of Architectures," which has since been published in a slightly revised version in Gerhard Mack, *Herzog & de Meuron 1978–1988, The Complete Works*, vol. 1, trans. Katja Steiner and Bruce Almberg (Basel: Birkhäuser, 1997), 204–6.
6   Lucius Burckhardt, *Der kleinstmögliche Eingriff*, ed. Markus Ritter and Martin Schmitz (Berlin: Martin Schmitz Verlag, 2013). Burckhardt originally wrote this text in the early 1980s.
7   „Wohnungsbau Basel 1915–1935", Seminar paper, winter semester 1976/77, ETH Zurich, 1977, led by Arthur Rüegg, Peter Quarella, and Klaus Dolder.
8   Jean-François Chevrier, *From Basel–Herzog & de Meuron*, (Basel: Birkhäuser, 2016), 172–3.
9   Le Corbusier's earliest sketches date to 1961.
10 See the review by Jordan Mejias, "M wie Minimalismus," *Frankfurter Allgemeine Zeitung*, November 30, 2012.
11 The Swiss company Lehni, for instance, coproduced Judd furniture with the artist in the 1980s.
12 Robert Venturi, *Complexity and Contradiction in Architecture* (New York: Museum of Modern Art, 1966).

Buildings and Projects
2005–2007

We traveled to Qingdao with Uli Sigg because we wanted to enlist the cooperation of Ai Weiwei on this unusual project —a gigantic campus for the Beijing Film Academy, which would one day rank on a par with Hollywood, its productions putting the Asian film industry on the world map.

The project was initiated, among others, by people who knew Weiwei from his days at film school. They showed us the location earmarked for this ambitious project. It was a marvelous site on the outskirts of the city: an open strip of land bordering the Yellow Sea, embedded between a rocky coastline to the north and one of the most beautiful beaches in China to the south. We envisioned the coming project in the course of prolonged walks on the sands flanked by craggy cliffs. There we found fascinating objects that had been washed ashore, bits of weathered wood, jumbled twigs, and pebbles that looked like nests.

For us, Qingdao is therefore associated with inspiring memories because we weren't simply traveling. We also had time to gaze in wonder at a place we had never seen before and to spend time with interesting people. But Qingdao is also associated with disappointment, with a situation that we faced when working on a number of other projects in China.

The disappointment: the project failed because of money. After an intense planning phase, our Chinese partners offered us a fee for detailed planning and execution that was one hundred times less than we would have received for a comparable project in the West.

The project was built after all but without our participation, although our architectural input had clearly exerted a sustained influence on our Chinese colleagues. Seen from far above on Google Earth, the finished project resembles our proposal. Obviously, our role was merely to supply initial proposals for the initiators of the project and to pave the way for its success by securing the goodwill of the authorities.

However, the Qingdao Project has also given us fruitful impulses, substantially influencing subsequent projects of our own, especially Actelion, VitraHaus and the residential tower on Leonard Street in New York. Faced with the challenge of understanding and working out plans for the colossal, sheer unmanageable size of the Film Academy, we resorted to a crude but extremely efficient method. We cut blocks out of paper and foam in different sizes and colors on a scale of 1:500, representing the diverse dimensions and functions of the entire project:

education, accommodation, administration, communication, etc. We ended up with a huge number of building blocks that could be arranged and moved about like dominoes. They could be laid out flat or superimposed in several layers; we tried square and rectangular arrangements, but nothing was really satisfactory, neither in form nor in spatial layout or functionality. So we took a different approach: we became playful, almost like being in kindergarten, but then became very serious again when we realized that by stacking the blocks, piling them up and taking them down, much more complex spatial and functional relations started to emerge among all the varied parts of the project. In addition, we were now able to compare them with each other. Using a micro camera that simulates a person's perception in real space, we moved through the resulting three-dimensional structures. We kept making corrections and adjustments as we followed the path of the camera. The forms of the building complex as a whole almost took shape by themselves—on one hand, extremely specific and unanticipated, on the other, with a perfectly natural logic and simplicity. It was as if we had come full circle, back to the nests of grass and twigs and weathered driftwood, shaped by the movement of the oceans, which we had discovered while walking on the beach at Qingdao.

Herzog & de Meuron, 2015

The Film Academy is to be built at one of China's most beautiful beaches with its driftwood and rock formations. The architects visit the site with Ai Weiwei.

269_SI_0502_036

269_EV_0503_015

269_RFNL_0502_016

269_RFNL_0504_046

Sketches, drawings, and photomontages show the layout of the buildings for the enormously complex brief of the Film Academy.

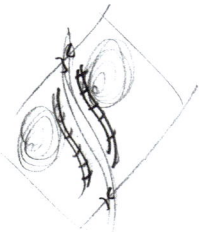

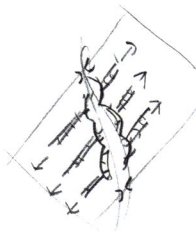

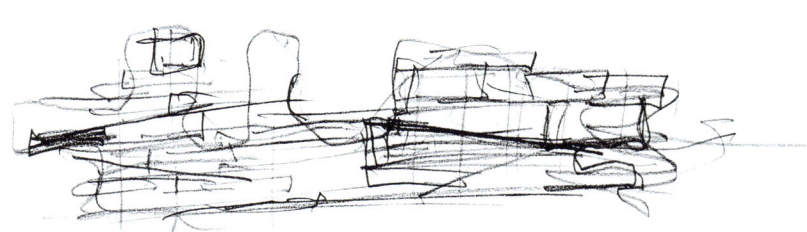

269_SK_0502_001_PdM

269_SK_0502_002_PdM

269_SK_0502_003_PdM

269_SK_0503_007

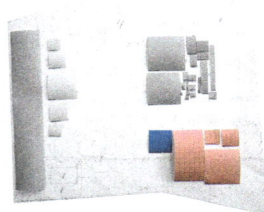

269_MO_0502_005

269_MO_0502_007

269_MO_0502_011

269_CI_0502_056

The specified elements are cut out of foam, laid out, and assembled in clusters.

269_MO_0503_048_K

269_CI_0505_008_REP

269_CI_0505_011_REP

269_CI_0505_009_REP

269_MO_0504_104_QIN

269_MO_0503_095_K

269_CI_0505_002_REP

269_MO_0504_06_AERIAL

Studies on the connections and structural engineering of the individual blocks.

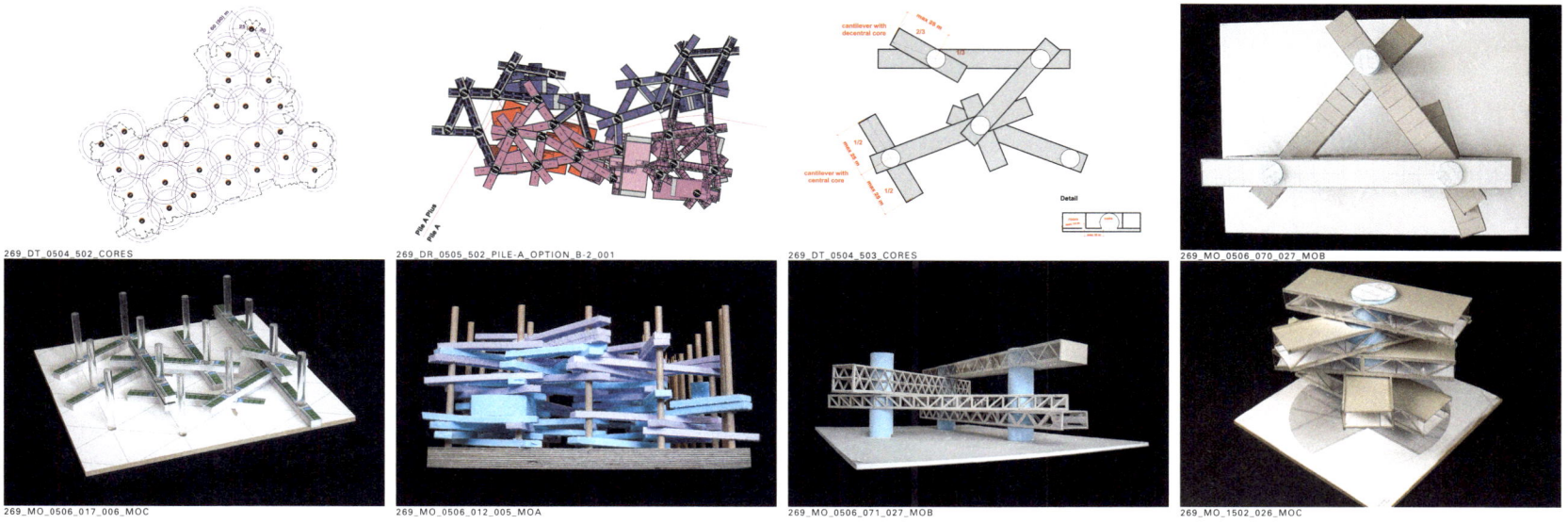

269_DT_0504_502_CORES

269_DR_0505_502_PILE-A_OPTION_B-2_001

269_DT_0504_503_CORES

269_MO_0506_070_027_MOB

269_MO_0506_017_006_MOC

269_MO_0506_012_005_MOA

269_MO_0506_071_027_MOB

269_MO_1502_026_MOC

The brief divided into three units; studies on pile A (bottom right) addressing important functions on the coast.

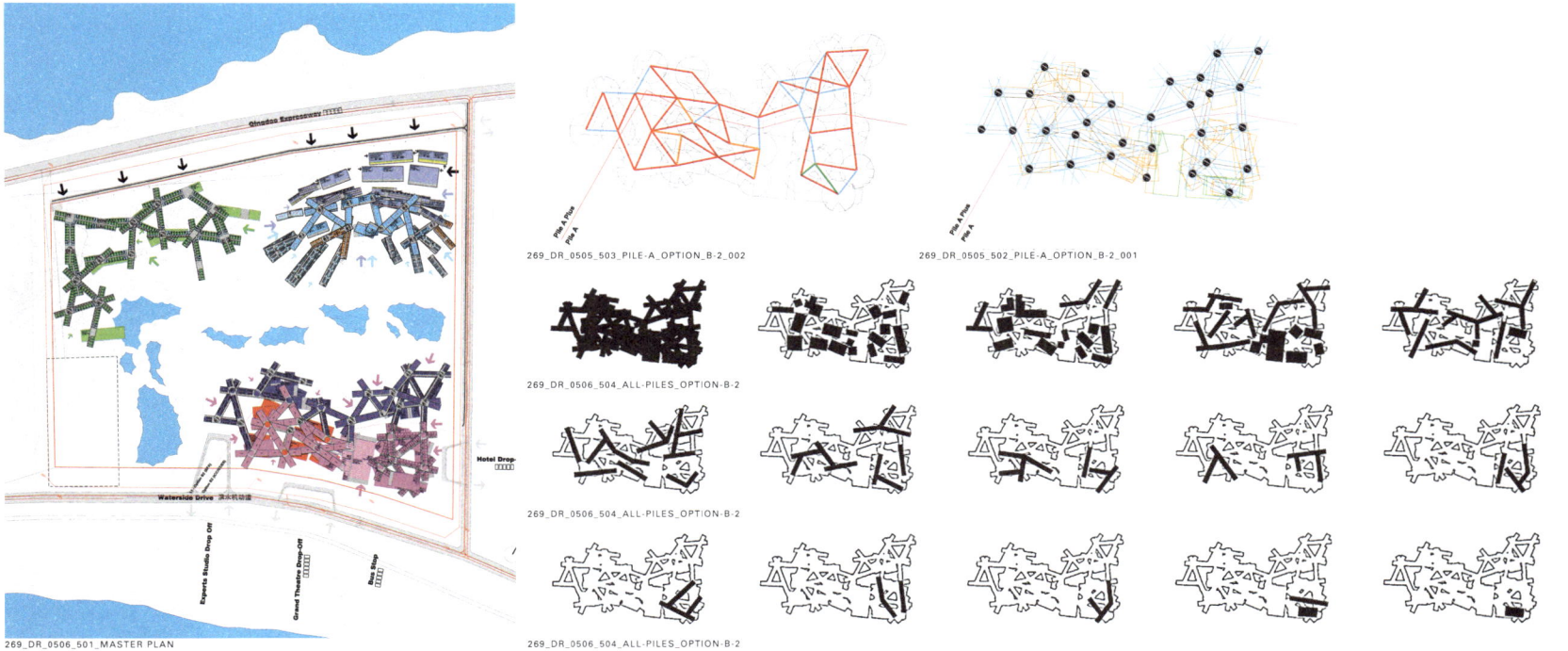

269_DR_0506_501_MASTER PLAN

269_DR_0505_503_PILE-A_OPTION_B-2_002

269_DR_0505_502_PILE-A_OPTION_B-2_001

269_DR_0506_504_ALL-PILES_OPTION-B-2

269_DR_0506_504_ALL-PILES_OPTION-B-2

269_DR_0506_504_ALL-PILES_OPTION-B-2

Cross section of pile A.

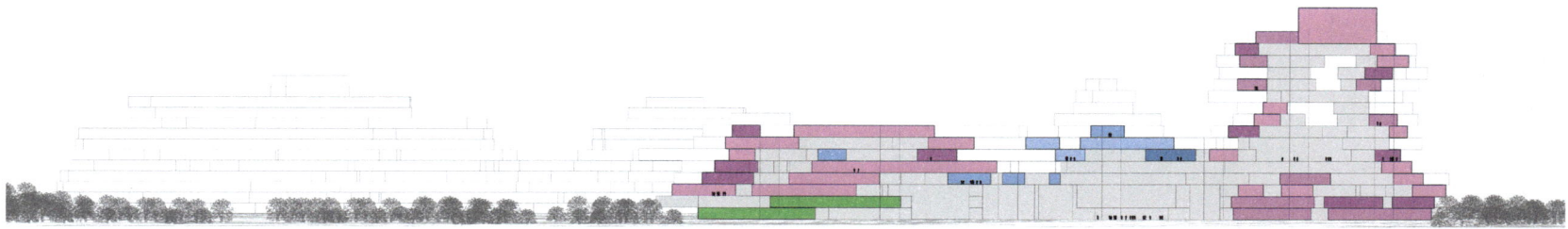

269_PA_0504_501_SECTELEV

Large-scale models. A micro camera provides realistic impressions of the interior.

269_PA_0504_500_3E2F

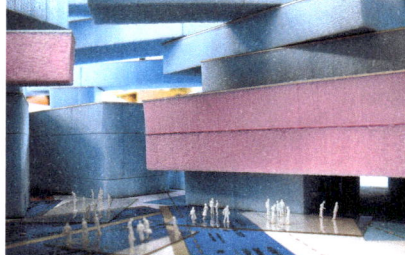

269_MO_0503_004

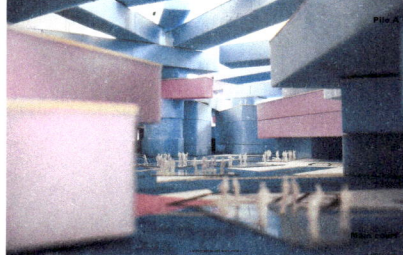

269_MO_0504_03_COURTYARD

269_MO_0504_500

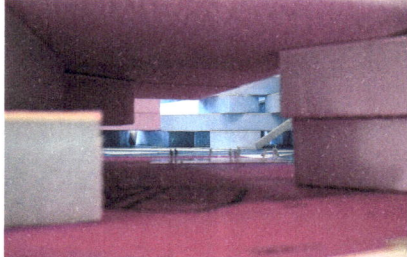

269_MO_0503_006

269_MO_0503_509_K

269_MO_0503_502

The project on concluding the feasibility study.

269_CI_0504_504_SOUTH

269_CI_0504_501_BIRD-EYE

269_CI_0504_502_EAST-STREET

269_CI_0504_505

Realization of the Film Academy by Chinese firms without Herzog & de Meuron, but based on their ideas.

269_RFCL_1410_702

269_RFCL_1107_701

269_SI_1701_002

The city of Qingdao, with a population of 7.6 million, lies in Shandong province. Its location on the Xuejiadao peninsula and its proximity to Haixi Bay and the China Sea make for an extraordinarily rich coastal setting. A master plan for the new Economic & Technological Development Zone involving ecologically protected areas, tourist infrastructure, apartments, and cultural facilities features a new campus for the Beijing Film Academy, set in the middle of the ecologically protected area and forming an anchor for future development. The 340,000-square-meter site is bounded to the north by the rocky coastline of the bay and to the south by one of China's most beautiful sandy beaches, known as Golden Beach. The program of the new Beijing Film Academy Qingdao School of Creative Media is highly ambitious. It has been conceived as a technologically cutting-edge center of cinematic art and television, allowing the students, who can reside on campus, to hone their skills in everything from computer-generated special effects to advertising, graphic design, and computer games, representing the full spectrum of the moving image in all its forms. In addition, it is intended as a center for the production and postproduction of technically sophisticated films and television shows.

Herzog & de Meuron's design embeds the wide-ranging facilities into the protected landscape. Early proposals included housing the various elements of the program, prescribed in detail right down to the room sizes, in single-story structures like a fishing village. The linear arrangement using traditional typologies such as the courtyard house would have allowed a flexible use of rooms, depending on function, without compromising the design as a whole. However, this solution would have occupied almost the entire site without giving the film academy the visibility that both the institution and the city wished it to have. In order to give the project an appearance that would reflect its national importance and its seaside location, it was necessary to focus on more expressive, vertically oriented architecture.

The architects retained the concept of using the individual elements of the program as building blocks, and distributed them over as many as six stories. Attempts to layer them in a single block, however, proved unsatisfactory, as did the division of functions into three elongated blocks for student accommodation, teaching, and communication. So the site was opened up and the focus placed instead on the individual building blocks and the spaces between them, optimizing the location's pleasant climate. In this way, the film academy takes on a man-made topography of its own that fits in with the natural landscape and communicates with it. The architects stacked the prescribed rooms into one, two, then three mounds with courtyards and passageways to provide a variety of urban spaces, but with an overall outward appearance reminiscent of hills or rocks, allowing the actual construction process to be undertaken in several stages. The largest building is in the southern, seaward area, with publicly accessible facilities on the side facing the beach. In addition to restaurants and stores on the ground floor, these include a theater above the entrance hall and a conference hotel that opens into a tower. A follow-up construction phase envisages the provision of studios for visiting specialists. To the rear, facing the campus, are the library and classrooms. The production facilities with large studio halls and student dormitories take up the two other large buildings on the north side of the site. These are easily accessed from the nearby highway.

The mound-like structures are enclosed by a dense landscape of newly created ponds and greenery that is already developing into palm forests, extending towards the beach and encompassing the pathways leading into the buildings themselves. What appears at first to be a random arrangement of volumes is actually optimized in terms of in-between spaces, passageways, and scale. Interior and exterior spaces, the built environment, and the cultivated environment engage and interact.

For the buildings, the architects devised a grid system of interconnecting and cantilevered beams based on the structural logic of stacking. They define a load-bearing grid of 7.80 by 8.80 meters that allows for fairly light ceilings. The maximum escape routes of 60 meters and the maximum projection of 25 meters determine the form of the vertical cores with their elevators and emergency stairs. Because they are round, the horizontal room units can be turned in any direction and combined according to spatial requirements. The load-bearing structure is designed to form single-strand typologies of south-facing rooms, with the access areas and corridors to the rear. Height and width vary according to the respective program and the number of stories. The load-bearing structure consists of diagonally placed steel beams at the sides and in situ concrete for the upper and lower sections. These rooms can be prefabricated on the ground and assembled by fixing them to the vertical core structures from top to bottom. They are not stacked one on top of each other: the load transfer is from the walls to the core.

The design for the film academy in Qingdao was not built. Although the investor was granted consent by the city authorities, he could not acquire the necessary funding. He is now building a structure that has atmospheric echoes of some of the design, such as the modular combination of building elements and additive stacking. Herzog & de Meuron have channeled the experience they have gained through their work on this project into a number of new designs. The concept of additive composition has long been an approach that they regard as equal to other more compact or holistic designs. They fully understand that its formal vocabulary is firmly rooted in the repertoire of modernist architecture. After all, the Neues Bauen movement itself also arose in response to industrial production processes. Similarly, Herzog & de Meuron's design for the Pilotengasse housing project in Vienna, Austria, can be seen in terms of this exploration of serial principles. Within the same period, in the early twenty-first century, they came up with their first design for the Parrish Art Museum as a collection of pavilions. The stacking of spaces, projecting outwards because there is no encasing facade, can also be seen shortly afterwards in the Leonard Street apartment building in Manhattan as well as in the Pérez Art Museum in Miami. Stripping away the facade, opening up the structure, putting the focus on the space itself—all of this finds its most eloquent expression in the Beijing Olympic Stadium.

This concept of stacking layers was implemented again soon afterwards by Herzog & de Meuron in their design for the headquarters of Actelion in Allschwil/Basel, where, on a smaller scale, they showed both expressive prowess and a wealth of ideas for the spatial organization of workplaces and communication zones, transitions from interior to exterior, courtyards and terraces. One year later, the structural principle for the VitraHaus in Weil am Rhein, Germany, was expanded: the block-like structure was given a pitched roof and the structural sobriety of an architecture pared down to its bare bones took on a strongly emotive visual aspect embracing the program of the building itself, while at the same time expanding the variety of intersections and spaces available.

The film academy in Qingdao, which marks the beginning of this series of designs, may be regarded as a contribution to an architecture that exploits the new technical possibilities of computer design in order to achieve previously unattainable complexity while at the same time, in the early years of the new millennium, applying this potential to expressive landmark buildings as well. Unlike most projects of this kind, the designs by Herzog & de Meuron are built on a continuing exploration of reduction. Buildings are constructed according to basic elements such as the simple block structure, using a modular concept that gains its vibrant sense of tension precisely from the fact that it combines simplicity and complexity within a single design.

Staatsoper Unter den Linden, Berlin
Germany
2005–2006

No. 274
Tristan and Isolde,
Stage Design

The stage sets created by architects or even by artists are perfectly dreadful—this was how we felt having been confronted with so many failed attempts. The pitfalls of simply transferring one's own style, one's typical trademark from construction site to proscenium stage seemed almost insurmountable. But since we try to avoid a signature style in our architecture and are more inclined toward experimentation, we found the invitation from the German State Opera in Berlin really quite fascinating: what an exciting challenge to design the stage set for Tristan and Isolde, *directed by Stefan Bachmann and conducted by Daniel Barenboim.*

It is in the nature of the stage to exert a magical attraction; it is a site of the imagination where time and space seem unbounded despite the clearly limited area of the stage and the length of the performance.

So the stage is a place for appearances. Everything is appearance. Which is precisely what invests stage design with so much potential. Above all for a Wagner opera, and most especially Tristan and Isolde, *as we envisioned it in our conversations with Stefan Bachmann. Wagner's music and the performers' voices are so exceptional that the stage set and the staging could easily be little more than an unwelcome distraction. We therefore wanted to generate an imagery that is neither illustrative nor confined to one single interpretation. The stage sets and the production would not represent the things themselves but rather their appearances. In other words, not simply emergence and fading but rather the appearance of emergence and the appearance of fading. The appearance of the hull of a ship, stairs, a cave or part of a body, a concrete form and identity, and the appearance of emptiness, of nothing, of a zero space.*

We did not want to use conventional technologies like video or slide projections in order to make things emerge, to magically whisk these appearances onto the stage. Instead we wanted to generate a tangible experience that would have a much more direct, physical impact on the spectators. This would also enable the singers to actively engage with the onstage image instead of merely being flanked by passive, projected images. The technical implementation of our ideas proved to be rather difficult and would have failed if it hadn't been for the extraordinary commitment of the stage technicians and our assistant Claudius Frühauf, who had already spent months in Basel experimenting with models and methods that would be able to generate the desired images. When we first tested the model and later conducted full-scale tests on stage, we found that what we had envisioned had indeed come true. Using negative pressure in a specially designed pressure chamber, it was possible to mold and shape a rubber membrane to create appearances that were constantly changing, breathing, imperceptibly overlapping, fading in and fading out. Thanks to the precision of the lighting, these appearances acquired an almost hallucinatory effect.

Herzog & de Meuron, 2006

Images sourced from paintings, films, and nature for the stage set of *Tristan and Isolde*. The objective is imagery that avoids realism and certainty.

274_RFCL_0510_804_ERASMUS-SAILS

274_RF_0507_001_FRIEDRICH

274_RF_0507_001_RUINE

274_RF_0509_005_SPONGIOSA

274_RF_0506_003_PP

274_RF_0506_001_TERMINATOR

274_RF_0511_017_CRASH

274_RF_0511_015_CRASH

Sketches of a rubber membrane into which backstage objects can be pushed. Cross section of the pump to create a vacuum behind the membrane.

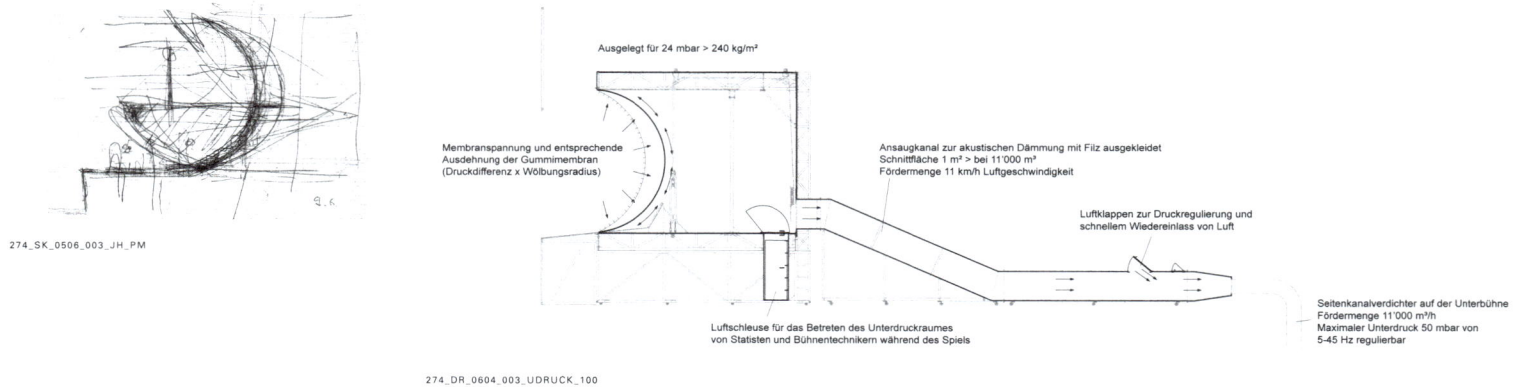

274_SK_0506_003_JH_PM

Ausgelegt für 24 mbar > 240 kg/m²

Membranspannung und entsprechende Ausdehnung der Gummimembran (Druckdifferenz x Wölbungsradius)

Ansaugkanal zur akustischen Dämmung mit Filz ausgekleidet Schnittfläche 1 m² > bei 11'000 m³ Fördermenge 11 km/h Luftgeschwindigkeit

Luftklappen zur Druckregulierung und schnellem Wiedereinlass von Luft

Luftschleuse für das Betreten des Unterdruckraumes von Statisten und Bühnentechnikern während des Spiels

Seitenkanalverdichter auf der Unterbühne Fördermenge 11'000 m³/h Maximaler Unterdruck 50 mbar von 5-45 Hz regulierbar

274_DR_0604_003_UDRUCK_100

Lighting tests with rubber, textiles, and various props.

274_MO_0506_007_GUMMI1

274_MO_0506_001_TEXTIL

274_MO_0506_001_TEXTIL

274_MO_0501_807_WORKSHOP

Testing the vacuum chamber on full-scale models.

274_MU_0512_005

274_MU_0512_007

274_CP_0604_194_CLOSEUP_AKT3_K

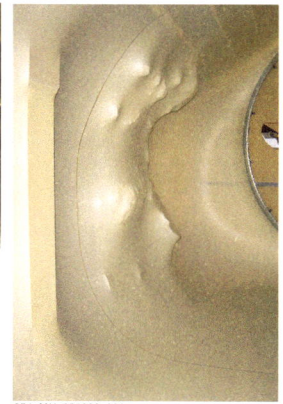

274_MU_051222_001

Working with rubber membrane during rehearsals.

274_CP_0604_013_BACKSTAGE

274_CP_0604_021_BACKSTAGE

274_CO_0604_001_BACKSTAGE

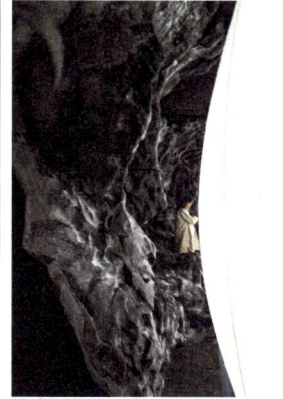

274_EV_0604_705_HDM

274_CP_0604_009_BACKSTAGE

274_CO_0604_012_BACKSTAGE

274_EV_0604_706_HDM

The visual presence of the membrane varies during the performance.

274_CP_0604_702_MR

274_CP_0604_159_CLOSEUP_AKT3_K

274_CP_0604_182_CLOSEUP_AKT3_K

274_CP_0604_739_MR

274_CP_0604_742_MR

274_CP_0604_726_MR

Verdi's Attila *captures a crucial time in the history of Italy when the old world, the world of ancient Rome, had collapsed, releasing energies that fueled a new world rising out of the ruins. Verdi composed his opera at another crucial moment in Italy's history, in the middle of the 19th century, at a time when the country, disunited since antiquity, began to merge into the nation of Italy.*

In designing the stage set, destruction as a prerequisite for renewal was more important to us than a possible historical analogy between the fall of ancient Rome and the rebirth of Italy. Closely aligned with Verdi, we devised two starkly contrasting images: the rubble and ruins of a devastated city in the prologue and an impenetrable forest in the three acts that follow.

Both images rise vertically before the audience like three-dimensional pictures: their depth is implicit but not physically accessible. Since the leeway for the singers and actors is limited, Pierre Audi's production focuses primarily on the music and under-plays the theatrical gesture. Both backdrops could reference any historical era: they are contemporary, like pictures from the daily news or the Internet but they are also reminiscent of times past, like pictures of archaeological digs. Miuccia Prada, who also collaborated on the stage set, created similarly ambivalent costumes that cannot be ascribed to a specific epoch.

The light keeps changing, especially in the forest, which remains in place for two acts until the end of the opera. This creates an ambiguous atmosphere, beautiful, eerie, and inescapable at the same time, like the fairytale world that Hansel and Gretel must have experienced, while simultaneously conjuring up the real world experienced by Roman legionaries in the forests of Germania or by American soldiers in Vietnam.

Herzog & de Meuron, 2010

Source images: catastrophes. Lighting effects in works by Dalí, Tiepolo, and Ruff.

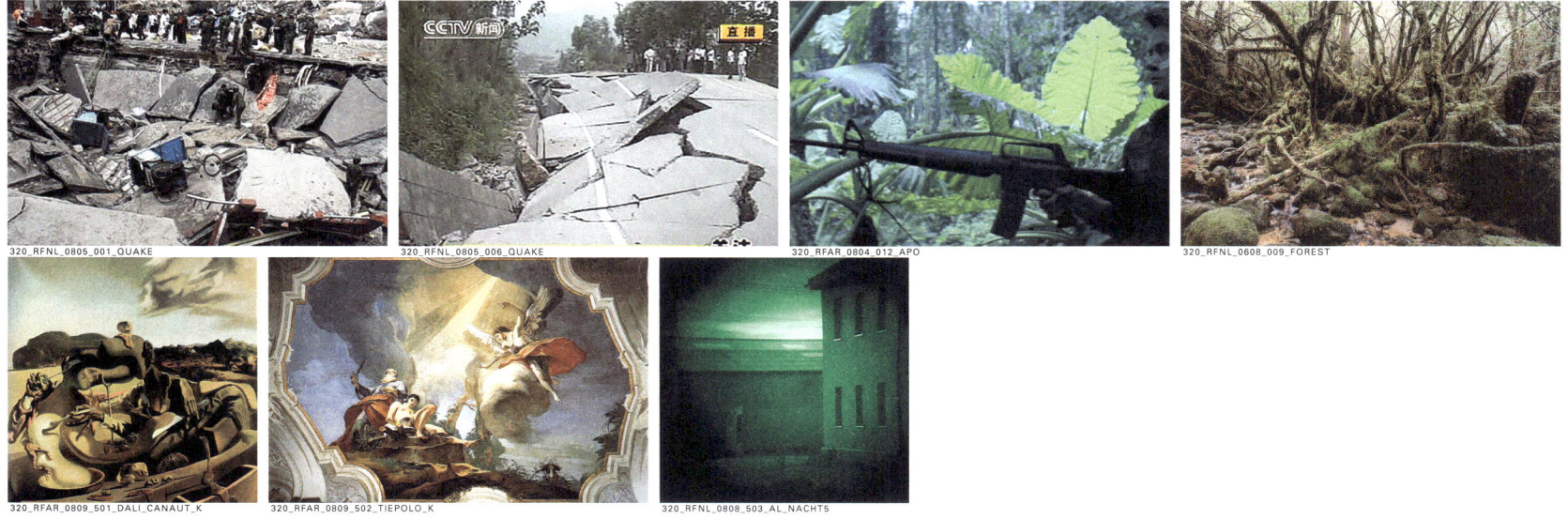

320_RFNL_0805_001_QUAKE

320_RFNL_0805_006_QUAKE

320_RFAR_0804_012_APO

320_RFNL_0608_009_FOREST

320_RFAR_0809_501_DALI_CANAUT_K

320_RFAR_0809_502_TIEPOLO_K

320_RFNL_0808_503_AL_NACHT5

Sketches of the stage set show a backdrop close to the audience and extending the entire height of the stage—like three-dimensional pictures of indefinable depth.

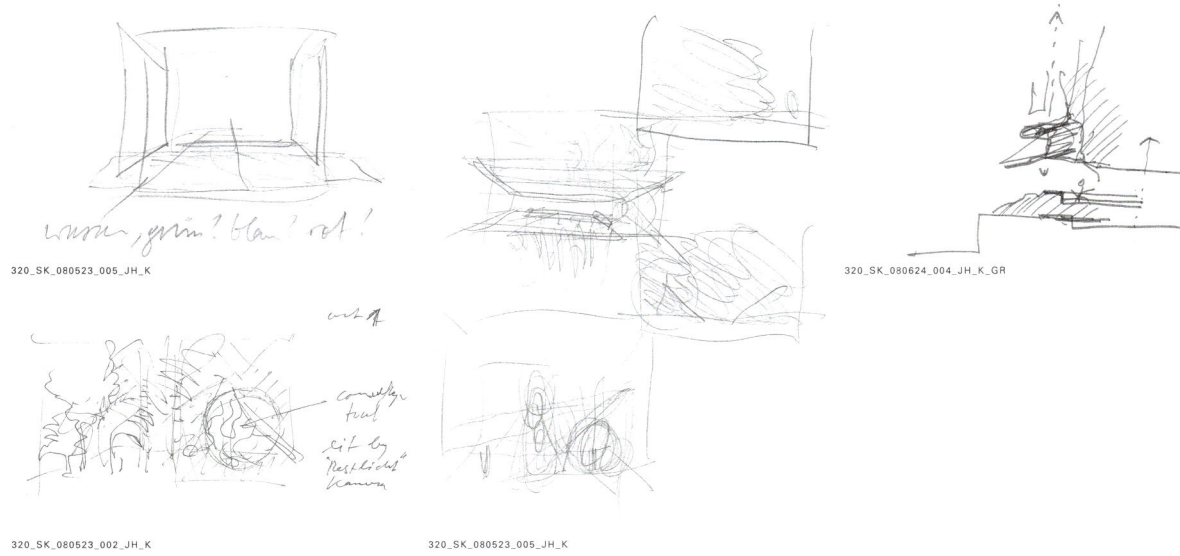

320_SK_080523_005_JH_K

320_SK_080624_004_JH_K_GR

320_SK_080523_002_JH_K

320_SK_080523_005_JH_K

The performance is bathed in deliberately artificial and complex lighting, as in a dreamscape.

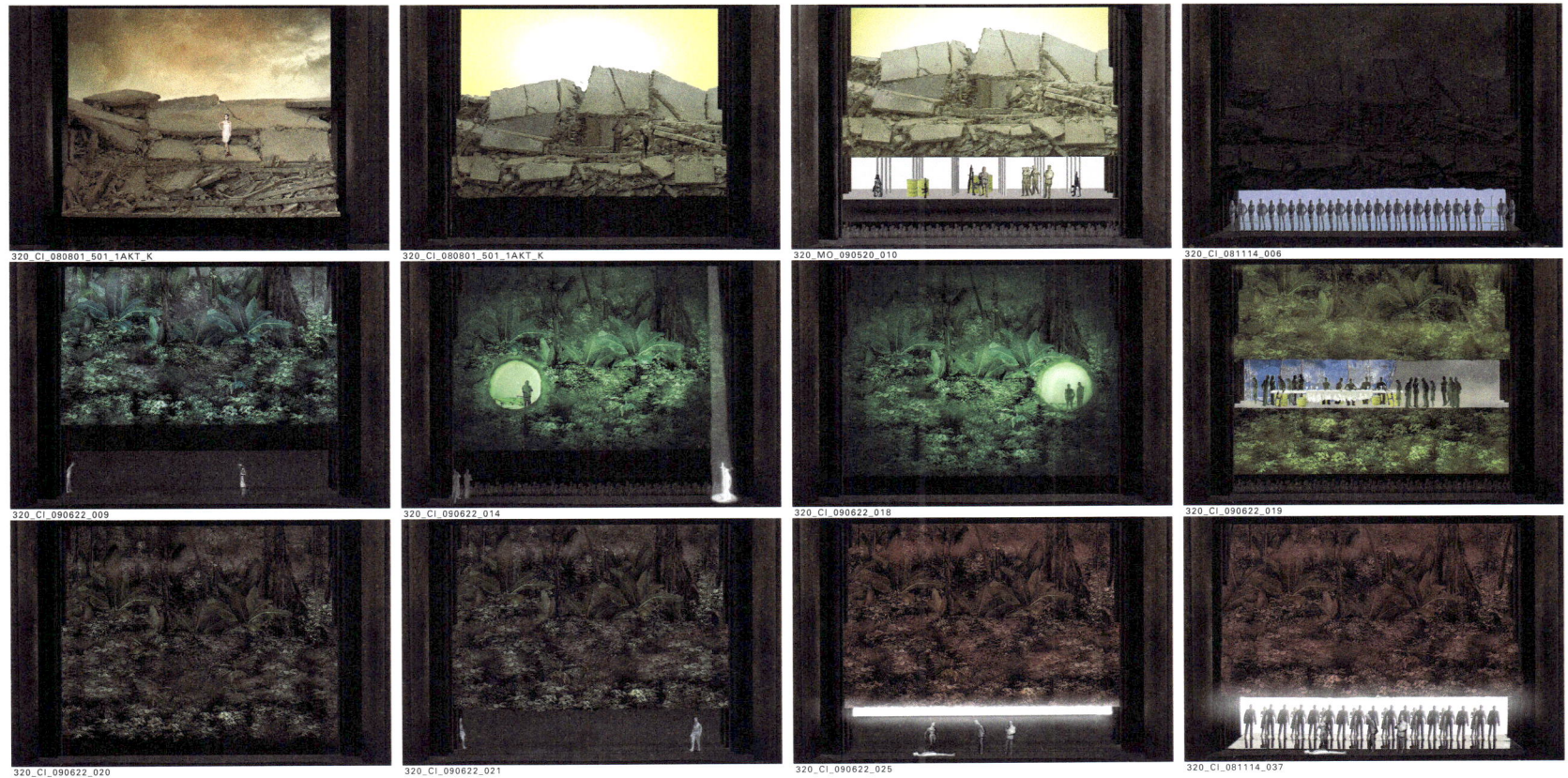

320_CI_080801_501_1AKT_K

320_CI_080801_501_1AKT_K

320_MO_090520_010

320_CI_081114_006

320_CI_090622_009

320_CI_090622_014

320_CI_090622_018

320_CI_090622_019

320_CI_090622_020

320_CI_090622_021

320_CI_090622_025

320_CI_081114_037

Models of the stage set in progress and full-scale mock-ups to test lighting and movement.

320_MU_090423_001

320_MU_090423_007

320_CI_081110_007_AAD

320_MU_0810_16

320_CI_081114_001

320_MO_080622_009

320_MO_080630_013

320_CI_080609_01

320_MU_0810_11

320_MU_0810_17

320_CO_1002_009_REHEARSALS

Impressions of the archaic, romantic atmosphere during the performance of the opera *Attila* at the Metropolitan Opera in New York.

320_CP_090219_701_IB

320_CP_1002_712

320_CP_090219_702_IB

320_CP_090219_711_IB

320_CP_100219_704_IB

Unlike the everyday world, the stage is a symbolic space. Everything that is seen on it, or happens on it, has a wider significance. This is something that the stage set of a theater has in common with the film set in cinema. However, in contrast to the techniques of the moving image, the possibilities for illusion are comparatively limited. The performance itself is always live. Director, cast, and audience willingly operate on both sides of the boundary line between constructing an event and imagining the world it is meant to portray. This is even more true of opera than it is of theater, since the former is highly implausible by definition while at the same time addressing issues that we all know from experience.

This ambiguous relationship between the symbolic and the factual has fascinated Herzog & de Meuron from the very beginning of their architectural journey. It can be seen, for instance, in the way they describe their everyday surroundings in cinematic terms, in the way they ponder how to translate the built environment into an exhibition format for their first exhibition at the Architekturmuseum Basel, or in their use of heightened visual and simulatory processes to combine buildings with images and imaging techniques as they do in their printed facade for the Eberswalde library or in their pixelated walls and cladding for the TEA on Tenerife and the de Young Museum in San Francisco. It can also be found in the way their apparent dissolution of reality contrasts with the otherwise manifest and tactile qualities of the architecture itself. In this regard, the two opera stage sets by Herzog & de Meuron are not simply a continuation of a tradition unbroken since Karl Friedrich Schinkel's 1816 design for Mozart's *Magic Flute*, at the latest. Instead, they have risen to the challenge of staking out an entirely new terrain for the pursuit of a lifelong endeavor that seeks to explore the ambiguous character of the spatial environment.

For the stage set of Richard Wagner's *Tristan and Isolde* at the Staatsoper Unter den Linden in Berlin, directed by Stefan Bachmann and conducted by Daniel Barenboim, they chose a reductive solution that many would see as a combination of minimalist mentality and postminimalist materiality—both Bruce Nauman and Eva Hesse had introduced rubber into contemporary art—together with a touch of the machine aesthetic rooted in Nouveau Réalisme and Op Art. The architects, perceiving opera as song accompanied by orchestral music, place the singers and their vocal development at the fore. The opulence so often associated with Wagner operas does not come into play. Places and spaces are merely hinted at. The audience has to imagine them based on the actions and characteristics of the performers. Wagner's *Tristan and Isolde* is particularly suited to such an approach. The first act in this tale of impossible love is set on a ship; the following acts are set in a castle garden and a cave. It is a tale that melds the mythical world of Arthurian legend with the romanticism of Novalis.

For this, Herzog & de Meuron created a pneumatic space using just one basic structure that could be adapted rapidly to each individual scene. A white rubber membrane forming a segment of a circle was stretched like a half-pipe right across the entire stage, and a pressure chamber was designed to apply negative pressure that could suction the elements positioned behind the membrane in order to illustrate the respective scene. These include the ropes of the rigging in the first act, wall sections, benches, steps, and passageways in the second act, and the rough interior of a cave with recesses in the third act. The inspiration for this approach was drawn from a variety of sources as diverse as Christo's wrapped buildings, the action film *The Terminator*, the Romantic paintings of Caspar David Friedrich, and the geological formations of weathered karst. Moreover, the vast white membrane focuses audience attention on the actors and

projects the sound forward into the auditorium. It is also an ideal way of using light to generate changing atmospheres and times of day. In a certain sense, this stage set is a new slant on the theater aesthetic of Wagner director Adolphe Appia, who, in the early years of the twentieth century, proclaimed space and light to be equal components in stage design. The breathing space that this affords in spatial terms allows architecture to follow the dream of a malleability that even the most advanced computer programs cannot achieve. And indeed, in the Berlin performance, the love between Tristan and Isolde remains a dream. Though the actors on the stage may be real, they appear like cinemascope images projected onto a screen. The entire plot unfolds within a setting so tactile that it resembles the moment of awakening from a dream, when the spatial and the visual converge, and the metaphor of pictorial space becomes tangible.

The fundamental approach of abstract concretion, as evidenced in the Berlin stage set, can also be found, in somewhat altered visual form, in a very different nineteenth-century opera: Giuseppe Verdi's 1846 work *Attila*, directed by Pierre Audi, with Riccardo Muti conducting for the first time at the New York Metropolitan Opera. Herzog & de Meuron collaborated here with fashion designer Miuccia Prada, whose flagship Prada store they created in Tokyo's Aoyama district. The production team turned this opera about the fifth-century conquest and sack of Rome by Attila, king of the Huns, and its analogies with the nineteenth-century Risorgimento that created modern Italy, into a timeless piece about destruction and new beginnings. Neither the great drama of history nor the analogies with contemporary events were visible. The stage set and the costumes avoided all concrete reference to specific epochs, events, nationalities, religions, or ethnicities.

As with *Tristan and Isolde* in Berlin, the huge stage at the Met was reduced to little more than the narrow confines of the proscenium and defined primarily by visual abstraction. In New York, however, this did not take the form of a completely transformable pneumatic chamber with minimalist undertones. Instead, the set design was based on two starkly contrasting and strongly evocative images that created a similarly ambiguous association with cinema as the Berlin design. For the prolog, they filled the stage with a gigantic pile of rubble, not only representing the destruction wrought by the king of the Huns in his conquest of Rome, but just as easily associated with Ground Zero or recent earthquakes. As in Berlin, albeit in a very different way, this was nonarchitecture capturing a moment of transition and unpredictability. The soloists had little room to move among the ruins. The following three acts of the opera, which are set in a forest near Attila's field camp or close to Rome, were framed by a wall covered in a jungle-like growth, reminiscent of such projects as the CaixaForum in Madrid and more like a relievo image than an actual space. For the chorus, the stage flats could be raised to create an empty space of varying height that allowed considerable scope for imaginative lighting. And indeed, the lighting itself did conjure the kind of atmospheric ambiguity that haunts the enchanted forests of fairy tales. The costumes were a blend of casual sportswear and uniform epaulettes in which the predominant materials, leather and fur, were enhanced by minimal accessories such as light diodes blinking on a helmet, shoulder strap, or diadem, underlining the multifaceted atmosphere of timelessness.

In both cases, the focus was firmly on the vocal and musical performance, with the stage design itself providing imagery rather than spatial definition. In doing so, they cultivated an artifice that brought opera into the realms of media forms such as installation or performance.

The client had lived in a castle in northern Germany for many years and now wanted to move farther south for a complete change of landscape in entirely different architectural surroundings. He had acquired a lakeside property near Munich with an old building on it.

The home for himself and his wife required a large library for the many books and rarities on the arts and sciences that he had collected with great passion from all over the world. In addition, as a painter, he needed a studio and, as a collector of sculptures, specially appointed rooms that would be almost like a museum.

The castle in northern Germany had accommodated other collections in countless spacious halls, including historic furniture and objects, which were then sold since there would be no room for them in the new location. The house at the lake would concentrate on the most important parts of the collection, and these were to be presented with great care. This is a concern that has been of great interest to us for years, for instance, while planning the de Young Museum in San Francisco.

We were fascinated by the idea of designing a home for all of these "facets" of living, but on our first visit we realized that the array of uses and the interests of the painter and his wife could not be assembled under a single roof. More than one building would be required, and we planned to lay them out on the property like a farmstead with barns and outbuildings.

Our initial design showed a shape somewhat like a leaf: a complex with several wings and a room for the library in the middle. Five wings would extend from the middle into the open space of the garden with its stand of old trees. This early version of the house was motivated by the idea of giving a distinct shape to each of the functions of living throughout the day—a wing for the bedrooms, for bathing, for living, for the collection, and for the library—echoing the conglomerative ground plan of the castle.

However, life at the lake was to be organized differently; everything would be closer together and overlapping under a shared roof. Only the library would remain in the middle, becoming the actual center of the home. From there hallways open up to other areas of the house. The interior is not simply a loft, as one might assume from outside; it contains separate "clumps of space," which lend rhythm to the whole and organize it, as strikingly demonstrated by the sculptural effect of the staircase. The fittings of the home are more sophisticated while the materials of the buildings on the property are homogeneous: wooden boards, corrugated Eternit and glass.

The rustic simplicity of the studio is related to the Parrish Museum, with its idea of additive "artists' studios," on which we also started working in the summer of 2006.

Herzog & de Meuron, 2015

First impressions of the lake, the property, and the sheds.

276_SI_0507_159

276_SI_0506_039

276_SI_0506_059

Preliminary studies for the home propose a leaf-shaped structure around a central hall with each function accommodated in a single leaf.

276_MO_0507_052

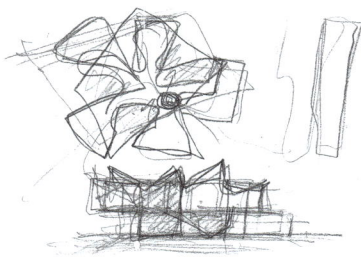

276_SK_0506_001

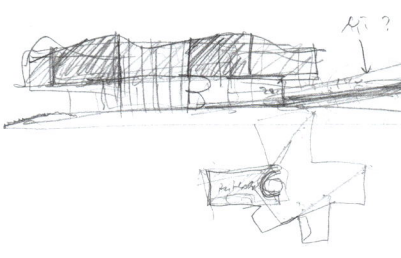

276_SK_0506_004

276_MO_0506_165

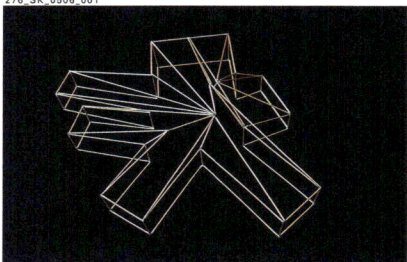

276_MO_0508_118

276_MO_0508_109

276_MO_0508_119

As the design develops, the functions are aligned in a linear sequence around the central two-story library.

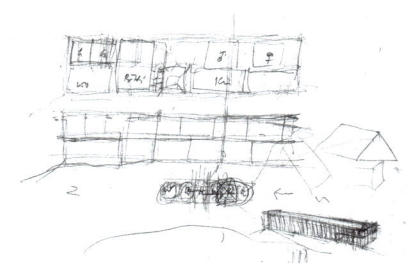

276_SK_0508_008_JH

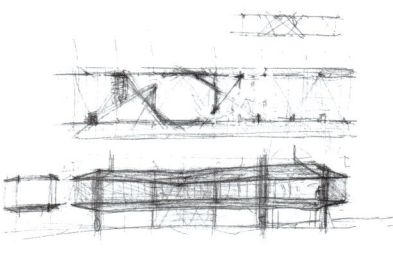

276_SK_0512_001_PdM

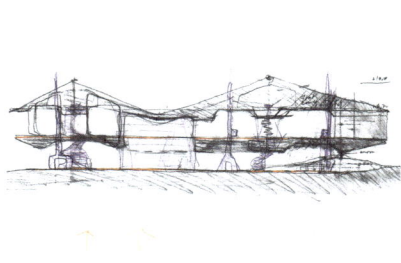

276_SK_0511_017_PdM

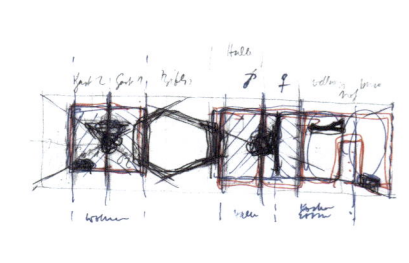

276_SK_0511_023_PdM

276_MO_0509_175

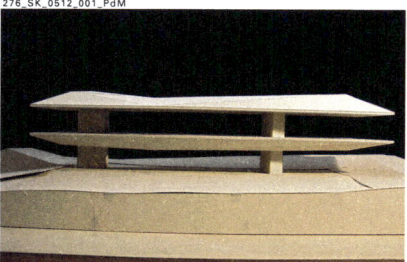

276_MO_0601_015

276_MO_0509_148

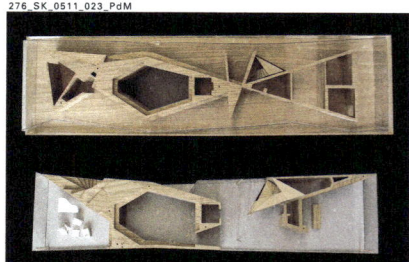

276_MO_0602_035

Studies for the load-bearing structure of the second floor and the roof.

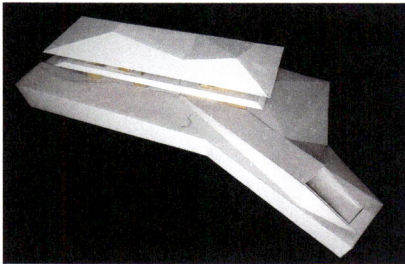

276_MO_0603_029

276_MO_0605_007

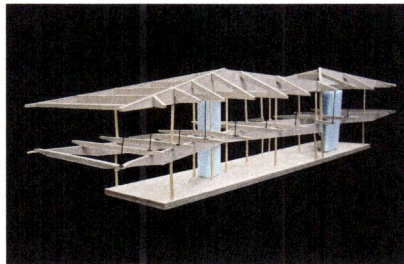

276_MO_0604_085

276_CI_0609_012

The central feature of the design is the hexagonal library.

276_EV_0702_009

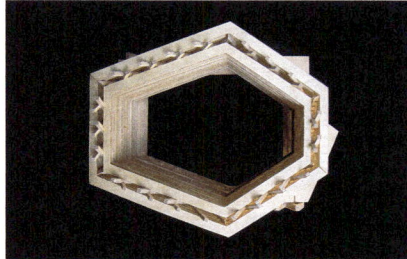

276_EV_0703_008_JH-PDM-RH_SITZUNG

276_MO_0602_040

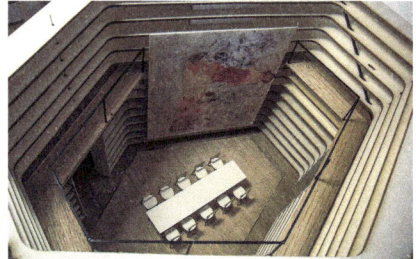

276_MO_0511_153

276_MO_0703_113

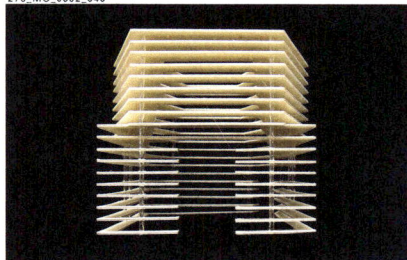

276_MO_0703_001

At an earlier stage, the stairs are cut out of a solid block, reminiscent of the architects' Jinhua sculpture.

276_MO_0510_006

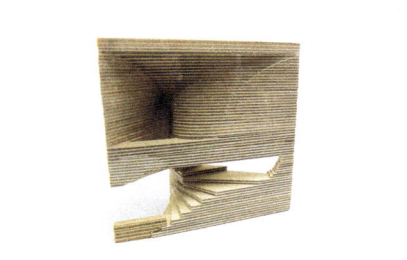

276_MO_0603_141

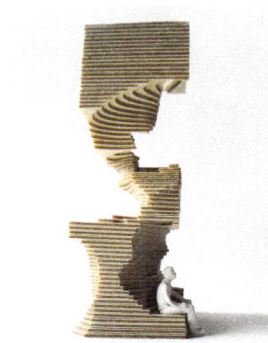

276_MO_0511_064

276_MO_0511_063

276_MO_0604_028

276_MO_0604_138

The two built staircases create a flowing space of their own that fills the triangular spaces remaining within the load-bearing structure.

276_MO_0701_099

276_MO_0610_127

276_CP_0811_714_RH

276_CP_0804_717_RH

276_CP_0811_744_RH

Studies for the print workshop and studio with light from the north.

276_MO_0605_002

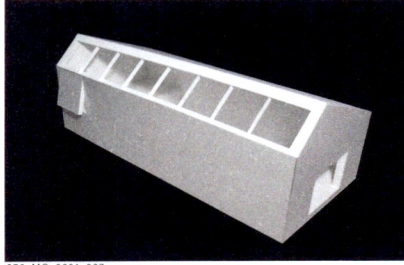
276_MO_0601_067

276_MO_0601_069

Full-scale tests in mineral-based materials and steel for the facade, and construction of the load-bearing structure with maximum use of wood.

276_CI_0606_006

276_MU_0605_009

276_CI_0711_012_SCREENSHOT

276_CO_0610_047

276_CO_0707_050

276_CO_0708_019

276_MO_0706_002

Home with glazed ground floor, patios and library, print shop and studio.

276_CP_0806_714_RH

276_CP_0806_701_RH

276_CP_0811_733_RH

276_CP_0804_742_RH

276_CP_0804_734_RH

276_CP_0806_705_RH

276_CP_0811_706_RH

276_CP_0811_721_RH

276_CP_0811_732_RH

276_CP_0804_741_RH

276_CP_0806_703_RH

276_CP_0806_718_RH

276_CP_0811_742_RH

276_CP_0811_741_RH

For a large site by a lake that was to be developed to create premises for a varied and diverse program, Herzog & de Meuron proposed a group of several buildings in the manner of a farmstead. The aim was to create a distinctive identity based on the rural character of the place with its open meadows, romantic little grove of trees, clusters of bushes, and a row of oaks. To this end, the individual buildings would be designed and arranged in a way that would form obvious links between them while at the same time providing a variety of outdoor spaces reflecting the traditional agricultural vernacular.

The focal point of the group is the residence itself, replacing an existing dwelling. In their initial design, the architects proposed a glass cube housing the kitchen, living area and library, with a star-shaped upper level in which the bedrooms, two guest rooms, office, and library extension fan out like five fingers. The library was to form the core of the house, extending over two levels. This basic concept of dividing the whole into variously public areas and a centrally positioned library was then retained in an otherwise radically reworked design that acknowledged the need for a clearer layout, and more shelter from outside gazes.

In the new design, a block runs from north to south through the row of oaks and, like the early Plywood House in Bottmingen near Basel, it has a sharp kink to protect an old tree root. Instead of simply aligning a row of rooms in the interior and opening it up with a southwest facing veranda, the ground floor is left as a more or less open space separated from the exterior only by a glass skin. Hovering above that, the upper level, with its own wraparound veranda, is cantilevered to the east and south so that its volume juts far out over the terrace below, sheltering it from the elements. The upper-level veranda can be closed off by automatically folding wooden shutters that ensure privacy while still affording views across the lake. Herzog & de Meuron had already deployed the concept of a continuous veranda as facade in their earlier apartment building along a dividing wall on Hebelstrasse in Basel. The two residential floors are covered by a pitched roof of corrugated fiber cement. The simple basic form of the block is interrupted by the complex geometry of a wooden paravent superimposed on a glass pavilion; the lightweight pitched roof conceals a complex load-bearing structure.

This, in turn, defines the inner structure of the building: the roof beams form two huge X shapes, allowing the ground floor to be more or less open, with the few required supports placed far into the interior. This also creates the basis for a triangulation of the spatial structure, dividing the building into two areas. The more public spaces incorporating a television room and guest rooms on the upper level are set to the northwest, while the kitchen and the family bedrooms are southwest-facing. Two stairways incorporated into the loadbearing structure provide separate, independent access to each zone. These are compressed or stretched into the sharply angled triangular structure, like expressive sculptures emphasizing the vertical movement.

The stairs give access to the library. This two-story room open to the roof appears at first sight as a porous shell of stacked shelves full of books. However, its representative character is then revealed by its spatial complexity: the floor plan is based on the double-X of the roof beams, but the rhomboid shape this creates is blunted at the tips to form a flattened, irregular hexagon. The room tapers upward and its sides are enclosed by a three-layered shell. Doorways turn it into a passageway that links both sides of the house. The central shelving area forms an inner space to walk around and reach books from the double-sided shelf behind. Steps lead up to a mezzanine around the inner space, accessing the higher-level shelves. The uppermost shelving area takes the form of a balustrade with additional floor space, separating the library from the surrounding bedrooms and guest rooms. Fireplace and television are integrated into the narrow end walls. A large painting is displayed on one of the wider walls. Even before walking in, a distinct indentation on the entrance facade lets an indication shimmer through that this room is the heart of the home.

The house is protectively surrounded by three further new buildings. On the eastern boundary of the site, a building for a sculpture collection stands adjacent to a previously existing shed. Inside, the space can be partitioned freely as required, while externally it provides protection from the gaze of neighbors higher up the slope or from the other two adjoining structures: a printing workshop continuing in the same line and a studio set at an oblique angle to the southwest. It is embedded into the hillside in a way that delineates between the woodland and the group of buildings in the southern part of the site and, as the largest structure, sets a distinctive landmark. The hillside topography allows for some spatial surprises: entering the studio from the plaza, one finds oneself on a mezzanine above a room that is some ten meters high. To the north, a ribbon of skylights in the pitched roof lets in daylight, while on the opposite side, just below the gable, there is a broad cluster of fluorescent tubes running in the direction of the eaves. At the end of the hall, a wide window offers panoramic views of the meadows and the lakeside woodland. Beneath the mezzanine, connecting rooms lead to the printing workshop, which forms a cohesive volume together with the studio on the lower level.

Externally, the three functional buildings are designed as a unit distinct from the house itself, with an architectural vocabulary redolent of a traditional barn: facade and roof are clad in corrugated fiber concrete, while the pitched roofs extend beyond the walls far enough to provide covered outside spaces; the studio's indented courtyard wall allows still more such space. The house echoes this vocabulary with a roof in the same material, reminiscent of a folded cardboard box set on top of the upper level, and deep overhangs forming veranda areas.

With its stairways, central library space, rooftop, and floating upper level and with its echoes of the rural vernacular of agricultural structures, this project combines a number of elements that have long been a hallmark of Herzog & de Meuron. The fascination of the expressive in the midst of such reductivist objectivity was already evident in their design for the Museum Küppersmühle in Duisburg, where it is also the stairway that adds this particular touch. Ever since, stairways in many variations have bored their way through projects whose rooms are at times startlingly pared-down and flexible. The architects combine two seemingly contradictory modernist approaches. Not as opposites, but as two contrasting ways of handling space, which, when experienced, actually complement one another. Similarly, the barn-like roof can be found in the implemented second variation of the Parrish Museum, which—also inspired by the regional vernacular—is effectively a barn for art. Herzog & de Meuron have repeatedly deployed an architectural element as an urban fulcrum point from their Kunsthaus in Aarau to their TEA in Santa Cruz de Tenerife. In this instance, the same effect is achieved by the central library space within a house. Separating the interior and the exterior by nothing but a glass shell is a detail to be found even in the very first design for the Kramlich House in California's Napa Valley, as is the load-bearing structure of a roof using triangular forms. The House above a Lake project is one that evokes the very questions Herzog & de Meuron keep on asking.

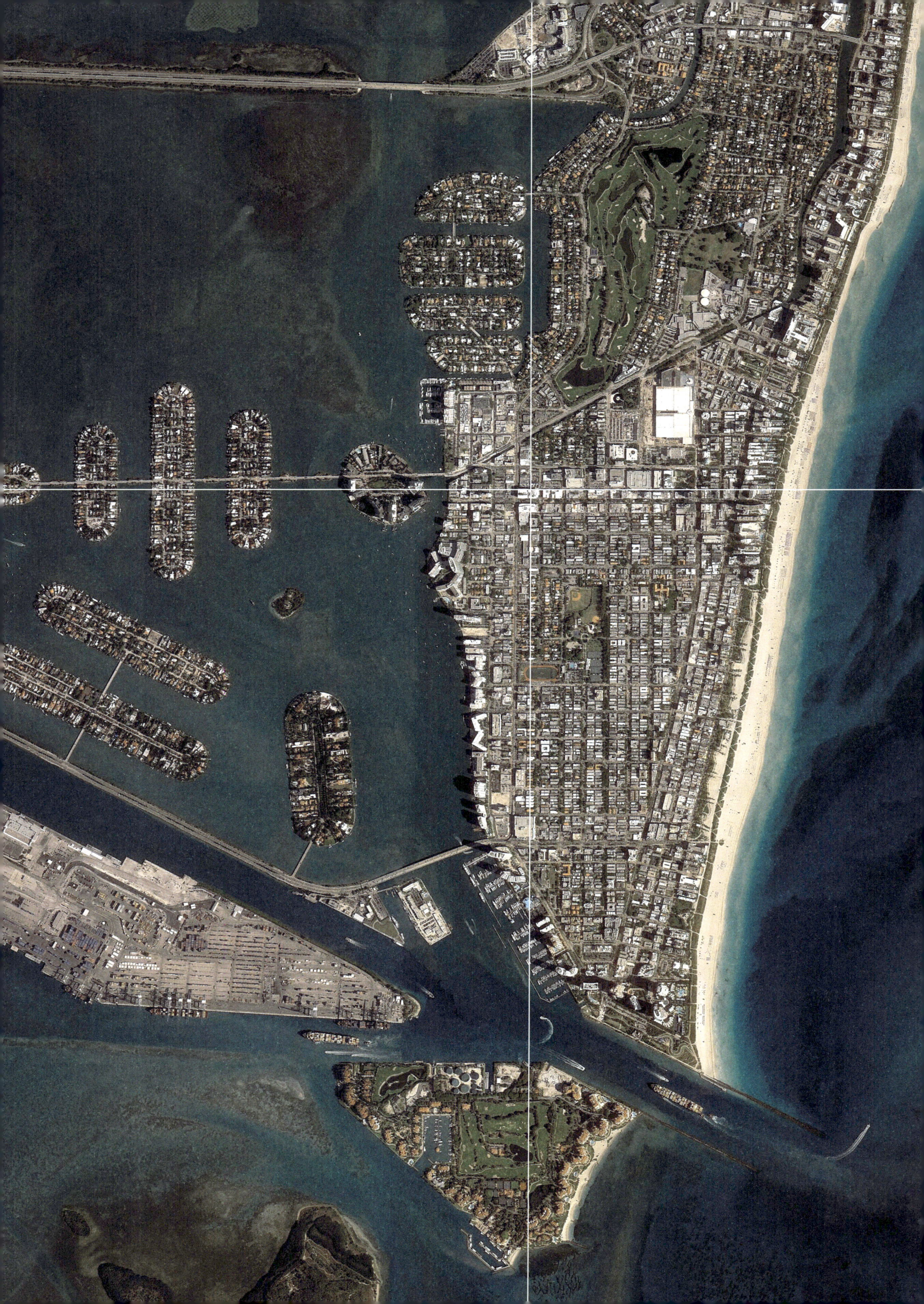

Cities change. Their transformation is relentless. Buildings and neighborhoods are repurposed, torn down, rebuilt, and occasionally wiped off the map altogether. When we first started working on 1111 Lincoln Road, while still doing research to collect relevant materials, we came across a picture of a dilapidated theater from Detroit's heyday in the 1920s; it was then being used as a garage: a compelling and expressive picture on the subject matter of our project.

We said to ourselves, if a theater can turn into a garage, why can't a garage turn into a theater, an urban theater for a variety of urban uses. Parties, dance performances, fashion shows, yoga, gastronomy, and accommodation could all be connected by a ramp, so that parking a car would become a very special experience.

That is what we wanted our project to achieve and that meant applying for variances of the building code, such as a modification of the specified building height. The client was always on hand when it came to negotiating with the authorities in Miami to acquire special permits for this entirely novel idea. There were some memorable moments in the course of these negotiations, as when the client fought for permission to make the building taller to match the height of the neighboring Sun Trust Bank, which we wanted to integrate as part of our project. He was prepared to fight for more height even though that didn't mean increasing the gross floor space. In other words, he was committing to much more expansive and therefore more expensive architecture without a corresponding increase in profits. Obviously, no one knew at the time that the project would meet with such success in the media. As an investor, he was willing to take the risk. He could also have built something more conventional, based on safe, time-tested market analysis. Our client's embrace of risk was, no doubt, an expression of his particular personality but it certainly also mirrored the mood of the times. Projects financed by private investors are a particularly good measure of the current zeitgeist, specifically whether a conservative, exclusively profit-oriented, speculative attitude prevails or whether it is a time of experiment and openness, which also affects the public life of a city.

An important requisite for the architectural attitude that we wanted 1111 Lincoln Road to communicate was inspired by several stays in Miami long before we were commissioned to do the project. We were so impressed by the natural beauty, the climate, and the vegetation and, at the same time, disappointed by the local architecture, which, though decorative and colorful, did not take advantage of the natural surroundings. The famous buildings in the Art Deco District, lined up side-by-side and decorated in pretty colors, are nothing but hermetic, air-conditioned shoeboxes with no relation whatsoever to the outside world, to the climate and the vegetation. Until well into the 1990s, there were practically no restaurants with a terrace where one might have eaten outside in the evening.

The arrival of Art Basel in 2002 has made an enduring impact on the city. Not only has art become more visible in the cityscape, the city itself has become generally more cosmopolitan. Miami is more European today and, at the same time, the South American influence is more evident than ever before in the city's urban culture. The garage on Lincoln Road illustrates this change. We wanted the building to be playful and theatrical, not by resorting to decoration but by focusing on radical simplicity. Structure, space, and sculptural expression form a unified whole. Everything is structure, structure that also generates spaces and is integral to the sculptural shape of the building: utterly naked architecture.

Instead of superimposing vertical columns, one on top of the other, we designed trapezoidal supports, like a house of cards that establishes a fragile balance. The floor slabs, cantilevered to varying degrees, reinforce the impression that every element is an indispensable constituent of the overall balance. Our building is an expression of balance and not of authoritative assertion like the neighboring Sun Trust building of the 1970s, with which the naked skeleton of the garage is now in dialogue: you may or may not like the somewhat brutalist architecture of the former bank, but the juxtaposition of the two types of architecture emphasizes their respective and distinctive sculptural qualities.

Variations in the shape of the wall panels are defined by the varied scenarios for the movement of cars and the arrangement of parking spaces. However, the architecture of the concrete skeleton has not been optimized to accommodate a maximum number of parking spaces; it is more like a vertical, urban landscape with small "leftovers": the unused spaces under stairs and ramps.

Precisely these places, the ones whose function is not clearly predetermined, proved to make a vital contribution to the quality of spending time in the building; they are places of the kind one might come across somewhere outdoors, for instance, by a boulder or under a tree. The garden in the penthouse underscores this impression. A densely planted carpet of bushes, trees, and grass merges with the concrete skeleton of the building, not only alluding to the subtropical environment that once dominated what is now a city, but also indicating how quickly nature could someday regain possession of the place.

Herzog & de Meuron, 2016

Subtropical flora is cleared on Lincoln Road in the course of developing Miami Beach.

279_SI_0602_501_1895

279_SI_0602_502_1927

279_SI_0905_503_1962

279_SI_0511_507_HDM

279_SI_0511_716_HDM

279_SI_0905_509_LINC-ALT_RD

Sketches and illustrations for mixed use of the garage.

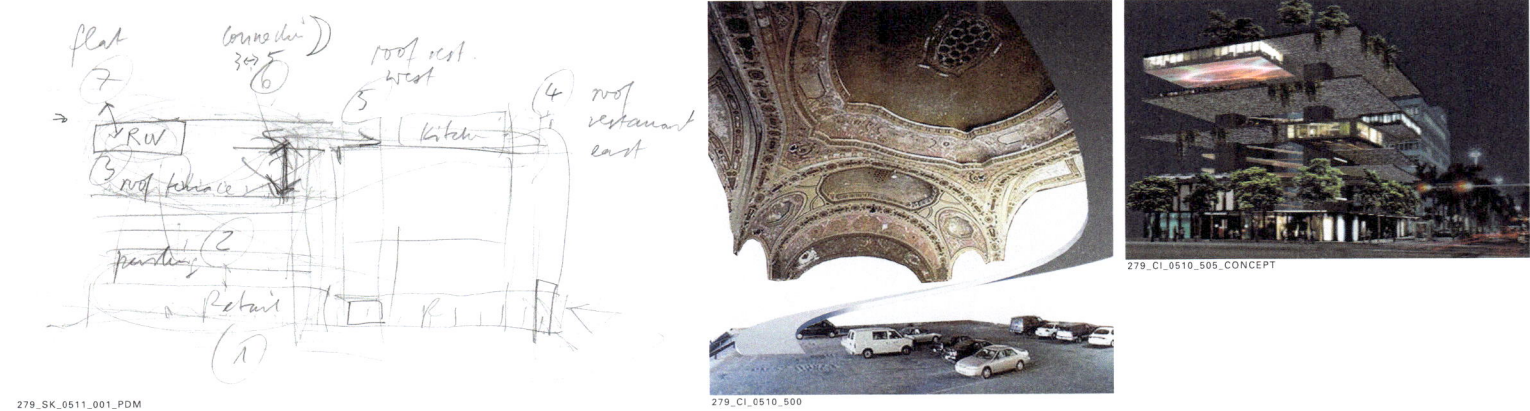

279_SK_0511_001_PDM

279_CI_0510_500

279_CI_0510_505_CONCEPT

Urban strategies to connect the pedestrian zone on Lincoln Road with the surroundings.

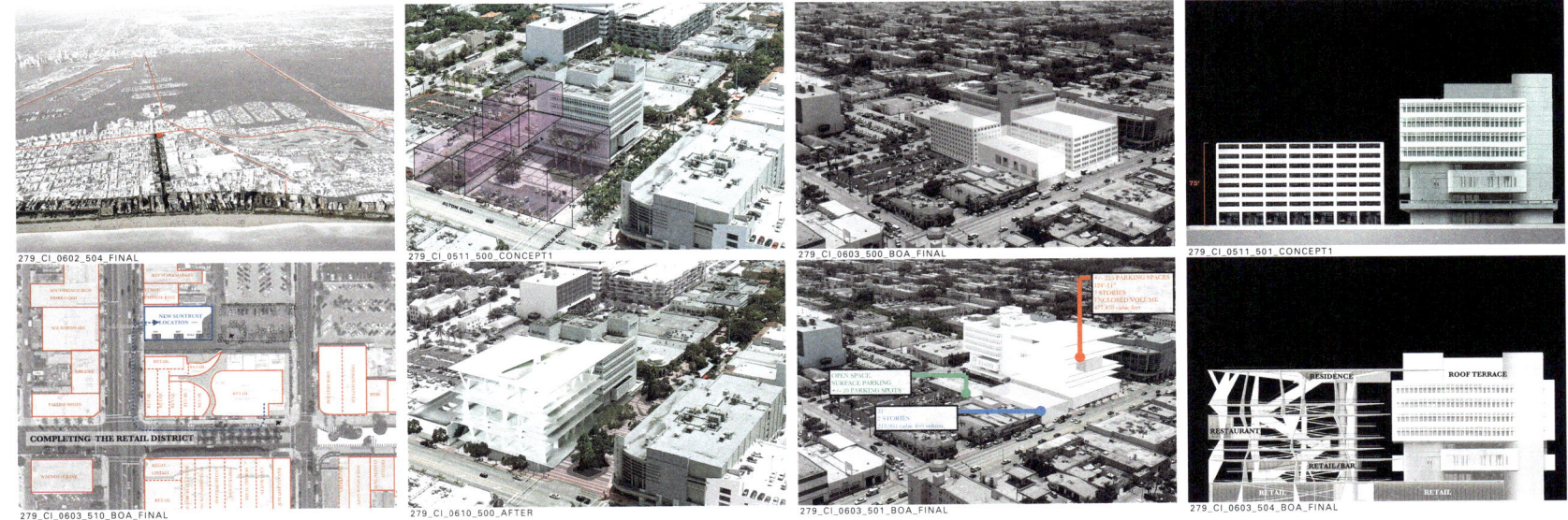

279_CI_0602_504_FINAL

279_CI_0511_500_CONCEPT1

279_CI_0603_500_BOA_FINAL

279_CI_0511_501_CONCEPT1

279_CI_0603_510_BOA_FINAL

279_CI_0610_500_AFTER

279_CI_0603_501_BOA_FINAL

279_CI_0603_504_BOA_FINAL

Relationship between program and structure.

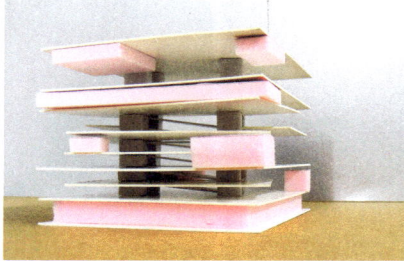

279_MO_0510_019

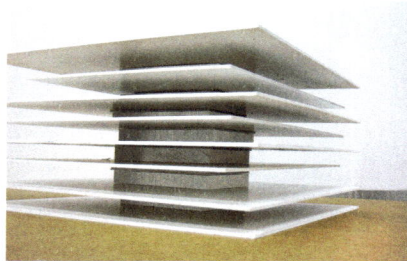

279_MO_0511_003_HEIGHT_K

279_MO_0602_019_007-MOA

279_MO_0602_022_008-MOA

279_MO_0602_020_007-MOB

279_MO_0602_071_024-MOB

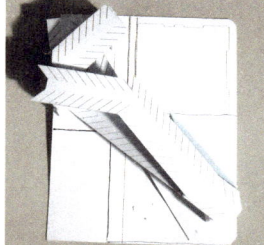

279_MO_0602_026_009-MOB

279_MO_0602_014_005-MOB

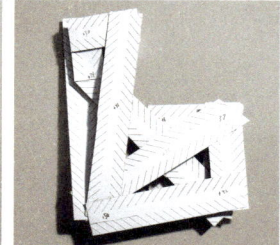

279_MO_0602_056_019-MOB

Studies for the load-bearing structure of the variously
cantilevered decks.

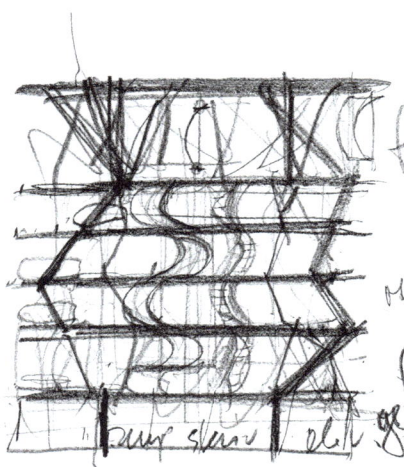

279_SK_0603_008_K

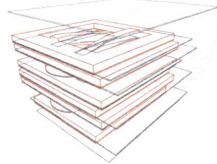

279_CI_0601_502_DIAGRAM

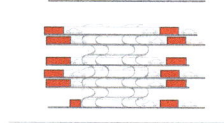

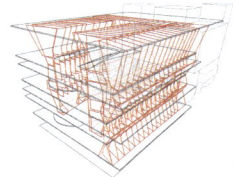

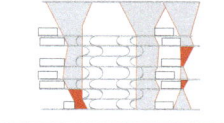

279_SK_0602_001_PDM

279_CI_0000_501_ALTON1_K

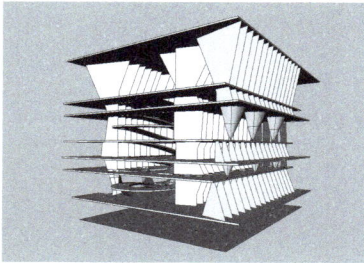

279_CI_0601_511_DIAGRAM

Testing the vertical supports.

279_MO_0000_502_INTERIOR_A_K

279_CI_0000_507_K

279_CI_0000_509_K

279_CI_0000_508_K

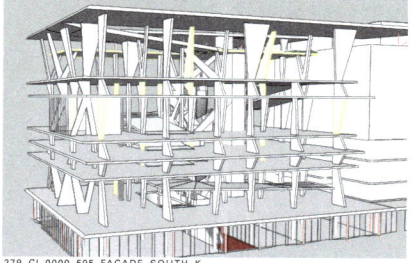

279_CI_0000_505_FACADE_SOUTH_K

279_EV_0605_018

279_MO_0609_005

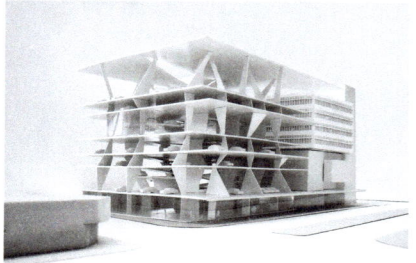

279_MO_0512_500_PERSP

44

A new plaza in front of the garage echoes the shaded
open-air architecture of the pedestrian zone.

279_CI_0704_500_SCHEM_ELEV

Full-scale tests of vertical supports and construction
of various forms.

279_MU_0810_035_ADD-CS

279_CO_0901_025

279_CO_0901_024

279_CO_0901_036

The stairs designed as a vertical pilgrimage for pedestrians.

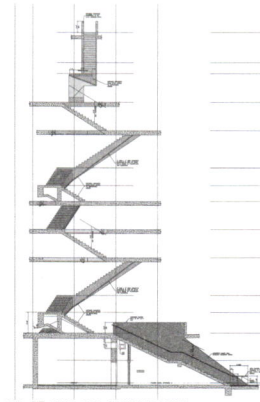

279_DT_0909_501_CENTRALSTAIR

279_CO_0909_085

279_CO_091129_723_IB_4324_H

279_CO_091129_718_IB_4213_U

Penthouse as a modernistic residence on top of the garage
and apartments in the lower building next door.

279_MO_0702_004

279_CP_1203_740_EO_40_DD_S

279_CP_1203_777_EO_14_S

279_CP_1203_778_EO_16_S

279_CO_0911_807_EO

279_CP_100904_004_ROHA_K

279_CO_1004_954_IB_6568_U

279_CO_1004_979_IB_6647_U

The open garage with views and multifunctional decks
of varying height.

279_CP_1004_612_IB

279_CP_110203_720_HC

279_CO_1004_808_IB_6235

279_CP_110203_725_HC

279_CO_1004_855_IB_6371

279_CP_1104_752_DM_9131

279_CP_1104_743_DM_1191

279_CO_0911_819_EO

279_CP_1004_759_IB

279_CO_091206_881_IB_4318

A popular venue for various events.

279_CO_091206_840_IB_4228

279_CO_091206_1013-14_IB

279_EV_1102_503

279_EV_1309_2683

A distinctive architectural sculpture as a landmark that
revitalizes a neglected neighborhood.

279_CP_110111_701_JW

279_CP_110203_709_HC

279_CP_1104_716_DM_0546

279_CO_110212_701_IB_M_7318

279_CO_1004_IB_703_MCHAP-PRI

279_CP_110203_730_HC

279_CO_091206_726_IB_3677

Parking garages in American inner cities are low-investment, low-maintenance money makers. So when Herzog & de Meuron were asked to design such a building in the center of Miami Beach, they redefined the genre. Instead of the usual ugly box for parking vehicles, they created an urban design instrument that energizes its surroundings. Lincoln Road Mall is one of the earliest, and still rare, pedestrian streets in the USA. Set on the edge of the historic Art Deco District around Ocean Drive in South Beach, its boutiques and restaurants, its pavilions in the style of South American modernism, its theaters and movie theaters, lend the area a Southern flair that invites tourists and hotel guests to stroll and linger outdoors all year round in the subtropical climate. At the time when Herzog & de Meuron were first approached, the mall was a place that ended abruptly within an ill-defined urban situation at the Alton Road intersection earmarked for the planned garage. The four plots that the client envisaged developing were occupied by two buildings and by two empty spaces: the bulky volume of the 1968 Sun Trust Bank building closed off from its neighbors, the parking lot behind it, bounding the Alton Road intersection, with its little no-man's-land patch of green, and the slender building next to it on Alton Road, forlorn and detached, set against the bank building to bracket a residual space that was also used as a parking lot.

Herzog & de Meuron shook up this entire situation, transforming the nondescript intersection into a distinctive landmark: the pedestrian mall of Lincoln Road was extended as far as Alton Road and the parking garage was constructed to a height that overshadows the surrounding buildings and makes it a counterpart echoing the tower on Washington Avenue at the other end of the mall's pedestrian zone. The small building was demolished, and the new design constructed further forward toward the street, with a connecting pathway from the street into the building, based on the idea of strolling in a warm climate.

A plaza has been created at the end of Lincoln Road, planted with trees salvaged from demolition sites within a hundred-kilometer radius. The resulting ambience, brightened by light-reflecting water basins, evokes the nearby Everglades and the lush vegetation of South Florida. Concrete benches encourage people to spend time in this space. A pavilion by Dan Graham echoes the architectural opulence of the Art Deco District.

The same sense of openness defines the parking garage, which the architects have designed as a mixed-use building. Because the city authorities approved plans for the structure to be taller than normal in the local area on condition of maintaining a certain maximum floor area, the ceiling heights of the seven floors can vary between the usual three meters and as much as nine meters. There are slender steel cables, barely visible from below, in place of the conventional white boundary markers. The ramps are interwoven in a way that guides traffic through the building, saving space and—like the open pedestrian stairs—resembling a meandering processional path. The shops on the ground floor are complemented by another on the fifth floor. The open parking decks with their breathtaking views of the city and the bay form a stunning public loggia that is used as a venue for photo shoots, film shoots, concerts and parties.

The nakedness of the pared-down structure makes the architecture of the building appear sculptural, much like the Olympic Stadium in Beijing. Having toyed initially with the idea of using steel, the architects eventually chose concrete, not only corresponding to the local vernacular, but also paying homage to Latin American modernism. For all its Nordic sharpness and angularity, the building has an almost musical rhythm. The decks taper toward the edges, giving a beveled finish like a perfectly hemmed garment. The fact that the decks also jut out onto Lincoln Road to varying degrees lends a certain softness to the overall facade. Inside, they lie like bookshelves on their supports although they are actually suspended. The columns themselves take the form of diagonally slanted individual supports or V-shaped buttresses, depending on their respective position and load-bearing capacity, which adds a further dynamism to the cantilevered slabs. The cables of the safety railings installed to protect people at the edges of the decks are drawn directly through the concrete supports, the sprinklers integrated into the load-bearing structure and the bumpers in front of the parking spots have been left in their three test colors. The use of uplighting throughout generates a softer, more genial environment.

On the whole, the 1111 Lincoln Road project is one of those designs that epitomize Herzog & de Meuron's ability to conquer the traditions of modernism with a light touch. Although they dropped their initially envisaged white in favor of exquisitely finished exposed concrete, the steel-cable railings still conjure images of Le Corbusier's railings and his vision of an ocean liner—aptly enough given the proximity of Miami Beach. The building can also be seen as a nod to Frank Lloyd Wright's spiral for the Solomon R. Guggenheim Museum in New York: whereas Wright adapted the parking garage ramp for the interior of a museum, Herzog & de Meuron have transformed the parking garage with its spiral ramp into a multipurpose space not only for cars, but also for art, a place to be seen, and to take in the urban vistas.

The airy openness of the parking garage also responds to the existing bank building. This bunker-like structure was built in 1968, at a time when the Miami area was infamous for its drug trade and race riots. The architects have retained the bank's brutalist style as an architectural document of its time, while transforming it for more openly accessible, contemporary use. Some of the floorplates of the parking garage jut into the closed structure, creating a physical connection between the buildings. The ground floor has a glazed, kinked storefront with commercial appeal. The rooftop restaurant with its spectacular views is accessed by an open stairway in one of the corner towers of the existing building.

The bank itself has been relocated to the new, unassuming building on Alton Road adjacent to the parking garage. Here, too, the mixed-use principle is applied: four identically proportioned apartments have been created as independent residences opening onto two landscaped inner courtyards.

The blend of urban and coastal landscape is a point of reference in its own right where the public building becomes a private space. On the seventh floor of the parking garage, the owner of the building has a penthouse that is barely discernible from below. The single-level 500-square-meter penthouse is, to all intents and purposes, a bungalow. In yet another nod to the tradition of classical modernism, its all-round glazing cites Mies van der Rohe's Farnsworth House and Philip Johnson's Glass House. The difference here, though, is that the residence is sheltered from noise and intrusive gazes not by extensive grounds, but by its location above the surrounding buildings. Because the facade is open to the north, the residents can enjoy the shade while the city bakes in the sun. To the south, there is a park-like garden with a surrounding roof structure. The 1500-square-meter area takes in a large proportion of the existing bank building, where a swimming pool for residents has been installed, allowing views of the seventh-story parking floor, while at the same time being screened by vegetation to ensure privacy. Anyone ascending to this rooftop will have noted the many and varied functions of the building, and the way it comes full circle: private living space as part and parcel of a far wider whole, linked with the natural environment that encompasses the plaza in front of the building. This parking garage combines living and driving in a whole new way as an icon for Miami, and as a benchmark for the American way of life.

This project is the outcome of the last of many trips that we had the privilege of taking with Rémy Zaugg. Significantly, we had gone to Courgenay, the little village in the Swiss Jura where Rémy grew up and went to school—a village on the edge of Switzerland that already belongs, geographically, to the Ajoie plains facing France. The proximity of France is culturally tangible here: Ronchamp with the Chapel Notre-Dame du Haut, which may well be Le Corbusier's most important work, and Ornans, the birthplace of Gustave Courbet, an artist deeply admired by Zaugg.

Rémy Zaugg and his brother Georges chose the untouched Jura pasture on a rise above their place of birth, Courgenay, as the future site of the Auditorium du Jura, with the explicit intent of establishing a "cultural triangle" between Ornans, Ronchamp, and Courgenay.

The auditorium would be an important cultural magnet in Switzerland and beyond—especially for music. Georges Zaugg approached us as a representative of the Festival du Jura and initiated the project, which was to be financed primarily by private sponsors with, at best, a modicum of federal funding. The project never materialized, despite Switzerland-wide sympathy for the marginalized and poor Jura Canton and the "seductive attraction" of the architecture, as we were repeatedly told. While the project for the Elbphilharmonie in Hamburg, launched in 2003, triggered a veritable wave of enthusiasm, what little hope there was for its country cousin in the Jura had to be abandoned upon the unexpected death of Rémy Zaugg in 2005.

While visiting the Jura in 2004, Rémy had shown us the village church, the Hôtel de la Gare restaurant, where the famous Gilberte de Courgenay hosted soldiers from the front during the First World War, the house in which he was born, and his own room where some of his early figurative paintings were still mounted on walls. He took us to the meadow on which he wanted to build the auditorium as one of the three pillars of his imaginary cultural triangle. The artist was not, however, directly involved in the architectural planning.

Standing alone, all by itself in the landscape—what kind of architecture could that be? After numerous failed attempts, the idea of a precise geometric shape gradually surfaced, based on the triangle of Zaugg's cultural vision as well as the much more mundane image of the pyramid-shaped triangulation points often found on summits in the Jura Mountains, for instance on the Hohe Winde. However, since we did not want the pyramid to be a pure and dominant element, we placed a dome inside, made up of several superimposed and twisted hexagons. Several stories within this hexagonal dome would provide additional space for the audience by leaning over the stage and the center of events. This most radically embodies our intention of almost inseparably connecting audience and event, an objective to which we aspire in all of our stadium projects and in the Elbphilharmonie as well. The sound reflector, suspended like a chandelier above the stage of the Elbphilharmonie, was originally meant to be accessible to the public, with seating for a few members of the audience.

The pyramid with its protrusions was to be built out of wood and clad with wooden shingles or carved wood paneling. From a distance the building would have something of the casual and self-evident appearance of a farmhouse. Only on coming closer would one realize that the mighty roofed pyramid was floating above a glazed, seemingly immaterial foundation. And only on entering would visitors discover the sunken arena with the tiers of seating and the stage. In short, the project was based on three entirely distinct architectural typologies, each with its own historical and cultural background, which we spontaneously named "Theater Syracuse," "Mies," and "Poelzig." The sunken topography of the tiers and the stage would establish a direct connection between the auditorium and the limestone earth of the Jura, much like the dramatic experience in the Greek theater of Syracuse. Suspended above the whole is the dome with its protrusions and depressions, reminiscent of Baroque or Moorish cupolas or Poelzig's stalactitic visions; in any case, it is architecture that allows for reference to natural shapes.

Between these two very physical typologies, we planned to open up the space by having a ground-floor entrance area all around, which we called "Mies," referencing the modernist longing to overcome the separation between inside and outside. This intermediate space, which was to be as immaterial as possible, would offer views of the surrounding Jura pasture lands and the Ajoie plains extending toward France.

Herzog & de Meuron, 2015

The concert hall on a hill near Courgenay.
The pyramid marks cultural points of reference.

280_SI_0510_008

280_SI_0510_004

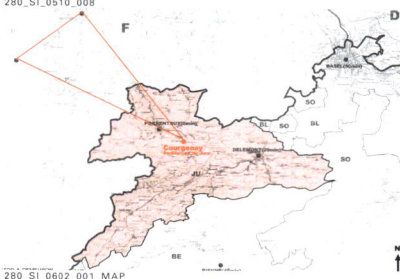

280_SI_0602_001_MAP

280_SI_0602_004_TOPVIEW

280_SK_060113_002A_PdM

280_MO_0512_523

The design incorporates ancient and modern building
typologies.

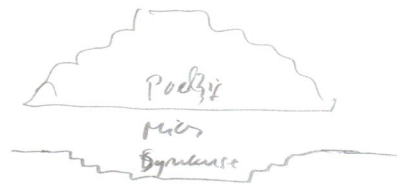

280_SK_0512_501_JH_K_SW

280_CI_0602_003_CONCEPT

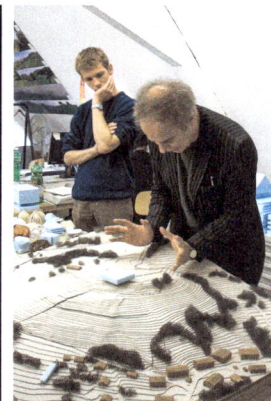

280_EV_051117_501_K

Models for the pyramid-shaped ceiling of the auditorium.

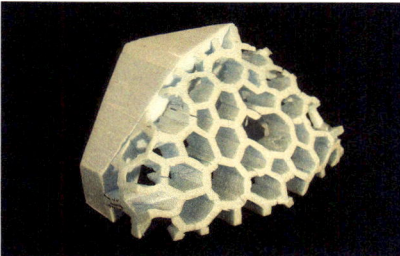

280_MO_0602_333_110-MOC

280_MO_0602_346_115-MOA

280_MO_1502_101-MOA

280_MO_1502_133-MOA

Inside the pyramid is a cupola of overlapping and tapered
hexagons.

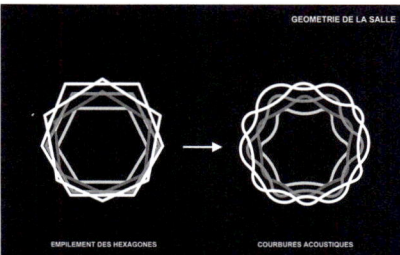

280_DG_0604_501_BW

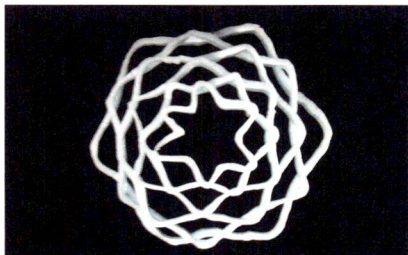

280_MO_0602_407_134-MOB

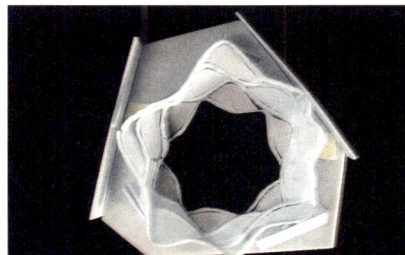

280_MO_0602_458_151-MOB

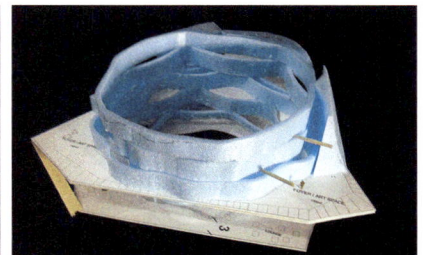

280_MO_0602_456_150-MOC

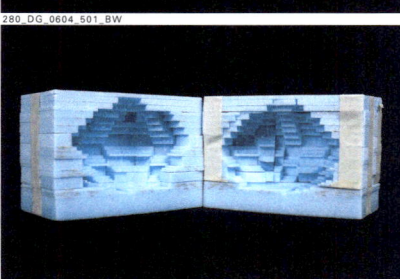

280_MO_1502_086_MOA

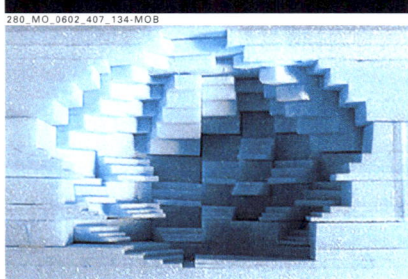

280_MO_0511_244

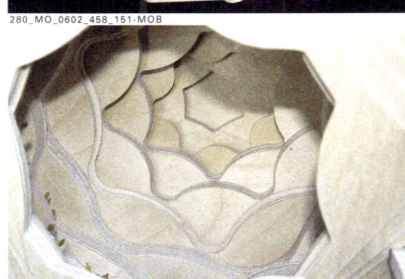

280_MO_0601_247

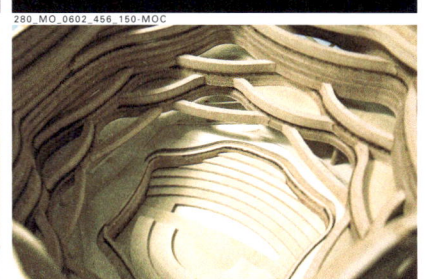

280_MO_0601_138_ALT

Sketches show the hybrid space generated by
combining the two typologies.

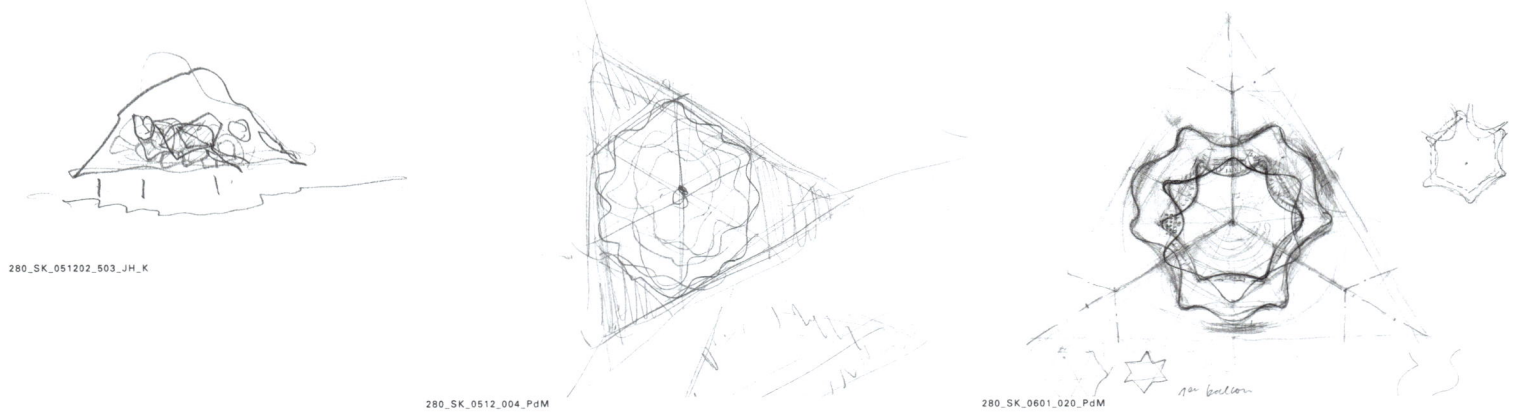

280_SK_051202_503_JH_K

280_SK_0512_004_PdM

280_SK_0601_020_PdM

Models show the interior pushing against the
outer shell like a textile membrane and forming
stepped configurations.

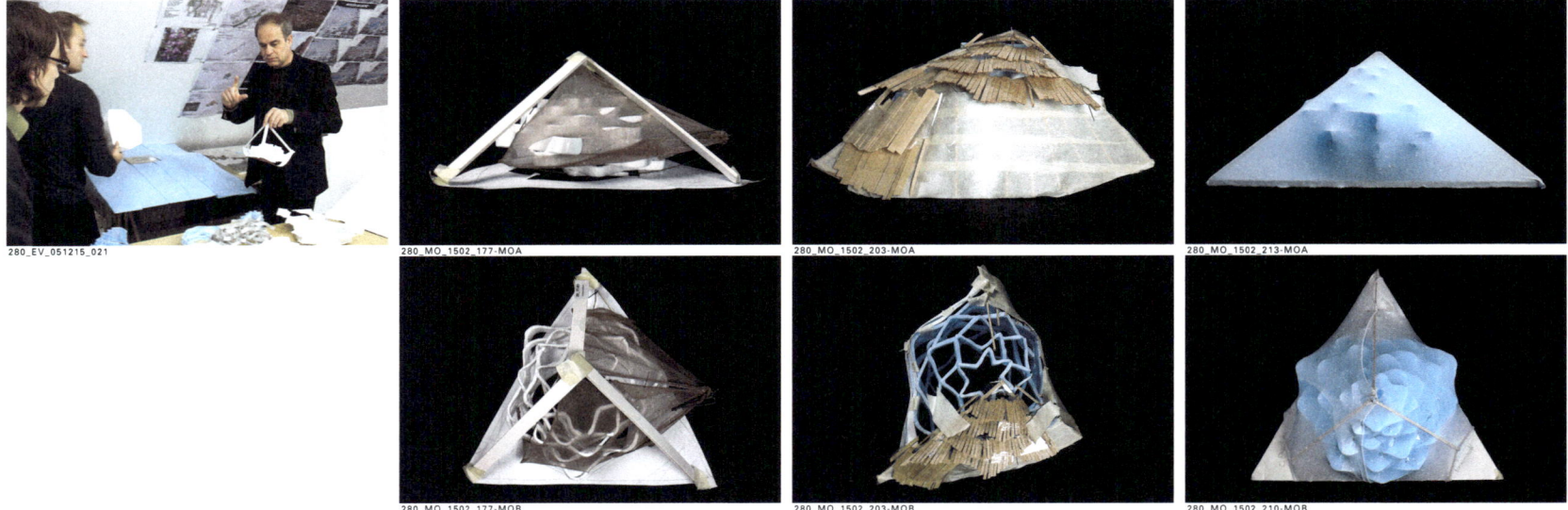

280_EV_051215_021

280_MO_1502_177-MOA

280_MO_1502_203-MOA

280_MO_1502_213-MOA

280_MO_1502_177-MOB

280_MO_1502_203-MOB

280_MO_1502_210-MOB

The auditorium can be seen from afar; a landmark in
the Jura countryside. Various uses include a concert hall,
lobbies and exhibition spaces.

280_CI_0602_007_NIGHTVIEW

280_CI_0602_004_SECTION

280_CI_0601_060

280_MO_0602_054B

280_MO_0602_012

280_CI_0602_005_VIEW

280_CI_0602_002B

VUE DEPUIS L'AMPHITHEATRE

280_RE_0602_20_K

280_RE_0602_19_K

VUE DEPUIS COURTEMAUTRUY

280_RE_0602_23_K

Rémy Zaugg (1943–2005) grew up in Courgenay, Switzerland, and, until the end of his life in 2005, took a profound interest in the history of the Swiss Jura region. He discerned in it the residues of the ancient kingdom of Burgundy, which had been such a powerful force in amalgamating its neighbors right up until early modern times, though later discord meant that its influence gradually fragmented and its potential was diminished. Zaugg found his creative inspiration in the paintings of Gustave Courbet, who had grown up near Ornans, and also in Le Corbusier's chapel of Notre-Dame du Haut in Ronchamp. This meeting of art and architecture was to culminate in a cultural triangle in combination with a House for Music. Envisioned at the same time as the controversial Swiss national exposition Expo.02, it proposed a creative topography that expanded the visual and acoustic realm into a multidimensional and almost synaesthetic entity of a kind long dreamt of by modernism, not least in the celebration of the gesamtkunstwerk. But how could this convergence of landscape and culture, of geographical and intellectual space, both contemporary and historical, possibly be translated into an architectural sign that would be worthy of such complexity and yet at the same time immediately comprehensible?

Rémy Zaugg and his brother Georges, artist and musician respectively, can be seen to personify this approach. Placing their focus firmly on the region of their childhood, they selected a hill in Courtemautruy, cradled amid gently rolling pastures. This was where the new Auditorium du Jura was to rise out of the landscape and hover above it. Herzog & de Meuron proposed that the outer form should be a triangular pyramid, combining the topography of the mind with the geographical coordinates of Ornans, Ronchamp, and Courgenay to create a landmark, visible from afar. The pyramid is the most conspicuous component of a geometric concept that combines three forms and three materials. The auditorium itself is based on a square, set into the hillside. Above its mineral base, elevated over three core access zones, there hovers a pyramidal triangle of wood interspersed by all-round glazing forming an irregular polyhedron. A hexagon embedded into the triangle of the pyramid forms the central auditorium with seating for an audience of 700. This interaction of divergent geometries lends the Auditorium du Jura its exciting sense of spatial tension.

Behind all this lies the question of how a concert hall should be designed. In principle, what we have are the classical box-like form and the shell-like form, such as the Amsterdam Concertgebouw or Hans Scharoun's Berlin Philharmonie. What Herzog & de Meuron are looking for—as with their stadium designs—is a way of bringing the performance as close as possible to the public. The best way to do that is by creating a communal space arranged concentrically around the orchestra in the middle, as in the Elbphilharmonie concert hall in Hamburg. Yet, for all their similarities, these two concert venues are based on principles that are almost diametrically opposed. Whereas the Hamburg venue, which has to seat a much bigger audience, has a distinctly sculptural feel, with the space seemingly hewn from a single block, the Jura venue is more tectonic: layer upon layer, volume upon volume, geometry upon geometry.

On the whole, the architects are somewhat closer here to Scharoun's Berlin Philharmonie concert hall. Scharoun chose a pentagon, to which he added further pentagonal arrangements, each turned by one side. Herzog & de Meuron have taken the hexagon as their basic form, turned three equally dimensioned hexagonal forms by one side, interwoven them like bands and inserted two smaller hexagons. These rings of hexagons are stacked story by story around the auditorium. The concept creates a textile quality that enhances the acoustics. The sharp ends of the hexagons are rounded so that the curves form concave and convex niches and pockets wherever

they intersect. It is there that most of the audience is seated, while other bays formed in this way are utilized for lighting.

The interwoven character of the design is further underscored by the choice of wood as the material for the pyramidal cupola. The outer cladding features wooden shingles that echo the regional vernacular of local agricultural buildings while at the same time recalling the wooden structure of the Théâtre du Jorat above Lausanne, which Jacques Herzog and Pierre de Meuron visited when they were students. Inside, bands of wood line the open space like the thin wooden casings used for soft cheese. From the outside, the bays of the hexagons appear as angular layered protrusions that jut through the surfaces of the pyramid's sides like objects pushed under a taut layer of fabric. In this way, the interior pushes out to the exterior, stretching the overall form and lending the cupola a stepped appearance redolent of mountain terracing.

This tectonic principle also has an archaeological dimension. The zone comprising the orchestra pit and the stalls is dug into the hill, as in the theaters of classical antiquity, such as the theater of Syracuse in Sicily. It is seamlessly linked with the foyer, which can be closed off by sound-insulating curtains during concerts, but which is otherwise separated only by a fully glazed partition. The protrusions of the cupola trigger associations with the interior of the Grosses Schauspielhaus in Berlin, remodeled by Hans Poelzig in 1919 using arcs of forms resembling pinecones and droplets. Moreover, the textile appearance of the wooden pyramid also recalls some of their own early designs for the Tate Modern extension in London, even though the materials deployed are different. And it foreshadows such buildings as the Leonard Street residential tower in New York and the Pérez Art Museum in Miami (PAMM), which have been designed from the inside out, dispensing with an all-encompassing facade skin. Architectural forms from across the epochs, incorporating the typologies of amphitheater, landscape, and cupola, all converge and unify in the Auditorium du Jura.

Inside, this sense of unity is achieved primarily by the open central space that incorporates all levels of the building. It links the lower level, housing the concert zone, dressing rooms, wardrobe, toilets, and technical service areas, with the ground floor foyer and terrace, the Rémy Zaugg Foyer on the first floor, and the balcony seating above. The upper foyer takes the form of a promenade giving access to the balconies and the ancillary open spaces formed by the interaction between the dual geometries of the concert auditorium itself and the three corners of the pyramid. Here, the work of Rémy Zaugg can be presented. This homage to the region's greatest twentieth-century artist combines various art forms under one roof and continues in the footsteps of earlier efforts to showcase contemporary art in the Swiss Jura. One particularly notable example of this is the restoration and conversion of an old patrician town house in the historic center of Porrentruy, for which Rémy Zaugg and Herzog & de Meuron drew up the initial concepts, which stalled on the death of the artist. The design for the Auditorium du Jura bears comparison with other projects by the architects. For instance, it rises from the ground like the Cottbus library in Germany and the Iglesia de la Natividad in Mexico, although it does not share their underlying concepts: the university library building evokes a castle founded on the virtual storage of knowledge while the church seems like a continuation of the mountain, forming a kind of celestial telescope. In contrast, the connection between the Auditorium du Jura and the earth is not immediately evident. In spite of its scale, the pyramidal cupola appears to hover above the earth, like a sign of the immaterial quality that pervades this predominantly rural landscape, but was previously invisible.

The collection of original works by Francisco Goya is not enough in size or quality to fill a new building and attract sufficient numbers of visitors in the long term. In addition, even the most attractive exhibition schedule of old and new art would not in itself be adequate motivation for people to travel to Zaragoza, given the growing competition of new and exciting high-style museums in Spain and in so many other places all over the world.

While thinking about this project, we therefore gave priority to the potential programming of the future Espacio Goya, fully aware that, in the competition phase, we would have to manage without conversing with the museum authorities in Zaragoza. Nonetheless, we chose to focus on this aspect since it was the only means of finding an approach that would allow for a genuinely new and suitable architectural solution.

On the basis of our experience with museums and exhibition venues, and especially our diverse collaborations with artists, we knew—even more so than in other museum projects— that a successful Espacio Goya would have to unite architecture, artwork, and location to form a distinctive, unique whole that is possible only in and for Zaragoza. It has become increasingly difficult to speak of an authentic place especially when it comes to museums, and yet we still aspired to the almost old-fashioned idea of an authenticity that is connected with a specific place, a place in which program and architecture are inseparably linked.

So we wanted to work out a concept for architecture that would not merely function as a container for art. Above all, we wanted to establish an exciting and dynamic relationship between architecture and art, a relationship between the old architecture and the new additions, and between old and new art: art by Goya and art about Goya. Our architectural and curatorial proposal for the Espacio Goya addresses the urgent, vital issues that confront architecture and art today: it is about reality and simulation and the processes of perception that are attendant upon that dichotomy. In particular, the proposal charts new territory in the encounter with Goya: it reveals his outstanding and enduring influence, brings to life some of his key works, and places them in an entirely different light.

The crucial element in our architectural, curatorial concept is a group of four Anchor Rooms, which have been built into the physical substance of the Escuela, like dropstones. Their presence recalls the cathedral that Charles V had built into the Great Mosque of Córdoba in the 16th century. The insertion of the four Anchor Rooms is essentially an act of violence because it destroys parts of the building, thereby disrupting its historical continuity and the layout of the rooms. But it is also a liberating act because it opens up a number of new perspectives and makes a vibrant, substantive addition to the historicist mix of Spanish and French styles that marks the Escuela building of 1908. The four Anchor Rooms are reconstructions of interiors for which Goya created in-situ works: the Aula Dei, the San Antonio de la Florida Chapel, the Quinta del Sordo, and the Real Academia where Goya taught. Along with five sites containing in-situ works by Goya in the environs of Zaragoza, it is here and only here, in one single city, that future visitors will have the opportunity to experience all of the rooms that Goya painted in full-scale. The Anchor Rooms do not contain the original works but their size and proportions create a physical experience that matches the original places. Furthermore, the four rooms do without stucco and decoration; they are all solid and homogeneous, built of the same smooth and jointless light-gray brick used for the facades of the Escuela and the museum. In this way a complete and seamless connection is established between the intruding spaces and the existing building. The discreet light-gray brick, an ideal background for both old and contemporary works of art, recalls famous buildings reconstructed after the war such as the Glyptothek or the Alte Pinakothek in Munich. Above all, the Anchor Rooms provide extremely flexible exhibition spaces as a meaningful complement to the somewhat stereotypical sequence of the existing rooms in the Escuela.

The unusual, irregular dimensions and shapes of the Anchor Rooms lend rhythm to the visitor's tour of the Espacio Goya. They form a specific topography within the Escuela's simple courtyard typology. Documentary material on each of the sites—photographs, drawings, maps, and texts—is laid out like a study center in the wide hallways that connect all the galleries.

The Anchor Rooms not only stand out as a distinctive group of spaces; they are also exceptional in terms of content and curatorial potential. As exhibition galleries, they revitalize the experience of Goya's absent originals, giving these extraordinary works a renewed currency in combination with contemporary art. Artists like the Chapman Brothers or Bruce Nauman have already addressed the work of this master. However, instead of acquiring finished works, it would be even more interesting to commission artists to create a direct response to the absent in-situ works in the four Anchor Rooms. The wide range of artistic strategies and methods, such as media art, photography, video, installations, or sculpture, could make such contemporary responses to Goya a new highlight within the future Espacio Goya.

Herzog & de Meuron, 2015

The Academy of Applied Arts is to be converted into a museum and connected with the adjacent historical museum. Both buildings were erected in 1908 for a Spanish-French exhibition.

282_RFSB_0611_022

282_RFSB_0611_005

282_SI_0611_129_MZ_INT

Herzog & de Meuron add four new Anchor Rooms to the future museum. Grand stairs connect the two buildings, and historical courtyards are restored.

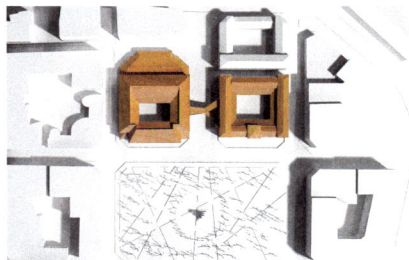

282_CI_0711_009

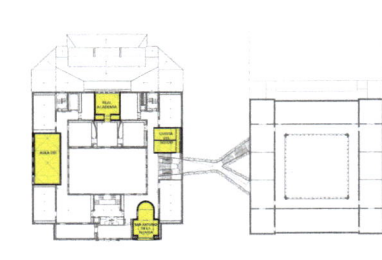

282_DR_0711_001

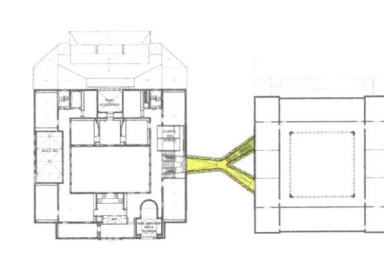

282_DR_0711_002

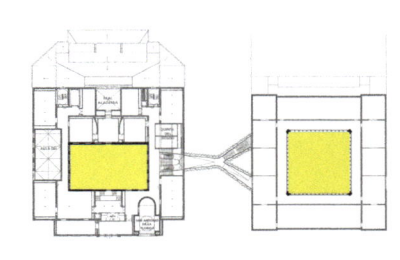

282_DR_0711_003

Models and studies for inserting the Anchor Rooms in the former Academy of Applied Arts.

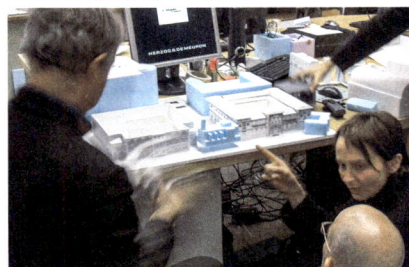

282_EV_0601_006

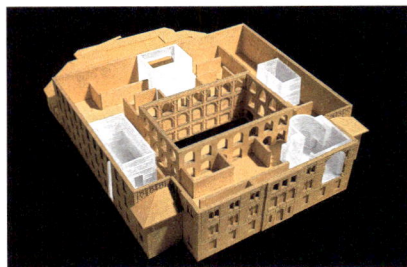

282_MO_0703_004

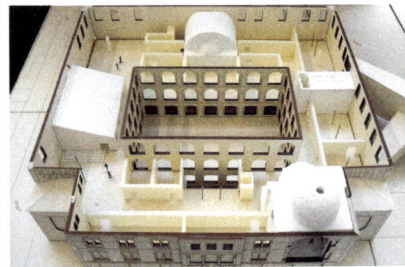

282_MO_0609_064

282_MO_0612_0037

For a new art museum, the architects reference four
locations in Spain to which Goya contributed.

REMOLINOS ● Iglesia de San Juan
● Iglesia Cartuja de Aula Dei
ZARAGOZA ● Basílica del Pilar
MUEL ● Iglesia de Na. Sa. de la Fuente
CALATAYUD ● Iglesia de San Juan el Real
FUENDETODOS ● Iglesia de La Asunción

○ Real Academia
MADRID ● Iglesia de San Antonio
● Iglesia de San Francisco El Grande
● La Quinta del Sordo

TOLEDO ● Catedral

282_DR_0704_013

Charterhouse of Aula Dei in Zaragoza.
Church of San Antonio de la Florida in Madrid.
Quinta del Sordo in Madrid.
Real Academia de Bellas Artes in Madrid.

282_RFSB_0000_501_AULA-DEI_K

282_RFSB_0612_068_AD

282_RFSB_0612_011_AD

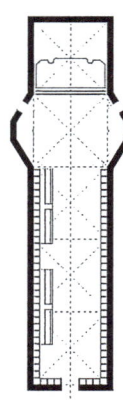

282_PP_060504_005_COMPETITION

282_RFSB_0607_050_SA

282_RFSB_0607_075_SA

282_RFSB_0607_032_SA

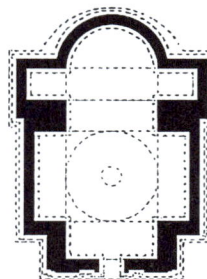

282_PP_060504_004_COMPETITION

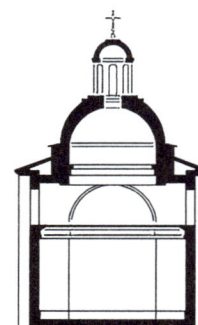

282_RFSB_DEL_SORDO_1930

282_RFAR_0511_019_1820-23

282_RFSB_0607_032_SA

282_RFSB_0608_001_RA

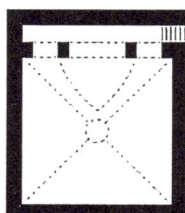

282_RFAR_0511_019_1820-23

Designing the Anchor Room after the Charterhouse of Aula Dei.

282_MO_0712_122_059-MOC

282_MO_0601_281_GOYA-SPACES_1-50

282_CI_0711_017_B

282_SK_0609_003_AULA DEI

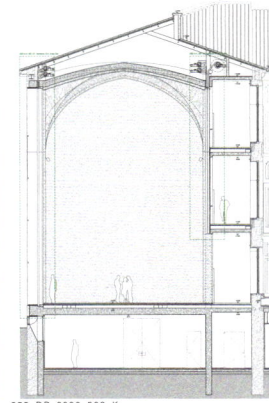

282_DR_0000_502_K

Designing the Anchor Room after the Church of San Antonio de la Florida.

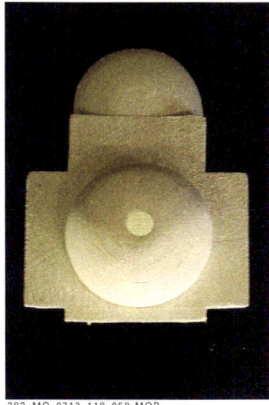

282_MO_0712_118_058-MOB

282_MO_0601_279_GOYA-SPACES_1-50

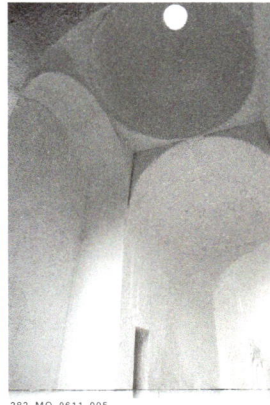

282_MO_0611_005

282_CI_0711_016

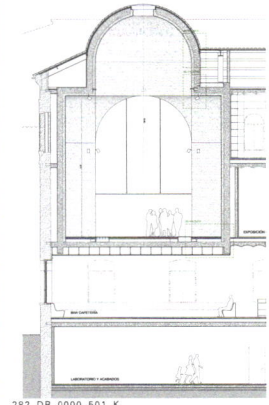

282_DR_0000_501_K

Designing the Anchor Room after the Quinta del Sordo.

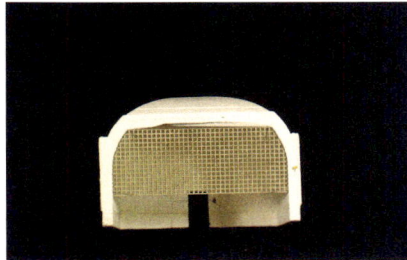

282_MO_0712_132_063-MOA

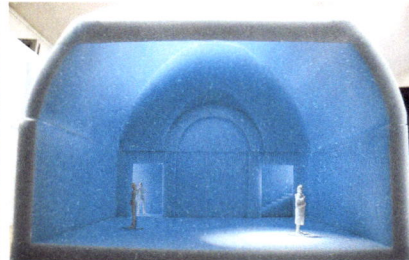

282_MO_0601_271_GOYA-SPACES_1-50

282_MO_0611_006

Designing the Anchor Room after the Real Academia de Bellas Artes de San Fernando.

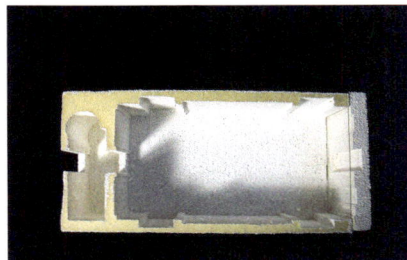

282_MO_0703_023_012-MOB

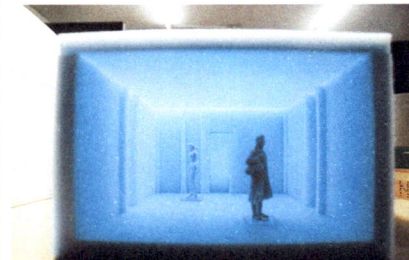

282_MO_0601_273_GOYA-SPACES_1-50

282_MO_0610_064

The grand stairs linking the two buildings as a load-bearing grid reminiscent of shadow architecture.

282_EV_0601_036

282_MO_0712_147_CONJUNTO-MOA

282_EV_0601_035

282_MO_0707_028

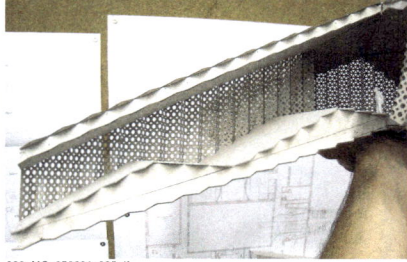

282_MO_070621_095_K

282_MO_0707_010

282_MU_0710_004

282_CI_0711_005

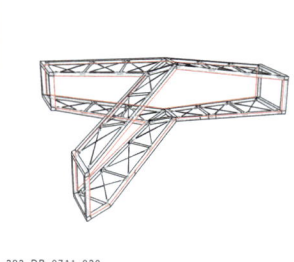

282_DR_0711_020

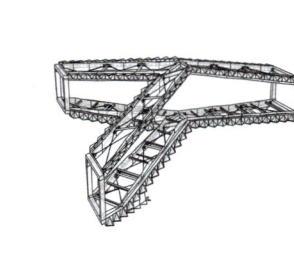

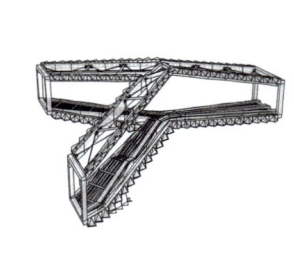

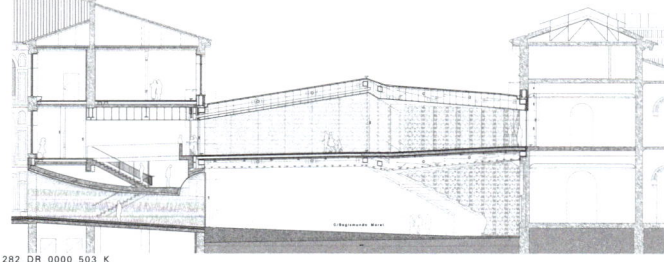

282_DR_0000_503_K

Newer additions inside the existing buildings are removed.

282_CI_0811_002_TIENDA

282_CI_0811_001_CAFETERIA

282_CI_0811_004_FOYER

282_CI_0709_016

Windows in the facades indicate the presence of the Anchor Rooms; the connecting structure creates a new entrance and a plaza.

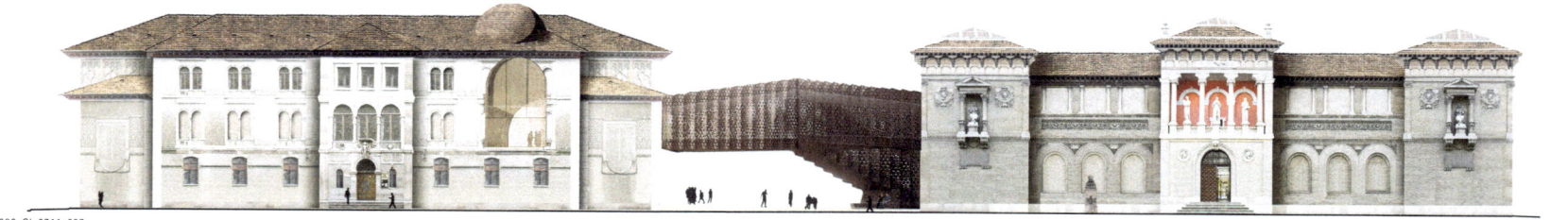

282_CI_0711_027

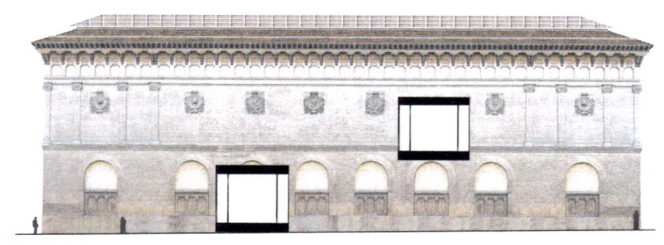

282_CI_0711_026

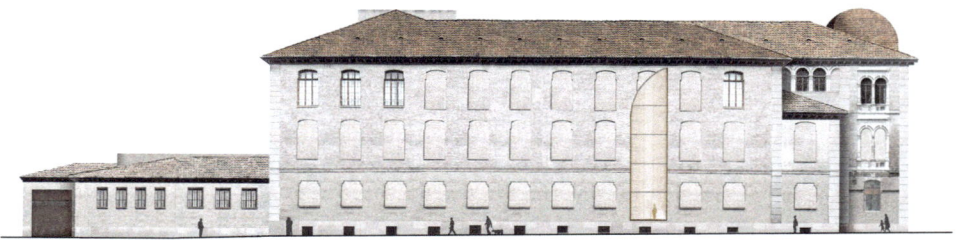

282_CI_0711_026

For Expo 2008, Zaragoza aimed to enhance its cultural appeal. The glory days of this former capital city of the kingdom of Aragón were long gone. Only some remnants of the original Roman colony and the Moorish palace of Aljaferia bore witness to its rich and storied history. There was not even one museum of any renown, in spite of the fact that Goya was born nearby. And so the city tendered a competition for the conversion and restoration of two buildings that had been built in 1908 for a Spanish-French exhibition commemorating the seige of Zaragoza by Napoleon. The two buildings, with their courtyard typology, both face onto the grand Plaza de los Sitios and blend into the nineteenth-century urban framework. The northernmost of the two was to house the new art museum: Espacio Goya. The school of art and applied arts previously based there was to move out. Its southern counterpart was to continue in its role as the home of the city's history and civic museums.

Herzog & de Meuron retained the substance of the neoclassical architecture, while at the same time restructuring it, respecting the pasticcio character of the brick structures. They had originally been built for exhibition purposes and were later converted into educational institutions. The historicist facades were inspired by the local Aragonese vernacular, with Moorish influences evident in the moldings and friezework, and roof beams reflecting the construction of baroque palaces of the sixteenth to eighteenth centuries. The architects proposed cleansing the inner courtyards of later additions and using the flow of loggias for access. Where required, closed openings were to be reinstated, while in other places many of the windows in the school were to be bricked up to optimize the exhibition space. Such wall areas were to remain visible, as at the Museum Küppersmühle in Duisburg, in order to retain the shape and memory of the original windows.

Most of the proposed alterations affected the future art museum. The existing rooms with their brick vaulting and cast iron columns were to be retained and enhanced by oak flooring, and the overall structure strengthened accordingly. Given that there was neither a substantial collection nor a dedicated team of curators in place, Herzog & de Meuron created distinctive spaces that would lend the future museum an identity clearly setting it apart from other buildings. On the first floor, each of the four wings was allocated a so-called Anchor Room—a concept devised by the architects for their 2006 exhibition "Perception Restrained" at MoMA in New York. These spaces follow the architectural dimensions of four rooms either designed by Francisco Goya or in which he lived or worked. These are, in Zaragoza, the charterhouse of Aula Dei, and, in Madrid, the dome of the church of San Antonio de la Florida, the ceiling of which he painted, the Quinta del Sordo (Villa of the Deaf), where he lived for a time, and the Real Academia de Bellas Artes de San Fernando, where he taught. The abstract handling of space is incorporated into the flight of rooms like a three-dimensional quotation, which is expressed on the exterior in the form of differently sized windows. A link is established by using the same pale gray brick of the old building for the new rooms, while their shape and size interrupt the rhythm of the original layout. Goya is present here, not in his works themselves, but in the rooms in which, or for which they were created. The spaces are now open to contemporary artists seeking an insight into the life of the master. As striking as the change inside the building may be, the urban statement made by the exterior is no less remarkable: the architects have created a link between the two buildings by deploying an X-form and a Y-form.

The project could not be implemented for Expo 2008 and later fell victim to the consequences of the financial crash and the real estate crisis. Architecturally, it is notable in two regards: first of all for the way that Herzog & de Meuron deployed an urbanistic tool to link the two buildings. The passageway is combined with a grand staircase of the kind often associated with prestigious buildings and the plaza is opened up. The dividing street that runs through here is transformed into a public space in its own right, incorporated into the existing Plaza de los Sitios and thus appealing to passers-by. In terms of restructuring an urban district, this approach is reminiscent of the design for the Kunsthaus in Aarau and the TEA in Santa Cruz de Tenerife. Rather than adopting an existing structure, the architects have spotted a gap that nobody before them had noticed. These are interventions on a meta-level, involving a whole new reading of the urban fabric and a recalibration of the threads that form it. An abstract, indeed almost virtual, gaze thus infiltrates the reality of the built environment in much the same way that the script of a computer program produces a perfect tool on a milling machine.

The Zaragoza project is a much more subtle intervention and on a much smaller scale. That demands a special eye for detail. Here, the fulcrum point is a sculptural issue. Early variations using brickwork indicate this, while later designs using steel look more like computer-generated machined parts. The proposed solution in the form of a massive grid that takes on the main functional load further emphasizes this figurative power. The bridge between the two neoclassical buildings plays on memories of shadow architectures, like Zaragoza's very own bridge of sighs, triggering a fata morgana of the imagination.

In this regard, it plays a direct role in relation to the key intervention: the spaces derived from the four Goya rooms. These, too, are places of the unreal and of simulation, albeit in a different way. The Goya rooms can be seen, in simple terms, as found spaces in contrast to invented ones, as simulated spaces in contrast to those originally built, as contemporary spaces in contrast to historical ones. These are spaces that none other than the coinventors of the White Cube themselves present as a contrast following its decontextualization. They set an anchor in the slowly clearing mists of postmodern society. For this, Herzog & de Meuron draw upon historical forms. Whereas the White Cube implied the dissolution of historicity in a radiant glow of modernist utopia, the room as simulacrum, the imagined space of Herzog & de Meuron, counters such vacuity with a contoured form, empty and yet filled by the imagination.

This concept can also be applied to other situations. On the one hand, when it comes to conferring an identity through architecture that a collection cannot provide because it does not yet exist or because it is too young and too indeterminate. When the Sardinian city of Cagliari wanted to build a museum, Herzog & de Meuron proposed a vertical structure with Anchor Rooms in which the prehistoric Nuraghe relics would play a key role. Spaces such as these can, by dint of their specific layout and central position, act as connecting hubs that guide not only visitors but also exhibitions in other directions. Or they can form a foundation on which to build exhibitions and acquisitions of contemporary art, as is conceptually the case with the Pérez Art Museum Miami (PAMM). In such cases, Anchor Rooms form primary cores where loaned collections, specific groups of works, or commissioned pieces can be presented as a condensed expression of the energy that radiates throughout the entire building. Conceptually expanded, the Park Avenue Armory in New York can be seen as an Anchor Room for the entire city. The building, with its ensemble of historical rooms dating from around 1900 is a landmark, not only within the museumscape, but throughout Manhattan and the wider urban area; it is a beacon in a sea of historically listless monotony. The concept of Anchor Rooms has arrived at the level of urban analysis.

**Allschwil
Switzerland
2005–2010; 2007–2010, 2009–2013**

**No. 284
Actelion Business Center
No. 318
Actelion Research
and Laboratory Building**

Actelion, a young company, needed more room for expanding operations: offices, conference rooms, restaurants, laboratories, and meeting places for researchers who come from all over the world to live and work in Basel. But instead of just putting up a building, Actelion wanted a building with "a face," a location with which people would identify. The company was looking for architecture that would express the experimental spirit, the openness, and the uncomplicated, forthright communicative attitude of the two founders.

Most of the buildings in the neighborhood had not had the stimulating input of a similarly inspired client. These utilitarian structures seem both random and cheaply built. For some incomprehensible reason, the building height in the up-and-coming Bachgraben neighborhood is dictated by the zoning plan of the Allschwil municipality, although there are no residents to complain about shadow impacts and it would make perfect sense to densify and concentrate building mass in an area that is destined to accommodate a cluster of life science companies and institutes.

That meant we were confined to a six-story perimeter block and a maximum height of 22.6 meters (a little over 74 feet) within which to build a business center that would embody the free and open architecture envisioned by the client. Our first step was to break down the program into simple prismatic beams, which we grouped around a traditional inner courtyard. But the arrangement did not convince us: the teams and work units would have been too far apart and the building would have been too rigidly split into a world geared toward the neighborhood outside and an insular, screened-off world within.

We tried out a number of other typographies working with both traditional and more unconventional patterns and layouts. We liked the most chaotic version best: prisms piled like a random bunch of pick-up sticks. But how would that work? And how could something like that be constructed? Could a rational order be devised that would give the heaped structure meaning and orientation? In the course of the emerging design, the four access cores therefore proved to require the most study, as illustrated by the numerous models of the project in our archives. These cores would determine the flow of the circulation within the building, which paths would lead in which direction, and which places within the building would be more or less frequented. We were convinced that we could ensure the quality and flexibility of the workplaces in this unusual building, but would the organization and the orientation function not only in the model but also in the built reality? When we saw the chaos of the naked steel supports of the skeleton structure, we began to wonder and our doubts were not allayed until the various beams of the building had been glazed and clad so that you could tell the difference between inside and outside. All of a sudden, you could make out the sequence of the rooms and throughout the building, unexpected, diverse lines of sight began to emerge.

The building functions like a three-dimensional grid with a varied architectural topography that reflects the diverse needs and types of work at Actelion. Like VitraHaus, the Actelion Business Center is conceptually related to the Beijing Film Academy Qingdao: beam-shaped elements seem to be placed every which way with clearly recognizable design intent. These "stacks," as we call them in our office, demonstrate that the same building typology can yield solutions specifically tailored to meet the needs of entirely different programs and local parameters.

At VitraHaus, the "beams" are glazed at the ends offering visitors a view of the surrounding landscape, while closed rooms inside draw attention to the objects on display. That situation is reversed at Actelion. The sides of the beams are open, offering panoramic views of the busy interior world of the building.

As a whole, VitraHaus, seen from the outside, does not evoke associations with anything familiar. It is simply a stack, but the parts of the stack can instantly be identified, for they have the simplest, most ordinary shape conceivable: a house with a pitched roof, closely resembling the houses in the residential neighborhoods nearby.

The way the stack works at Actelion is the exact opposite in this respect as well: the single elements are far from figurative. Indeed, the white glazed beams are almost abstract, protruding in all possible directions and without end, were it not for the fact that they have been cut off vertically along a single line, as if sliced by a knife. This abrupt boundary imposed by the right-angled shape of the property forces the stacked beams into an overall rectangular shape, like a cake that can rise only as *much as the baking tin allows. Thus sliced off, the cut surface looks entirely different on each of the four sides of the stacked building: random fragments of a facade for an otherwise facade-less building, invigorated entirely by its sculptural shape.*

Herzog & de Meuron, 2016

A piece of property in a commercial area near the French border is available as a site of innovation to accommodate new company headquarters. Initial site overview.

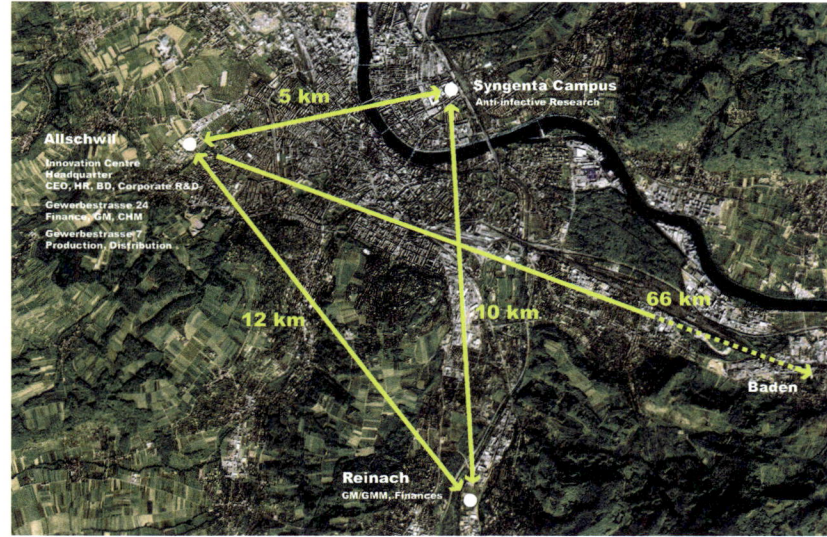

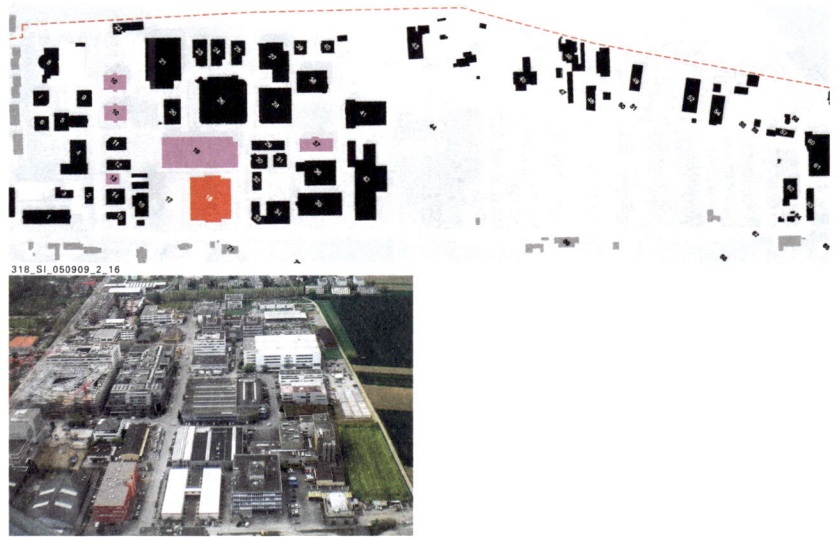

284_SI_050909_2_25

318_SI_050909_2_16

318_SI_0905_001_ACT FROM TOP

Meeting with the company founders and first sketches for an open, communicative building.

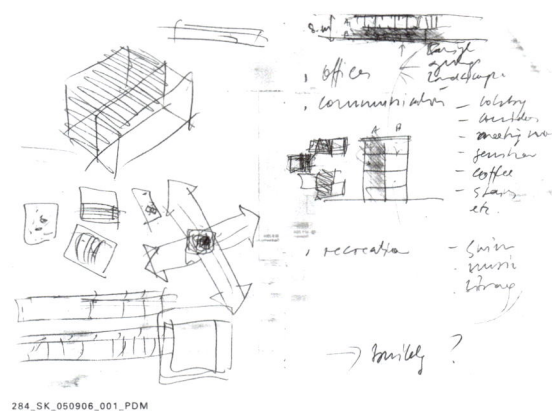

284_EV_0512_001

284_EV_0609_020

284_SK_050906_001_PDM

Horizontal layout of the program and inquiry into the potential of a dense structure to foster direct communication.

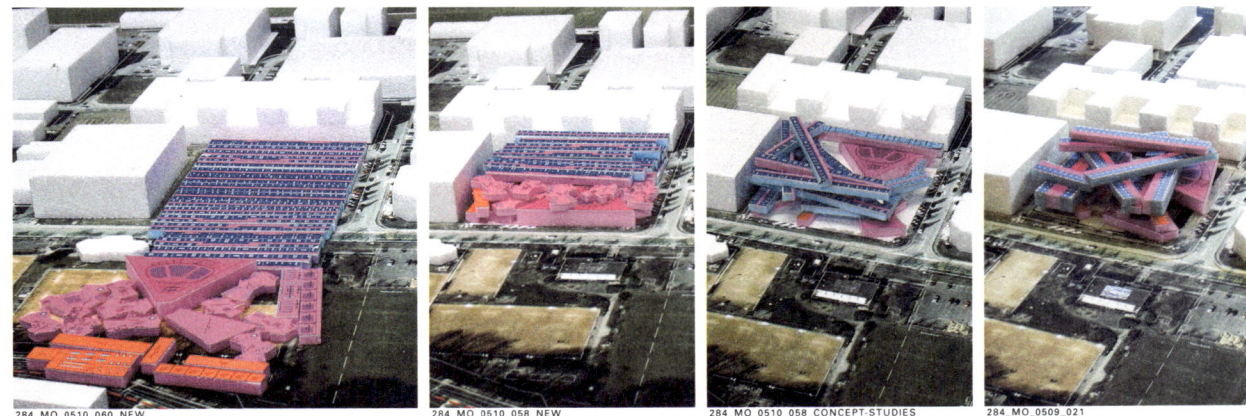

284_MO_0510_060_NEW

284_MO_0510_058_NEW

284_MO_0510_058_CONCEPT-STUDIES

284_MO_0509_021

Linking the floors above four open cores to create a
maximum of direct connections.

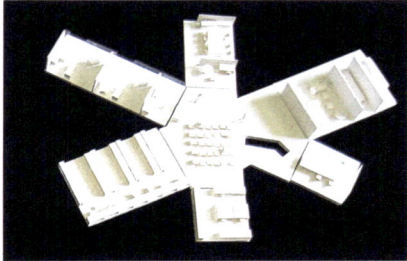

284_MO_0509_097_ALL_4

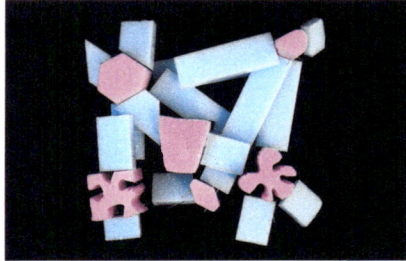

284_MO_0000_501_K

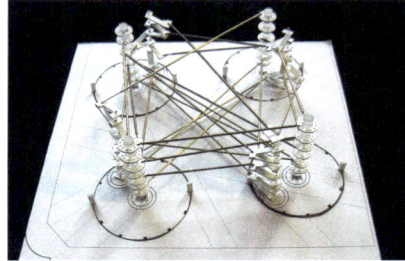

284_MO_0510_010_B

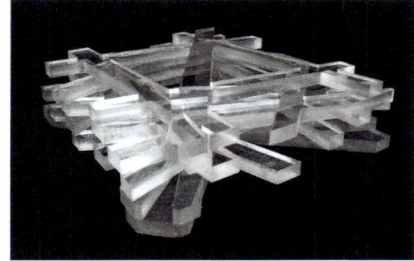

284_MO_0509_137

The vertical cores are used for structural purposes, HVAC
and circulation; they mediate between the floors that point
in different directions.

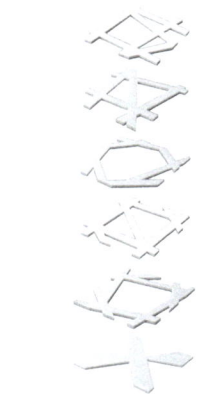

284_MO_0605_001_ISOMETRIE

284_CI_0705_003

284_MO_0811_049

284_MO_0606_070_GHOST

The forces of the bridge structure form trees that rest on a
few supports in the underground carpark. The direction and
tilt of the glass facades depend on location and function.

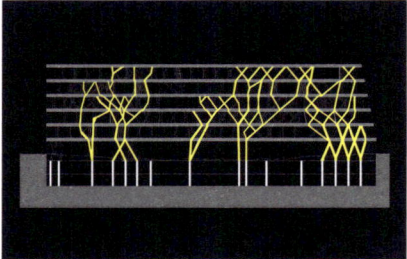

284_CI_0608_012_STRUCTURE

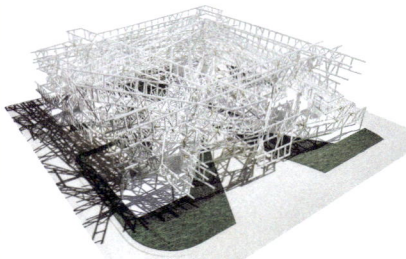

284_MO_0806_004_STRUKTUR_W

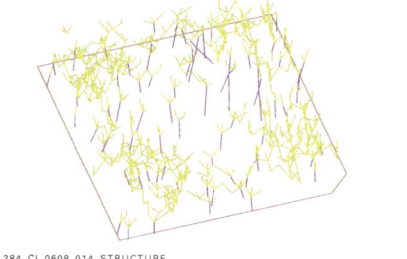

284_CI_0608_014_STRUCTURE

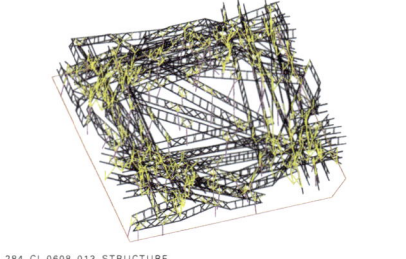

284_CI_0608_013_STRUCTURE

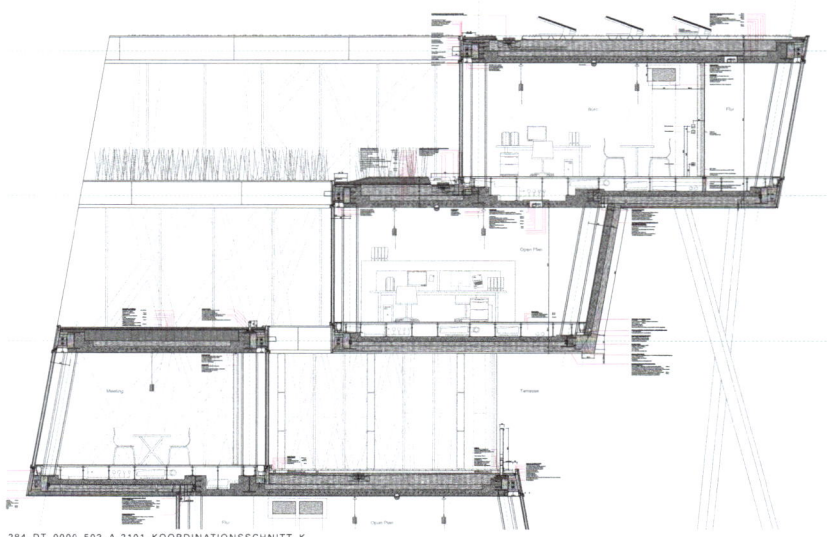

284_DT_0000_503_A-2101_KOORDINATIONSSCHNITT_K

On-site assembly of prefabricated steel elements.

284_CO_0805_036_0506

284_CO_0806_140_0624

284_CO_0901_751

284_CO_1003_093

284_EV_0802_107

284_CO_0812_100_1209

284_CO_0901_006_0106

284_CO_1001_107

The sequencing of the rooms emphasizes the link between indoors and outdoors; the struts indicate the force flow.

284_CO_1011_821_IB_1440

284_CP_110201_943_IB_U_1298

284_CP_110201_818_IB_H_0697

284_CP_110201_894_IB_H_0975

284_CP_110201_761_IB_U_1409

284_CP_1012_270

284_CP_110201_701_IB_U_1662

284_CP_110201_742_IB_U_1045

The shape of the research and laboratory building is defined by two adjacent plots of land.

No. **318** Actelion Research and Laboratory Building

284_CP_130425_794_IB_U_1992

318_MO_0705_033

318_MO_0912_502_SITE

Two separate volumes become a single building with setbacks in keeping with the lighting profile.

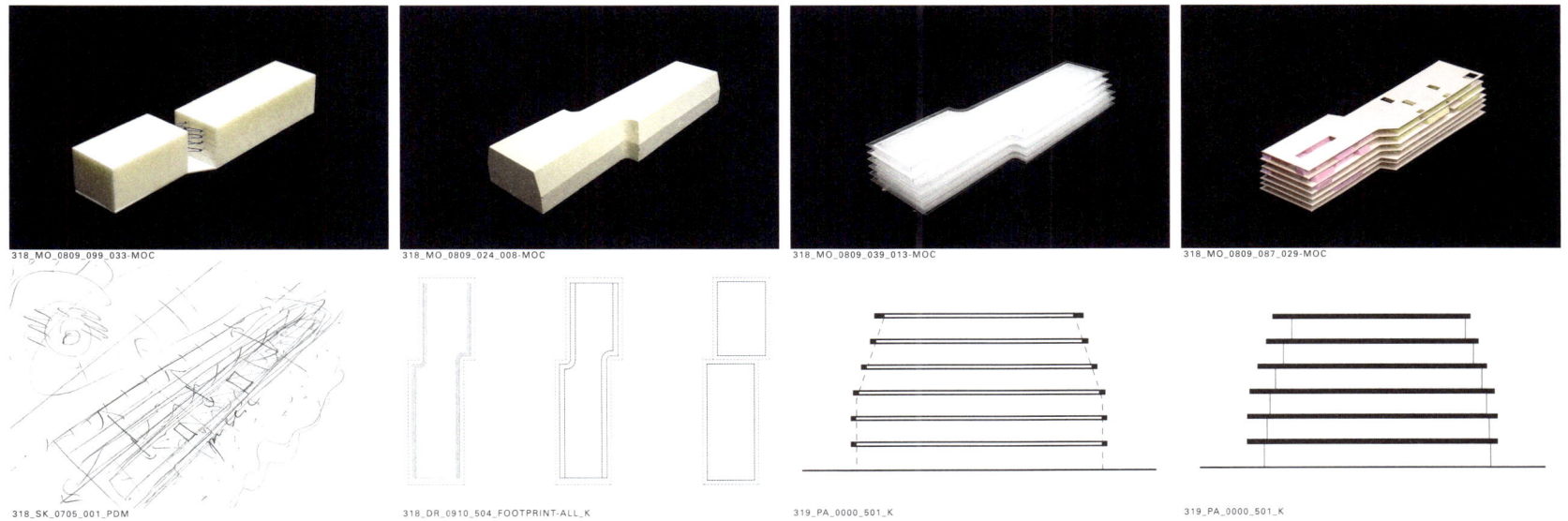

318_MO_0809_099_033-MOC

318_MO_0809_024_008-MOC

318_MO_0809_039_013-MOC

318_MO_0809_087_029-MOC

318_SK_0705_001_PDM

318_DR_0910_504_FOOTPRINT-ALL_K

319_PA_0000_501_K

319_PA_0000_501_K

Two spiral stairwells, each different in shape, provide
zones of communication at either end of the building.

318_SK_0809_001_PDM

318_CI_0804_010

318_SK_0812_002A_JH

318_MU_1007_007

318_CO_1007_035

318_CO_1011_0187

318_CO_0910_151

318_CO_1005_128

318_CO_1004_113

318_CO_1006_183

Steel elements integrated into waves of concrete allow
for a vertical load transfer for large cantilevers.

318_CI_0805_046

318_MU_0902_204

318_CI_0809_011

318_CO_1003_115

318_EV_0906_015

318_CO_1007_128

318_MU_0903_096_III

318_CO_1007_135

Flowing landscapes of rooms with spacious balconies
for research and administration.

318_CP_1309_729_IB_H

318_CP_1309_704_IB_H

318_CP_1309_730_IB_H

318_CP_1309_706_IB_H

318_CP_1309_722_IB_H

318_CP_1309_726_IB_H

318_CP_1309_705_IB_H

Actelion has experienced a meteoric rise. This biotechnology company founded in 1997 by former employees of the Swiss pharmaceutical giant Roche initially rented space at a center for innovative start-ups in Allschwil near Basel. The industrial estate on the French border was aiming to become a high-tech park, and Actelion provided an important push in that direction. The company needed a new business HQ for its staff of 350. A site covering 80 by 80 meters was available next to a laboratory building they had already constructed. What the client was now looking for was an iconic landmark that would stand out from its otherwise bland surroundings and give the young business its own architectural identity. At the same time, spatial and visual communication between the team members was to be a key priority. Informal meeting points and quality workspaces were deemed to be more important than the use of upscale materials.

Herzog & de Meuron initially presented the 17,000-square-meter program on a level field, layering it according to different concepts. The industrial estate permits a building height of 20 meters. Perimeter block housing and pectinated structures offer little visual contact, while block structures with a central corridor and offices on either side do not provide appealing contact zones. So the architects decided to cut open the block structure and to stack five levels with workspaces on one side of a corridor. In order to create as many contact points as possible, the blocks are not simply juxtaposed, but are openly linked across four core areas which, though not structurally significant, do contain the vertical traffic zones. The beam alignment varies from level to level, providing a variety of vistas both upward and downward. The intersections reflect this sense of flexibility in motion. The stairways all begin in the direction of one block and culminate in the alignment of the next level, creating a turn that is made possible by vertically stacked intermediate landings. The intersections between the load-bearing elements create sculpturally defined zones that are open enough to invite informal communication as well as more formal communication zones with pigeonholes for mail, meeting rooms and tea kitchens on alternate floors.

Structurally, after initially trying out the idea of concrete wall slabs, the architects decided on a bridge support system of steel. The load distribution is such that the flows of forces are spread out like trees whose finely ramified branches in the upper levels are channeled into a few supports that are aligned with the grid of the two-story underground parking garage. How this works can be clearly seen in the lateral framework: X-type bracing elements indicate where the load is distributed downward, while straight posts are sufficient for projecting elements, with a sequence of K-type and V-type bracing as well as tapered supports between them, ensuring that each office space looks different. The structure is given a triple-glazed facade with integrated sun shading. Depending on the direction of orientation of each block, the glazing is either tilted slightly outward to maximize daylight or slightly inward to minimize heat inflow. For temperature control, the concrete slabs between each floor are fitted with a thermo-active building system (TABS). The combination of steel construction and glass facade lends the building a crystalline, almost grid-like look, in contrast to the VitraHaus, which was developed on the basis of the same concept, but where the choice of concrete and the house-shaped elements create a much more tactile spatial effect.

For the Actelion Business Center, Herzog & de Meuron have created a unique environment that is not only evident from the outside, but also feels like a world of its own on stepping inside. The ground floor, unlike the structure of criss-crossed volumes stacked above it, is a large open space with room for up to a thousand employees, a communicative interim zone extending outward in a cruciform plan whose four slightly upward-sloping arms house a variety of functions: an auditorium, a theater-like seating staircase, café, and restaurant. A section of the floor is folded up to give access

to the underground parking garage. The landscape and planting concept by the artist Tita Giese underlines the seamless transition between outdoors and indoors. Islands of palms grow high to form a jungle-like canopy that connects the two uppermost levels with their rooftop gardens that are open to employees.

Otherwise, the interior design is muted. The use of simple white and tinted glazing put the focus on the individual. The flooring throughout is anhydride screed, while the offices are carpeted. Only the auditorium is furnished with parquet flooring. Small details add a softer, more comfortable touch. Wooden door handles lend warmth to the offices. Curtains provide privacy in the individual offices and can also be used to divide the open-plan office areas into smaller units. The fireproof cladding on the steel beams is rounded at the corners.

Shortly afterward, the company's runaway success was developing at such a pace that it required further laboratory and office space. A site adjacent to the existing research center was available, and an opportunity arose to acquire another at the start of the planning phase. Herzog & de Meuron quickly dismissed the idea of two separate buildings and instead designed a cohesive volume whose floor plan reiterates the slight discrepancy between the outlines of the two sites. The floor slabs are stacked in a way that tapers in size upward, while echoing the clearance heights of the neighboring building. There are no angled supports. At the same time, in order to avoid the large overhangs that would be necessary in a perpendicular flow of forces, steel load-transfer elements are embedded in the floor slabs and clad in a meter-thick wave of concrete. The protruding slabs provide passive sun-shading to the south, so that the setback facades need to be shaded only by awnings.

Inside, the rooms have been kept as simple as possible. The ceiling heights and laboratory typologies of the neighboring building have been replicated, the walls painted white and the ventilation and lighting fixtures integrated into the ceilings. The concrete wave conceals the upper edge of the glass facade. The laboratory levels have uniformly wide central corridors, while the administrative levels have uniformly deep office spaces. At either of the narrow ends, as in the Roche Building 92, there are communication zones with two different spiral staircases adding a distinctive note. The staircase on the north side cuts a cylinder through the floor slabs like a drill. While the circumference remains stable, the actual stair newel swings in the space, broadening and narrowing, offering vistas below. The height of the balustrade varies so that the user feels at times enclosed and at other times exposed. The staircase on the south side, by contrast, describes a path through the building. On its way, it takes a little detour to accommodate a passageway to the neighboring building, divides into a secondary route, and loops like a textile ribbon around both cores. The two stairways are far more than just expressive fulcrum points: they are explicitly designed to animate the employees to move between floors. And, with this in mind, they also lead to the roof terraces, where the coverings reiterate the same forms.

In the buildings for Actelion, two possible forms of expression meet, both of which can be found to some degree in various phases of the oeuvre of Herzog & de Meuron. In the Business Center, the open stacking of architectural volumes is realized for the first time. This, together with the VitraHaus completed soon afterward, may be seen as the interim culmination of an ongoing evolution. The laboratory building, on the other hand, indicates a new direction in its return to a more subtle syntax that will later imbue future designs. The inventors of the Swiss Box are not so much returning to their roots here, but instead discovering the potential that lies in their own early and historical design formulations, and, with that, the possibility of responding to a definitively changed global situation in a time of multiple crises.

The Park Avenue Armory has become an internationally renowned cultural venue, hosting events in contemporary music, dance, performance, fine arts, and architecture. Completed in 1881, the building looks back on a venerable history as a prestigious military facility and, after the mid-1900s, as a social club for the elite of New York.

The Armory has therefore always been perceived as an important monument in New York City—a historical building, whose renovation and technical retrofitting has acquired increasing urgency in recent years.

In addition, the Park Avenue Armory is not simply one of many important buildings but, in fact, the most important incarnation of American historicism, the Aesthetic Movement. All the major representatives of this eclectic movement and its incredibly sophisticated craftsmanship were involved in adopting and adapting neo-Renaissance, Gothic, Baroque, and any number of hybrid styles in their design of the interiors: Louis Comfort Tiffany, Stanford White, Herter Brothers, and Pottier & Stymus. The roster of names demonstrates how closely this location was associated with the history of art in the United States. At the same time, it was the hub of social, military, and political events. Until recently, the police departments and the army continued to use the Drill Hall, the last time in 2001 as a center of operations during the 9/11 catastrophe.

It is therefore especially surprising that we, as European architects, were contacted in 2006 regarding the renovation of the Head House with its sumptuous Company Rooms and colossal Drill Hall, a challenging task of immense art historical and psychological significance. One might compare it to the local authorities in Basel contacting a New York architect regarding the restoration of the Basel City Hall with its centuries-old frescoes and intricate architectural embellishments.

Restoration of such a prestigious monument naturally raises several questions. How is restoration to be interpreted? Restoration of what: a return to the first and earliest state of the building? And what does "renovation" mean? Does it mean renewal as if there had been no history, as if there had been no decades of ceaseless technical and social change? There are no clear-cut answers to these questions. Where there are doubts of this kind and divergent approaches to past and present, wide-ranging cultural and psychological patterns are inevitably brought to bear as well.

The extreme ends of the scale are as follows: don't change anything, leave it as it stands today with all the traces of time, the additions and extensions, and the technically necessary modifications; or: change everything, go back to the original state as on the first day, with no traces of time and history.

Many of the artists who had the opportunity to set up their studios or put up temporary installations in the Company Rooms of the Park Avenue Armory, sympathized with the former approach and advocated changing as little as possible.

In the United States, however, the prevailing practice in conservation tends toward the latter extreme: restoration to the "original state," as on the first day. This is achieved by covering the current state of the building, like makeup, behind which all the historical layers can be hidden and preserved: in other words, a simulation of what is assumed to be the original state. In this way, the original layers are preserved but a new architectural space is created that simulates the historical space and ignores the temporal aspect of the monument, thus making it look like an alien body.

There are other approaches as well. Particularly striking and contrary are those of John Ruskin and Eugène Viollet-le-Duc, who were both working in Europe when the Armory was built in New York.

Viollet-le-Duc's philosophy was to add new architectural components to the old, creating a mix that completely changed the expression of the original building. He was interested in new spaces, which meant transforming the original work and incorporating it into a new whole. Starting with the historical substance, he came up with new architecture for a new age, the dawning age of industrialization.

Ruskin, on the other hand, emphasized the significance and inviolability of the original, especially the Gothic monuments of the Middle Ages as embodiments of a philosophical and political message that he wanted to convey. From his point of view, the medieval unity of architectural concept, craftsmanship, and spiritual, rather than economic orientation, was fundamental to the creation of great works and the ideal of a social order that had once prevailed and should now be restored. He considered certain neo-Gothic buildings, which were under construction in the 19th century, as steps on the way to reviving those times.

But what they lacked in comparison to the Gothic originals was, he felt, the equivalent of an ideal social order, whose loss he lamented.

These different approaches to dealing with historical architecture do not give us insight into which path would be meaningful, but they do indicate how relevant architecture is in relation to its time, that is, the extent to which it mirrors the contemporary psychology and mood, and thus itself becomes a transient part of history. We can never start with a blank slate; something is always there to begin with and it is imperative to take those givens, the concrete surroundings, into account. No two architectural tasks are ever identical; each one requires a singular strategy of its own, much like medical intervention into a living organism.

Working in close collaboration with conservationists at the Park Avenue Armory, we wanted to chart a path of our own and work out tailored approaches not only for each room but also for specific states and conditions within them. Some of them, like the Board of Officers Room, had undergone little structural change and therefore only needed to be cleaned, stabilized, and technically updated to meet contemporary standards. Crucial issues were the lighting and the heating, which were originally provided by gas lamps and fireplaces. Although they contributed substantially to the architectural expression of each of the rooms, we chose not to restore the old technologies. Basically, we were neither able nor did we want to return to the "original" state of the rooms because the technical prerequisites were no longer available, having been lost or destroyed in renovation. But in some cases, for instance the Company D room, we proceeded as if we were restoring the Sistine Chapel: dirt and subsequent layers were meticulously removed in order to reveal the original painting of the walls and ceiling. This original painting had, in turn, been overpainted several times (the final layer being a monochrome light green) and partially damaged or destroyed altogether. We decided not to completely repaint and reprint these damaged patches to look as if they had never changed. Nor did we want to leave spots as if to pit the old against the new, like the "honest" intervention, as espoused by the still prevalent dialectical method introduced in Europe after the Second World War.

Having identified the background color, we used it throughout to restore the original expression and coherence of the room. In addition, both the damaged and intact patches were printed with a pattern borrowed from the existing wall pattern.

We used copper-based pigments and the original method of stenciling to apply the pattern to the wall. Copper and other metal pigments, introduced in the mid-19th century, make surfaces look iridescent and almost ethereal. Copper, in many different shapes and forms, would become a recurring theme in our work on the architecture at the Park Avenue Armory: we used it for light fixtures, handles, and as cladding on the wall of the elevator. The material is a kind of leitmotif that does justice to the different rooms and yet also functions as a unifying factor. Where copper pigment has been applied to the original substance, it can be removed again at some point should the eternal questions of renovation, restoration, or simulation be revisited.

Herzog & de Meuron, 2016

Park Avenue Armory with head house and drill hall in the year 1881 shortly after it was inaugurated, and in 2006 when Herzog & de Meuron first saw it.

293_SI_0803_EXT-HIST_026

293_SI_0807_238_DH

293_SI_0902_CO-D_1880

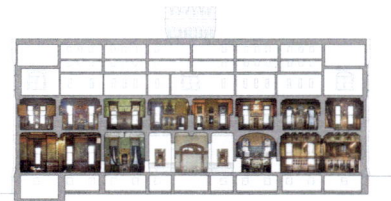

293_RE_110715_DD_03

293_SI_0811_EXTERIOR_001

293_SI_070619_151_4E4_DH

293_SI_0902_CO-D_EK

293_RE_090225_100-DD_DH_2010

This prestigious building for the upper classes was variously restored and remodeled. The architects meticulously mapped all of these phases.

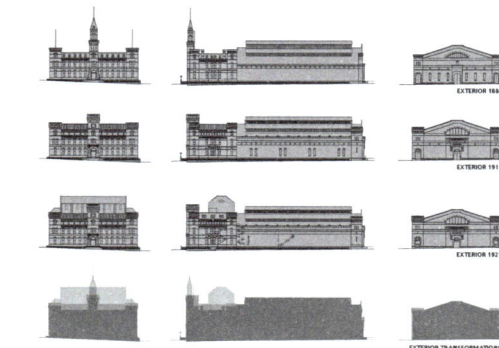

EXTERIOR 1860

EXTERIOR 1911

EXTERIOR 1927

EXTERIOR TRANSFORMATIONS

293_RE_1007_INTRO_P-071

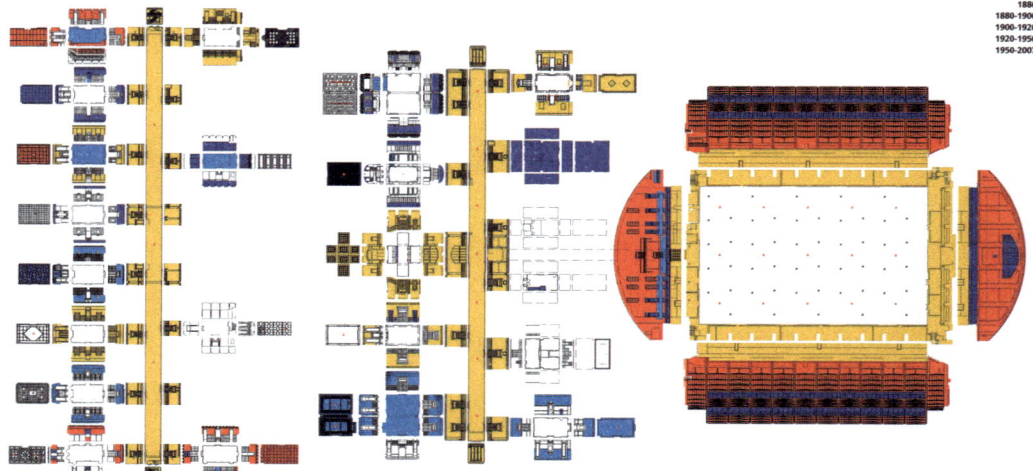

1880
1880-1900
1900-1920
1920-1950
1950-2007

HEAD HOUSE 2ND FLOOR

293_PA_090401_1950-2007

HEAD HOUSE 1ST FLOOR

DRILL HALL

1880

Company D was one of the first period rooms to be restored in 2011.

293_CI_091130_801_COD_SEQUENCE-WALL

293_CO_110407_CO_D_JE_07

293_CP_110705_CO_D_JE_4592

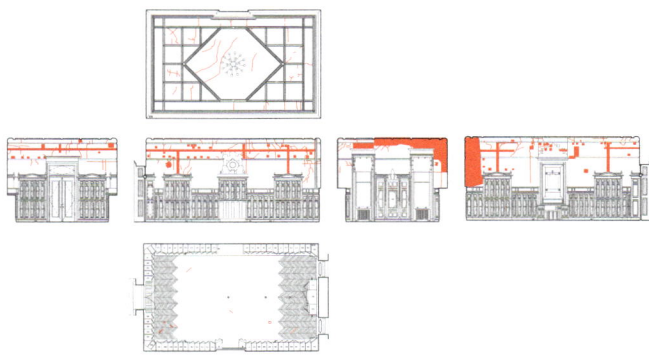

293_CI_091107_801_COD_DAMAGES

293_CO_110210_005_COD

293_CO_1105_PAA_CO_D_JE_28

293_CO_1104_706_JE_H

Modifications were necessary to accommodate new uses and to meet technical and security requirements. These, as well as the replacement of missing elements, evolved by thoughtfully weighing the balance between on-site conditions and a contemporary syntax.

293_CP_111024_740_IB_0559_H

293_CP_111024_739_IB_0558_H

293_CO_1101_119_COD_WOODWORK

293_CP_1109_726_JE_COD_H

293_CP_1108_PAA_CO_D_JE_6048

293_CO_110329_047_COD-CHANDELIER

293_MU_1009_023_D-GLOBE

293_CP_1109_718_JE_COD_H

293_CP_110824_002_CO_D_JE

293_CI_1201_801_CHANDELIER_K

To improve vertical access, the artists designed a copper-clad elevator which is large enough to be used for artistic events as well.

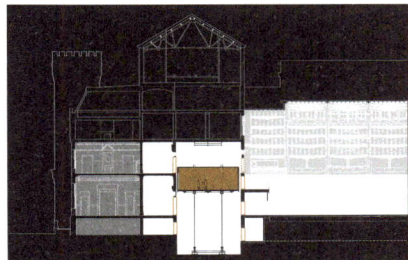

293_DR_0902_054A_SEC-N4_BLACK

293_MO_0906_031_MV

293_CI_0906_015_HHMV_DH

293_CI_1109_002A_MV-OPEN

75

The drill hall hosted social events. Its industrial character has been restored.

293_SI_0603_039_DH-HIST

293_SI_0603_751_HIST

293_MO_0908_006_DH

293_CI_0902_115C_CAFE

The sumptuous Veterans Room is one of the few rooms designed by Louis C. Tiffany to survive in its entirety.

293_SI_0804_702_1880_VT

293_SI_0603_744_HIST

293_SI_1107_JE_VET_01

Meticulous historical restoration of every detail in the Veterans Room, from lighting fixtures to wallpaper patterns, was completed in 2016.

293_CO_1601_499_VET

293_CO_1508_011_VET

293_CO_1601_507_VET

293_CO_1601_030_VET

293_CO_1601_361_VET

293_CO_1601_360_VET

293_CP_160223_723_JE_H

293_CI_140929_801_VET

WALLPAPER: HAND PAINTED LAYERS

293_DR_150901_002-VET-WALLPAPER-HAND-PAINT

WALLPAPER: STENCIL LAYERS

293_DR_150901_001-VET-WALLPAPER-STENCIL

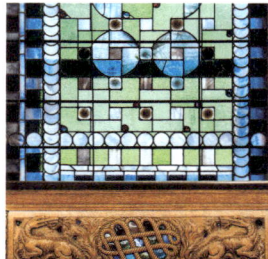

293_CO_1506_013_VET

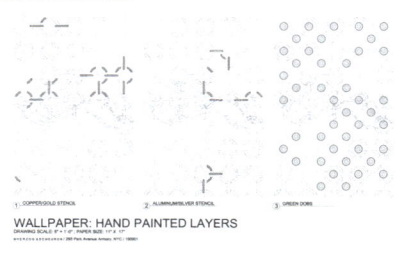

293_CP_160223_704_JE_H

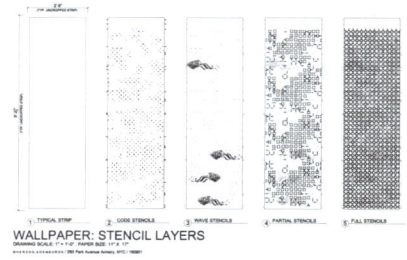

293_CP_160223_707_JE_H

293_CP_160223_735_JE_H

293_CO_1601_373_VET

293_CP_160223_727_JE_H

293_CP_160223_701_JE_H

Park Avenue Armory is one of the key architectural monuments of the American Aesthetic Movement. Louis Comfort Tiffany, Stanford White, the Herter Brothers, and many other outstanding artists of the day collaborated here to create entire ensembles. The massive red-brick building, which occupies an entire block between Park Avenue and Lexington Avenue, was constructed between 1877 and 1880 to plans by architect Charles W. Clinton and was, for a long time, one of the central meeting points of New York's upper class. This was where the scions of leading families trained in the Seventh Regiment of the New York Guard, and the place where glittering society balls were held. Like the grand railroad stations of the era, Park Avenue Armory combines a palatial head house with an industrial-style hall behind, its barrel-shaped roof resting on huge columns. With its three-story facade, mansard roof, and corner towers, the building recalls an Italian palazzo as much as it does a fortress. When Herzog & de Meuron were called in, the building was in a dilapidated state in spite of its historical significance. It was to be refurbished with the aim of hosting cultural events that would play an important role in New York's social life.

The architects took a sensitive approach to this architectural monument. They did not want to create a contrast between old and new, but instead to define the building as a "found space" at the heart of the city, rather like the oil tanks of Tate Modern. They felt that by preserving its historical identity, it would be possible to create a place distinctly set apart from the anonymity of global architecture. Observing tradition, a requirement for historical buildings, is primarily an architectural issue.

With this in mind, the first measures were to cleanse the facade of all later additions, to reopen bricked-up window apertures, and to restore the diversity of the interior rooms. The representational rooms and the rooms dedicated to the individual companies in the head house of the Armory are all very different. The divisions competed with one another to achieve the best look and so they constantly renovated their rooms to keep up with changing tastes and technical innovations. In some of the rooms, the Neo-Renaissance style had already been replaced by Neo-Gothic as early as 1892. Electrification of the building in 1897 involved the first major intervention, though many more were to follow. However, it was a subsequent lack of upkeep that eventually led to considerable damage. Herzog & de Meuron found rooms there that were like palimpsests of their own history. From the flooring to the wall coverings to the ceilings, furnishings, fixtures, and lighting, Herzog & de Meuron set about determining the details that gave the rooms their distinctive identity and developed a strategy that would allow them to take a consistent approach to the changes that would be made. Wherever possible, the original state was restored and stabilized. Damage was repaired, and areas beyond repair were colored in the tones of the dominant original paintwork. In a third stage, the overall historical mood of each room was enhanced without eradicating the traces of change. As it turned out, much of the wooden paneling and many of the built-in elements such as lockers were found to be well preserved and in need of little more than careful cleaning, whereas the walls and ceilings had undergone the greatest changes. This approach differed considerably from prevailing standards in the United States, which generally involve simulating an earlier state.

The architects developed a range of tools by which to integrate the existing patchwork into an aesthetically cohesive whole. Where the findings beneath several historical layers proved to be too heterogenous or too severely damaged, the wall was overprinted in a filigree pattern abstracted from the original floral decor into circular and other forms. The new layer thus combines the existing differences into a finely woven network. The copper hue echoes the metallic paints that can be found residually in many of the rooms. These metallic paints were new at the time the Armory was built and they gave the rooms a special sheen, depending on light conditions, though this faded over the years due to oxidization.

Copper is a material that Herzog & de Meuron have used in many of their own projects, from the cladding of the Signal Box in Basel to the facade of de Young Museum in San Francisco. They appreciate its changing appearance: it can be matte or shiny, luminously red or brackish green, it ages well and it can be used both as cladding and as a material. Copper thus became a unifying element used throughout many of the rooms. It can be found in the ventilation grilles for the lockers of the company rooms, in the tonality of the mirrors that replicate their predecessors over former fireplaces, in chain curtains and furnishings newly designed for various functions and, above all, in the new lighting fixtures.

Light is another important element that lends cohesion throughout the individual rooms. Since most of the chandeliers and wall lights had been lost, Herzog & de Meuron developed their own language of lighting. On the one hand, they sought to reinstate the original lighting mood, while on the other they did not wish to conceal the addition of an element from their own era. One of the crucial aspects in defining the overall spatial impression was the size and dynamic of the original chandeliers. For instance, for Company D Room, the architects devised an equivalent using copper piping that not only echoes the functional language and additive structure of the original but also allows for further lighting fixtures as needed. In Company E Room, by contrast, a contemporary chandelier of simple rectangular tubing was installed as an infrastructural element allowing a variety of lighting solutions to be incorporated as required. In addition to reinstating the individual rooms, the architects have restructured the inner circulation of the building as a system of streets. On the ground floor, they have freed up passageways that directly connect the four most representative rooms on Park Avenue. And the central staircase in the middle of the head house has regained its significance and purpose: connecting the original three stories and illuminating the corridors through its skylight. That was lost in 1909 when a fourth story was built into the attic level. Moreover, in 1984, a partition wall was inserted to block off the staircase from the third story, which was being used as a center for the homeless, which is still one of the identifying features of the Armory. Herzog & de Meuron moved this sheltering facility to the fourth floor and opened up the staircase to reinstate the cohesion of the original, historical three-story unit. In place of the lost skylight, they installed lighting fixtures into the paneling on the underside of the stairs, with sheet copper coverings, providing infinitely variable lighting for the stairway and corridors. Windows that had previously linked ancillary rooms with the staircase were reopened wherever possible. The corridors on the first three floors, corresponding to each other with sequentially diminishing ceiling heights, were given a coordinated design.

Separate and distinct from the imposing Head House building is the Drill Hall. The architects treated it in the same way as the head house, but turned the huge hall into an open stage, revealing its industrial character. Later additions built into the hall were removed to reveal the arched roof beams. The ceiling and ribbon skylighting were restored to complement the overall atmosphere of the space. Ventilation and other technical services required for its multipurpose usage as a performance and exhibition space have been discreetly relegated to the background and colored dark green. Instead of decor, naked structure predominates here.

Thanks to this sensitive restoration and refurbishment, the Armory remains not only a significant American historical monument, but has also become a unique venue for contemporary arts and culture in the heart of New York.

In planning a project, it is rare for one of the earliest design proposals to be the final outcome. The initial idea hardly ever survives subsequent weeks and months of study within the team and in exchange with the client. But that is exactly what happened in the case of VitraHaus. The very first sketch already contained the basics of the final design—an assemblage of stacked houses.

Exchange with the client was extremely close, intense, and efficient. The client was one person: Rolf Fehlbaum. He had already carried out building projects with a number of architects and yet, with his inquisitive mind, he was always prepared to learn about something new and different. As young architects, we had traced his development of the Vitra Campus with a mixture of curiosity and jealousy, and we were really looking forward to our exchange with him. Above all, we admired the location that he had created over the years on the threshold of Basel, especially because his campus contributed to consolidating the idea of a metropolitan city, the city of Basel, covering territory in Switzerland, France, and Germany. The interpretation of Basel as a metropolitan city is one of our main concerns and has been a driving force behind our work for decades. VitraHaus gave us the opportunity to add an important building block to that idea.

VitraHaus aptly designates the project but the name was not determined until the building had been finished. Starting with the idea of creating a complement to the Vitra Design Museum, devoted to the history of design and architecture, the client wanted to build a new space for currently available design classics and the collection of Vitra Home. It was to be as close as possible to the existing museum. But where? He wanted the new building to be equivalent to the museum and close to the main entrance but without overshadowing Frank Gehry's architecture—no hint of vain one-upmanship. In consequence, the new building should not be too close to the museum because it would be taller and designed to communicate with the landscape.

The buildings on the campus have been placed in surroundings of their own so that spaces in between have never been a concern. Each building stands alone, possibly out of respect for existing neighbors or perhaps simply because there was enough room to sidestep spatial issues. In this case, however, care had to be taken to leave enough room for both buildings. Moreover, they provided an opportunity to create a recognizable main entrance to the campus—on the one hand, the singular gesture of the architect embodied in the overall sculptural presence of the Vitra Design Museum and, on the other, the conceptual stack of the VitraHaus: these two in combination now define the main entrance.

As mentioned, the first sketch shows the stack and its basic element: a simple house. It has a gabled roof like most of the houses in the somewhat staid neighborhood around the campus. The traditional shape of the house is suitable architecturally because the building is used by Vitra to organize changing presentations of its Home Collection. It therefore made sense to build on a scale that is more in the nature of a private home than an exhibition space in a museum.

In each of the houses in the stack, a linear sequence of furniture, carpets, and lamps is assembled to show a variety of interiors. Visitors move horizontally from one end of the house to the other, and at the fully glazed end of each house, they see a different section of the surrounding landscape: the silhouettes of the buildings in Basel, the plain of the Rhine with the mountain peaks of the Vosges, or the orchards on the slopes of the Black Forest foothills nearby.

The houses, stacked one on top of the other, are like telescopes facing different directions and each capturing a specific view of the landscape. In addition, a vertical dimension was required to fully appreciate the landscape and to offer viewers another experience of space that is not confined to the horizontal level of presentation.

When the individual houses of the stack meet, they create a sculptural interface. The houses are pushed into each other, generating a number of possible slices. We studied these options and selected what we considered the most suitable and the most beautiful. Both the computer and the physical model were the tools used in making the selection and defining the form. We did not take a proactive approach governed by the vagaries of our design mood; it was more like a screening or a selection procedure. The result is therefore the consequence of an artifice we have devised through which diversity and beauty emerge as if by themselves, for free, as it were. It might be compared to lying on a meadow watching the clouds pass by overhead and waiting until we see one that depicts something we want to keep—more in the nature of a conceptual strategy rather than an individually drafted design.

In consequence, complex cultural spaces emerge basically on their own at the intersections caused by pushing the houses into each other. There, at those interfaces, staircases wind their way through the stack of houses, following an irregular, seemingly random course.

The spaces formed by these cuts bring to mind non-places of the kind found underneath the stairs or the sloping roofs in a private home. They call for and also facilitate presentations of the Home Collection that are entirely different from the linear and lofty sections with the large windows facing the landscape.

Herzog & de Meuron, 2015

The VitraHaus at the entrance relates to the surroundings like a multiple vector.

294_CP_130425_720_IB_5428

294_CP_130425_772_IB_5563

294_CP_130425_750_IB_5524

The shape of the building was developed by defining the spatial needs and experimenting with their layout.

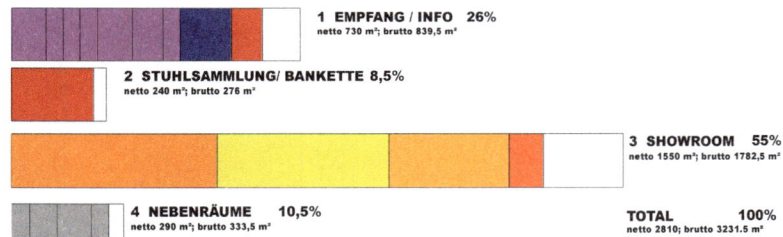

1 **EMPFANG / INFO**   26%
netto 730 m²; brutto 839,5 m²

2 **STUHLSAMMLUNG/ BANKETTE** 8,5%
netto 240 m²; brutto 276 m²

3 **SHOWROOM**   55%
netto 1550 m²; brutto 1782,5 m²

4 **NEBENRÄUME**   10,5%
netto 290 m²; brutto 333,5 m²

TOTAL   100%
netto 2810; brutto 3231.5 m²

294_CI_0703_003

294_MO_060519_038_PROGRAM_K

294_MO_060519_035_PROGRAM_K

294_MO_060519_PROGRAM_063

294_MO_060519_055_PROGRAM_K

294_MO_060529_004

294_MO_0606_004_PROGRAM

Early studies of stacked volumes and the emerging shape of a house.

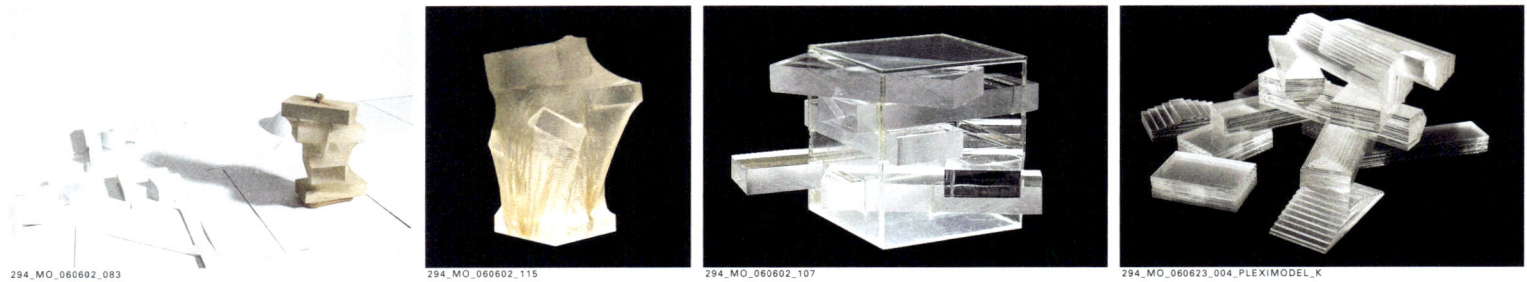

294_MO_060602_083

294_MO_060602_115

294_MO_060602_107

294_MO_060623_004_PLEXIMODEL_K

Sketches of stacked and intersecting house-shaped volumes.

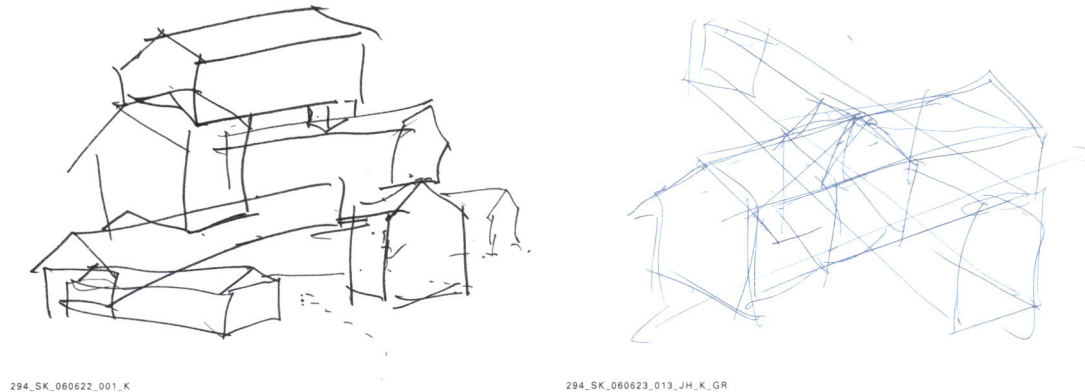

294_SK_060622_001_K

294_SK_060623_013_JH_K_GR

Systematic investigation of variations on intersecting, intercut, and pivoted forms, based on existing and abstract house-shaped buildings.

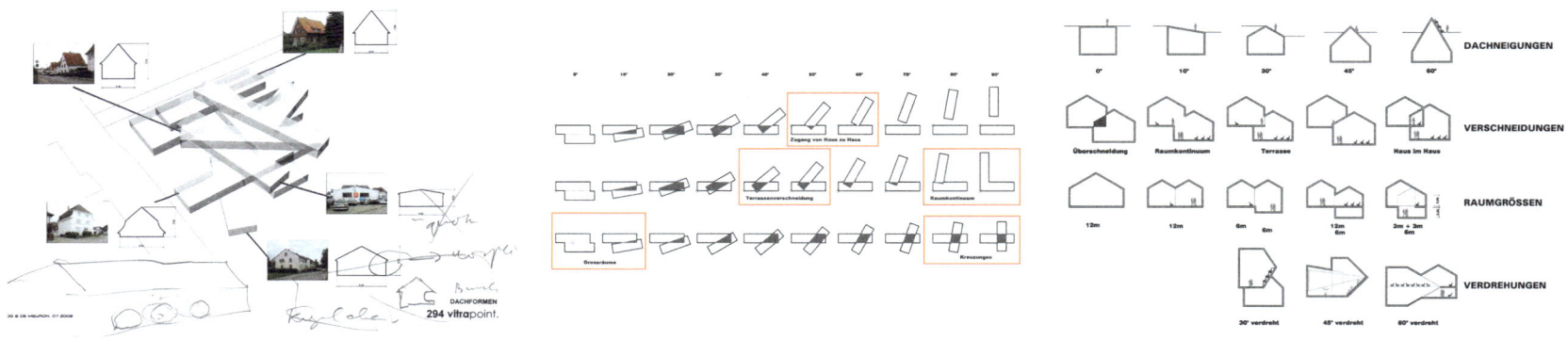

294_SK_0607_002-TM-060726

294_CI_0703_005

294_CI_0703_006

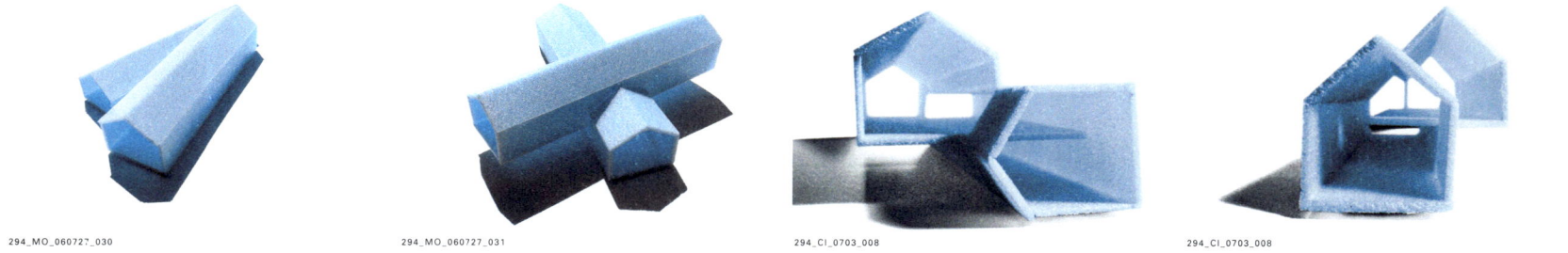

294_MO_060727_030

294_MO_060727_031

294_CI_0703_008

294_CI_0703_008

Jacques Herzog, Rolf Fehlbaum and Pierre de Meuron study the intersecting forms.

294_EV_060623_023

294_MO_0608_098

294_MO_070202_099

294_MO_070202_162

At three interfaces, staircases create special places
and specific routes through the showrooms.

294_MO_0608_024

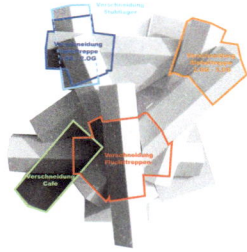

294_MO_0610_061_VRSCHN_K

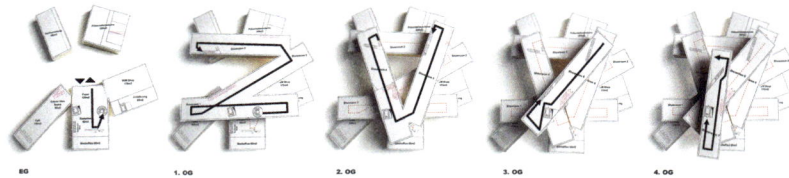

294_CI_0703_011

Models and drafts of staircases as distinctive, biomorphic
shapes set into the largely open interior.

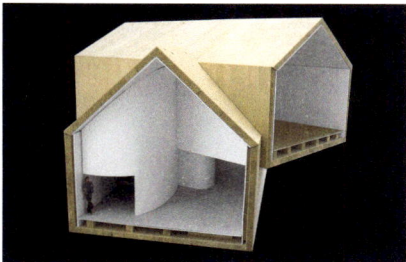

294_MO_0906_063_112-MOA

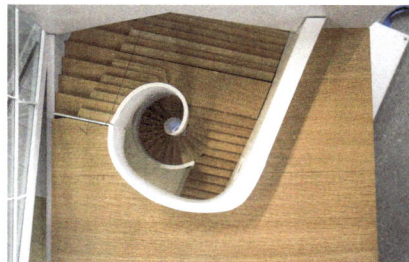

294_MO_090225_162

294_MO_070214_013

294_MO_0710_021

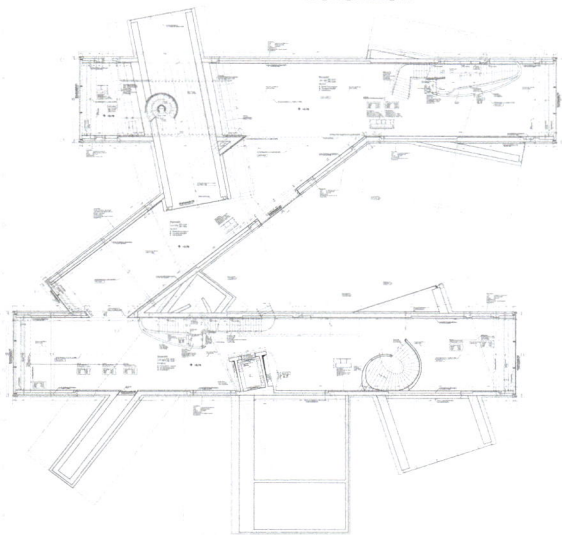

294_DR_0908_502_A-103_LEVEL1_K

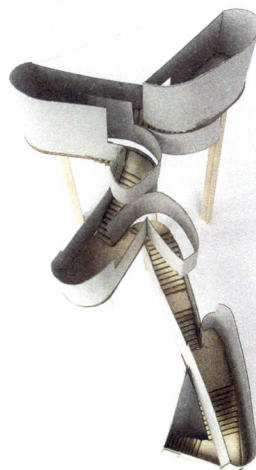

294_MO_0710_002

Models, sketches, and drawings of benches that
could be in a living room although they are industrially
integrated into the construction of the walls.

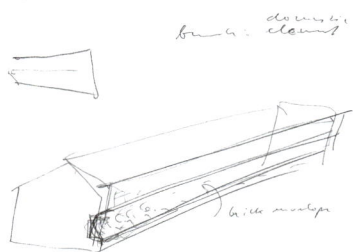

294_SK_060623_501_JH_K

294_MO_090218_040

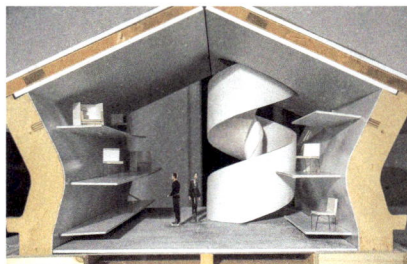

294_MO_090921_10

294_EV_090313_21

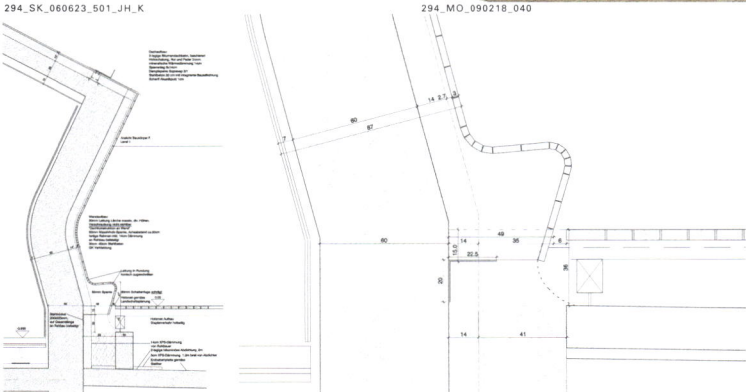

Schnitt Wand E2 (hofseitig)
1:20
294_DT_0910_702_K

Schnitt Wand E1 (wiesenseitig)
1:20

294_EV_070329_001_TM_K

294_CO_0801_33

Architects and client on-site, checking out materials, lighting, and the colors of the walls.

294_CO_0810_003_RF

294_EV_080401_502_K

294_EV_090219_42

294_CO_090922_186

Concrete construction of the labyrinthine building, poured in situ.

294_CO_0808_004_VITRA

294_CO_0810_723_RW

294_CO_0810_157

294_CO_0810_726_RW

294_CO_0810_749_RW

294_CO_0810_724_RW

294_CO_0810_099

Upon completion, VitraHaus presents an exciting flow of spacious and narrow interiors and becomes a luminous beacon in the landscape.

294_CP_1001_702_IB_4853

294_CP_1001_745_IB_3187_K

294_CP_1003_728_DM_028-1914

294_CP_1001_714_IB_5065

294_CP_1001_870_IB_2747_K

294_CP_1001_722_IB_2631

294_CP_1001_724_IB_3582

294_CP_1001_1078_IB_3600_K

294_CP_1003_732_DM_032-1846

294_CP_1001_728_IB_2877

294_CP_1001_717_IB_3660

294_CP_1001_729_IB_3700

Since it was founded in 1950, Vitra has been known as a leading manufacturer of high-end office furniture. In 2004, the company diversified by launching its Home Collection of iconic classics and contemporary products aimed at design-aware private individuals. However, Vitra did not have a showroom, either on its own premises in Weil am Rhein or in any specialist outlet, suited to presenting its range. Although they had inaugurated their own Design Museum in 1989, this was run by an independent foundation and dedicated entirely to exhibitions on themes of architecture and design. Even the company's unparalleled collection of chairs could only occasionally be seen here. So in 2001 they approached Herzog & de Meuron, asking them to propose a concept for an extension of the museum. In an initial study, they suggested converting an existing production hall located directly opposite the museum and building a bridge to link the two. The idea was that it could be used both as a storage depot and as an exhibition space.

However, as the company honed its Home Collection, the discrepancy between the requirements of an exhibition space and a commercial showroom became increasingly evident. What was actually needed was an entirely new type of building that could function as a showroom, museum, library, and experimental base, complete with shop, café, and conference rooms, making it a publicly accessible place. A strip of land was duly acquired for the construction of the new VitraHaus in front of the factory grounds, adding a third new building to complement Tadao Ando's Conference Pavilion and Frank O. Gehry's Vitra Design Museum in a contemporary take on the tradition of architectural follies. Moreover, thanks to its prominent gateway position as well as its scale, the building was to become a visual landmark for Vitra.

In 2006 Herzog & de Meuron were entrusted with planning this building, the first new one to be erected by Vitra in sixteen years. They proposed a design that combines simplicity and complexity, creating a highly expressive architectural icon: twelve houses of varying lengths and widths arranged around an open courtyard, stacked five stories high to some 21 meters. The building, whose plasticity recalls the 2004 Jinhua Structures, looks different from every angle and, with its vertical orientation, sets a counterpoint to the horizontal sprawl of the factory grounds. It achieves all this without competing with the buildings of other prominent architects on the Vitra Campus. Indeed, the new monolith is set a considerable distance from the much smaller museum by Frank O. Gehry for this very reason.

In developing the overall structure of the building, the architects went back to the basic ur-form of the house with pitched roof, floor, and walls, which they had also used in previous projects. Visitors are indeed prompted to think of a home; after all, they are choosing furniture for their own private living space. As early as 1979, in their very first new building project, the Blue House in Oberwil, the architects also chose to follow the traditional typology familiar to all of us since childhood. In an era in which the flat roof and cuboid forms of modernism had already become the norm, the young architects chose to test the limits of traditional forms and their capacity not only to comply with building regulations but also to meet contemporary expectations of the spaces we live in. The pale blue wash of that first project, the slightly off-center porthole window, and its allusion to the films of Jacques Tati all added a lighter touch, breaking with prevailing convention. In 1985, this ur-type of house reemerged in a model for a touring Lego exhibition and provided an art collector in the Swiss municipality of Therwil with the outer framework in which to incorporate various spatial configurations. In 1997 it took shape as a concrete structure in Leymen, on the Franco-Swiss border, rising like a sculpture set on a plinth in the quiet countryside of the Upper Rhine. At the Schaulager, which opened in 2003, for the collection of the Emanuel Hoffmann Foundation in Münchenstein near Basel, it features in the form of a small gatehouse mediating between the huge volume of the building behind it and the housing on the opposite side of the street.

In the case of the VitraHaus, this assimilation of tradition and alienation takes on a new quality. Here, the architects have treated the gabled house form as an abstract volume, alternately extruding and compressing it, and stacking it up over five levels. The connotations and associations between this approach and the mechanical production process of furniture-making are entirely deliberate. The individual volumes all share the same basic shape of the ur-house, but the length, height, and width as well as the pitch of the roof vary. The ground-floor modules are shorter and wider, while those on the upper levels cantilever out; some as far as 15 meters. Where they intersect, the building volumes penetrate each other and where they are superimposed, they pierce through roof spaces. The resulting outward appearance is that of an architectural sculpture whose abstract form is further emphasized by the dark umber finish of the external rendering. Even the thermal insulation system seems to fit the buildings like warm and cozy socks. The walls, floors, and roofs become such an indistinguishable jumble that the load-bearing strategies underpinning the entire in situ concrete structure fade into the background. This is because it is not, as it appears to be, a random stack of houses piled up on one another, but instead an architecture based on a complex underlying system of interconnected tubing in varying thicknesses specifically adapted to the respective loads and forces. A similar structural system of load-bearing tubing, albeit visible and accessible, was deployed for the Prada building in Tokyo's Aoyama district, which also features the ur-house as an autonomous spatial structure within its glass shell.

The principle of stacking has been a recurrent theme in the Herzog & de Meuron approach to architecture ever since their design for the Ricola company's storage facility. In that particular early example, it was applied almost two-dimensionally to the facade. By 2005 it was being deployed as a means of spatial organization. For the business center of Actelion in Allschwil near Basel, for instance, volumes were not arranged as open-plan areas, but as scattered and stacked "office beams." Then, in 2006, the architects proposed a stack of rectangular layers in the form of a massive pyramid as an extension for Tate Modern. Yet the gabled ur-house form actually makes the VitraHaus considerably more complex. From the intersections between the house forms to the varying pitch of the rooftops, there is a precision in play that demands optimum attention to detail. What may appear to be a pile of randomly dropped pick-up sticks is in fact the product of exact calculation.

On the inside, the structure creates a diversity of spatial impressions, from the intimate to the commodious, all generated entirely by the use of volume and the refusal to conceal awkward quirks and edges. Walls and ceilings are painted white throughout, while rough-sawn oak-plank flooring lends a cozy, home-style atmosphere. The ground floor with its conference area, exhibition space for the Vitra chair collection, reception, shop, and café, embraces an inner courtyard with wood paneling that stretches up the walls, morphs into seating benches, and extends all the way to the café garden, creating an intimate and yet open and thoroughly inviting plaza. In this respect, the VitraHaus is very much the reception building for the campus. Inside, rather like the much larger Roche tower, it is arranged as a vertical city. Visitors can access the uppermost floor by taking the elevator in the single connecting circulation core of the building and can walk back down spiral stairways softening the angularity of the building with their organically rounded geometry that opens up individual spaces and vistas throughout the entire length and height of the building.

Perception proves to be a recurrent theme in this design. The fully glazed end walls afford outward views. The individual modules are almost like telescopes honing in on surrounding landmarks. By night, the direction of view is reversed, turning the building into a massive showcase. The VitraHaus, together with the Fondation Beyeler and the Schaulager, forms part of a new triangle of cultural institutions in the Basel area and, as such, an important element of the trinational agglomeration that has been a crucial concern to Herzog & de Meuron since completing their urban study, *Basel – A Nascent City?*, in collaboration with Rémy Zaugg.

Burgos—a stop on the pilgrimage route to Santiago de Compostela—has a mighty Gothic cathedral that towers above the city like a mountain and still dominates the skyline today. Although there are a few industrial parks, the city is surrounded by endless fields of wheat as it has been for centuries. So when we visited Burgos for the first time, we wondered why there was so much construction under way on the outskirts.

Our astonishment was justified. The countless high-rise apartment buildings that were mushrooming in the early 2000s had been financed by cheap loans. The result was a real estate bubble and the beginning of a prolonged economic crisis in all of Spain and beyond. Our project for the Bulevar in Burgos gave us an idea of the extent and cause of the crisis and, at the same time, allowed us to work out a sustainable project without any bells and whistles, a solution that does not even involve an architectural contribution in the conventional sense of a building.

We felt that the Bulevar provided a unique and unexpected opportunity to give the city a new urban backbone that would develop and progress in the years to come, thus forging a new urban dimension as a complement to the existing and incredibly impressive historical image of the cathedral.

The project was sparked off by plans to build a new railroad track to the north of the city, outside of the settlement area, in order to accommodate the Spanish high-speed rail network AVE. This meant that the old tracks, cutting straight through the densely populated city from west to east, could be repurposed. We were commissioned to study the consequences of this relocation on the city as a whole, and to propose a master plan. Our plan has been accepted and is now officially binding.

Our next step was to make plans for repurposing the former railroad tracks. In collaboration with traffic planners and landscape architect Michel Desvigne, we defined the elements required for a boulevard: plants, trees, and surfacing; spaces for pedestrians, bicycles, cars, and a future streetcar. We made drawings of bridges, park benches, streetlamps, and bus stops. We even specified building zones, defining both height and size of the buildings, which would one day shape the appearance of the new urban location. The Bulevar had always been on the "wrong" side, flanked by the usual fire walls and not particularly appealing backyards, much like the areas around trains pulling into the main station of many cities. We wanted to reverse all that: we wanted to turn the back side into a front side, to turn an inaccessible dividing line into a public area accessible to all residents and visitors to the city.

There has been no new construction because of the above-mentioned crisis but even so, the newly created area was rapidly appropriated and has become a vibrant part of the city.

We wanted all of the new elements of the Bulevar—from indigenous trees to park benches and streetlamps—to feel familiar and natural, rather than introducing the sleek contemporary design that often characterizes newly built pedestrian zones in European cities. We therefore used familiar, existing forms for such elements as wooden benches. The design of the latter responds to the specifics of the Bulevar only through their unusual length and curved shape, while the streetlamps are strung diagonally across the street like large drops of water on a clothes line.

The bus stops are the only exception. They instantly attract attention for they look like sculptures in public space and can, in fact, be interpreted as such. Instead of art, for which there was not enough money, we created a small group of oddly shaped, almost absurd bus stops, which we had not designed but copied. The originals are Modernist leftovers from the collapse of the Soviet Union. They now stand abandoned in the landscape of Armenia, where they were discovered and photographed by the artist Ursula Schulz-Dornburg, thanks to whom they ended up on Christine Binswanger's drawing table. Schulz-Dornburg's photographs communicate the sadness and abandonment of waiting in the loneliness of an empty landscape. Here in Burgos, the black-and-white photographs have become real objects again. We translated the photographed images into three-dimensional objects, built models, and designed seating for them so that waiting in the new Bulevar is also an architectural experience.

Herzog & de Meuron, 2016

Burgos lies on the pilgrimage route to Santiago de Compostela and is a city of churches.

266_RE_0612_501_K

266_SI_0603_501_GREEN1_BIRD_L

266_SI_0501_001_HISTORICAL

295_CP_1206_1499_EO_U

266_SI_060727_502

266_RE_0612_522_K

The high-speed railway connects Burgos to
the Paris-Madrid line and stops at Bilbao.

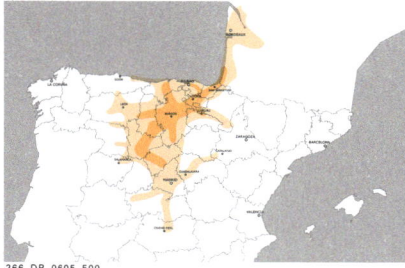

266_DR_0605_500

266_RE_0612_503_K

266_RE_0612_507_K

295_SI_0412_141_EC

266_RE_0612_505_K

295_SI_0412_183_EC

266_RE_0612_528_K

295_SI_0603_500_GAMONAL_L

A three-step master plan. First step: thanks to the
new railroad line, 12 km of inner-city railroad bed have
been freed up for a boulevard. Second step: the
neighborhoods are densified. Third step: new neighborhoods emerge on the edge of the city.

266_RE_0612_508_K

266_SI_0506_019

266_SI_0504_261_VISIT3-KPK

295_SI_0605_155_ESPOLONCI

271_CI_0703_006_CITYMAP1

266_RE_0612_516_K

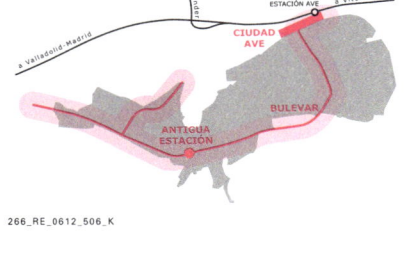

266_RE_0612_516_K

266_RE_0612_506_K

BARRIO NEIGHBOURHOOD	POBLACIÓN INHABITANT	AREA AREA (km2)	DENSIDAD DENSITY (inh./km2)
JUAN XXIII	5.090	0,104	48.900
GRANDMONTAGNE	16.350	0,341	47.900
GAMONAL	4.760	0,136	35.000
A. DEL CID - A. DE CANTABRIA	13.236	0,427	31.000
G-9	10.850	0,381	28.500
BDA. INMACULADA	2.335	0,084	27.800
AVE (+40% USO TERCIARIO) (+40% TERTIARY USE)	EXPECTED 5.085	0,183	27.800
SAN ESTEBAN FERNÁN GONZÁLEZ	3.290	0,120	27.400
ATALAYA DE LA QUINTA	EXPECTED 3.470	0,144	24.100
REYES CATOLICOS	6.160	0,235	26.200
LOS VADILLOS	5.860	0,224	26.200
AVDA. DEL ARLANZON	7.350	0,297	25.400
LAS TORRES	4.470	0,183	24.400
SAN AGUSTÍN	3.840	0,163	23.600
VEGA BARRIÓ GIMENO (+ USO TERCIARIO CONSIDERABLE) (+ SUBSTANTIAL TERTIARY USE)	4.180	0,197	21.200

266_RE_0612_510_K

BARRIO NEIGHBOURHOOD	POBLACIÓN INHABITANT	AREA AREA (km2)	DENSIDAD DENSITY (inh./km2)
ANTIGUA ESTACIÓN (+42% USO TERCIARIO) (+42% TERTIARY USE)	EXPECTED 3.370	0,163	20.700
STA. AGUEDA	960	0,047	20.400
SAN GIL SAN JUAN	4.540	0,237	19.200
EL CARMEN	1.180	0,062	19.000
SAN ZOLES	EXPECTED 2.668	0,150	17.900
SAN PEDRO DE LA FUENTE	4.860	0,278	17.500
TERRAZAS DEL HOSPITAL DEL REY	EXPECTED 2.215	0,130	17.000
CAUCE DE VILLARGÁMAR	EXPECTED 5.270	0,313	16.800
POZANOS VILLATORO	4.640	0,280	16.600
SAN PEDRO Y SAN FELICES	7.040	0,436	16.200
PINAR DE VILLACIENZO	EXPECTED 2.797	0,175	16.000
SANTA CLARA SAN PEDRO DE CARDEÑA	7.890	0,497	15.900
CAPISCOL	1.780	0,163	15.800

The proposal for the Burgos Bulevar is presented at an exhibition in Burgos.

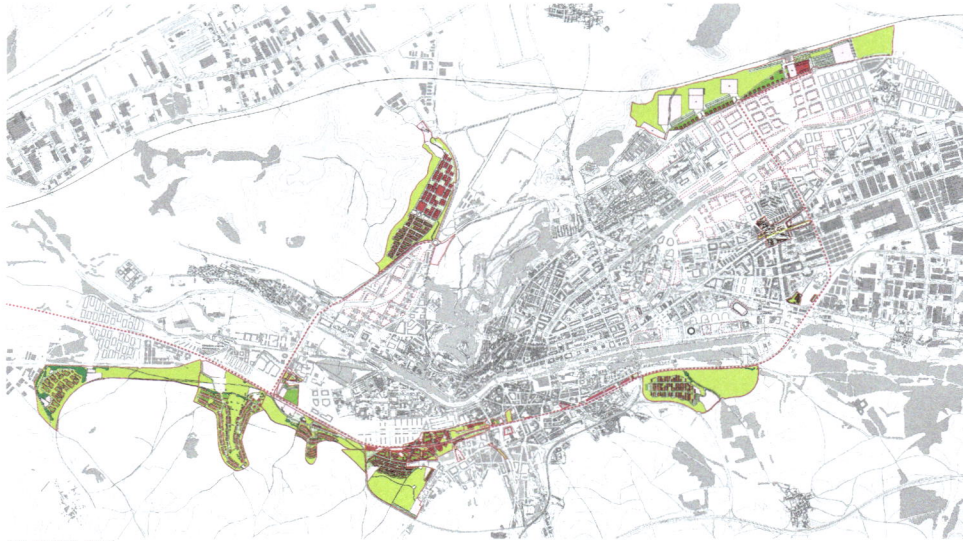

266_RE_0612_546_K

295_EV_0610_015_EXHIBITION

266_MO_0603_001

Specific locations before and after converting the railroad line into a boulevard. They link extremely diverse neighborhoods.

295_SI_0504_043_EC

295_SI_0412_116_EC

295_SI_0412_109_EC

295_SI_0412_132_EC

295_CP_1206_0721_EO

295_CP_1206_1295_EO

295_CP_1206_1317_EO

295_CP_1206_1093_EO

For the public squares, the architects have designed drop-shaped lamps, which are already in use at the Plaza de España in Tenerife.

295_CI_0608_125_LIGHTING

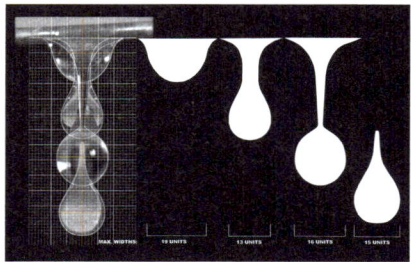

295_DR_0608_043_LIGHT

295_MU_0611_068_TRANSPARENT

295_MU_0706_501_K

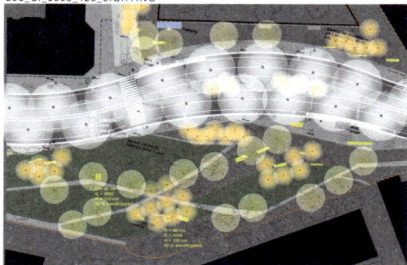

295_CI_0701_148

295_MO_0703_223_PASARELLA

295_CP_1206_0723_EO

295_CP_1010_006

The boulevard brings the landscape back into the city; local stone chips give the asphalt a natural touch.

295_SA_0704_029_ASPHALT

295_CP_1103_015_AN

295_EV_1103_132

295_CI_0710_080

Proposal for public pathways and greenery, in collaboration with Michel Desvigne.

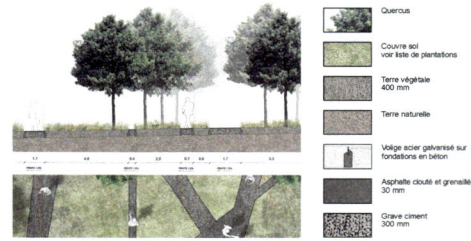

295_RFCL_0000_059_MD_PARIS

Quercus
Couvre sol voir liste de plantations
Terre végétale 400 mm
Terre naturelle
Volige acier galvanisé sur fondations en béton
Asphalte clouté et grenaillé 30 mm
Grave ciment 300 mm

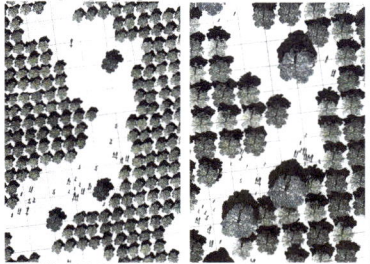

295_CP_110325_575_131

295_PP_0710_074_K

295_CP_0903_010

295_RFNL_0000_100

295_CP_1206_1187_EO

295_CP_1206_1268_EO

To design the bus stops, the architects have taken inspiration from bus shelters in Armenia and Saudi Arabia.

295_RFAR_0000_502

295_CO_1106_BUSHALTESELLTEN

295_CP_1206_0701_EO

295_CP_1206_0813_EO

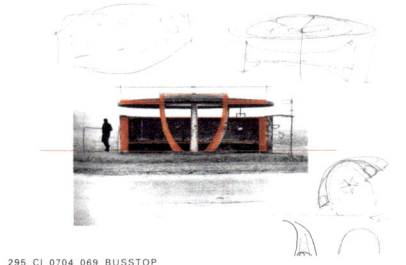

295_CI_0704_069_BUSSTOP

295_CO_1102_083

295_CP_1206_0738_EO

295_CP_1206_1353_EO

The park benches reference typologies in Central Park, New York.

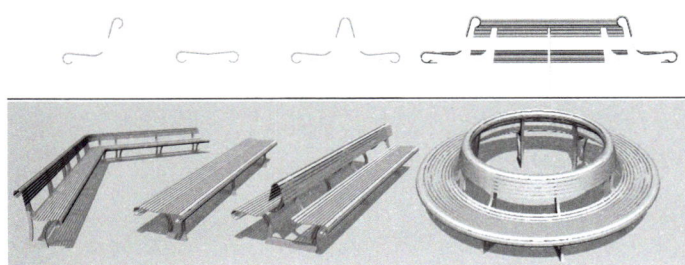

295_CI_0000_501_K

295_CO_0907_4092

295_CP_1206_1314_EO

The road bridge over the Rio Arlanzón is divided, illuminating the terrain underneath and creating meeting places.

295_SI_0506_017_QUINTA

295_MO_0706_017_BRIDGE

295_MO_0000_501_K

295_CP_1206_0852_EO

295_CP_1206_0707_EO

295_EV_120412_PDM_001

295_EV_120412_PDM_012

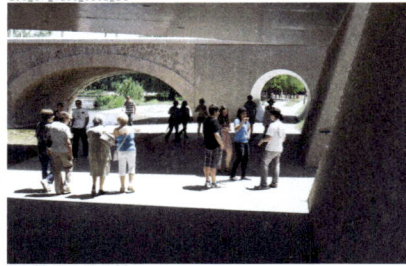

295_CP_1206_0866_EO

A network of public squares on the new boulevard connects the once separated neighborhoods to the right and left of the railway line.

295_CP_120625_ZOB

295_CP_1103_022_AN

295_EV_1103_198

295_CP_120630_701_DM

295_CP_1206_1070_EO

295_EV_1103_197

295_CP_0903_006

295_CP_1206_0736_EO

295_CP_1206_0725_EO

295_CP_1103_046_AN

295_CP_1010_007

Burgos is connected to Europe's high-speed rail network via the Paris-Madrid route. With its population of 170,000, Burgos is also a major highway hub as well as being an important station on the historic pilgrimage route known as the Camino de Santiago. In the year 2004 alone, more than 60,000 pilgrims stayed overnight in the city. Churches, convents, and monasteries are an important part of the urban fabric, and the Gothic cathedral draws as many as 300,000 visitors each year. Madrid, some 250 kilometers to the south, is about a 75-minute commute, while Bilbao to the north can be reached within the hour. San Sebastian, Navarra, Logrono, and Valladolid are even closer. All of this, coupled with low prices, a leisurely pace of life, and a beautiful historical center, makes Burgos a very appealing place to live. Set at an altitude of 850 meters, the town is an administrative center capable of attracting other branches of industry to complement its existing automotive and agricultural sectors.

A new master plan was needed to adapt the urban layout to the changes required by the AVE high-speed rail connection. This included considering future building developments as well as devising a comprehensive new traffic system. The master plan also called for a 12-kilometer-long boulevard to replace the existing railway route. The track for the high-speed AVE line, with a new railway station, will run through the northern area of the city, bordering on its surrounding agricultural zone, thus freeing up the track network that previously ran from east to west.

Herzog & de Meuron drew up a master plan that was implemented in 2007. It included new residential zones and involved redeveloping the city center by creating a new boulevard with two distinct focal points. In providing these new developments, careful consideration was given to both building density and public space as key criteria. A large proportion of the new residential area would be centered primarily around the new high-speed railway station, forming a contemporary counterpoint to the historical core of the city. A number of mixed-use high-rise buildings would be constructed between the northern periphery and the ancient Roman Via Aquitania, making the new railway line widely visible. Because the area is already well served by public transport, a further development phase will include a new stadium and bullring just outside this line.

The master plan also allows for increased development of the existing districts in the east and west of the city. In previous decades, low-rise buildings, wide streets, and oversized squares had resulted in an atmosphere of emptiness rather than urban density. A more human scale is introduced to the area by means of new zoning and additional buildings. A similarly thoughtful approach has been taken with regard to the creation of new residential developments in the surrounding area, to ensure that these are vibrant, livable places, while at the same time respecting the topography and avoiding further urban sprawl that would encroach on the landscape.

In the center, the historic landmarks are treated as points of orientation and their visibility enhanced by enlarging the public spaces around them. These landmarks include not only buildings such as churches and monasteries associated with the Camino de Santiago, but also the San Amaro university campus and the Hospital del Rey, as well as historical examples of architecture relating to the agricultural industry. In addition, new high-rise buildings at selected points define the new boulevard as a further axis complementing the Camino de Santiago and the Río Arlanzón. The largest available site in proximity to the city center is around the old railway station, which has been freed up due to the relocation of the tracks. Thirteen high-rise buildings on an 800-meter-long section of the new boulevard frame it as an urban artery, enlivened by the publicly accessible lower floors with a mix of uses. Their polygonal forms and the spaces between them respect the lines of view between the castle, cathedral, old railway station, Las Huelgas monastery, and the surrounding hills. The potential of this strategy is exemplified by the

Torres Burgos: two residential towers, 14 to 15 stories high, define the street space, with a pavilion nestled behind. The metal facades of the outer shell echo the delicate structures of northern Spanish winter gardens and at the same time they are reminiscent of the shutters of the Basel residence on Schützenmattstrasse and the apartment buildings on the Rue des Suisses in Paris. The pattern is derived from the forms of the three floor plans, similar to the approach taken for the apartment building beside the parking garage in Miami Beach. Behind this, an inner glass facade forms a series of balconies, as in the apartments of the Helsinki Dreispitz in Basel. A park leads to the former locomotive shed. The towers form part of a large-scale connection between the historical center, the river, the old railway station, and the viewing tower on the hill.

So far, what has already been completed of the master plan is the transformation of the old railway tracks into the new boulevard. The boulevard improves access to the city center while alleviating it of traffic. Above all, however, it forms an integral part of the concept of public space. With exemplary attention to detail, Herzog & de Meuron show here just how much the redevelopment of urban space is a question of patience and of having the courage to proceed one small step at a time. What is immediately evident is that the boulevard runs like a ribbon through very different kinds of neighborhoods, both old and new, both central and peripheral. In the past, the railway tracks divided them. Now, the boulevard offers the possibility of reuniting them.

The architects have adapted the number of lanes and the width of the sidewalks to the varying volume of traffic. They have chosen traffic lights rather than roundabouts, for the benefit of pedestrians, and they have divided the lanes according to direction of travel by planting rows of trees to minimize the impression of a vast area of asphalt. The asphalt itself is mixed with a high volume of crushed local stone to give a more natural look. Each situation has its own specific solution. The urban space of the boulevard is intended to be more personal and more varied than envisaged in many late modernist designs. Herzog & de Meuron depart from late modernism even in their choice of street furniture. Instead of inventing a new design, they look to older forms that appear to come from a different time. The boulevard is illuminated by lamps like those developed for the Plaza España in Santa Cruz de Tenerife: droplike glass forms suspended from a network of cables. The bus stops recall photographs taken by the artist Ursula Schulz-Dornburg in 1997 of the architecture of waiting areas in Armenia and Saudi Arabia. The architects have appropriated these strange structures that look like a parasol or a lidded trophy, and have created social sculptures where people congregate. There are no billboards, and the timetables and ticket machines are positioned separately nearby. The benches form circles or long rows that mark the boundary between asphalt and grass. As in New York's Central Park, they invite people to linger, sometimes in large groups. Social structures are created instead of design.

Finally, the architects have also combined infrastructural requirements with the need for green spaces. The landscape, with its hills, its castle mount, and its two rivers, reaches deep into the heart of the city. Herzog & de Meuron have complemented this factor on a grand scale. The new boulevard, with its thousands of newly planted trees, creates additional green space. A meadow-like park links the back of the now-defunct former railway station, its tracks dismantled, with the urban space. A new bridge channeling traffic across the Río Arlanzón has lanes that are separated so that light falls between them, making the space below more welcoming to pedestrians. The old railway bridge is reserved for cyclists. The park meanders beneath the bridge. In a place that was once inaccessible to people, the architects have created a linked-up and socially inclusive boulevard. Further development has been stalled by the economic crisis.

**Hong Kong
China
2006–2018**

**No. 296
Tai Kwun,
Centre for Heritage & Art**

*The former Central Police Station was constructed by
the British in the mid-19th century as the most important police
headquarters in the colony: a walled-in rectangular compound
containing a dense layout of buildings to accommodate administrative offices and jails. Between the buildings there are both
extremely confined and more open spaces: narrow lanes, a police
parade ground, and a prison courtyard at the southern end of
the premises.*

*The central police station is a city within the city. Seen
through European eyes, the compound is the closest thing to
an old town in all of Hong Kong, although it was never open to the
public and few people had been there.*

*Nonetheless, in the multiyear planning process, the loca-
tion, which has contributed substantially to the history of the city,
proved to be particularly sensitive when it came to remodeling and
modifying the long familiar cityscape. This is no different from
what happens in other cities, but we were still surprised at the vehe-
mence and commitment of the reactions in the neighborhood,
and the responsiveness of the client and the authorities to the
critical voices.*

*The former police headquarters of the British colonial
powers were to be remodeled and rebuilt as a center of art
and culture. If there are places in cities that might be compared
to acupuncture points in the human body, then the police
station compound is certainly such a place for the people of
Hong Kong—even more so because it was not just a question of
remodeling and rebuilding. The project meant creating a
public site for art and culture in a city that had never known anything of that kind. For decades, the cultural and social life
of Hong Kong has been dominated by trade, commerce, and
finance. But in 2006 the Hong Kong Jockey Club, which makes
its money on betting and organizing horse races and invests
some of its profits in charitable projects, contacted us regarding a
mixed-use site that would accommodate galleries, shops,
and restaurants, as well as locations for fine art, music, and performances. That was a few years before Art Basel decided in
2011 to expand to Asia and selected Hong Kong as its strategic
site, rather than Beijing or Shanghai despite their incompa-
rably larger art scenes.*

When we won the competition in 2013 for M+, a museum for visual culture, Hong Kong had already become a different city. Major international galleries had opened branches there, and every spring, Art Basel Hong Kong lends the city a Western art-world flare, at least for a few days.

The Central Police Station was our first project in this built city with its incredibly dense architecture, in this ocean of towers and high-rise buildings. We therefore set to work with a completely free hand and without the usual restrictions regarding height and density.

Our first design was a towering skyscraper: steel skeletons rising up like gigantic bamboo scaffolding or unfinished high-rise buildings, limited only by the incidence of light. These skeletons would be covered with plants and fitted with vertical gardens. The building's uses were nestled in between like treehouses: exhibition venues and platforms for public life as an expression of the city's burgeoning cultural and intellectual life.

This first design failed, and so did the second—a beam floating above the compound—because of the resistance of the local community and restrictions in height that had been introduced by the Town Planning Board.

As a result, we had to radically rethink our approach to this cultural quarter of the future. We abandoned the idea of an overarching architectural form and realized that there was considerable potential in the scale and small patchwork nature of the existing compound. We studied the brickwork of the wall around the compound, the openings in it, the frames around the entrances, the steep staircases, the differences in the adjoining streets, and the locations on Old Bailey Street and Arbuthnot Road best suited as new entrances to the compound.

We recognized the potential of the former prison courtyard as a future plaza: we would plant greenery on the high wall towards the south that closes off the courtyard like a cliff face, in order to emphasize the natural character of Hong Kong's distinctive hilly topography. The plaza lies between the two new buildings erected in the southwest and southeast corners of the compound, with venues for exhibitions, music, and performances as well as restaurants and bars. They supplement the spaces reserved for cultural functions in the remodeled old buildings. The Central Police Station—renamed Tai Kwun, Centre for Heritage & Art—will feature white cubes and found spaces, *making the location even more attractive and flexible for both artists and visitors.*

In other words, we concentrated exclusively on determining the qualities of the existing site and bringing them to the fore. Since hardly anyone had ever been in this once locked and forbidden place in the city, it was vital to create a permeable site by making the narrow lanes and little squares, the broad staircases, the large plazas, and all the different, architecturally distinct old and new buildings accessible on foot. Opening up this compound is something special here in Hong Kong, quite unlike the repurposing of a derelict industrial site in a European city. Tai Kwun will be a place where visitors can stand with their own two feet on public ground—in a city where people ordinarily go from one place to another by negotiating a confusion of sky bridges and semi-public lobbies in department stores.

Herzog & de Meuron, 2016

An initial concept is based on the maximum building volume permitted by capacity and solar access regulations. The scaffold-like structure allows for various uses and the cultivation of vertical gardens.

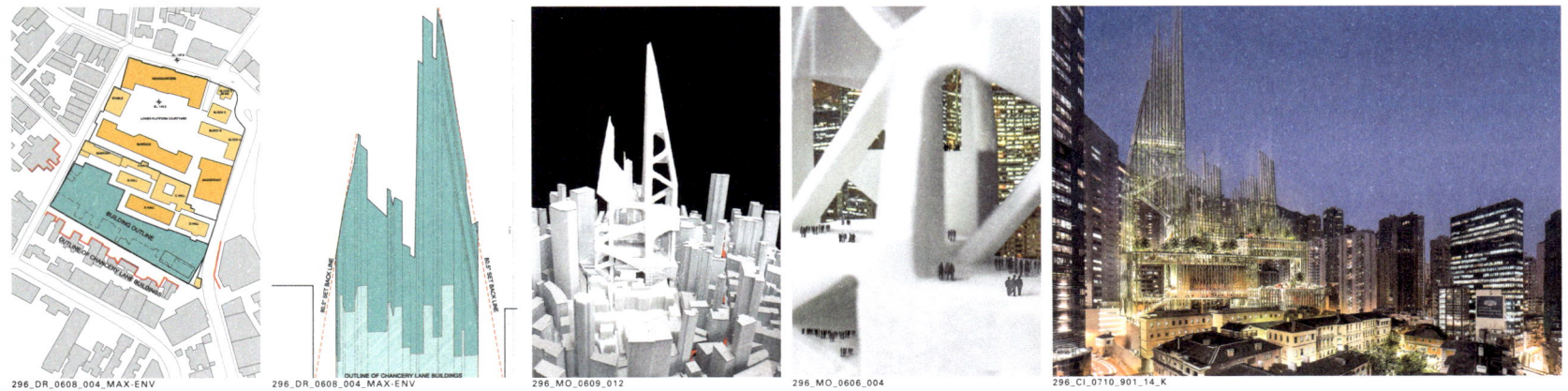

296_DR_0608_004_MAX-ENV

296_DR_0608_004_MAX-ENV

296_MO_0609_012

296_MO_0606_004

296_CI_0710_901_14_K

A second design proposes placing a horizontal block, structured like a bridge on top of the existing buildings.

296_MO_0905_026_28

296_MO_0905_090

296_MO_0907_025

296_MO_0907_054

296_MO_0910_521

296_MO_0912_021

296_MO_0910_504

296_MO_0910_512

The former police station is one of the most important
architectural vestiges of British rule.

296_SI_090324_022_HK_MTG_K

296_SI_060523_502_K

296_SI_1012_501

296_PA_1010_501_2COURTYARDS

296_CI_0712_703_AERIAL

296_SI_0707_003_WY

296_SI_0606_034_AM

296_SI_0604_124_HK

296_SI_0606_021_ENTRANCE

The final design includes a new passageway that opens
up the compound to the surroundings and turns the former
prison yard into a plaza, flanked by new buildings facing
Arbuthnot Road and Old Bailey Street.

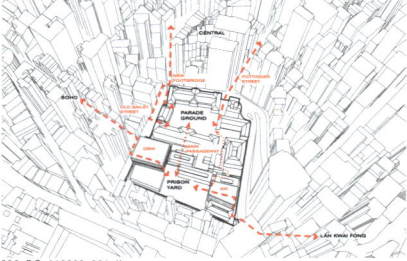
296_DG_110920_001_K

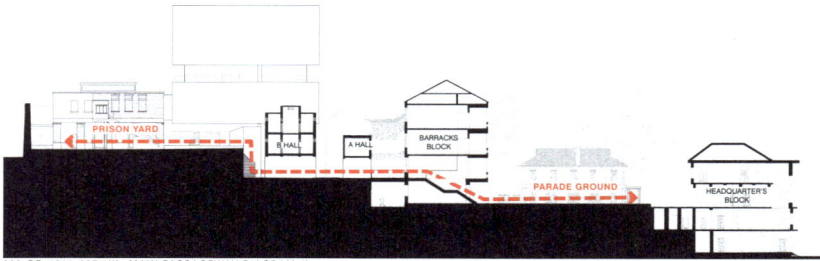
296_DR_1211_007_HK_ MAIN PASSAGEWAY DIAGRAM_K

296_MO_1010_009

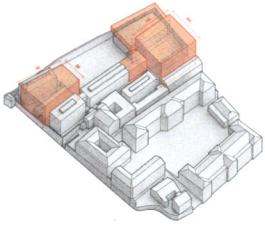
296_DR_1007_044_ZONING

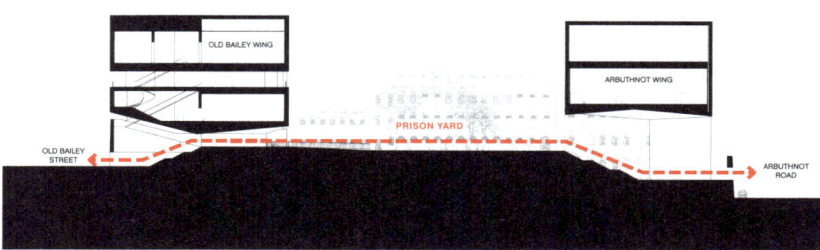
296_DR_1012_502

Volumetric studies for the two new buildings to be inserted
within the existing complex. Staircases form unique
spaces that can also be used as performance venues.

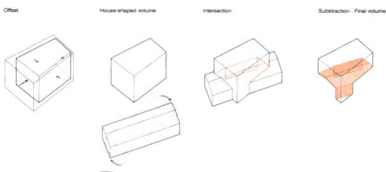
296_DR_1007_037_CONCEPT-VOL

296_MO_1106_086_COURTYARD_K

296_MO_1010_015

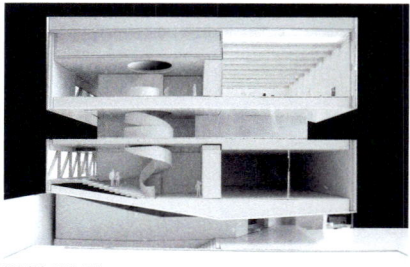
296_MO_1102_087

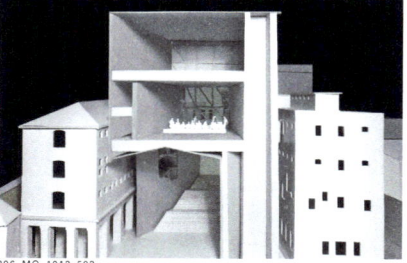
296_MO_1012_503

296_MO_1012_504

296_CI_1106_144_AW_LAUNDRY-YARD_K

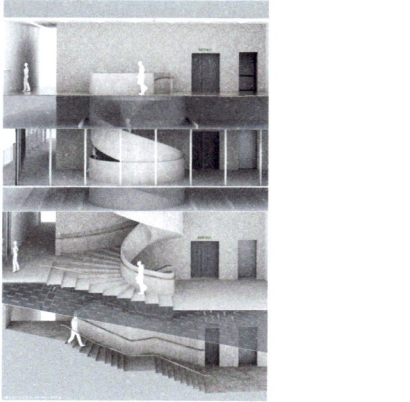
296_CI_1210_072_OBW_STAIR_A1

Aluminum elements for the facades: color, shape and size of the modules are designed to reference the stone walls.

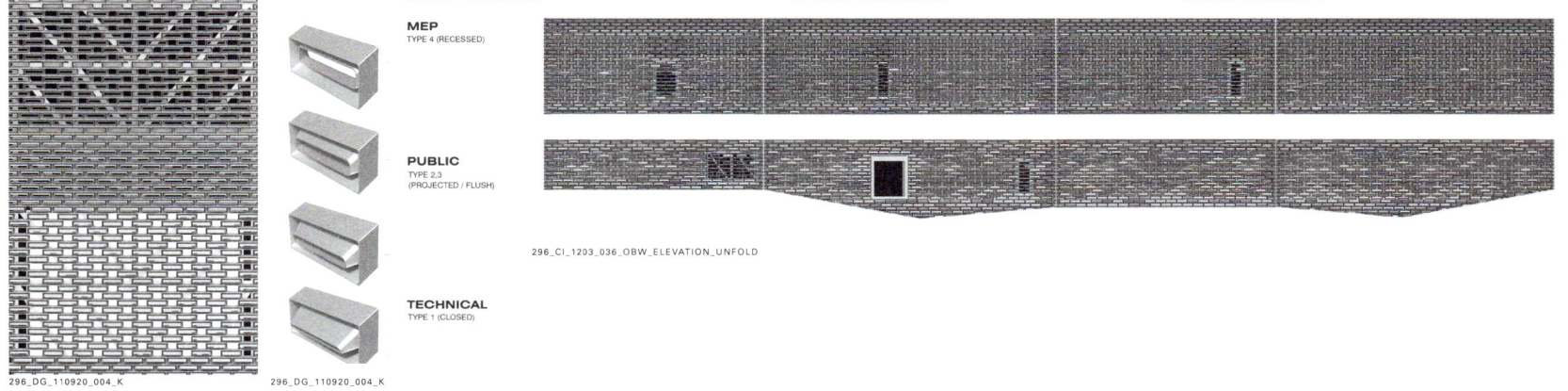

296_RFMT_0000_503_K

296_CI_1104_158_FCD-SCALE_K

296_MU_1105_003_FCDUNIT

296_RFMT_0000_504_K

296_MU_1109_501_MOCKUP2_K

296_MU_1201_502_K

296_MU_1106_018

296_CI_1106_069_FU-UPDATE

296_MU_1112_023_REVIEW

296_MU_140226_030_CASTING

296_MU_141112_037_AW_K

MEP
TYPE 4 (RECESSED)

PUBLIC
TYPE 2,3
(PROJECTED / FLUSH)

TECHNICAL
TYPE 1 (CLOSED)

296_CI_1203_036_OBW_ELEVATION_UNFOLD

296_DG_110920_004_K

296_DG_110920_004_K

The elements of the numerous interventions are poured in situ based on mock-ups; a finish is selected for them that is in keeping with their location.

296_EV_1305_012

296_MU_140430_150_AM_K

296_MU_140430_209_AM_K

296_MU_140512_045_K

296_MU_1201_029

296_DR_1604_141_AW-STAIR_K

296_CO_151123_058_OBW_SITE-UPDATE_K

296_CO_160417_097_OBW_K

296_CO_150518_003_OVERALL-SITE_AW

296_CO_160417_134_SITE-UPDATE_OBW-HQ

Construction of the complex combining old and new buildings.

296_CO_151123_029_BLK-6-7-STAIR

296_CO_151123_044_AW-FACADE

296_CO_170505_007_OBW_K

296_CO_160308_001_BARRACKS-BRIDGES

296_CO_170505_008_AW_K

296_CO_160504_017_AW_K

296_CO_170508_004_AW_K

296_CO_170505_007_B-YARD_K

Views and impressions of the Arbuthnot wing.

296_SA_161118_036_AW_K

296_CO_161012_026_AW_K

296_CO_161128_011_AW_LAUNDRY-YARD_K

296_CO_170505_002_AW_K

296_CO_150401_043_AW-STAIRS_K

296_CO_160118_037_AW-STAIR_K

296_CO_160118_041_AW-STAIR_K

Facade and the interior of the Old Bailey wing.

296_CO_170505_002_OBW_K

296_CO_160417_061_OBW_K

296_CO_160504_011_OBW_K

296_CO_160504_019_OBW_K

296_CO_170508_002_OBW_K

296_CO_160504_005_OVERVIEW

The former Central Police Station and Victoria Prison compound (CPS) is located on Hollywood Road in the heart of Hong Kong's historic center. It forms a city within a city, shielded from its surroundings by a high stone wall and dividing the vibrant districts of SoHo and Lan Kwai Fong from each other. When the compound was built in 1841 under British colonial rule as a seat of magistracy, judiciary, and correction, the steeply sloping hillside was barely developed and so the central command edifice held an imposing position, set on a narrow riverbank above the city with breathtaking views of Victoria Harbour. In 2005 it was decommissioned and taken over by the Hong Kong Jockey Club with the aim of restoring this historical monument. As the biggest charitable organization in the city, they contacted Herzog & de Meuron to propose an initiative that would revitalize the compound's sixteen historical buildings arranged around two courtyards and create a complex that would be able to pay its own way within twenty years.

Herzog & de Meuron have considerable experience in the refurbishment of heritage sites. In London, for instance, their Tate Modern project transformed the defunct Bankside Power Station into a catalyst for urban renewal throughout the surrounding area. Unlike Tate Modern, however, their 2006 plan for the Central Police Station, now the Tai Kwun, Centre for Heritage & Art, envisaged not only revitalizing the existing fabric of the building, but complementing it with a 200-meter, grid-like high-rise structure intended to house spaces for exhibitions, theater, restaurants, and gardens. But this concept of generously expanding the small-scale character of the compound into the vertical was rejected by popular vote. In 2010 a second proposal featuring a 100-meter-tall structure spanning the rear area of the Tai Kwun like a bridge fell afoul of new building-height regulations restricting new developments to 80 meters above the Hong Kong reference height. The third variation, which was accepted and realized, complies with these guidelines and preserves the village-like character of the compound by undertaking interventions into the existing fabric while at the same time adding new buildings to the two upper corners of the site, the only areas permitted for development.

In all three of these concepts, Herzog & de Meuron placed great emphasis on restoring the historical fabric while opening up the compound to the urban environment. As a key symbol of colonial rule and one of the very few remaining historical buildings in Hong Kong, the Tai Kwun is of unique significance. On the other hand, it should not be allowed to become either a Disneyland or a moribund monument. The architects do not regard the treatment of historical architecture as a matter of conservation, but as an opportunity to interpret the history of the urban environment itself and the role it plays in crafting identity. To implement the details of this, Purcell Architects of London were commissioned.

This is particularly evident in their approach to the fabric of the complex. The CPS evolved over a lengthy period. Each part of the compound has its own idiosyncrasies and different materials. Whereas the perimeter walls are built mainly of granite blocks, most of the buildings themselves are constructed of bricks from varying sources and in differing colors. Herzog & de Meuron cleaned the wellpreserved stonework, removing as many as twenty layers of paint that had been applied over the course of 170 years, restored damaged masonry, and replaced cement-filled repairs with new bricks specially produced in the UK from similar clay sources as the originals. The magistracy on Hollywood Road that is the most recognizable face of the compound was repainted. The color used was as close as possible to the original hue. For the roof, which had to be completely renewed, a variation on the traditional local semicircular terracotta tiles was chosen, and anchored by a stormproof central concrete spine.

Inside, the existing rooms are restored to their original state as far as possible. Bricked-up throughways are opened up again and their original proportions reinstated. The ceilings are opened up to the attic, its wooden cladding painted the original beige and its metal substructure unveiled. The now rare window and door framing of kapur wood has been restored wherever possible, painted brown on the outside and varnished on the inside. Existing wooden floors have been cleaned and repaired where necessary. Health and safety standards have been stringently but subtly adhered to: the stair rails, for instance, have been given additional uprights in a slightly heavier gauge, but in the same color. Historic fragments gradually uncovered during the building work, such as the royal coat of arms or the wall painting of a former chapel, have been restored.

The historical architecture, from the small corner buildings to the grand courtroom, comprise a wide variety of spaces that the architects have converted to other uses. The former grand parade ground has been given over to stores and restaurants, while the more intimate upper courtyard, formerly used as a prison yard, has become a venue for arts and culture, performances, lectures, theater, installations, and exhibitions, as well as some restaurants. A few of the cells and other original loci defining the history of the Tai Kwun have been retained as a documentation of its past, while the two new wings mark the conversion and opening-up of the compound.

The two new buildings fit into the existing family of buildings like long-lost relatives, their block-like volumes hovering over the historically listed surrounding wall to form a sheltering entrance area. They stand as close to the neighboring structures as houses in a huddled village and are linked inside by bridges and shared usages. The wing on Old Bailey Street provides two floors for exhibitions of contemporary art, with a restaurant level sandwiched in between. Their lofty ceiling heights and skylights complement the rough spaces of the adjacent cellblock and its columns. The second tower, on Arbuthnot Road across from the former prison yard, houses a multipurpose space with seating for 220. Like the CaixaForum cultural center in Madrid, it is set on only two pillars and the communication core above a new space accessed by a broad stairway that can also be used as an auditorium for open-air screenings. The bridges and communal stairway link the new wing with the earlier prison buildings that flank it on either side. To the south, there are dressing rooms and other facilities for performers, while the former cells to the north have been fitted out as offices or rental spaces.

There is a sense of affinity with the original as well as a sense of self-awareness in the architects' approach to these two new wings. This is immediately evident, even in the facade. Herzog & de Meuron have created a modular form based on the granite blocks of the perimeter wall in the Tai Kwun together with recycled aluminum, lending a warm champagne tone that fits perfectly with the heritage buildings while at the same time drawing attention to itself. The mold-cast elements form a self-supporting structure that appears both monolithic and porous at once. With its apertures in four different sizes, the facade adapts to the various usages. Derived from this, as in the Schaulager in Basel, is the paneling of the multipurpose hall.

The two extensions with their covered passageways form building blocks that connect the compound to the wider urban space. Carefully calculated wall apertures create a new east–west connection via the former prison yard. On the north–south axis the organic jumble of alleyways and tiny courtyards combines to form a meandering historical pathway. Bridges and new shortcuts through the buildings link the prison yard with the parade yard below. A pedestrian bridge leads from the public escalator bringing commuters from the Central District downhill directly to the parade yard. What was once an enclosed area has now become a focal point of the urban fabric, tying together the surrounding districts and forming an integral part of the city's everyday life.

The Museum of Modern Art, New York
New York, USA
21 June–25 September 2006

No. 300
Artist's Choice: Herzog & de Meuron,
Perception Restrained

When the Museum of Modern Art invited us to contribute to their Artist's Choice series in 2006, we knew from the start that we would concentrate on the perception of art per se rather than foregrounding our artistic preferences. Everybody knows that the quantity, quality, and density of the MoMA holdings are unparalleled. So how were we supposed to cherry pick the gems, when gems were all we had to choose from?

The museum's problem is not a lack of world-class art, but a lack of perceptive attention on the part of museum visitors despite the spectacular galleries of the new extension. The art is there but not visible, although the panorama presentation and professional lighting makes it impossible to overlook. Our project was an attempt to offer a spatial alternative to the existing galleries for a limited period of time and within a limited area, a place of heightened concentration and density that would function like a kind of perception machine, where perception becomes more sustained, selective, and individual by the very virtue of being made more difficult.

The idea behind our exhibition reversed the usual presentation in the galleries of the MoMA. We confined older media like painting, sculpture, drawings, prints, and design to a smaller area than usual while placing more emphasis on film and video, or rather specific fragments thereof. This did not reflect an artistic bias of Herzog & de Meuron but rather a general redistribution in our visual universe in recent years. The moving picture with explicit studies in violence, drama, and sex has attracted increasing attention, while the traditional visual media of painting, drawing, or sculpture require a special effort or special, potentially blockbuster exhibitions in order to attract attention. Seen in this light, our installation did not represent the medial disposition of the museum but that of the world at large. At the same time the installation gave some thought to the distinctions and categories established by the MoMA and maintained to the present day, that is, the classification of artistic media in five departments: Painting & Sculpture, Prints & Illustrated Books, Photography, Film & Media, and Architecture & Design. Most of the galleries obey the dictates of these categories; presentations are still relatively rare, which are based on a mix of artistic media, generating fruitful friction between them and offering viewers new insights and new perceptive potential.

Herzog & de Meuron, 2006

In an early phase, a salon-style hang was tested in the gallery.

300_DR_051018_001

300_MO_051018_114_HDM

300_MO_051018_120_HDM

The exhibition area was precisely framed through division into one rectangular room and two niches.

300_SI_0509_002_CL

300_SI_0509_003_CL

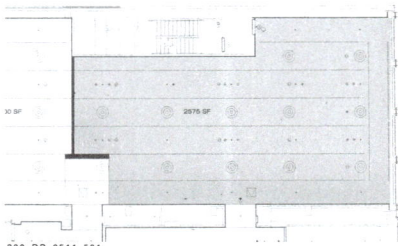

300_DR_0511_501

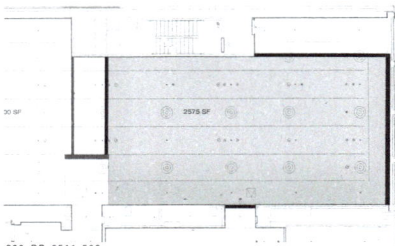

300_DR_0511_502

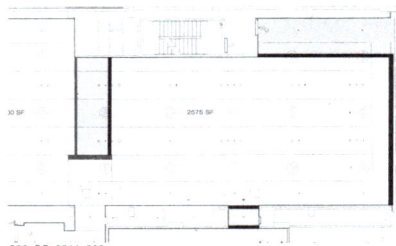

300_DR_0511_503

Different ways of distinguishing the character of the main space from the niches with their reduced range of vision.

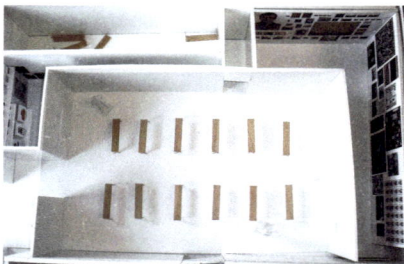

300_MO_060420_001

300_MO_060512_005

300_MO_051024_106_HDM

300_MO_051024_122_HDM

300_MO_051018_134_HDM

300_MO_051102_105_HDM

Development of the visual slit for the niches.

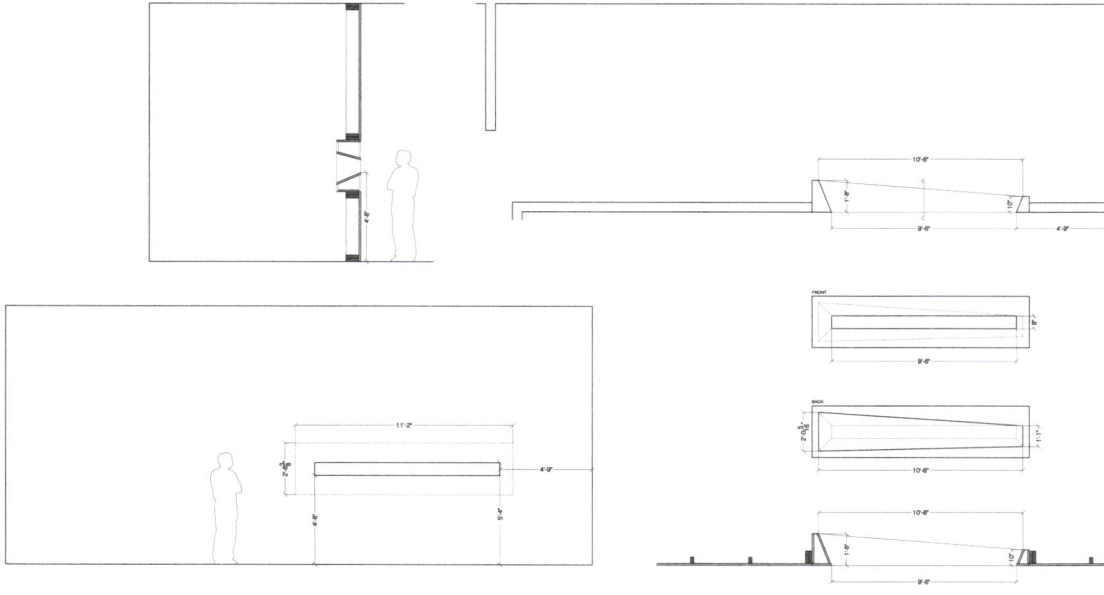

300_DR_060523_502_05-03_K

Painted ceilings as source images for projecting films and videos on the ceiling of the main gallery.

300_RFSB_051114_501_ZILLIS_K

300_RFCL_050921_003_ZILLIS_K

300_RFCL_050925_005_CEILING_K

300_MO_050928_511_HDM

300_MO_051018_125_HDM

300_MO_051102_103_HDM

300_MO_051018_128_HDM

Source images for hand mirrors to watch the moving images on the ceiling.

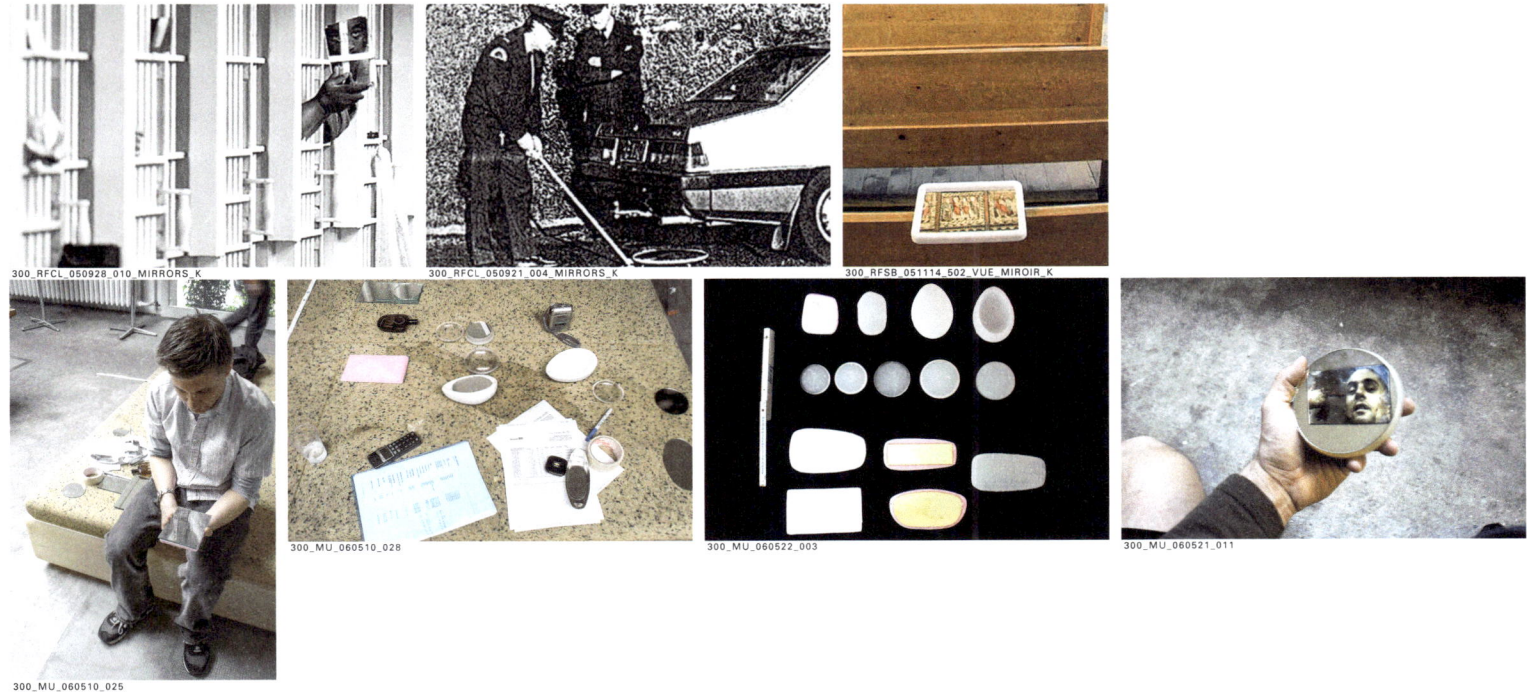

300_RFCL_050928_010_MIRRORS_K

300_RFCL_050921_004_MIRRORS_K

300_RFSB_051114_502_VUE_MIROIR_K

300_MU_060510_028

300_MU_060522_003

300_MU_060521_011

300_MU_060510_025

Layout of the main gallery and three niches for works from the MoMA collection.

PHOTOGRAPHY

ARCHITECTURE and DESIGN

FILM and MEDIA

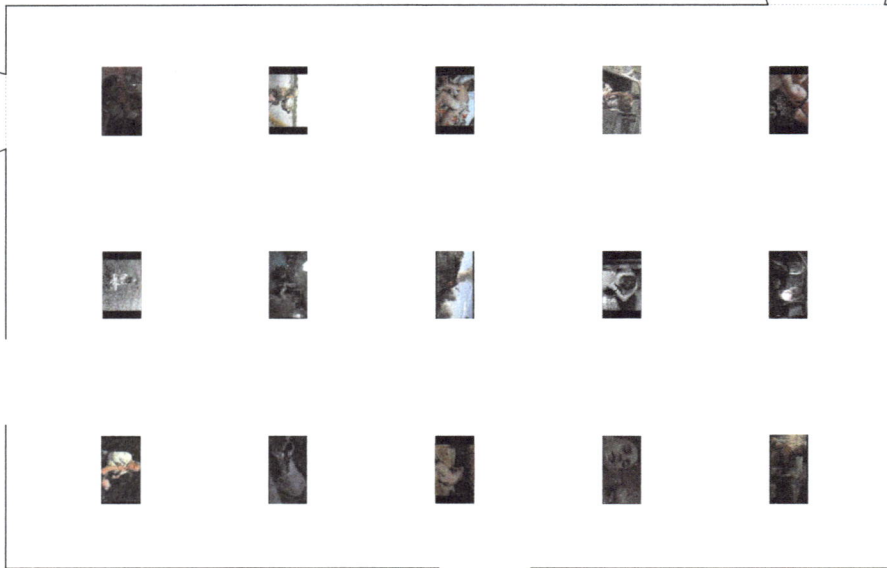

PAINTING and SCULPTURE

300_DG_060714_501_OVERVIEW-MAP_K

Views of the four exhibition spaces after the opening.

300_CP_0606_709_MP

300_CP_0606_705_MP

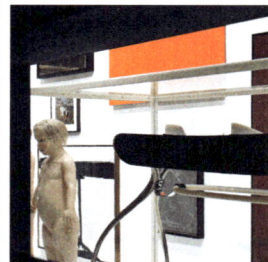

300_CP_0606_704_MP

300_CP_0606_703_MP

300_EV_060620_518_HDM

300_EV_060620_519_HDM

300_CP_0606_712_MP

In 1989 the Museum of Modern Art (MoMA) in New York invited the sculptor and performance artist Scott Burton to select works from their collection and use them to curate an exhibition on a theme he considered particularly important. Burton, who died in December of the same year, chose Constantin Brâncuşi and used his works to address the relationship between the sculpture and the base. This marked the beginning of a loosely connected series of exhibitions known as Artist's Choice to which many renowned artists have since contributed. The aim of the series is to show the institution's collection from a different perspective, introducing visitors to an artist's personal viewpoint, while the museum itself is freed from curatorial responsibility.

By inviting Herzog & de Meuron, in the summer of 2006, to curate a show in the series with works from its collection, MoMA was breaking new ground. Until then, such an opportunity had been offered only to artists. Surely it was to be expected that if architects were asked to participate in this experiment, they would place the focus on their own field. However, that was not how Herzog & de Meuron responded to the challenge. Tasked with selecting works from the various departments of the collection, they set about addressing the compartmentalization of the museum's holdings: the four areas of Film & Media, Painting & Sculpture, Photography, and Architecture & Design were each given their own dedicated, but conceptually linked rooms. This was achieved by means of the overarching concept of "perception restrained" addressing an inherent aspect of art. It has been a central category in the architectural thinking of Herzog & de Meuron right from the start. They see buildings and urban interventions as accelerators of perception, lend fluidity to the materially rigid urban form in moving film images, and always reflect in their exhibitions on how forms of presentation determine the appearance and perception of projects. That begins with the 1988 exhibition *Architektur Denkform* at the Architekturmuseum in Basel, where screenprints on the glass facades of a modern building underlined the immateriality and transparency of architecture. It continues in many other major exhibitions. A few of them hint at the spectrum: anyone leaning over the tables covered in plans, sketches, and images that were lined up in rows by Rémy Zaugg at the Centre Georges Pompidou in 1995 was adopting a study mode more like that of a medieval monk poring over a psalter than an art aficionado in a contemporary gallery. The exhibition cocurated by Philip Ursprung in 2002 at the Canadian Centre for Architecture (CCA) in Montreal presents the archive as archaeological material, which, like other remnants of human history, can be understood and interpreted only partially. In 2004 the major presentation of archive materials from Herzog & de Meuron at Schaulager for the collection of the Emanuel Hoffmann Foundation in Münchenstein/Basel saw this material spread out as though on market stalls. Each time, a different facet of architecture comes to the fore. Each time, we look at it differently.

The fact that we look at all is a challenge in itself these days. The oppressive visual overkill and the lack of concentration we afford it is constantly lamented. Everybody knows the rapid pace at which visitors lope through museums. Basically, this situation can be highlighted only by changing the exhibition format and, with that, the visitors' behavior. Herzog & de Meuron have devised a special space to refocus the gaze, describing it as Anchor Room. The aim is to heighten perception by making it more difficult. "Perception restrained" has echoes of a series of strongly performative films created by sculptor, performance artist, and filmmaker Matthew Barney under the title *Drawing Restraint*. In the films, he works with hurdles and barriers that his body has to overcome by means of climbing, contortions, or counterbalances, and which make drawing difficult.

As a former football player, Barney reckons that progress comes only by overcoming difficulties and he introduces this idea into his art as a performative element.

In their Anchor Room Herzog & de Meuron combine various strategies of rendering perception more difficult. They do so first of all by dividing off the various areas of the exhibition space with partition walls and using the resulting niches as closed display showcases with horizontal viewing apertures as narrow as embrasures or the little slits for peepshows at some old-fashioned fairground. While the main room is painted entirely black, the display niches are steeped in brilliant white, so that they stand out from the wall section like a picture made up of a collage of other things. Inside them are selected objects from three MoMA departments, presented in an extremely dense alignment. In the case of the paintings and photographs, the density of the array is reminiscent of the so-called Petersburg style of presentation in some nineteenth-century museums or the curiosity cabinets in a baroque painting. At the same time, the architects eschew all judgment or favor-based selectivity. At most, some universal themes can be discerned: in photography, these are images of people from the 1950s onward in which an existential sense of loss is framed by nature, landscape, and the urban environment. The selection of paintings and sculptures indicates an oscillation between the abstract and the representational that is not so much a commentary on the struggle between two twentieth-century dogma but more about outlining divergent attitudes, endangerment of life, utopian ideals and their failures. Beuys's felt suit hangs below a portrait by Francis Bacon, Andy Warhol's mock-up of a box of Campbell's soup cans stands next to human figures by artists ranging from Charles Ray to Alberto Giacometti. The design niche presents the diversity of everyday life on a span from the Thonet chair to Tupperware for home-made ice cream. All in all, these niches are also reminiscent of the concept of the Schaulager built by the architects.

While these traditional genres are crowded together and the visitor has to view them through a slit, like a cheap voyeur, the main gallery space is devoted to film. Although film is indeed represented in the MoMA collection, it has to date received very little public exposure. Yet it has long become established as the leading visual medium of our time. Hollywood drives our fears and yearnings and, with that, our view of the world. We no longer check whether a film reflects our experience, but instead check whether our experience chimes with the images produced by the film studios. The architects created a dedicated darkroom, almost like some den of vice, a place of eccentricity and shame, but at the same time a cult place of the uncannily sacred, where they installed five rows of monitors, three to a row, on the ceiling, showing clips from such cinematic classics as *Goodfellas*, *Flesh*, *Apocalypse Now*, and *Taxi Driver*, like the ceiling frescoes of our time. The clips feature scenes of sex and violence, which, for the curators, increasingly determine the way we see the world. An ever-accelerating society can only focus its attention on the brief kicks provided by these two archaic drives. And when we are offered these scenes only as clips, that perception is heightened still further. We see a scene and make associations with the rest of the film and its world, at least in terms of atmosphere. There is no time for anything else. As we watch, we sit on simple wooden benches like those we might find at a street festival or in a schoolroom, and view the clips reflected on palm-sized, hand-held mirrors. Perhaps this return to the hand, to the body, which is so important to Matthew Barney as well, triggers a reflex that slows the acceleration. Perception as an opportunity to reflect and observe more intently. That is what such Anchor Rooms offer, and what the architects intend to develop further in future.

Our first high-rise project in New York is devoted to urban living: living high above the earth, not on the ground where gardens and courtyards might offer individuality and intimacy. That means living on top of one another and not next to one another, where neighbors could make contact more easily through chance encounters than in a tower, the latter conventionally consisting of single, hermetically sealed units on each floor. Our aim was to design a kind of vertical residential neighborhood.

So we set ourselves the task of finding an alternative to high-rise buildings, in which the base plate is ordinarily just repeated and extruded as far as zoning allows, and then simply cut off or embellished with some kind of decorative finish at the top.

We wanted to design a basic unit for the tower comparable to a single brick in a wall, in order to achieve a coherent and yet diversified conglomerate of individual, recognizable parts.

The outside and the inside, the structure and the vertical arrangement from bottom to top, floor by floor: all of this would obey the same simple set of rules. These rules define the natural basic unit of the whole, the single room, which can be assembled to form various types of residences and penthouses. Although very few apartments are identical, the rules we devised still apply: rooms for different purposes and of different sizes are organized around a central core, like large flagstones. The arrangement is different on every floor. One stone is placed on another, as it were; it is as if a natural topo-graphy of protrusions and cantilevers had formed the balconies and terraces. The sculptural expression is extremely vibrant and decorative, but it is the result of a programmatic, static structure and not of arbitrary design.

The sculptural impression of the tower is most con-spicuous at its base and toward the top. The cantilevered cubes in the lower part of the building react to the small scale of the components in the neighboring buildings, while the boldly canti-levered spaces of the penthouse apartments toward the top offer spacious platforms as terraces for a new residential experi-ence in the sky above New York. The innovative aspect of these lofty locations is their topographical character, reminiscent of rock overhangs or caves, which offer a uniquely intimate and individualized atmosphere in contrast to conventional *balconies or alcoves. As in Actelion and VitraHaus, this topo-graphy is generated by the sculptural and structural strategy of the stack. Although the principle of these stacks is very simple, effectively imitating the gesture of children playing with building blocks, it can produce an astonishing variety of projects, almost contrary in architectural expression and for the most diverse places and uses.*

Herzog & de Meuron, 2016

A residential tower in Lower Manhattan features three zones in response to the architecture and street grid of the neighborhood.

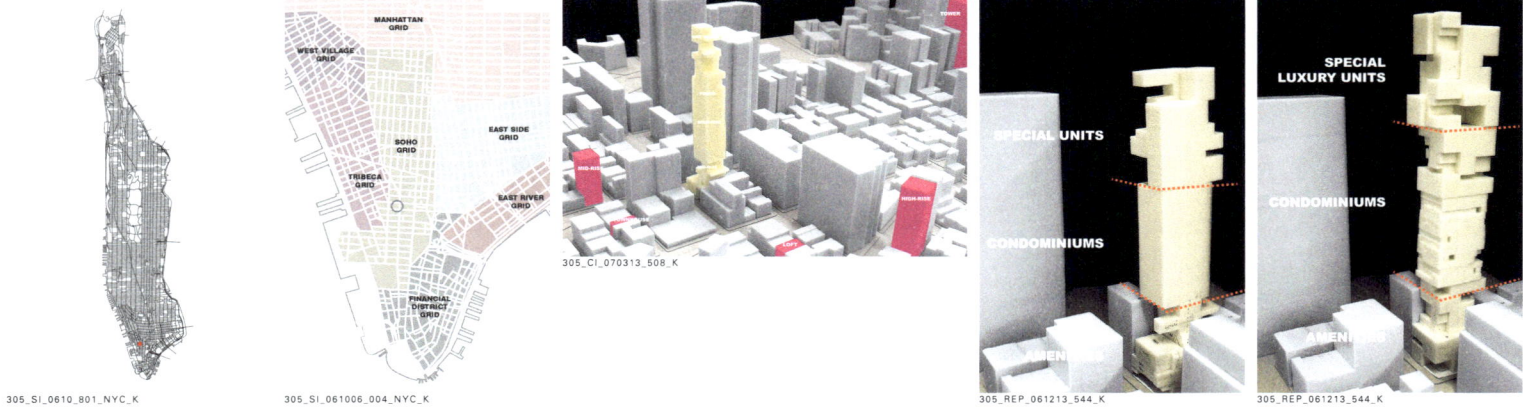

305_SI_0610_801_NYC_K

305_SI_061006_004_NYC_K

305_CI_070313_508_K

305_REP_061213_544_K

305_REP_061213_544_K

The units are a composite of rooms typical of New York real estate and are grouped like pixels around a central core. The mix generates individual apartments and stories.

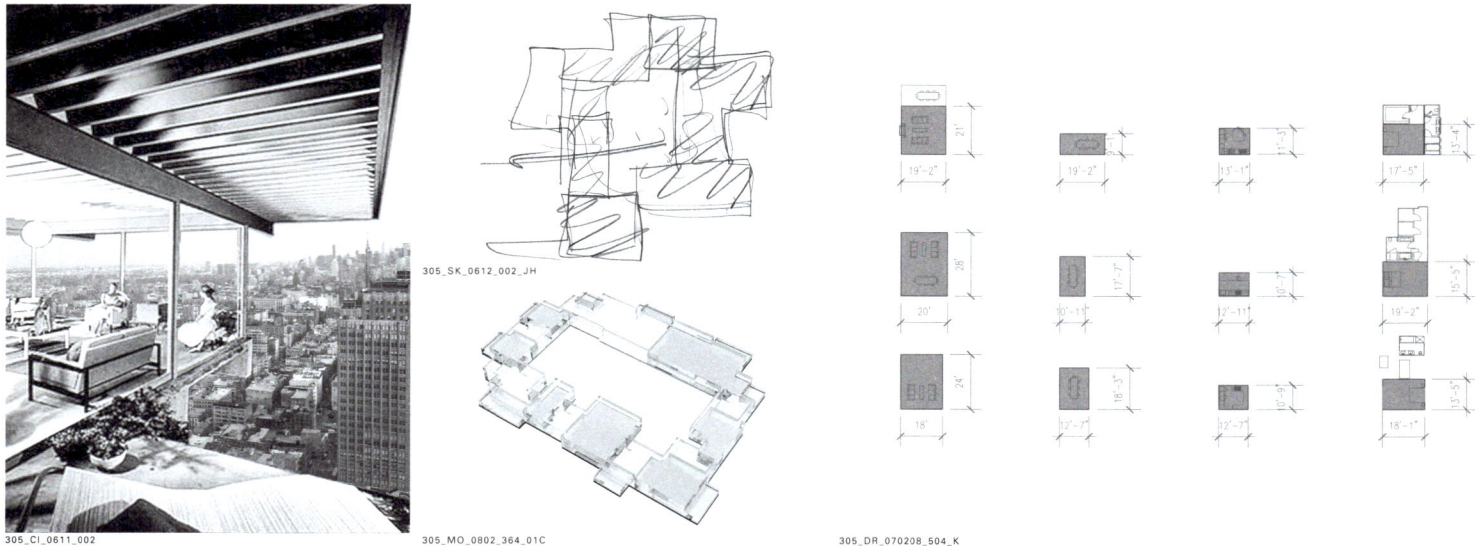

305_CI_0611_002

305_SK_0612_002_JH

305_MO_0802_364_01C

305_DR_070208_504_K

The combination of different types of units and precisely planned setbacks heightens the sense of perspective from the outside.

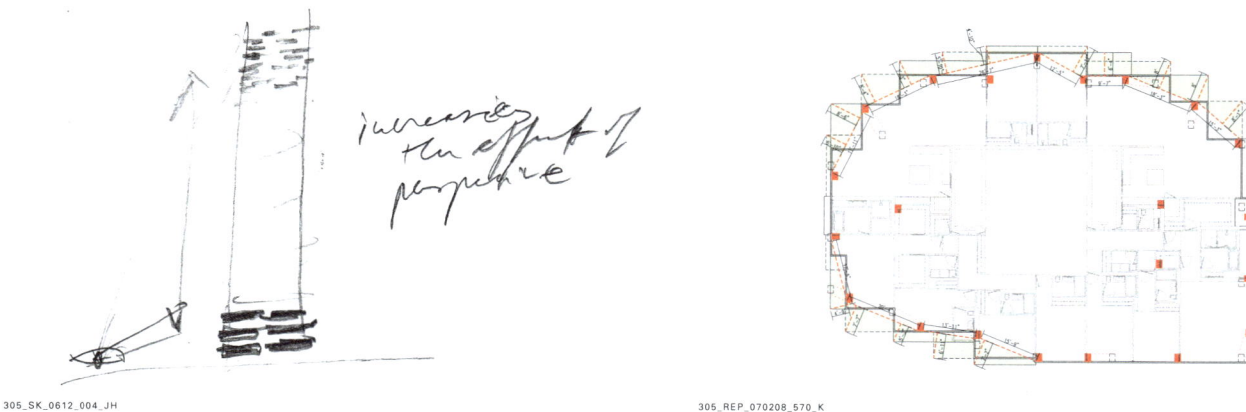

305_SK_0612_004_JH

305_REP_070208_570_K

Studies for the shape and surface structure of the tower:
from a square to an oval ground plan.

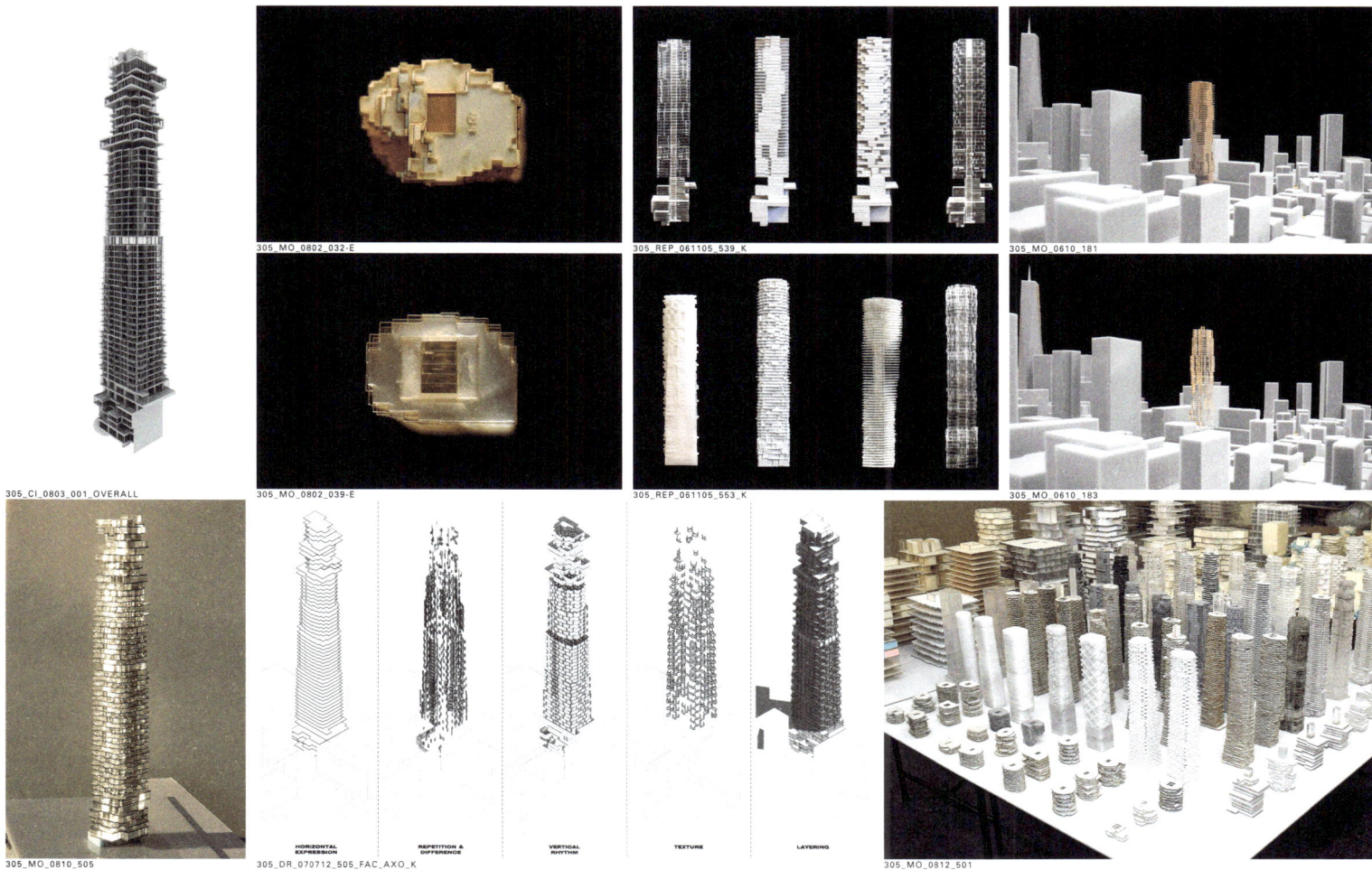

305_CI_0803_001_OVERALL

305_MO_0802_032-E

305_REP_061105_539_K

305_MO_0610_181

305_MO_0802_039-E

305_REP_061105_553_K

305_MO_0610_183

305_MO_0810_505

305_DR_070712_505_FAC_AXO_K

HORIZONTAL
EXPRESSION

REPETITION &
DIFFERENCE

VERTICAL
RHYTHM

TEXTURE

LAYERING

305_MO_0812_501

Variations on stacked volumes. The base of the building
contains general uses and relates to passers-by; a
sculpture by Anish Kapoor commands the open space
next to the lobby.

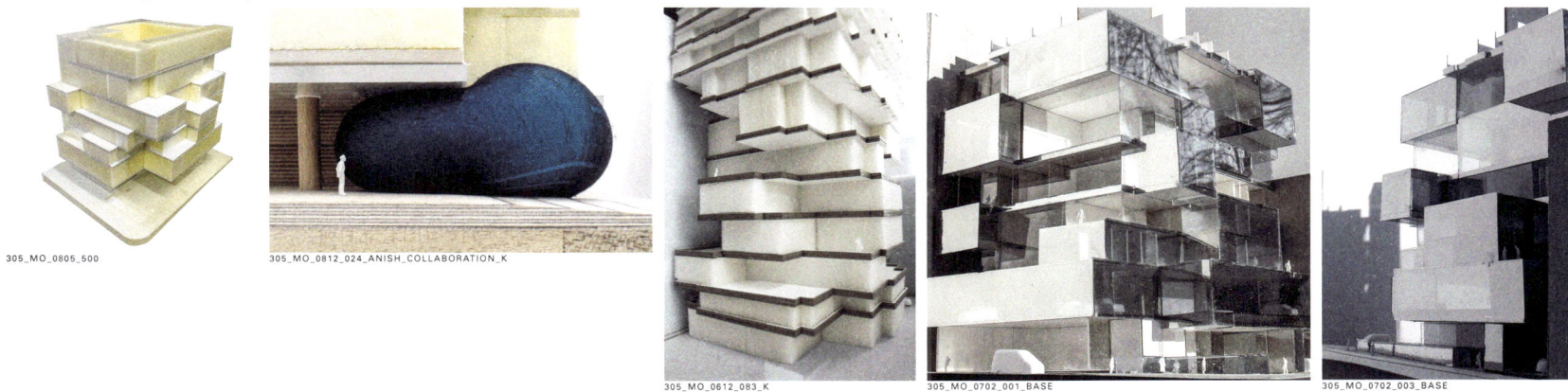

305_MO_0805_500

305_MO_0812_024_ANISH_COLLABORATION_K

305_MO_0612_083_K

305_MO_0702_001_BASE

305_MO_0702_003_BASE

The apartments are like homes in the sky, reminiscent of
modernist villas. Variations in the layout of the stories
allow for spacious terraces and facades set back from the
slab edges.

305_REP_061213_515_K

305_MO_0703_113_TOP-VIEW

305_CI_0810_514

305_REP_061213_536_K

305_REP_061213_575_K

305_CI_0711_100

Studies for the material of the ceilings. Custom-designed
kitchen, living area with fireplace, and bathroom.

305_MU_0706_015_CONC

305_MU_0704_206

305_MU_0706_010_WET

305_MU_0802_248

305_MU_0711_500_MB

305_MU_0712_056

305_MU_0806_014_KITCHEN

The detailing of stairs and interiors echoes the oval shape
of the transfer columns.

305_CP_1705_722_HC

305_CP_1705_714_HC

305_CP_1705_706_HC

305_CP_1705_501_VO_K

The residential tower in its urban context.

305_CP_1610_1130_IB_H_3802

305_CO_150903_027_GLAZING_K

305_CI_0810_508

305_CP_1610_1338_IB_H_4588

305_CP_1610_1612_IB_H_5503

305_CP_1610_0989_IB_H_3164

305_CO_150831_739_MG

305_CP_1610_0837_IB_H_2515

305_CP_1610_1196_IB_H_4034

The Tribeca neighborhood in Lower Manhattan has retained a largely heterogeneous demographic comprising a mix of middle-class families, artists and their studios, and small businesses. Traditional red-brick town houses stand here next to seven-story apartment blocks, industrial buildings, and former warehouses that have been converted into lofts. When Herzog & de Meuron were asked to design a residential tower on peripheral Leonard Street, they wanted to integrate the building fully into this colorful environment. New York skyscrapers tend to be anonymous entities with little to distinguish between them, and whether they are residences, offices, hotels, or a mix of all those functions is often difficult to discern from the outside. Yet they still make their mark on the public space.

Right from the start, Herzog & de Meuron were determined to make the new tower an integral part of the neighborhood, giving the residents a sense of security, comfort, and home. So they explored the local situation to come up with a bundle of strategies. One of their starting points for this was the unusual legal situation that applied to the site itself. The investor had been able to procure the air rights of the surrounding buildings from the directly adjacent law school, thus providing scope for a taller volume. In addition, the standard regulations for staggering and setbacks in towers were waived. Normally, a streetfront is prescribed to a height of 85 feet (26 meters) to ensure continuity for pedestrians, with a clear setback above that as the tower rises. This development site also has a setback, albeit starting considerably lower at about 15 feet (4.5 meters) and stepping back gradually, that allows the tower to transition downward and visually anchor itself in the ground.

In designing the form of this tower, Herzog & de Meuron started with the apartments it was meant to accommodate. An analysis of existing residential towers showed that, for all the individualization that might be offered depending on purchasing power, a largely homogenous typology of bedroom, living room, kitchen, and bathroom prevailed. Herzog & de Meuron treated these components as three-dimensional pixels that could be freely combined and juxtaposed in many variations on each floor, according to the requirements of the investors. In this way, the volume of the building is shaped additively from the inside out by the rooms themselves, which are legible on the outside. Each floor has varying cantilevers and setbacks, offering outdoor terraces and overhangs that provide shade from the sun. Albeit more reticently than in the Pérez Art Museum Miami (PAMM), the architects have created a structure that openly shows itself, instead of taking the conventional route of covering them with a facade skin.

This extreme diversity has been brought together into one single large corpus. The site has an almost square outline, bounded on one side by a windowless industrial high-rise, but offering fantastic views across the city on the other three sides. Herzog & de Meuron start with a massing whose outer dimensions shift from a right-angled base to an oval at the top of the tower. For this, they have adopted conventional New York skyscraper construction techniques—a skeleton frame of concrete floor slabs and supports around a central service core—while adapting the interior to the needs and requirements of the investors. The investors were to determine the size and number of rooms in the apartments, based on market feasibility; many layout variations are possible within the building. However, countless experiments with models indicated that instead of mixing specific types of units like a Rubik's cube, it would be better to arrange them in zones, with smaller units on the lower levels, standard sizes in the middle segment, and penthouses at the very top, to create vertical neighborhoods. The floor slabs in each of these three zones are cut back slightly to create jagged forms with the cumulative effect of forming an oval. On financial grounds, the client requested window walls between stories instead of a curtain wall facade. The architects took this as an opportunity to make the residential purpose of the building more clearly evident to the outside gaze. On each floor, the window walls define an inner boundary and the glass balustrades an outer one. Within structural limitations, the layout of the rooms and terraces is freely variable. Of the 146 apartments, only five are repeated.

Each of the three zones has its own distinct character. The plinth maximizes the use of cantilevered and recessed elements, engaging with passers-by and, in addition, provides a further attraction: the free space on street level next to the relatively small lobby and the parking access is not rented out as a business space, as is so often the case, but is reserved instead for a sculpture that the architects have developed in collaboration with artist Anish Kapoor. A blob of stainless steel, so typical of his oeuvre, marks one corner of the tower and mirrors the surrounding environment. Its startling effect is enhanced by the way it cuts deeply into the floor above. Over that, there are smaller apartments and two town houses. The two upper floors of the plinth accommodate pool, spa, event space, cinema, and other facilities shared by all the residents. The midsection of the tower seems comparatively modest in outward appearance; it has to function for the residents. A subtle sense of movement is created by the alternating rhythm of the balconies. The top of the tower comprises a vertical stack of ten penthouses. Their boldly cantilevered elements lend them a potent expressiveness that redefines the iconic form of the skyscraper as a visible conglomeration of volumes rather than an ornamental ziggurat.

For the residential tower to exude the coziness of a home, meticulous attention has been paid to the handling of detail and painstakingly crafted finishes with finely tuned structural variations. Rubber molds inserted at the ends of the formwork have given the slab edges a concave curve, while at the same time strengthening them, making them more easily legible as horizontal lines and distinguishing the appearance of the skeleton frame from that of an unfinished building. Even the undersides of the balconies have a touch of elegance: a film integrated into the formwork adds a sheen to the concrete surface and makes them almost dissolve visually in bright daylight. For the window walls, conventional industrially manufactured components of champagne-colored extruded aluminum have been deployed.

This adherence to the concept of fine detail continues inside the building with high-quality fittings. As in their first New York apartment building at 40 Bond Street, Herzog & de Meuron have undertaken the interior design themselves. The apartments are, for the most part, a fluid sequence of spaces bringing the outdoor and indoor worlds together. One contributing factor is the flooring, which consists of a trinity of white oak for the living areas, beige-tinted concrete slabs with the appearance of wooden planks for the balconies and rectangular travertine tiles for the bathrooms. The open-plan kitchens are integrated into the architectural design. The built-in cupboards have white and matte silver glass surfaces that contrast with the black granite and piano lacquer finish of the kitchen island with its mirrored lamp above echoing the glazing of the facade. There are also other sculptural elements: the extraction hood above the cooking area is installed under a bulge in the wall that protrudes like a nose. In the penthouses, it is suspended like a bag over the freestanding stove. In these spacious apartments, the open fireplaces are designed as independent spaces with a sculptural effect. In the bathrooms, the oval floor tiles are a variation on those in the foyer, subtly connecting the semipublic space of the entrance area with the intimacy of the private home; they indicate that the residents have been in their own personal sphere here all along. They have found their home in the sky.

When we went to see the Miami Art Museum at its former location on Flagler Street in downtown Miami, we were much sobered on two counts: Architecturally the building of 1984, designed by Philip Johnson, was nothing but an inconsequential box facing an empty forecourt; a black glass door separated the hot and humid outdoors from the refrigerated atmosphere indoors. We were even more sobered when we entered the building and discovered the scanty holdings inside. This was especially disappointing in a city like Miami, which is home to a number of well-heeled art collectors, who have amassed impressive, sizable collections in recent years and have repeatedly made their collections accessible to the public during Art Basel Miami Beach. So why a new museum when important private collections can be seen in private exhibition spaces? This question was posed by some of the private collectors themselves. By putting up a new building, the museum authorities naturally wanted to bind new collectors to the museum and to interest other social circles in contemporary art, in particular a younger generation.

How can something like that succeed? Given these circumstances, it seemed even more important than in other museum projects to ensure that the holdings, acquisitions policy, exhibition program, and architecture come together to form a distinctive, unified whole. Terry Riley, whom we had already met when he was still at the Museum of Modern Art in New York, represented the client with regard to all of these crucial issues. Such a radical reinvention of the entire institution would not have been possible without his indefatigable commitment. Together we aimed to start with a completely honest, unsparing, and open-minded study of all the above factors.

There were too many gaps in the holdings to present a chronological narrative of art in the 20th and 21st centuries. But when we started planning, there were already several strong points in the collection and these would be reinforced even more, for instance, the circle around Wifredo Lam or other artists from South America and the Caribbean. This imbalance gave us the impetus to propose a museum topography based on the "ideal" museum, whose advantages we had explored long ago with Rémy Zaugg (Rémy Zaugg: "The Art Museum of My Dreams or A Place for the Work and the Human Being," 1987/2013).

Essentially, it consists of closed volumes arranged like single buildings in a village. A flowing space in between would link them and permit viewers to walk about freely without having to follow a linear enfilade. In other words, we proposed two contrary types of spaces that seemed eminently suited to the needs of the Miami Art Museum.

The open, flowing area is an excellent space in which to spread out the holdings and fill possible gaps with documentary material as in a library or study center. The atmosphere in this spatial sequence is informal, almost like a spacious living room with wall-sized glazing facing Biscayne Bay and Museum Park.

The "buildings" in between accommodate a "Focus" or "Project Gallery," suitable for a selected theme, a single collection, or a specific artist. These galleries contain only a few strategically placed windows; they have the usual plaster walls as well as walls of fair-faced concrete; they are essentially classical museum spaces. The hall for temporary exhibitions is also a separate "building" that can be subdivided.

When we began working on the Miami Art Museum, the 1111 Lincoln Road garage project was already under way. So we had already spent some time studying the architecture in Miami and some of the city's fundamental issues and problems. In view of the public nature of the museum and the intention of attracting many people to this new location, we wanted to design architecture that is not only a stage for art but also for the natural environment and the people who use it. As in 1111 Lincoln Road, we wanted to take advantage of Florida's climate and vegetation. We wanted architecture that could offer the experience of walking through a sculpture with spacious terraces and staircases down to the park and the bay, and with canopies controlling direct sunlight like treetops, not blocking it altogether but playing with it. Relief from the intensity of the sunlight and the heat in the air is provided by a filter of wooden slats and hanging plants all around the inner world of the museum.

All the elements of the architecture are visible and equal: every support, every wall, every level, every plank of concrete or wood, every slat, every screw. That even includes the cars, visibly parked on the ground underneath, as well as the visitors, who can use the stairs as seats, and the seats as stairs. PAMM—the new name of the Miami Art Museum in honor of an important donor—is naked architecture. Nothing is hidden, not even the auditorium, which is a triumphal staircase in addition to its main function as a theater. There are several levels but none is privileged over the other. The level above the ground floor is perforated; it is no more a hermetic platform than the trellis-like roof supported by slender columns, as if by crutches. As mentioned, every component of the architecture is an equal, visible, and independent part of the whole. This applies to the materials as well: the concrete, wood, glass, and plaster. All of the materials take different shapes: raw or polished, sawn or planed, shiny or matte. Surfaces can be identified as self-support-ing or as layers applied in varying thicknesses; supports are taken apart, reinforced, and screwed together because the bending stress requires a "crutch" of that kind—and naturally, because by borrowing this detail from orthopedics, we were able to introduce other proportions and modifications of scale.

Herzog & de Meuron, 2016

The offshore stilt houses of Miami, trees and support structures as point of reference.

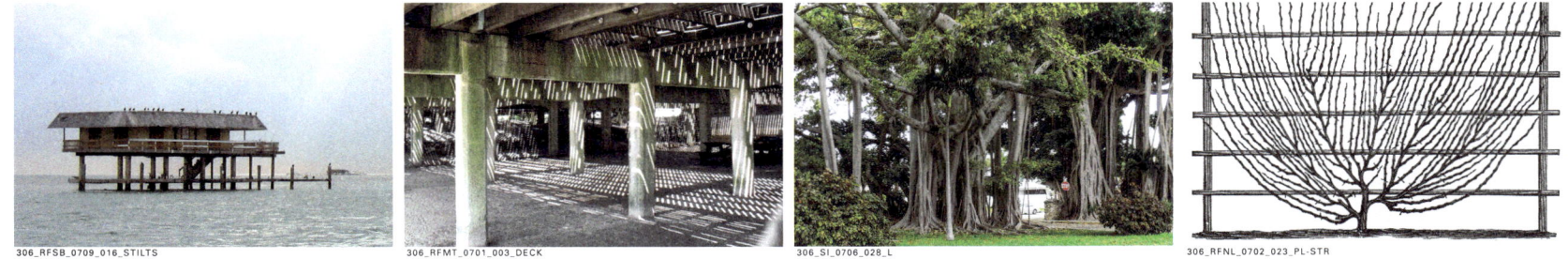

306_RFSB_0709_016_STILTS

306_RFMT_0701_003_DECK

306_SI_0706_028_L

306_RFNL_0702_023_PL-STR

One of the few public pieces of land along Biscayne Bay is available for a new art museum; the adjoining Bicentennial Park is to be revitalized.

306_SI_0610_021_AERIAL

306_CO_1101_704

306_SI_0709_001

Within two days, preliminary concepts are drawn up, proposing different types of volumes.

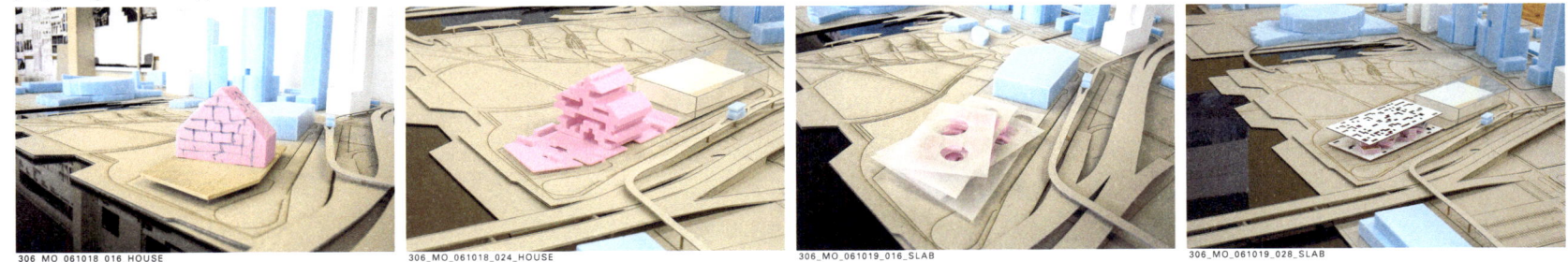

306_MO_061018_016_HOUSE

306_MO_061018_024_HOUSE

No._MO_061019_016_SLAB

306_MO_061019_028_SLAB

Diverse exhibition spaces loosely arranged within a basic layout determine the shape of the museum.

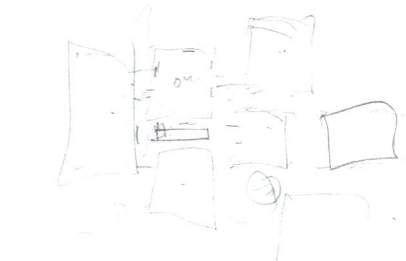

306_SK_0610_007

306_MO_061109_015_A

306_MO_080409_003_SW-3A

306_CI_1302_003_LEVEL_2

The exhibition floors of the museum are raised above ground to avoid flooding. They form an open, floating structure between ground and roof area.

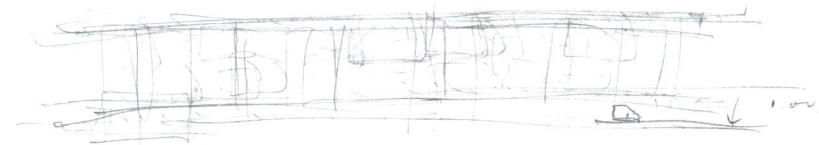

306_SK_0610_020A-HI

306_MO_061109_040_CR

306_EV_070111_016_A

306_MO_070211_015_PHASE-2-A

306_AN_0710_501_03-01-01_FRONT

306_MO_0801_128_QUARTER

Layers of the building: parking level, two floors of exhibition spaces, offices, and roof structure.

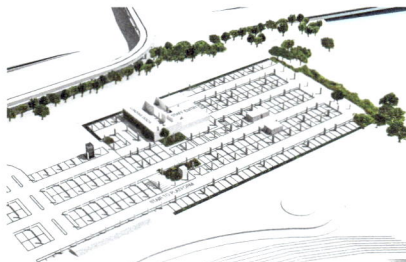

306_DR_0910_001_PROG_ISO

306_DR_0910_002_PROG_ISO

306_DR_0910_003_PROG_ISO

306_DR_0910_006_PROG_ISO

Studies for incorporating local vegetation and a hanging garden into the museum and the veranda.

306_CI_070312_001_CHMBR-F

solar_influence_max
0.00 10.0 20.0 30.0 40.0 50.0 60.0 70.0 80.0 90.0 100.

306_DR_0910_501_SHADING_K

306_MO_070219_014_SELECT

306_MO_0708_033_FINAL

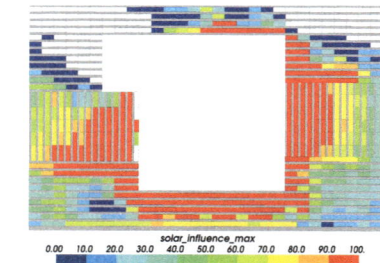

306_DT_1206_001_HANGING_GREEN_CATCHMENT

306_EV_1206_003_TREES

306_MU_0906_042

Auditorium and stairs form a multifunctional space between the two exhibition floors.

306_CI_1001_502_AUDITORIUM-SEAT-DIAGRAMS-1

306_CI_0909_259_AUDIT

306_CI_1204_041

306_MU_1210_192

306_MU_1210_135

306_CO_121113_708_DA

306_CP_140205_726_ROHA

Concrete is used in a variety of ways, partially in response to the subtropical coastal climate: poured (A), planed (B), roughened (C), polished (D).

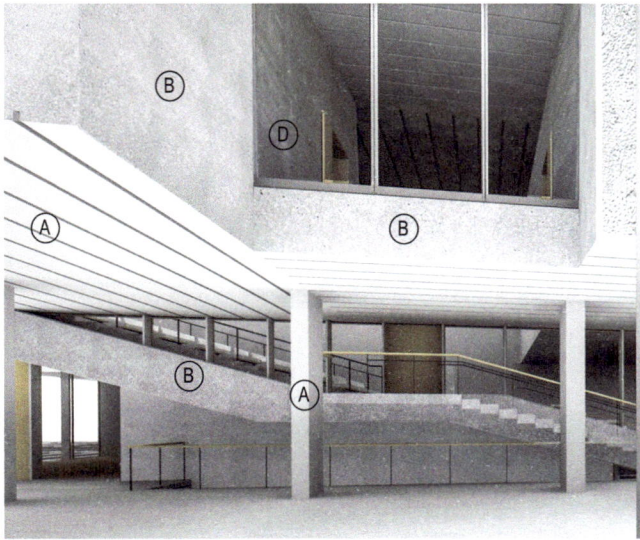

306_PP_130411_033_K

306_MU_1008_501_K

306_MU_1008_180_K

306_MU_1008_025_K

306_MU_1008_080_K

A mock-up is made to test concrete surfaces, exhibition spaces, and materials.

306_MU_1007_053

306_MU_1007_151

306_MU_1104_096

306_MU_1104_085

306_MU_1104_104

306_MU_1112_049

306_MU_1006_131_WOOD_FLOOR

Building the load-bearing structure of concrete elements with supports up to two stories high.

306_CO_1202_054

306_CO_121221_720_IB_2172

306_CO_121221_747_IB_1757

306_CP_131203_729_IB_H

306_CO_1209_201

306_CO_130824_712_DA

306_CO_120528_002

In its completed form, PAMM is a facade-free building that can be accessed from all four sides.

306_CP_140806_706_DA_4

306_CP_140205_702_ROHA_H

306_CP_1401_107

306_CP_1311_704_DIGITAL_EO

306_CP_140205_745_ROHA_H

306_CP_131205_979_IB_5065

In the new museum, hybrid, flowing zones for reception, exhibitions, restaurant and lectures, embedded galleries and the intimate reading niches throughout create a diversity of spatial experiences.

306_CP_140111_724_DM_1715_H

306_CP_131203_720_IB

306_CP_131203_719_IB

306_EV_140709_708_WREYE

306_CP_140111_734_DM_2277_H

306_CP_140205_759_ROHA

306_CP_140205_753_ROHA

306_CP_140205_772_ROHA_H

306_CP_140205_719_ROHA_H

306_CP_131203_706_IB_H

306_CP_140205_718_ROHA

120

Miami is home to a number of internationally renowned private collections of contemporary art, some of which are shown in their own dedicated spaces. However, for a very long time, the city had no art museum of its own. Then, in the early years of the new millennium, it was decided that the city's Bicentennial Park, which was inaugurated in 1976, should be revitalized and that this somewhat neglected green space on Biscayne Bay in downtown Miami should incorporate a number of cultural and sporting facilities to revive its appeal. The redevelopment master plan put forward by Cooper, Robertson & Partners also envisaged two new museum buildings with a shared plaza on the northerly strip of land designated Museum Park. The Pérez Art Museum Miami (PAMM) by Herzog & de Meuron and the Patricia and Phillip Frost Museum of Science by Nicholas Grimshaw were designed to screen the park from the MacArthur Causeway that links the mainland with Miami Beach. Moreover, Herzog & de Meuron came up with a museum concept that would open onto the newly greened park and become an attractive community meeting point in its own right.

The design is based on two horizontal parameters prescribed by the topography: the museum should be situated above the maximum high-water level likely to occur during a hurricane and it should not be so high as to block the waterside view of the Adrienne Arsht Center for the Performing Arts by César Pelli. Herzog & de Meuron responded to these stipulations by formulating two levels linked by a forest of supports distinguishing the pavilion-style structure of the PAMM from the randomly placed apartment and office blocks of the downtown district. The concrete building is set on an elevated platform and is capped by a roof area of approximately the same dimensions. The combination of upright and horizontal slatted elements generates a pixelated impression of closures and apertures, forming various zones of shading and cooling that make an important contribution to the climate conditioning of the building. In between, the space is defined by rectangular volumes stacked alongside and on top of one another, some on supports so slender that they appear to float, rather like Le Corbusier's Villa Savoye, and often receding far beneath the roof canopy. The entrance level combines public functions and exhibition spaces, as does the level directly above. Research and administrative facilities occupy the outer areas of the third level. The structure of the building appears to be stripped bare, unadorned by even the flimsiest of wraps. The initial idea of an undulating glass wall around the volume, such as the one developed for the Kramlich Residence in Napa Valley, was soon abandoned. The museum, like no other, is thus uniquely open to its surroundings.

However, the innovative visual impact of the design is actually derived from a tried and tested typology. The utilization of concrete, wood and glass as materials lends it a clarity of syntax that sets it apart from the ornate boxes of the Art Deco District. The elongated structure cites Mies van der Rohe's Neue Nationalgalerie in Berlin and references the temple of the Parthenon, from which Mies took his inspiration. But underneath it there is neither a rocky outcrop nor a solid base of exhibition galleries. Instead, the platform covers an open-air parking level and consists in part of narrow concrete planks with gaps between them that let the daylight filter through to the lower level. The stilt-like supports that elevate the platform echo the simple stilt shacks out in Biscayne Bay that were once used by fishermen. And the museum is no elite enclave, but a public building. The wide stair leading from the waterfront up to the museum platform forms an attractive place to meet and relax by the bay, and transitions to a covered veranda beneath the roof. A formulaic grand architectural device is thus transformed into a set piece of pop culture. And one that enters into dialogue with nature.

Two strategies are deployed here. On the one hand, the park with its bushes and trees encroaches on the building from outside.

And then, nature is accorded its own dedicated spaces in which greenery climbs up from the floor of the parking area, spreads out across the platform or hangs down from the ceiling. For this, artist and botanist Patrick Blanc designed tubes of up to 15 meters in length, covered in felt and planted with a variety of different species. In concert with the tall and slender concrete columns that support the cantilevered exhibition galleries of the upper level and the roof, they generate a vibrant aesthetic energy. Nature thus takes on an architectural accent, while architecture becomes part of the landscape. In this respect, the PAMM may be regarded as the pinnacle, so far, of the longstanding efforts by Herzog & de Meuron to incorporate elements of nature into their architecture. Other outstanding examples include the greening of the Fünf Höfe in Munich, the Ricola Marketing Building, and the de Young Museum.

This feeling of openness toward the surrounding environment continues inside the PAMM. The platform is accessible from all four sides. Anyone entering the PAMM from the park does not step straight into a lobby, but into a hybrid space that functions as a distribution hub for ticket sales, shop, café, and restaurant, and which is also used for exhibitions as well as connecting to various galleries. It flows into a large stairway that acts as a topographical fulcrum point, social meeting place, auditorium, and screening room for video projections. The upper section has fixed upholstered rows of seating, while the lower section has double-height steps on which people can sit freely. The actual stair takes the form of a strip of steps along one wall with a handrail. A system of sound-insulating curtains with almost cozy pleating in a sophisticated color palette ranging from brown to gray allow all three zones to be separated or opened up to form a single auditorium. This core feature of the building is a variation on the large outdoor stair, bringing art presentation, movement, and communication together as one.

The first floor is devoted entirely to art. Here, the typology of the exhibition gallery comes fully into its own. A fluid, open space forms wide expanses and narrow corridors, which can be combined in various ways, with huge swaths of glass wall offering breathtaking views over the bay, the park, the downtown area, and the MacArthur Causeway. The Overview Zone incorporates the Focus and Anchor Galleries for the presentation of individual themes, artists, and commissioned works. Two large rooms for temporary exhibitions add a fourth gallery type.

Variations in materials make each of the different galleries distinct. While the ceilings are all uniformly composed of the smooth, light-reflecting undersides of concrete beams that bridge the shorter widths, with recessed fluorescent tubes, tracks for spotlights, sensors, and sprinklers, as in the Schaulager in Basel, the floors and walls have individual combinations of fair-faced concrete, glass, wood, and gypsum. The Overview Galleries and the two rooms for temporary exhibitions on the first floor have concrete floors and plasterboard on the concrete walls. In the island-like Focus Gallery rooms, by contrast, the concrete walls are exposed and mark a contrast with the wooden flooring and the deep wooden jambs of the doorways and windows. The built-in window seats made of wood are, like most of the furnishings, designed by the architects. The double-height Anchor Room spanning two floors is entirely in concrete.

With the PAMM, as with so many of their other projects, Herzog & de Meuron have tested the typology of museum architecture to the limit. In Miami, they have placed it on a pedestal, only to deconstruct this image immediately. It is neither a monolithic figure like Tate Modern, nor a treasure chest like the Schaulager in Basel, but exudes instead the fragility of Miami's multicultural society and the distinctive appeal of Latin American modernism. Something open to creative interpretation.

When the client, Unibail, operator and owner of Paris Expo, contacted us, a study had already been made that proposed two medium-height towers along with several other buildings. Overall, it was a banal, commercial development: it might have generated more income for the fairgrounds from rents on the property leased from the city, but would have contributed nothing to improving the urban landscape at this location on the Boulevard Périphérique near Porte de Versailles.

We persuaded Unibail that in addition to the commercial benefits, their objectives also had considerable urban potential that could be a great asset not only to the immediate neighborhood but to the entire metropolitan area.

The urban problem was obvious: over the decades, large sprawling halls had proliferated on the fairgrounds, creating an urban blockade that cut the 15th arrondissement off from the suburbs of Issy-les-Moulineaux and Vanves. That problem was aggravated by the fact that trade fair buildings are filled with life for just a few weeks per year, remaining empty and unused the rest of the time. The street life typical of the small patchwork nature of central Paris is impossible in a location of that kind.

The Porte de Versailles may sound attractive but it is perceived as little more than an insignificant spot on the map in the urban fabric of Paris.

We wanted to address both the blockade and the anonymity of the Porte de Versailles in a single urban gesture: one tall building with a simple but unmistakably distinctive triangular shape would cut through the fairgrounds like a knife and open up the site to the neighborhood. This would reanimate the historical axis—from the Place de la Porte de Versailles via Avenue Ernest Renan—that connects the 15th arrondissement with its suburbs.

For a building of that nature to win political approval, it was essential to open it up to the neighborhood and to the public. Initially, we entertained an even more radical concept: a high-rise building, like a vertical urban neighborhood, consisting of large and small clusters, with main axes and side streets, with vertical links via elevator to apartments and offices, and with diagonal elevators to publicly accessible platforms. The platforms would have themes and would be curated and run as branches of the Centre Pompidou or another art institution in Paris. However, not only financial expectations but also serious and growing threats to public safety led to modifications in the program and in plans for public access to the building.

What has not changed is the client's obligation to dispense with the idea of the usual monofunctional office tower and make the building accessible to both visitors and residents of Paris. Stores, restaurants, bars, and neighborhood facilities will be accommodated in the base along Avenue Ernest Renan and also in the entrance atrium at the Place de la Porte de Versailles. In addition, there will be two elevators along the diagonal edge of the building to access the observation deck and restaurant on top.

In short, we did not want a high-rise building with the usual monocultural program, nor did we want the standard repetition of identical stories. Our goal was a tall object, a so-called urban topography that would lend visibility to the Porte de Versailles as a gateway between Paris and the adjoining suburbs.

The triangular shape of the building is dictated first and foremost by logical considerations: it is an architectural version of the geometrical diagram that casts the smallest shadow on the buildings in the neighborhood. In other words, it did not start out as a design decision, but we did like the fact that the provocative and historically venerable shape of a pyramid had emerged without any effort on our part. That was especially appealing to us in a city like Paris, with its crystalline urban planning. For centuries and up to the present day, monuments have been placed in this city with exceptional precision, which is indebted to the unusual architectural obsession of absolutist kings, emperors, and mayors.

Architecture is inseparable from any city's history, but in Paris it has always been more than that. It is the driving force behind a vision of perfection and absolute beauty, embodied in the potentially infinite axial system of boulevards and streets. Monuments like the Arc de Triomphe, the Opéra, and the Dôme des Invalides are fixed stars on the intersections of that axial system, providing orientation in the dense and uniform urban fabric. Seen at night from above, these intersections look like "étoiles" in a milky way. One can observe a noticeable decrease in the density of the stars south of the Seine, as if the obsessive design energy of Paris had gone missing there.

The Tour Triangle, as the tower is called, is now inscribed in the southern part of the city. As a new fixed point visible from afar, the building will offer an axial perspective. The stars of Paris are like the acupuncture points in the human body that release energy. This is what the Tour Triangle is meant to achieve.

Can this goal be fulfilled? For several years, the question was hotly debated by advocates and detractors of the project.

It even featured as a bone of contention during the 2014 mayoral campaign between the right-wing UMP candidate Nathalie Kosciusko-Morizet, who opposed the project, and the socialist Anne Hidalgo, who was in favor of it. The seductive "beauty" of the building also figured in the debate. Could the transparency and diversity of changes in appearance on all sides, as seen in the renderings, actually be implemented or was it just an illusion? Why take the risk? Why hazard the museum-like beauty of the city for another monument imposed by the "classe politique"? To a certain extent, the ideological battle against high-rise buildings in this almost unrealistically beautiful city is understandable. The homogeneity of Paris within the Boulevard Périphérique, with no high-rise buildings, is incontestable—with the exception of the much-despised Tour Montparnasse, frequently belabored as a conspicuous deterrent. What is the point of new high-rise buildings if they threaten the homogeneous beauty of the city and, as if that were not enough, portend environmental and economic disaster? As in parliaments all over the world, there was abundant debate that remained unheard and did not change minds in one way or another—until the last moment, that is, until the last decisive vote in the summer of 2015 when those in favor under the leadership of Hidalgo outvoted the opponents, 87 to 74, paving the way for the realization of the project.

Herzog & de Meuron, 2016

The land, on trade fair premises to the south of Paris,
is located on the inside margin of the ring road.

307_SI_0710_501_AERIALSITE

307_SI_0000_501_K

The design takes its cue from the axes that radiate from key
monuments in Paris.

915_RFCL_0000_501_K

915_RFCL_1410_LES_AXES_002

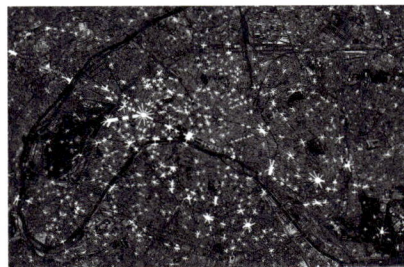

915_RFCL_0000_502_K

307_SI_1010_801

A 2002 feasibility study with three buildings. Herzog &
de Meuron propose one single building.

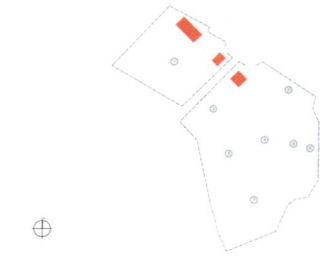

307_DR_0706_005_DIAGRAMS

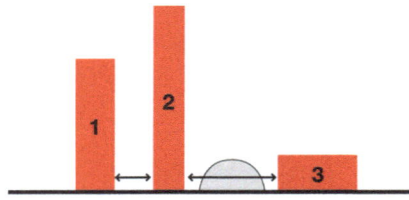

307_DR_0706_001_DIAGRAMS

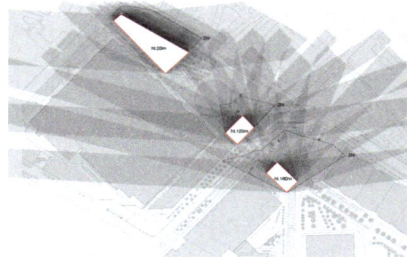

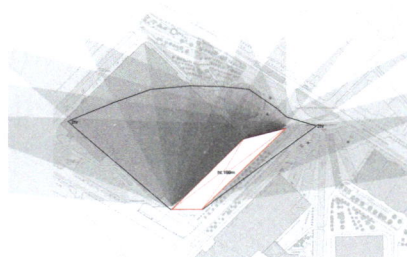

307_CI_100426_507_K

307_RF_0000_501_FIRST-PROJECT_K

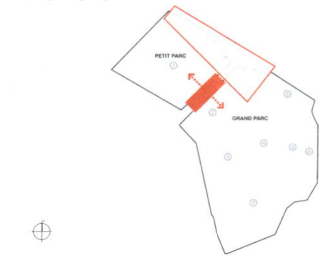

307_DR_0706_008_DIAGRAMS

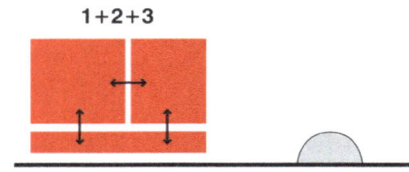

307_DR_0706_001_DIAGRAMS

307_CI_100426_507_K

307_MO_070618_061

Shaped like a pyramid, the building is laid out as a vertical
city of streets, plazas, and viewing axes; it refers to the
monuments of Paris and provides zones for various uses.

307_RFCL_0901_003

307_1410_015_505_ARSENALE-TABLE

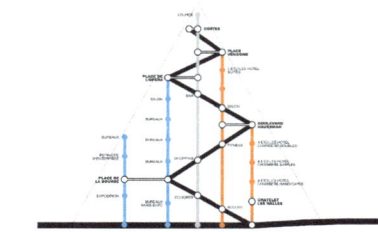

307_DR_0706_502_METRO_K

307_DR_0706_506_VERT_CITY_PRG_E

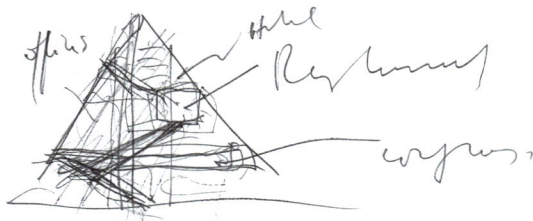

307_SK_0702_015_JH

307_DR_0706_501_DIAG_GREEN_K

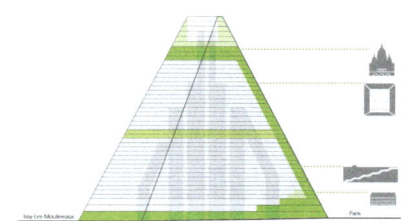

307_DR_1410_509_PUBLIC-PROGRAM_K

Studies and models of volume, circulation, and
load-bearing grid.

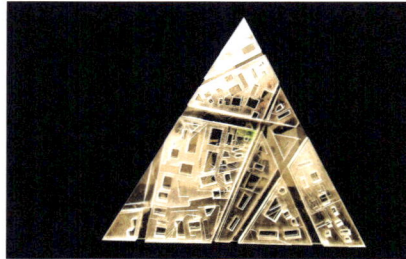

307_MO_0706_010_MOA

307_MO_0702_072_MOA

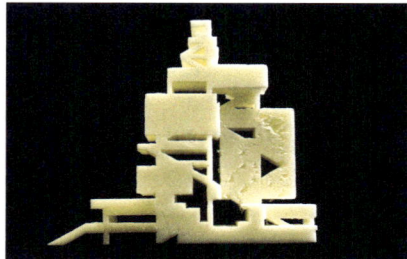

307_MO_0702_048_MOA

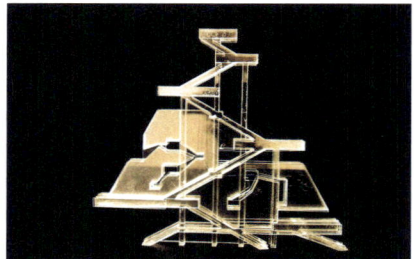

307_MO_0000_501_K

307_MO_0706_013_MOA

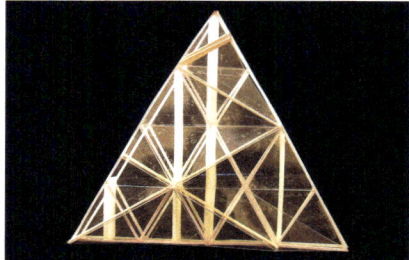

307_MO_0706_019_MOA

307_MO_0706_004_MOA

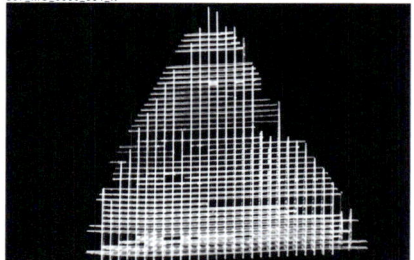

307_MO_0706_093_MOA

307_MO_0706_022_MOA

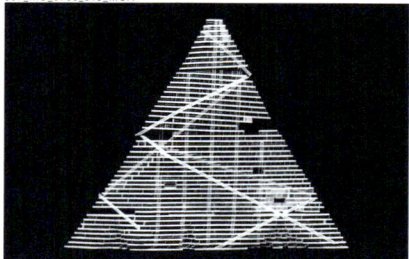

307_MO_0706_090_MOA

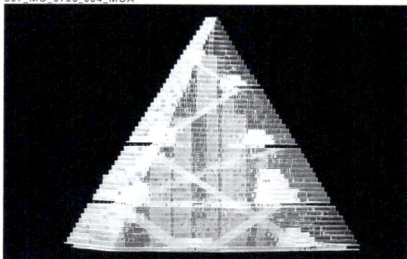

307_MO_0710_041

307_MO_1003_001_MIPIM

Volume studies: the design of the building is based on the incidence of light; the ground plan is twisted into a trapezoid.

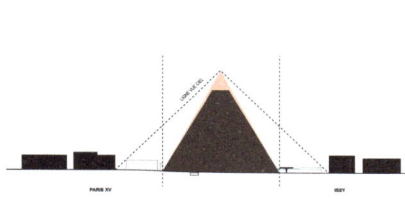

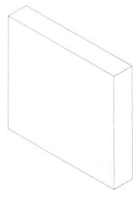

307_DR_1410_507_DIAGRAMS_K

307_MO_1410_505_WOOD_K

Volumétrie simple: limitant l'impacte au sol

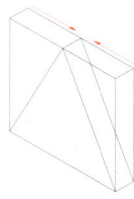

Forme triangulaire: favorisant les angles de vues du ciel

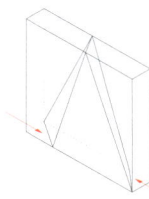

307_DG_1410_001

307_MO_0612_027_K

Plan trapézoïdale: en retrait du boulevard Périphérique et du Palais des sports

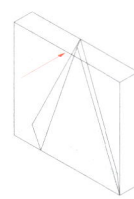

Pointe en retrait de l'avenue Ernest-Renan

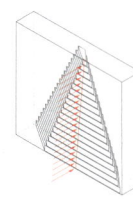

307_DG_1410_001

307_MO_070605_014

Découpe en retrait successif à chaque niveau d'échelles reconnaissables

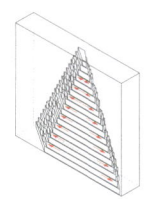

Insertion de redents d'échelles reconnaissables

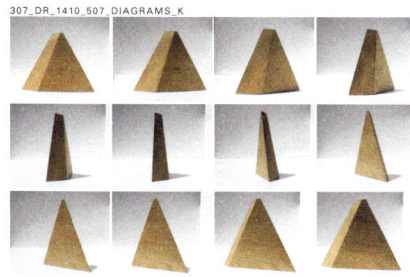

307_DG_1410_001

307_CI_1206_505_K

The architects add a public zone to the specified functions of a convention center, hotel, offices, and restaurant.

307_SK_0702_019_PDM

307_MO_070605_024_COLLAGE

307_CI_111019_299

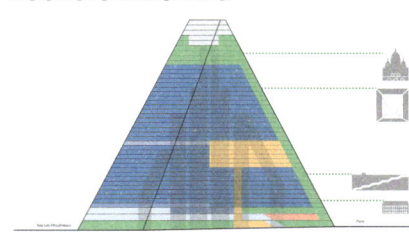

307_CI_0706_502_PROGRAM_OVERALL_K

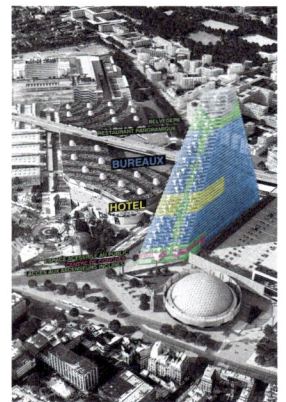

307_DR_1502_030_ELEVATION-DIAGRAMME

307_CI_0000_502_K

Spaces for offices or galleries jut out from the crystalline facade singly or in clusters to form outside zones.

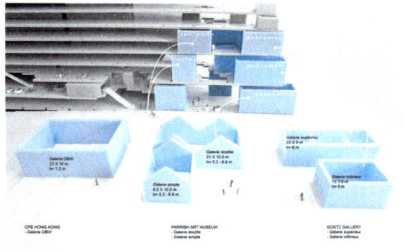

307_DG_111020_045

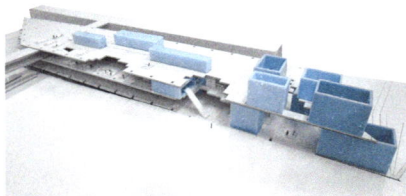

307_CI_111012_127_ENTRANCE

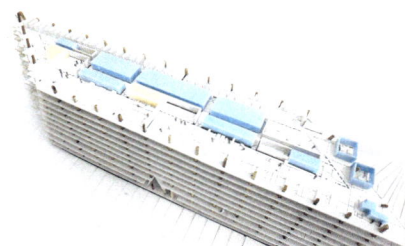

307_CI_111012_206_OFFICES

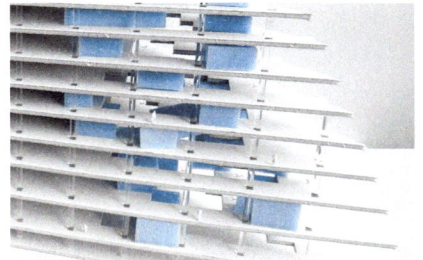

307_DG_111020_039

307_CI_111012_183

307_CI_120328_508_FAC_REDANS-2B_K

307_DR_120228_190_APS-PLUS_K

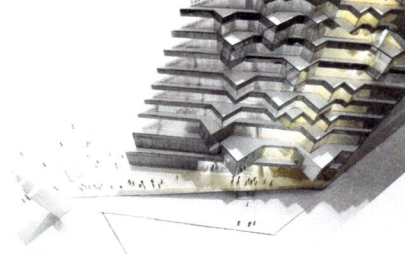

307_PC_141028_033_K

307_MO_1111_502

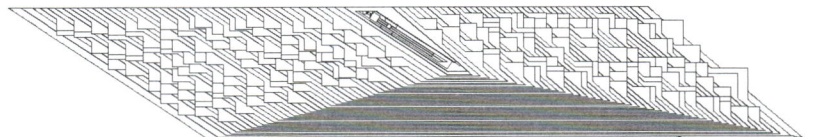

307_PC_141028_013_K

The design includes a public, multistory lobby for the arts.
An elevator accesses the panoramic terrace.

307_DG_111020_043

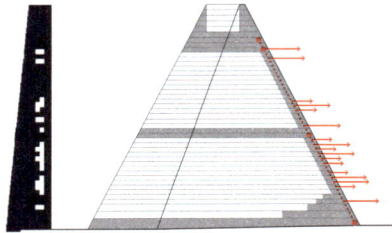
307_DR_1410_508_ASCENSEUR_K

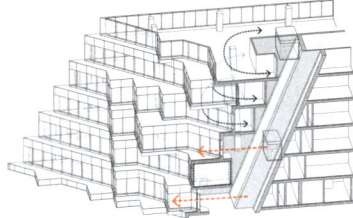
307_DR_1202_137_IE_COUPE-DETAIL-AXO

307_MO_1003_503_CITY-MEETING_K

307_CI_0000_501_BELVEDERE

307_CI_1112_086_LOBBY

Full-scale mock-up for the facade including elements of
reflecting glass, and computer studies of the entire facade
with its pixel-like, protruding spaces seen at different
times of day.

307_MO_1204_006_12.00_ANGLE

307_MO_1204_010_13.00_ANGLE

307_MO_1204_022_16.00_ANGLE

307_CI_0000_504_K

307_CI_0000_506_K

307_CI_0000_505_K

Renderings of the building outside and inside for public
debate on the project.

307_CI_1502_014_PLACE

307_CI_100308_008_A

307_CI_150212_004_SKYBAR

307_CI_1502_015_PORTE-VERSAILLES_NUIT

307_CI_1502_004_HOTEL-SKY-BAR

307_CI_141030_004_PRI

307_CI_141030_006_PRI

The Boulevard Périphérique in Paris is a ring road that divides the city into an inner and an outer zone, which differ in many respects. Former mayor Bertrand Delanoë wanted to bridge the gap between them. To that end, he proposed building high-rises at selected points in what would effectively continue in the tradition of the Grands Travaux initiated by President François Mitterrand, redefining the Paris skyline both symbolically and architecturally. One of the sites chosen for this was the Paris Expo trade fair grounds at the Porte de Versailles in the south of the city, where the 15th arrondissement meets the communities of Issy-Les-Moulineaux and Vanves without any clear urban framework to mark this encounter. The Expo grounds lie between these neighborhoods like an alien body, separating them, and intersected by the Avenue Ernest Renan.

An initial feasibility study conducted in 2002 envisaged marking the meeting of these neighborhoods by creating two towers; one on either side of the Avenue Ernest Renan at the Porte de Versailles. These were to provide hotel accommodation and office space for the trade fair grounds, with an additional low-rise building on an adjacent unoccupied site offering conference facilities and visually connecting with the nearby Dôme de Paris – Palais des Sports, based on a design by Buckminster Fuller. A gateway formulation such as this would merely have further emphasized the divide between the inner city and its outer environs. Herzog & de Meuron came up with an alternative solution, proposing a solid block whose length would trace the line of the Avenue Ernest Renan instead of countering it. This block would be capable of housing all the required functions, while at the same time its sheer bulk would anchor the site as a landmark on the city skyline. Viewed from the city of Paris, the building appears narrow; viewed while driving along the Périphérique ring road, by contrast, it appears like a giant billboard. What is more, within its immediate environs, it actually unites the two halves of the Expo site and considers the public transport hub there. The ground-floor stores and restaurants provide a sense of continuity to the outdoor life of the neighboring boulevards, interrupted only by the Avenue Ernest Renan. Between Hall 1 and the Boulevard Victor a newly landscaped garden area extends an already existing small green space. In addition, the shadow cast by the building, unlike the initially proposed towers, falls primarily on the trade fair site itself rather than on neighboring apartment buildings.

The tower's form is derived from the angles of incidence at which the sun's rays hit the building. By plotting 45-degree lines from the neighboring buildings, the architects have calculated the maximum point at a height of 180 meters, from which the lines then rebound to the outer margins of the site. The footprint of this triangular segment is then stretched to form a trapezoid and the volume extended upwards to a height of 200 meters. The appearance of the resulting pyramid thus alternates between extremes of depth and slenderness. For the facade, Herzog & de Meuron have adopted the three-dimensional mineral texture that is the hallmark of much Parisian architecture, and have translated this into a pixelated relievo skin of glass from which offices and hotel rooms protrude either individually or in clusters, forming outdoor spaces and balconies. The overall layout is arranged so that the lower part of the building is occupied by the conference center and trade fair offices, while the south-facing part of the midsection is reserved for mixed-use office spaces available to rent, and the remaining central and upper zones, including the tip of the pyramid, house hotel and restaurant facilities with views toward the city.

In addition to fulfilling the client's specifications, the architects have included the further element of a public space. A high-rise with such a defining urban function as other Paris landmarks should also be accessible to the public. With this in mind, Herzog & de Meuron have developed a public pathway that leads diagonally through the pyramid from the atrium up to a large room at the very top. On the way, it incorporates stopping-points at different height levels, each referencing a Paris landmark: the buildings of the Haussmann boulevards at 28 meters, then the Centre Pompidou, the Grande Arche de la Défense and, at 148 meters, the basilica of Sacré-Cœur. To stroll along this promenade is to stroll through a familiar slice of Paris, albeit in the vertical, with public spaces, terraces, museums and galleries, restaurants, and shops just as might be expected on the horizontal boulevards of the city.

In the interests of financial feasibility, some aspects of the project had to be pared down. At that time a hotel was unlikely to be profitable in this location, so the area initially allocated to that proposal was turned into office space instead. Moreover, the investors felt that public facilities were given too much prominence. The zigzag line of the promenade would have to be screened by a fireproof wall, creating an unattractive concrete tunnel. The tip of the pyramid could not be utilized, and the facade was too complex. Herzog & de Meuron retained the pyramid form, but reduced the facade overlooking the trade fair grounds to a perpendicular wall, thereby expanding the upper segment of the tower to accommodate the central technical services. The load-bearing structure follows the structure of the pyramid, with the floor slabs and supports, many of them angled, connected to form a solid grid. The internal circulation cores are positioned at the center so that there are always zones featuring individual cells on one side and open-plan spaces on the other, and each level can be individually rented out. The facade looking toward the city is recessed incrementally from floor to floor, which has the effect of reducing the sense of monumentality to a more human scale for passers-by on the street. The projecting triangular volumes proposed in the initial design have been expanded to form squares that can accommodate meeting rooms with space for outdoor terraces. The glazing of the facade, like the Elbphilharmonie concert hall in Hamburg, has a silver-colored imprint.

For the public, two diagonal elevators are to be installed on the Paris-facing side of the building to carry people from the plinth up to the panoramic restaurant at the top. In this, the architects have used the fire regulations for office buildings to optimum advantage: the 180-meter-long base actually requires three fire zones. Dividing the building into two zones results in empty triangles in the corners of the pyramid, which add up to provide public space. On the city side of the building, visitors can either access the elevators to the office floors through a sky lobby reached via the main entrance, or they can go up a ramp to the public spaces that can be used by museums for exhibitions and take the elevators from there to the belvedere.

The Triangle project was initially halted by political change at the upper echelons of Parisian local government. A public ballot rejected the investors' wide-ranging reduction of publicly accessible facilities. After the investors revised their plans, the project was given another chance. For Herzog & de Meuron it offers the opportunity of exploring the concept of urban density in a new type of tower building that embodies the notion of a vertical city with a mix of public and private spaces by developing the European urban fabric upward and incorporating a variety of districts, zones, connections, internal pathways, houses within a house, and entire communications networks. The Triangle tower is like a city map tipped up into the vertical, with its corridors, escalators, and elevators resembling a diagram of a public transport system. The monotony of uniformly stacked identical floors is broken here. Instead, spatial and structural variety cater to the new requirements of today's workplace organization, living situations, and expectations of hotel accommodation. A combination of clusters and individual rooms allows for individual use as well as meeting the needs of entire corporate units. In the Roche Building 1 office tower on the grounds of the pharmaceutical company in Basel, Switzerland, this has been achieved in a form that is tailor-made to the needs of the client.

The area known as the Dreispitz has seen substantial change since the turn of the century, evolving from a place unrelated to the life of the city into an "up-and-coming neighborhood." Due to the unusual givens of the site—its history, ownership, and political jurisdiction—it has proved to be an ideal laboratory for urban transformation.

Covering some fifty hectares, it is a piece of city with a single owner, the Christoph Merian Foundation. Originally used for warehouses and later as a customs depot, its development was governed by idiosyncratic rules, leading to a fascinating hodgepodge of architectures and uses, both ugly and beautiful. The streets bear the names of cities from all over the world, such as Oslo-Strasse, Florenz-Strasse, and Helsinki-Strasse.

Sites of that nature are uncommon in Switzerland and when we were asked in 2001 to conduct an urban study on transforming the site into an open, mixed-use neighborhood, we were, of course, happy to accept the commission. We wanted to work out stages of planning that would not be dictated by a rigid master plan but instead subject to an open-ended process with the goal of fostering the existing urban diversity and allowing for a substantial increase in density. In contrast to a tabula rasa, we proposed a combination of various architectural typologies and uses, enabling small, unassuming structures to remain side-by-side with large-scale objects. This is best illustrated by the Schaulager, an art institution of international renown, located at the southern end of the Dreispitz next to ugly workshops, offices, and bourgeois apartment buildings. The institution, inaugurated in 2003, has been one of the neighborhood's prime agents of transformation.

An important step in encouraging a diversity of uses was the relocation of the Academy of Art and Design, with some 1000 students and teachers, to the Dreispitz in summer 2014. The university is housed in both existing industrial buildings and new facilities. In addition, the House of Electronic Arts has also moved into an existing building, and the Transitlager, a former transit warehouse, is constructed with spaces for cultural activities in the base of the building as well as numerous apartments above.

The Dreispitz urban study and its political implementation were of special interest to us because it was the largest test area to date where we have actually been able to apply the research we have been doing for years in relation to our repeated calls for border-crossing development of the city of Basel, with the long-term goal of a trinational metropolitan region. One of our concerns has always been to develop new and border-crossing neighborhoods, where people from France, Germany, and Switzerland can plan the everyday reality of their lives together, without the entrenched defensive reactions that still reflect the political animosities of the past.

Following our urban study of the entire area, we finally wanted to execute a concrete architectural project and therefore initiated and developed the Helsinki Dreispitz project, a warehouse for our own archives topped by 41 apartments. The master plan originally specified a building height of 20 m, which would have been just enough for our archives. As authors of the master plan, we appealed to the authorities and the owners of the land, requesting a building height of 40 m so that the density and vibrancy of the neighborhood to which we aspired could be set in motion by providing housing there.

The warehouse contains the archives of Herzog & de Meuron, accumulated since the firm was founded in 1978: plans, documents, sketches, drawings, samples of materials, models, and fragments of models to test scale and execution. So far these diverse sources had been stored in a number of different locations, making it cumbersome to do research, to work with the material, and to study it, for instance, for publications or exhibition projects. Now, at Helsinki Dreispitz, all of these holdings have been assembled in one building and can be viewed in purpose-built display cases and storage shelves that meet today's logistic and conservatorial needs. The works by artists with whom we have collaborated over the years are also preserved in the same location as well as the photo collection of Peter and Ruth Herzog, which we had the opportunity to acquire. This extremely extensive and important collection of historical photographs and family albums of great social historical significance; the art collection; and the models, drawings, and plans of Herzog & de Meuron are each concentrated in a cabinet of their own. The whole, collectively named the "Jacques Herzog und Pierre de Meuron Kabinett," was established as a charitable foundation in 2015.

The main task will be the storage and maintenance of the archives. After being digitized, the extensive collection of photographs will be available for exhibition projects, in particular to meet the needs of the Kunstmuseum Basel and provide a potential cornerstone for a future department of photography. Making the holdings of the Jacques Herzog und

*Pierre de Meuron Kabinett publicly accessible for research
and study is one of several scenarios currently under
consideration. Scenarios of that nature are especially important
to us because they will complement and support the activities
of the Academy of Art and Design and other cultural institutions,
whose relocation was initiated by our urban study.*

*The Dreispitz is such a hodgepodge of buildings that
we found no significant urban or architectural points of reference
that might have been of use when we first started thinking
about the Helsinki Dreispitz project. But we did like some of the
existing buildings because they are so direct and basic, their
design is of an innocence that we found fascinating. That was
something we could not imitate, but we could certainly aim
for the discreteness and self-sufficiency manifested by every one of
them, some of which had even been built without an architect.
We soon decided to concentrate on a freestanding, simple,
raw structure, like a cliff or a palazzo, with few openings in the base,
which would contain the archives, and a more permeable
facade above for the apartments. The base and the units on top are
clearly discrete but made of the same raw concrete that gives
the building a monolithic appearance both inside and outside.
Although it seems symmetrical and almost brutal at first
sight, a closer look reveals variations and nuances, to which we
gave meticulous attention in the course of the project.
These variations on the symmetry, on rectangular or straight lines,
were not, however, arbitrary formal decisions made by us as
authors but primarily governed by technical, functional, or
regulatory parameters. The east side of the base is curved,
generating an asymmetry and forming a kind of "main facade"
facing the Campus des Bildes (Campus of the Image).
The curve in the base is a sculptural gesture that is meaningful and
appeals to us especially because it was practically forced on
us due to the old tracks of the freight trains that run adjacent to
the building site. The curve also enlarges parts of the
cantilevered apartments placed like a basket on top of the base.
This necessitated local reinforcement of the cantilever with
brackets, also of concrete, which further distinguishes the base from
the building on top. The slanted walls of the base and of
the balconies in the "basket" on top actually enhance the legally
stipulated incident angle of light. The slanted walls also
create irregular trapezoid shapes at the sides of the building in the
concrete grid of the balconies—an intricate, technical, and
geometrical challenge because the integrated sunshades run on
parallel, vertical tracks. This meant that the farther away the
supports are from the middle, the more we had to bend them so*

that the metal tracks could still be attached to and concealed by the concrete support. Numerous historical analogies can be found in masonry, friezes, and foundations to this increase in the distortion of supports the closer they are to the edge of a building. However, the actual spatial and physical on-site consequences are even more interesting than these historical examples. The irregularity in the concrete columns makes them thicker, thereby increasing their physical presence. Because the balconies around the edges of the basket turn the corner of the building, the outside area is more open and unprotected; this is now compensated by the more massive concrete columns.

Herzog & de Meuron, 2016

The development of the duty-free depot at the Dreispitz-areal on the fringes of Basel.

204_SI_1924_LBS_MH01-005462

204_SI_0200_503

204_SI_0200_501

There were several types of logistics buildings on the premises.

204_REP 030204_BUCH_059_K

204_SI_0000_081_K

204_SI_0000_080A_K

204_SI_0000_079_K

Potential development of the site with the new building at one side of the university campus.

312_DR_0811_521_GREEN

312_CI_0805_005

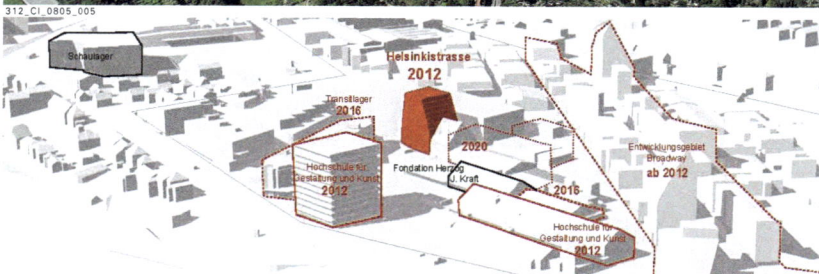

312_CI_0805_007A_RED

Plans and models show how the shape of the building is extruded from the ground plan of the site.

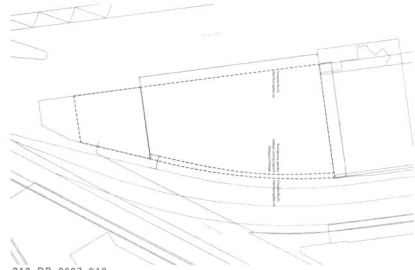

312_DR_0807_010

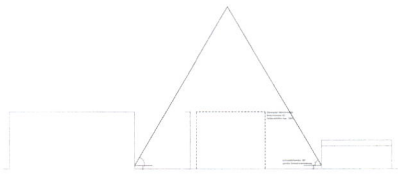

312_DR_0807_008

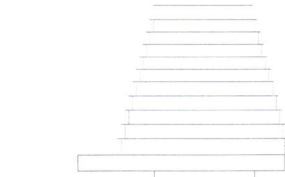

312_DR_0807_012

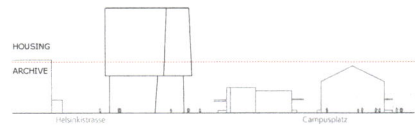

HOUSING
ARCHIVE

312_RE_140826_021_K

312_CI_0807_010

312_CI_0807_012

312_CI_0807_013

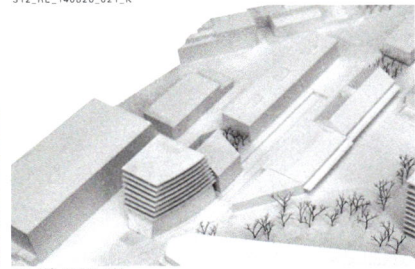

312_MO_081211_036

Development and construction of the solid base for the office archive.

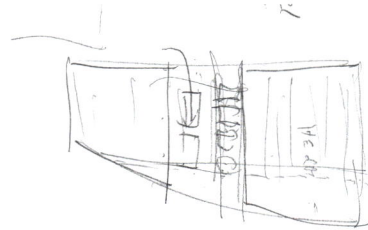

312_SK_0000_JH_504

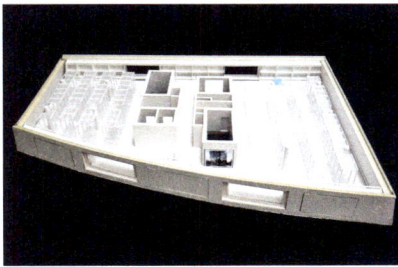

312_MO_0909_002

312_MO_1005_033_011-MOC

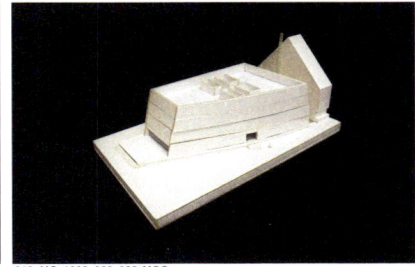

312_MO_1005_069_023-MOC

312_CO_1208_054_BAUGRUBE_BAUMEISTER

312_CO_120909_089

312_CO_1304_333

Layered "shelves" of the building on top and development of the distinctive grid of concrete supports.

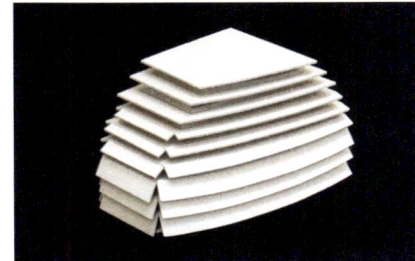

312_MO_1005_027_009-MOC

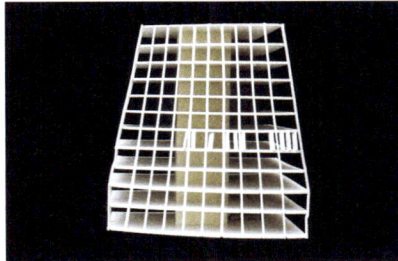

312_MO_1005_049_017-MOA

312_MO_0909_164

312_MO_0912_012_FACADE-OPT

312_EV_120823_722_H

312_CO_1305_005

312_MU_111017_016

312_CP_150603_740_IB_6726

The new office and apartment building is a striking addition to the heterogeneous logistics buildings in the neighborhood.

312_CO_1409_8996_TG

312_CP_150618_701_IB

312_CP_150618_736_IB

312_CP_1507_726_RH

312_CP_150618_742_IB

312_CP_150618_721_IB

The flowing spaces, freestanding supports, understated colors, and pared-down materials of the apartments echo the industrial aura that can be seen from the balconies.

312_CP_1507_727_RH

312_CP_150604_764_IB_H

312_CP_150604_835_IB

312_CP_1602_5398_JH

312_CP_150604_809_IB

312_CP_141028_707_AZ_H

312_CP_141028_710_AZ_H

312_CP_141028_702_AZ_H

312_CP_1410_711_RH

312_CP_141028_715_AZ_H

Workshop bay with courtyard, project space with garden, and archive with custom-designed elements for storage.

312_CP_1507_721_RH

312_CP_150619_770_IB

312_CP_150619_784_IB

312_CP_1602_5392_JH

810-11_CP_150609_002

312_CP_150619_797_IB

312_CP_150619_800_IB

Herzog & de Meuron wanted to bring their archives together in one central place where the wide range of different materials could be stored in accordance with today's best-practice conservational standards and also be more easily accessible to their own team and to researchers on request. To this end, the architects developed a project for the Dreispitz, a former goods storage area and later customs depot on the outskirts of Basel. The Christoph Merian Foundation has acquired the site with the intention of having it gradually merge with the existing urban fabric. This made the 45-hectare site the biggest development area in Basel. In 2001 Herzog & de Meuron accordingly drew up an urban planning concept for the development under the title Vision Dreispitz. Their focus was on transforming the area from one dominated by transport and warehousing functions into a varied and vibrant urban neighborhood.

As an anchor for this opening-up of the urban space, the architects proposed a Campus of the Image, with the Hochschule für Gestaltung und Kunst (HGK) at its center and the Schaulager forming a landmark at its southern extremity. The HGK school of design moved into its new premises in 2014 and is already complemented by a variety of facilities for arts and culture, thus creating a broader campus. The archives of Herzog & de Meuron add to this by spanning a bridge between the HGK and the Schaulager to form a triangle of cultural knowledge. The site is located at the end of the built-up area of Helsinki-Strasse in direct proximity to the campus.

In a phased approach, Herzog & de Meuron, together with the Merian Foundation and the local authorities, put forward a new development plan that provides optimized usage of the narrow gap between two existing buildings. The permitted building height has been doubled to 40 meters. The little transit hub at the end of the street is too small for such a densely developed neighborhood and its demolition will allow that area to be redesigned as a private space. The new building stands apart from the adjacent gabled building and the resulting in-between space is used as an internal courtyard. The planned building is set back somewhat from the row and at the same time forms its conclusion as an imposing head house. The architects used this prominent situation to extend the program by including residential apartments in a pioneering revitalization of this semi-industrial area.

The form of the new twelve-story building is developed out of the characteristics of the local situation. The angle at which light falls into the plaza and the surrounding buildings demands that the volume should be tapered, narrowing upward. An amendment to the building regulations allows for volumetric continuity. Initially, Herzog & de Meuron designed an open structure of stepped floor slabs and supports, in the manner of a gigantic bookshelf. Later, however, they decided to divide the volume in two, with a predominantly closed plinth for the archive anchoring the building on the ground and a more open structure for the apartments above. The apartment levels are thus shielded from the noise and bustle of the street with its freight and goods traffic, while offering the residents magnificent panoramic views on all four sides over Basel and the surrounding countryside. For the residential apartments, Herzog & de Meuron teamed up with a second client, Senn Resources. The two areas of use are accessed by separate entrances with a shared service core for elevators.

The floor plan of the plinth follows the outline of the site and describes a slight curve in the direction of the HGK. The structure of the floors and supports is legible on the facade of the massive volume, with interim fields slightly staggered or perforated by the occasional large window that lets natural light flow into the workspaces. Herzog & de Meuron have housed their archives in two basement levels and three aboveground levels. A custom-built system of shelving, showcases, and open areas accommodates the varying functions and requirements of the holdings, combining cutting-edge conser-

vation techniques with maximum accessibility, as in the Schaulager, which the architects designed for the art collection of the Emanuel Hoffmann Foundation. Separate storage areas have been designated for the collection of works by artists who are friends of the architects and have collaborated with them on many occasions. An open studio space on the ground floor is graced by a huge panoramic window overlooking the new gardens to the southern end of the site and provides amenities for many functions, from presentations to exhibitions. This space is echoed on the opposite side by a cathedral-like hall that incorporates the first basement floor and so allows room for the construction of large-scale models. By recessing the building in this way, natural light is allowed to flow in and the adjoining forecourt that fronts the neighboring building can also be used for outdoor projects. On the upper levels, workplaces have been aligned along the window areas of the facade. This is where the Jacques Herzog und Pierre de Meuron Kabinett foundation stewards an extensive archive.

The plinth is superimposed with a suite of Herzog & de Meuron offices and seven residential levels. The floors and supports, as envisaged in the early prototype design, determine an inner structure that is delimited, rather than enclosed, by a glass shell. Wherever outdoor terrace areas are required, these are drawn inward almost like a curtain, somewhat redolent of the design for the apartment block on Leonard Street in Manhattan. Around this inner box-like formation, the architects have created a layer of balconies that cantilever out so that they are structurally distinct from the interior space. These are surrounded by a floor-to-ceiling grid whose weight is supported by the plinth via diagonal consoles. The clearances between the vertical supports are determined by the size of the wooden roller blinds, which provide shading and privacy as in the apartment complex on the Rue des Suisses in Paris. The tracks of the blinds thus remain hidden from the outside gaze, as do the rainwater pipes and the fixtures for the surrounding railings with their wooden handrail. The horizontal elements are wide enough to conceal the rolled-up blinds.

Inside, the 41 apartments of nine varying types have a semi-industrial look. The rooms flow into one another to create a kind of loft atmosphere. The materials are clear and simple: exposed concrete flooring, raw concrete ceilings and white walls. The supports are freestanding and angled slightly inward to meet structural requirements. Only the oak frames of the large windows and the wooden built-in cupboards add a hint of bourgeois comfort, which is echoed in the gentle curve of the corridor walls with their stucco lustro rendering.

The apartment complex and archive building can be seen as a liberal interpretation of the brutalist architecture of the 1950s and 1960s. Viewed from the Campus of the Image, the building initially appears as a bulky concrete entity with its closed plinth topped by a massive concrete grid converging into an angular overall form. On closer inspection, however, a subtle play of contrasts emerges in which the ponderous mass seems to dissipate. The volumetric form of the building is made up of two geometrical approaches. The plinth follows the outline of the site, with three right angles and a curve sweeping toward Freilagerplatz. The superimposed structure forms a trapezoidal pattern of straight lines. Because the narrow ends of the building taper upward, whereas the longer facades are perpendicular, the overall visual effect is one that counters perspectival foreshortening and gives an impression of the building leaning outward on the right. The consoles between the two areas have to balance out these differences, so the eye constantly perceives minor variations in the grid. Similarly, the vertical supports of the concrete grid, with their alternating positions and widths, generate an almost imperceptible sense of movement, concealing the divisions between the apartment balconies and allowing a right-angled sequence of blinds.

When we received an inquiry from a private client in Culiacán, Mexico to build a church, we were happy to accept. However, since we were not familiar with Culiacán, the staid atmosphere of the area in which the church would be located took us by surprise. This gated residential neighborhood built in a traditionalist architectural style was home to a community of Catholics for whom the church was to be built. A Brave New World. We had doubts, though not morally, about whether the client would be willing to engage with the project as a contemporary architectural challenge. Wouldn't they prefer something consistent with the usual pattern of cheaply built, faceless boxes?

Our first conversations, in which we spoke about our impressions and initial ideas, were encouraging. We wanted radical architecture—religious architecture that would attract both believers and nonbelievers.

For modernist architects, a major contribution has consisted in reinventing church architecture. They have had ample opportunities to practice: the growth of the population and a flourishing economy after 1945 generated the need for many new residential neighborhoods. After the war, architects of modernism continued their crusade to build enlightened architecture for an enlightened society. But did that work for religious architecture as well? Whatever the case, it frequently led to bizarre results. Crosses were modified almost beyond recognition and church towers took every conceivable shape, their sculptural contortions like caricatures that still dot the landscape today.

Doesn't religious architecture necessarily require a different approach from, say, offices or apartment buildings? Not formally, but philosophically. Not enlightened, but aware. For example, being aware of how the great embodiments of premodern religious architecture affected visitors. No architect can resist raving about the earthy weight and mass of Romanesque churches, about the transcendental nature of diaphanous coloring in Gothic cathedrals, or the sumptuous pomp of Baroque churches in Rome. No less impressive is the sparseness and modesty of the adobe churches built by Spanish Mexican settlers on the border of the United States and Mexico.

A small but conspicuous hill in the middle of the residential neighborhood had been earmarked for the church. We wanted to take advantage of the geography and studied alternative scenarios: floating above the hill or growing out of it.

Based on the above thoughts about church architecture, we finally settled on a project that could clearly be identified from afar as a conventional church with a cruciform ground plan but with a topographical or biomorphic component, characterized by the way in which the building grows out of the hill like the trunk of a mighty tree.

No direct lines of sight were planned from inside the church. But we did test a version in which the tall, tapered space would rise up from inside the hill, its top cut off abruptly to form a window to the sky in the shape of a cross. In another version, we cut a cross out of the folded eastern wall of the church. When we built models and illuminated them with strong lamps to simulate the searing sun of Culiacán, the cross took on the appearance of a brand.

In our Culiacán project, we actually tried to achieve the hallucinatory, religious radiance of early church architecture, which enthralls not only the faithful. The client decided against these ideas and chose not to pursue the project.

Herzog & de Meuron, 2016

Church architecture in Mexico shows great diversity from the early settlement churches in the northwest to the Baroque cathedrals of the 16th and 17th centuries.

317_RFSB_0805_004_PUEBLO

317_RFSB_0805_034_OCOTLAN

317_RFSB_0805_050_TECA

317_RFSB_0805_016_CAPILLA

The site of the new cathedral is a landfill hill 10 meters (ca.33 ft.) in height directly opposite the main entrance to the new settlement that is planned to the south of Culiacán.

City center

317_DR_0805_001_CULIACAN

317_SI_0805_004_AERIALSITE

317_SI_0805_008_CULIACAN

317_SK_0805_003

317_SK_0805_004_ALL

Early volumetric sketches and models that include the hill.
The second version is detailed.

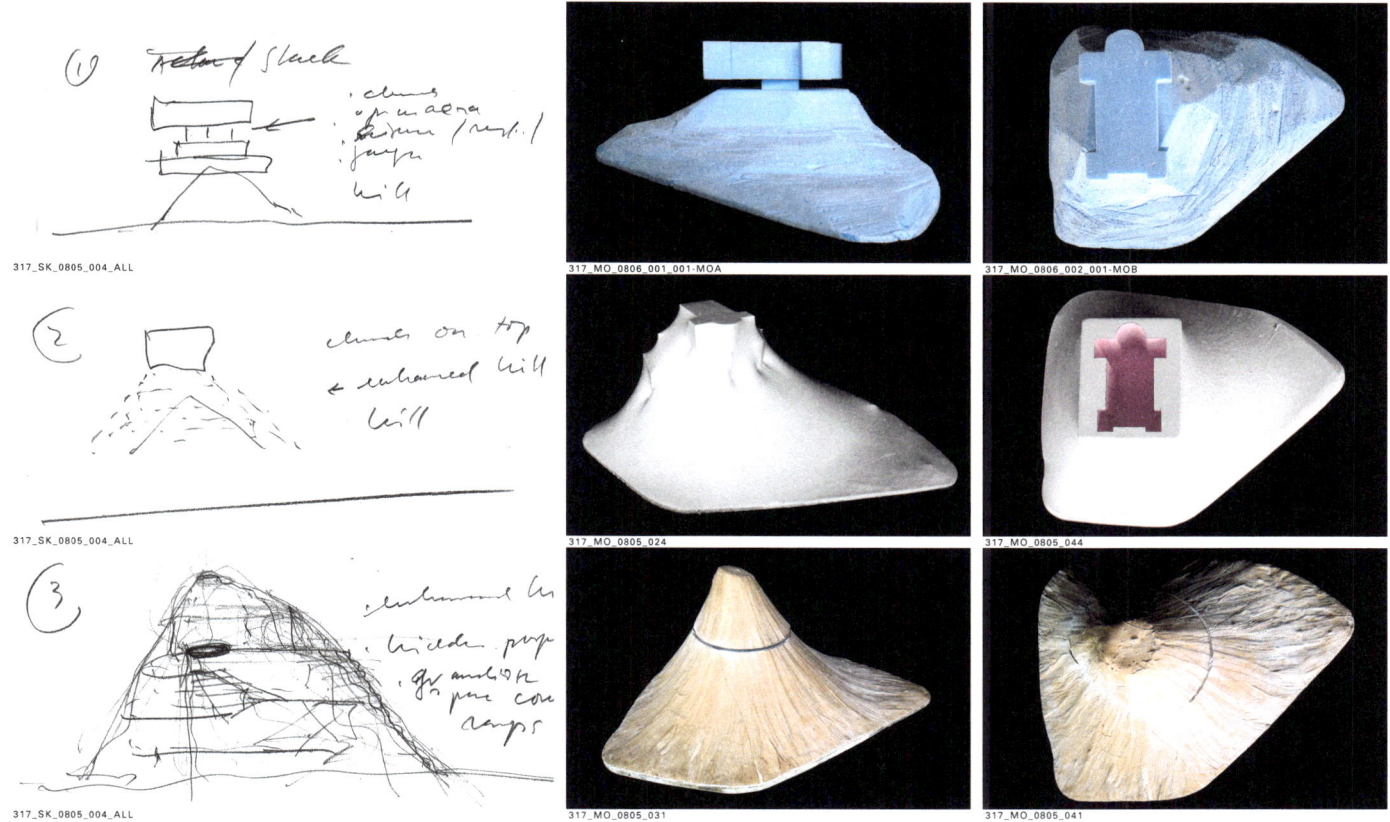

317_SK_0805_004_ALL

317_MO_0806_001_001-MOA

317_MO_0806_002_001-MOB

317_SK_0805_004_ALL

317_MO_0805_024

317_MO_0805_044

317_SK_0805_004_ALL

317_MO_0805_031

317_MO_0805_041

The volume, in the shape of a cross, becomes an
artificial extension of the hill.

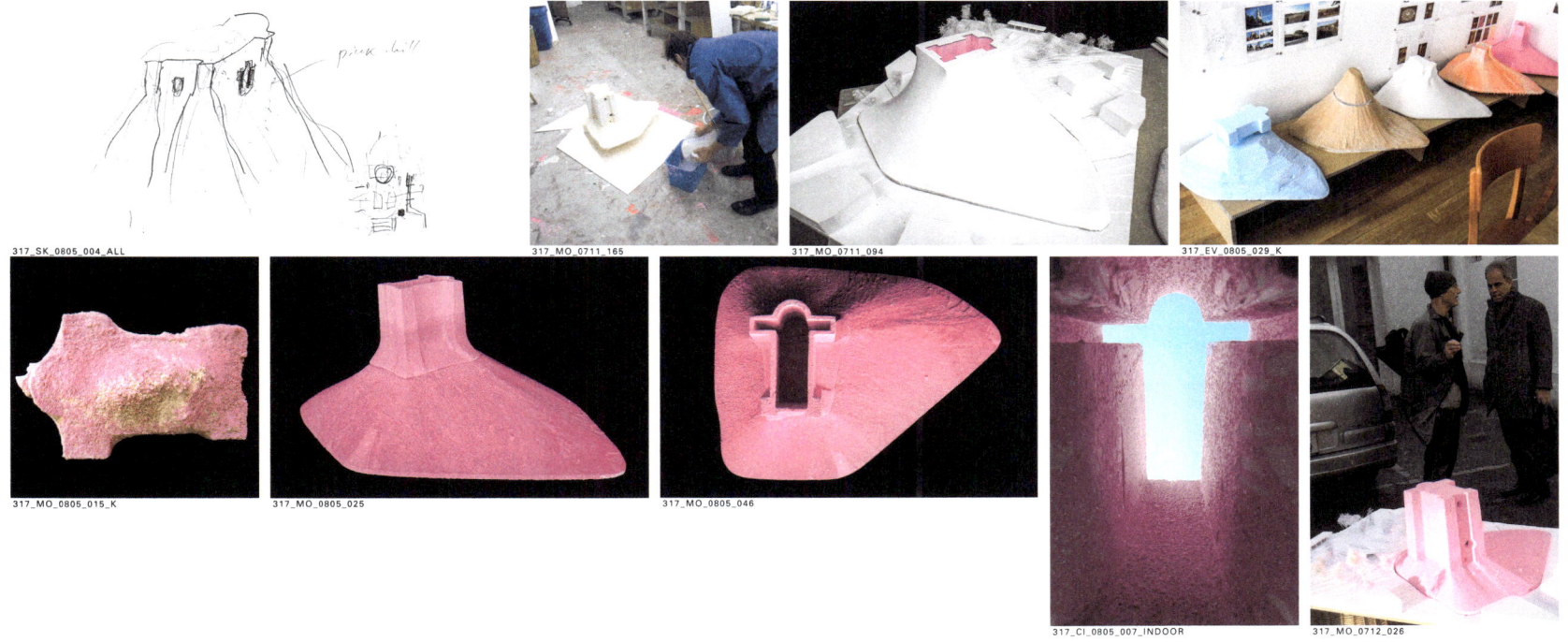

317_SK_0805_004_ALL

317_MO_0711_165

317_MO_0711_094

317_EV_0805_029_K

317_MO_0805_015_K

317_MO_0805_025

317_MO_0805_046

317_CI_0805_007_INDOOR

317_MO_0712_026

Elaboration of the cross shape as a vertical, largely open
interior: procession-like path from the parking garage in
the hill up to the nave of the church with suspended crypt.

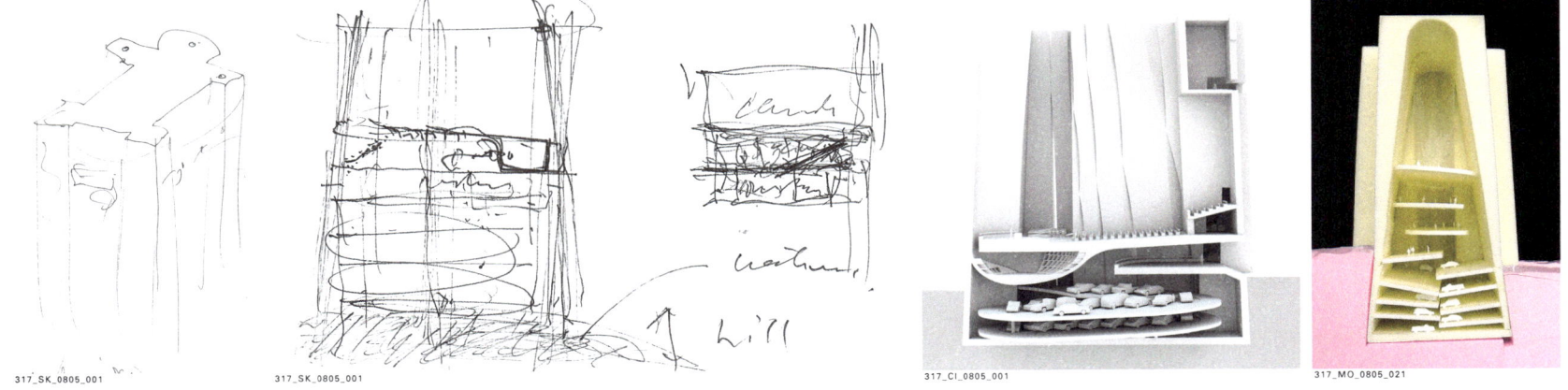

317_SK_0805_001

317_SK_0805_001

317_CI_0805_001

317_MO_0805_021

Ground plans of the four public stories: parking garage, crypt, church, meeting rooms.

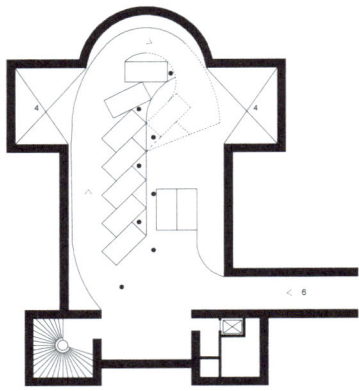

317_DR_0000_504_LEVEL-3_K

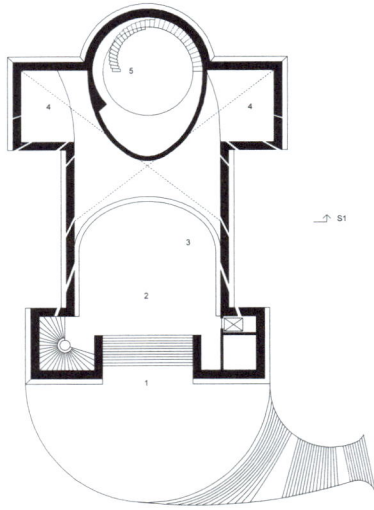

317_DR_0000_501_LEVEL0_K

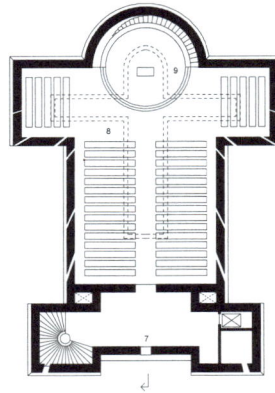

317_DR_0000_502_LEVEL1_K

317_DR_0000_504_LEVEL3_K

The last model that was proposed shows an archaic shape rising out of the hill, with daylight falling through the arms of the cross, through window slits and a skylight. In the nave, monitors replace the conventional images of colorful, stained-glass windows.

317_MO_0712_009

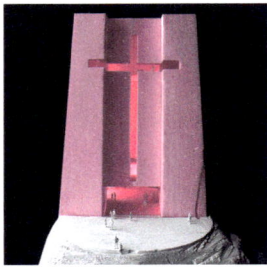

317_CI_0805_021

317_CI_0805_025

317_CI_0805_019_PARKING

317_MO_0804_033

317_CI_0805_018_PARKING

317_EV_0805_026_K

317_CI_0805_008_INSIDE_HIGH

The function of the fortress-like building is indicated by the cross cut into the facade. The arms of the cross contain a terrace with a panoramic view; it is accessed from the meeting rooms.

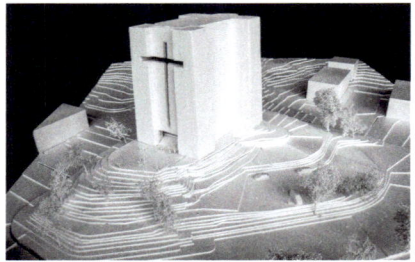

317_CI_0805_027

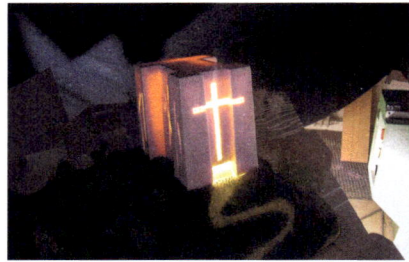

317_MO_0801_022

317_MO_0801_083

317_CI_0805_004_NIGHT COPY

317_CI_0804_014

317_CI_0805_005_ENTRANCE

A group of private investors purchased ten thousand hectares of land to the south of Culiacán with the aim of developing a new urban district there. Culiacán, capital of the state of Sinaloa in Mexico, is situated on the Pacific coast at the confluence of three rivers. It has excellent transport connections and a diverse demographic with a high proportion of immigrants from all over the world. For many years, however, it had been known as a hotbed of narcotics feuds between rival drug cartels, costing hundreds of lives each year. The master plan developed by PBR Architects in 1993 designated the new Primavera district as a gated community offering 100,000 residents a secure home. That amounts to one-sixth of the Culiacán population. While most of this scheme is aimed at the upper-middle classes, a number of affordable properties and tiny plots of land are available for lower-income families. Kindergartens, schools, higher-education facilities, stores, and restaurants provide the necessary infrastructure for everyday life. A newly developed 270-hectare lake, a country club, and a golf course cater for rest and recreation. An area of land on the periphery has been earmarked for a small industrial estate. Almost all the facilities are privately operated. In addition to roads, there are also pathways for pedestrians and cyclists.

The central building envisaged by the investors in this little slice of paradise is a church serving the predominantly Catholic population of the new settlement, but open to other visitors as well, and setting an architectural landmark. The proposed site of the church is an area opposite the main entrance in the northern sector of the development. At 66 meters above sea level, this site lies some 10 meters above the rest of the otherwise flat terrain, presumably because this is where the material excavated when creating the lake was deposited. By the time Herzog & de Meuron were approached by members of the family to submit a planning concept, streets and parking lots had already begun to take shape, snaking up the slopes of the little hill.

The clients wanted a church capable of accommodating as many as one thousand attendees, with seating for five to six hundred. For many of the faithful, the church is also a social hub where christenings, weddings, and communions are celebrated with many guests. The gallery above the main entrance would provide space for a large choir to accompany religious services. The main, south-facing entrance would provide shade, while an air-conditioning system would be installed to ensure a pleasant indoor climate. Culiacán has three hundred days of sunshine annually, with temperatures reaching up to 40°C (104°F) in the shade during five months of the year. The altar would portray the Nativity, featuring as many figures as possible. The church would be dedicated to this central biblical event, as in most other places of worship in this region. Special sound systems for the church interior, indirect lighting, accommodation for the priest, a crypt for community burials, and a parking garage under the church would also be included in the program. Pedestrian walkways over nearby streets would provide safe access.

This was the first time Herzog & de Meuron had designed a Catholic church. The competition to design a Greek Orthodox church in Zurich had taken place in 1989, with a very different focus. In that instance, the young architects had taken the icon, which is central to the Orthodox faith, and sought to translate it visually into a contemporary space. For the church in Culiacán their approach had another starting point. Not only does Catholic liturgy have its own quite distinctive form in Mexico, but the country also has a rich tradition of religious architecture that is much easier to link up with than in the case of a center for the Orthodox community in the Swiss diaspora. What the two projects do have in common, however, is an almost instinctive quest to tap into the very core of the respective liturgy and its archaic formulation.

Herzog & de Meuron began by meticulously researching the history of the symbolism used in Christian church architecture and its geometry. The circle representing the divine and the square representing the mortal realm are superimposed and lead in a developmental sequence to a cruciform layout on an east–west axis forming what is known as a *cruz latina* temple, evoking the body of Christ on the cross with arms outstretched. The narthex symbolizes the earthly sphere, with an archway formulating the transition into the spiritual realm, while the two corner towers represent the Old and New Testaments. The domed ceiling represents the celestial vault, while the nave symbolizes Noah's Ark and the altar in the central crossing forms the fulcrum point of mediation between the earthly and heavenly realms, translating the religious cosmos into an architectural space. Herzog & de Meuron implemented the evolutionary development of this fundamental framework, while reflecting the distinctive vernacular of church architecture in Mexico. But instead of basing their design primarily on the modern basilica, the neoclassical purism of Puebla, or the flamboyant baroque to be found throughout the country, Herzog & de Meuron have taken their cue from the small settler churches that can be found mainly in the north of Mexico, where Culiacán is also located. With their compact layout of nave and tower, it is sometimes hard to tell whether the building is part of a fortress or a monastery. Built as centers of Christianization, their architectural syntax speaks as much to the cultural difference that prevails as it does to the hostility of the climate and the desert landscapes. San Estevan del Rey de Acoma, dating from the mid-seventeenth century, is a case in point: its facade and dual towers soar skyward like some archaic stronghold.

In successive stages, Herzog & de Meuron have combined this sense of the archaic with the human dimension of the cross shape. By layering the programmatic design in several building volumes on the hill, they have devised a church that becomes part of the hill itself, as though growing out of it, rising over the topography like a man-made mountain. The towers and the nave form a monolithic whole. The interior follows the cruciform plan, with an initial variation opening toward the sky, though later taking the form of a closed baldachin symbolizing the heavens. The tapered extrusion lends the interior space a further upward dynamic, adopting a fluidity of movement not unlike that of Le Corbusier's cathedral in Firminy.

All the required facilities are housed within this earthen body of meter-thick adobe walls. The basement floors set into the plinth of the building provide a parking garage with direct access to the open atrium above, which overlooks it, and where visitors arriving by foot enter the church. From there, they enter the sanctuary with its soaring 34-meter-high ceiling and its floor sloping gently toward the altar. The chancel is elevated and pushed into the apse so that square and circle converge. Beneath that, the crypt is suspended like an oval shell and connected to the earth by a column. Light falls into the sanctuary through slits in the walls developed from cracks formed as the adobe dried. These add a note of vulnerability that contrasts with the perfection of the floor plan, evoking the wounds of Christ's flagellation and reminiscent of Lucio Fontana's Concetti spaziali. In addition, a cross cut almost full height into the front facade makes a clear outward statement of the building's function, while the transversal arms provide a viewing terrace for the community room that stretches across the entire width of the building.

The design combines both archaic and modern aspects of church architecture, bringing them together in a space that is as open to abstract spirituality as it is to traditional Catholic worship. However, the clients felt the design departed too far from the conventional regional notion of a church to which most future residents of the Primavera community belong. The project has been suspended.

Work on a swimming pool for Riehen near Basel has always been on our agenda, ever since the early days of our career. Over 30 years went by between the first competition project to the inauguration of the "Bädli" in 2015. The natural swimming pool is the outcome of the fourth attempt to build a new pool in Riehen, following aborted projects for an outdoor and indoor swimming pool (1979/81–1982), an outdoor swimming pool on the meadow in front of the site where the Fondation Beyeler now stands (1986–1987, 1990–1992), and a project for the old bathing area at the Schlipf, as the slopes of the nearby hills are called.

The four projects differ considerably and give an insight into various phases in our approach to architecture.

The project for an outdoor and indoor swimming pool was the first competition (1979) we ever won. We could hardly believe it. It was of considerable importance, and had been noted and debated far beyond Basel. Ernst Gisel and Dolf Schnebli, Switzerland's most famous architects in those days and much admired by their younger colleagues, had set the tone in the jury. Gisel liked the organic and figurative appearance of our project. He saw affinities with Aalto and Scharoun, architects that we had studied with great care at the time. The proposed materials—plywood, sheet copper, and slabs of asphalt—had been inspired by the preferences of these Nordic masters, although we were even more fascinated with the mystical, material universe of such artists as Joseph Beuys. The Photographic Studio Frei in Weil am Rhein, the Blue House in Oberwil, and the competition for Visp illustrate our interest in using new, architecturally unorthodox materials. It was an attempt to set ourselves off against contemporary architects and prevailing preferences for certain materials and forms. We loved soaking plywood in tar pigments so that it smelled like old garden fences; we loved the informal, almost shabby aesthetics of roofing paper; and we deliberately applied paint hastily, unprofessionally, as if by an amateur.

This project for an indoor and outdoor swimming pool was voted down by the people of Riehen because of the cost and probably also because of the energy consumption. Nonetheless, we were commissioned to make further plans, but only for an outdoor swimming pool in the same location.

The second project had nothing to do with the first one. In the meantime, we had discovered other issues of interest beyond questions of material. The figurative, almost romantically naïve architecture of the first project had disappeared. We stopped looking for visual analogies and focused on expressing what a pool actually is, with no detours. We started with the physical structure, the basin out of concrete and the water it contains. Instead of making it flush with the ground, as is usually done, a big object would be placed in the landscape. Variations in the dimensions of the pools would be apparent and, in contrast to the pools in a conventional facility, the size of the pools could be identified at first sight. We liked the idea of making something visible that is ordinarily invisible, of turning a negative shape into a positive one. The depths of the different pools and how much water they contained were now revealed in the height of freestanding objects. Bathers would have moved about on the platforms of these raised basins as on the deck of a ship, with a corresponding view of the beautiful wetlands along the nearby Wiese River.

This was one of the early projects in which we literally tried to dig up the latent potential in order to come up with a simple device that would make it easy to see and practical to use. Unfortunately this project failed as well.

Finally, the location on unbuilt land was abandoned but not the intention of building a new swimming pool. We were now permitted to plan a project to remodel an old building and construct a new one on the site of the existing swimming pool at the foot of the "Schlipf." Once again we wanted to dig up the basin and turn it into an object with a sundeck in place of the old, shady facility. This also inspired the idea of building a bridge across the street to access a beautiful location next to the Wiese River, which had so far been used as a parking lot. Soon all those involved in the project began thinking: why not move the entire facility across the street, where it's sunnier and the landscape is much more attractive? Since the so-called Zollfreistrasse (Duty-Free Street), a tunnel connecting the German towns of Weil am Rhein and Lörrach, would pass underneath the old facility in Riehen, the relocation made even more sense—with the additional advantage that Germany would help to finance the relocation.

This project, now the fourth one, therefore had political support as well. Called upon to emphasize sustainable, environmentally friendly planning with a view to landscape preservation, we had the opportunity to take an entirely *different approach: as little architecture as possible, above all water and landscape. No conventional pools but rather a huge pond or lake; no conventional bathing pavilions but rather spacious fencing like a protected garden open to the river; as little mechanical and chemical purification of the water as possible; instead biological filters using corresponding plants and microorganisms; a cosy "Bädli," as it is called, accommodating a maximum of 2000 visitors; no large-scale facility like the existing municipal swimming pools.*

The fence is an all-timber construction that integrates all the functional facilities: changing rooms, showers, admissions, and maintenance as well as a restaurant and the lawn. It was therefore built largely by joiners and carpenters. The "Bädli" is reminiscent of older baths at lakes and rivers such as the popular "Rhybadhüsli" Breite or St. Johann am Rhein in Basel, and has less in common with conventional municipal swimming pools especially since the basin was designed and built to be a lake, its shores lined with gravel, sand, and plants. The water feels soft and smells natural because of the biological filtering plant, which we situated at the foot of the Schlipf slope as a publicly accessible landscape park.

Like the preceding swimming pool projects, the landscape park is also linked to the early history of Herzog & de Meuron. We had already wanted to build a park of that kind as a water purification plant in 1989, albeit much bigger and more radical because it would have replaced the municipal purification plant in Barcelona. In both projects, Barcelona and Riehen, we were particularly fascinated by the possibility of combining a functional necessity—cleaning polluted water—with an expansive, publicly accessible park facility containing plants, animals, and bodies of water. The alternative is to house technical equipment for such facilities as purification plants and processing plants in isolated buildings, which are ordinarily relegated to the outskirts of cities, like criminals that have to be locked away and made as invisible as possible. Seen in this light, the natural swimming pool represents the attempt to integrate all the functions, needs, and requirements of the project, and also all processes attendant upon it, into one single architectural landscape, where everything becomes a visible and necessary part of the whole.

Herzog & de Meuron, 2016

Earlier projects for public outdoor baths in Riehen.

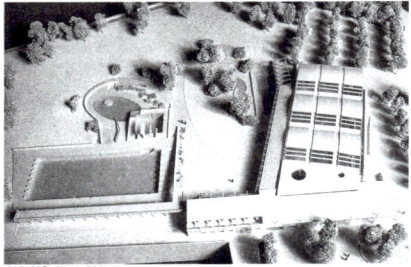
007_MO_8111_502

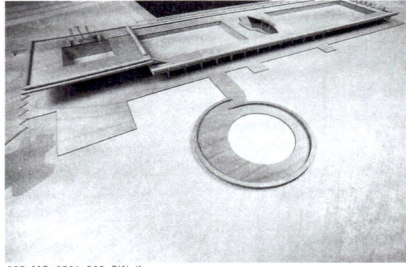
037_MO_8701_503_BW_K

085_CI_9201_001

Location of the new bath and several types of baths in Basel.

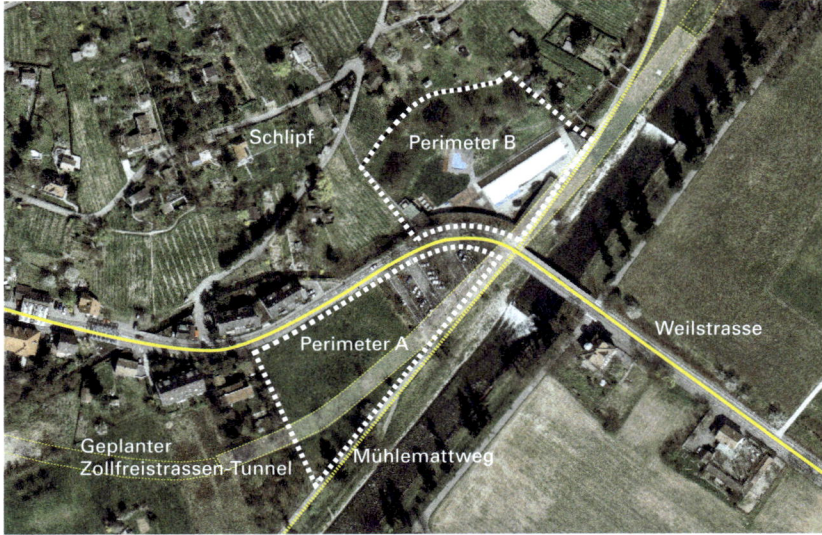
Schlipf
Perimeter B
Perimeter A
Weilstrasse
Geplanter Zollfreistrassen-Tunnel
Mühlemattweg
319_PP_0802_001-BHS-HRES 7

319_RFCL_0000_501_FOTO HÄGI_SCHWIMMBAD_1918

319_SI_0808_001

319_RFCL_0000_502_K

319_RFCL_0000_503_K

319_RFCL_0000_501_K

Development of the pool with zones of natural vegetation.

319_MO_0712_018

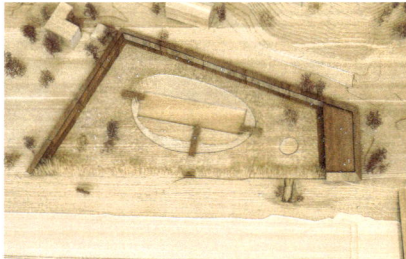
319_MO_0802_034

319_MO_1002_006

319_MO_1002_005

319_MO_1002_004

319_MO_0802_028

The enclosure ensures privacy and is architecturally detailed to accommodate several functions.

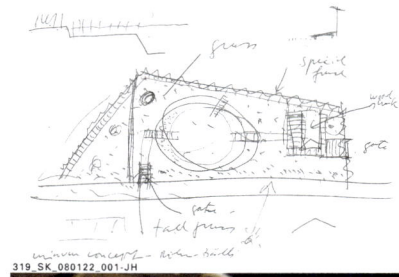

319_SK_080122_001-JH

319_MO_0802_046

319_MO_0903_041

319_MO_1111_044

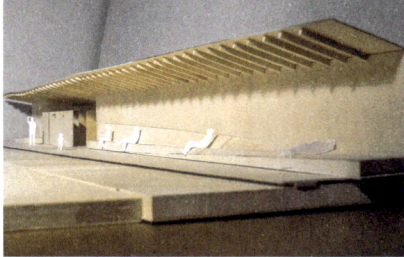

319_MO_0811_022

319_MO_0811_015

319_MO_0812_022

Cross section of the project, showing the dimensions.

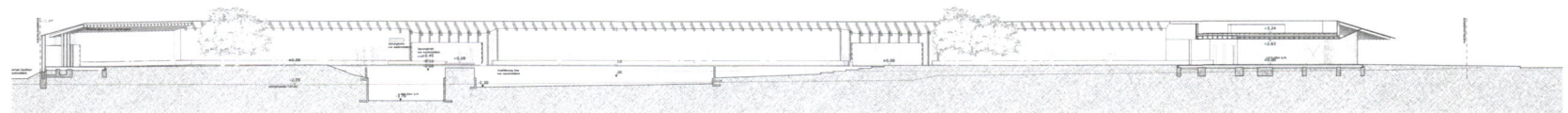

319_DR_1201_503_LAENGSSCHNITT_A_100_K

The timber architecture makes use of traditional crafts and recalls earlier baths along the Rhine.

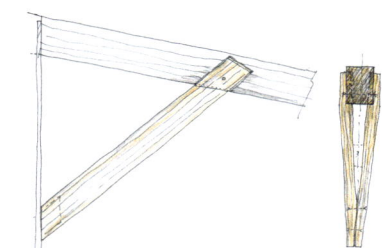

319_SK_111018_503_DACHSTUETZE_MB_K

319_SK_111020_EINGANGSSTUETZE_MB

319_MO_1111_043

319_CO_130827_001

319_CO_130827_004

319_CO_130827_006

319_CO_1310_001

319_CO_1311_032

319_CP_140614_004_MB_H

319_CO_1405_002

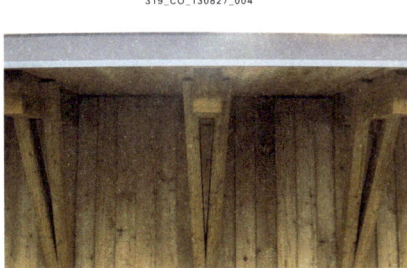

The pool, placed in natural surroundings, is purified with vegetation and gravel.

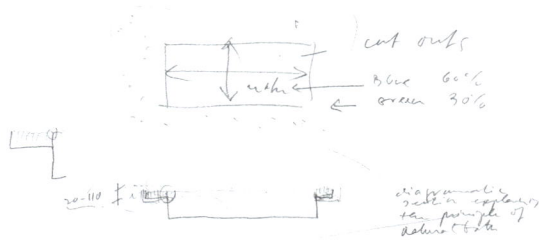

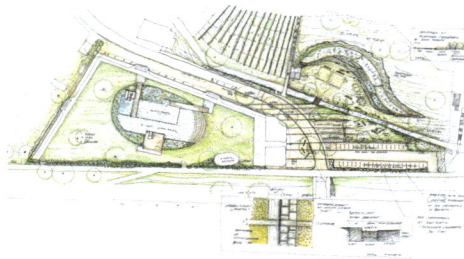

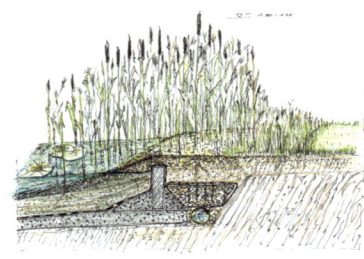

319_SK_071114_001_JH

319_SK_120522_504_SITE-PLAN_MB_K

319_SK_110910_501_BECKEN-RAND_MB_K

319_CO_130409_020_SAD_GRBK

319_CO_1403_027

319_CO_1401_062_E3

319_CP_140619_0848_IB_3226_H

319_CP_140619_1089_IB_3799_H

319_CP_140619_0772_IB_3069

319_CP_140619_1070_IB_3772_H

The wooden enclosure protects the natural bath from the street and remains open to the river.

319_CP_140619_0987_IB_3579_H

319_CP_140619_1123_IB_3877

319_CP_140619_0706_IB_2919

319_CP_140614_006_MB_H

Entrance, changing rooms, showers, and restaurant are integrated into the wooden enclosure, ensuring a sheltered, private atmosphere for bathers.

319_CP_140619_1023_IB_3665_H

319_CP_140619_1041_IB_3710

319_CP_140619_0795_IB_3112

319_CP_140619_0824_IB_3172

319_CP_140619_0817_IB_3158

319_CP_140619_0782_IB_3087_H

319_CP_140619_0727_IB_2968_H

319_CP_140619_1070_IB_3772

For all the many different types of construction projects that Herzog & de Meuron have realized over the years, the Naturbad Riehen was their first swimming pool—even though they had already twice submitted proposals for a pool for the municipality of Riehen, on the outskirts of Basel, very early on in their career. Indeed they came top in two competitions for a swimming pool design, but on both occasions the local residents voted against their proposals. In 1979–82 they designed a combination of indoor and outdoor pool for Riehen; four years later the project was reviewed and reduced to just an outdoor pool in view of the changed conditions in the investment market. The striking designs of both projects reflected the mood of the 1970s and 80s, when public pools were largely seen as sports facilities; both projects were eye-catching—from the cool, underwater world of the indoor pool (illustrated in Herzog & de Meuron's first video simulation), the welcoming gesture of the two "arms" of the building, and the undulating roof of the indoor pool to the more abstract language of the later megastructure in a meadow, containing all three pools—a supertanker that had run aground in Riehen.

Anyone comparing those earlier designs and the Naturbad as it now exists cannot help but be struck by the differences wrought by changed social attitudes. These days ecological considerations shape many aspects of daily life and the spread of technology has, by definition, reawakened a yearning for nature. Bathers love pools in "natural" settings. So Herzog & de Meuron consulted Claus Schmitt in Bamberg—a leading expert in swimming pool design—regarding the fundamental requirements of outdoor bathing. They drew on the experiences we all have of swimming but also on the history of outdoor swimming seen in pictures throughout the ages. Medieval woodcuts and contemporary images alike show people swimming in ponds, rivers, and the sea. The latter are the stage and the bathers are the protagonists, who require showers and toilets, a restaurant and reception area, sun decks and purified water.

Herzog & de Meuron considered these basic requirements in light of the local parameters. The new pool was to be at the edge of Riehen on a plot of land that takes a "bite" out of German territory; a customs-free road passes through a tunnel underneath it. On two sides of the site there are roads, on the third side it is separated from the Wiese River and the meadows beyond it by a farm lane. Herzog & de Meuron came up with a design that gives bathers the desired feeling of protection but still allows them to enjoy the view out into the countryside. The entrance, with the reception area and restaurant, occupies the narrow end of the site and is integrated into the timber fence that marks the perimeter, hiding the road and the neighboring field. A hedge marks the perimeter line by the lane that runs parallel to the river.

The untreated larch wood fence recalls aspects of earlier projects. However, the fence does more than shield bathers from prying eyes; it is also designed as a space in its own right, with a canopy roof. On the outside it is fitted with bicycle racks; on the inside it morphs into a continuous, two-meter-deep bench, which extends the areas where visitors can lounge and relax. In their first swimming pool design the architects integrated the changing areas into a similarly protective exterior structure and in their second design they integrated the changing facilities into the wall of the "supertanker." The pragmatic simplicity of the overall design recalls the traditional river pools along the Rhine, dating back to the late nineteenth century, which consist simply of railings, walkways, and timber changing facilities.

In Riehen the pool itself is an oval pond surrounded by grass. With the exception of the toddlers' paddling pool near the restaurant, all the different bathing areas interconnect, giving swimmers the feeling that they are bathing in real open water. The surface of the pool is only broken by short metal markers set into the concrete edges of the twenty-five-meter pool, the diving pool, and the shallow pool. Each of the three interconnected "pools" has its own wooden jetty. The gravel bed in the shallow areas and the green film covering the concrete bed of the main swimming area (1.8 meters deep) reinforce the impression swimmers have that this is an entirely natural pond.

The pool water is purified in an entirely traditional method. The river meadows, where the pool has been created, are part of the water protection zone from which Basel draws its groundwater, partly through the artificial percolation of river water. The same principle is used for the swimming pool. The first filter process occurs along the edges of the grass, which are separated from the bathing pool, laid with a border of loess, and planted with reeds in the water. From there pumps take the water to a site at the foot of the Schlipf hill, diagonally behind the swimming pool, where two filter terraces have been built into the natural curvature of the slope. The water passes through a two-meter-deep layer of gravel and a green filter. The Naturbad Riehen can accommodate 2,000 guests per day, and when the pumps are working at full capacity the water can be fully filtered twice a day. The water quality is monitored and the readings are transmitted to an external quality-control center, which constantly adjusts the computer-operated pumps. The natural bathing experience has a high-tech support system. The pool uses natural filtering processes and thus becomes part of the landscape. In essence the Naturbad Riehen implements a concept that the architects originally came up with in 1989 for the Avenida Diagonal in Barcelona.

This bathing pool by the Schlipf is something of a homecoming for the architects. Besides elements from earlier proposals it also has an unusually detailed finish. Despite its size the architecture almost has the air of a piece of furniture. For a start, there is precision joinery. And then there is the underlying principle, that is to say, the subtle exploitation of the intrinsically linear nature of timber construction. The timbers of the perimeter form a fence; at the same time their vertical repetition creates the impression of a series. The pairs of posts buttressing the canopy grasp the roof beams like fingers. The drainpipes from the canopy are accommodated in the spaces between the roof supports. Showers, toilets, and changing areas are all accommodated in three conch shapes that sweep elegantly outward. A simple concrete wall shields these from view and enters into sculptural dialog with the wood. The showers, which are attached to the concrete wall, heighten the ambivalence of this interplay of functionality and carefully staged, minimalist beauty. The showers look like simple water pipes; the hot showers are only identifiable by the fact that two pipes come up out of the ground together.

In this project Herzog & de Meuron rediscovered lovingly executed craftsmanship as a strategy for contemporary architecture. They had already demonstrated their interest in craft skills in some of their early projects, such as the house for a veterinary surgeon in Dagmersellen, the conversion and extension for Alfred Richterich in Laufen, and the plywood house in Bottmingen. In their most recent proposals Herzog & de Meuron give craft-based solutions an additional edge, which wards off any hint of eco-sentimentalism. The Naturbad Riehen thus takes its place alongside the new depot and production facility for Ricola in Laufen, the Bergstation on the Chäserrugg, and the barn-like blocks for the Parrish Art Museum—all examples of a rural minimalism that combines advanced construction skills and conceptual abstraction with regional traditions and global awareness.

Our design for the new headquarters of the BBVA attempts to create a new neighborhood in the city of Madrid. It has no freestanding towers with plazas and a sculpture after the model of modern building in Madrid and other major cities; it has no blocks of buildings typical of the 19th century; and it has no sprawling complexes like the Fiat plant in Turin or the Karl-Marx-Hof in Vienna. It is a neighborhood on the outskirts of Madrid, not far from the airport, in an uninviting, almost desert-like but increasingly built-up landscape with no recognizable order. In other words, it is a project in a location with no urban identity and none of the vibrant, daily street life that is omnipresent elsewhere in Madrid. Architecture and urban planning cannot conjure up that kind of vitality out of nothing, but some urban models do foster and reinforce such life more than others.

An urban typology that encourages public life and simple, spontaneous communication among people is what we wanted to achieve. Basically it is a natural form of exchange among people that was once perfectly self-evident in the lanes and squares of towns and villages, especially in southern Europe. We proposed a model of that kind in our competition project, and the jury was obviously persuaded that something of that nature could succeed in the headquarters of a major corporation.

The BBVA, a Spanish bank of international reach, wanted to create workplaces for 6,000 employees. The client was a single firm, not a campus for several different companies, nor a building for a community or municipal administration. Nonetheless, our first thought was not of the company and its identity but of a "city," a new patch of city and the potential urban identity that could be forged there.

In keeping with that thought, we designed a carpet of low-rise buildings, three stories high, spread out over the entire premises. This carpet originally consisted of eleven, and in the subsequent project of eight elongated buildings, like fingers on the property. In between, there is a system of gardens and lanes as in a Moorish or southern Spanish city, echoing the way of life in such locations: windows and doors of the offices can be opened as in an apartment, and people gather outdoors for meetings or lunch or coffee. The strong sunlight in Madrid is relieved by plants, water in the gardens, sunshades above the lanes, and the raw, naked structures of concrete in the otherwise largely open and glazed buildings.

The "rawness" of the architecture proved to be a salient feature of the project and represents a radical departure from the corporate architecture ordinarily featured by a major bank. We wanted to bare the concrete as we had done in the first building phase that involved integrating an erratic scattering of half-finished buildings into our project. It seemed obvious to incorporate those buildings into our plans since they were included in the client's acquisition of the land. However, we did not want to compromise our overall concept by adopting their conventional inner layout and organization. So we decided to separate them, to saw through them, turning their insides out and their outsides in. We literally incorporated them and, by so doing, exposed their concrete structure, which we found interesting and fitting for the site. This in turn influenced the design and construction of our new finger-shaped buildings. The lanes that we sawed out of the existing buildings are at a slight diagonal and do not fit into the geometrical grid of the rest of the project. One cannot help thinking of a medieval town. An urban form had fallen into our laps, as it were, without our having to function as form-giving authors. As a result, it had become quite conceivable that the new premises—now occupied by the BBVA as the only landlord—could one day function as the nucleus of a mixed-use urban neighborhood. The public plaza also contributes to this potential; its almost circular shape, cut out of the surrounding carpet of buildings and gardens, has simply been upended to yield a building slab some 100 meters (330 feet) tall in the exact same shape as the plaza. What started out as a somewhat playful experiment in the competition phase, about which we were far from certain, survived and proved to be a welcome urban gesture that makes the new headquarters of the bank a landmark visible from afar.

The distinctive brise-soleils lend the entire compound the character of a closed campus or a cloister. A facade was required to close off the premises from the outside in contrast to the fenestrated finger buildings in the interior, whose lighting and climate is regulated by the narrow lanes and gardens. Architects have long been reluctant to employ brise-soleils, perhaps because they were a Le Corbusier trademark. Given the inhospitable location of the project, where buildings and people *are often exposed to extreme heat, we wanted to return to this interesting architectural element and update it. Because a brise-soleil juts out so far from the facade, it creates an additional space in front of the office window, almost like an uninhabited room. Our analyses of physical data such as solar radiation, brightness inside and at the workplace, angle of view, etc., yielded several innovative options, on the basis of which we had the brise-soleils specifically tailored to meet the needs of the BBVA. The shape on which we decided allows for different inter-pretations and does not instantly elicit specific associations.*

We ended up producing smaller elements with a single axis for short distances and larger ones that protrude farther on two axes for larger offices and conference rooms. Variations on the facade thus reveal differences in the use of the rooms inside the building. This makes for an extremely lively facade, enhanced even more by the movement of the architecture which traces the natural slope of the topography.

Herzog & de Meuron, 2016

The design of the company headquarters echoes the squares and lanes of the Mediterranean city and its public life.

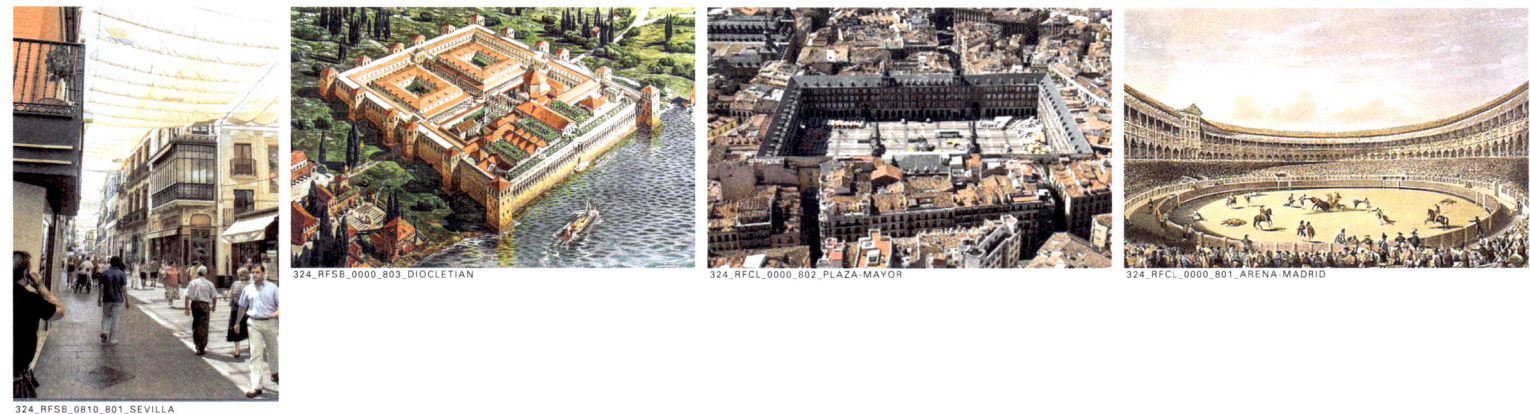

324_RFSB_0810_801_SEVILLA

324_RFSB_0000_803_DIOCLETIAN

324_RFCL_0000_802_PLAZA-MAYOR

324_RFCL_0000_801_ARENA-MADRID

Initial sketches proposed building fingers that follow the topography. Initial competition models integrated the existing rows of buildings, into which a plaza with a high-rise building was incised.

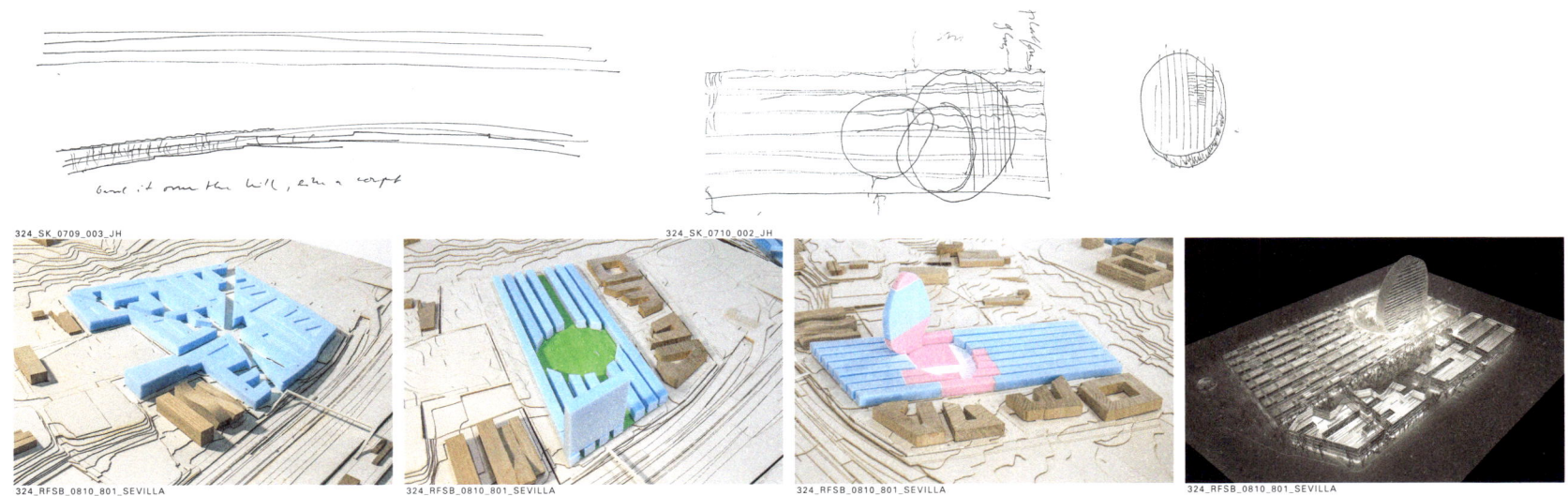

324_SK_0709_003_JH

324_SK_0710_002_JH

324_RFSB_0810_801_SEVILLA

324_RFSB_0810_801_SEVILLA

324_RFSB_0810_801_SEVILLA

324_RFSB_0810_801_SEVILLA

The shallow depth allows for a direct link to the outside; the levels follow the topography.

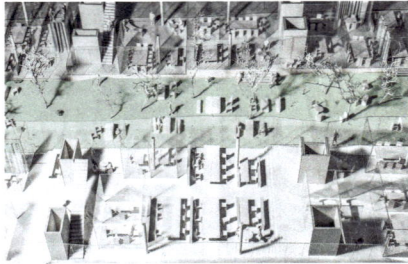
324_MO_0812_042_VERDE

324_MO_0000_001

324_CI_0712_320

324_MO_0812_302

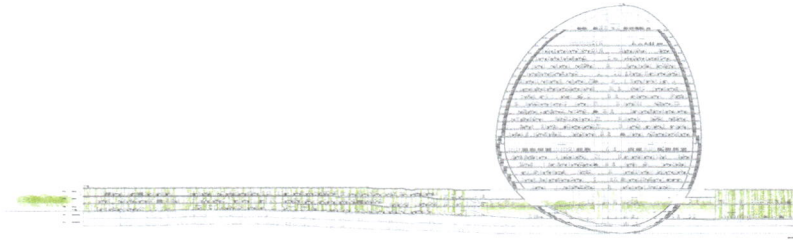
324_DR_0712_SEC-LONG

324_DR_0812_011_TOPOGRAFIA

The existing buildings were stripped down to their original structure, new elements added, and the whole integrated into the overall architectural tapestry.

324_SI_0712_001

324_SI_0708

324_CO_1006_017_DEMO_W

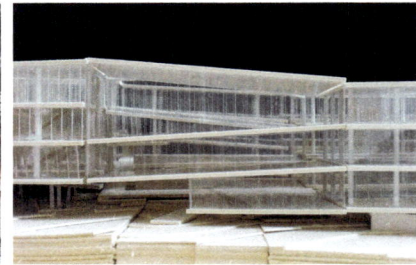
324_MO_0811_133

324_CO_140428_501_K

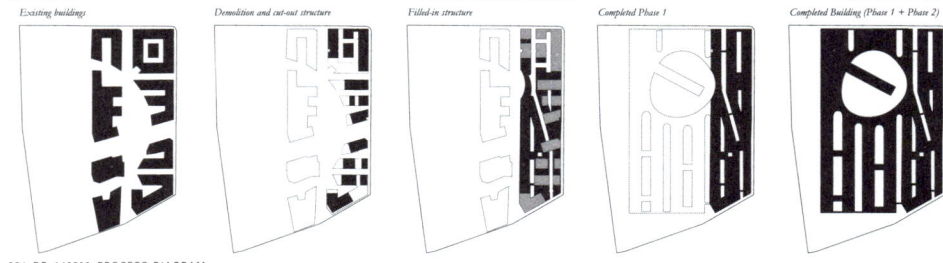
Existing buildings   Demolition and cut-out structure   Filled-in structure   Completed Phase 1   Completed Building (Phase 1 + Phase 2)
324_DR_140509_PROCESS-DIAGRAM

The brise-soleils regulate the incident light and shut off the complex from the outside world. Installed between the existing ceilings, they are custom-sized to each location.

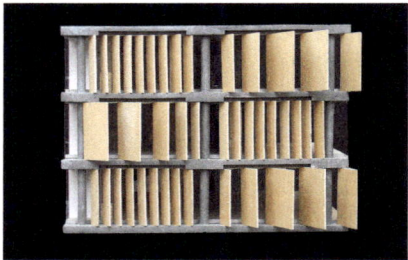
324_MO_090420_FINAL012

324_MO_0910_303

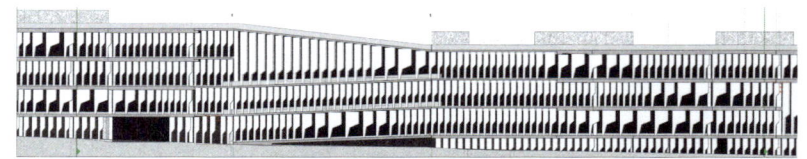
324_DR_1002_F1-PE-4_3004_R01

324_MU_080326_008_PP

324_MO_0910_300

324_MO_0908_079

324_RFAR_0908_036_E-KELLY

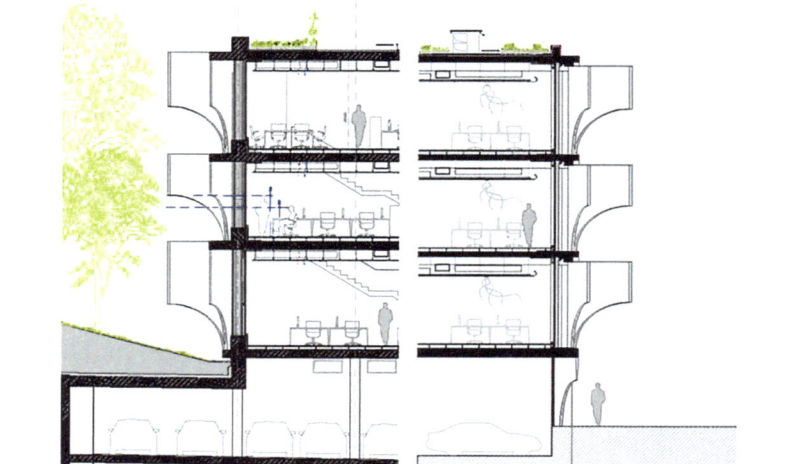
324_CI_0000_801_K

The shape of the central plaza, cut out of the carpet of buildings, was upended to form a tower.

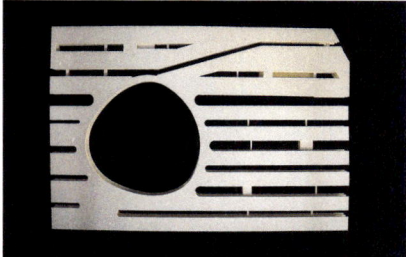

324_MO_0910_017_006-MOB

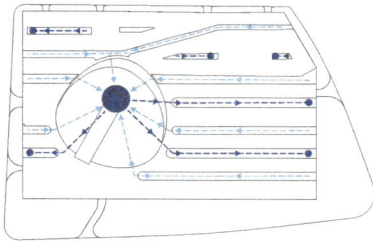

324_DG_1411_WATER

324_MO_0902_030

324_MO_0712_027_1-500

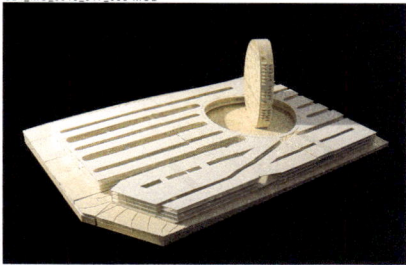

324_MO_0901_076

324_CI_0712_321

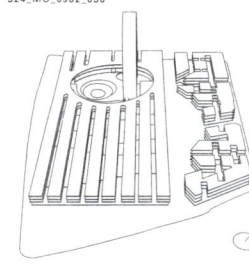

324_DG_1411_022

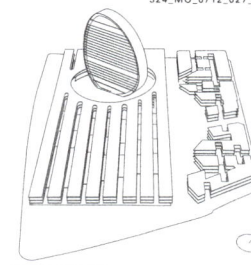

324_DG_1411_023

The shallow depth and oval shape allows for circulation and spatial effects reminiscent of Piranesi.

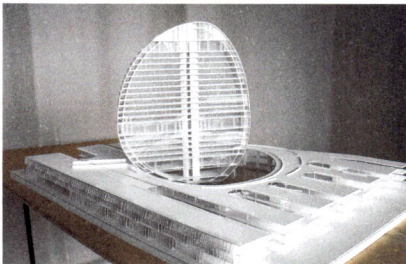

324_MO_0904_069

324_MO_0903_019

324_MO_0902_005

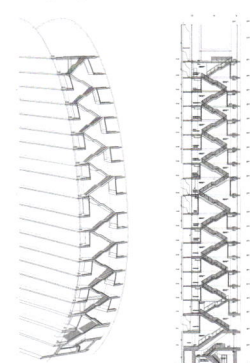

324_DR_1010_F2-EV-PE_4600.01-00-0

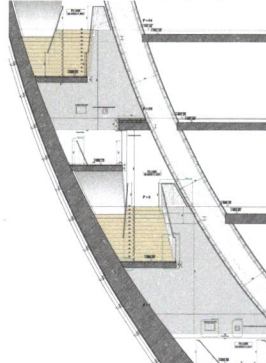

324_DR_1010_F2-EV-PE_5601.00-00-0

324_CO_140305_724_IB_0676_H

324_CO_131114_614

Construction of the tower.

324_CO_1309_002_K

324_CO_1312_574

324_CO_1401_998

324_CO_1401_136

324_CO_1410_006_094057

324_CO_131122_738

324_CO_140305_717_IB_0506_H

324_CO_1401_992

324_CO_1407_CHB_022

The high-rise building sets a landmark for this complex, which is sheltered from its surroundings by solar sails.

324_CO_150527_1170_IB_H_3087

324_CP_1601_852_IB_1914

324_CO_150527_921_IB_H_2382

324_CO_150527_1144_IB_M_3018

324_CP_1608_801_RPB

324_CO_150527_782_IB_M_3571

324_CO_150527_805_IB_M_3631

324_CO_140305_703_IB_0297_H

The shallow depth of many structures allows for frequent vistas through the buildings and onto the city.

324_CP_1603-04_793_DH_H

324_CP_1603-04_723_DH_H

324_CP_1601_763_IB_1646

324_CP_1601_775_IB_1681

324_CP_1603-04_760_DH_H

324_CO_140305_729_IB_0826_H

Squares, courtyards, gardens, paths, passages, and stairs create a compact urban atmosphere in the interior.

324_CP_1601_164_IB_2947

324_CO_150527_1056_IB_2782

324_CP_1601_242_IB_3136

324_CO_150527_986_IB_H_2578

324_CO_150527_708_IB_H_3390

324_CO_1508_501_K

324_CO_150527_965_IB_2511

324_CP_1603-04_712_DH_H

324_CO_1506_014

The Banco Bilbao Vizcaya Argentaria (BBVA), Spain's second-biggest credit institute, had various offices scattered across Madrid, and was looking for a site where it could bring them all together under one roof to form a single operative headquarters for a staff of 6,000. They chose a site on the northern periphery of the city, directly by the A1 highway in Las Tablas, one of the new urban districts that had been built from scratch during the housing boom, with an unrelated mix of company headquarters, undeveloped land, and residential blocks. The financial crisis had left gaps that would still have to be linked to form a cohesive whole over the next few decades.

In a nod to autistic modernism, Herzog & de Meuron at first seemed to close the new headquarters off from its inhospitable environment. Inside, however, they designed the complex as a city, providing a wide variety of spaces and an exemplary sense of openness. They placed a three-story structure of parallel fingers on the site, which slopes down by 8 meters from the highway at its southern end to the northern perimeter, spreading over the topography like a carpet, and reiterating the height differences so that the buildings themselves form a man-made topography: 290-meter-long blocks alternate with streets, lanes, and gardens, all interwoven by lateral axes into a dense tapestry.

This concept meets one of the key requirements of the client: when the bank launched a competition inviting designs, eight unfinished buildings by various investors were occupying the site, some of them with the facades already mounted. The client wished to retain at least 60 percent of these buildings in order to have them turnkey-ready two years before completion of the complex as a whole. Herzog & de Meuron demolished four of the buildings in the middle and integrated the other four into a serial pattern. These were pared down to just their supports and floor slabs, and their irregular geometries were partially altered and partially adopted, so that the individual structures were incorporated to form fingers. That involved separating some elements to create a linear alignment and extending others. The height differences are reflected in the connecting elements, while the new parts are legible in the grid of supports. Incisions into the existing structures transform the underdrafts of the existing floor slabs into capitals and the posts into columns, thereby strengthening the archaic character of the volumes themselves. The architects have embraced this by allowing the load-bearing structure to come to the fore and by placing the floor-to-ceiling glazing behind the outer row of supports so that it appears more as a permeable skin than as a closure. The building fingers are separated by narrow lanes greened here and there by the firm of Vogt Landscape Architects. One of these lanes utilizes a segment of the existing development to break through the linear grid and, like a miniature Broadway, drives along the entire length of the complex with a little diagonal kink. The fingers have a shallow depth of only 15 meters, which means that the workers can enjoy natural daylight and vistas to either side throughout the entire depth of the campus, as far as to the brise-soleils which frame the overall complex as massive white entities spanning two or more floors, offering both shade and panoramic views.

This interaction between interior and exterior space continues in the new section of the campus. For reasons of efficiency, the finger-like office blocks have been reduced from the originally planned eight to just four and have been widened to a depth of 19.45 meters. The broader exterior spaces have been utilized as a combination of green spaces and pathways. Although the emergency services access route marks a boundary between the first and second construction phases, the company headquarters comprise a uniformly structured and coherent whole with which every individual member

of staff can identify. Paradoxically, this coherent whole actually fragments into a number of separate buildings. On the ground floor, transverse connections and pathways ensure easier communication, while gangways and corridors on the upper levels structure the in-between spaces. The workforce of 6,000 can thus be integrated into a cohesive complex while at the same time inhabiting a kind of city that has its own almost domestic surroundings and sense of orientation.

A major factor in creating this sense of an urban identity is the central plaza incised into the northern edge of the tapestry of buildings. All the fingers of the office buildings point toward this plaza, which takes the form of a compressed circle hewn from a shift in the central axis. In its scale and openness it exudes the fundamental principle of a southern architectural culture that consciously couples internal and external spaces. In each of the fingers there are flights of stairs drilling down toward the plaza. A wraparound loggia on the first floor not only ties the building blocks together but at the same time provides a space to stroll outdoors or sit on one of the many benches for respite and relaxation.

Jutting out at an angle from the center of this tapestry of buildings is a structure that rises 99 meters to command the skyline of Madrid. It takes the form of an even more compressed circle with a maximum width of 80 meters, so that it looks like a cutout slice of the plaza itself, especially given that its shallow depth of just 13 meters echoes the height of the three-story building tapestry. Through the structural design of an oval volume with integral floor slabs and a central service core, this disk-shaped tower achieves a subtle balance between movement and stability. It is firmly anchored, yet seems likely to roll away at any moment. The plaza flows beneath it on the ground level and an outdoor ramp leads up from the central entrance of the complex to the first-floor lobby or to the promenade around the plaza. The nineteen floors of differing heights are divided in two by the central service core. The dimensions, the wide-open spaces, the visibility of the concrete shell, the flooring of oak, terrazzo, and carpet, all exude the spaciousness of a factory floor. The panels of the fully glazed facades are aligned so that the fixtures are concealed, allowing light and space to dominate. The south-facing orientation means that the north facade needs no sun-shading and most of the south side can be shaded by the cantilevered floor slabs and framing. The fire escape further condenses the spatial ambiguity of the building. Depending on the angle of the curve, it is situated either on the inside or the outside of the concrete shell, creating an impression worthy of a work by Piranesi. Approaching the complex, one might see this disk as a kind of head house, much like the combined storage and residential building found in the Helsinki Dreispitz project on the grounds of the former bonded warehousing facility in Basel. Both buildings, after all, share in common a reduction of the design to the bare structural bones, with little or no adornment.

It is the subtle details that set the tone. That includes the tension between the contemporary office architecture of concrete and glass and the narrow lanes within the remodeled buildings and the use of cobblestones that are unusual in Spain but quite commonplace in Portugal. It also includes the alternation between the brise-soleil elements and the greenery strung across the lanes. Finally, the rounded forms of the service cores, the floor slabs, and the glazing in many of the fingers add a further hint of spice to the building as a whole. It is almost like being party to a landscape view in a historical diorama. The architects achieved something similar on a smaller scale in their design for the de Young Museum in San Francisco. In the BBVA this interplay is taken to a whole new level.

Plans

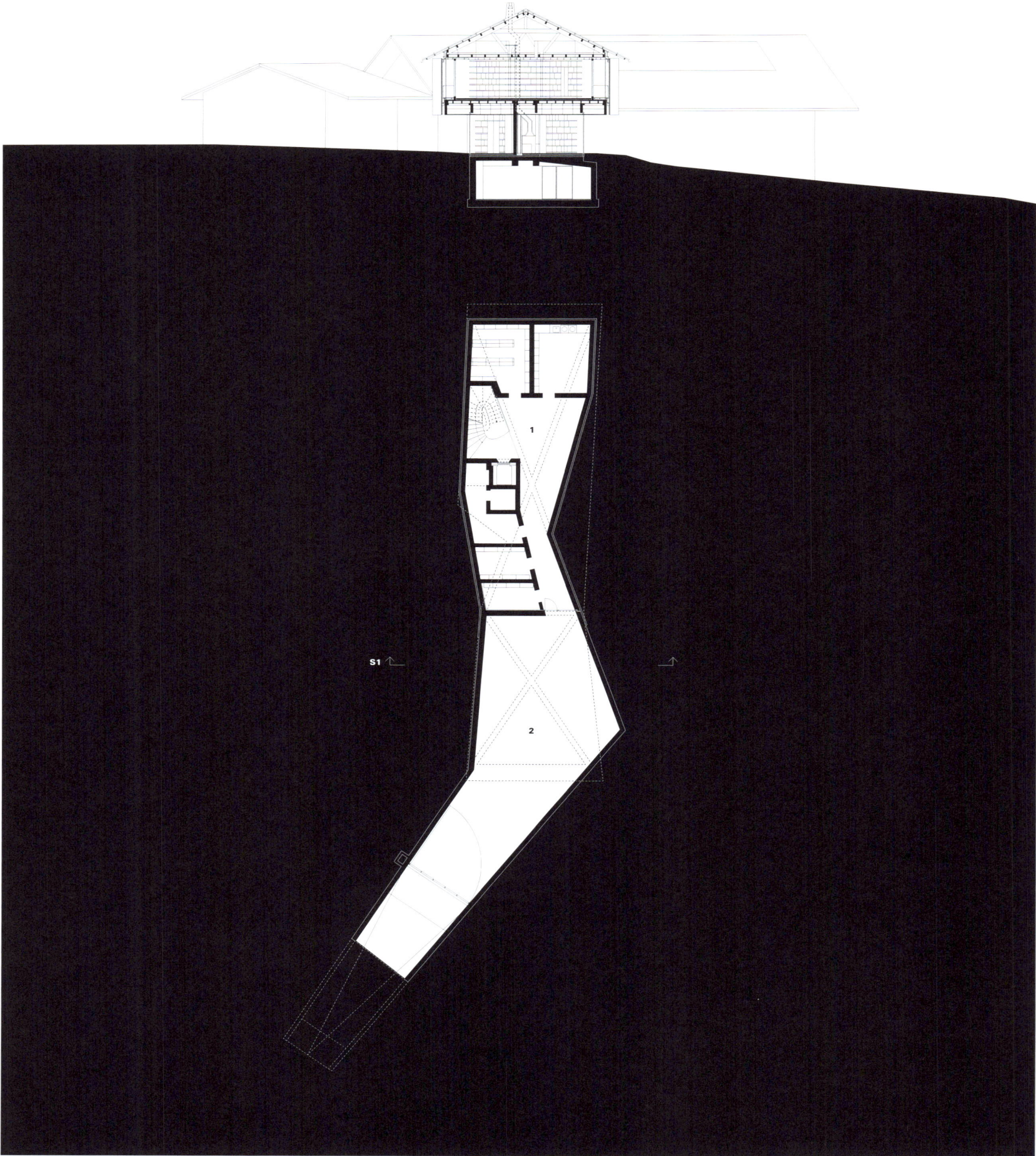

N

1:350

S1

1

2

0   5   10

Section S1: through living room facing library
Basement plan: ¹ foyer ² garage

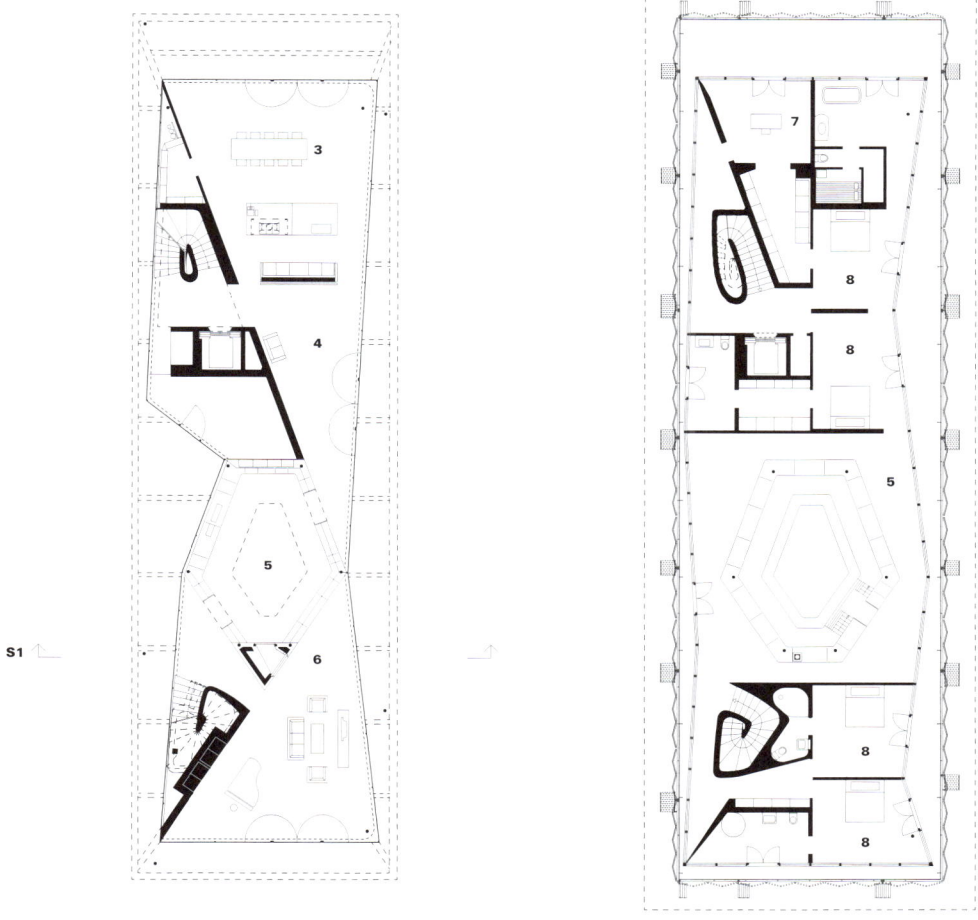

N

1:350

S1

3

4

5

6

7

8

8

5

8

8

0   5   10

Ground floor plan: ³ kitchen/dining room ⁴ hall ⁵ library ⁶ living room
1st floor plan: ⁵ library ⁷ office ⁸ bedroom

163

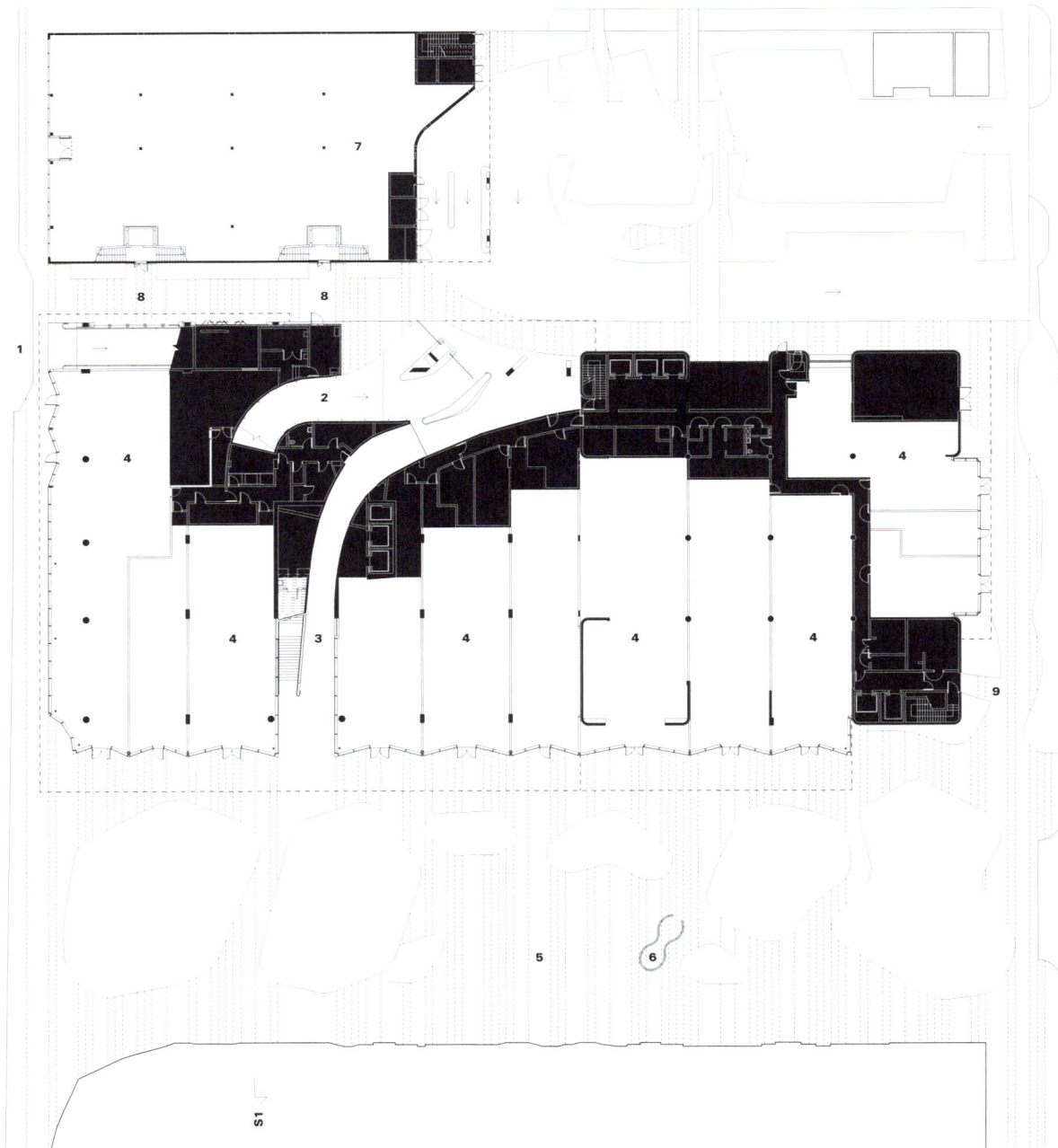

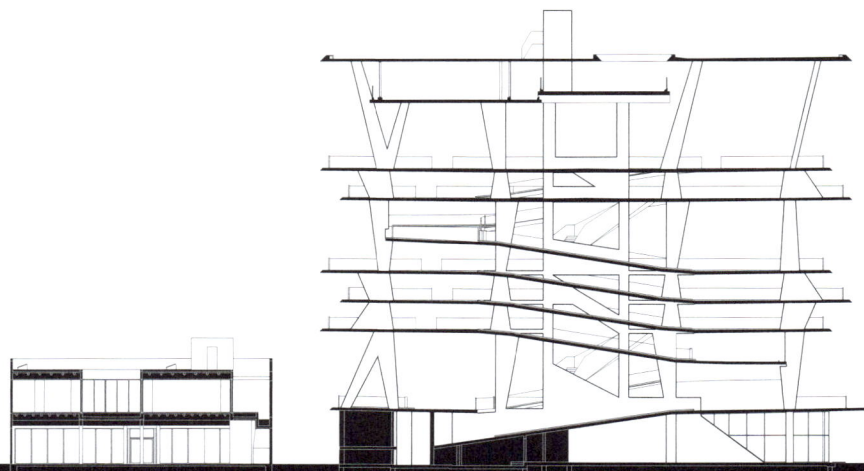

0   5   10
1:700

Ground floor plan: ¹ car entrance ² car exit ³ pedestrian access/passage ⁴ retail ⁵ public plaza ⁶ pavilion ⁷ bank
⁸ entrance to courtyard residences ⁹ entrance to rooftop restaurant
Section S1: through bank, courtyard residences building and parking structure

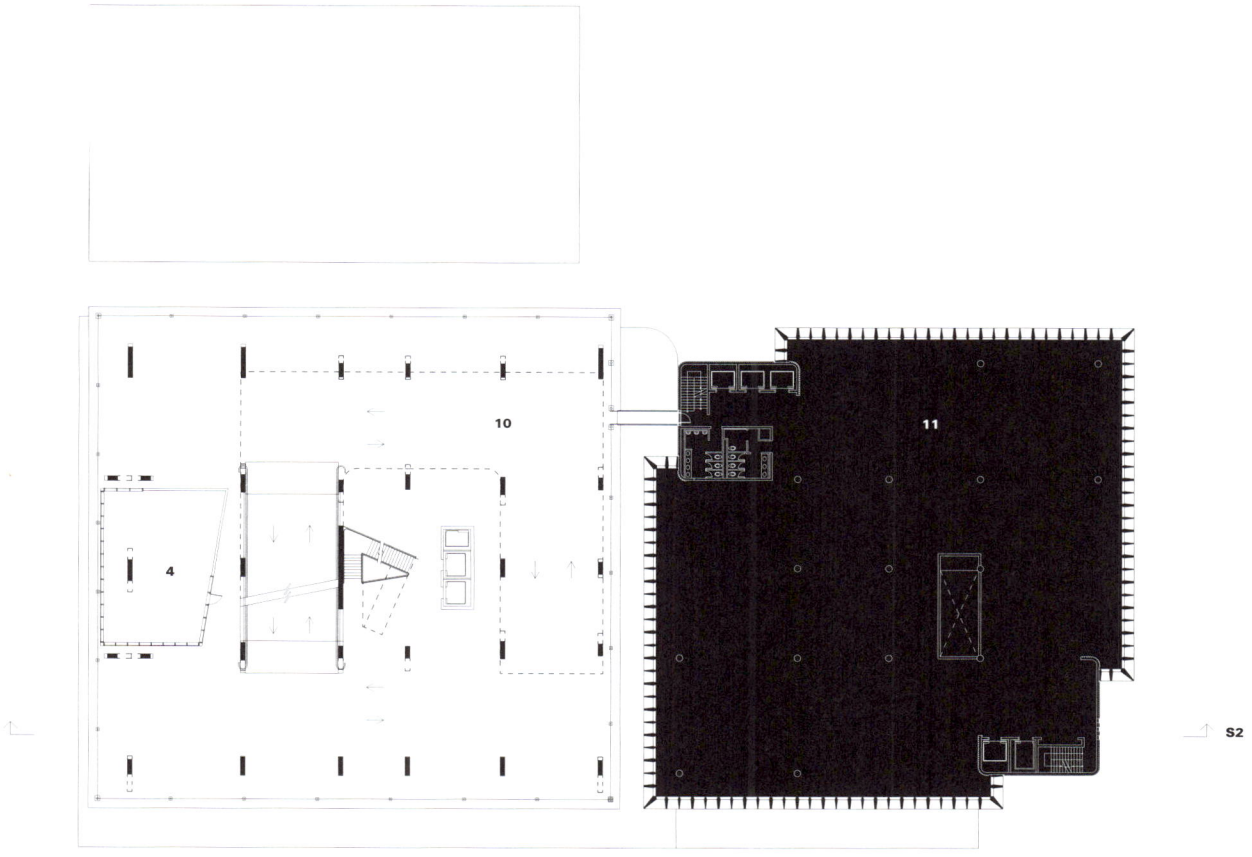

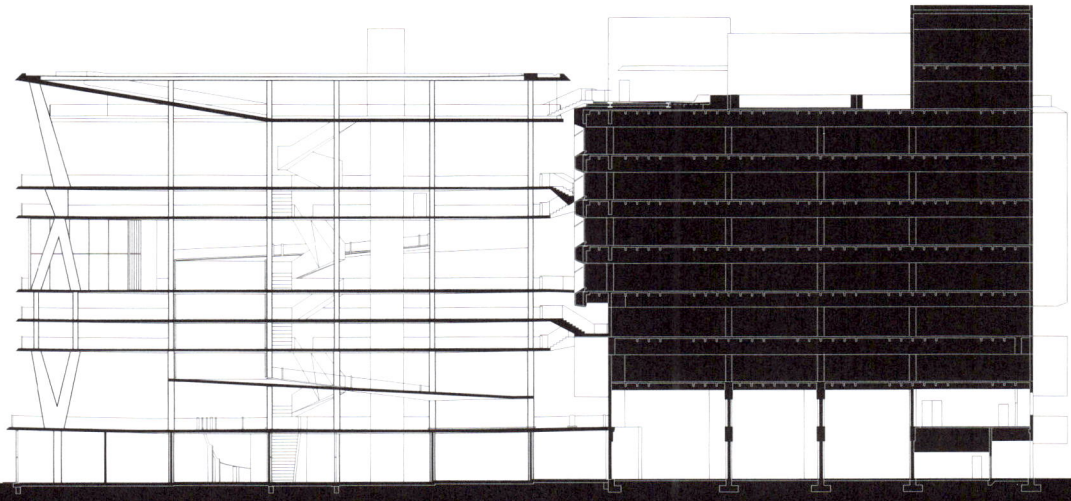

10

11

4

S2

0   5   10

1:700

5th floor plan: ⁴ retail ¹⁰ parking ¹¹ office
Section S2: through parking structure and existing office building

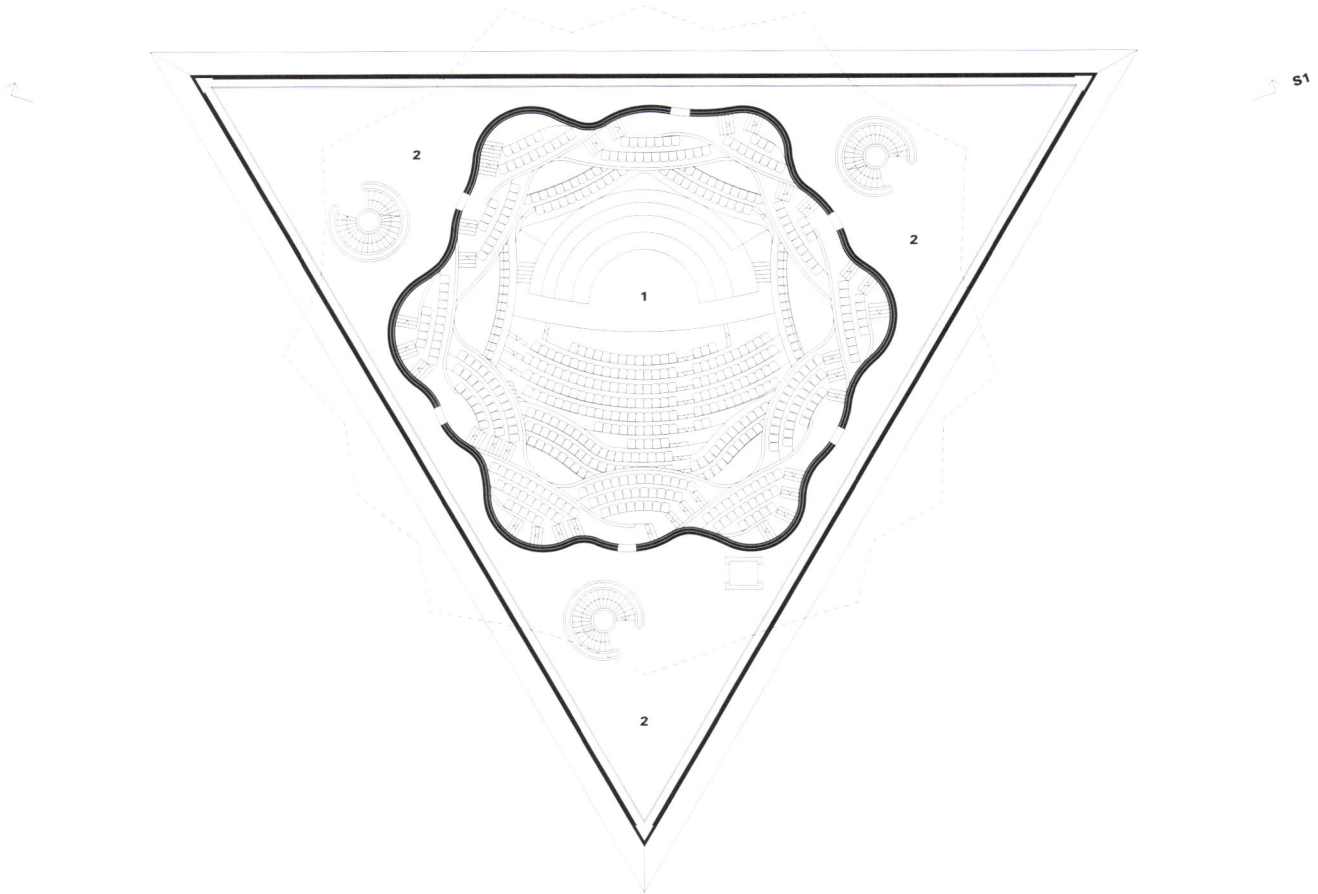

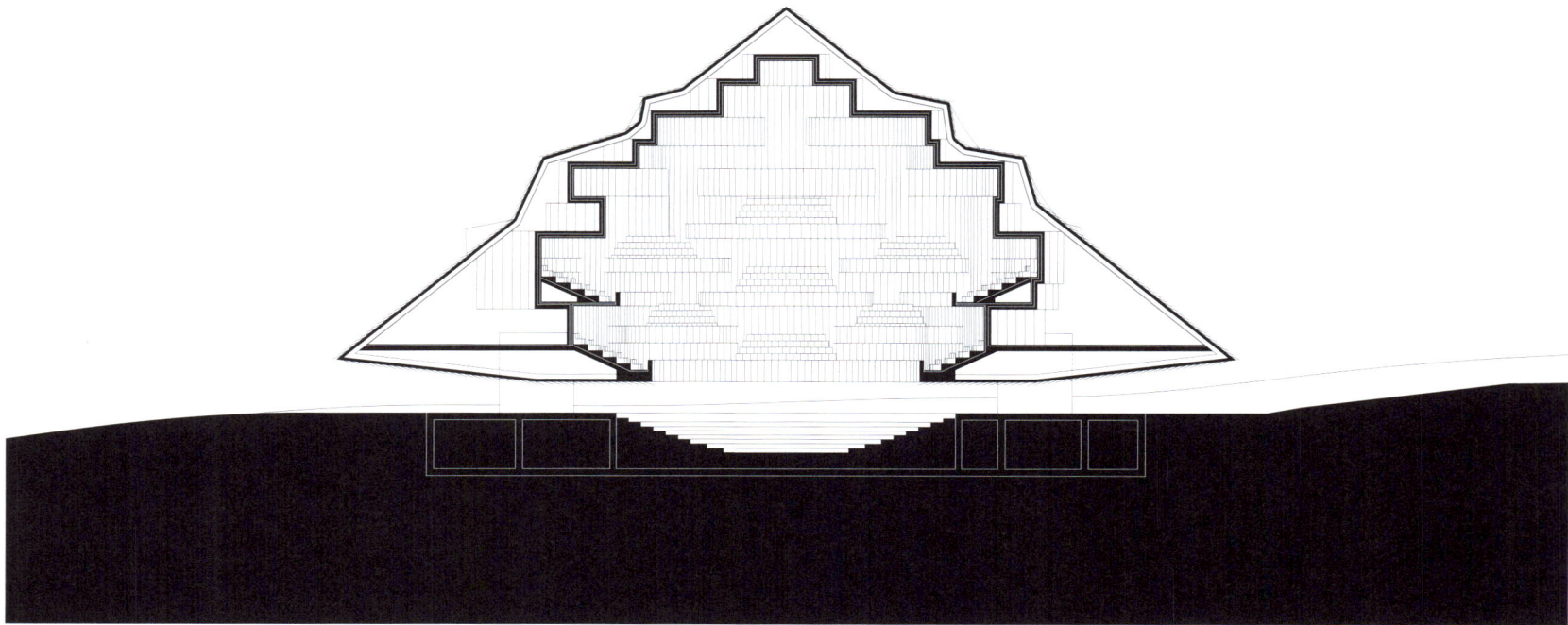

S1

1:500

1st floor plan: ¹ auditorium ² foyer Rémy Zaugg
Section S1: through auditorium

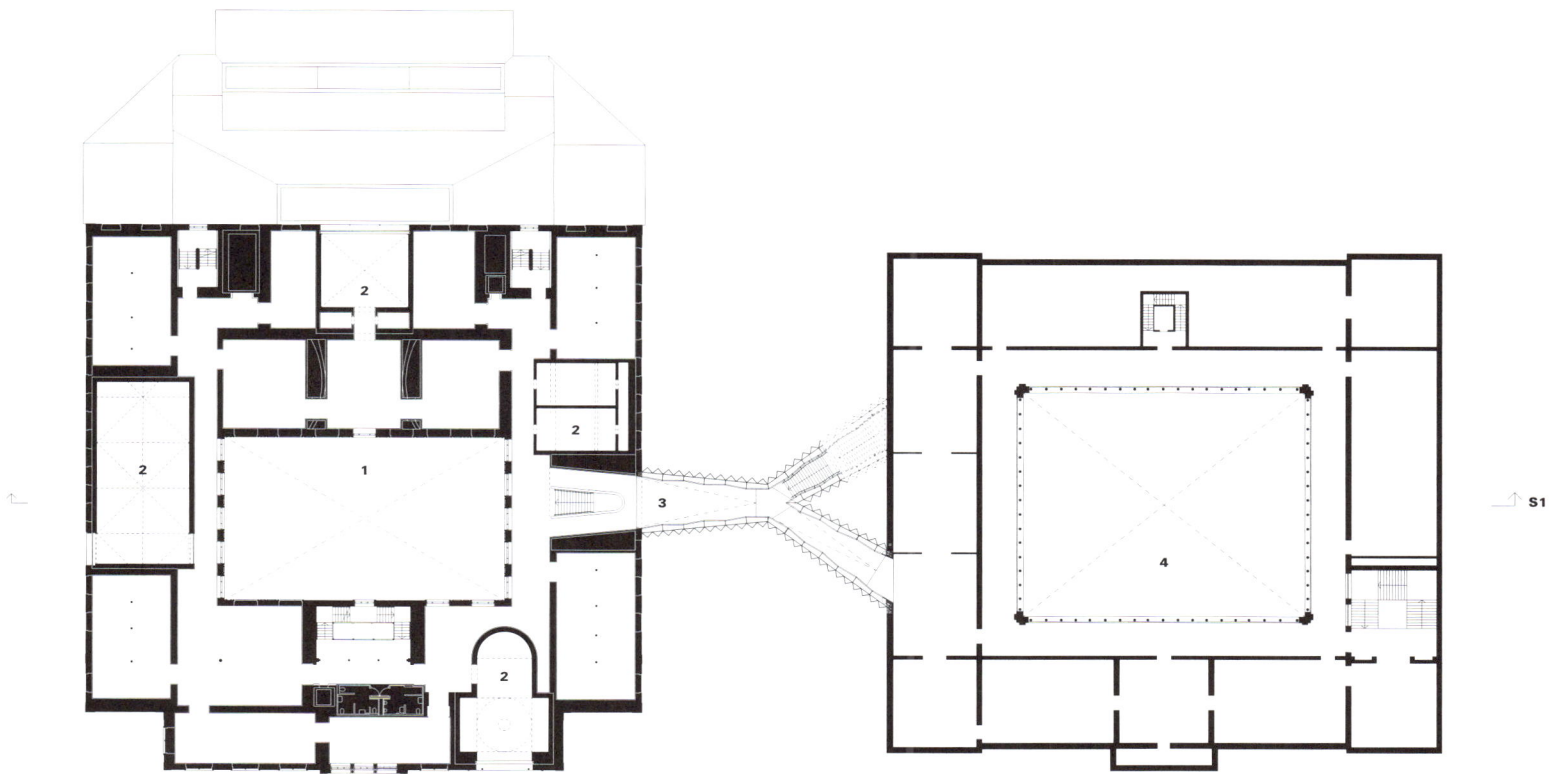

0   5   10

1:750

1st floor plan: ¹ **Espacio Goya** ² **Anchor Room** ³ **grand stairs** ⁴ **Museo de Zaragoza**
Section S1: through Anchor Room, courtyard and grand stairs

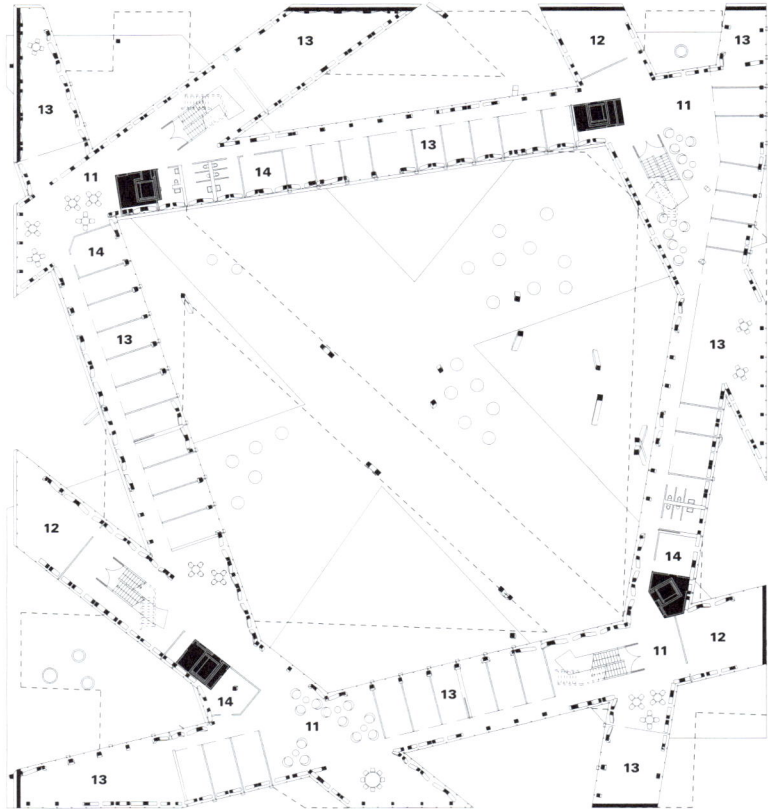

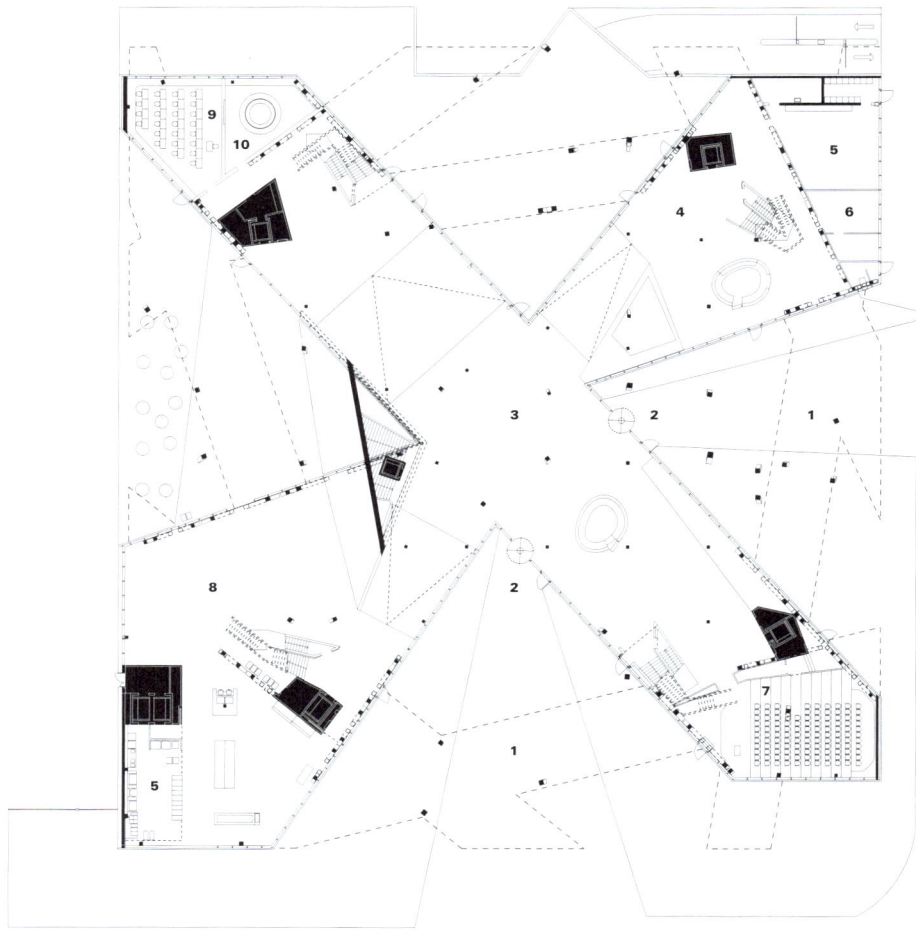

1st floor plan: [11] communication area [12] meeting room [13] office [14] technical room
Ground floor plan: [1] courtyard [2] main entrance [3] foyer [4] café [5] kitchen [6] back office [7] auditorium
[8] restaurant [9] classroom [10] boardroom

0   5   10

1:750

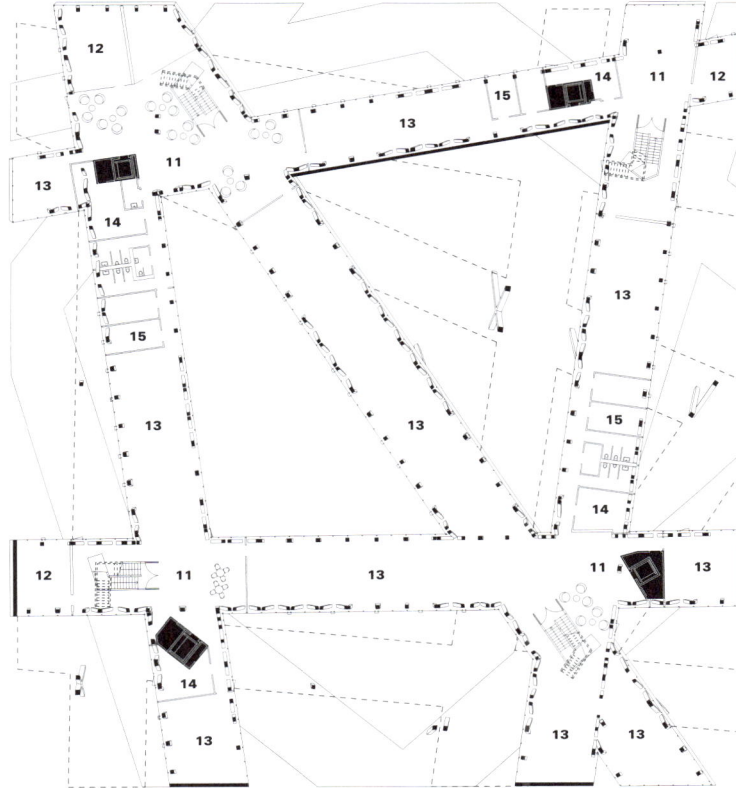

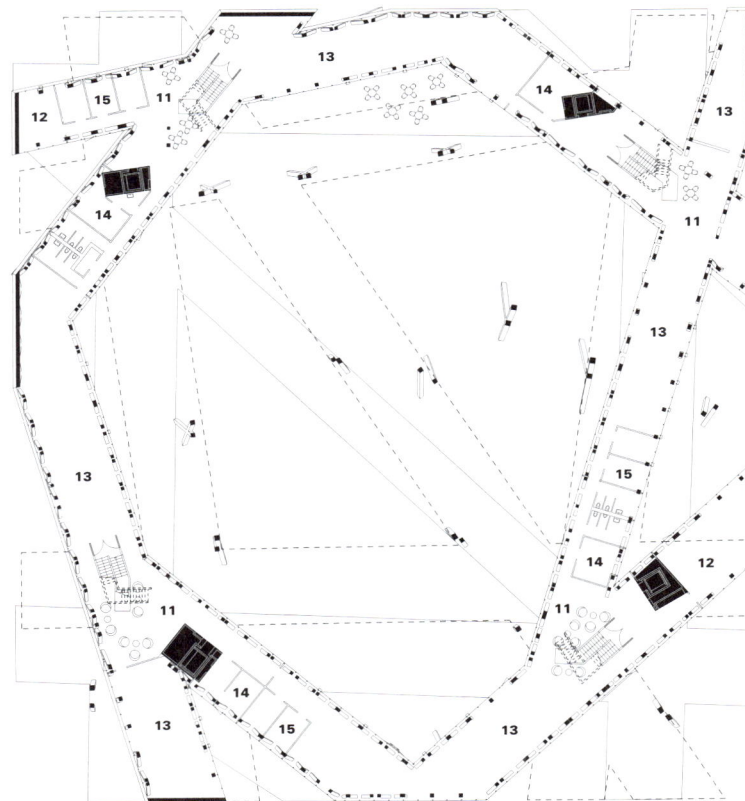

0   5   10

1:750

4th floor plan: [11] **communication area** [12] **meeting room** [13] **office** [14] **technical room** [15] **quiet room**
3rd floor plan: [11] **communication area** [12] **meeting room** [13] **office** [14] **technical room** [15] **quiet room**

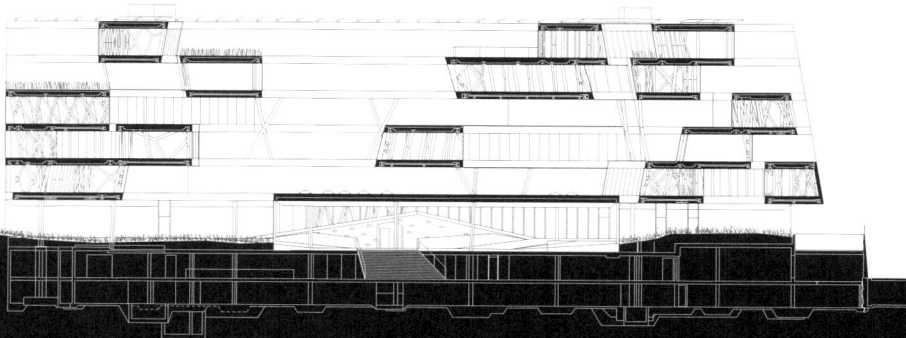

1:750

5th floor plan: ¹¹ communication area ¹² meeting room ¹³ office ¹⁴ technical room ¹⁵ quiet room ¹⁶ terrace
Section S1: through foyer, offices, meeting rooms and terraces

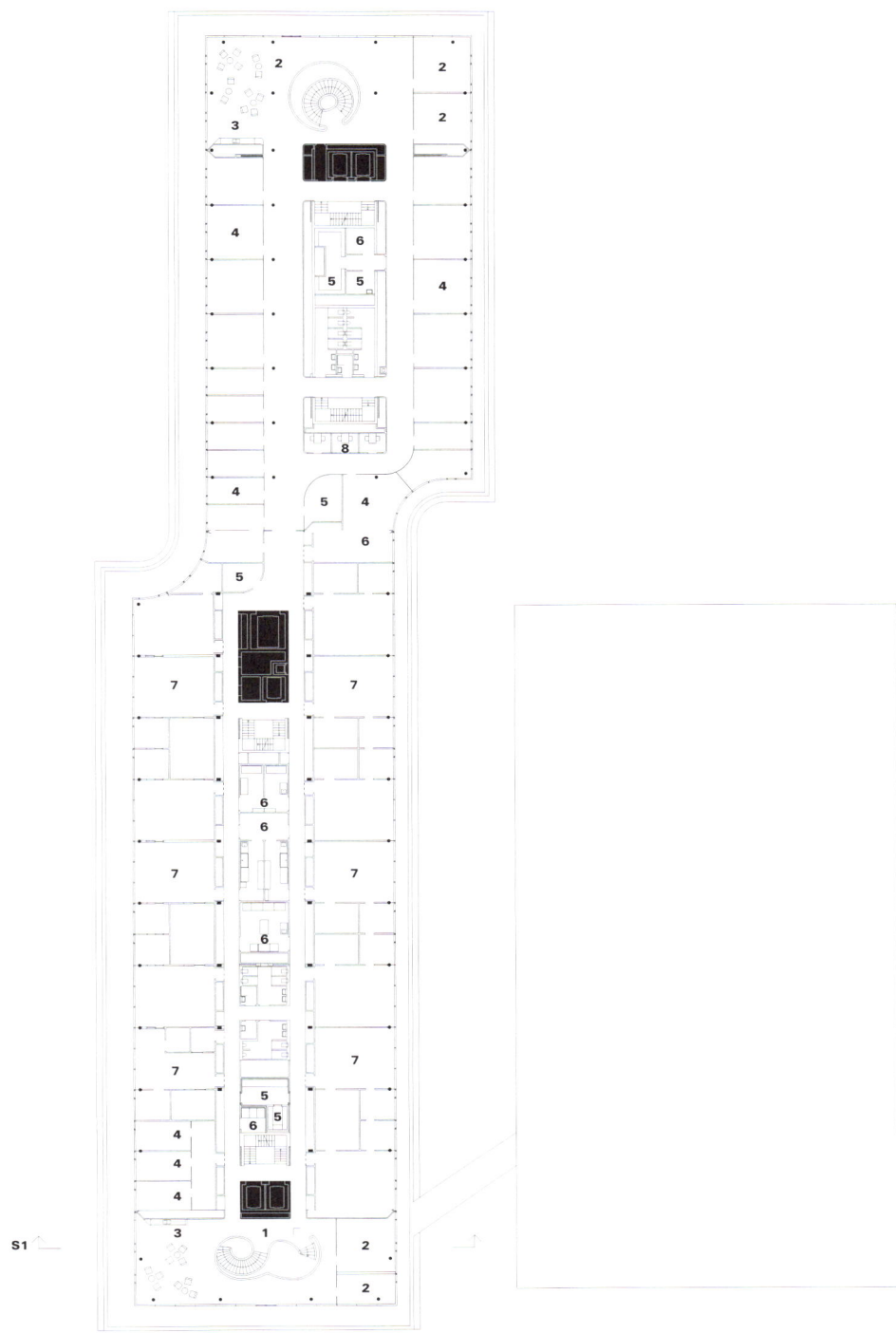

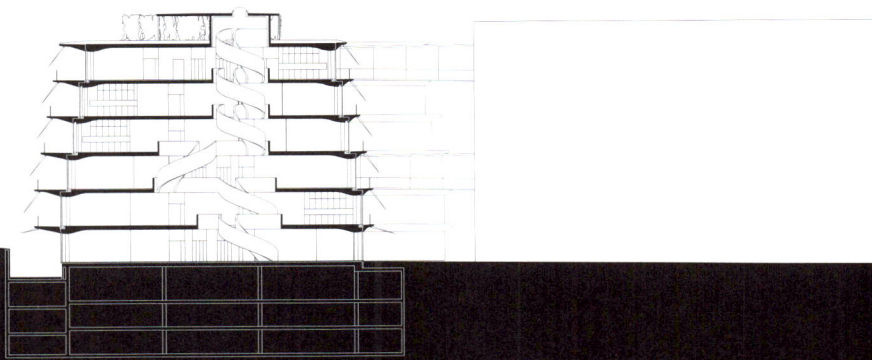

1:750

3rd floor plan: ¹ communication area ² meeting room ³ kitchenette ⁴ office ⁵ service room ⁶ technical room ⁷ laboratory
Section S1: through helical stairs

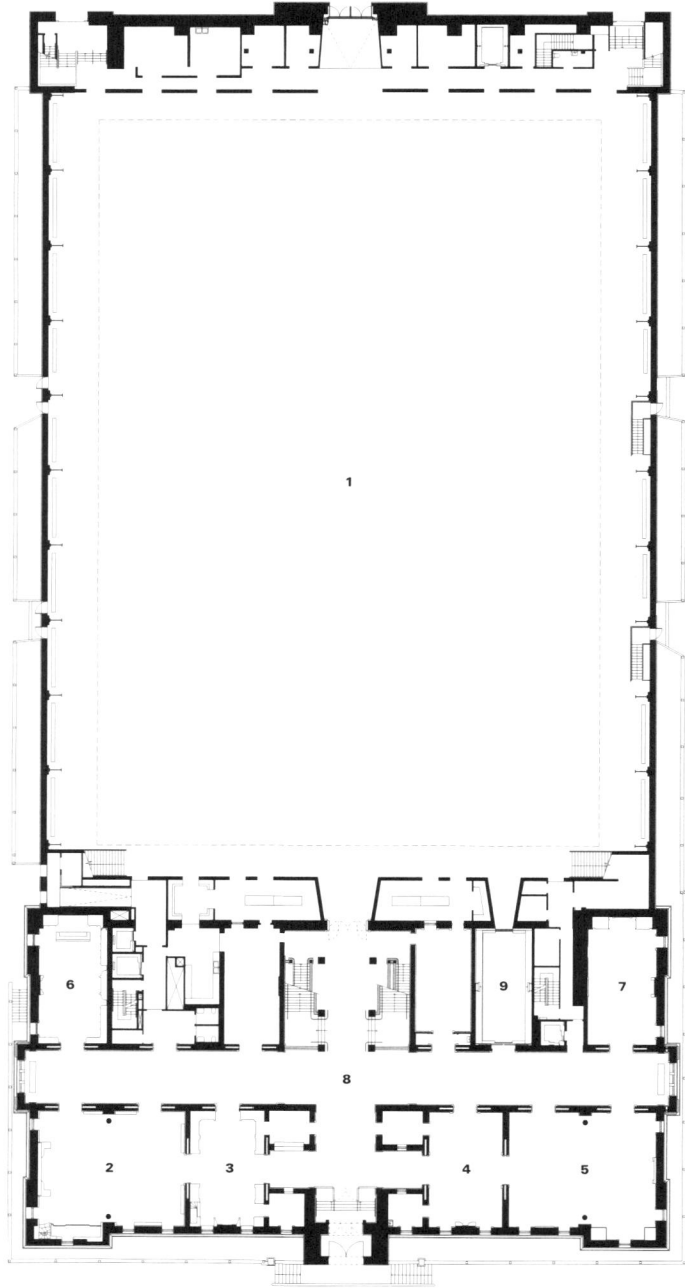

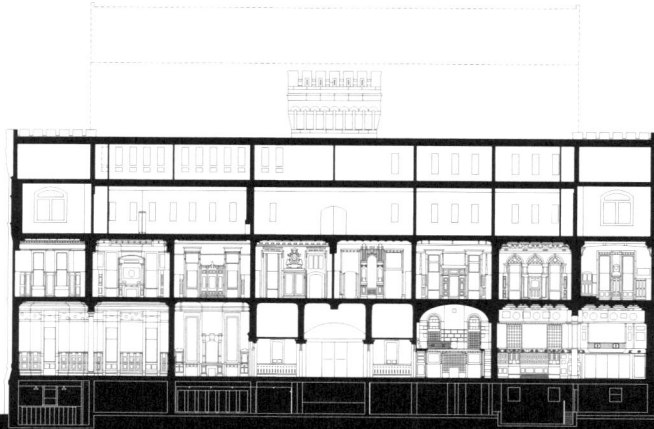

1:750

1st floor plan: ¹ Drill Hall ² Veterans Room ³ Library ⁴ Reception Room ⁵ Board of Officers Room ⁶ Field & Staff Room
⁷ Colonel's Room ⁸ circulation ⁹ Megavator
Cross section S1: through head house

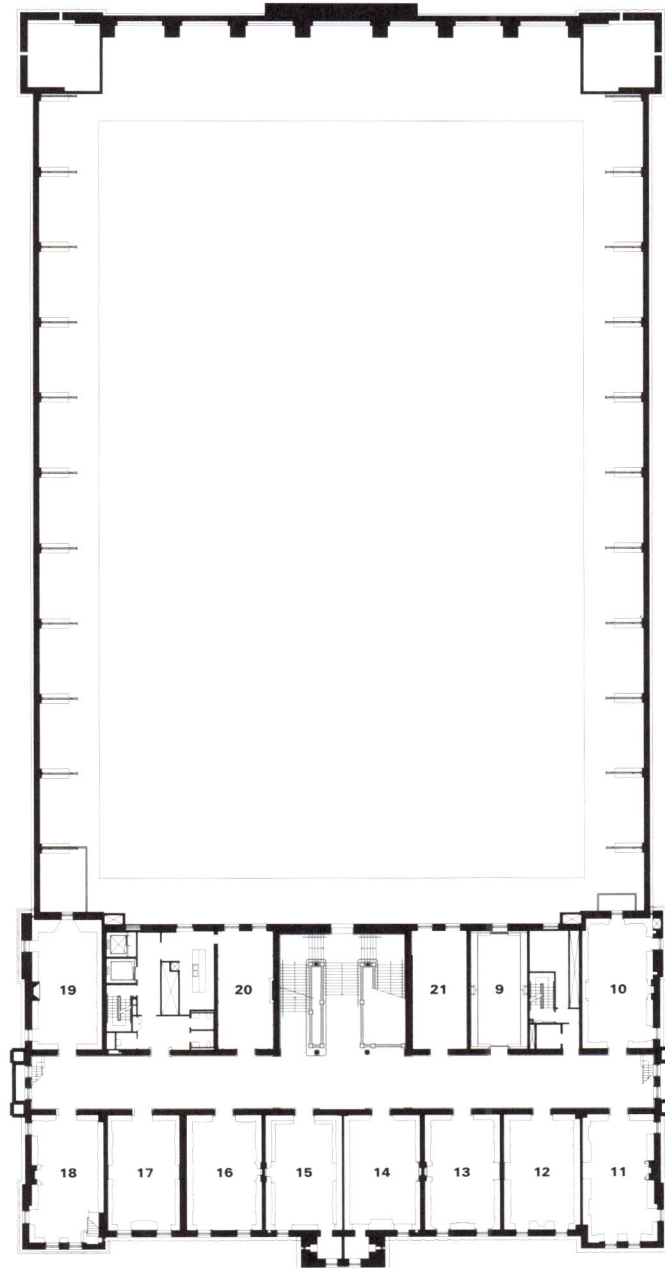

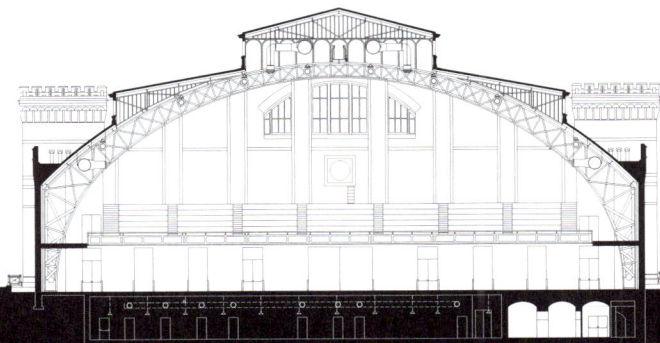

1:750

2nd floor plan: ⁹ Megavator ¹⁰ Company A ¹¹ Company B ¹² Company C ¹³ Company D ¹⁴ Company E ¹⁵ Company F ¹⁶ Company G ¹⁷ Company H ¹⁸ Company I ¹⁹ Company K ²⁰ Company L ²¹ Company M
Cross section S2: through drill hall

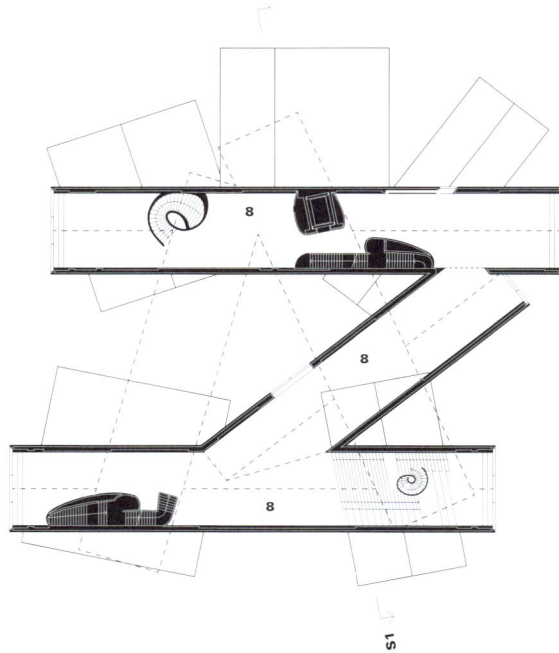

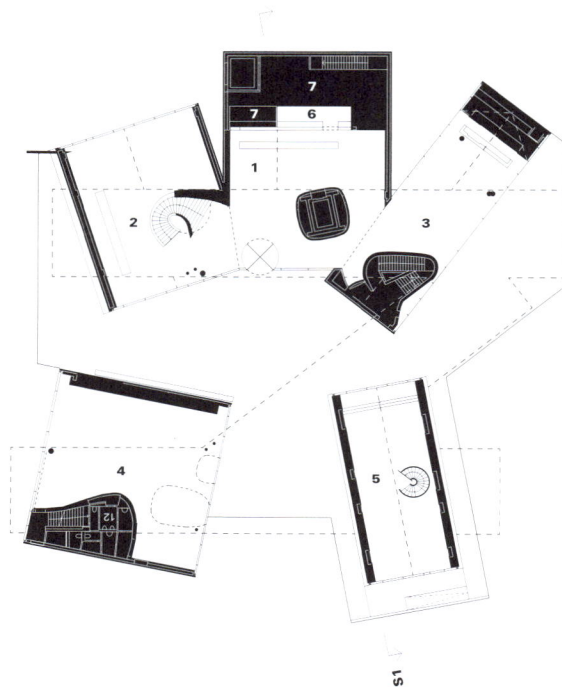

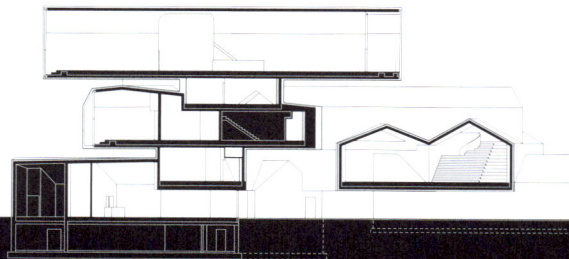

1:750

1st floor plan: [8] showroom
Ground floor plan: [1] reception [2] shop [3] café [4] business lounge [5] exhibition vitrine [6] cloakroom [7] delivery
Section S1: through reception and top-floor showroom

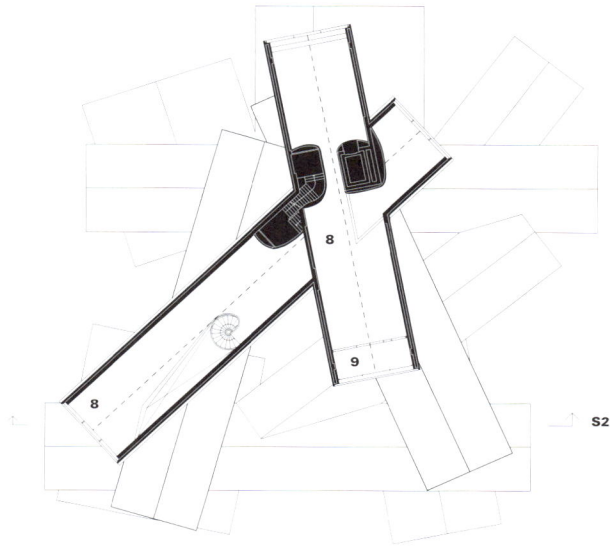

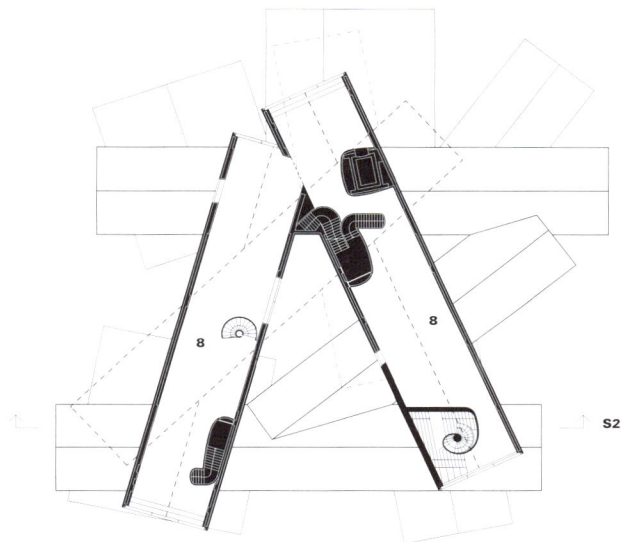

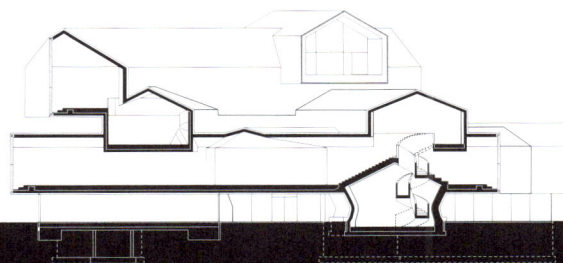

S2

8

8

9

S2

8

8

0   5   10

1:750

4th floor plan: [8] showroom [9] terrace
2nd floor plan: [8] showroom
Section S2: through showroom, exhibition vitrine and stair

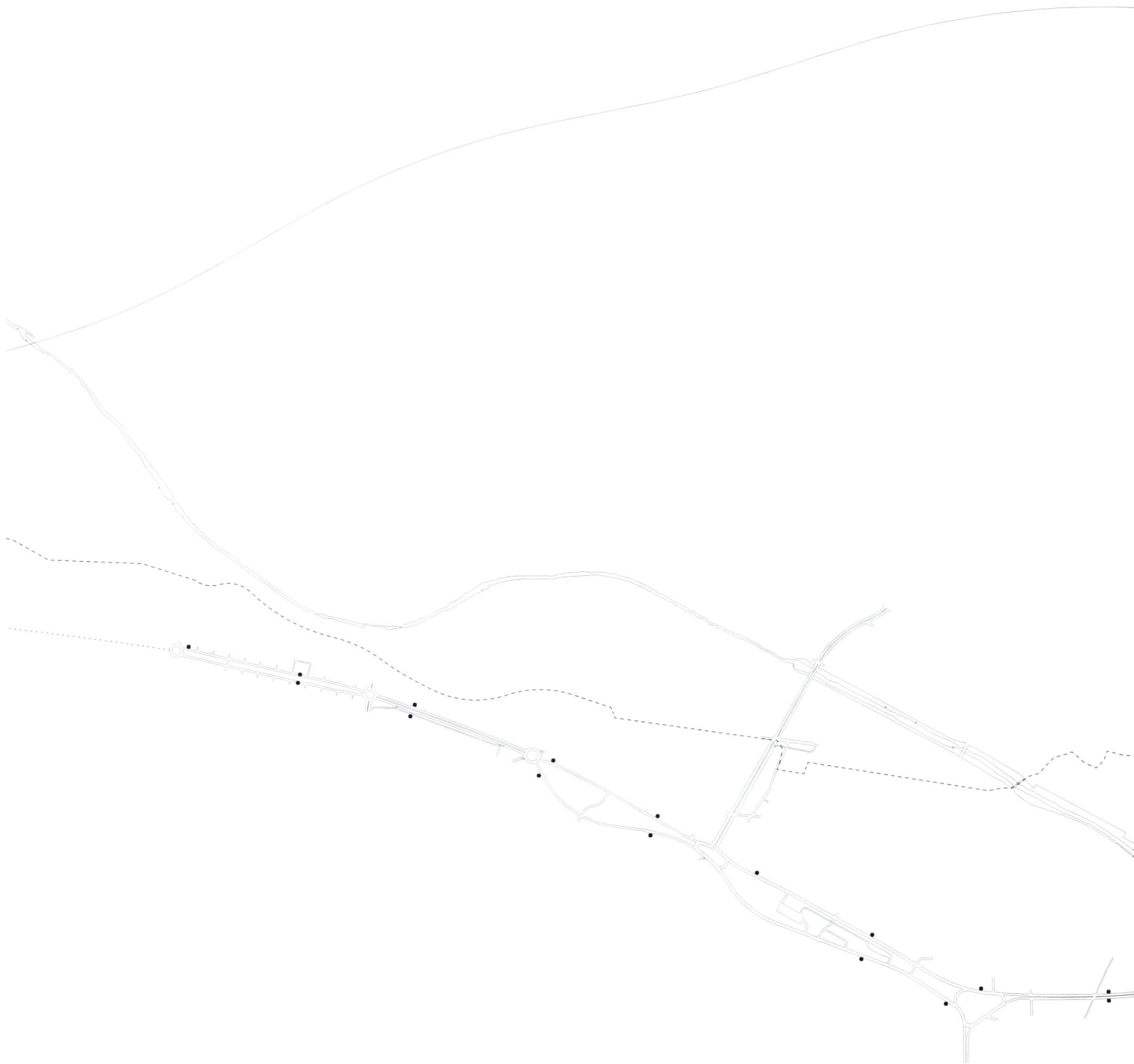

N

0   100   500

1:20000

General plan: ¹ **Arlanzón River** ² **Camino de Santiago** ³ **Burgos Bulevar** ⁴ **new high-speed railway** ⁵ **cathedral** ⁶ **bus stop**
⁷ **old train station** ⁸ **new train station**

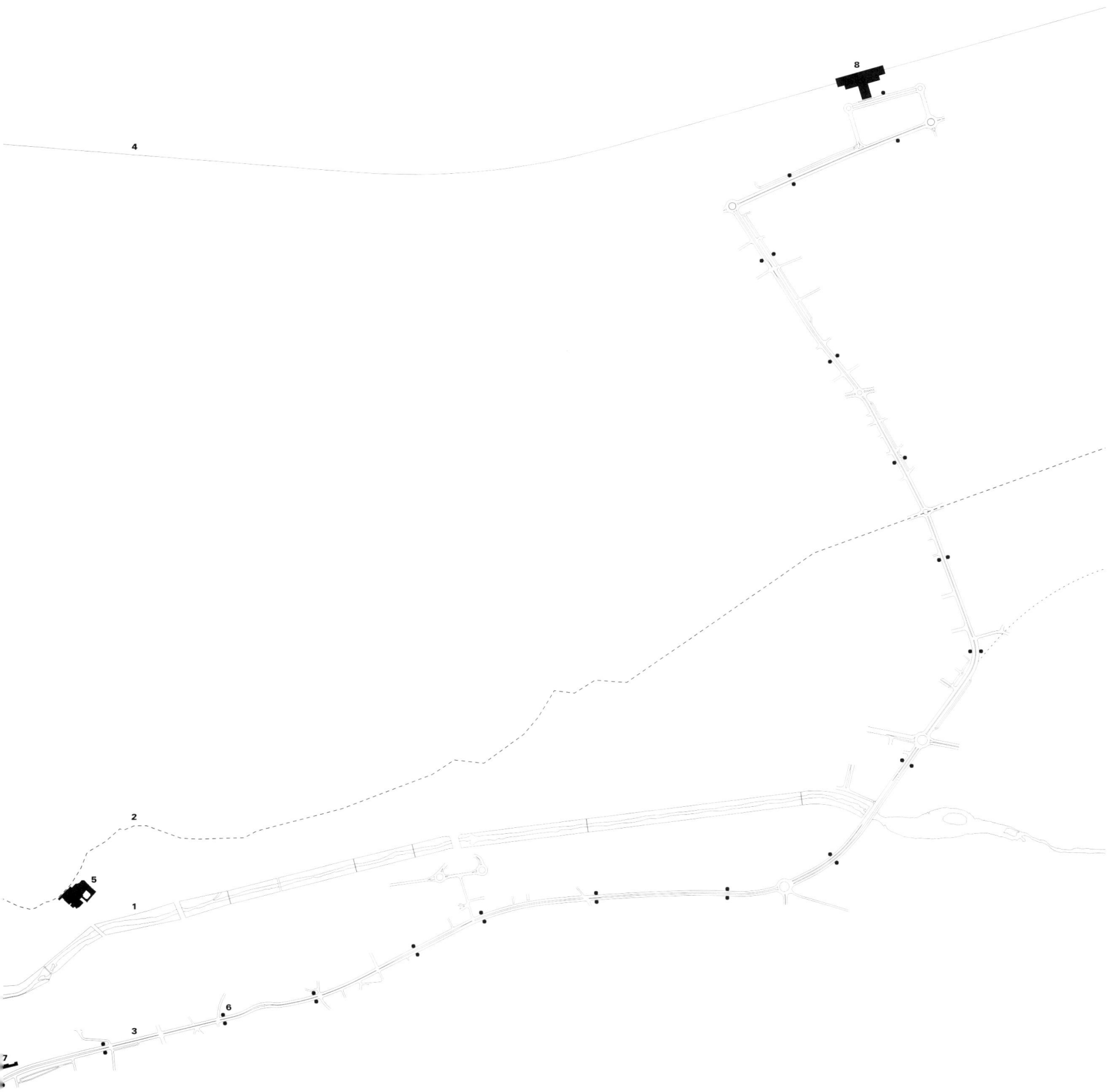

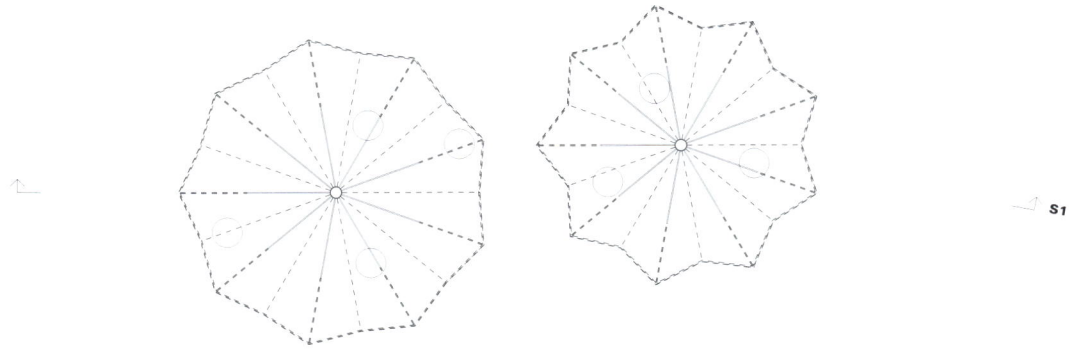

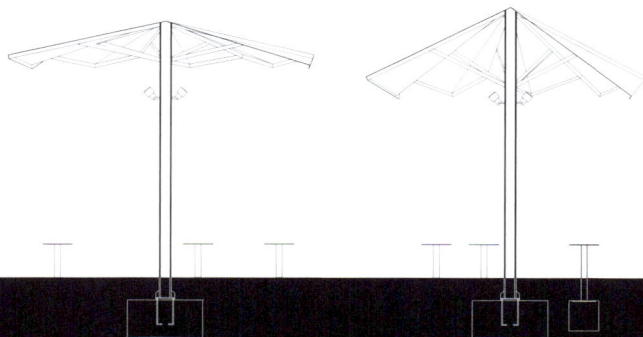

1:100

0   1

S1

Ground plan: bus shelter
Section S1: through bus shelter

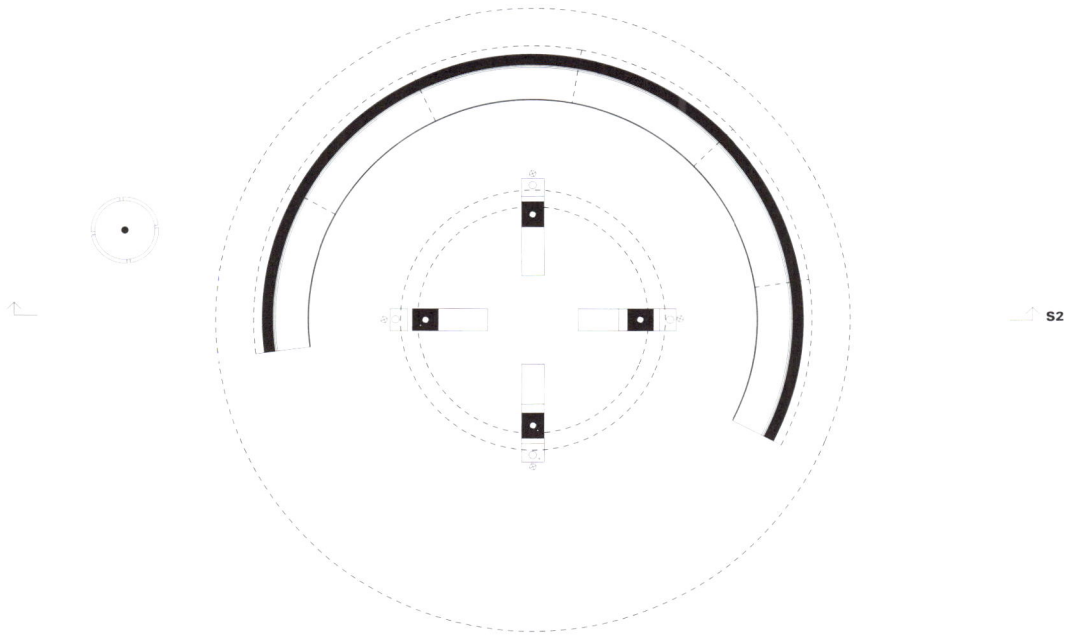

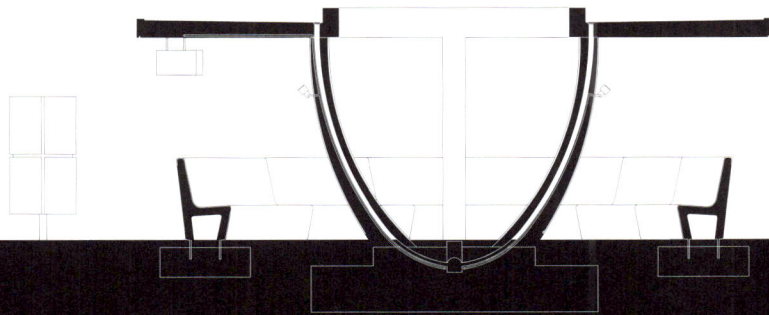

1:100

S2

Ground plan: bus shelter
Section S1: through bus shelter

0 — 1

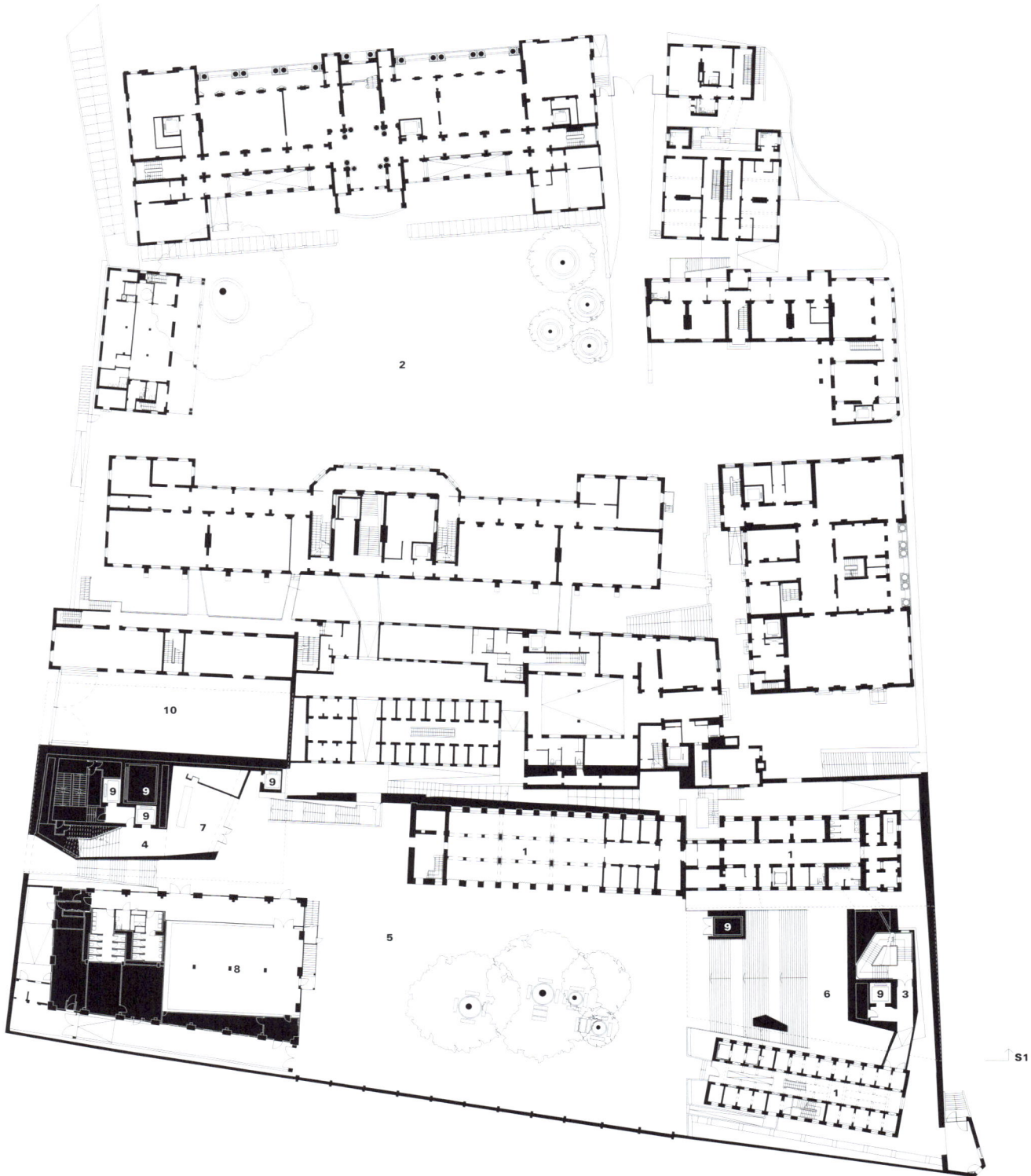

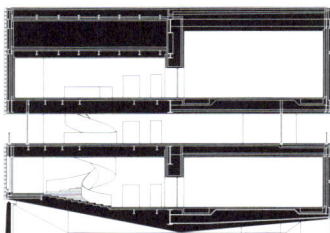

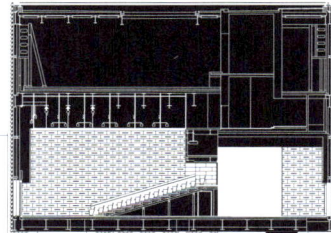

1:750

Ground floor plan: **¹ existing buildings ² Parade Ground ³ Arbuthnot Wing ⁴ Old Bailey Wing ⁵ Prison Yard ⁶ Laundry Yard stair ⁷ reception ⁸ event space ⁹ elevator ¹⁰ delivery**
Section S1: through new buildings Old Bailey Wing and Arbuthnot Wing

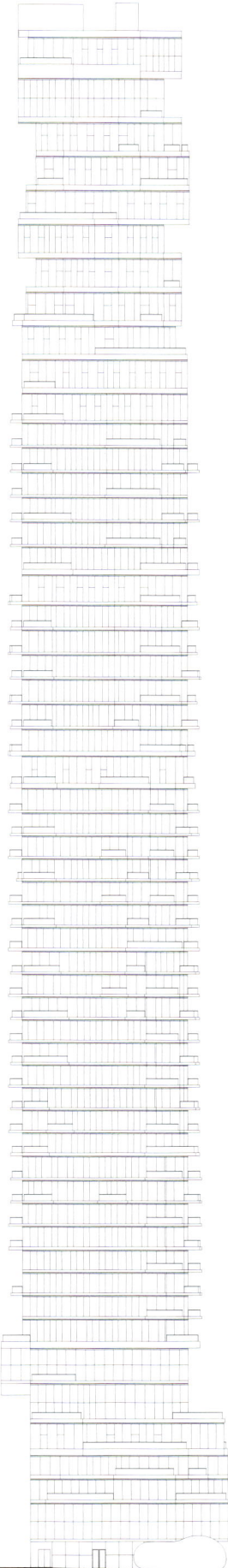

1:1000

0   5   10

5
4
3
3
3
2
1

<u>Elevation East :</u> **¹ lobby and retail ² parking ³ residences ⁴ lounge and amenities ⁵ pool and gym**

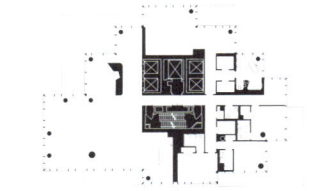 49
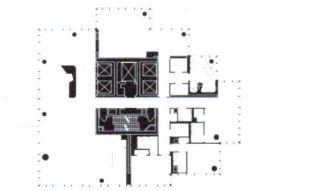 50
 51
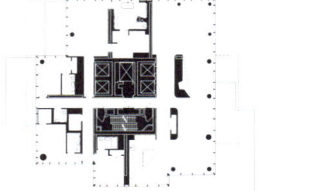 52

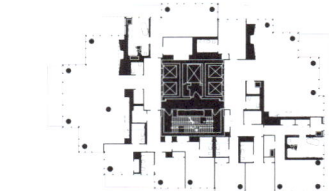 41
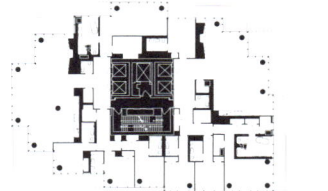 42
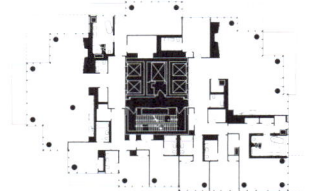 43
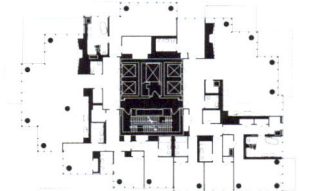 44

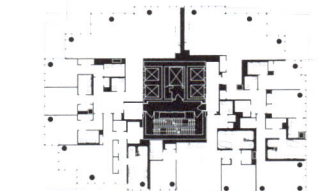 33
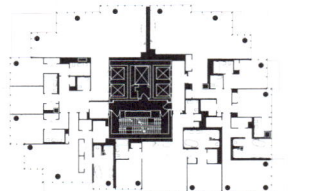 34
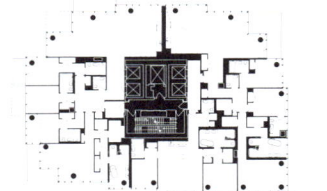 35
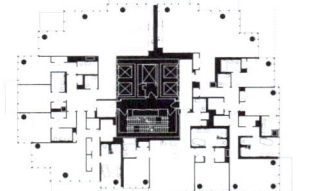 36

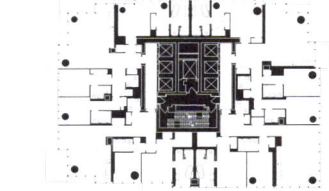 25
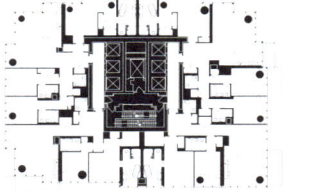 26
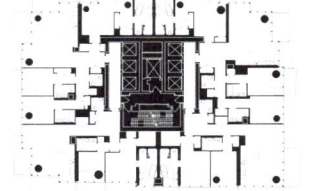 27
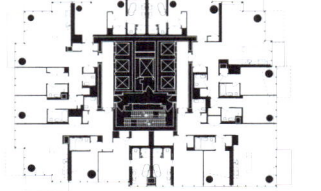 28

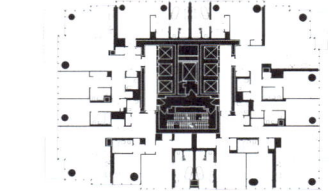 17
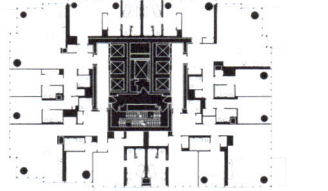 18
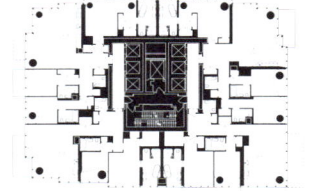 19
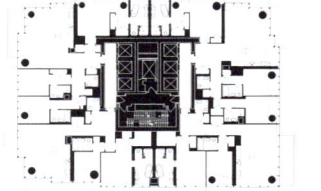 20

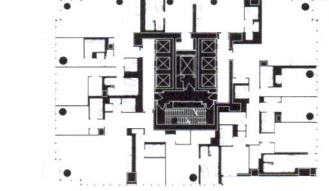 9
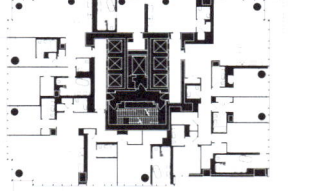 10
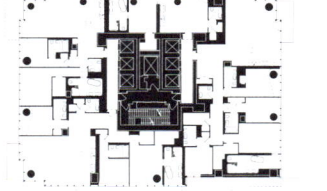 11
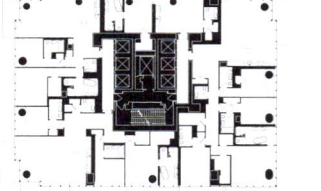 12

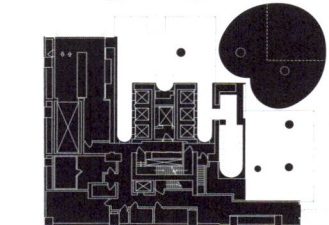 1
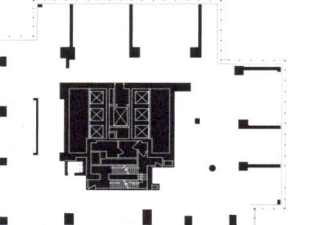 2
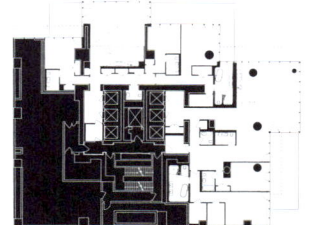 3
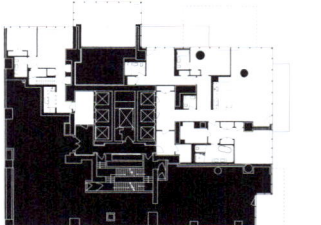 4

0   5   10

1:1000

Ground floor to 56th floor plans: ¹ **lobby and retail** ² **parking** ³⁻⁵ **residences** ⁶⁻⁷ **amenities** ⁸⁻⁵⁶ **residences** ³²/⁴⁶/⁵⁶ **technical rooms**

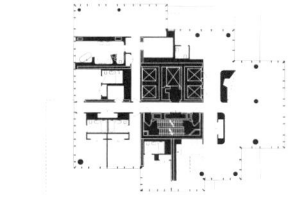

53

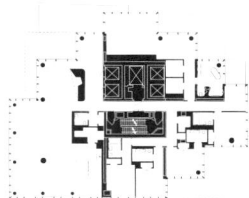

54

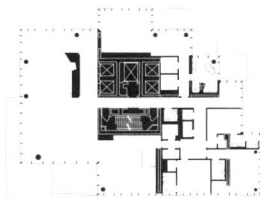

55

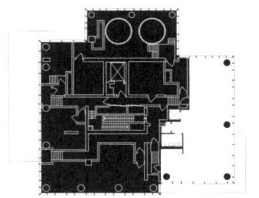

56

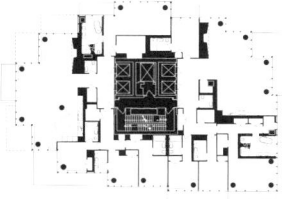

45

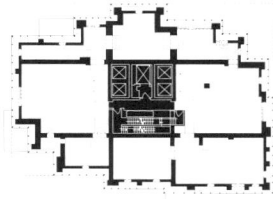

46

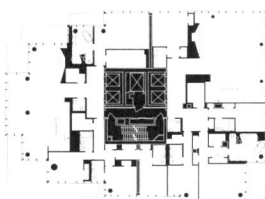

47

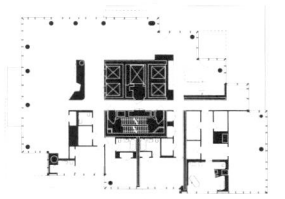

48

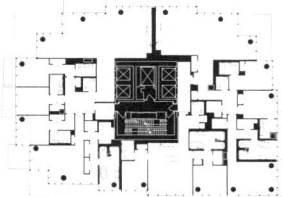

37

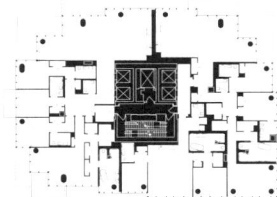

38

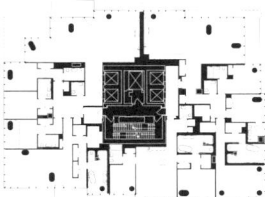

39

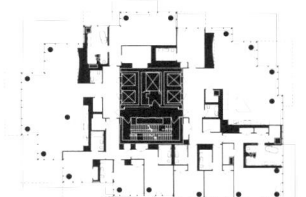

40

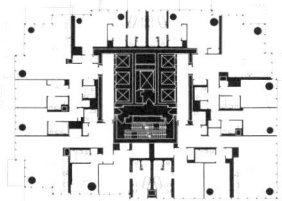

29

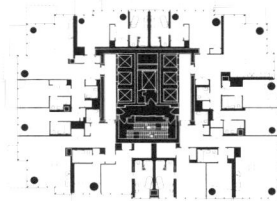

30

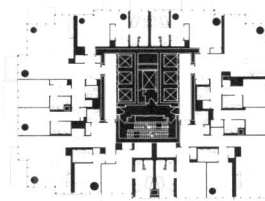

31

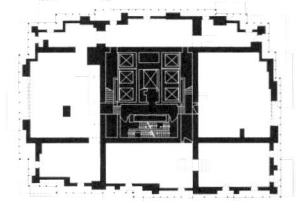

32

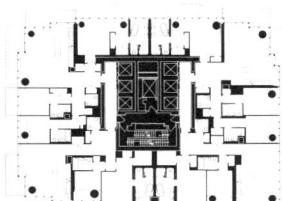

21

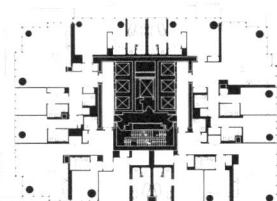

22

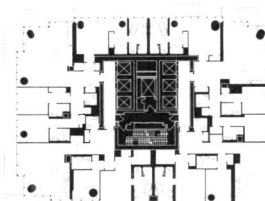

23

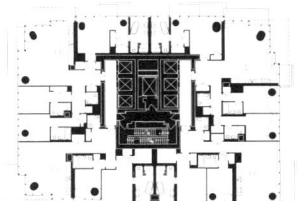

24

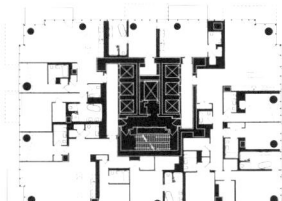

13

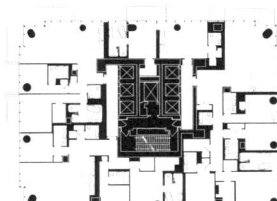

14

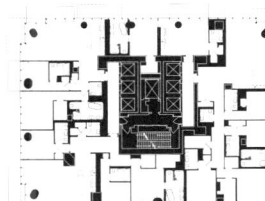

15

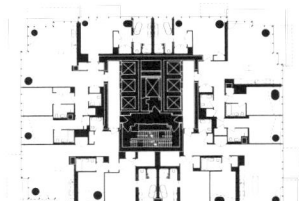

16

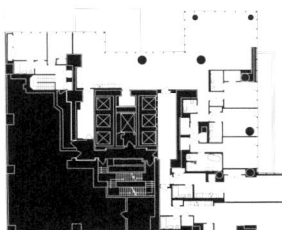

5

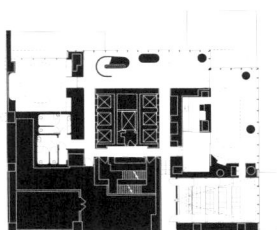

6

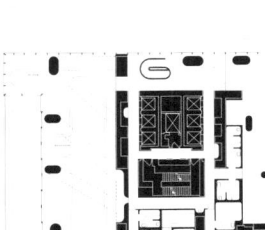

7

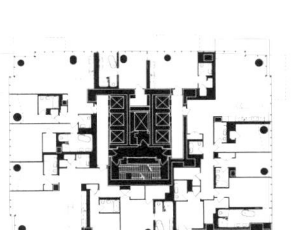

8

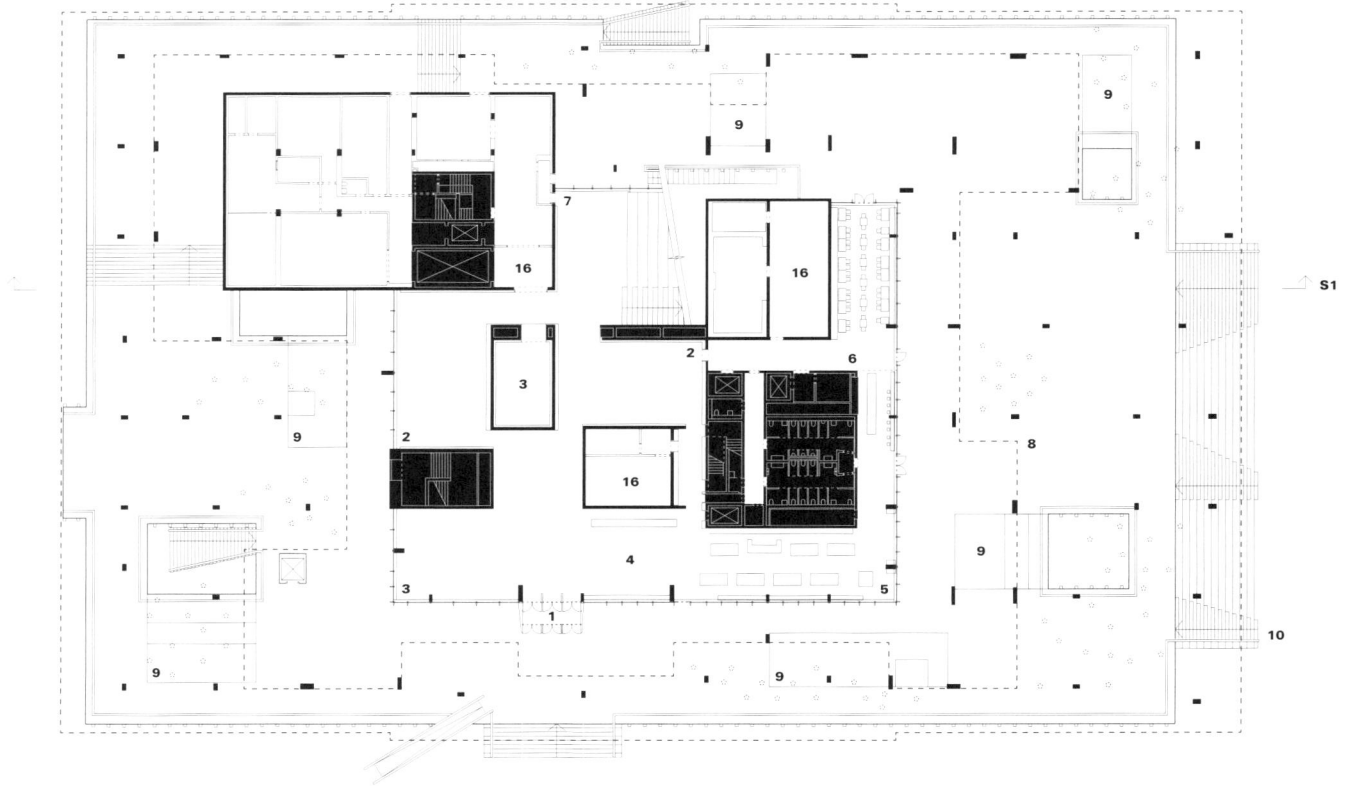

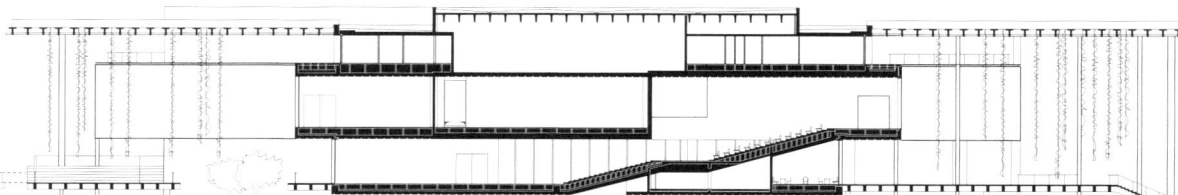

1:750

1st floor plan: ¹ main entrance ² overview gallery ³ project gallery ⁴ lobby ⁵ shop ⁶ bar/restaurant ⁷ education theater ⁸ porch ⁹ planter ¹⁰ bayside stair ¹⁶ back of house
Section S1: through auditorium, restaurant and bayside veranda

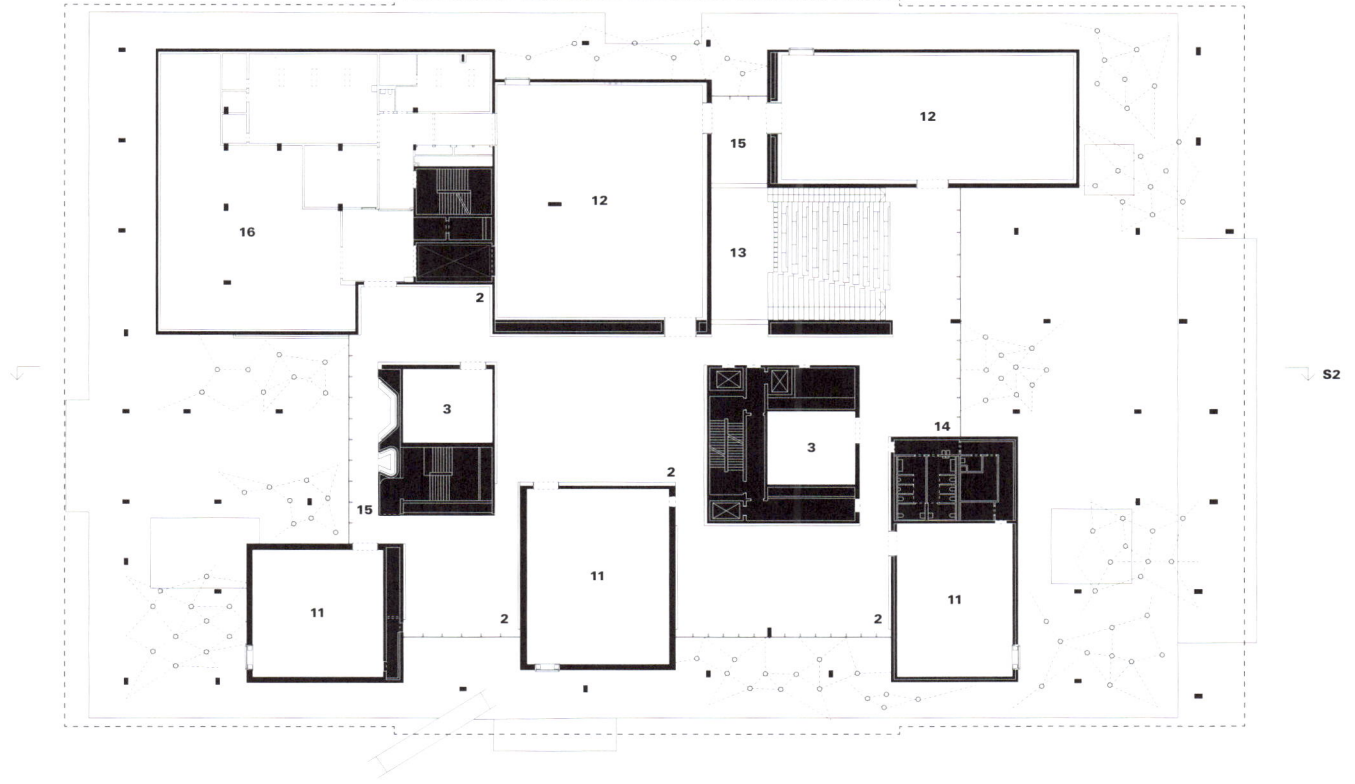

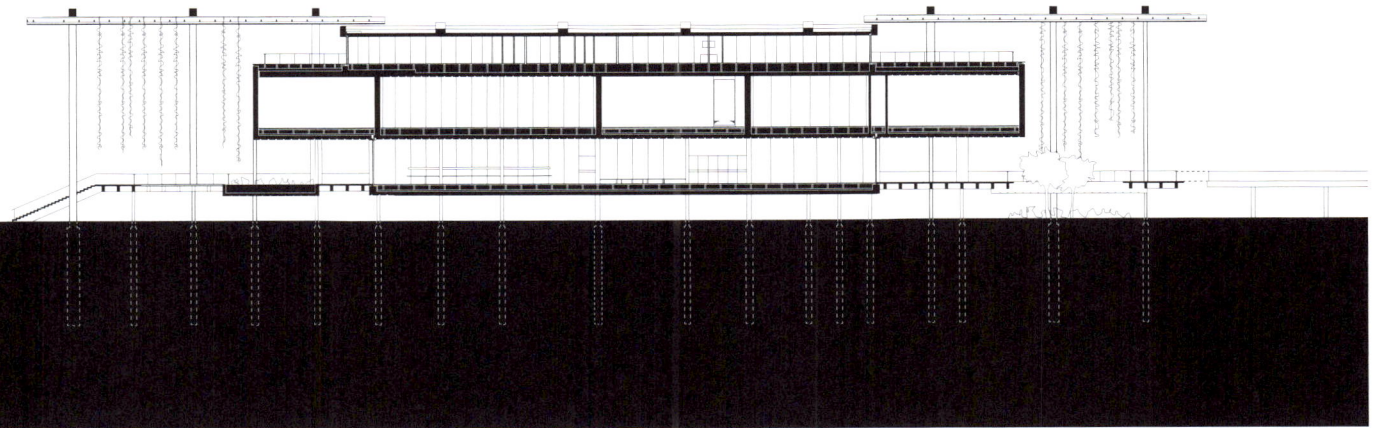

1:750

2nd floor plan: ² overview gallery ³ project gallery ¹¹ focus gallery ¹² special exhibition gallery ¹³ auditorium
¹⁴ special events bay ¹⁵ visitors' gallery ¹⁶ back of house
Section S2: through lobby and overview galleries

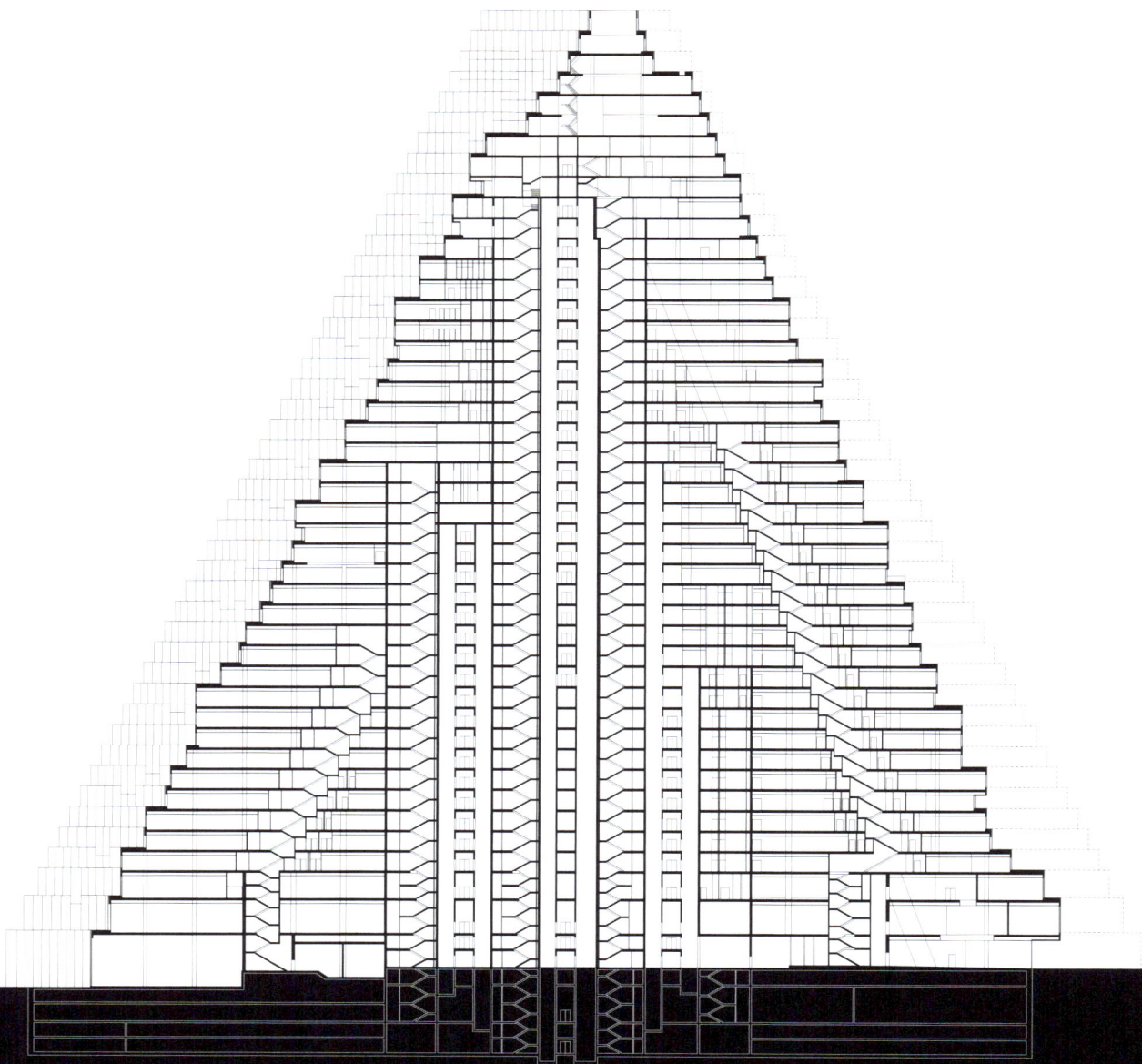

0   10   20

1:1250

Section S1: through lobby and cores

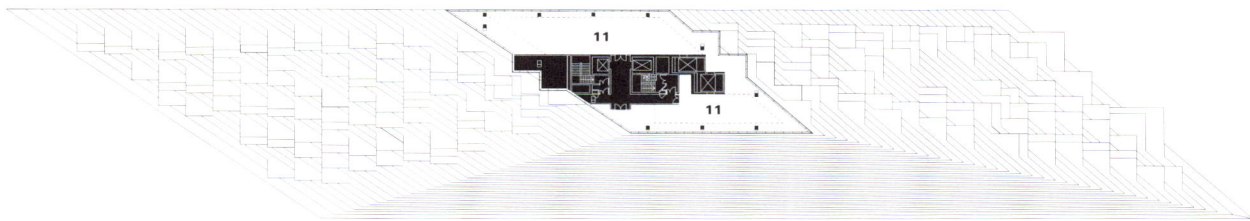

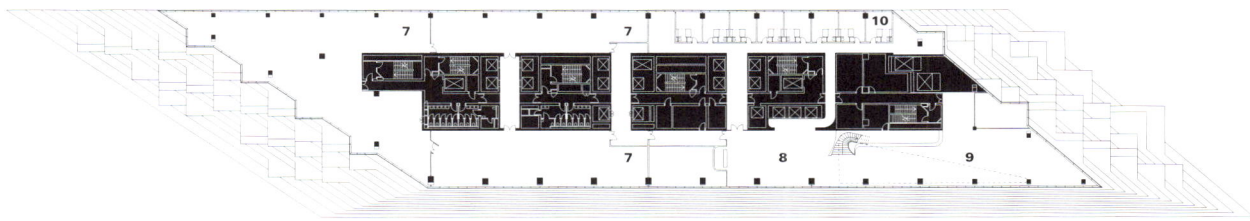

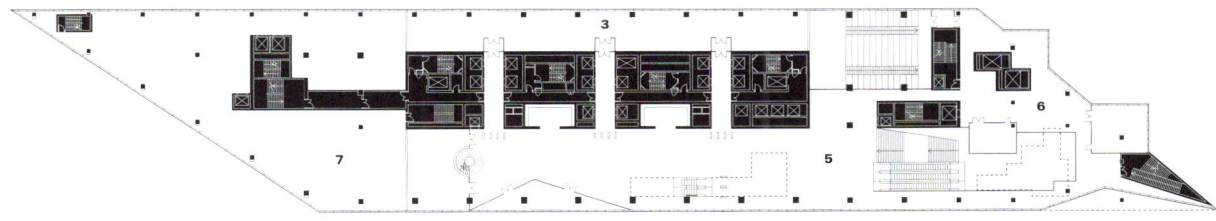

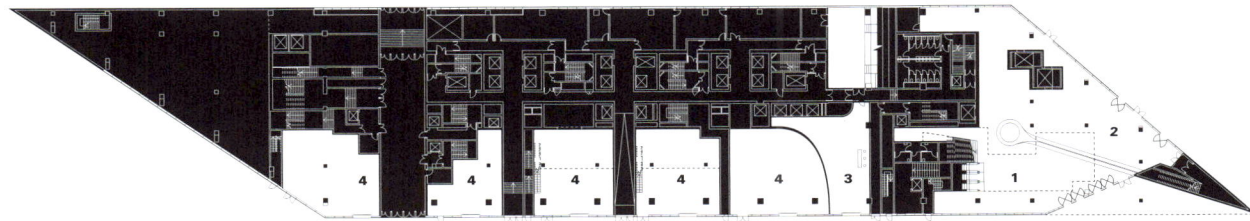

0   10   20
1:1250

37th floor plan: [11] public belvedere
12th floor plan: [7] offices [8] hotel lobby [9] restaurant [10] hotel room
1st floor plan: [5] offices foyer [6] congress center [7] offices
Ground floor plan: [1] office entrance [2] belvedere entrance [3] hotel entrance [4] retail

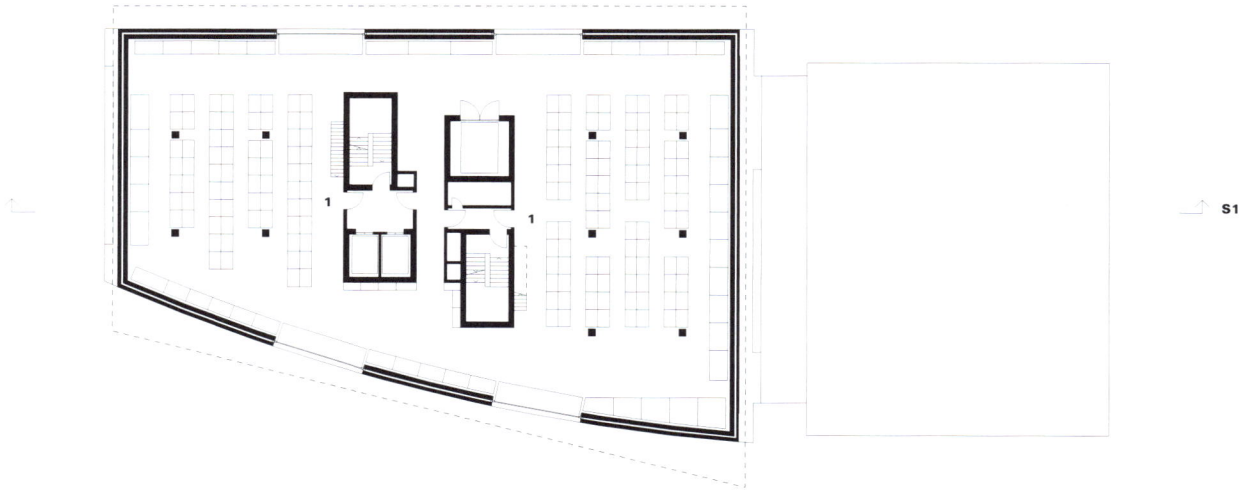

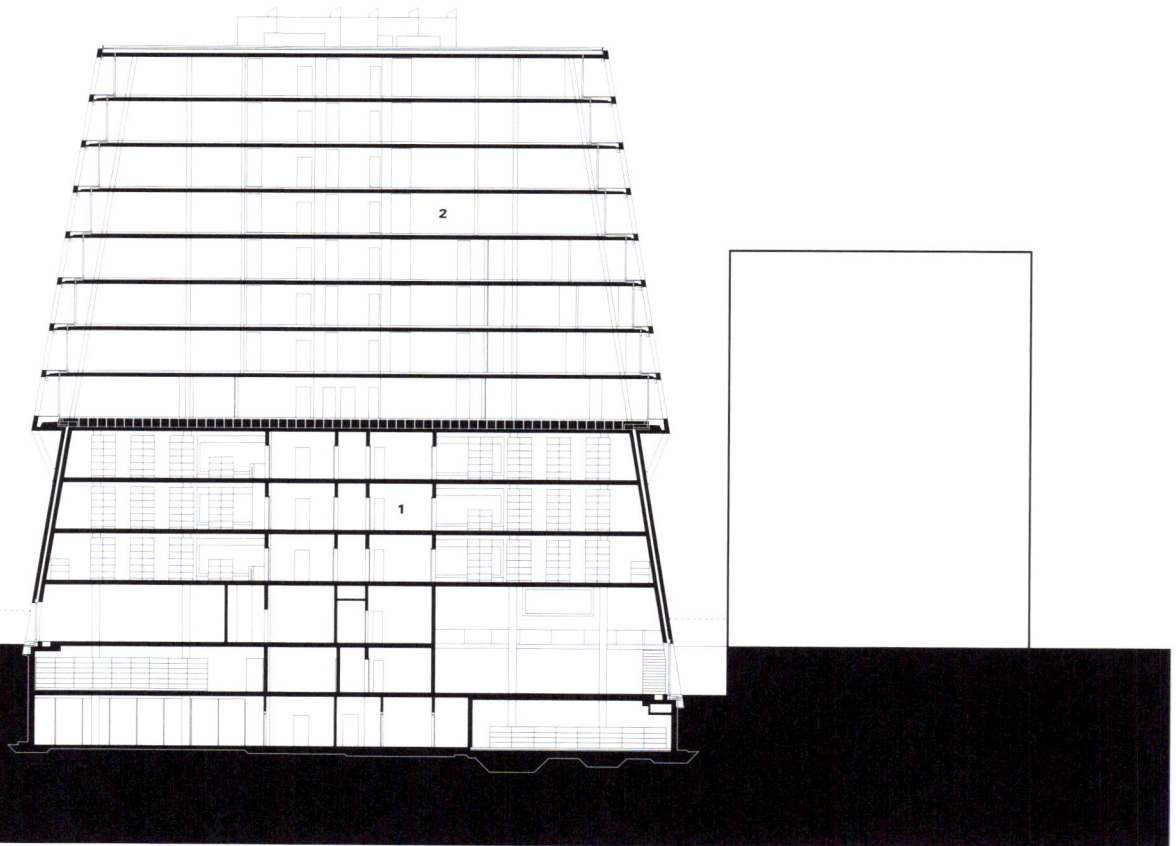

S1

1:500

1st floor plan: [1] archive
Section S1: through [1] **archive and** [2] **apartments**

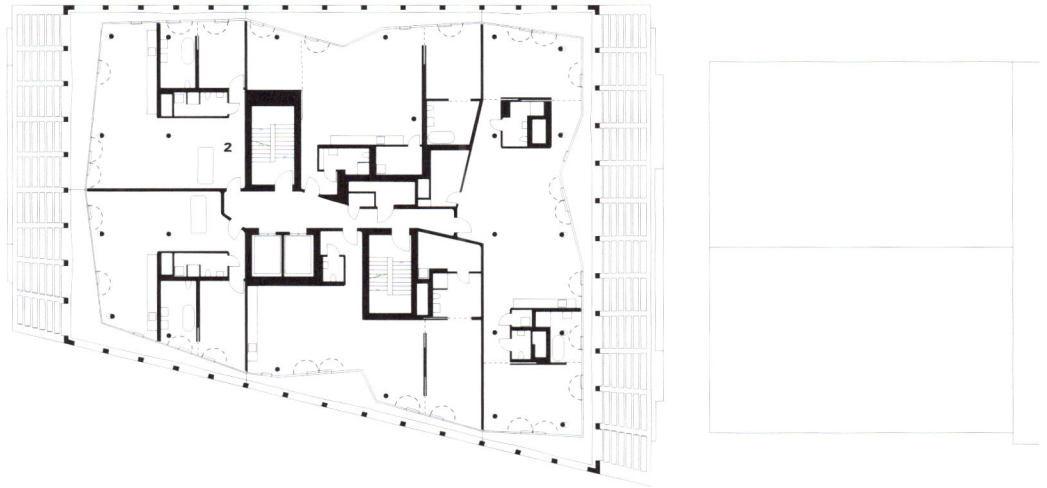

1:500

0   5   10

10th floor plan: ² apartments
Elevation South

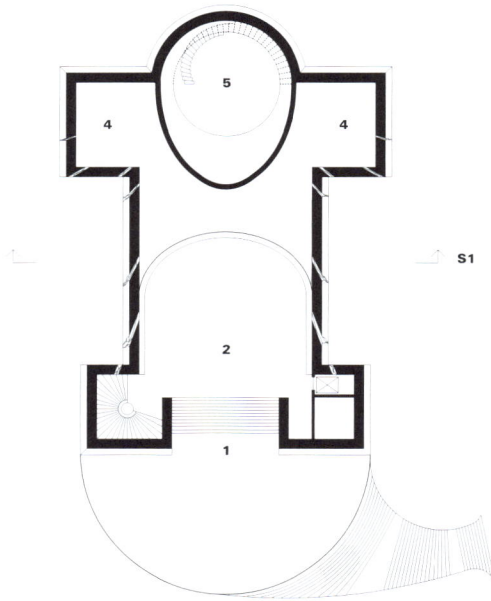

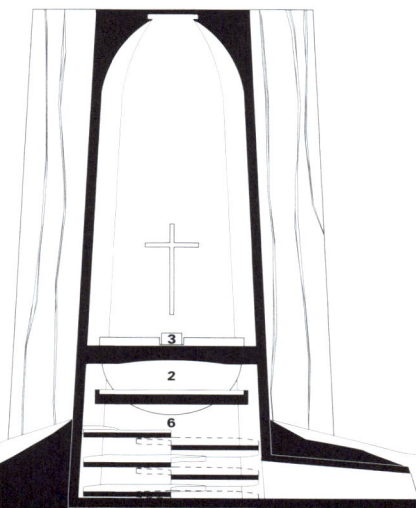

1:750

5

4   4

2

S1

2

1

3

2

6

1:750

Ground floor plan: ¹ entrance ² atrium ⁴ void ⁵ crypt
Section S1: through nave ² atrium ³ altar ⁶ parking

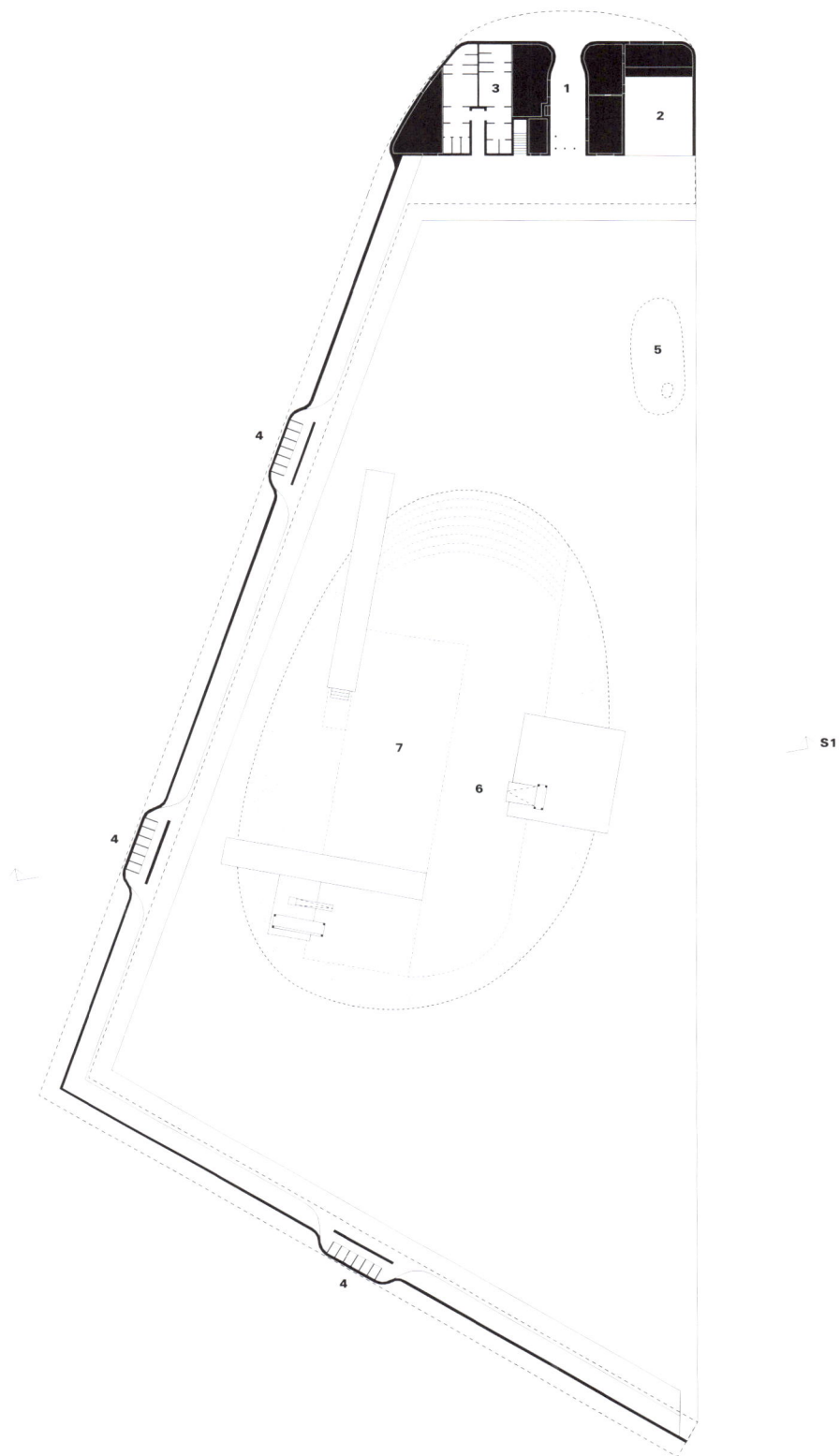

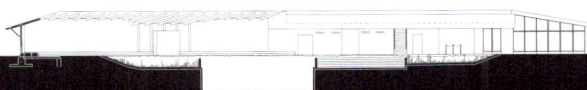

1:750

Ground floor plan: ¹ entrance ² café ³ changing rooms ⁴ showers ⁵ children's pool ⁶ non-swimming pool ⁷ swimming pool

Section S1: through pools

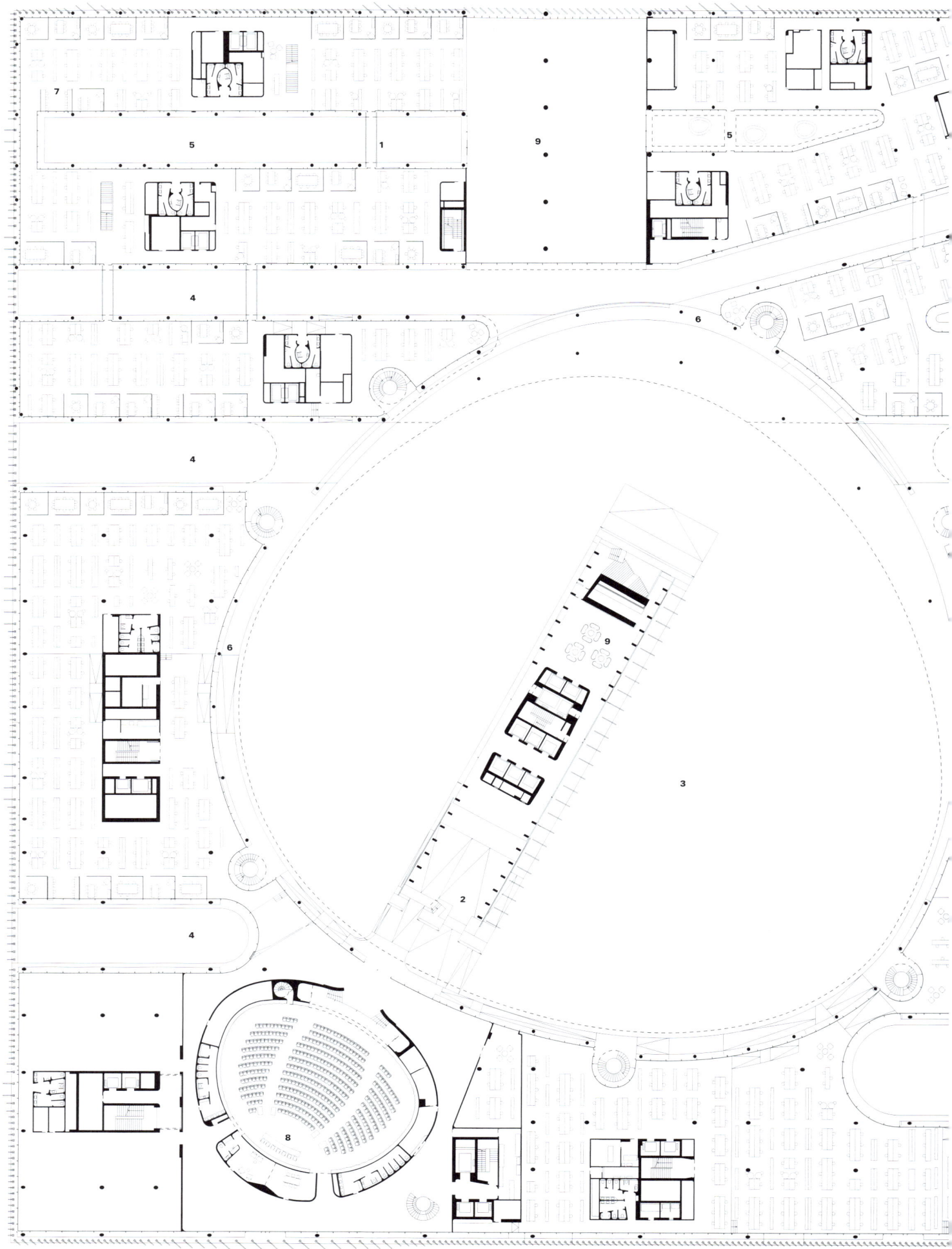

N

0   5   10
1:750

1st floor plan: [1] bridges [2] ramp to the tower [3] plaza [4] streets and gardens [5] patio [6] ring [7] office [8] auditorium [9] restaurant [10] trading room

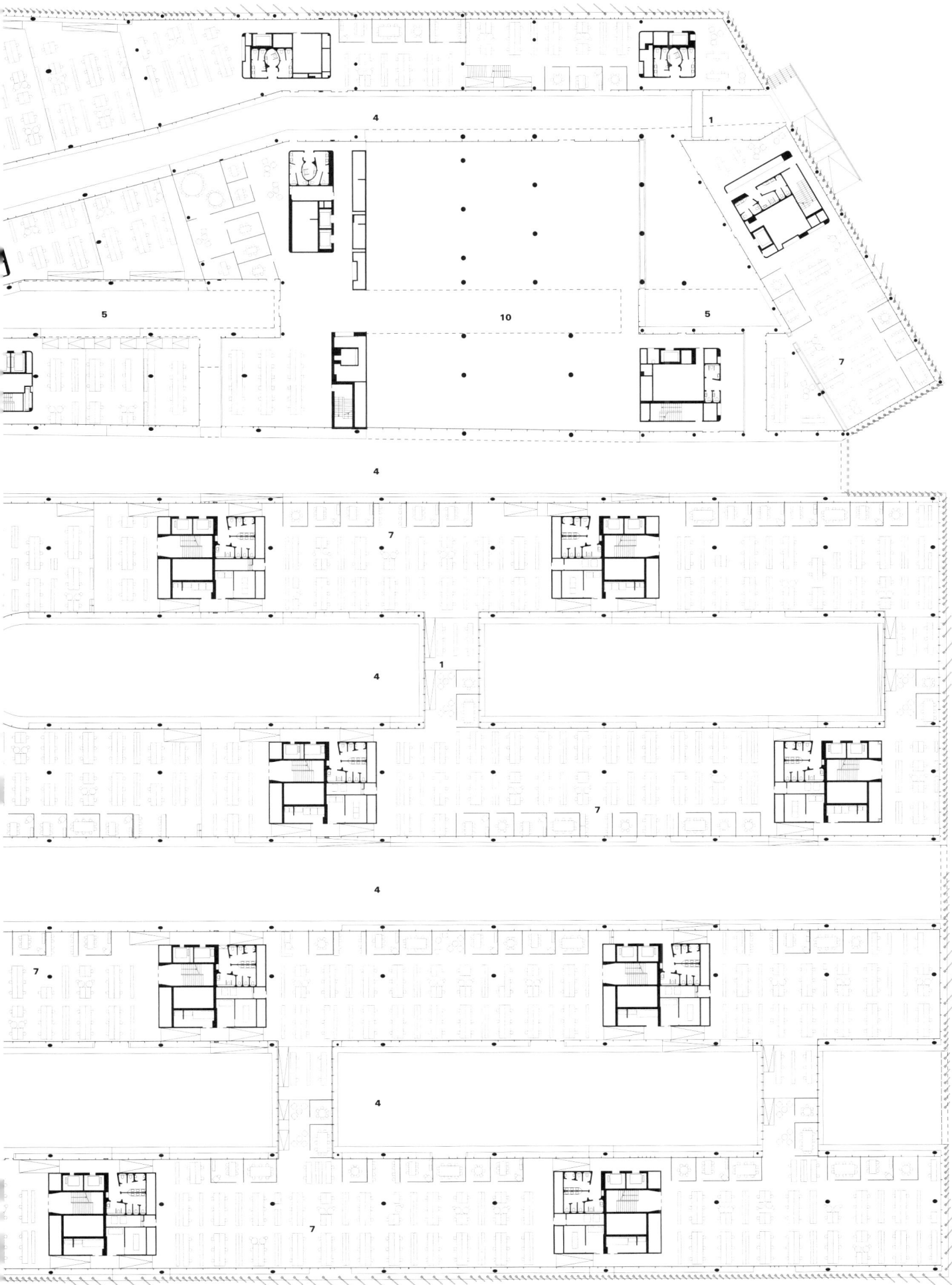

4

1

5   10   5

7

4

7   7

4   1

4

7   7

4

S1

7

4

7

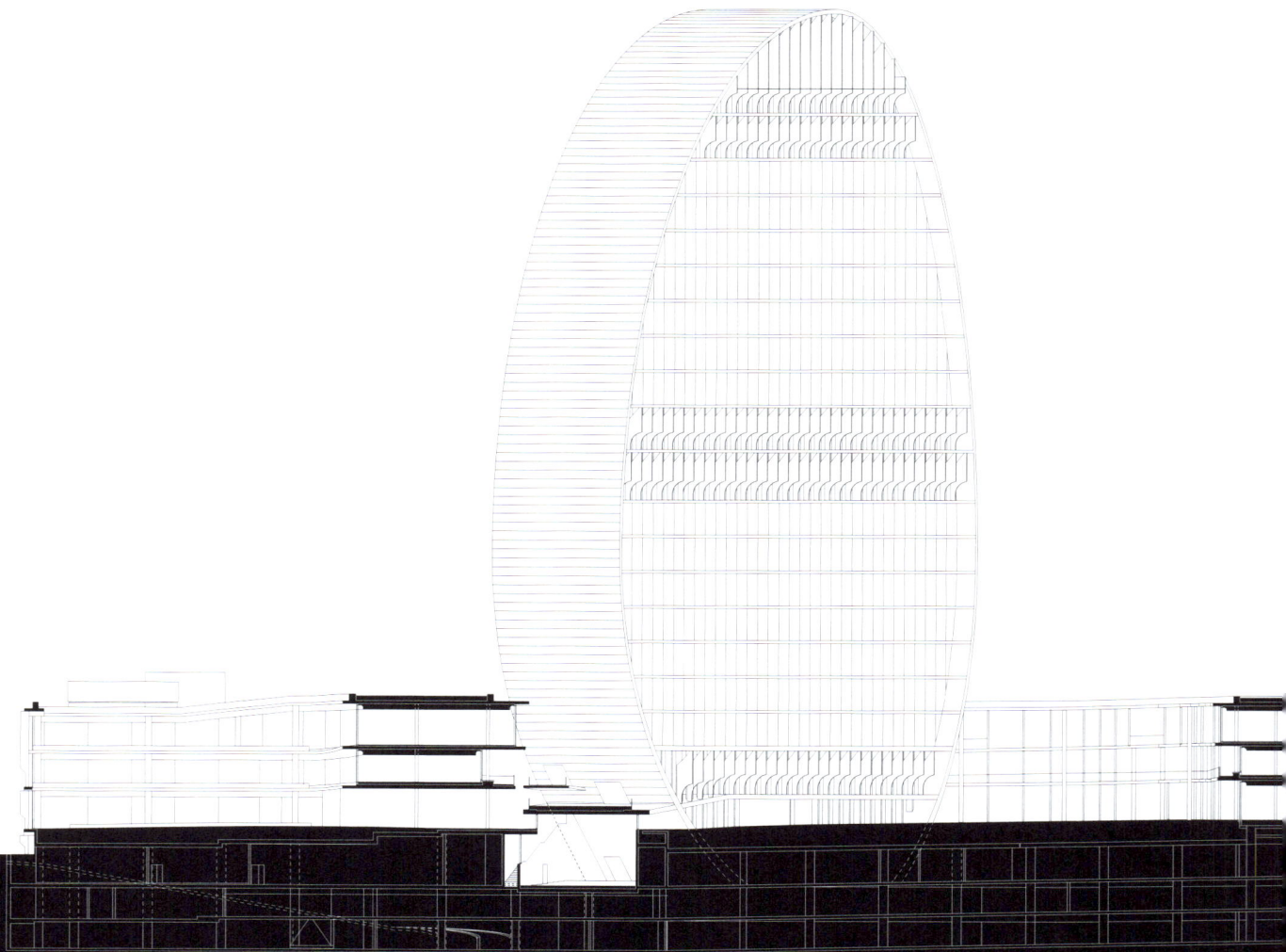

0 5 10

1:750

<u>Longitudinal section S1</u>: through plaza and offices

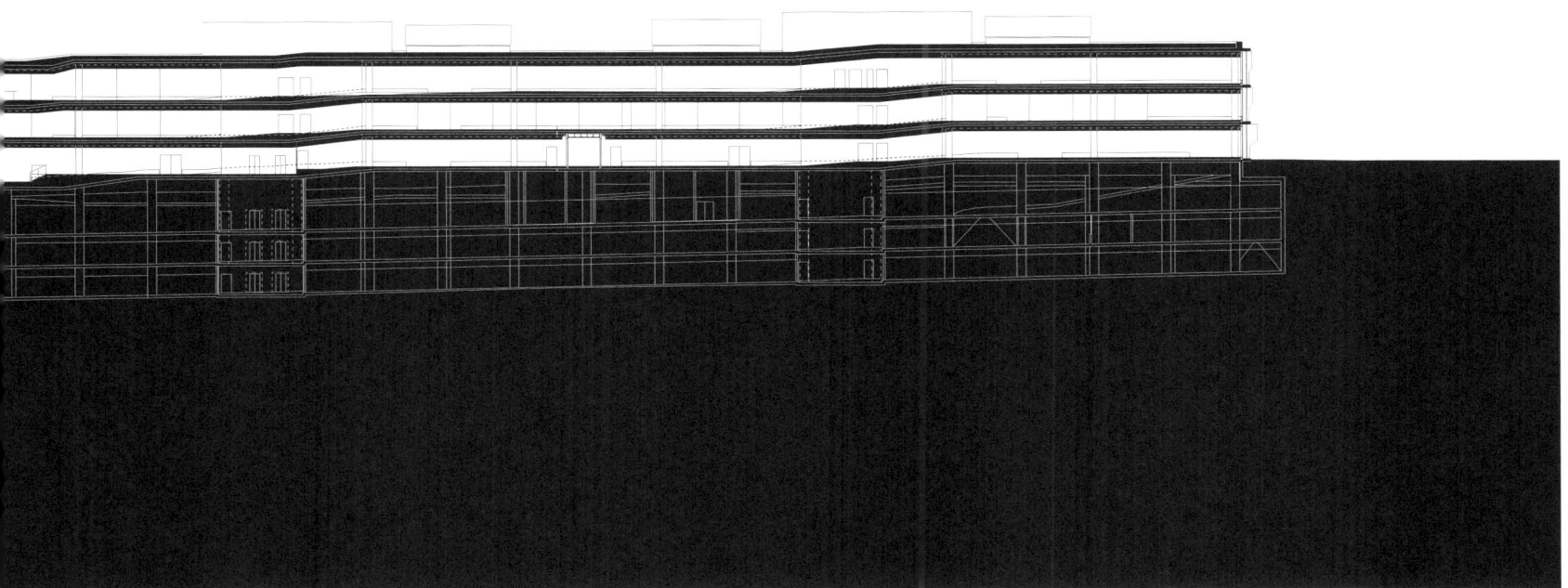

Texts

Herzog & de Meuron

p.199

**Restoration,
Renovation,
Reconstruction,
Simulation**

p.203

**Not Knowing
vs. Knowing**

p.205

**On Transcending
the Boundaries
of Architectural
Thinking**

Restoration, Renovation, Reconstruction, Simulation

Jacques Herzog in conversation with Gerhard Mack on the strategic role of the Armory in Herzog & de Meuron's approach to architecture

Gerhard Mack

Herzog & de Meuron are restoring the Park Avenue Armory in Manhattan, a building that is vital to the history of New York. Looking back at what you have done so far, one realizes, of course, that working with existing volumes is seminal to your work; you might call it part of your DNA. You have always attached great importance to it. Your career actually started with various refurbishment projects. Here you are, two young architects in the early 1970s and instead of predictably dreaming of building something new, you say to yourselves, let's look and see what's already there and what we can do with it. And let's do it in a way that is different from postmodernism's schematic reaction to modernism's permanent call for something new. That was the impetus of your earliest work. Do these beginnings have a historical significance that goes beyond the pragmatic requirements that young architects have to meet?

Jacques Herzog

Our early refurbishment projects really were pragmatically motivated. In the second half of the 1970s, modernism suffered a major economic crisis. It was a time marked by recession following the economic boom after the Second World War, the oil crisis, the Club of Rome with the first call for caution regarding the world's resources, and the realization that resources are not unlimited. Renovation was almost the only available work and it applied to regular buildings that were not necessarily of great historical significance. The recession had an ideological component as well. The enthusiastic, optimistic nature of modernism began to crumble. Modernism thought of history as an impediment to the goal of creating a new tradition, a new future, a new society. The existing world had to be overcome. That is certainly an option. But as a result of the crisis, the advisability of sweeping everything away to have a tabula rasa was questioned. That was the point of departure for our biography. If we had been born ten years earlier, we would have been more profoundly influenced by an intact modernism. But as it was, this historical break enabled us to develop our own issues.

Mack

By the time you started building, postmodernism had already taken a retrospective turn.

Herzog

Postmodernism developed a nostalgic interest in the highlights of history. History became a model instead of an impediment. Architects like James Stirling, Richard Meier, and Mario Botta—in fact the Tendenza movement as a whole—believed that you shouldn't abandon the old on your way to a new society. But since we were not familiar with the old that they were referring to, it meant nothing to us. We have to look at the world we are living in and deal with it; that was our everyday reality. And there certainly was a lot of "world." This is what lies behind the approach that has been crucial to our work throughout: to look at the world with which we are confronted, regardless of era, regardless of whether or not it is highly regarded. In the early years, we did attic extensions and renovated facades, and much later the conversion of a former power plant into Tate Modern. This is about concrete and conscious involvement with something that comes from another age and needs to be updated, and it's also about overcoming taboos or preferences that tend to extinguish the dimension of time, which is ultimately essential to architecture. At the time, even in very small projects, we learned that architecture is something constructive and constructed, which in turn produces constructions and is therefore also subject to change. In contrast to ETH Zürich where we were both employed as assistants at the same time, all the key issues of architecture were exemplified in concrete objects.

Mack

How would you describe your approach in terms of Tate Modern?

Herzog

We "discovered" the potential of the Turbine Hall and made it the centerpiece of our design. It's like the nave of a church. It was obvious to us that the architect, Sir Giles Scott, had envisioned a cathedral for machines. We tuned into this idea and reinforced it: we took everything out of the hall and lowered it, making it even bigger and mightier. At the time I compared this strategy to aikido, a Japanese martial art that involves absorbing and appropriating the energy of one's opponent. We built our Plywood House around a tree, to draw attention to the tree. The Ricola warehouse in Laufen deliberately draws attention to the cliff directly behind it. So we make people aware of what is already there: the form that we produce brings out the properties and qualities of the world around it. At Tate Modern, the context is larger: the huge space and the precise placement of the building within the urban fabric forms a counterpoint to St. Paul's Cathedral on the other side of the Thames. This relationship was barely perceptible; it had been overwhelmed by urban growth.

Mack

The Museum der Kulturen in Basel is a very recent urban example of the way you incorporate existing environs. The museum lies hidden in the Old Town just below the Cathedral. How did you go about giving the building a new visibility?

Herzog

We used several strategies. To begin with, we turned the previously neglected courtyard in the rear into the new entrance. This reversal unites medieval buildings with the rear facades of 19th-century buildings, without any intervention on the part of the architects. We wanted people to experience this area as a space where various components are interrelated. The first thing we did was to lower the courtyard so that it is now level with the lowest story of the museum. That way, when you enter the courtyard, you don't have to decide whether to go up or down. We wanted all of the stories to be equivalent. Secondly, we use plants to unify the surfaces in the courtyard. They come as a surprise; they look exotic; and since they change with the seasons, there is also something temporary and fragile about them. As a result there was no need to make any major modifications in the buildings. Besides, some of the buildings were already overgrown with ivy and wild grape vines so the new vegetation connects with what is already there.

Mack

You also replaced the roof of the Museum.

Herzog

Our initial mandate was to plan an exhibition space for temporary presentations. We placed this extension on the roof and deliberately made it clearly visible from outside to draw attention to the Museum's new entrance. At the same time, we wanted to integrate the new roof into the existing roofscape. That's why we covered it with glazed tiles, similar to those already used in the historical context. On one hand, it's an invasive modification, and on the other, it's an almost tender gesture because it resonates with the shapes and materials of the Old Town. And it is, of course, the key architectural element in transforming the former backyard into the new entrance.

Mack

You took a much more explicit approach in the historic center of Madrid, when you converted an old industrial structure opposite the Royal Gardens into the CaixaForum. There you can sense a certain lack of respect toward the existing substance of the building. It was almost completely destroyed. What is the rationale behind that?

Herzog

True, not much of the building has survived. In contrast to Tate Modern in London, the interior did not provide space suitable to the demanding program that called for doubling the existing volume. What was really worth preserving was the extremely compact masonry of the building, consisting of delicate bricks, reminiscent of ancient Rome. We were extremely impressed by the powerful physical presence of these walls in the narrow alleyways of the historic center and we wanted to heighten that presence. Paradoxically we managed to do that by cutting off the bottom of the building, so that it hovers above the ground, which gives it more weight and the bricks more visibility. This impression was much more vital to us than preserving the appearance of the building before we got involved. In addition we wanted to create an area where people can meet and enter the premises without having to stand in line in an alley. The public space underneath the CaixaForum is analogous to the Turbine Hall at Tate Modern. It is appreciated not only by visitors but also as a meeting place for other people who do not plan to enter the building.

Mack

Your approach to the industrial structure was therefore much influenced by the requirements of its use as a cultural center. You focus on the material of the historical substance. Do you often use this strategy?

Herzog

In this particular case it simply had the greatest exploitable potential. But it could have been an interior room as well. If we had started with the question of preservation, we could have said, okay we will restore the existing hall, we will renovate and stabilize it and make do with the limited volume. But as architects we have a client and specifications. The extent of intervention is determined by the preservation authorities. If it is very limited, you do a different project.

Mack

Is the substance of the building a kind of Ping-Pong partner that you use to bat your ideas back and forth as they develop?

Herzog

Ping-Pong sounds a little frivolous. But we do, of course, go back and forth, thinking about what to preserve and what to tear down. If that weren't the case, it would mean returning to an approach that breaks off the process before it's been thought through to the end. As I said, we are interested in the world as a world that exists, not as an ideal, fictional, or empty world on which we are setting foot for the first time like an astronaut on the Moon. Modernism tried to do that and was tripped up by the resistance of the ordinary, by the habitual nature of everyday life. That doesn't mean that we love it but we have accepted it as the material of our lives and our work. Our designs and projects mold or modify what is already there. Anything new comes from our projections on what already exists and not from an untouched, innocent world. But the means of projection are purely mental; we do not want to tie them in with established values and taboos. That's why the methods we use to put our thoughts into practice are as diverse as possible, ranging from reconstruction to simulation.

Mack

A project in progress that pools a number of strategies is the expansion of the Musée Unterlinden in Colmar, a world-famous museum because of Matthias Grünewald's Isenheim Altarpiece.

Herzog

It's a fascinating and very challenging project. It changes the urban fabric of the location by adding a new piece of architecture that evokes historical forms. It's challenging because we want to avoid the pitfalls that have made lots of experiments with historical forms less than successful. The project integrates disparate elements of urban development in Colmar. The museum consists of a monastery with neo-baroque baths nearby. In between there is a parking lot and an old canal that has been covered over. An extension will provide more space for contemporary art.

Mack

Actually you are radically changing the urban situation.

Herzog

We're restoring the canal that used to be there and is still uncovered in other parts of Colmar. That completely changes the situation of the existing buildings. In addition, we are dividing the large plaza—now a bus terminal—into two sections. The neo-baroque baths no longer have to match the monastery; they will stand alone. We are also introducing a smaller scale that is more appropriate to a medieval town than the large plaza, which was just a place to park cars. We emphasize that by reconstructing a gatehouse based on old documents that we found in the archives. The monastery as a self-contained unit is upgraded, as it were, while the neo-baroque baths and the extension form a new complex in counterpoint to the monastery premises. The new building for temporary exhibitions is therefore essential from both an urban and a curatorial point of view.

Mack

How does that work?

Herzog

The size and the three-dimensional quality of the new extension for contemporary art correspond to the monastery church of the medieval complex. The analogy is intentional because all our experiments with a modernist volume and modernist appearance were not subtle enough: too obviously old versus new. We replaced the vertical ribbon windows of the original competition with windows that have pointed arches reminiscent of the early Gothic windows in the churches of Mendicant Orders. The slits that we initially planned would have broken up the facade too much. We wanted to find a window shape that is defined and not a slit that cuts through the whole wall, so we came up with the idea of using pointed arches. In the model they looked like ghosts. We thought that was interesting and wanted to explore that. But to avoid simple emulation, we worked out a way of relating them directly to the construction of the wall so that you only realize from close-up how new and different they are from the manual craftsmanship of Gothic construction.

Mack

Could that be described as simulation that revamps an old, familiar image in a new and disconcerting way?

Herzog

We did not want simulation in the sense of a reconstruction; we wanted to generate a specific constructive reality that would evoke in the minds of viewers a certain (historical/Gothic) form. It's like the experience of looking at a photograph close-up and studying all the pixels as opposed to standing back to make the image come into focus as a whole.

Mack

You also apply that phenomenon to the facades of the de Young Museum in San Francisco and the TEA on Tenerife.

Herzog

Yes, we did think about that at first, about pixel versus image and image versus pixel. But then the pixels evolved into real elements of copper or poured concrete, so that the original visual idea was no longer relevant. That's as it should be. Architecture should be an open-ended system, so that it can be perceived in various ways and not confined to the image the architect has in mind.

Mack

Could one say that you use the historical substance in Colmar as a sculptural mass?

Herzog

We have no ideal image in mind. We are more interested in "optical illusions" or rather in subverting ideal images. Perception lures us into believing what we see. The images that architecture can evoke are only appearances and like almost everything else on this planet, they are subject to the deceptive nature of sensory perception. We try to counteract that with architecture that involves all of the senses. That's the crux of what architecture can achieve. The medieval shape of the windows in Colmar and the local materials establish a link between the new and existing buildings. At the same time, from close-up you can see the construct behind this impression, which in turn establishes distance again. Constructing and deconstructing the perception of architecture has always interested us. Ideally, that should work as well in architecture as it does in nature; nature is, so to speak, the prototype of the existing world that we were talking about before.

Mack

The Musée Unterlinden focuses less on such effects but even so, I think that in many cases your approach to the existing world is highly sculptural. It is an artistic strategy and you use it to find out how a built substance might be gutted, dissected, elevated, or modified, as you have done for instance at Tate Modern, the CaixaForum, and especially in your proposal for the Casa Museo de Goya in Zaragoza. We detect shades of Gordon Matta-Clark but also a certain lack of respect toward historical substance.

Herzog

The competition for the Museum in Zaragoza gave us an opportunity to try out something radically new.

Mack

You take a very exciting concrete approach. In the historical building you have inserted four rooms that are reconstructions of rooms that Goya had painted in other buildings. They do not relate to the museum architecturally but only to Goya, to the subject matter of the building.

Herzog

We really hope to be able to execute this project when Zaragoza has recovered from the economic crisis. It means a great deal to us because, on one hand, the proposal is very precisely conceived, virtual and imagined in the truest sense of the word, and on the other, the physical, concrete, spatial, and constructed proposal is already so clearly defined.

The idea is to reconstruct rooms painted by Goya within the building that is to be refurbished as the Espacio Goya. These rooms, for instance the one located in the church of San Antonio de la Florida in Madrid, will be physically and mentally present but not as in the national museums of the nineteenth century, which actually removed murals and spolia and reassembled them in the capital city. We are only interested in the reconstructed, empty room as an abstract and yet very concrete shell, in its reconstruction as brickwork that is inserted into the building of the Espacio Goya. Originally we planned to project Goya's paintings onto the walls but then we suggested doing without space-filling simulative projections. Instead of marking the presence of Goya and his oeuvre through illusion, it would be marked by the physical presence of the room in combination with documentary information like books, small-format reproductions, text, diagrams, etc., somewhat like a study center. That would make the rooms devoted to Goya more neutral and give curators the opportunity to present other artists as well.

Mack

Your inserts are spaces of absence that brilliantly leave room for a host of ideas about presence, history, and interpretation. Does that imply a certain critique of society?

Herzog

In our society, the interplay of what exists and what is new has become extremely convoluted. It's become a mishmash, almost a free-for-all. There is no interest in getting to the bottom of things and uncovering truths. Even terms like *truth* and *fact* have lost their currency; they seem to belong to a past age. It is easier to pursue particular interests when things can't be distinguished, when issues are blurred, as they are, for instance, in referendums. This applies even in such a small, straightforward country like Switzerland.

Mack

Does your critical attitude toward these social tendencies fuel the more radical thoughts embodied in your architectural and urban models, somewhat like modernism being fueled by tabula rasa fantasies?

Herzog

We all know, of course, that the tabula rasa as a model for renewing society didn't work. But we have reached the point where a bit of plastic surgery here and there will no longer do; it really is time for radical change and that means addressing issues of energy, food, mobility, in other words, issues crucial to the urbanization of our planet. We are also going to have to find more radical responses to urban planning and transformation. Work on a single architectural object may seem almost ridiculous in view of such concerns—but it isn't. We always take the singular building seriously as part of a larger fabric, as part of daily life that involves the participation of many people. For instance, cutting off the bottom of the CaixaForum building is a radical, transformative statement both for the location and the people who meet there and use the building. There's something liberating about that. But in relation to society as a whole, such an incisive step has much greater consequences.

Mack

You are responsive to modernism's destructive tendencies and its tabula rasa fantasies and yet you yourselves basically practice something else. As you said, you work with what exists and exploit its energy. In the case of the Park Avenue Armory, you practically fade into the wallpaper of the building's history. You opted for a micro surgical approach diametrically opposed to the way monuments are ordinarily reconstructed in the United States.

Herzog

The Armory is not a footnote; it is a stunning memorial to American history. The foremost families of New York society celebrated themselves there. In the period rooms, you walk into sacred territory. The rooms are the creations of the best designers that were to be had in those days. It would be utterly inappropriate for us to force a contemporary spirit on such a monument. We wanted to revitalize the original concept of these rooms, which cannot be found anywhere else. In this case, consideration and respect have priority over making an authorial statement. Incidentally, simulative, reconstructive models and total restoration are not mutually exclusive although the complete restoration of a whole room is of no interest to us as architects, and it's not necessary either. And, of course, total restoration also entails total destruction and extinction of the very thing you're trying to bring back to life!

Mack

It never ceases to amaze me: Even in New York, a city of permanent renewal, the Holy Grail of modernism, you have reacted with almost "unmodern" delicacy and discrimination. Your proposal for the expansion of the Museum of Modern Art showed great respect for previous phases of construction—a far cry from complete demolition.

Herzog

New York is no longer a city of permanent change and hasn't been for a long time. The MoMA competition was, in fact, a drastic demonstration of that. The MoMA extension does not reflect the spirit of expansive modernism; instead it is a tribute to a finished, historical period. Our proposal was different although it did respect the environs. As I said before, because of our background, it has always been a crucial concern of ours to pay attention to what is already there—including modernism. But that's not a moral motivation; we're just convinced that it makes for better projects. We have also begun working in places where there is nothing for us to tie in with, nothing that might be preserved. In those cases, the tabula rasa is a promising strategy. But even in central European society we have reached a problematic point where there is just too much mediocrity. So we also explore the possibility of destruction instead of extension, in other words an iconoclastic strategy, in order to find a new openness and new movement again. The methods may then be different from those of modernism or from countries like China and India. Modernism wanted to manifest as an image of itself. Modernism was also a style. We now try to look at a site from a different point of view, which means trying to institute change through a focus on perception. There's a famous German song that says we see but half a moon, and yet it is so round and fair. And so it is that many things we safely mock because we see them not.

Mack

Doesn't a subversive mind-set play a decisive role as well? In Colmar and Zaragoza you haven't torn down the old buildings. Instead, you changed the character of the place by giving them a thematic twist, by assigning new positions to them within the ensemble. You never changed the architecture of the rooms in the Museo de Goya, but the four inserts give them an entirely different syntax. You clean up the courtyard, you put the building on display as it were, and you change it through just one radical, sculptural gesture.

Herzog

That's true, to a certain extent. In those cases we used the potential of simulation and disguise. But on the other hand we already took a tabula rasa approach in some very early projects. For the exhibition *Berlin morgen* in 1991, on which we collaborated with Rémy Zaugg, we suggested using mountain-like wall slices to mark the middle of the reunited city. Our demolition in this case took the shape of heightening, of adding something. The idea reappears in our proposal for urban development in Basel along the Rhine River. We echo the specific structure of the historical, riverside city, by establishing a similar relationship between the urban architecture and the river in the northern and eastern parts of the city, but in radically contemporary form. Paradoxically, the application and repeti-

tion of the existing situation leads to a completely different and yet still familiar city. That approach is not entirely unlike the one we have taken in refurbishing the Armory, but the result could not be more different.

Jacques Herzog, Gerhard Mack: "Restoration, Renovation, Reconstruction, Simulation… Jacques Herzog on the strategic role of the Armory in Herzog & de Meuron's approach to architecture," in: Gerhard Mack (ed.), Herzog & de Meuron Transforming Park Avenue Armory New York, Basel 2014, pp. 300–306.

Not Knowing
vs. Knowing

In the early 1970s we studied under Aldo Rossi. It was a time of fading belief. Most of the architects practicing at that time did not realize that they were facing the end of modern utopian thinking and essentially the end of their influence on city planning. The arrival of two seminal books – Rossi's *L'architettura della città* and Robert Venturi's *Complexity and Contradiction in Architecture* – created a deceptive certainty about how one should perceive and plan the contemporary city. They marked the beginning of postmodern culture, which shaped the thinking of our generation. We were fascinated by them. Rossi, Venturi and Denise Scott Brown made us believe that they *knew* what a city was, or should be. Rossi believed that cities are based on permanence and typological patterns that one should repeat. He suggested tracing historical patterns or re-creating them in other locations, much like the ancient Romans did when they built their cities across the Empire. Venturi and Scott Brown uncovered the informal quality of the American city, especially of "Main Street," emphasizing the importance of iconography in architecture. They observed and described cities, and presented them as a model. This has played a major role in the way we or other architects of our generation initially approached urban design.

However, while Rossi, as well as Venturi and Scott Brown, envisioned how the city should be, it became obvious to us that we had to live without manifestos. While they presented models of cities, we realized that we had to do without models and start with an unprecedented lack of theory. We embraced the freedom of this uncertainty as a unique opportunity. We were fascinated by the sheer fact of the city and tried to face it with as much openness as we could, with a kind of pragmatic naïveté. Our approach was based on *not* knowing what we might rely on rather than knowing or believing; it is the same approach that we apply to our work on the design of buildings.

Specific vs. Generic

The term *genius loci* could hardly be a more fruitless and irrelevant means of describing a city. Cities become more specific rather than more generic under the pressure of globalization and as a consequence of aging. In this respect they are a bit like human beings. You become more "you" the older you get: more "you" in the way you move, speak, and look, more "you" in your obsessions, failures, and successes. Your life shapes you and conversely you shape your life. Our analysis of Switzerland has revealed the specific nature of the city, not in the sense of a romantic idea of "locus" but rather as an inevitable fate. A kind of illness. A slow process during which patterns emerge, often unconsciously, becoming insurmountable obstacles to change and real transformation.

A comparison of two German cities and their evolution since World War II dramatically illustrates one hypothesis of the ETH Studio Basel. Both Frankfurt and Munich were practically razed to the ground. Bombed out. Frankfurt opted for a tabula rasa strategy in the tradition of modernism, whereas Munich decided to rebuild by imitating and simulating the old structures and reconstructing the local architecture. The Munich approach has proven to be more successful; the city has become one of the most attractive locations for younger generations. Interestingly, Munich has re-created the fake, simulated Italian Renaissance imported by King Ludwig in the 19th century, whereas Frankfurt has remained true to its sober, democratic and purist architecture cultivated by the local *Bürgergemeinde*. One could say that today Frankfurt has become even more Frankfurt and Munich even more Munich than ever before – despite the bombing – or because of the bombing?

Architecture vs. Urban Planning

Since the end of the 1960s and early 1970s architects have been eliminated from city planning and urban design. The lack of utopia has consolidated the process of establishing technocratic city planning based on an ideology of democracy and participation. The highlights of that period are the numerous pedestrian zones, especially in German cities, and the motto of the socialists *die Stadt ist gebaut* (the city is built), which means that no major transformation should question or rethink the already built fabric of the city. A kind of standstill.

In the late 1970s Pierre de Meuron and myself started analyzing Basel, the city where we live and work. We started on our own doorstep, so to speak. Later we involved Rémy Zaugg, the artist whose work is based on perception and language, and our collaboration led to an approach to cities that was certainly new and appropriate to the abovementioned lack of utopia and models. It is based on a kind of intentional naïveté that rejects all a priori thinking and all ideological pretensions and preferences. We started by observing the artifact of the city and all of its underlying economic, social, and psychological processes and transformations. We worked out a method that not only enabled us to reveal threats but also to discover the potentials of a city and give them names that everybody could understand and act on. This has exerted significant political influence and has, for example, consolidated the *integration* of trinational metropolitan planning processes in Basel. The highly critical portrait of Switzerland, which we undertook at the ETH Studio in Basel in collaboration with Roger Diener, Marcel Meili, and Christian Schmid was, in many ways, a continuation of the Basel project and has created remarkable media hype in a country that is normally rather reluctant to discuss its own urban structures.

In recent years we have witnessed an interesting new trend, which is probably independent of our urban studies on Basel and Switzerland: we (Herzog & de Meuron) have been commissioned to carry out numerous projects for large-scale master plans and even entire cities in China, Germany, Spain, and the U.S. We are currently working on a master plan for the entire city of Burgos, Spain, and for the largest piece of land ever developed in Las Vegas. In other words: not only we – the architects – cherish the city as an object of desire, but conversely the city has rediscovered the architect and architecture as the driving force for its reinvention and rejuvenation. Both developers and ambitious politicians have discovered iconic architecture designed by architects of renown to be the most attractive, the most effective and the most profitable tool to build cities.

We see our approach to city planning as a possible accumulation of difference, while in reality it is often reduced to a kind of accumulation of built icons and symbols, like a collection of artworks stored in a "Schaulager." You can visit it on demand and with special permission only.

Therefore, in recent projects, such as the Forum in Barcelona or the National Stadium for the 2008 Olympic Games in Beijing, we have tried to convince politicians to integrate new programs and public spaces as integral parts of the buildings. We see those buildings as possible trigger points of the contemporary metropolis, comparable to acupuncture points in the human body.

Translation of: Jacques Herzog, "Not Knowing vs. Knowing", in: *Cities. Architecture and Society*, La Biennale di Venezia, 10. Mostra Internazionale di Architettura, Vol. 1, Venice, pp. 70–71.

On Transcending the Boundaries of Architectural Thinking

Jacques Herzog in conversation with Hans Ulrich Obrist and Ezra Petronio

Hans Ulrich Obrist

For starters, let's talk about the stadium in China. An important question is the issue of complexity in such a project. Andreas Hug talks about "iconomania" taking over the world. Would something as large and complex as this project be less likely to lend itself to the effortless mass-consumption of icons?

Jacques Herzog

To answer your question with another question, how did this iconic transformation come about to begin with? How was it possible for architecture to become an object of mass consumption?

Architecture has become an increasingly popular media item since the 1980s. People are much more aware nowadays of important buildings and who built them, and cities use architecture to set themselves apart from other cities. That's not new, of course, but when modernism introduced the idea of democratic architecture and a binding architectural idiom, that certainly did not encourage competition. The rebirth of iconomania is a consequence of a paralyzing modernism that bows to the global market and a changing economy. In this sense, architecture is a little bit like a seismograph that keeps track of the economic and political changes around the world. As architects we are part of this seismographic perception. Our projects are both the expression and consequence of these worldwide changes. So they are also instruments of perception that actually allow us to develop credible buildings in so many different places all over the world. Our conceptual approach to the process of architectural design is helpful in this respect.

Architects who have a typical, easily recognizable style may be quicker in working out proposals but there's also the risk that the design may not really suit the specific conditions of the given location or that it will even be rejected.

People are quick to accept "beauty." But what is that? Architects tend to use "form" in order to produce beauty: iconic form, in fact, as demonstrated in recent years. We are somewhat hesitant in that respect because we want to avoid being dependent on "iconic form." We do not want to be immediately recognized as authors. We need the freedom to approach each project from scratch without being loaded down with the baggage of earlier works.

It's not always easy to sustain that kind of freedom. Take the competition for Gazprom in St. Petersburg: the most famous architects in the world were invited to make a proposal. The client clearly wanted something iconic enough to eclipse everything else around it. That objective did not benefit the quality of the submitted projects.

Obrist

Can you elaborate on this? There were five finalists in St. Petersburg. How did you deal with the situation?

Herzog

Gazprom's specifications and wishes required a gigantic building. Given the building height of over 300 meters, our project would have impacted the skyline, just like the others. Since we did not want to create a vertical "monster," we decided to shift most of the weight to the horizontal axis and complement with a very light and spiky vertical axis. We thought that design was better suited to the urban character of St. Petersburg. What impressed us there was the typical separation between the horizontal city and the vertical "needles" of the churches and palaces that tower into the incredibly beautiful skies of St. Petersburg. So our idea was to create the impression of a thin needle rather than a real building. In other words, the iconic impression is a consequence of conceptual considerations rather than of form.

Obrist

Looking at your work, I have the feeling that it's always a negotiation between the local and the global. What's your perspective on this? The work we see here can hardly be reduced to one signature.

Herzog

Exactly. As mentioned, we're not aiming for a typical H&deM style. We want to avoid that. We want to probe the possibilities of architecture today and use its potential for a project. Whatever the style, materials, forms, spaces, specifications…

But there are, of course, themes that we return to or that we elaborate on. Taken together, they might form a group. You can't reinvent yourself every time you do another project, nor is it necessary. But one thing is clear, our work has conceptual roots—something that we were probably not fully aware of at first. We've always worked that way, from the very first designs. Initially just Pierre and me, later with additional partners. We often work as a team. Talking, trying to put into words what it is we are looking for is fundamental to understanding a project. There are texts—often written in tandem with working on a competition design—that are more incisive, more to the point than the architectural draft itself. It's only in the course of elaborating on these ideas that a concrete project rises above its linguistic shell and sheds the now meaningless cocoon.

The research of conceptual thinking was more radical in modernist art than it was in modernist architecture. Architecture didn't have intellectuals like Picabia or Duchamp, or radical abstract thinkers like Reinhardt or Judd, or reinventors like Richter or Wall. But today you do find a small group of international architects exploiting the field of architecture more radically.

Obrist

An important topic uniting art and architecture is the museum. Two years ago we talked about your incredible Walker Art Center. Two years have passed, and many other museum projects have come your way: the Goya Museum in Zaragoza, the CaixaForum in Madrid, the Pérez Art Museum Miami (PAMM). Can you tell me about your experiences?

Herzog

All those projects have completely different needs and specifications so they forced us to do really thorough inquiry into the museum per se. What is a museum? Why do we need them? How do you exhibit art? What is ideal? We have always said that it's time to abandon the postmodern quirkiness of our predecessors, like Hollein, Stirling, or Meier and we shared the radical view advanced by Rémy Zaugg's *The Art Museum of My Dreams or A Place for the Work and the Human Being* (1987/2013). We worked with Zaugg on some early projects and learned a great deal from his incredibly rigorous and yet extremely open-minded approach. The idea of museums as spaces that are more or less "ideal," more or less like white cubes, had basically served its purpose.

Trying to think of other possibilities, we came up with what we call "Anchor Rooms," which we first introduced for a temporary project at MoMA New York. We have now also incorporated that idea in the design of the Espacio Goya in Zaragoza, the Parrish Art Museum, and PAMM in Miami. An Anchor Room is a kind of anti-white cube, a gallery space where architecture and art are interlocked in an essentially archaic and holistic way. No abstract, neutral architecture but a specific room with a history and character of its own, which therefore also becomes part of perceiving the works of art. Materiality, smell, sound, and form are of greater significance than in a white cube, and in combination with the artworks, they contribute to the experience of the space, somewhat like a chapel or a temple.

An Anchor Room is highly specific as opposed to the white cube, which remains flexible, unspecific, and receptive to changing presentations. Anchor Rooms provide new ways of creating a specific architectural and curatorial topography. They have become the intellectual backbone of our most recent museum projects. As mentioned, we first tested and developed the concept of an Anchor Room in our *Artist's Choice* exhibition at MoMA New York. So it was temporarily mounted in a museum with the one of the world's richest collections of 20th century art, which is paradoxical, since the concept is, in fact, most effective for places that have no collections or only poor ones to start with.

In Goya's birthplace Zaragoza, for example, we proposed inserting an "Espacio Goya" in the 19th century building of the museum there, further developing our architectural concept of Anchor Rooms.

The museum in Zaragoza has no works of significance by Goya. But as a young artist, Goya created in situ works in and around Zaragoza and later painted some important murals outside of Zaragoza, like the famous Chapel San Antonio de la Florida in Madrid. We suggest bringing all these works together in Zaragoza by creating computer simulations of the relevant chapels, rotundas, etc., reproducing them in full scale and then building them into the existing museum of brick and mortar, exactly like all the other rooms of the museum. A kind of rape but also an enrichment. The museum is housed in an eclectic Beaux-Arts building, a hodgepodge of different architectural styles. The reconstructed in situ rooms will be integrated into the sequence of existing rooms, adding another historical dimension to the building and establishing an immediate, unique reference to Goya's oeuvre. Only the architecture will be replicated but not the murals, the artworks themselves. But these may occasionally be projected onto the walls and accompanied by photographs, films, and texts. The same rooms, the Anchor Rooms, can also be used for contemporary art, like commissioned works that relate to Goya. An example might be the Chapman Brothers, who have addressed Goya in their work. So the Anchor Rooms in Zaragoza are kind of physical and mental crossroads where Goya's work, the in situ spaces, works by contemporary artists, the Beaux-Arts building, and the specific perception of viewers all come together.

Obrist

How about the bigger museums, the expansion of the Tate. Will they have Anchor Rooms as well?

Herzog

Yes, the sheer size of the completed Tate will require a kind of curatorial-architectural topography.

Obrist

Last time we met, you showed me a perfume. Let's talk more about smell in architecture, and how you came to make a perfume.

Herzog

We have always felt that architects should create perfumes, rather than film stars, actors, or even fashion designers. Smells are intimately related to our memories. A smell may instantly evoke a specific memory of a room or a place or a city we've been to. It's like a spirit, like a pure, immaterial architectural idea. Our perfume is therefore an architectural statement, an experiment that has no intention of being a player in the fashion market. It's more like a magician's experiment: perfume is incredibly effective when we open it and smell it again after a long time. For a brief moment, it unleashes perception and awareness of a time in the past. Then it evaporates again and disappears forever. That's why there is also something sad about perfume. Like photographs, it makes me think of times that are gone, of things that don't exist anymore or that can never come back.

Obrist

I have another question about museums. Everything in art and architecture seems to be expanding. What about smaller projects; are they big ideas in smaller portions? What about the VitraHaus?

Herzog

VitraHaus is the smallest one of our "stack-projects." There are also very big ones, like our proposal for the Qingdao Film Academy or the high-rise building on Leonard Street in New York. What interests us about VitraHaus is the combination of abstraction and figuration. On the one hand, stacking is a neutral, sculptural device that's been known and used for ages. And children are great "stackers"; they love it. On the other hand, you see the concrete shape of a house with a gabled roof, like those in the neighborhood around VitraHaus. The rudimentary shape of a house is one of the few recurring typologies in our work. It goes back to the 1980s—the Blue House in Oberwil, for instance, and the house for a veterinary surgeon in Dagmersellen, both in Switzerland, or the house in Leymen, France.

Obrist

Another important question to me concerns your research projects. Art and architectural schools are in a crisis of sorts these days. Knowledge in architectural firms is increasingly produced bottom-up rather than instructed top-down. I meet people all over Europe who are in some way connected with you, who are part of your knowledge network. How does that network materialize? What is your vision there?

Herzog

There were a number of reasons why we wanted to set up a research center for urban planning in Basel in the late nineties. The main reason, though, was that we were really interested in doing something else in addition to the work in our office, and in collaboration with Marcel Meili and Roger Diener. Together we founded a kind of research garage which then became the ETH Studio Basel, an urban research institution, which is small but still inspiring and with an interesting information network. The first project was a four-year in-depth study of Switzerland that led to a book of three volumes, which caused quite a splash in cultural and political circles in Switzerland: *Switzerland, an Urban Portrait*. We had great fun doing it, but it was also extremely hard work. Astonishingly, some of the fundamental insights that we arrived at have been well-received in federal departments in Switzerland and they have become vital aspects of official land-use planning. Urban research can be frustrating but it opens new doors to our own way of thinking and looking.

Obrist

What have you been investigating?

Herzog

After the Swiss book we reorganized Studio Basel so that we can conduct two studies per year, side by side, one led and inspired by Roger and Marcel, and the other by Pierre and myself. This split allows us also to involve our Harvard students in the same topics that we explore in Basel. Studies on Naples, Paris, St. Petersburg, and the Canary Islands generated new material, part of which is being post-produced over the years. This postproduction (books, films, web), which is about making research material available, is the really tough thing to do. But it is also where the knowledge or the value of an urban study becomes visible and useful. The book on Switzerland became very successful in Switzerland. It made a strong political impact and a similar political impact is being generated through our ongoing urban research on the trinational metropolitan area of Basel, a study that we started around 1990 with artist Rémy Zaugg. It crosses borders and brings things together which otherwise would be neglected or planned separately.

Obrist

It's fascinating because I'd never thought about the fact that Basel is a trinational city. Where I grew up in Kreuzlingen it was the same, leading to a daily crossing of boundaries, a sort of biographical thing.

Herzog

I feel that way, too. As a child, I was more familiar with the "German side" of Basel, like Lörrach and Weil, than I was with a lot of neighborhoods on the Swiss side. The tram went straight from where I lived to the market across the border in Lörrach. A strong psychological component is involved in cities and city planning. The lives and destinies of urban residents have an effect on the city in which they live and conversely—for generations, in fact. There's often talk of cities being "generic," but they never are and never will be; they are all different and each have a very specific character of their own.

Ezra Petronio

Are you often frustrated?

Herzog

When you're trying out new things, you know that they may not always turn out the way you want them to. But I wouldn't call it frustration, but rather impatience.

Obrist

Where do you have your space in terms of thinking and drawing and creativity?

Herzog

I'm not sure I have a space of that kind ... sometimes in bed or in the bathroom or just somewhere. The ETH studio or Harvard studio are not more intense "thinking spaces" than our Herzog & de Meuron offices, where we are surrounded by so many talented people. Personally, I find that very inspiring, more so than when I

focus on only one theme and work only with a small group of students full of expectations. That's interesting because it contradicts the assumption that smaller offices tend to be more creative than big ones.

Petronio

What are the limitations? Do you reach a point when your mind cannot focus enough? Do you envision that as something scary?

Herzog

The design of our company is as important for us as the design of our projects. We have recently posed that question a lot. How did we work in the past, how do we want to work in the future? How do we want to organize ourselves and how does that impact our firm?

Obrist

Can architecture offices function like a brand and can that brand function without the founding architect?

Herzog

There are many different examples of effective management succession. Firms have to keep reinventing themselves in order to keep on living. Like downsizing or growing, focusing on technologies or specializing. It's like soccer: a team is successful when the talent of the players influences the system of play, and not conversely.

Obrist

In an earlier interview we discussed the possibility of an architectural practice having a very specific premiere line and then having a secondary line.

Herzog

That doesn't work in architecture. We have thought a great deal about the possibility of giving young partners greater leeway. But the premiere line would always overshadow the secondary line, as implied by the words themselves. Why would a private collector have his art museum produced by the H&deM factory, when his greatest rival, who is also a collector, can buy a tailor-made project designed by Jacques Herzog and Pierre de Meuron? And the converse would be even worse for us as an architectural office: namely, why not simply take the design offered by the H&deM factory design if it's cheaper and looks just as good as the tailor-made product? That may work in the fashion world where the product is clearly defined and reproducible. You can easily combine designer fashions with clothes bought off the rack. Architecture functions somewhat differently.

Edited version of conversation between Jacques Herzog, Hans Ulrich Obrist and Ezra Petronio (Basel, 12 July 2007). First publication: Jacques Herzog / Hans Ulrich Obrist / Ezra Petronio, *On Transcending the Boundaries of Architectural Thinking*, in: *Self Service* 27, 2007, pp. 348–351, 393.

Work
Chrono-
logy

Herzog & de Meuron

Work Chronology

PROJECTS 1–47 ARE PRESENTED
IN VOLUME 1 HERZOG & DE MEURON
1978–1988.

NO.1 ATTIC CONVERSION
Riehen, Switzerland
Project 1978,
realization 1978

NO.2 HOUSE CONVERSION
Basel, Switzerland
Project 1979,
realization 1979

NO.3 REDESIGN OF THE MARKTPLATZ
Basel, Switzerland
Competition 1979,
project 1982,
1983, 1985, 1987

NO.4 CONVERSION AND RENOVATION
OF AN APARTMENT BUILDING
Basel, Switzerland
Project 1979,
realization 1980

NO.5 BLUE HOUSE
Oberwil, Switzerland
Project 1979,
realization 1979–1980

NO.6 URBAN STUDY ROSSHOF QUARTER
Basel, Switzerland
Competition 1979

NO.7 INDOOR AND OUTDOOR
SWIMMING POOL AM MÜHLETEICH
Riehen, Switzerland
Competitions 1979, 1981,
project 1982

NO.8 APARTMENT EXTENSION
Laufen, Switzerland
Realization 1980

NO.9 GASTHOF ZUM BAD,
APARTMENT CONVERSION
Schönenbuch, Switzerland
Realization 1980

NO.10 MURUS GALLICUS UNDERGROUND
EXHIBITION SPACE
Basel, Switzerland
Project 1980

NO.11 RENOVATION OF THE KASERNE
EXHIBITION SPACE
Basel, Switzerland
Project 1980,
realization 1981

NO.12 URBAN STUDY KLÖSTERLI
QUARTER
Bern, Switzerland
Competition 1981

NO.13 APARTMENT BUILDING
CONVERSION
Basel, Switzerland
Realization 1981–1982

NO.14 FREI PHOTOGRAPHIC STUDIO
Weil am Rhein, Germany
Project 1981,
realization 1981–1982

NO.15 APARTMENT AND OFFICE BUILDING
CLARAGRABEN
Basel, Switzerland
Competition 1982

NO.16 ST. ALBAN-TAL HOUSING
Basel, Switzerland
Competition 1982

NO.17 STONE HOUSE
Tavole, Italy
Project 1982,
realization 1985–1988

NO.18 PARISH CENTRE
Lenzburg, Switzerland
Competition 1983

NO.19 CONVERSION OF OFFICES
FOR RICOLA
Laufen, Switzerland
Realization 1983

NO.20 CONVERSION AND RENOVATION
OF AN APARTMENT BUILDING
Basel, Switzerland
Realization 1983

NO.21 FARM EXTENSION
AND RENOVATION
Rocourt, Switzerland
Realization 1983, 1986

NO.22 HOUSE FOR A VETERINARY
SURGEON
Dagmersellen/Lucerne, Switzerland
Project 1983,
realization 1984

NO.23 VISP THEATRE
Visp, Switzerland
Competition 1984

NO.24 CONVERSION AND RENOVATION
OF AN APARTMENT BUILDING
Basel, Switzerland
Project 1984,
realization 1985

NO.25 APARTMENT AND COMMERCIAL
BUILDING SCHÜTZENMATTSTRASSE
Basel, Switzerland
Competition 1984–1985,
Project 1991,
realization 1992–1993

NO.26 CONVERSION AND RENOVATION
OF AN APARTMENT BUILDING
Birsfelden, Switzerland
Project 1984,
realization 1985

NO.27 PLYWOOD HOUSE
Bottmingen, Switzerland
Project 1984,
realization 1985

NO.28 LEGO HOUSE: ONE SPECIFIC ROOM.
CONTRIBUTION TO THE EXHIBITION
L'ARCHITECTURE EST UN JEU...
MAGNIFIQUE
Centre Georges Pompidou, Paris, France
Exhibition 10 July – 26 August 1985

NO.29 APARTMENT BUILDING ALONG
A PARTY WALL, HEBELSTRASSE
Basel, Switzerland
Competition 1984,
realization 1987–1988

NO.30 RESTAURANT FOR THE BASEL ZOO
Basel, Switzerland
Competition 1985

NO.31 APARTMENT AND OFFICE BUILDING
SCHWITTER
Basel, Switzerland
Competition 1985,
project 1985,
realization 1987–1988

NO.32 CONVERSION AND RENOVATION
OF A BUILDING IN THE HISTORIC
CENTRE OF LAUFEN
Laufen, Switzerland
Project 1985,
realization 1986

NO.33 CONVERSION AND RENOVATION
OF LABORATORY BUILDING 91
FOR SANDOZ
Novartis Industrial Area, Basel, Switzerland
Project 1985,
realization 1986

NO.34 HOUSE FOR AN ART COLLECTOR
Therwil, Switzerland
Project 1985,
realization 1986

NO.35 E, D, E, N, PAVILION, HOTEL EDEN
Rheinfelden, Switzerland
Competition 1986,
realization 1987

NO.36 CLADDING FOR A HOUSE
Fischingen, Germany
Partial realization 1986

NO.37 OUTDOOR SWIMMING POOL
AM MÜHLETEICH
Riehen, Switzerland
Project 1986–1987

NO.38 RICOLA STORAGE BUILDING
Laufen, Switzerland
Project 1986,
realization 1987

NO.39 CONVERSION AND RENOVATION
OF TWO HOUSES
Basel, Switzerland
Project 1986,
realization 1987

NO.40 MUSEUMS COMPLEX
Vienna, Austria
Competition 1987

NO.41 ARCHAEOLOGICAL MUSEUM
Neuchâtel, Switzerland
Competition 1987

NO.42 SANDOZ OFFICE BUILDING 430
Novartis Industrial Area, Basel, Switzerland
Project 1987

NO.43 HOUSING PILOTENGASSE
Wien-Aspern, Austria
Project 1987–1988,
realization 1989–1992

NO.44 APARTMENT BUILDING
AND NURSING HOME SCHWARZPARK
Basel, Switzerland
Competition 1987–1988

NO.45 REFURBISHMENT
OF THE GABA BLOCK
Basel, Switzerland
Project 1982, 1983, 1985, 1988

NO.46 SANDOZ TECHNOLOGY
DEVELOPMENT CENTER
Novartis Industrial Area, Basel, Switzerland
Projects 1988, 1991,
realization 1993

NO.47 ARCHITEKTUR DENKFORM
Architekturmuseum, Basel, Switzerland
Exhibition 1 October–20 November 1988

PROJECTS 48–79 ARE PRESENTED
IN VOLUME 2 HERZOG & DE MEURON
1989–1991.

NO.48 RAILWAY ENGINE DEPOT
AUF DEM WOLF
Basel, Switzerland
Project 1989,
realization 1991–1995

NO.49 SIGNAL BOX AUF DEM WOLF
Basel, Switzerland
Project 1989,
realization 1991–1994

NO.50 SUVA HOUSE,
EXTENSION AND ALTERATION
OF AN APARTMENT
AND OFFICE BUILDING
Basel, Switzerland
Project 1988–1990,
realization 1991–1993

NO.51 PARK FOR THE AVENIDA DIAGONAL
Barcelona, Spain
Competition 1989,
project 1989

NO.52 LUZERNERRING APARTMENT
BUILDINGS
Basel, Switzerland
Competition 1989

NO.53 RICOLA FACTORY ADDITION
AND GLAZED CANOPY
Laufen, Switzerland
Project 1989,
realization 1989–1991

NO.54 DESIGN MUSEUM
Basel, Switzerland
Project 1989–1990

NO.55 PFAFFENHOLZ SPORTS CENTRE
Saint-Louis, France
Project 1989–1990,
realization 1992–1993

NO.56 GOETZ COLLECTION,
GALLERY FOR A PRIVATE COLLECTION
OF MODERN ART
Munich, Germany
Project 1989–1990,
realization 1991–1992

NO.57 GREEK ORTHODOX CHURCH
Zurich, Switzerland
Competition 1989

NO.58 EXTENSION OF HEAD OFFICES
FOR HELVETIA
St. Gallen, Switzerland
Competition 1989,
project 1990–1991

NO.59 INTERPRETING THE PLACE
9H Gallery, London, UK
Exhibition 6 October–12 November 1989

NO.60 MASTER PLAN FOR THE
UNIVERSITÉ DE BOURGOGNE
Dijon, France
Project 1989–1990

NO.61 EXTENSION OF OFFICES,
STORAGE AND LABORATORY, SOLCO
Basel, Switzerland
Project 1990–1991

NO.62 RAILWAY BUILDING SERVICES
CENTRE AUF DEM WOLF
Basel, Switzerland
Project 1990

NO.63 ARCHITEKTUR DENKFORM
Swiss Federal Institute of Technology (ETH),
Zurich, Switzerland
Exhibition 27 April–10 May 1990

NO.64 ANTIPODES I, STUDENT HOUSING,
UNIVERSITÉ DE BOURGOGNE
Dijon, France
Project 1990,
realization 1991–1992

NO.65 ELSÄSSERTOR OFFICE
AND CARGO BUILDING
Basel, Switzerland
Competition 1990

NO.66 FLOWTEC OFFICE AND LABORATORY
BUILDING
Reinach, Switzerland
Project 1990

NO.67 ALTES FLUGFELD, URBAN DESIGN
Karlsruhe, Germany
Project 1990

NO.68 TWO CARPETS DESIGNED
FOR TEPPICHFABRIK MELCHNAU
Langenthal, Switzerland
Project 1991

NO.69 HERZOG & DE MEURON
Col·legi d'Arquitectes de Catalunya,
Barcelona, Spain
Exhibition 16 October–9 November 1990

NO.70 CONTRIBUTION TO THE EXHIBITION
OUVERTURES
Arc en Rêve, Centre d'Architecture,
Bordeaux, France
Exhibition 22 October 1989–6 January 1990

NO.71 BERLIN ZENTRUM, CONTRIBUTION
TO THE EXHIBITION BERLIN MORGEN
Deutsches Architekturmuseum,
Frankfurt a. M., Germany
Exhibition 26 January–24 March 1991

NO.72 ALFRED RICHTERICH COLLECTION
Laufen, Switzerland
Project 1991

NO.73 VIESENHÄUSER HOF URBAN DESIGN
Stuttgart-Mühlhausen, Germany
Competition 1991

NO.74 ARCHITEKTUR VON
HERZOG & DE MEURON
Kunstverein München, Munich, Germany
Exhibition 1 March–7 April 1991

NO.75 ARTS CENTER
Blois, France
Competition 1991

NO.76 ARCHITECTURE OF HERZOG &
DE MEURON. PHOTOGRAPHED BY
MARGHERITA KRISCHANITZ,
BALTHASAR BURKHARD,
HANNAH VILLIGER AND THOMAS RUFF.
5. Mostra Internazionale di Architettura,
Swiss Pavilion, Venice, Italy
Exhibition 8 September–6 October 1991

NO.77 "EINE STADT IM WERDEN?"
URBAN STUDY
Basel, Switzerland
Project 1991–1992

NO.78 SILS-CUNCAS SETTLEMENT DESIGN
Sils, Engadin, Switzerland
Competition 1991

NO.79 ANTIPODES II, STUDENT HOUSING,
UNIVERSITÉ DE BOURGOGNE
Dijon, France
Project 1991

PROJECTS 80–152 ARE PRESENTED
IN VOLUME 3 HERZOG & DE MEURON
1992–1996.

NO.80 BEUNDENFELD URBAN DESIGN
Bern, Switzerland
Project 1991–1992

NO.81 ONE BUILDING FOR THE MUSEUMS
OF THE 20TH CENTURY
Munich, Germany
Competition 1992

NO.82 STUDIO FREI
Weil am Rhein, Germany
Project 1992

NO.83 ALTERATIONS TO HOTEL ADMIRAL
Basel, Switzerland
Project 1992

NO.84 LABORATORY BUILDING,
NEW FACADE FOR BUILDING 411,
CIBA-GEIGY AG
Basel, Switzerland
Project 1992

NO.85 OUTDOOR SWIMMING POOL
IM SCHLIPF
Riehen, Switzerland
Project 1990–1992

NO.86 FRANKFURT OSTHAFEN,
URBAN STUDY:
CONTRIBUTION TO THE EXHIBITION
Deutsches Architekturmuseum,
Frankfurt a. M., Germany
Exhibition 20 June–26 July 1992

NO.87 BERLIN PULVERMÜHLE,
HOUSING PROJECT
Berlin, Germany
Competition 1992

NO.88 CONTRIBUTION TO HANOVER
EXPO 2000
Hanover, Germany
Competition 1992

NO.89 TWO EXHIBITION SPACES
FOR CONTEMPORARY ART,
MUSÉE DE SEMUR-EN-AUXOIS
Semur-en-Auxois, France
Project 1992

NO.90 TWO LIBRARIES,
UNIVERSITÉ DE JUSSIEU
Paris, France
Competition 1992

NO.91 COMMERCIAL BUILDING
AND MASTER PLAN FOR SBS-PERREY
Delémont, Switzerland
Competition 1992

NO.92 APARTMENT BUILDING
ON THE RHINE RIVER
Basel, Switzerland
Competition 1992

NO.93 PRODUCTION BUILDING,
FLOWTEC SA
Cernay, France
Project 1992

NO.94 RICOLA-EUROPE SA,
PRODUCTION AND STORAGE BUILDING
Mulhouse-Brunstatt, France
Project 1992,
realization 1993

NO.95 MASTER PLAN
FOR THE KRUPPGELÄNDE
Essen, Germany
Competition 1992

NO.96 KOECHLIN HOUSE
Riehen, Switzerland
Realization 1993–1994

NO.97 THREE APARTMENT BUILDINGS
Starnberg, Germany
Project 1993

NO.98 LIBRARY AND MASTER PLAN
OF THE COTTBUS TECHNICAL UNIVERSITY
Cottbus, Germany
Competition 1993

NO.99 KEMPINSKI RESIDENCE,
COMMERCIAL BUILDING AND HOTEL
Dresden, Germany
Competition 1993

NO.100 ROCHE PHARMA-RESEARCH
BUILDING 92
Roche Basel Site, Basel, Switzerland
Project 1993–1995,
realization 1998–2000

NO.101 COOP SHOPPING CENTER,
HOTEL AND APARTMENTS
ON THE WARTECK-AREAL
Muttenz, Switzerland
Competition 1993–1994

NO.102 DORNACHERPLATZ COMMERCIAL
AND APARTMENT BUILDING
Solothurn, Switzerland
Project 1993, 1995, 1997,
realization 1998–2000

NO.103 CONTRIBUTION TO THE EXHIBITION
DIE BANK
Deutsches Architekturmuseum,
Frankfurt a. M., Germany
Exhibition 3–29 September 1994

NO.104 ROCHE ADMINISTRATIVE
AND TRAINING BUILDING
Sisseln, Switzerland
Project 1994

NO.105 EBERSWALDE
TECHNICAL SCHOOL LIBRARY
Eberswalde, Germany
Project 1994–1996,
realization 1997–1999

NO.106 EBERSWALDE TECHNICAL
SCHOOL SEMINAR BUILDING
Eberswalde, Germany
Project 1994–1995,
realization 1996–1997

NO.107 APARTMENT AND COMMERCIAL
BUILDING FOR THE DRESDNER BANK
Eberswalde, Germany
Project 1994, 1997

NO.108 HYPO-BANK THEATINERSTRASSE,
MIXED-USE COMMERCIAL QUARTER
Munich, Germany
Competition 1994,
project 1995

NO.109 RAILROAD BRIDGE
ACROSS THE RIVER RHINE
Basel, Switzerland
Competition 1994

NO.110 NEUSTÄDTER FELD,
REDEVELOPMENT OF A DISTRICT
OF PREFABRICATED HOUSING
Magdeburg, Germany
Project 1994

NO.111 AMPHITRYON, TWO OFFICE
BUILDINGS FOR THE BAYERISCHE
HYPOTHEKEN- UND VEREINSBANK
Frankfurt a. M., Germany
Competition 1994,
project 1995, 1997–1998

NO.112 EXTENSION OF KOHLENBERG-
HOLBEIN-GYMNASIUM
Basel, Switzerland
Competition 1994

NO.113 LANDOLT HOUSE
Riehen, Switzerland
Project 1994,
realization 1994

NO.114 VISCHER HOUSE
Basel, Switzerland
Project 1994,
realization 1994

NO.115 PRIVATE RESIDENCE
Basel, Switzerland
Project 1994,
realization 1994–1995

NO.116 SWISS PAVILION AT THE BIENAL
INTERNATIONAL DE SÃO PAULO
São Paulo, Brazil
Project 1994,
realization 1994

NO.117 SONNENHALDE SANATORIUM
Riehen, Switzerland
Competition 1994

NO.118 URBAN DESIGN FOR THE
SITE OF THE METALL
GESELLSCHAFT REUTERWEG
Frankfurt a.M., Germany
Study 1994

NO.119 CENTRAL SIGNAL BOX
Basel, Switzerland
Competition 1994,
project 1995,
realization 1998–1999

NO.120 HERZOG & DE MEURON.
DAS NEUE SUVA-HAUS IN BASEL
1988–1993
Architekturgalerie Luzern,
Lucerne, Switzerland
Exhibition 25 September–30 October 1994

NO.121 GEORGSPLATZ
COMMERCIAL BUILDING
Dresden, Germany
Feasibility study 1994

NO.122 SITE SANTA FE, MUSEUM
AND CULTURAL CENTER
Santa Fe, New Mexico, USA
Study 1994

NO.123 DREIROSENBRÜCKE,
TWO-LEVEL HIGHWAY-BRIDGE
Basel, Switzerland
Competition 1994

NO.124 RHEINHAFEN WESTQUAI,
HOUSING PROJECT
IN A HARBOUR AREA
Basel, Switzerland
Project 1994

NO.125 BORNEO AMSTERDAM,
HOUSING PROJECT
IN A HARBOUR AREA
Amsterdam, Netherlands
Project 1994

NO.126 TATE MODERN
London, UK
Competition 1994–1995,
project 1995–1997,
realization 1998–2000

NO.127 ENKA SCHOOL
Istanbul, Turkey
Project 1994

NO.128 HOUSE IN LEYMEN
Leymen, Ht. Rhin, France
Project 1996,
realization 1997

NO.129 DRESDNER BANK PARISERPLATZ
Berlin, Germany
Competition 1995

NO.130 HERZOG & DE MEURON,
UNE EXPOSITION,
CONCEIVED BY RÉMY ZAUGG
Centre Georges Pompidou, Paris, France
Exhibition 8 March–22 May 1995

NO.131 CARICATURE AND
CARTOON MUSEUM,
CONVERSION AND NEW BUILDING
Basel, Switzerland
Project 1994,
realization 1994–1996

NO.132 INSTITUTE FOR HOSPITAL
PHARMACEUTICALS, ROSSETTIAREAL
Basel, Switzerland
Project 1995,
realization 1997–1998

NO.133 STUDIO RÉMY ZAUGG
Mulhouse, France
Project 1995,
realization 1995–1996

NO.134 WOOD HOUSE
Stuttgart, Germany
Project 1995

NO.135 HOUSE IN ARLESHEIM
Arlesheim, Switzerland
Project 1995

NO.136 WHITE FOUNTAIN
AT THE RÜDENPLATZ, URBAN STUDY
Basel, Switzerland
Competition 1995,
project 2000

NO.137 DOMINUS WINERY
Yountville, California, USA
Project 1995,
realization 1996–1998

NO.138 UNIVERSITY PSYCHIATRY CLINIC
Basel, Switzerland
Project 1995

NO.139 EXPANSION OF EURO AIRPORT
BASEL-MULHOUSE-FREIBURG
Mulhouse, France
Competition 1995

NO.140 SATELLITE SIGNAL BOX
Basel, Switzerland
Project 1995–1996,
realization 1998–1999

NO.141 SCHAUSPIELHAUS ZÜRICH,
CULTURAL CENTRE,
THEATRE WORKSHOPS AND MUSEUM
Zurich, Switzerland
Competition 1996

NO.142 HERRNSTRASSE COMMERCIAL
AND APARTMENT BUILDING
Munich, Germany
Project 1996,
realization 1998–2000

NO.143 FÜNF HÖFE, FIVE COURTYARDS
FOR THE MUNICH CITY CENTRE
Munich, Germany
Project 1997–1998,
realization 1999–2003

NO.144 ST. JAKOB STADIUM
Basel, Switzerland
Project 1996

NO.145 ART BOX BONN,
MUSEUM FOR THE GROTHE COLLECTION
Bonn, Germany
Project 1996 – 1997

NO.146 SITE STUDIES
FOR THE GABA-AREAL
Basel, Switzerland
Project 1996

NO.147 CONTRIBUTION TO
LA BIENNALE DI VENEZIA
6. Mostra Internazionale di Architettura:
Sensing the Future: The Architect as
Seismograph, International Pavilion,
Venice, Italy
Exhibition 15 September–17 November 1996

NO.148 ST. JAKOB-PARK BASEL, FOOTBALL
STADIUM, COMMERCIAL CENTRE AND
RESIDENCE FOR THE ELDERLY
Basel, Switzerland
Project 1996, 1998,
realization 1998–2002

NO.149 RUE DES SUISSES APARTMENT
BUILDINGS
Paris, France
Competition 1996,
project 1997–1998,
realization 1999–2000

NO.150 THE OBERRHEINGRABEN
Region Oberrhein, Germany
Study 1996–1997

NO.151 KÜPPERSMÜHLE MUSEUM,
GROTHE COLLECTION
Duisburg, Germany
Project 1997,
realization 1997–1999

NO.152 THE VIRTUAL HOUSE
New York, New York, USA
Project 1996–1998

PROJECTS 153–172 ARE PRESENTED
IN VOLUME 4 HERZOG & DE MEURON
1997–2001.

NO.153 EXPANSION OF THE AARGAUER
KUNSTHAUS
Aarau, Switzerland
Competition 1996–1997,
project 1998–1999,
realization 2001–2003

NO.154 RICOLA MARKETING BUILDING
Laufen, Switzerland
Project 1997,
realization 1998–1999

NO.155 EXPANSION OF THE MUSEUM
OF MODERN ART
New York, New York, USA
Competition 1997

NO.156 HERZOG & DE MEURON:
ZEICHNUNGEN DRAWINGS
Peter Blum Gallery,
New York, New York, USA
Exhibition 31 May–31 July 1997

**NO.157 ARCHITECTURES OF
HERZOG & DE MEURON.
PORTRAITS BY THOMAS RUFF**
TN Probe Exhibition Space,
Tokyo, Japan
Exhibition 22 November 1996–9 January 1997
**NO.158 KRAMLICH RESIDENCE
AND COLLECTION**
Oakville, California, USA
Project 1997–2003, 2004–2007,
realization 2007–2017
NO.159 CRYSTAL RING
Realization 1997
NO.160 LABAN DANCE CENTRE
London, UK
Competition 1997,
project 1998–1999,
realization 2000–2003
NO.161 MULTIPLEX CINEMA HEUWAAGE
Basel, Switzerland
Competition 1997–1998,
project 1998, 2000
**NO.162 TRADE FAIR BASEL,
NEW TOWER AND SQUARE**
Basel, Switzerland
Competition 1998
NO.163 PUERTO DE SANTA CRUZ
Santa Cruz de Tenerife,
Canary Islands, Spain
Competition 1998,
project 1999–2004,
realization 2007–
**NO.164 TEA, TENERIFE ESPACIO
DE LAS ARTES**
Santa Cruz de Tenerife,
Canary Islands, Spain
Project 1999–2007,
realization 2002–2008
**NO.165 REHAB BASEL, CENTRE FOR
SPINAL CORD AND BRAIN INJURIES**
Basel, Switzerland
Competition 1998,
project 1998–1999,
realization 1999–2002
**NO.166 IKMZ BTU COTTBUS,
INFORMATION, COMMUNICATIONS AND
MEDIA CENTRE, BRANDENBURG
UNIVERSITY OF TECHNOLOGY**
Cottbus, Germany
Competition 1993,
project 1998–1999, 2001,
realization 2001–2004
NO.167 HOUSE ABOVE LAKE CONSTANCE
Lake Constance, Switzerland
Project 1998–2005,
realization 2001–2005
**NO.168 HELVETIA, EXTENSION OF HEAD
OFFICE, SOUTH AND EAST WING**
St. Gallen, Switzerland
Competition 1989,
project 1998–1999,
realization 2000–2002
**NO.169 SCHAULAGER,
LAURENZ FOUNDATION**
Münchenstein/Basel, Switzerland
Project 1998-1999,
realization 2000-2003
**NO.170 REFURBISHMENT
OF AN OFFICE FLOOR**
Basel, Switzerland
Project 1998
**NO.171 JACK S. BLANTON
MUSEUM OF ART**
Austin, Texas, USA
Competition 1998
NO.172 STUDIOS FOR TWO ARTISTS
Düsseldorf, Germany
Project 1998–2000,
realization 2000–2002
NO.173 DE YOUNG MUSEUM
Golden Gate Park,
San Francisco, California, USA
Competition 1999,
project 2000–2002,
realization 2002–2005
**NO.174 HELVETIA, EXTENSION
OF HEAD OFFICE, NORTH WING**
St. Gallen, Switzerland
Competition 1989,
project 1999–2001,
realization 2001–2004
NO.175 WALKER ART CENTER, EXPANSION
Minneapolis, Minnesota, USA
Project 1999–2002,
realization 2003–2005
NO.176 RÉFECTOIRE
Pomerol, France
Project 2001,
realization 2002
NO.177 ASTOR PLACE HOTEL
New York, New York, USA
Project 2000–2001
NO.178 PRADA AOYAMA
Tokyo, Japan
Project 2000–2002,
realization 2001–2003
NO.179 SCHÄLLEMÄTTELI URBAN STUDY
Basel, Switzerland
Competition 2000
**NO.180 ELSÄSSERTOR II,
OFFICE AND COMMERCIAL BUILDING**
Basel, Switzerland
Project 2000,
realization 2002–2005

**NO.181 OFFICE BUILDING
IN NORTHWESTERN SWITZERLAND**
Switzerland
Project 2000–2001,
realization 2002–2003
NO.182 PLAZA DE ESPAÑA
Santa Cruz de Tenerife,
Canary Islands, Spain
Competition 1998,
master plan 1999–2001,
project 2002–2005,
realization 2006–2008
**NO.183 HERZOG & DE MEURON.
ARCHÉOLOGIE DE L'IMAGINAIRE**
Canadian Center for Architecture,
Montreal, Canada
Exhibition 23 October 2002–6 April 2003
**NO.184 PRADA LE CURE,
PRODUCTION CENTRE AND WAREHOUSE**
Terranuova, Arezzo, Italy
Project 2000–2001
**NO.185 PRADA NEW YORK,
HEADQUARTERS PRADA USA**
New York, New York, USA
Project 2000–2002
**NO.186 HERZOG & DE MEURON:
IN PROCESS**
Walker Art Center,
Minneapolis, Minnesota, USA
Exhibition 4 November 2000–11 February 2001
**NO.187 PRADA LEVANELLA,
WAREHOUSE AND DISTRIBUTION CENTRE**
Montevarchi, Arezzo, Italy
Project 2000–2002, 2004
**NO.188 CONCERT HALL,
EUROPEAN MONTH OF MUSIC**
Basel, Switzerland
Project 2000–2001,
realization 2001
NO.189 HOSANNA WINERY
Pomerol, France
Project 2001–2003
NO.190 FORUM 2004 BUILDING AND PLAZA
Barcelona, Spain
Competition 2000,
project 2001–2002,
realization 2002–2004
**NO.190.2 MUSEU BLAU,
MUSEU DE CIÈNCIES NATURALS
DE BARCELONA**
Barcelona, Spain
Project 2009–2010,
realization 2010–2012
NO.191 TATE MODERN, MODIFICATIONS
London, UK
Project 2001,
realization 2001–2002, 2005
**NO.192 OSLOSTRASSE
PHOTOGRAPHIC COLLECTION**
Münchenstein, Switzerland
Project 2001,
realization 2001
**NO.193 ST. JOHANNS-VORSTADT,
OFFICE CONVERSION**
Basel, Switzerland
Project 2001,
realization 2002
**NO.194 WORKS IN PROGRESS:
PROJECTS BY HERZOG & DE MEURON
AND REM KOOLHAAS/OMA**
Fondazione Prada, Milan, Italy
Exhibition 2 March–8 April 2001
NO.195 ST. JOHANNS-RHEINWEG
Basel, Switzerland
Project 2001–2007,
realization 2005–2007
**NO.196 EXPANSION OF THE
KUNSTMUSEUM BASEL**
Basel, Switzerland
Competition 2001
NO.197 URBAN STUDY
Germany
Project 2001
NO.198 HOUSE ON LAKE TEGERNSEE
Tegernsee, Germany
Project 2001
**NO.199 EXPANSION OF THE CANTONAL
LIBRARY AARGAU**
Aarau, Switzerland
Project 2001–2002
NO.200 MUSEUM DER KULTUREN
Basel, Switzerland
Project 2001–2010,
realization 2008–2010
NO.201 CAIXAFORUM MADRID
Madrid, Spain
Project 2001–2003,
realization 2003–2008
NO.202 URBAN STUDY
Basel, Switzerland
Project 2001–2005
NO.203 DAVINES HEAD OFFICE
Parma, Italy
Project 2002–2003
**NO.204 BASEL DREISPITZAREAL,
URBAN STUDY**
Basel, Switzerland
Project 2001–2002, 2003
NO.205 ALLIANZ ARENA
München-Fröttmaning, Germany
Competition 2001–2002,
project 2002–2004,
realization 2002–2005
NO.206 SWISS CHURCH
London, UK
Project 2001

**PROJECTS 207–266 ARE PRESENTED
IN VOLUME 5 HERZOG & DE MEURON
2002–2004.**

NO.207 HOTEL ASTORIA LUZERN
Lucerne, Switzerland
Project 2002,
realization 2005–2007
NO.208 PRIVATE RESIDENCE
Bottmingen, Switzerland
Project 2002
NO.209 HIGH-RISE STUDY
Basel, Switzerland
Project 2002
NO.210 FELDMÜHLEPLATZ
Düsseldorf, Germany
Project 2002
**NO.211 PALACIO DE LA MUSICA
Y LAS ARTES ESCÉNCIAS**
Vitòria, Spain
Competition 2002
NO.212 CENTRE DE SERTISSAGE
Cormondrèche, Switzerland
Project 2002
NO.213 MESSE BASEL – NEW HALL
Basel, Switzerland
Project 2004–2012,
realization 2010–2013
NO.214 SÜDPARK BAUFELD D
Basel, Switzerland
Competition 2002,
project 2004–2011,
realization 2008–2012
NO.215 NATURAL HISTORY MUSEUM
Los Angeles, California, USA
Competition 2002
**NO.216 THE SHAIK ZAYED BIN SULTAN
AL NAHYAN MOSQUE**
Abu Dhabi, UAE
Project 2002
NO.217 MERCURY VILLAGE
Moscow, Russia
Project 2002
NO.218 PROJECT STUDY
Switzerland
Project 2003–2004
**NO.219 STUDY HOCHSCHULPLANUNG
BASEL**
Basel, Switzerland
Project 2002–2003
NO.220 PRIVATE RESIDENCE
London, UK
Project 2002–2003,
realization 2003–2004
**NO.221 CONTRIBUTION TO
LA BIENNALE DI VENEZIA**
8. Mostra Internazionale di Architettura:
Next
Arsenale, Venice, Italy
Exhibition 3 September–3 November 2002
NO.222 URBAN STUDY
Basel, Switzerland
Project 2002
NO.223 URBAN STUDY
Shantou, China
Project 2002–2003
**NO.224 ANTWERP DRY DOCKS,
CULTURAL CENTRE**
Antwerp, Belgium
Competition 2003
NO.225 ROCHE BUILDING 95
Roche Basel Site, Basel, Switzerland
Project 2003–2005,
realization 2004–2006
**NO.226 NATIONAL STADIUM,
THE MAIN STADIUM
FOR THE 2008 OLYMPIC GAMES**
Beijing, China
Competition 2002–2003,
project 2003–2005,
realization 2003–2008
NO.227 SCHATZALP
Davos, Switzerland
Project 2003–2005
NO.228 URBAN STUDY
Shantou, China
Project 2003
**NO.229 EXPANSION ENGINE DEPOT
AUF DEM WOLF**
Basel, Switzerland
Project 2003
NO.230 ELBPHILHARMONIE HAMBURG
Hamburg, Germany
Project 2001–2014,
realization 2006–2016
NO.231 ST. ANDREAS
Cham, Switzerland
Project 2003–2005
NO.232 GREENGATE HOUSE
London, UK
Project 2003–2005
NO.233 HOSPITAL DE LA ALBAIDA
Córdoba, Spain
Project 2003–2004
NO.234 COUNTRY HOUSE
Ascott, UK
Competition 2003
NO.235 AVIC-PLAZA HIGH-RISE BUILDING
Shenzhen, China
Project 2003
**NO.236 JINDONG
NEW DEVELOPMENT AREA**
Jinhua, Zhejiang, China
Project 2003–2006

NO.237 PRIVATE FOUNDATION
Porrentruy, Switzerland
Project 2003
NO.238 PROJECT STUDY
Austria
Project 2003–2004
**NO.239 LONDON OLYMPICS
MASTER PLAN 2012**
London, UK
Competition 2003
NO.240 CIUDAD DEL FLAMENCO
Jerez de la Frontera, Spain
Competition 2003,
project 2004–2006,
realization 2005–
NO.241 CENTRE POMPIDOU METZ
Metz, France
Competition 2003
NO.242 SAINT-LOUIS URBAN STUDY
Saint-Louis, France
Project 2003–2004
**NO.243 HELVETIA,
EXTENSION OF HEAD OFFICE,
WEST WING**
St. Gallen, Switzerland
Competition 1989,
project 2003–2004
**NO.244 UNIVERSITY CHILDREN'S
HOSPITAL BASEL**
Basel, Switzerland
Competition 2003
NO.245 ST. JAKOB TOWER
Basel, Switzerland
Project 2003–2005,
realization 2006–2008
NO.246 URBAN STUDY
London, UK
Project 2003
NO.247 TREE VILLAGE CAMPUS
Beijing, China
Project 2003–2004
NO.248 PRIVATE HOUSE
Bickleigh, UK
Project 2003–2005,
realization 2005–2006
NO.249 NEW STADTCASINO BASEL
Basel, Switzerland
Competition 2003
**NO.250 HERZOG & DE MEURON:
NO. 250. AN EXHIBITION**
Schaulager, Münchenstein/Basel, Switzerland
Exhibition 8 May–12 September 2004
NO.251 OFFICE BUILDING REVALUATION
Basel, Switzerland
Project 2004–2008
NO.252 HOUSE ON THE CLIFF
Ibiza, Spain
Project 2004–2005
NO.253 40 BOND, APARTMENT BUILDING
New York, New York, USA
Project 2004–2005,
realization 2006–2007
NO.254 NATIONAL MUSEUM OF CHINA
Beijing, China
Competition 2004
NO.255 HOCKER
Basel, Switzerland
Realization 2004
**NO.256 SWEET DREAMS, LANDSCAPE #1
AND TOOLS #1, EDITION 1**
Basel, Switzerland
Edition 2004
NO.257 MAAG TOWER
Zurich, Switzerland
Competition 2004
NO.258 TPT, THREE PARTNERSHIP TOWER
Beijing, China
Project 2004–2005
**NO.259 LEARNING CENTRE,
ÉCOLE POLYTECHNIQUE FÉDÉRALE
DE LAUSANNE**
Ecublens, Switzerland
Competition 2004
NO.260 ST. PAUL'S WAY
London, UK
Project 2004–2007
NO.261 JINHUA STRUCTURE
Jinhua, China
Project and realization 2004–2005
NO.262 CASINO LAS VEGAS
Las Vegas, Nevada, USA
Project 2004
NO.263 THE TATE MODERN PROJECT
London, UK
Competition 2005,
project 2005–2012,
realization 2010–2016
NO.264 DONAU CITY TOWER 2
Vienna, Austria
Project 2004–2005
NO.265 RINDERHALLEN ST. MARX
Vienna, Austria
Project 2004
NO.266 BURGOS MASTER PLAN
Burgos, Spain
Project 2004–2006,
planned completion 2008–2020

No.267
Private Residence
Riehen, Switzerland

2005–2006

In 1921 the homeowners' cooperative Gartenfreund built a large number of properties at the edge of Riehen, with dwellings in different sizes but all drawing on traditional materials, typologies, and styles – including pitched roofs. One of these houses might be demolished by its new owner. Instead the architects propose careful renovation and the construction of a separate extension, which will enter into respectful but bold dialogue with the existing structure. The pitched roof thus continues in the extension and, with what looks like a generous entrance arch on the ground floor, the extension preserves the spectacular view looking west that the original loggia has always had of the city of Basel. However, in its execution, the extension departs as far as possible from traditional craft techniques. In accor-

dance with proximity regulations the new extension is built very close to the old house, but does not touch it. Its main feature is a turret staircase that is developed entirely digitally and cut from wood using the latest technology. A geometric template is created on the basis of human motion sequences and dimensions; this virtual template is then applied to the drawings. Lines are defined according to need. The resulting pattern is implemented three-dimensionally and generates the shapes of windows, niches, doors, seating areas, and the pattern of the doorscreen in front of a glass door. The turret, which was split into four sections in the factory, is delivered to the site and reassembled. It now stands like a peg in the shared, reinforced-concrete foundations of the old house and the new extension. The rest of the new extension is a lightweight construction on a steel frame, which is attached to the turret. Wood and loam floors provide a comfortable interior ambience. The architects have already tested this combination of digital design, precision cutting, and on-site assembly in their inhabitable Jinhua sculpture; here it has evolved into a dwelling space with internal rooms.

Project Phases

Concept Design
2005

Schematic Design
2005

Design Development
2005

Construction Documents
2005–2006

Construction Services
2005–2006

Project Team

Partner
Jacques Herzog
Pierre de Meuron

Project Team
Philippe Fürstenberger
(Associate)
Ines Huber
Roman Aebi, Renata
Arpagaus, Lukas Baumann,
Volker Helm, Daniela Hofer,
Julian Löffler, Mario Meier,
Günter Schwob, Thomas
Strebel, Iwan Zanzotti,
Claudia Zipperle

Planning

Architect
Herzog & de Meuron,
Basel, Switzerland

Executive Architect
Herzog & de Meuron,
Basel, Switzerland

Construction Management
Proplaning AG,
Basel, Switzerland

Electrical Engineering
Herzog+Kull AG, Beratende
Energie-Ingenieure,
Basel, Switzerland

HVAC Engineering
Waldhauser Haustechnik,
Basel, Switzerland

Landscape Design
August Künzel
Landschaftsarchitekten AG,
Basel, Switzerland

Plumbing Engineering
Bogenschütz AG,
Basel, Switzerland

Structural Engineering
WGG Schnetzer
Puskas Ingenieure,
Basel, Switzerland

Specialists/Consultants

Geotechnics
Kiefer & Studer AG,
Reinach, Switzerland

Timber Construction
Steiner Jucker Blumer AG/
Creation Holz,
Herisau, Switzerland

Building Data

Site Area
2,177 sqm

Gross Floor Area
400 sqm

Building Footprint
157 sqm

Gross Volume
1,300 cubic meters

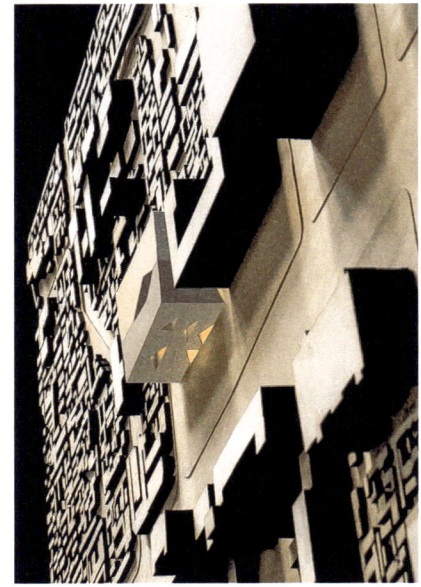

No.268
MK2, City of Image and Sound
Beijing, China

2005

French cineaste Marin Karmitz, founder of the production company and movie theater chain MK2, champions independent cinema; for many years now he has also fostered connections between his venues and other cultural institutions such as libraries, lecture theaters, and cafés. He has joined forces with the Chinese enterprise group BBMG in the construction of a multiplex cinema as part of the City of Image and Sound on the prestigious Chang'an Avenue, close to the Forbidden City. The new cultural center in this prime location will comprise fourteen movie theaters, exhibition spaces for photography, cafés, and office buildings for the headquarters of BBMG. Herzog & de Meuron create two distinct realms with different

functions. Fronting the avenue are the public movie theaters, stacked in three layers. Behind them there are seven stories of retail units and offices. Between the two realms there is a thirty-meter-high central lobby, spanning both sets of buildings and with openings looking out in different directions. The triangular shapes of the openings are derived from the geometry of the movie theater auditoriums with their raked seating; they look like negative volumes that have been removed from the solid block – almost like eyes in a pumpkin lantern. Inside the movie complex these voids serve as lobbies for different movie theaters and as freely accessible terraces, and a photography gallery is inserted into the office complex. In addition to the movie theaters and the offices, the whole complex also has a third geometric structure, which contains a loft space and a "cave." This archaic-looking project combines sculptural elements with an early version of stacked volumes. However, development work on the project came to an end when the authorities refused to grant the client the lease for this site.

Project Phases

Concept Design
2005

Project Team

Partner
Jacques Herzog
Pierre de Meuron

Project Team
Mia Hägg (Associate)
Vladimir Pajkic

Client
MK2, Paris, France
BBMG, Beijing, China

Building Data

Site Area
7,000 sqm

Gross Floor Area
50,000 sqm

Building Footprint
3,000 sqm

2005

No. 269
Beijing Film Academy Qingdao
Qingdao, China

Project Phases	
Concept	
2005	

Stephan Achermann,
Anna Jach, Sunkoo Kang,
Philipp Schaerer, Iva
Smrke, Thomas Wyssen

Bibliography • MK2, City of Image and Sound, in: a+u 2006.

Project Team	
Partner	
Jacques Herzog	
Pierre de Meuron	
Project Team	
Stefan Marbach (Associate)	
Yong Huang, Dieter Mangold,	
Roland Rossmaier, Xinyuan	
Wang, Thomasine Wolfens-	
berger, Pim van Wylick	
Collaboration	
Ai Weiwei, Beijing, China	

Client
Qingdao Omnipresent
Culture Development
Corporation Limited,
Qingdao, China

Bibliography • Beijing Film Academy Qingdao, in: a+u 2006 • Escuela de Comunicación Audiovisual, Qingdao, School of Creative Media, Qingdao. Herzog & de Meuron, in: AV Monographs 109/110, 2004.

Gross Volume
189,000 cubic meters
Building Dimensions
Length 105m
Width 60m
Height 30m

Planning
Architect
Herzog & de Meuron,
Basel, Switzerland
Mechanical Engineering
Waldhauser Haustechnik AG,
Basel, Switzerland
Structural Engineering
WGG Schnetzer
Puskas Ingenieure AG,
Basel, Switzerland

Building Data
Site Area
340,000 sqm
Gross Floor Area
228,480 sqm

2005

No. 270
Urban Study Heuwaage
Basel, Switzerland

Ever since the first Celtic settlement in this area, the Birsig River has crucially influenced the development of the Old Town in Basel. Nowadays, in the historical center of the town, it has been channeled and banished underground. Herzog & de Meuron have proposed a series of projects for Marktplatz, Rüdenplatz, and Stadtcasino that would see the river reemerging below the Münsterhügel as the focal point of this valley town; however, their proposals have not found favor with the local politicians.

Project Phases	
Concept	
2005	

Project Team	
Partner	
Jacques Herzog	
Pierre de Meuron	
Project Team	
Astrid Peissard (Associate)	
Lara Semler	

Client
Baudepartement des
Kantons Basel-Stadt,
Hochbau- und Planungsarnt,
Basel, Switzerland

Their Urban Study Heuwaage is yet another attempt to instigate a small-scale improvement. In the area near Basel Zoo the Birsig still flows in full view in its own river bed, before disappearing underground until the point where it joins the Rhine. The transition between the two sections is an ugly conglomeration of residual spaces between the City Ring, an exit ramp, and a parking lot. Herzog & de Meuron suggest extending the zoo and the green strip along the river further toward the city center. This extension would terminate in a small park, which would also accommodate the turning loop needed by the trams. Small structures, including an aviary and a café bar, would mark the point where the river disappears from view; the parking lot would be removed. The architects have previously developed a proposal for a Heuwaage multiplex cinema at this awkward juncture.

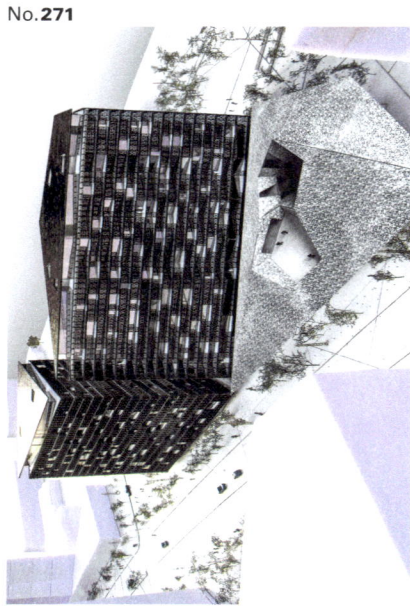

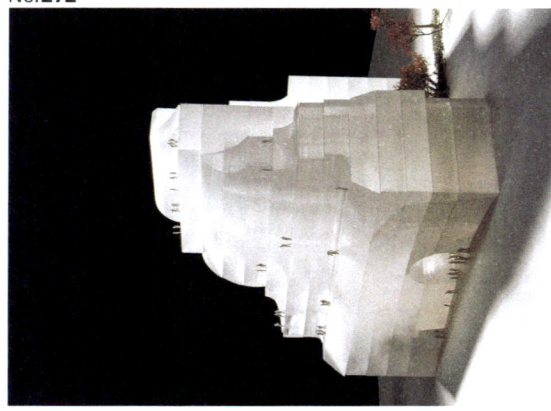

2005–2007

No. 271
Torres Burgos
Burgos, Spain

Project Phases

Concept Design
2005–2006

Schematic Design
2006

Design Development
2006–2007

Construction Documents
2007

Client
Consorcio para la Gestión
de la Variante Ferroviaria
de Burgos, Burgos, Spain

Project Team

Partners
Jacques Herzog
Pierre de Meuron
Christine Binswanger

Project Team
Peter Ferretto (Associate)
David Koch (Associate)
Miquel Rodríguez (Associate)
Key Portilla-Kawamura
Marta Alonso Yebra, Thomas
Arnhardt, Benito Blanco
Avellano, Francisco de
Freitas, Eric Frisch, Silvia Gil,
José Gómez Mora, Ursula
Hürzeler, Martin Knüsel,
Natalia Miralles, Jaume
Prieto, Nuno Ravara, Ana
Maria Santos Lima, Mónica
Sedano Peralta, Miguel Silva
Ortiga, Gee Ghid Tse,
Thomas de Vries

Planning

Architect
Herzog & de Meuron,
Basel, Switzerland

**Electrical Engineering,
Mechanical Engineering,
Plumbing Engineering**
R. Urculo Ingenieros
Consultores,
Madrid, Spain

Structural Engineering
NB35 Ingeniería,
Madrid, Spain

Cost Consulting
Idom, Bilbao, Spain
Integral SA,
Barcelona, Spain

Specialists/Consultants

Facade Engineering
ENAR, Madrid, Spain

Fire Protection
Estudi GL Francesc Labastida,
Barcelona, Spain

Geology
Eptisa, Burgos, Spain

Building Data

Site Area
5,201 sqm

Gross Floor Area
49,597 sqm

Building Footprint
3,980 sqm

Gross Volume
175,000 cubic meters

Number of Levels
18 aboveground
3 belowground

Building Dimensions
Pavilion:
Length 64 m
Width 43 m
Height 8 m
West Tower:
Length 68 m
Width 28 m
Height 54 m
East Tower:
Length 53 m
Width 30 m
Height 54 m

Bibliography • Herzog & de Meuron trazará un Proyecto heterogéneo acorde con la Forma de Vida y la Gente de Burgos, in: El Correo de Burgos 10.02.2005 • Belén Delgado, El Bulevar tendrá siete Estilos adaptados al entorno urbano en sus 11 Kilómetros, in: Diario de Burgos 10.02.2005.

2005

No. 272
New Court
London, UK

A private bank wants to build new headquarters on the same site that it has long occupied in the heart of London. The cramped, rather small site has to be put to best use; the building itself has to reflect the status of this exclusive banking business. Although the existing structures can be demolished, the numerous remnants of a long history of building significantly reduce the scope for laying the foundations for a new building. Herzog & de Meuron, exploiting the maximum volume allowed by local planning regulations, develop a body that has the massive presence of a block of ice but that also lets light flood in. Taking inspiration from Christ

Church, Spitalfields by Nicholas Hawksmoor, Herzog & de Meuron stack different volumes and use sculptural techniques to create recesses and other details. The entrance from the single-lane street is at the apex of a shallow curve inward so that visitors can alight from vehicles in comparative privacy. Another entrance echoes the barrel vaults of an earlier building and similar arches in the surrounding area. An internal courtyard affords a view of St. Stephen's Church (on the neighboring plot) and forms a light court that extends the full height of the building, bringing daylight into the offices inside. A spiral staircase rises upward through the publicly accessible levels and creates vertical communication zones for the bank's employees. Recesses are used as terraces. Two passages connect the bank (a closed unit for security reasons) with its surroundings. The skilled use of space means that this twelve-story design provides over 14,000 square meters for the six hundred bank employees, more than the specified minimum of 12,000 square meters.

Project Phases

Competition
2005

Client
NM Rothschild, London, UK

Project Team

Partner
Jacques Herzog
Pierre de Meuron
Harry Gugger

Project Team
Michael Casey (Associate)
Iela Herrling, Heeri Song

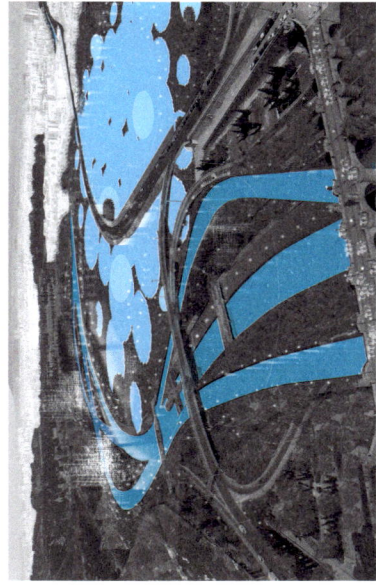

No.273
Rio Manzanares
Madrid, Spain

2005

As part of its urban renewal project the city of Madrid rerouted a section of its inner ring road underground. The road previously ran alongside the Rio Manzanares and the newly regained ground is to be used to increase the small amount of greenery in the Spanish capital. In their competition entry Herzog & de Meuron aim not only to create new green spaces but also to relate these to the wider context of the city. An analysis of the city's development showed that the Rio Manzanares in fact connects two natural landscapes with ample water, whereas Madrid itself is situated atop the Castilian desert plateau. Herzog & de Meuron's proposal echoes the way that the plateau in effect forms a bridge between the Sierra de Guadarrama in the north and the Rio Tajo—the longest river on the Iberian peninsula—in the south. The new green spaces relate Madrid to its wider geographic situation. The vegetation will also connect vertically with the huge, subterranean lake that lies under much of the Castilian plateau. Wherever the lake surfaces, settlements have sprung up like oases. Madrid is itself just such an oasis. The architects suggest liberating the river from its canal-like confines, which it was forced into for practical reasons during the nineteenth century, and restoring its earlier state with numerous tributaries. These would interconnect, creating islands and dry zones in the summer. At various points along the river, existing structures would be enhanced and given new uses. At the Royal Palace a new fountain would reference the subterranean reservoir, as would a new lake with bubbling springs at the Atlético Madrid stadium, which the city is planning to relocate. Buildings that once housed abattoirs provide space for cultural events and a bridge will become a whole new building. Far beyond the green spaces it will nurture, the liberated river would also play an important part in the urban landscape, as the city rejoins it and discovers new connections. In the midterm, as soon as the present utilization of industrial zones changes, the green strip could be extended to become a ring.

Project Phases

Competition
2005

Project Team

Partner
Jacques Herzog
Pierre de Meuron
Christine Binswanger

Project Team
David Koch (Associate)
Tomislav Dushanov
Blanca Castaneda, Yichun
He, Lara Semler, Masato
Takahashi, Pim van Wylick

Client

Ayuntamiento de Madrid,
Madrid, Spain

Planning

Architect
Herzog & de Meuron,
Basel, Switzerland

Hydrology Engineering
NB35 SL, Madrid, Spain
Surge Estudios Hidráulicos
e Hidrológicos SL,
Madrid, Spain

Bibliography • Herzog & de Meuron, Concurso Internacional Madrid Rio Manzanares, in: AV Proyectos 11, 2005.

No.274
Tristan and Isolde, Stage Design
Staatsoper Unter den Linden, Berlin, Germany

2005–2006

Project Phases

Project
2005–2006
Premiere
8 April 2006

Project Team

Partner
Jacques Herzog
Pierre de Meuron

Project Team
Claudius Frühauf

Client

Staatsoper Unter den
Linden, Berlin, Germany

Planning

Set Design
Herzog & de Meuron
Conductor
Daniel Barenboim
Director
Stefan Bachmann
Chorus Master
Eberhard Friedrich
Costume Design
Annabelle Witt
Dramaturgy
András Siebold
Light Design
Andreas Fuchs

Die Architekten Herzog & de Meuron stecken Wagners "Tristan" an Berlins Staatsoper in eine Unterdruckzelle, in: Die Welt 10.04.2006 • Benjamin Herzog, Willkommene Musik zum Tod, in: Basler Zeitung 10.04.2006 • Elenore Büning, Saug mal wieder, Macht der Pumpe! Liebe hinter Herzog & de Meurons Gummiwand, in: Frankfurter Allgemeine Zeitung 10.04.2006 • Robert Braunmüller, Im Nebel des Traums, in: Abendzeitung 10.04.2006 • Tristan mit Herzog & de Meuron, in: Münchner Merkur 09.04.2006 • Jörg Königsdorf/Jacques Herzog, Tristan in der Vakuumpumpe, in: Süddeutsche Zeitung 08.04.2006 • Hubertus Adam, In der Druckluftkammer, in: Archithese 3/2006 • Herzog & de Meuron, Tristan und Isolde. Ein Bühnenbild, in: Tristan und Isolde. Handlung in drei Aufzügen von Richard Wagner, Berlin 2006.

Bibliography • Luis Fernández-Galiano, Attila and Tristan, the Romantic Imagination, in: AV Monographs 157/158, 2012 • Ulrich Amling, O, sink hernieder, Nacht der Liebe, in: Partituren 16, 2008 • Basler Liebestod in Berlin. Herzog & de Meurons Bühnenbild für Tristan und Isolde, in: Baumeister 1/2007 • Tristan and Isolde, Stage Set, in: a+u 2006 • Die vakuumverpackte Oper, in: Art 6/2006 • Georg-Friedrich Kühn, Sorgen und Halluzinationen. Tristan mit Herzog & de Meuron und die Nöte der Berliner Opernstiftung, in: Neue Zürcher Zeitung 11.04.2006 • Wolfgang Schreiber, Das Erscheinen des Nullraums. Barenboim, Bachmann, Herzog & de Meuron meistern den "Tristan" in Berlin, in: Süddeutsche Zeitung 10.04.2006 • Kai Luehrs-Kaiser, Epochale Klassenfahrt ins Nichts.

No.**275**
Hotel Casino
Las Vegas, Nevada, USA

2005

At the height of the real estate boom, Las Vegas is seen as something of a gold mine. With themed hotels appealing to families and changing the reputation of the city in the desert, the aim is now that the city should trade on its weather, its range of entertainment, and its favorable tax laws to attract more permanent residents. The client wants to develop a huge plot of land, with three different complexes combining casino, hotel, and apartments. Herzog & de Meuron come up with a range of proposals that reinterpret the tradition of themed hotels with their instant recognizability. The first proposal "Leaning Slab" consists of two planes, opened like pages of a book, which give access to a plaza and a sunken pool area that stretches out in front of them, and is contained by a corso with retail outlets and a casino. The second proposal "Deck" envisages a second level (above the casino, pools, and hotel towers) with apartments grouped in smaller units, like a village, and enjoying wonderful, panoramic views. A "Pool Garden" is matched by a "Sky Garden." The architecture–indebted to both science fiction and archaeology–generates abstract images that combine surreal aspects of both the city and the desert. The archaism of the natural environment in Nevada is reflected most clearly in the third proposal "Fold." The horizontal plane containing public facilities, such as shops and a casino, is flipped up, like the screen of a laptop. In the fold there are plazas, beach zones, and open courts. Huge canyons and arcs are cut into the plane with its hotels and apartments. The complex, with its echoes of the desert, boasts gold-tinted glass facades of the kind that were later to become so popular in Las Vegas.

Project Phases
Concept
2005

Schematic Design
2005

Design Development
2005

Construction Documents
2006–2007

Construction Services
2006–2008

Project Team
Partners
Jacques Herzog
Pierre de Meuron
Ascan Mergenthaler

Project Team
Mia Hägg (Associate)
Mark Loughnan (Associate)
Vladimir Pajkic
Roman Aebi, Philip Fung,
Anna Jach, Sunkoo Kang,
Dirk Peters, Philipp Schaerer,
Chasper Schmidlin, Günter
Schwob, Iva Smrke, Pim
van Wylick

Client
Harmon Koval Partners LLC,
Las Vegas, Nevada, USA

Planning
Design Consultant
Herzog & de Meuron,
Basel, Switzerland

Associate Architect
Klai Juba Architects,
Las Vegas, Nevada, USA

Structural Engineering
WGG Schnetzer
Puskas Ingenieure AG,
Basel, Switzerland

Climate Engineering
Transsolar,
Stuttgart, Germany

Building Data
Site Area
83,600 sqm

Building Height
150 m

No.**276**
House above a Lake
Germany

2005–2008

Project Phases
Concept
2005

Project Team
Partner
Jacques Herzog
Pierre de Meuron
Robert Hösl

Project Team
Wolfgang Hardt (Associate)
Christoph Röttinger
Roman Aebi, Ida Basic, Lucas
Fernandez-Trapa Chias,
Mario Gasser, Yuko Himeno,
Katharina Mayr, Katja
Mezger, Günter Schwob,
Jochen Seelos, Kai Strehlke

Planning
Architect
Herzog & de Meuron,
Basel, Switzerland

Partner Architect
Muck Petzet Architekten,
Munich, Germany

**Electrical Engineering,
HVAC Engineering,
Plumbing Engineering**
Teuber + Viel
Ingenieurgesellschaft,
Munich, Germany

Landscape Design
Erdmann Kicherer,
Munich, Germany
Vogt Landschaftsarchitekten,
Zurich, Switzerland

Structural Engineering
WGG Schnetzer Puskas
Ingenieure AG,
Basel, Switzerland
Zilch und Müller Ingenieure,
Munich, Germany

Specialists/Consultants
Building Physics
PMI, Munich, Germany

Facade
R & R Fuchs,
Munich, Germany

Geometrician
Karner Ingenieur
Vermessung,
Munich, Germany

Geotechnics
Kraft + Dohmann Geotechnik,
Munich, Germany

Lighting
Andreas Heiland,
Munich, Germany

Building Data
Site Area
17,209 sqm

Gross Floor Area
Residence: 1,250 sqm
Studio: 1,145 sqm
Annex: 820 sqm

Gross Volume
Residence: 6,020 cubic meters
Studio: 4,440 cubic meters
Annex: 3,335 cubic meters

Building Dimensions
Residence:
Length 41 m
Width 12 m
Height 11 m
Studio:
Length 31 m
Width 14 m
Height 11.5 m

No.**277**
Parrish Art Museum
Water Mill, New York, USA

2005–2008

Ever since the late nineteenth century, the landscape at the far end of Long Island has been valued by artists for its especially bright light. Over the years artists have set up studios in old farm buildings and sheds. The Parrish Museum celebrates this local tradition and has a remarkable collection of around 2,600 works that significantly add to the overall picture of American art. The home in Southampton that Samuel Longstreth Parrish created for the collection in 1897 has long been too small. However, the museum board decided against a simple extension. Instead a new museum is to be built in Water Mill, around two miles away on land once used as a tree nursery, between the Montauk Highway and the tracks of the Long Island Rail Road. Herzog & de Meuron create a design that does justice to the spirit of this place, with its flat, austere landscape, its traditional agriculture and farm buildings, the sharp light, and the proliferation of artists' studios. They develop a concept consisting of a cluster of buildings, each fulfilling a particular function—from galleries and storage spaces to cafés, educational facilities, and more: a village where the houses are all interrelated but have their own individual, crystalline forms, arranged irregularly but interlinked by a network of connecting routes. The various buildings all have similarly textured, concrete exteriors (cast in situ) and large, deep-set windows that constantly create new links to the landscape (similar windows are seen in the refectory of a vineyard in Bordelais). Their shapes adapt freely to the layout of artists' studios in that area. The various exhibition spaces all have their own individual dimensions and lighting conditions. Four Anchor Rooms recall studios once used by William Merritt Chase, Fairfield Porter, Willem de Kooning, and Roy Lichtenstein, who are regarded in the Parrish Art Museum as particularly important for the development of the local art scene. A different project (No. 349) was eventually realized.

Project Phase
Competition
2005
Schematic Design
2006
Design Development
2006–2007
Construction Documents
2007–2008

Project Team
Partner
Jacques Herzog
Pierre de Meuron
Ascan Mergenthaler
Project Team
Jayne Barlow (Associate)
Michael Bekker
Dieter Mangold
Nathan Barnhart, Simon Demeuse, Daniel Johansson, Savannah Lamal, Severin Odermatt, Miquel Ortiga, Uta Schrameyer, Iva Smrke, Camia Young

Client
Parrish Art Museum,
Southampton, NY, USA

Planning
Design Consultant
Herzog & de Meuron,
Basel, Switzerland
Executive Architect
Handel Architects LLP,
New York, NY, USA
Electrical Engineering, Mechanical Engineering, Structural Engineering
Buro Happold,
New York, NY, USA
Civil Engineering, Environmental Engineering
Nelson & Pope
Engineers & Surveyors,
Melville, NY, USA
Furniture Design
KGID, Konstantin Grcic
Industrial Design,
Munich, Germany
Landscape Design
Herzog & de Meuron,
Basel, Switzerland
Landscape Executive Architect
Reed Hilderbrand
Landscape Architecture,
Watertown, MA, USA
Project Management
F.J. Sciame Construction
Co. Inc., New York, NY, USA

Specialists/Consultants
Acoustics
Shen Milsom Wilke,
New York, NY, USA
Facades
R.A. Heintges & Associates,
New York, NY, USA
Geotechnics
Langan, New York, NY, USA
Lighting
Arup Lighting,
New York, NY, USA/
London, UK
Security
Ducibella Venter & Santore,
North Haven, CT, USA
Fire Protection
Rolf Jensen & Associates, Inc.,
Chicago, IL, USA
Concrete Consulting
Reginald D. Hough,
Rhinebeck, NY, USA
Climate Engineering
Transsolar,
Stuttgart, Germany

Building Data
Site Area
56,000 sqm
Gross Floor Area
Phase 1: 3,900 sqm
Phase 2: 5,760 sqm
Building Footprint
Phase 1: 3,530 sqm
Phase 2: 5,110 sqm
Building Dimensions
Length 137 m
Width 76 m
Height 11 m

Bibliography • Parrish Art Center, in: Arkitekten 112, 2010 • Museo de Arte Parrish. Parrish Art Museum, in: AV Proyectos 25, 2008 • Javier Montes. Ampliación del Museo Parrish de Herzog & de Meuron, in: Arquitectura Viva 117, 2007 • Kate Taylor, The Parrish readies an expansion, in: The New York Sun 17.07.2007 • 277, in: Building Review 340, 2007 • Robin Pogrebin, The New Parrish Art Museum Was Designed With Light in Mind, in: The New York Times 23.07.2006 • Carol Vogel, Architect for the Parrish, in: The New York Times 05.08.2005.

No.**278**
Housing Study
Herrliberg, Switzerland

2005

The potential of a built-up plot in the heart of a residential district in a municipality on Lake Zurich is to be maximized. In a feasibility study Herzog & de Meuron explore the possibility of either converting and extending the existing dwelling houses, or of rebuilding more densely on the site. The architects investigate the potential for retaining the existing buildings and creating two or three new units from them. The alternative proposal, dubbed "Rebberg" ("vineyard"), involves terracing the slope. New polygonal structures interlock in rows and form a rhythmical sequence of lower and taller structures. The dense configuration of southern mountain villages provides visual inspiration.

→

No.**279**
1111 Lincoln Road
Miami Beach, Florida, USA

2005–2010

Project Phases	
Concept Design	
2005	

Planning	
Architect	
Herzog & de Meuron,	
Basel, Switzerland	

	Project Team
Partners	
Jacques Herzog	
Pierre de Meuron	
Harry Gugger	
Project Team	
Catherine Preiswerk	

Building Data	
Site Area	
1,488 sqm	
Gross Floor Area	
372 sqm	
Building Footprint	
190 sqm	

Project Phases	
Competition	
2005	
Schematic Design	
2005–2006	
Design Development	
2006	
Construction Documents	
2006–2008	
Construction Services	
2008–2010	

Client	
MBeach1 and	
Robert Wennett,	
Miami Beach, FL, USA	

	Project Team
Partners	
Jacques Herzog	
Pierre de Meuron	
Christine Binswanger	
Project Team	
Jason Frantzen	
Mark Loughnan (Associate)	
Nils Sanderson	
Charles Stone (Associate)	
Karl Blette, Christopher	
Haas, Yong Huang, Yuichi	
Kodai, Savannah Lamal,	
Paul Martinez, Mehmet	
Noyan, Caro van der Venne	

Planning	
Design Consultant	
Herzog & de Meuron,	
Basel, Switzerland	
Mechanical Engineering	
Franyie Engineers Inc.,	
Miami, FL, USA	
Structural Engineering	
Optimus Structural Design,	
Miami, FL, USA	
Landscape Design	
Raymond Jungles,	
Miami, FL, USA	
Civil Engineering	
Kimley Horn and Associates,	
Miami Beach, FL, USA	
Architect of Record	
Charles H. Benson &	
Associate Architects,	
Miami Beach, FL, USA	
Branding Consultant,	
Signage Concept	
Wolff Olins, London, UK	
Signage	
Tom Graboski Associates,	
Miami, FL, USA	
Pavilion	
Dan Graham	

Specialists/Consultants	
General Contractor	
G.T. McDonald	
Enterprises Inc.,	
Miami Beach, FL, USA	

Building Data	
Site Area	
Car park: 2,510 sqm	
Existing: 1,950 sqm	
Bank: 1,115 sqm	
Building Footprint	
Car park: 2,125 sqm	
Existing: 1,620 sqm	
Bank: 980 sqm	
Gross Floor Area	
Car park: 22,575 sqm	
Existing: 12,635 sqm	
Bank: 1,980 sqm	
Number of Levels	
Car park: 7, 1 mezzanine	
Bank: 2	
Building Dimensions	
Car park:	
Length 51.5 m	
Width 49.4 m	
Height 37.8 m	
Existing:	
Length 45.7 m	
Width 45.7 m	
Height 41.1 m	
Bank:	
Length 45.7 m	
Width 24.4 m	
Height 9.8 m	

Bibliography • Maria Shollenbarger, In Faena Fettle, in: Supplement, Financial Times 01.08.2015 • Finn Canonica, Man kann eine Stadt nicht einfach lassen, wie sie ist, sonst stirbt sie, in: Supplement, Das Magazin 25.04.2015 • Rowan Moore, Two Decades of Herzog & de Meuron, in: The Architectural Review 3/2015 • Till Briegleb, Sie machen die Ausnahme zur Regel, in: Häuser 2/2015 • Raymond Ryan, Herzog & de Meuron in Miami, in: Whitewall, Winter, 2015 • Marc Kushner, Can you get married in a parking garage?, in: The Future of Architecture in 100 Buildings, New York 2015 • Lincoln Road, Miami, USA, in: Pin-Up 17, 2014 • Jean-François Chevrier, Nature, Model of Complexity, in: The Return of Nature. Sustaining Architecture in the Face of Sustainability, New York 2014 • Urban Juxtapositions, in: CLOG: Miami, New York 2014 • Daniel Riera, The Dark Side, in: T. International Herald Tribune Style Magazine 16.03.2013 • Cedric van der Poel, Le Parking selon Herzog & de Meuron, in: Tracés 30.01.2013 • Vera Grimmer/Tadej Glažar/Jacques Herzog, Architecture is made by and for the People. Arhitekturu rade ljudi za ljude, in: Oris 79, 2013 • 1111 Lincoln Road, in: Car Parks, Hong Kong 2013 • Marie-Douce Albert, Le Parking Silo bouscule les Usages, in: Le Moniteur 11/2012 • Multiple desde varias Perspectivas, in: Summaand 125, 2012 • 1111 Lincoln Road, 2005–2010, Miami Beach (EE UU), in: AV Monographs 157/158, 2012 • Herzog & de Meuron. 1111 Lincoln Road, Miami Beach. Museum der Kulturen, Basilea, in: Plot 6/2012 • Cloe Piccoli, Interpretando as Cidades, in: Casa Vogue Brasil 318, 2012 • Philip Jodidio, Herzog & de Meuron. Raymond Jungles. Plaza de España. 1111 Lincoln Road, in: Architecture Now, Köln 2012 • Judith Paine McBrien, Miami Art Museum. 1111 Lincoln Road, in: Pocket Guide to Miami Architecture. New York/London 2012 • Jean-Marie Duthilleul, 1111 Lincoln Road, Miami Beach, United States, in: Circulate. When our Movements shape Cities, Paris 2012 • 1111 Lincoln Road, in: Details, Technology, and Form, New York 2012 • Benedikt Kraft, Rafael Moneo, una reflexion sobre el estilo, in: Arquitectura Viva 147, 2012 • Deutsche Bauzeitschrift 4/2011 1111 Lincoln Road, Miami Beach, von Herzog & de Meuron, in: Deutsche Bauzeitschrift 4/2011 • Gerhard Mack, Wer hier nur sein Auto parkt, ist selber schuld, in: Werk, Bauen+Wohnen 4/2011 • Christian Gänshirt, Architekturkritik und das Elend der Welt, in: Archithese 4/2011 • Silo Automóvel 1111, Lincoln Road, Miami Beach, in: Arqa 90/91, 2011 • Susanne Kippenberger, Schöner Parken, in: Der Tagesspiegel 30.01.2011 • Michael Barbaro, A Miami Beach Event Space. Parking Space, too, in: The New York Times 24.01.2011 • Maciej Lewandowski,

Parking 1111 Lincoln Road Miami Beach. Architektura poprzez technike. in: Architektura Murator 1/2011 • Miami Beach, USA, 1111 Lincoln Road, Parking, in: Iwan Baan. Around the World. Diary of a Year of Architecture, Hyères/Paris 2011 • Enrique Dominguez Uceta, Herzog & de Meuron, in: Descubrir el Arte 7, 2011 • Jörg Häntzschel, Ankommen und abfahren. Tour de Force aus Beton und Intelligenz, in: Süddeutsche Zeitung 15.12.2010 • Multi-storey Time. A tired Miami strip now houses the world's most beautiful parking lot, and more, in: Wallpaper 140, 2010 • Mario Carpo, Gli Scaffali per la Città. City Shelving, in: Abitare 506, 2010 • Tanya Homleid, The Art of Parking, in: Civil Engineering 10/2010 • 1111 Lincoln Road, Miami Beach, Florida, USA 2010, in: a+u 480, 2010 • Jean-François Lejeune, Die Mehrzweck-Parkgarage 1111 Lincoln Road, Miami Beach. Private Infrastruktur, öffentliche Architektur. The 1111 Lincoln Road Mixed-Use Parking Garage on Miami Beach. Private Infrastructure, Public Architecture. in: Architektur Aktuell 366, 2010 • Marie-Douce Albert, La Revue des Projects Parkings. Stationnement Sculptural. Sculptural Parking, in: L'Architecture d'Aujourd'hui 379, 2010 • Paul Goldberger, Wheelhouse. Herzog & de Meuron reinvent the Parking Garage, in: The New Yorker 09.08.2010 • Intelligent Architecture, in: Tabloid/Miami Art Museum 10, 2010 • 1111 Lincoln Road, in: Details, Seoul, 22, 2010 • Beth Broom, House of Cars. Herzog & de Meuron strips down in Miami Beach with a revealing new Parking Garage, in: Architectural Record 198, 2010 • Linda Lee, Is it finished? Herzog & de Meuron glorify the raw esthetics of the parking garage, in: Mark 26, 2010 • Silvio Carta, Let's go to the Parking Garage, in: C3, Seoul, 310, 2010 • Architekturszene, in: Architektur & Technik 6/2010 • James Cornetet, Die Schönheit des Parkens, in: Bauwelt 28.05.2010 • Mihail Moldoveanu, Caprice Suisse à Miami Beach?, in: Architecture Intérieure Créé 346, 2010 • Leen Creve/Pierre de Meuron, Een Tempel voor de Zintuigen, in: Knack Weekend 10.03.2010 • Edwin Heathcote, I spent a lot of time around the scruffy end of Lincoln Road, in: Icon 81, 2010 • Tim Barber, 1111, in: Intersection 17, 131, 2010 • 1111 Lincoln Road, in: El Croquis 152/153, 2010 • Virgilio Gutiérrez, Obra desnuda, in: Arquitectura Viva 130, 2010 • Edwin Heathcote, Grand Step Auto. A Car Park? Seriously? Architects Herzog & de Meuron say Yes, Seriously, in: Financial Times 19.12.2009 • Jacques Herzog/Lori Conner, Living Architecture, in: Nikki Style 23, 2007 • Andres Viglucci, Miami Beach: Famed architects add unique flair to garage plans, in: The Miami Herald 04.12.2005.

No. 280
Auditorium du Jura
Courgenay, Switzerland

2005–2006

Project Phases
Concept Design
2005–2006

Project Team

Partners
Jacques Herzog
Pierre de Meuron

Project Team
Mia Hägg (Associate)
Hans Focketyn
Roman Aebi, Jeroen
Hagendoorn, Sabine Hansky,
Mario Meier, Charlotte
von Moos, Vladimir Pajkic,
Dirk Peters, Günter Schwob,
Kai Strehlke, Benjamin
Wiederock

Client
Fondation Auditorium
du Jura,
Porrentruy, Switzerland

Planning

Architect
Herzog & de Meuron,
Basel, Switzerland

Structural Engineering
WGG Schnetzer
Puskas Ingenieure AG,
Basel, Switzerland

Cost Consulting
Proplaning AG,
Basel, Switzerland

Specialists/Consultants

Acoustics
Nagata Acoustics,
Tokyo, Japan

Fire Protection
Schweizerisches Institut
zur Förderung der Sicherheit,
Zurich, Switzerland

Scenography
dUCKS scéno,
Villeurbanne, France

Building Data

Site Area
157,680 sqm

Gross Floor Area
4,740 sqm

Building Footprint
2,016 sqm

Building Volume
27,930 cubic meters

Number of Levels
3

Building Dimensions
Length 48 m
Width 42 m
Height 30 m

Bibliography • Auditorium du Jura, in: Trou 18, 2008 • Herzog & de Meuron: Pirámide para el Jura, in: Arquitectura Viva 106, 2006 • Jacques Houriet/Michel Cattin, Je me sens frustré de ce que l'on fait de la Médecine, in: Le Quotidien Jurassien 17.06.2006 • Un Auditorium au Coeur du Jura, in: Batir 16.06.2006 • Rahel Marti/René Hornung, Zwei Klangfeuer entfacht, in: Hochparterre 6/2006 • Anna Schindler, Ein Markstein in der "stillen Zone", in: Sonntags-Zeitung 14.05.2006 • Hubertus Adam, Kultureller Triangulationspunkt, in: Neue Zürcher Zeitung 05.05.2006 • Caspar Schärer, Pyramide von Courgenay, in: Tages Anzeiger 05.05.2006 • Axel Simon, Schwebende Pyramide, in: Basler Zeitung 05.05.2006 • Monique Keller, Un Auditorium signé Herzog et de Meuron dans le Jura, in: Tribune de Genève 05.05.2006 • Pierre de Meuron, Nous défendons l'Idée du Fédéralisme, in: Tribune de Genève 05.05.2006 • Un merveilleux Projet d'Auditorium du Jura, in: Jura pluriel 49, 2006 • Marco Guetg, Ein Musentempel ist gelandet, in: Kultur & Gesellschaft 5/2006.

No. 281
ARTEM–Quartier Haussonville-Blandan
Nancy, France

2006

A former military site south of Nancy is to be repurposed in phases to accommodate various educational institutions—from a research center for nanotechnology to an art school. The different spatial requirements of these facilities might seem to suggest that each should have its own building, thus perpetuating the patchwork placement of the old barracks on the site. Herzog & de Meuron instead suggest concentrating the educational institutions in one place, thus releasing as much of the site as possible for use as parklands. According to their vision, this once

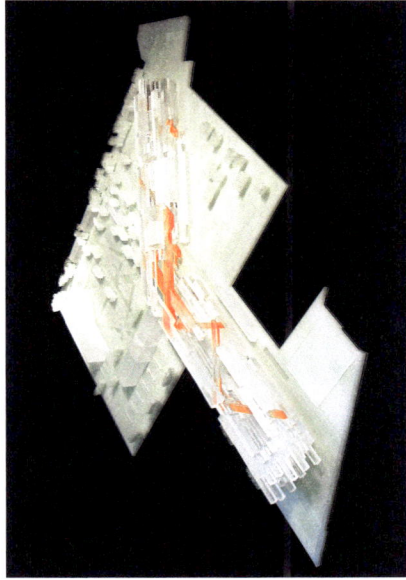

secluded site should become a place that connects with the surrounding residential districts and brings them closer together again. The first step would be to accommodate the École des Mines and the Jean Lamour Institute in the same building, which would set the tone on the grand scale. Two bodies, responding both to the urban setting and also to its natural boundaries, are joined together, forming an obtuse angle. They provide space for both institutions. At the intersection are the entrances to both buildings, also giving access to communal areas and an exhibition space. On their short sides, the two institutions look out toward the surrounding buildings. Here the units that make up the overall structure—like the multiple units of the Film Academy in Qingdao—are cantilevered outward. With its throughways, the building connects two plazas and contains within it a rich array of public facilities—restaurant, café, retail units, and a library—that are separate from the teaching and research facilities.

Project Phases
Competition
2006

Project Team

Partners
Jacques Herzog
Pierre de Meuron
Harry Gugger

Project Team
Mia Hägg (Associate)
Guillaume Delemazure
(Associate)
Nicolas Grosmond, Anna
Jach, Yuichi Kodai, Vladimir
Pajkic, Masato Takahashi,
Zachary Vourlas

Client
Solorem–Société Lorraine
d'Economie Mixte
d'Aménagement Urbain,
Nancy, France

Planning

Architect
Herzog & de Meuron,
Basel, Switzerland

**Construction Management,
Electrical Engineering,
Mechanical Engineering,
Cost Consulting**
Sirr Ingéniérie,
Metz, France

Landscape Design
WEST 8, Urban Design
& Landscape Architecture BV,
Rotterdam, Netherlands

Structural Engineering
WGG Schnetzer
Puskas Ingenieure,
Basel, Switzerland

Specialists/Consultants

Acoustics
Echologos,
Livry-Louvercy, France

Renderings
Philipp Schaerer,
Zurich, Switzerland

Sustainability
Tribu, Paris, France

Bibliography • Richard Scoffier, Artem, nouvelle école de Nancy? in: D'Architectures 159, 2006 • Concours Artem Nancy, in: AMC Le Moniteur Architecture 164, 2006.

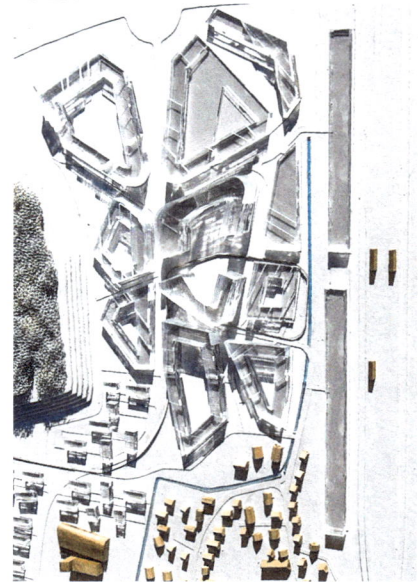

2005–2007

No.**282**
Espacio Goya
Zaragoza, Spain

Project Phases

Competition
2005–2006

Schematic Design
2006

Design Development
2006–2007

Construction Documents
2007

Project Team

Partners
Jacques Herzog
Pierre de Meuron
Christine Binswanger

Project Team
Peter Ferretto (Associate)
Carlos Gerhard (Associate)
Andreas Fries
Benito Blanco, Sergio Cobos
Álvarez, Heitor García
Lantarón, Silvia Gil, Andrea
Landell, Maria Ángeles Lerin
Ruesca, Diego Martínez
Navarro, Mateo Mori Meana,
Argel Padilla Figueroa, Maki
Portilla, Fran Rojo, Mónica
Sedano Peralta, Agustín
Solórzano

Competition Phase

Partners
Jacques Herzog
Pierre de Meuron
Christine Binswanger

Project Team
Tomislav Dushanov
Javier Artacho, Lara Semler,
Masato Takahashi, Thomas
de Vries

Client
Gobierno de Aragón,
Zaragoza, Spain

Planning

General Planning
Herzog & de Meuron,
Basel, Switzerland

Partner Architect,
Cost Consulting
Integral SA,
Barcelona, Spain

Electrical Engineering,
HVAC Engineering,
Mechanical Engineering,
Plumbing Engineering
Estudio PVI Ingeniería SL,
Barcelona, Spain

Structural Engineering
NB35 SL, Madrid, Spain

Specialists/Consultants

Acoustics
Estudi Acústic H. Arau,
Barcelona, Spain

Facade
Enar SL, Madrid, Spain
Jaume Avellaneda,
Barcelona, Spain

Fire Protection
Estudi GL
Francesc Labastida,
Barcelona, Spain

Lighting
Arup Lighting, London, UK

Building Data

Site Area
4,606 sqm

Gross Floor Area
14,924 sqm

Building Footprint
3,696 sqm

Gross Volume
55,192 cubic meters

Number of Levels
4

Building Dimensions
Length 80m
Width 57m + 25m (bridge)
Height 19m

Bibliography • Espacio Goya, in: AV Monographs 2012 • Espacio Goya, in: El Croquis 152/153, 2010 • Herzog & de Meuron, Not another new Museum, in: Casabella 768/8, 2008 • Javier Montes, Arte aguado. Una Colección al Aire libre, in: Arquitectura Viva 117, 2007 • Radical Minimalism, in: Fun Palace 1, 2007 • Roberto Miranda, Herzog: La Arquitectura tiene que penetrar el Arte de Goya, in: El Periódico de Aragón 03.04.2007 • Mariano García, Herzog y de Meuron suavizan su diseno para el edificio del futuro Espacio Goya, in: Heraldo de Aragón 07.02.2007 • Esperanza Pamplona, Creada una fundación para comprar, promocionar y divulgar la obra de Goya, in: Heraldo de Aragón 25.01.2007 • Rob Gregory, Herzog & de Meuron. Museum, Zaragoza, Spain, in: The Architectural Review 1319, 2007 • David Cohn,

Zaragoza prepares a Garden of Architectural Delights for 2008 World's Fair, in: Architectural Record 11/2006 • El Espacio Goya de Herzog & de Meuron, in: Arquitectura Viva 106, 2006 • Aluvión de Inauguraciones y Actos para celebrar el Día de los Museos, in: Heraldo de Aragón 19.05.2006 • Belén Boloqui, Traición a la Exposición 1908, in: Heraldo de Aragón 14.05.2006 • Mariano García, La exposición de los proyectos para el Espacio Goya despierta poco interés, in: Heraldo de Aragón 11.05.2006 • Mariano García, Cultura se mantiene firme en el proyecto de Espacio Goya, in: Heraldo de Aragón 10.05.2006 • Mariano García, Los arquitectos suizos Herzog y de Meuron diseñarán el futuro Espacio Goya, in: Heraldo de Aragón 06.05.2006.

2005–2006

No.**283**
Pôle de Développement Gare Ouest Technoport
Saint-Louis/Hésingue, France

On the French periphery of greater Basel, an area between the train tracks and the highway has been identified for development. The site, comprising gravel pits and wasteland, has extremely advantageous transport links: it is in close proximity to Basel-Mulhouse Airport, and a direct road link to Saint-Louis rail station is planned for the future. Accordingly, the large central zone at the site is not to be built up. Herzog & de Meuron propose that this area should become a golf course, for which they can already identify potential investors. They locate the new built areas at

either end of the development site and identify them with names. The "Cité des Affaires" is close to the airport. It is protected from the railway by apartment blocks that are fronted with buildings of various heights. The "Quartier de Lys" connects with the railroad station at Saint-Louis and is linked to the existing city by tree-lined boulevards and a new tram route. The overall configuration of the new structures, defined by thoroughfares and differentiated by ownership, takes the form of a flower, with distinctive views, heights, and public spaces in its various compo-nents. A nearby landfill site will become a green space. The architects' master plan proposes an alternative vision to the isolated modernist blocks, undefined green spaces, and shopping malls that characterize much of Saint-Louis. Ultimately, how-ever, the difficulties plaguing the efforts of the various communities to collaborate see this proposal founder, despite the evident appeal of the site's proximity to the center of Basel.

Project Phases

Concept
2005–2006

Project Team

Partners
Jacques Herzog
Pierre de Meuron

Project Team
Guillaume Delemazure
(Associate)

Client
Communauté de Communes
des Trois Frontières,
Saint-Louis, France

Planning

Architect
Herzog & de Meuron,
Basel, Switzerland

Partner Architect
Sutter+Laburte,
Saint-Louis, France

Specialists/Consultants

Traffic
Gruner AG,
Basel, Switzerland

Judit Chapallaz-Laszlo,
Samir Tarek El Kordy,
Charlotte von Moos,
Zachary Vourlas,
Benjamin Wiederock

Collaboration
Hans Wirz Raumplanung,
Basel, Switzerland

No. 284
Actelion Business Center
Allschwil, Switzerland

2005–2010

Project Phases	Project Team	Client	Planning	Specialists/Consultants	Building Data
	Partners	Actelion Pharmaceuticals	**Architect**	**Acoustics**	**Site Area**
Concept Design	Jacques Herzog	Ltd, Allschwil, Switzerland	Herzog & de Meuron,	Büro für Bau- und	7,611 sqm
2005	Pierre de Meuron		Basel, Switzerland	Raumakustik,	**Gross Floor Area**
Schematic Design	Stefan Marbach		**Partner Architect**	Langenbruck, Switzerland	27,469 sqm
2005–2006	**Project Team**		Proplaning AG,	**Building Physics**	**Building Footprint**
Design Development	Martin Fröhlich (Associate)		Basel, Switzerland	Zimmermann+Leuthe GmbH,	3,192 sqm
2006	Michael Fischer (Associate)		**General Planning,**	Aetigkofen, Switzerland	**Gross Volume**
Construction Documents	Enzo Augello, Peter Becker,		**Construction Management**	**Catering**	104,502 cubic meters
2006–2009	Gabriela Bertozzi Werner,		Arge GP Headquarters	Hosta AG,	**Facade Surface**
Construction Services	Martin Bittmann, Laetitia		Actelion, Basel, Switzerland	Basel, Switzerland	15,024 sqm
2007–2010	Buchter, Stephan Burger,		Herzog & de Meuron,	**Facade**	**Number of Levels**
	Oliver Franke, Thomas von		Basel, Switzerland	Emmer Pfenninger	6 aboveground
	Girsewald, Nikolai Happ,		Proplaning AG,	Partner AG,	2 belowground
	Fabienne Hoelzel, Debora		Basel, Switzerland	Münchenstein, Switzerland	**Building Dimensions**
	Hummel, Yasmin Kherad,		**General Contractor**	**Fire Protection**	Length 80 m
	Manuel Lucas Klauser,		Anliker AG	Swiss Institute of	Width 80 m
	Martin Krapp, Benno Lincke,		Bauunternehmung,	Safety and Security,	Height 21 m
	Sebastian Lippert, Kenan Liu,		Emmenbrücke, Switzerland	Zurich, Switzerland	
	My Long, Lush Manrecaj,		**Electrical Engineering**	**Geometrician**	
	Adriana Müller, Chasper		Karl Schweitzer AG,	Jermann	
	Padrutt, Michel Pauli, Ella		Allschwil, Switzerland	Ingenieure+Geometer AG,	
	Ryhiner, Gabriele Schell,		**HVAC Engineering**	Binningen, Switzerland	
	Hee-Jun Sim, Hendrik		Stokar+Partner AG,	**Geotechnics**	
	Steinigeweg, Moritz		Basel, Switzerland	Kiefer–Studer AG,	
	Thierfelder, Fabio Verardo,		**Landscape Design**	Reinach, Switzerland	
	Xinyuan Wang, Thomasine		Tita Giese,	**Irrigation System**	
	Wolfensberger, Daniel		Düsseldorf, Germany	Gysi+Berglas AG,	
	Zielinski		**Mechanical Engineering**	Baar, Switzerland	
			Transsolar,	**Security**	
			Stuttgart, Germany	Gruner AG	
			Plumbing Engineering	Ingenieure und Planer,	
			Locher, Schwittay	Basel, Switzerland	
			Gebäudetechnik GmbH,	**Traffic**	
			Basel, Switzerland	Rapp Infra AG,	
			Structural Engineering	Basel, Switzerland	
			WGG Schnetzer		
			Puskas Ingenieure AG,		
			Basel, Switzerland		

Bibliography • Actelion Business Center in Allschwil, CH, in: Ark 2/2012 • Actelion Business Center, in: Arper, Treviso 2012 • Douglas Murphy, Actelion Business Center, in: Icon 102, 2011 • Etappensieg für Actelion. Rechtsstreit in den USA, in: Basler Zeitung 25.10.2011 • Spencer Bailey, By creating inner harmony out of a chaotic exterior Herzog & de Meuron proves that appearances can be deceiving, in: Surface 10/2011 • Elisabeth Blum/Peter Neitzke, Kontrollierter Rausch, himmelstürzende Perspektiven, in: Baumeister 10/2011 • Katharina Marchal, Transparenz und Dynamik, in: Architektur Aktuell 378, 2011 • Katharina Marchal, Neu in Allschwil (CH). Actelion Business Center, in: Deutsche Bauzeitung 08/2011 • Astrid Rappel, Herzog & de Meuron. Siège Social d'Actelion, Allschwil, in: AMC Le Moniteur Architecture 207, 2011 • Patrick Valli, Gestapelte Ganzglas-"Bürobalken," in: Fassade 2, 2011

• Andres Herzog, Stapel zum Spektakel. Herzog & de Meuron stapeln Raumbalken zu einem imposanten Gebilde und stellen das inszenierte Chaos zur Schau, in: Hochparterre 4/2011 • Jacques Herzog: Stapeln als Prinzip, in: Hochparterre 4/2011 • 15n de l'Architecture Contemporaine. Un immense Appétit d'Architecture, in: Espaces Contemporains 4/2011 • Barras apiladas, Actelion Business Center, Allschwil, Basilea, in: Arquitectura Viva 134, 2010 • Heinrich Schnetzer: Wirkungsvoll kombiniert, in: Tec 21 15.01.2010 • Laurent Miguet, Un Centre d'Affaires traité comme un Jeu de Mikado, in: Le Moniteur 02.10.2009 • Herzog & de Meuron signent un manifeste de l'innovation, in: Le Moniteur 06.03.2009 • Markus Schär, Wir sind die letzten wahren Entdecker, in: SonntagsZeitung 08.06.2008.

2005

No. 285
Scandia Las Vegas
Las Vegas, Nevada, USA

At the height of the construction boom in Las Vegas, a plot of land on one of the main highways, parallel to the Las Vegas Strip, is to be developed. It will accommodate a mixture of casinos, retail outlets, hotels, and condominiums. Herzog & de Meuron come up with a solution that the client can implement in separate stages. An extensive base supports four towers, creating an uneven, atmospheric topography that recalls the weathered mountains and vertical rock formations of the nearby desert. The design combines two functionalities: in the base, between the towers, there are the public areas with shops and casinos, meanwhile the towers have parking levels with see-through, metal skins creating a cave-like feel, and lighting that almost makes parking into a pleasurable experience. The base and the towers together constitute a world of their own, with bars, restaurants, and a wide range of residential accommodation. A pool area is directly accessed from private, terraced homes (with direct links to the parking garage), which seem to collect at the feet of the residential towers like boulders in the foothills. Atriums, which evolve naturally from the geometry of the parking lot and the shape of the various sites, reach down into the parking zone like craters. The whole complex is conceived as a city of towers that translates geological formations into a habitable landscape.

Project Phases

Concept Design
2005

Project Team	**Client**
Partners	Ian Schrager Company,
Jacques Herzog	New York, NY, USA
Pierre de Meuron	
Ascan Mergenthaler	
Project Team	
Mia Hägg (Associate)	
Vladimir Pajkic	
Anna Jach, Sunkoo Kang,	
Dirk Peters, Stefano Rabolli	
Pansera, Zachary Vourlas	

Planning	**Building Data**
Design Consultant	**Site Area**
Herzog & de Meuron,	32,500 sqm
Basel, Switzerland	**Height**
Partner Architect	168m
Friedmutter Group,	
Las Vegas, NV, USA	

2005–2008

No. 286
Compendio Minerario di Monteponi
Iglesias, Sardinia, Italy

The Sardinian government is keen to develop a new kind of tourism that can flourish without new builds directly by the seashore. An old mine not far from the coast, which fell out of use in the 1980s and is now to be redeveloped, provides the perfect opportunity to exemplify the government's aspirations. A new tourist center will be built on a site where iron ore had once been mined by the Phoenicians. This new center will provide for a wide range of interests and will also be open to the local population. Dwellings for the locals and a wide range of hotels—from budget accommodation to five-star luxury—will rub shoulders with a local history museum, a conference center, and a university. The authorities stipulate that the total volume of the built structures on the site must not be increased. Having surveyed the existing structures, Herzog & de Meuron present a concept study proposing the restoration of viable buildings and the construction of a new horizontal block and a tower, which will echo and extend the existing structures. The positioning of the new buildings will create two new squares and open up views of points of interest in the landscape, in much the same way as the elongated, stacked blocks of the VitraHaus in Weil am Rhein. The facades, created by superimposing designs taken from existing facades around the site, will have recesses that can be used as niches. The subterranean world of caverns left by the mines will be accessible from both squares; the luminous red earth contaminated by heavy metals will be sealed off and incorporated into a golf course. A change of government halts the project.

Project Phases

Concept Design	Schematic Design
(Master Plan)	2007–2008
2005–2006	

Project Team	
Concept Design	**Schematic Design**
(Master Plan)	**Partners**
Partners	Jacques Herzog
Jacques Herzog	Pierre de Meuron
Pierre de Meuron	Stefan Marbach
Stefan Marbach	**Project Team**
Project Team	Thomasine Wolfensberger
Jayne Barlow (Associate)	(Associate)
Peter Ferretto (Associate)	Joana Anes, Dara Huang,
Stefano Rabolli Pansera	Andrea Landell, Betty Ng,
Jeroen Hagendoorn,	Sara Secci, Agustín
Sara Secci, Thomasine	Solórzano, Fumiko
Wolfensberger	Takahama, Claudia Zipperle

Client
IGEA SpA, Campo Pisano,
Iglesias, Italy

Planning	**Building Data**
Architect	**Site Area**
Herzog & de Meuron,	27,300 sqm
Basel, Switzerland	**Gross Floor Area**
Partner Architect	55,412 sqm
Studio Professionisti	
Associati srl, Cagliari, Italy	

Bibliography • Giuseppe Centore, Monteponi, Progetto di Qualità, in: La Nuova Sardegna 01.04.2008 • Giuseppe Centore, A Monteponi la nuova Porto Cervo, in: La Nuova Sardegna 14.03.2008 • Cinzia Simbula, Monteponi meglio di Porto Cervo, in: L'Unione Sarda 14.03.2008

• Giuseppe Centore, Miniere, ventiquattro mesi per le bonifiche, in: La Nuova Sardegna 13.03.2008.

No.**287**
Cultural Sports Park
Taipei, Taiwan

2005–2006

Not far from Taipei 101, at the time the tallest building in the world, a large area of parkland is to be developed for a variety of uses. In the center of the site there is an old tobacco factory, now partly overgrown by a profusion of tropical plants. Herzog & de Meuron want to retain this special atmosphere and base their concept on the courtyard of the deserted factory. In order that the site will not be fragmented by the new built structures, they create a functional, perimeter wall. The back of the stands in a baseball stadium adjoins the wall; the stadium itself faces the park. Another large structure—a block with apartments jutting out toward the road like pixels—is also placed directly on the perimeter. Existing buildings are repurposed: the hall where tobacco leaves were once dried will become a design school; the defunct warehouse will house performance spaces. Other buildings will contain cutting-edge retail outlets and a large lecture theater. A change of government stops the project in its tracks.

Project Phases	**Client**
Concept Design	Xue Xue Institute,
2005–2006	Taipei, Taiwan

Partners
Jacques Herzog
Pierre de Meuron
Stefan Marbach

Project Team
Tobias Winkelmann
Edman Choy
Tomislav Dushanov, Henrike
Elsner, Philip Fung, Henrik
Gruss, Jeroen Hagendoorn,
Volker Helm, Stefan Hörner,
Yong Huang, Yuichi Kodai,
Julian Löffler, Xiaojing Lu,
Jad Silvester, Xinyuan Wang,
Christian Zöllner

Planning	**Building Data**
Architect	**Site Area**
Herzog & de Meuron,	180,000 sqm
Basel, Switzerland	**Gross Floor Area**
Associate Architect	530,000 sqm
Fei Cheng & Associates,	**Building Dimensions**
Taipei, Taiwan	Length 357 m
Structural Engineering	Width 450 m
WGG Schnetzer	Height 57 m
Puskas Ingenieure,	**Height Stadium**
Basel, Switzerland	83 m

No.**288**
Prada Improbable Classics, Temporary Store
Basel, Switzerland

2006

Herzog & de Meuron have masterminded numerous projects for Prada. At the height of the luxury goods boom before the global financial crisis, the fashion house and the architects toy with the idea of extreme "dumping." They decide that in June 2006, during Art Basel, they will run a shop for one week that will epitomize everything Prada consistently avoids, i.e., it will be immediately at hand, like the blankets of immigrants in Italy peddling copies of Prada items, and random, like clearance stock being sold by a dealer from the back of his van. Moreover, the shop will be in a purely functional building like a garage, with no identity as such. A suitable venue is identified close to the architects' main office. The stock, specially manufactured for this event, is laid out on trestle tables, stacked in boxes, dangled from wire hangers. There could hardly be a greater contrast to Prada's flagship store in the Aoyama district of Tokyo, designed by the architects, and completed in 2003, as a "glass house" for the perfect staging of consumption as an iconic act. Yet there is also a connection between the two as expressions of a zeitgeist that always bows to the passing moment.

Project Phases	**Client**
Concept Design	Prada S.p.A.,
2006	Milan, Italy
Construction Services	
2006	
Temporary Store	
12 June–19 June 2006	

Partners
Jacques Herzog
Pierre de Meuron
Stefan Marbach

Project Team
Wolfgang Hardt (Associate)
Catherine Preiswerk
Bernhard König, Sara Secci

Building Data
Gross Floor Area
200 sqm

Bibliography • Herzog & de Meuron, Prada Improbable Classics—Prada Temporary Store, in: a+u 433, 2006 • Sithara Atasoy, Miuccia Prada überrascht während der Art, in: Bolero 9/2006

• Carol Vogel, At Basel Fair, High Rollers and Blue-Chip Artists, in: The New York Times 15.06.2006.

No.**289**
Roche Building 97
Basel, Switzerland

A line of six interlinked, north-facing buildings shields the Roche Basel Site from the apartment blocks on the opposite side of Wettsteinallee. In 2002 Herzog & de Meuron conduct a site study showing that there is scope here for a stepped structure: eighteen meters in height on the street side rising to forty meters in height on the side facing the center of the site. Since the company has to be flexible in its response to the challenges of the pharmaceuticals industry, the architects propose that the redevelopment plan should comprise a sequential series of individual buildings. Together with the planning authorities in Basel they devise principles that permit the under- or overoccupation of individual plots as long as the allowable gross internal floor space is not exceeded and minimum distances between buildings are preserved. Working with three basic shapes—box, shoe, and spreading

mushroom—the architects meet these conditions. In order to provide for a wide range of uses the first new structure, Building 97, takes advantage of the air rights of its future neighbor. The work in Building 97 will combine research and the manufacture of medicines in small batches for use in clinical trials. However, since the laboratories, production zones, and offices all have to serve different needs, the architects create a layer-cake structure: open layers with uninterrupted ribbon windows and external sun protection alternate with fully enclosed layers housing technical facilities. The latter are finished with smooth, white render and extend markedly further than the "open" floors. Inside, the infrastructure and small rooms are in the center with the larger rooms along the perimeter. The higher structures at the rear of the site can accommodate large halls that occupy the full width of the building. The varied cubature and the abstract, almost dematerialized appearance of the building give this sober structure—seemingly effortlessly—both strength and composure. Occasional design touches—the rounded entrance with a light shower, the supports, and ceilings made from fine, perforated metal—give the building a certain elegance.

Project Phases
Schematic Design
2006–2007
Design Development
2007
Construction Documents
2007–2008
Construction Services
2008–2011

Project Team
Partners
Jacques Herzog
Pierre de Meuron
Robert Hösl
Project Team
Stefan Segessenmann
(Associate)
Kord Büning-Pfaue
Roger Huwyler
Volker Jacob
Richard Wickli

Mark Bähr, Alexander
Bartscher, Axel Beck, Hans
Sebastian von Bernuth, Oke
Hauser, Wilhelm Heusser,
Deborah Hummel, Luis
Játiva, Gemma Koppen,
Lush Manrecaj, Klaus Marek,
Marcel Neuse, Tilmann
Noller, Jacqueline Pauli, Dag
Thies, Claudia Winkelmann,
Monika Zecherle, Maximilian
Zielinski

Client
F. Hoffmann–La Roche AG,
Basel, Switzerland

Planning
**Architect,
Construction Development**
Herzog & de Meuron,
Basel, Switzerland
Electrical Engineering
KIWI Systemingenieure
& Berater,
Dübendorf, Switzerland
Mechanical Engineering
M+W Process
Industries GmbH,
Nürnberg, Germany
Plumbing Engineering
IB Albrecht,
Gross Gerau, Germany
Cost Consulting
Proplaning Architekten AG,
Basel, Switzerland
Laboratory Planning
Dr. Heinekamp
Labor- und Institutsplanung,
Karlsfeld, Germany

Specialists/Consultants
Acoustics
Martin Lienhard,
Langenthal, Switzerland
Building Physics
Zimmermann+Leuthe,
Aetigkoven, Switzerland
Facade
Emmer Pfenninger
Partner AG,
Münchenstein, Switzerland
Geometrician
Roche (Ammann AG),
Basel, Switzerland
Security, Fire Protection
Sicherheitsinstitut,
Zurich, Switzerland

Building Data
Gross Floor Area
22,705 sqm
Building Footprint
1,691 sqm
Gross Volume
97,027 cubic meters
Facade Surface
6,729 sqm
Number of Levels
12
Building Dimensions
Length 61m
Width 30m
Height 40m

Bibliography · Susanne Sailer, Hell, modern und stimulierend, in: My Roche, Basel 2011
· TR & D Bau 97. Roche Forschungs- und Entwicklungsgebäude an der Wettsteinallee, Basel,
in: Das Baustellenbuch. Bauphase: Sommer 2008 bis Sommer 2011, Basel 2011.

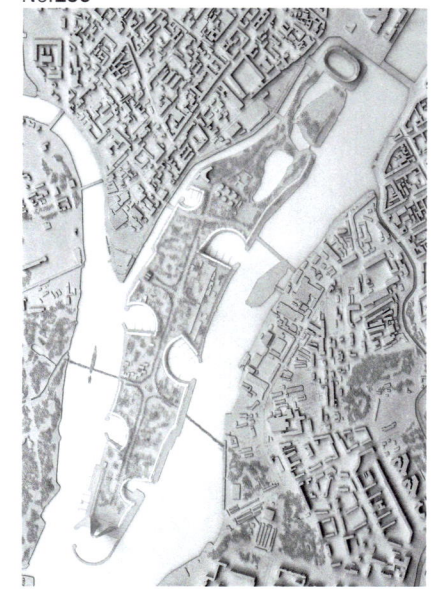

No.**290**
Petrovsky Island
St. Petersburg, Russia

When Herzog & de Meuron were commissioned to draw up a master plan for Petrovsky Island, they had already engaged with the architecture of St. Petersburg in connection with their teaching at Harvard University. This elongated island in the Neva delta is home (at its east end, closest to the city) to St. Petersburg's Zenit football club; it also has a number of factories and some contaminated wasteland. The majority of the island is unoccupied. The clients want to build high-value apartments and a limited number of office spaces on this island, taking advantage of its location at the edge of the historical city. Herzog & de Meuron treat the main con-

necting street as the central axis, marking it with a substantial, arched, office building that stands as a counterpart to the stadium. The island's considerable expanses of woodland and meadows are largely preserved; the apartments will be concentrated along the shoreline for economic reasons. Contaminated ground will be excavated at the same time, allowing polluted soil to be disposed of at minimum cost. The reclaimed areas can be used for marinas and promenades, surrounded by built structures up to fourteen stories high, of the kind seen in the South of France. The local inspiration for this concept is an early-twentieth-century marina at the Baltic Sea end of the island and older areas given over to agriculture. Private residences and villas will be sprinkled like sugar cubes on the green center of the island. A similar plan to combine the removal of contaminated substances with the creation of new urban areas, is seen in the architects' proposal for a water city to replace a landfill site in the Swiss city of Solothurn.

Project Phases
Concept Design
2006

Project Team
Partners
Jacques Herzog
Pierre de Meuron
Project Team
Mia Hägg (Associate)
Tomislav Dushanov
Yuichi Kodai, Young Lee,
Katharina Penner

Client
DLG Securities Ltd.,
Nikosia, Zypern
Nevsky Capital Partners,
St. Petersburg, Russia

Planning
Architect, General Planning
Herzog & de Meuron,
Basel, Switzerland

Building Data
Site Area
1,255,300 sqm
Gross Floor Area
1,509,642 sqm
Building Footprint
214,660 sqm
Number of Levels
1–50

No.**291**
Project Study
Nagoya, Japan

Following the Prada flagship store in Tokyo, this office tower is Herzog & de Meuron's second project in Japan. The site straddles the boundary between small-scale dwellings and tall, urban structures. Much like the process that would later lead to the first proposal for the expansion of the Central Police Station Compound in Hong Kong, the architects treat the maximum buildable volume as an objet trouvé,

marginally modifying it and adjusting the largest possible shape to harmonize with the scale of the neighboring buildings. The result is a jagged building–reminiscent of a peaked mountain–with a fractured, pointed base, like a fissured rock. At street level there is an open zone with retail outlets and a lobby that leads out to a new plaza. Three access cores take visitors to various facilities, including a vertical parking garage. The office spaces are designed with maximum flexibility in mind and can be leased, floor by floor, to multiple occupants. Externally, the glass facade gives the building an abstract air by revealing the main flow lines of the building's grid structure and concealing individual floors. A mild curvature toward the city sees the cityscape mirrored in the facade. The angles of reflection are specifically calculated to ensure optimum energy efficiency.

2006

Project Phases
Concept Design
2006

Project Team
Partners
Jacques Herzog
Pierre de Meuron
Stefan Marbach

Project Team
Mia Hägg (Associate)
Kentaro Ishida
Daniel Johansson, Yuichi
Kodai, Chasper Schmidlin

Client
Nihon Sekkei Inc.,
Tokyo, Japan

Planning
Architect
Herzog & de Meuron,
Basel, Switzerland

General Planning
Nihon Sekkei Inc.,
Tokyo, Japan

Cost Consulting
Shimizu Corporation,
Nagoya, Japan

Mechanical Engineering
Transsolar,
Stuttgart, Germany

Structural Engineering
WGG Schnetzer
Puskas Ingenieure,
Basel, Switzerland

Building Data
Site Area
2,365 sqm

Gross Floor Area
20,614 sqm

Building Footprint
1,400 sqm

Facade Surface
16,730 sqm

Number of Levels
22

Building Dimensions
Length 58m
Width 33m
Height 112m

No.**292**
Neuer Bürobau Basel
Basel, Switzerland

Roche's determination that its main site should remain in Basel has meant that it continually has to ramp up its occupation of the land it owns by the Rhine. A new tower will bring together numerous departments that are currently scattered throughout the city in rented properties. Their relocation to the main campus will greatly ease communications. Herzog & de Meuron start by stacking single "boxes"; then they adjust the overall shape, which calls to mind the Film Academy in Qingdao. The idea of making the different sizes of departments externally visible

soon gives way to a flowing, rounded form, because the spatial needs of different sections are frequently subject to change. Multistory clusters are connected by direct, internal stairs. In addition to oval elevator shafts and three emergency stairwells, there are two differently graded access routes spiraling up the facade like internal roads, which turn circulation routes into a design feature. At the four points where these intersect, creating the impression of a double helix, there are views of the city and opportunities for informal meetings, as in the Actelion Business Center. Changes to the brief, which now stipulates that fifty percent of the open-plan office spaces has to be readily convertible into individual offices, plus a request that the building should be less flamboyant and more in keeping with the identity of the unique industrial complex designed by Otto Rudolf Salvisberg, lead to a radical reworking of the design. Nevertheless, the concept of a vertical city, with communication zones and multistory units, is retained.

2006–2008

Project Phases
Concept Design
2006–2008
Schematic Design
2008

Project Team
Concept Design
Partners
Jacques Herzog
Pierre de Meuron
Robert Hösl
Stefan Marbach

Project Team
Stefan Segessenmann
(Associate)
Volker Homeier
Thomas Polster
Alexander Bartscher, Judit
Chapallaz-Laszlo, Corina
Ebeling, Hans Focketyn,
Marcin Grala, Volker Helm,
Anna Jach, Hauke Jungjohann, Sunkoo Kang, Hamit
Kaplan, Lorenz Lachauer,
Adriana Müller, Jacqueline
Pauli, Dirk Peters, Sebastian
Reinhardt, Hannes Scheutz,
Jennifer Schmachtenberg,
Uta Schrameyer, Claudia da
Silva, Kai Strehlke, James
Wong

Schematic Design
Partners
Jacques Herzog
Pierre de Meuron
Stefan Marbach

Project Team
Stefan Segessenmann
(Associate)
Volker Homeier
Thomas Polster
Aurélien Caetano, Chris
Christen, Cecilia Dantas,
Stefan Dobnig, Hans
Focketyn, Oliver Franke,
Marcin Grala, Volker
Helm, Hamit Kaplan, Evert
Klinkenberg, Lorenz
Lachauer, Gabriel Mörsch,
Dominik Nüssen, Nina
Renner, Johannes Scheutz,
Hendrik Schikarski, Ralf
Schwaller, Jakob Seyboth,
Agustin Solórzano, Kai
Strehke, Moritz Thierfelder,
Gerd Wetzel, James Wong,
Barbara Zeleny

Client
F. Hoffmann–La Roche AG,
Basel, Switzerland

Planning
Architect
Herzog & de Meuron,
Basel, Switzerland

General Planning
Drees & Sommer, Stuttgart,
Germany (Concept Design)

Electrical Engineering
KIWI, Dübendorf, Switzerland

HVAC Engineering
Transsolar,
Stuttgart, Germany
(Concept Design)
Henne+Walter,
Reutlingen, Germany
(Concept Design)
DS-Plan,
Stuttgart, Germany
(Schematic Design)
Bures+Voith Klima Planing AG,
Basel, Switzerland
(Schematic Design)

Specialists/Consultants
Facade
Emmer Pfenninger
Partner AG,
Münchenstein, Switzerland
(Concept Design)
DS-Plan, Stuttgart, Germany
(Schematic Design)

Geotechnics
Pfirter, Nyfeler,
Basel, Switzerland

Traffic
Gruner AG,
Basel, Switzerland

Fire Protection
HHP Berlin,
Berlin, Germany

Building Data
Site Area
4,600 sqm

Gross Floor Area
84,000 sqm

Height
154 m

Number of Levels
42 aboveground
3 belowground

Structural Engineering
WGG Schnetzer Puskas,
Basel, Switzerland
SBB Schlaich Bergermann,
Stuttgart, Germany
Gruner, Basel, Switzerland
(Schematic Design)

Bibliography • Silva Maier, Vorerst setzt Roche kein Wahrzeichen, in: Baublatt 05.12.2008 • Birgit Voigt, Der Turmbau zu Basel wird vertagt, in: Neue Zürcher Zeitung am Sonntag 30.11.2008 • Victor Weber, Humer stellt Humilitas vor Hochmut, in: SonntagsZeitung 30.11.2008 • Res Strehle, Woran der Roche-Turm letztlich scheiterte, in: Tages Anzeiger 29.11.2008 • René Staubli, Sie haben die Bodenhaftung verloren, in: Tages Anzeiger 26.11.2008 • Michael Heim / Patrick Marcolli, Der Roche-Turm hatte zu viele Nebenwirkungen, in: Basler Zeitung 25.11.2008 • Patrick Marcolli, Schade um den Turm, in: Basler Zeitung 25.11.2008 • Michael Heim / Felix Erbacher, Es wird ein hohes Gebäude geben, in: Basler Zeitung 25.11.2008 • Jörg Becher, Mekka der Meisterarchitekten, in: Bilanz 14, 2008 • Christoph Keller, Hoch über Basel, in: Das Magazin 10.05.2008 • Victor Weber, Der Turm

zu Basel droht zu kippen, in: SonntagsZeitung 11.03.2007 • Rob Gregory, Herzog & de Meuron. Roche Tower, Basel, Schweiz, in: The Architectural Review 1319, 2007 • Neuer Turm in Basel, in: Baublatt 28.12.2006 • Patrick Marcolli, Tradition als Standortfaktor, in: Basler Zeitung 11.2006 • Funde. Aku Aku in Basel, in: Hochparterre 11/2006 • Extension verticale pour Roche, in: Le Moniteur 13.10.2006 • Roche baut das Höchste, in: Baublatt, 19.09.2006 • Peter F. Frey, Eine Spirale als neues Basler Wahrzeichen, in: Tages Anzeiger 15.09.2006 • Neuer Turmbau zu Basel, in: Neue Zürcher Zeitung 15.09.2006 • Andrea Drescher, Turm schraubt sich in den Himmel, in: Badische Zeitung 15.09.2006 • Victor Weber, Neuer Stammsitz für Roche, in: SonntagsZeitung 10.09.2006 • Patrick Marcolli, Roche will 160-Meter-Turm bauen, in: Basler Zeitung 26.08.2006.

No.**293**
Park Avenue Armory
New York, New York, USA

Since 2006

Project Phases

Concept Design
2006–2009

Schematic Design
2008–2009

Design Development
2009–2010

Construction Documents
2010–

Construction Services
2009–

Realization Lexington Facade
2009–2010

Realization Upper Drill Hall
2009–2010

Realization Pilot Rooms Company D and Company E
2010–2011

Realization Park Avenue Facade
2011

Realization Board of Officers
2013

Realization South Core and 5th Floor MER
2013–2014

Realization Veterans Room
2015–2016

Client
Park Avenue Armory,
New York, NY, USA

Project Team

Partners
Jacques Herzog
Pierre de Meuron
Ascan Mergenthaler

Project Team
Charles Stone (Associate)
Marija Brdarski
Sara Jacinto
Dieter Mangold
James Richards
Caroline Alsup, Philip
Berkowitsch, Evan Chakroff,
Edman Choy, Christopher
Cornecelli, Peter Dougherty,
Silja Ebert, Eik Frenzel,
Evangelina Goula, Sara
Jardim, Daniel Johansson,
Sunkoo Kang, Samir Tarek
El Kordy, Evert Klinkenberg,
Ana Maria Santos Lima,
Savannah Lamal, Julian
Loeffler, Donald Mak,
Jonathan Muecke, Mehmet
Noyan, Ben Olschner,
Jeremy Purcell, Martha
Rawlinson, Sebastian
Reinhardt, Nils Sanderson,
Joem Elias Sañez, Philip
Schmerbeck (Associate),
Leo Schneidewind, Günter
Schwob, Jakob Seyboth,
Melissa Shin

Planning

Design Consultant
Herzog & de Meuron,
Basel, Switzerland

Executive Architect
Platt Byard Dovell
White Architects LPP,
New York, NY, USA

Landscape Design
Mathews Nilsen
Landscape Architects,
New York, NY, USA

Mechanical Engineering
AKF, New York, NY, USA

Structural Engineering
Robert Silman
Associates, P.C.,
New York, NY, USA

Fire Protection
Arup Fire,
New York, NY, USA

Building Physics (Concept)
Transsolar,
New York, NY, USA

Construction
Tishman Construction,
New York, NY, USA

Elevator Consulting
Pat Bosch, Miami, FL, USA

Exterior Restoration
Walter B Melvin Architects,
New York, NY, USA

Restoration Consulting
Building Conservation
Associates,
New York, NY, USA

Specialists/Consultants

Acoustics
Akustiks, South Norwalk,
CT, USA

Sustainability
Steven Winter Associates,
New York, NY, USA

Vertical Circulation
IROS Elevator Design
Services,
East Rutherford, NJ, USA

Lighting
FMS, New York, NY, USA

Code
Jam Consultants,
New York, NY, USA

Kitchen/Restaurant
Architects for Aid,
New York, NY, USA

Quantity Surveyor
Stuart-Lynn Company,
New York, NY, USA

Theater
Fisher Dachs Associates,
New York, NY, USA

Signage
CoDe. New York Inc.,
New York, NY, USA

Light Fixtures
Auroral Lampworks,
Brooklyn, NY, USA

Metalwork
Amuneal,
Philadelphia, PA, USA
Argosy Designs,
Brooklyn, NY, USA
McKay Lodge Laboratory
Fine Art Conservation,
Oberlin, OH, USA

Building Data

Site Area
7,767 sqm

Gross Floor Area
17,652 sqm

Building Footprint
6,596 sqm

Building Dimensions
Length 122 m
Width 61 m
Height 43 m

Wood Restoration
R. Mark Adams,
East Lempster, NH, USA
Fine Wood Conservation,
New York, NY, USA

Plaster/Paint Restoration
Evergreen Architectural Arts,
Brooklyn, NY, USA
Foreground,
Hudson, NY, USA
Stone/Tile Restoration
ICR-ICC, New York, NY, USA
**Stained Glass & Wood
Window Conservation**
Femenella & Associates, Inc.,
Branchburg, NJ, USA

Bibliography • Michael Shnayerson, The fabulous (second) life of the Park Avenue Armory, in: Departures 5/2014 • Herzog & de Meuron/Park Avenue Armory, Herzog & de Meuron Transforming Park Avenue Armory New York. Edited by: Gerhard Mack, Basel 2014 • Julie I. Iovine, A Tale of Two Histories, in: The Wall Street Journal 15.10.2013 • Roberta Smith, Ornate Peek at a Refreshed Gilded Age, in: The New York Times 19.09.2013 • Anna Foppiano, Herzog & de Meuron. Park Avenue Armory, New York. Subtle yet Substantive, in: Abitare 520, 2012

• Suzanne Stephens, Pattern Language. Park Avenue Armory, New York City, in: Architectural Record 2/2012 • Margaret Shakespeare, A Salute to U.S. Armories. Once abandoned, the nation's historic armories are being rediscovered and restored, in: Preservation 1/2012 • Viva l'Arte, abbasso la Guerra, in: GCasa 12/2011 • Pia Catton, Firm shares $200 Million Plan for reinforcing Armory, in: The Wall Street Journal 06.10.2011 • Robin Pogrebin, Fixer-Upper with Unique Challenge, in: The New York Times 06.10.2011.

No.294
VitraHaus, Vitra Campus
Weil am Rhein, Germany

2006–2009

Project Phases
Concept Design
2006
Schematic Design
2006
Design Development
2006–2007
Construction Documents
2007–2009
Construction Services
2007–2009

Project Team
Partners
Jacques Herzog
Pierre de Meuron
Wolfgang Hardt
Project Team
Guillaume Delemazure
(Associate)
Charlotte von Moos
Thomasine Wolfensberger
(Associate)
Katharina Rasshofer,
Harald Schmidt, Sara Secci,
Nicolas Venzin, Isabel
Volkmar, Thomas Wyssen

Client
Vitra Verwaltungs GmbH,
Weil am Rhein, Germany

Planning
Architect
Herzog & de Meuron,
Basel, Switzerland
Site Management
Mayer Baehrle,
Lörrach, Germany
**Construction Management,
Electrical Engineering,
Mechanical Engineering,
Plumbing Engineering**
Krebser und Freyler
Planungsbüro GmbH,
Teningen, Germany
HVAC Engineering
Krebser und Freyler
Planungsbüro GmbH,
Teningen, Germany
Stahl und Weiss Büro
für Sonnenenergie,
Freiburg i. Br., Germany
Landscape Design
August Künzel
Landschaftsarchitekten AG,
Basel, Switzerland
Structural Engineering
ZPF Ingenieure AG,
Basel, Switzerland

Specialists/Consultants
Facade
Frener & Reifer Metallbau
GmbH/Srl, Brixen/
Bressanone, Italy
Curtain Design
Création Baumann
Weberei und Färberei AG,
Langenthal, Switzerland
Acoustics, Building Physics
Horstmann und Berger,
Altensteig, Germany
Fire Protection
IBB Grefrath Ing. Büro,
Sallneck, Germany
Lighting
Ansorg GmbH, Mühlheim an
der Ruhr, Germany
Graphics
Graphic Thought Facility,
London, UK
Interior Fit-out
Visplay International GmbH,
Weil am Rhein, Germany
Multimedia
Zihlmann Electronics GmbH,
Freiburg i. Br., Germany

Building Data
Site Area
12,349 sqm
Gross Floor Area
4,126 sqm
Building Footprint
1,324 sqm
Gross Volume
22,755 cubic meters
Facade Surface
7,800 sqm
Number of Levels
5 aboveground
1 belowground
Building Dimensions
Length 57 m
Width 54 m
Height 21 m

Bibliography • J. Christoph Bürkle, Häuser im Haus, in: Archithese 1/2011 • Michele Nastasi, VitraHaus. Dentro il grande Giocattolo. Inside the Large Toy, in: Lotus International 146, 2011 • Adrien Buchet, Vitra Campus. Les Clés d'une Réussite, in: L'Information Immobilière 106, 2011 • La Casa Vitrina, VitraHaus, Weil am Rhein, in: Arquitectura Viva 134, 2010 • VitraHaus Weil am Rhein. Herzog & de Meuron, in: L'Arca 259, 2010 • Herzog & de Meuron. VitraHaus. Weil am Rhein, Germany 2006–2009, in: a+u 477, 2010 • Oliver Creutz, Wenn Riesen Mikado spielen, in: Stern 12.05.2010 • Nico Ros, Spaziergang der Kräfte, in: Tec 21 07.05.2010 • Robert Thiemann, Mecca am Rhein, in: Frame 74, 2010 • Justin McGuirk, The First Time I saw the VitraHaus it was made of Gingerbread, in: Icon 82, 2010 • Jonathan Bell, Pitch Perfect. Herzog & de Meuron's new addition to Vitra HQ is our kind of glorious pile, in: Wallpaper 133, 2010 • Robert Thiemann, Stacking with Herzog & de Meuron, in: Mark, Another Architecture 25, 2010 • Francesco Pagliari, VitraHaus, Vitra Campus – Weil am Rhein, Germany. Herzog & de Meuron, in: The Plan 41, 2010 • Hubertus Adam, Weil am Rhein. Präsentationsgebäude, in:

Deutsche Bauzeitung 4/2010 • Meret Ernst, Home Sweet Home, in: Hochparterre 4/2010 • Cornelia Tapparelli, Herzog & de Meuron. VitraHaus. Weil am Rhein, in: Casabella 788, 2010 • Ulrike Schettler, Vitra Showroom in Weil am Rhein, in: AIT 3/2010 • Chantal Hamaide, Carambolage au Cordeau. A Calculated Pileup, in: Intramuros 147, 2010 • Alice Rawsthorn, A New Dash of Color at Vitra's Eclectic Site. Laboratory of Hues adds to the Design Company's Allure as a Destination, in: International Herald Tribune 15.02.2010 • Cyrille Poy, VitraHaus. Compression Verticale d'une Forme Archétypale. Vertical Compression of an Archetypal Shape, in: L'Architecture d'Aujourd'hui 376, 2010 • Karin Leydecker, Herzog & de Meuron. VitraHaus, in: Deutsches Architektur Jahrbuch 2010/11, Munich 2010 • Mathias Remmele, Vielfalt und Komplexität. Der Vitracampus, in: Modulor 3/2009 • VitraHaus de H&dM, Apilamientos Domésticos, in: Arquitectura Viva 128, 2009 • Luis Fernández-Galiano, Ernsthafte Spielerei, in: Projekt Vitra, Basel 2008.

2006–2012

No.295
Burgos Bulevar
Burgos, Spain

Project Phases

Concept Design
(No.266 Burgos Master Plan)
2004–2005

Schematic Design
2006

Design Development
2007

Construction Documents
2007–2009

Construction Services
2008–2012

Project Team

Partners
Jacques Herzog
Pierre de Meuron
Christine Binswanger

Project Team
Peter Ferretto (Associate)
Miquel Rodriguez (Associate)
David Koch (Associate)
Miguel Chaves Gentil
Alexa Nürnberger
Javier Artacho Abascal,
Benito Blanco Avellano,
Margaux Eyssette, Cristina
Génova, Silvia Gil, Patricio
Guedes Barbosa, Wilhelm
Heusser, Fabienne Hoelzel,
Marie Kellermann, Tanjo
Klöpper, Martin Knüsel,
Cristina Limiñana, Duarte
Lobo Antunes, Jonas Marx,
Maki Portilla Kawamura,
Stefano Rabolli Pansera,
Pedro Ramalho, Joana
Simoes

Client
Consorcio para la Gestion
de la Variante Ferroviaria
de Burgos, Burgos, Spain

Planning

Architect, General Planning
Herzog & de Meuron SL,
Barcelona, Spain

**Executive Architect,
Electrical Engineering,
Mechanical Engineering,
Plumbing Engineering,
Structural Engineering**
MBG Ingeniería y
Arquitectura SL,
Burgos, Spain

Landscape Architect
Michel Desvigne Paysagiste,
Paris, France

Lighting Structure
BOMA SL,
Barcelona, Spain
NB35 SL,
Madrid, Spain

Bridge Structure
Manuel Villameriel Fernández,
Valladolid, Spain

Tram Stop Structure
Juan Manuel Manso
Villalaín, Burgos, Spain

Specialists/Consultants

Fire Protection
Estudi GL
Francesc Labastida,
Barcelona, Spain

Lighting
ICON, Paris, France
Salvi, Barcelona, Spain

Local Landscape Specialist
Hydra, Burgos, Spain
Jorge Villalmanzo,
Burgos, Spain

Tram
Kummler & Matter,
Zurich, Switzerland

Building Data

Site Area
1,800,000 sqm

Length Boulevard
12,000 m

Bibliography • Bulevar de Burgos, in: AV Monographs 157/158, 2012 • Burgos, in:
L'Architecture d'Aujourd'hui 391, 2012 • Héctor Jiménez, Hoy inauguracion, primer Tramo
del Bulevar, in: Diario de Burgos 15.12.2011 • J. Maiques, Lacalle retoma el Proyecto de
un "Transporte singular" para el Bulevar, in: El Correo de Burgos 27.04.2011 • R. Travesi, La
Competencia del Espolón, in: Diario de Burgos 27.03.2011 • Alvaro Melcón, Ya somos uno.
Inauguración del primer Tramo urbano del Bulevar, in: Diario de Burgos 26.03.2011 • Ignacio
Camarero Julián, Dibujos de Ciudad. Asi, si, in: Diario de Burgos 26.03.2011 • La nueva gran
Arteria urbana, in: Bulevar, Supplement, Diario de Burgos. 25.03.2011 • Gilles A. Tiberghien,
A Landscape Deferred, in: Intermediate Natures. The Landscape of Michel Desvigne,

Basel/Boston/Berlin, 2009 • Héctor Jiménez, El Bulevar costará 95 Millones y comenzará
a urbanizarse en 2009, in: Diario de Burgos 29.09.2006 • Pierre de Meuron/Héctor Jiménez,
Esta es una Oportunidad que se le da a una Ciudad una Vez en una Generación, in: Diario
de Burgos 29.09.2006 • El Bulevar se convertirá en el tercer Corredor verde de Burgos, in:
Gente Burgos 374, 2006 • Belén Delgado, El Bulevar tendrá siete Estilos adaptados al Entorno
urbano en sus 11 Kilómetros. Burgos emprende su mayor Transformación urbanística, in:
Diario de Burgos 10.02.2005 • Pierre de Meuron/Belén Delgado, Esta gran Columna puede ser
un Eje de Transporte publico, in: Diario de Burgos 10.02.2005.

2006–2018

No.296
Tai Kwun, Centre for Heritage & Art
Hong Kong, China

Project Phases

Concept Design
2006–2009

Schematic Design
2010

Design Development
2010–2011

Construction Documents
2011–2012

Construction Services
2011–2018

Project Team

Partners
Jacques Herzog
Pierre de Meuron
Ascan Mergenthaler

Project Team
Vladimir Pajkic (Partner)
Edman Choy (Associate)
Chi-Yan Chan
Raymond Jr. Gaëtan
(Associate)
Abdulfatah Adan, Roman
Aebi, Maximilian Beckenbauer,
Aurélie Blanchard, Emi
Jean Bryan, Alexander Bürgi,
Soohyun Chang, Julien
Combes, Massimo Corradi,
Duarte De Azevedo Coutinho
Lobo Antunes, Dorothee
Dietz, Peter Dougherty,
Piotr Fortuna, Luis Gisler,
Carl Kristoffer Hägerström,

Client
The Hong Kong Jockey Club,
Hong Kong, China

Planning

Design Consultant
Herzog & de Meuron,
Basel, Switzerland

Executive Architect
Rocco Design Architects Ltd,
Hong Kong, China

Conservation Architect
Purcell, London, UK

Construction Management
Gammon Construction Ltd,
Hong Kong, China

Structural Engineering
Arup, Hong Kong, China
Arup, London, UK

**Environmental &
Archaeology**
ERM, Hong Kong, China

Landscape Consulting
AECOM, Hong Kong, China

Specialists/Consultants

Building Physics
Transsolar,
Stuttgart, Germany

**Civil Engineering, Facade
Engineering, Geotechnics,
Security, Fire Protection, IT**
Arup, Hong Kong, China

Lighting
Arup, Hong Kong, China
Arup, London, UK

Art Advisor
David Elliott,
Berlin, Germany

Acoustics, AV
Shen Milsom & Wilke Ltd,
Hong Kong, China

Sustainability
Hyder Consulting Ltd,
Hong Kong, China

Building Data

Site Area
Compound: 14,500 sqm

Gross Floor Area
Compound: 27,000 sqm
Old Bailey Wing: 4,100 sqm
Arbuthnot Wing: 3,100 sqm

Building Footprint
Compound: 10,500 sqm
Old Bailey Wing: 800 sqm
Arbuthnot Wing: 550 sqm

Building Envelope
Old Bailey Wing: 4,200 sqm
Arbuthnot Wing: 3,300 sqm

Number of Levels
2–4

Kelvin Ho, Justin Hui,
Kentaro Ishida, Anna Jach,
Sara Jardim Manteigas,
Hauke Jungjohann, Anssi
Kankkunen, Rina Ko,
Johannes Rudolf Kohnle,
Dannes Kok, Pawel
Krzeminski, Jin Tack Lim,
Mark Loughnan (Associate),
Jaroslav Mach, Donald
Mak, James Albert Martin,
José Ramón Mayoral
Moratilla, Olivier Meystre,
Lukas Nordström, Cristian
Oprea, Leonardo Pérez-
Alonso, Thomas Polster,
Maki Portilla Kawamura,
Tom Powell, Günter
Schwob, Oana Stanescu,
Kai Strehlke, Fumiko
Takahama, Zachary Vourlas,
Kenneth Wong, Sung
Goo Yang, Daniela Zimmer

MEP Engineering
J Roger Preston Ltd,
Hong Kong, China
Quantity Surveyor
Rider Levett Bucknall Ltd,
Hong Kong, China

Metallurgist
C M Whittington &
Associates Pty Ltd,
Melbourne, Australia
Planning Submission
Townland Consultants Ltd,
Hong Kong, China
Retail Operation
Knight Frank,
Hong Kong, China
Scenography
dUCKS scéno,
Villeurbanne, France
Signage
Marc & Chantal Design,
Hong Kong, China
Theater
Hong Kong Academy
of Performing Arts,
Hong Kong, China
Traffic
MVA, Hong Kong, China
Tree Survey
Professor C Y Jim,
Hong Kong University,
Hong Kong, China
Facade
Josef Gartner & Co (HK) Ltd.,
Hong Kong, China
Aluminium Brick Facade
Hycast Metals Pty Ltd.,
Sydney, Australia
Exposed Concrete
United Soundfair
Engineering Co. Ltd.,
Hong Kong, China
Historical Facades
Stonewest Ltd., London, UK
**Historical Roofs, Windows
and Doors**
Harvest Century Holdings
(HK) Ltd., Hong Kong, China

Building Dimensions
Compound:
Length 140 m
Width 110 m
Height 50 m
Old Bailey Wing:
Length 33 m
Width 25 m
Arbuthnot Wing:
Length 32 m
Width 20 m
Height 31 m

Bibliography • Central Police Station. Herzog & de Meuron, in: Progettare 6, 2011 • Suzanne Miao/Ascan Mergenthaler, Full Steam ahead. Filling the Void, in: Perspective 11/2011 • Ma Hak, Cityspeak XX: The 'New' Central Police Station, in: South China Morning Post 20.01.2011 • Susan Schwartz, Vanilla Skyline, in: South China Morning Post 26.11.2010 • Stephen Siu Yu Lau, Blurring the Boundary between Local and International – Hong Kong's

Void City Syndrome, in: Space 10/2010 • Arresting Vision for Police Station Project, in: South China Morning Post 18.01.2008 • Central Police Station Compound Conservation and Revitalisation Project, in: South China Morning Post 07.01.2008 • Lynne Jackson, Herzog & de Meuron. Central Police Station Compound, Hong Kong, in: The Architectural Review 1319, 2008.

No.**297**
Betile Museum
Cagliari, Italy

2006

The city of Cagliari wants to build a museum by the harbor, with a department combining early history, modern history, and contemporary art. The proposed site at the harbor is close to the football stadium and social housing, but has no real connection to the city center. As part of their competition entry, Herzog & de Meuron therefore suggest that a green belt should be planted – inspired by Joseph Beuys's *7,000 Oaks* project – which will create a promenade linking the new museum to the city center. The museum building would also contribute to the creation of a new

hub. Taking full account of the good visibility of this site from the ferry, the architects design a vertical structure that references the Nuraghe artifacts associated with the early history of Cagliari, which are among the few local items in the city collection. An open stack of spatial volumes appears to dissolve as it rises upward. There is no encasing facade; a similar strategy is seen in the later Pérez Art Museum Miami. The closed structural units made from concrete formwork flap open at their short ends, not unlike the main facade of the Miu Miu store in the Aoyama district of Tokyo. In the open ground floors, visitors will be welcomed by an atrium, a shop, and a library. On the next level an open storage display leads out onto a viewing terrace. The exhibition spaces on the upper floors are grouped around Anchor Rooms which will not only house items from the Nuraghe collection but also act as circulation nodes and give the museum a distinctive ambience.

No. 298

Project Phases

Competition
2006

Project Team

Partners
Jacques Herzog
Pierre de Meuron
Stefan Marbach

Project Team
Jayne Barlow (Associate)
lela Herrling
Henrike Elsner, Francisco
de Freitas, Andreas Fries,
Stefano Rabolli Pansera,
Maria Ángeles Lerin Ruesca,
Sara Secci, Claudia Zipperle

Client
Regione Autonoma della
Sardegna, Cagliari, Italy

Planning

Architect
Herzog & de Meuron,
Basel, Switzerland

Partner Architect
SPA architects,
Cagliari, Italy

Mechanical Engineering
Stokar & Partner,
Basel, Switzerland

Structural Engineering
WGG Schnetzer
Puskas Ingenieure,
Basel, Switzerland

Building Data

Site Area
40,000 sqm

Gross Floor Area
11,660 sqm

Bibliography · Museum für mediterrane nuraghische und zeitgenössische Kunst in Cagliari,
I-Sardinien, in: Wettbewerbe aktuell 1/2007 · Herzog & de Meuron, in: Domus 899, 2007.

No. 298
Wasserstadt Solothurn
Solothurn, Switzerland

2006–2007, 2011

The city of Solothurn has to clean up a landfill site that was in use from 1935 to 1976. A private investor suggests removing the landfill and disposing of it properly. However, instead of the ensuing pits being filled in again, they would be flooded with water and landscaped to create a new residential district, which would finance the reclamation of the site. Advice is sought from Herzog & de Meuron, who conduct a concept study exploring the potential for waterside living that would attract new commuters to Solothurn, which has convenient access to Basel, Bern, and Zurich.

Herzog & de Meuron propose a two-stage development, creating a new loop in the River Aare–thus recalling the original meandering course of the river before it was straightened. The new island created by this loop would be planted and provide an open landscape for local residents. The outer bank of this river loop would become a new residential district with homes for over ten thousand people. With exclusive residences close to the riverbank and more urban, six-story apartment blocks further inland, the new district would form a series of arcs echoing the reshaped course of the Aare. A catalogue details different sizes of plots and styles of housing. The district is accessed via the existing road network. In addition to an external feeder ring, there will be a garden ring and a waterside promenade for the sole use of residents. The rows of houses will be interspersed with neighborhood squares. Bathing facilities, moorings, and a varied promenade will enhance the vibrant shoreline.

Project Phases

Concept Design
First Phase 2006–2007
Second Phase 2011

Project Team

Concept Design

First Phase

Partners
Jacques Herzog
Pierre de Meuron
Harry Gugger

Project Team
Julian Löffler
Catherine Preiswerk
Hee-Jun Sim

Concept Design

Second Phase

Partner
Jacques Herzog
Pierre de Meuron
Robert Hösl
Christine Binswanger

Project Team
Martin Fröhlich (Associate)
Salomé Gutscher
Mark Bähr, Frederik Bojesen,
Christoph Jantos, Benjamin
Krüger, Christopher Lunde,
Mika Zacharias

Client
Wasserstadtsolothurn AG,
Solothurn, Switzerland

Planning

Project Architect
Herzog & de Meuron,
Basel, Switzerland

Landscape Design
Vogt Landschaftsarchitekten,
Zurich, Switzerland

Structural Engineering
BSB+Partner,
Oensingen, Switzerland

Specialists/Consultants

Civil Engineering, Traffic
BSB+Partner, Switzerland

Energy, Sustainability
Regio Energie Solothurn,
Solothurn, Switzerland

Gastronomy, Hotel
Volkartberatung,
Solothurn, Switzerland

Geology
SolGeo AG,
Solothurn, Switzerland

Hydraulics
Hunziker, Zarn & Partner AG,
Aarau, Switzerland
AquaPlus, Zug, Switzerland

Building Data

Site Area
427,600 sqm

Gross Floor Area
111,000 sqm

Bibliography · Daniel Gerny, Herzog & de Meuron planen in Solothurn, in: Neue Zürcher
Zeitung 28.12.2013 · Schritt vorwärts für "Little Venedig", in: Solothurner Zeitung 04.11.2010.

No. 299

Tour Phare, La Défense
Paris, France

2006

High-rise office construction projects abound in Milan and London, but Paris lags behind. An investor wants to construct a 300-meter office tower in the La Défense district. Herzog & de Meuron prepare a competition entry that reacts to the artificiality of that area. The site is a "leftover" plot where existing train tracks and roads make it difficult to construct the foundations of any new building. The architects design the footprint of the building according to the available patches of ground and leave the rest of the site unbuilt. Their proposed tower relates to Paris in various ways. It has a gentle curve on its north side, closely matching the line of the road; on its south side, looking toward a square, it is slightly angled. Inside it the ground floor, with gardens and pools, connects with both the artificial and natural topography of the area. A circular tunnel is cut into the building for the road that will run through it. The access cores take account of the vistas out across the city. The occupants of the flexible office suites that are arranged along the perimeter of the building can see out to the Louvre, the Eiffel Tower, and Sacré-Cœur. At the narrow extremities of the tower, the ceilings do not always extend full length, creating open shafts connecting several stories, which will be used as vertical gardens. This slim tower appears transparent at either end. The structure takes the form of a grid that also animates the skin of the building. The north facade is smooth, the south facade is textured: the window panes on this side are equipped with solar convectors. When they are angled downward, these panes provide reflection-free city views.

Project Phases	Project Team	Client	Planning	Specialists/Consultants	Building Data
Competition	**Partners**	Unibail, Paris, France	**Architect**	**Security**	**Site Area**
2006	Jacques Herzog		Herzog & de Meuron,	Veritas, Paris, France	4,600 sqm
	Pierre de Meuron		Basel, Switzerland	**Elevator Consulting**	**Gross Floor Area**
	Ascan Mergenthaler		**Cost Consulting**	Jappsen, Berlin, Germany	180,000 sqm
	Project Team		Davis Langdon,	**Visualizations**	**Building Footprint**
	Guillaume Delemazure		London, UK	Philipp Schaerer,	2,800 sqm
	(Associate)		**Mechanical Engineering**	Zurich, Switzerland	**Number of Levels**
	Kentaro Ishida		Transsolar,		72
	Roman Aebi, Piotr Fortuna,		Stuttgart, Germany		**Building Dimensions**
	Thomas von Girsewald,		**Structural Engineering**		Length 135m
	Volker Helm, Daniel		WGG Schnetzer		Width 35m
	Johansson, Daniel Kiss,		Puskas Ingenieure AG,		Height 280m
	Andrea Landell, Xiaojing Lu,		Basel, Switzerland		
	Günter Schwob				

Bibliography • Phare Tower Competition in Paris. La Défense, Paris, France 2006, in: a+u 440, 2007. • "Tour Phare" im Hochhausviertel La Défense in Paris/"Phare Tower" at La Défense in Paris, in: Wettbewerbe Aktuell 4/2007 • La lama sottile/The Thin Blade, in: L'Arca 224, 2007 • Richard Scoffier, Puissance de l'Objet. Concours pour la Tour Phare à la Défense, in: D'Architectures 161, 2007 • Catherine Séron-Pierre, Concours Tour Phare Unibail, in: AMC 167, 2007.

No. 300

Artist's Choice: Herzog & de Meuron,
Perception Restrained
The Museum of Modern Art, New York, New York, USA

2006

Project Phases	Project Team	Client	Specialists/Consultants	Project Data	MoMA Collection
Project	**Partners**	The Museum of Modern Art,	**Mechanical Engineering**	**Exhibition Area**	**Artworks**
2005–2006	Jacques Herzog	New York, NY, USA	Altieri Sebor Wieber LLC,	240 sqm	124 artworks from 5
Exhibition	Pierre de Meuron	**MoMA Team**	Norwalk, CT, USA		Department Collections:
21 June–25 September 2006	Esther Zumsteg	Terence Riley, Peter Reed,	**Film Editing**		45 Architecture & Design
	Project Team	Christian Larsen	International Digital Center,		36 Photography
	Nils Sanderson		New York, NY, USA		28 Painting & Sculpture
	Mario Meier, Anna-Lisa				14 Film & Media
	Nemeth, Christoph Röttinger				1 Prints & Illustrated Books

Artists represented in the exhibition • Alvar Aalto, Robert Adams, Diane Arbus, Roy Arden, Francis Bacon, Balthus, Matthew Barney, Ruodi Barth, Maria Luisa Belgiojoso, Mario Bellini, Joseph Beuys, Oliver Boberg, Louise Bourgeois, Margaret Bourke-White, Bill Brandt, Marco Breuer, Alexander Calder, Harry Callahan, Paul Cézanne, Larry Clark, Franco Clivio, Joel & Ethan Coen, Francis Ford Coppola, Gregory Crewdson, David Cronenberg, Salvador Dalí, Peter Danko, Rudolph de Harak, Denominator Company, Inc, Philip-Lorca diCorcia, Rineke Dijkstra, Christopher Dresser, Charles Eames, William Eggleston, Walker Evans, Kaj Franck, Lee Friedlander, Adam Fuss, Alberto Giacometti, Eileen Gray, Robert Gober, Konstantin Grcic, Andreas Gursky, Jitka Hanzlová, Werner Herzog, Herzog & de Meuron, Josef Hoffmann, Gene Hurwitt, Arne Jacobsen, Jacob Jensen, Jasper Johns, Donald Judd, Frida Kahlo, Karlsson & Nilsson, Perry King, Franz Kline, Willem de Kooning, Jeff Koons, Robert James Leonetti, Raymond Loewy Associates, Man Ray, Robert Mapplethorpe, Henri Matisse, Piet Mondrian, William Morris, Paul Morrissey, Umberto Nason, Bruce Nauman, Floris M. Neusüss, Barnett Newman, Simone Nieweg, Eliot Noyes and Associates, Verner Panton, Arthur Penn, Pablo Picasso, Jackson Pollock, Richard Prince, Dieter Raffler, Charles Ray, Ad Reinhardt, Gerhard Richter, Gerrit Rietveld, Mark Rothko, Thomas Ruff, Timo Sarpaneva, Stephen Scheer, Collier Schor, Martin Scorsese, Cindy Sherman, Vilgot Sjöman, Frederick Sommer, Ettore Sottsass, Philippe Starck, Joel Sternfeld, Thomas Struth, Richard Süssmuth, Hiroshi Sugimoto, Walter Dorwin Teague, Gebrüder Thonet, Earl S. Tupper, Massimo Vignelli, Wilhelm Wagenfeld, Andy Warhol, Gillian Wearing, Hans Wegner, Michael Wesely, Brett Weston, Edward Weston, Frank Lloyd Wright, Eva Zeisel, Elyn Zimmerman.

Bibliography • Shonquis Moreno, Treasure Hunt: Herzog & de Meuron in New York, in: Frame 53, 2006 • Andrea Köhler, Der vielfach gebrochene Blick. Herzog & de Meuron als Gastkuratoren im MoMA, in: Neue Zürcher Zeitung 01.07.2006 • Roberta Smith, Two Spurned Architects Bite the Hand That Didn't Feed Them, in: The New York Times 30.06.2006 • Daniel Kunitz, Seeing MoMA through an Architect's Eye, in: The New York Sun 22.06.2006.

No. 301

2006–2011

MKM Museum Küppersmühle, Extension
Duisburg, Germany

When Herzog & de Meuron converted the former Küppersmühle into a museum for the Grothe Collection in 1997, they made an important contribution to the cultural regeneration of the area around Duisburg's inner harbor. Now additional space is needed, following the amalgamation of the Ströher Collection and the Grothe Collection; this also provides an opportunity for the museum, which has hitherto mainly been frequented by art professionals, to raise its public profile. The proposed site for the extension is situated between the old silos of the Küppersmühle and the raised roadways of the motorway. Regulations governing the distance to adjoining roadways mean that the site is too small for the required expansion.

Herzog & de Meuron therefore position the extension directly on top of the silos. The semitranslucent, two-story box has a lightness that recalls the glass superstructure on Tate Modern and gives the Museum Küppersmühle an eye-catching "logo" that will be immediately visible to pedestrians in the inner harbor area and to drivers passing by on the motorway. The silos plus the box look like a huge hammer. Inside, the silos are cut open to create shell-shaped rooms; the four corners of the building will house two elevators and two spiral staircases. There are various proposals for the interior design of the box. It is to accommodate both new forms of art and a mixture of art storage and display; this is also referenced in the exhibition *Perception Restrained* curated by the architects in 2006 for the Artist's Choice series at the Museum of Modern Art, New York. The steel frame of the "exhibition box" is constructed, but proves to be not correctly welded; the manufacturer goes bankrupt. A new, replacement project sees a smaller extension being constructed adjacent to the silos.

Project Phases
Concept Design
2006–2007

Schematic Design
2008

Design Development
2008

Construction Documents
2008–2011

Construction Services
2009–2011

Project Team
Partners
Jacques Herzog
Pierre de Meuron
Stefan Marbach
Wolfgang Hardt
Robert Hösl

Project Team
Michael Bär
Christian Zerreis
Claudia Zipperle
Fabian Dieterle, Tobias Fritzenwenger, Judith Funke, Debora Hummel, Benno Lincke, Jonas Marx, Marcel Neuse, Roland Schreiber, Jochen Seelos, Douwe Wieers

Client
Stiftung für Kunst und Kultur e.V., Bonn, Germany
GEBAG Duisburger Gemeinnützige Baugesellschaft AG, Duisburg, Germany

Planning
Architect
Herzog & de Meuron, Basel, Switzerland

Partner Architect
Mayer Bährle Architekten, Lörrach, Germany

Construction Management
Mayer Bährle Architekten, Lörrach, Germany
WSP CBP Projektmanagement GmbH, Germany

Electrical Engineering
a.p.-plan, Düsseldorf, Germany

HVAC Engineering
VIKA Ingenieure GmbH, Aachen, Germany (Planning)
Delta-i Ingenieurgesellschaft mbH, Berlin, Germany (Planning)
Ingenieurbüro Dr. Bleiker GmbH, Datteln, Germany (Construction)

Structural Engineering
LWS Ingenieure, Duisburg, Germany (Feasibility Study)
Ingenieurbüro Dipl. Ing. Wilfried Hippe, Essen, Germany (Project)

Specialists/Consultants
Building Physics
ISRW Klapdor GmbH, Düsseldorf, Germany

Civil Engineering
GFP Ingenieurbüro für Geotechnik, Duisburg, Germany

Facade Engineering
IGF Zimmermann, Mülheim, Germany

Security
Henseleit + Partner, Waldkirch, Germany
Streif Baulogistik GmbH, Essen, Germany

Fire Protection
Oekotec Sachverständige, Schwalmtal, Germany

Energy Consulting
Ingenieurbüro P. Jung, Cologne, Germany

Facade Lighting
Bartenbach Lichtlabor, Aldrans, Austria

Project Management
WSP CBP Projektmanagement GmbH, Germany

Wind Expertise
Wacker Ingenieure, Birkenfeld, Germany

Building Data
Site Area
3,830 sqm

Gross Floor Area
Silo: 1,909 sqm
Extension: 2,936 sqm

Building Footprint
320 sqm

Gross Volume
Silo: 9,332 cubic meters
Extension: 27,705 cubic meters

Facade Surface
4,500 sqm

Number of Levels
6

Building Dimensions
Silo:
Length 19.4 m
Width 15.5 m
Height 36.2 m
Extension:
Length 55.3 m
Width 29.4 m
Height 17.3 m

Bibliography • Die Mühle und der Schrott, in: Architektur & Technik 2/2012 • Marian Manten/Michael Schulz, Der Duisburg-Effekt, in: Bauwelt 29, 2011 • Jörn Esser, Pannenserie an der Küppersmühle, in: Westdeutsche Allgemeine 15.11.2010 • Hans Jürgen Krolkiewicz, Spektakuläre Kiste. Erweiterung Museum Küppersmühle, Duisburg, in: Beratende Ingenieure 1/2010 • Museum Küppersmühle wird erweitert. Museum Küppersmühle to be enlarged, in: Innenstadt Duisburg Entwicklungsgesellschaft, Duisburg 2009 • Vom Feinsinn zum Unsinn, in: Deutsche Bauzeitung 1/2009 • Hayke Lanwert, Ein Hingucker für den Hafen, in: Westdeutsche Allgemeine 21.11.2008 • Thomas Becker, Kunst über den Wolken, in: Westdeutsche Allgemeine, 21.11.2008 • Lothar Schröder, Duisburg klotzt mit Kunst, in: Rheinische Post 21.11.2008 • Peter Klucken, Eine "radikale Lösung", in: Rheinische Post 21.11.2008 • Projekt ohnegleichen: der "Hammer", in: Neue Ruhr Zeitung 21.11.2008 • Jens Dirksen, Die Küppersmühle will hoch hinaus, in: Neue Ruhr Zeitung 21.11.2008 • Herzog y de Meuron, vuelta al Küppersmühle, in: Arquitectura Viva 123, 2008 • Frank Maier-Solgk, Erweiterung MKM – Museum Küppersmühle, Duisburg. Leuchtkörper am Innenhafen, in: Nordrhein-Westfalen baut auf Kultur: Projekte und Visionen, Düsseldorf 2008.

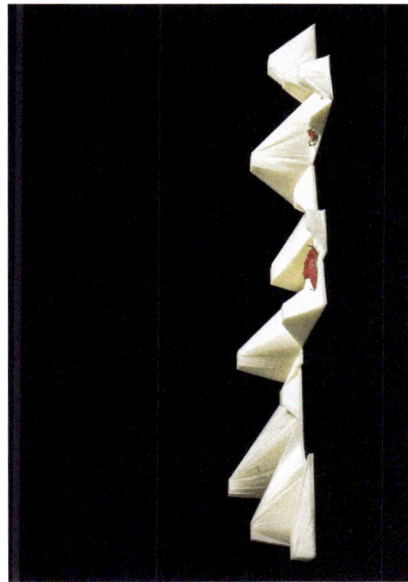

2006

No.**302**
Gazprom-City
St. Petersburg, Russia

Having decided to relocate its headquarters from Moscow to St. Petersburg, the energy company Gazprom announces a competition for a 300-meter office tower, to be constructed on a small site directly by the River Neva on the outskirts of the historical city. The planned infringement of the existing height regulations (set at 21 meters, that is, the "eaves height" of the Hermitage Museum) arouses fierce opposition, and UNESCO threatens to revoke the city's status as a World Heritage Site. Herzog & de Meuron understand the company's ambitions for its new tower and translate these into an elegant, dialogic structure that will integrate into the city around it. Taking into account the way that the Hermitage interacts with the fine, around it. Taking into account the way that the Hermitage interacts with the fine, 123-meter spire of the Baroque Cathedral of Saints Peter and Paul on the other side of the Neva, the new office tower both echoes the spire of the cathedral and relates to the Baroque Smolny Convent on the opposite bank of the river. The tower also adopts and develops the principle of stacking that is seen in traditional Russian Orthodox churches. It is to be as slim as possible at the same time as forming multi-level clusters. This allows its occupants to see other floors from above and below, so that they almost have the feeling of being in a town, rather than floating in isolation far above the ground. Each workspace has a spectacular view of the city. Two competing principles are combined by means of circular forms. The central access core—progressively narrowing as it rises up to its full height of 336 meters—is encircled by successive levels of discs, which transmit their loads to the central core. The tower is not dissimilar to twisting stacks of coins terminating in a single circle. In order to both engage local residents with the building and to meet extremely strict health and safety regulations, an external shuttle connects with the rooftop viewing platform. The spiral structure of this project is related to the first design for the tower for Roche, the Neuer Bürobau Basel, although the latter derives its form from redevelopment, whereas the Gazprom project is defined by spatial units.

Project Phases

Competition
2006

Project Team

Partner
Jacques Herzog
Pierre de Meuron

Project Team
Mia Hägg (Associate)
Tomislav Dushanov
Hans von Bernuth, Massimo
Corradi, Eik Frenzel, Volker
Helm, Anna Jach, Srdjan
Jovanovic, Yuichi Kodai,
Samir Tarek El Kordy, Judit
Laszlo, Young Lee, Masato
Takahashi, Sung Goo Yang

Client
Gazprom Neft,
St. Petersburg, Russia

Planning

Architect
Herzog & de Meuron,
Basel, Switzerland

**Structural Engineering,
Civil Engineering,
Facade Engineering,
Traffic, Fire Protection**
Arup, London, UK

Building Data

Site Area
41,850 sqm

Gross Floor Area
75,000 sqm

Building Footprint
1,672 sqm

Building Dimensions
Length 57 m
Width 57 m
Height 336 m

As Gazprom's realization appears certain, Russians rail against modern monuments, in: Architectural Record 1/2007 • Ellen Bennett, Gazprom jury walk-out, in: Building Design 1750, 2006 • Andrew Bolger, UK Architect to design Gazprom HQ, in: The Financial Times 02.12.2006 • Marina Rumjanzewa, Bedrohtes Stadtbild. Ein Hochhaus-Streit in St. Petersburg, in: Neue Zürcher Zeitung 17.11.2006.

Bibliography • Gazprom Headquarters Competition in St. Petersburg, Russia, 2006, in: a+u 440, 2007 • David Nauer, Gazprom möchte der schönsten Stadt der Welt ein neues Gesicht verpassen, in: Tages Anzeiger 20.03.2007 • Gazprom-City of Architecture Competition, in: Concept 94, 2007 • Symbolische Flamme, in: Architektur & Wohnen 2/2007 • Ellen Bennett, Rem demands Boycott, in: Building Design 1752, 2007 • Paul Abelsky, St. Petersburg dispatch:

2006

No.**303**
New Las Vegas
Las Vegas, Nevada, USA

After Herzog & de Meuron developed the design for Scandia Las Vegas, the client secured another plot of land by the highway for a major development project. The site is so large that it can accommodate a whole city district, equivalent to an entire neighborhood along the banks of the Rhine in inner Basel. In their first concept studies the architects focus on this vast scale and develop a whole range of building types, from modest dwelling houses to mountainous megastructures; they also consider various access routes and public spaces. Towers are connected by bridge systems, which can themselves be inhabited or used as public zones, for jogging routes, for instance. The close proximity to the highway means that planning regulations will allow the construction of a new silhouette. However, the unfolding real estate crisis prevents the project from progressing beyond this initial, exploratory stage.

Project Phases

Concept Design
2006

Project Team

Partners
Jacques Herzog
Pierre de Meuron
Ascan Mergenthaler

Project Team
Mia Hägg (Associate)
Sunkoo Kang, Chantal
Reichenbach, Nils
Sanderson, Jad Silvester

Client
Ian Schrager Company,
New York, NY, USA

Building Data

Site Area
266,000–515,000 sqm

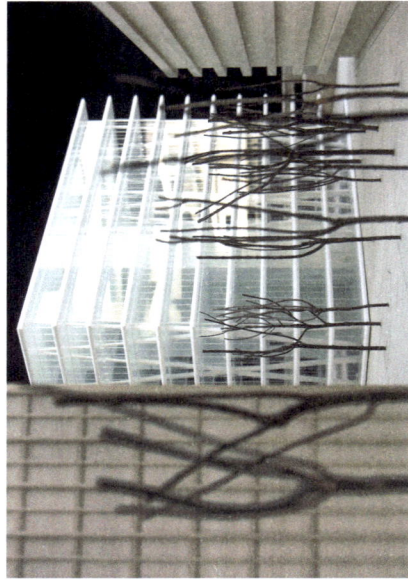

2006–2007

No.**304**
CityGate Basel
Basel, Switzerland

Diener & Diener Architects' design for the redevelopment of the site previously occupied by MIBA (Milchverband Nordwestschweiz), close to the motorway network, railroad tracks, and St. Jakob stadium in Basel, envisages four buildings arranged so that an old villa and the majority of the existing trees are preserved. A road constructed in the nineteenth century establishes a diagonal orientation. A number of different architectural practices are engaged to design the various buildings. Herzog & de Meuron are allotted the tallest building – forty meters in height. The Basellandschaftliche Pensionskasse, the client for this building, has requested a mixed-use design incorporating offices, a laboratory, and a hotel. The architects develop a concept that combines the desired flexibility with maximum economy. All ten stories will conform to the regulation laboratory ceiling height of four meters; the services will shift from the external walls to the center, creating maximum floor areas around the perimeter of the building, which can be variously subdivided in different stories and individually leased. The core serves as the main load-bearing structure, but there are also slightly angled supports around the outer edges of the building. The prefabricated balconies facing south and west take advantage of the sun; cantilevers on the motorway side reduce the traffic noise. Decentralized ventilation systems prevent the need for large ducts; the accommodation of pipe systems in spaces in the ceilings facilitates the rapid conversion of individual floors. The rounded shapes of the balconies along with the continuous glass facade give the building an elegant air. However, indications of a likely future surplus of accommodation in Basel prompts the client to abandon this project.

Project Phases

Concept Design
2006–2007

Client
Basellandschaftliche
Pensionskasse BLPK,
Liestal, Switzerland

Project Team

Partners
Jacques Herzog
Pierre de Meuron
Harry Gugger

Project Team
Michael Fischer
Kasia Jackowska, Luis
Játiva, Marie Kellermann,
Claudia Zipperle

Planning

Architect
Herzog & de Meuron,
Basel, Switzerland

Cost Consulting
Baukostenplanung Ernst AG,
Basel, Switzerland

HVAC Engineering
Amstein+Walthert AG,
Zurich, Switzerland

Landscape Design
August Künzel
Landschaftsarchitekten AG,
Basel, Switzerland

Structural Engineering
WGG Schnetzer
Puskas Ingenieure,
Basel, Switzerland

Specialists/Consultants

Acoustics
Gruner AG,
Basel, Switzerland

Facade
Emmer Pfenninger
Partner AG,
Münchenstein, Switzerland

Building Data

Gross Floor Area
11,500 sqm

Building Footprint
1,114 sqm

Gross Volume
56,545 cubic meters

Facade Surface
4,883 sqm

Number of Levels
10 aboveground
2 belowground

Building Dimensions
Length 52 m
Width 30 m
Height 40 m

2006–2017

No.**305**
56 Leonard Street
New York, New York, USA

Project Phases

Schematic Design
2006–2007

Design Development
2007

Construction Documents
2007–2008, 2012

Construction Services
2012–2017

Client
Alexico Group,
New York, NY, USA

Project Team

Partners
Jacques Herzog
Pierre de Meuron
Ascan Mergenthaler

Project Team
Philip Schmerbeck
(Associate)
Mehmet Noyan (Associate)
Vladimir Pajkic (Associate)
Caroline Alsop, Iwona
Boguslawska, Marija
Brdarski, Mark Chan, Simon
Filler, Josh Helin, Dara
Huang, Sara Jacinto, Jin Tack
Lim, Mark Loughnan,
Jaroslav Mach, Donald Mak,
Hugo Miguel Moura, Jeremy
Purcell, Martin Raub, Chantal
Reichenbach, James
Richards, Joem Elias Sanez,
Heeri Song, Charles Stone,
Kai Strehlke, Zachary
Vourlas, Jason Whiteley,
Sung Goo Yang, Daniela
Zimmer, Christian Zöllner

Planning

Design Consultant
Herzog & de Meuron,
Basel, Switzerland

Executive Architect
Goldstein, Hill & West
Architects LLP,
New York, NY, USA

Construction Management
Lendlease, New York,
NY, USA

Client Representative
Hines, New York, NY, USA

Mechanical Engineering
Cosentini Associates,
New York, NY, USA

Structural Engineering
WSP Cantor Seinuk,
New York, NY, USA

**Polished Stainless Steel
Sculpture**
In collaboration with
Anish Kapoor

Specialists/Consultants

Facade
Gordon H. Smith Corporation,
New York, NY, USA

Lighting
Schwinghammer Lighting
LLC, New York, NY, USA

Vertical Circulation
Jenkins & Huntington Inc,
Avon, CT, USA

Acoustics
Shen Milsom & Wilke LLC,
New York, NY, USA

Concrete
Reginald D. Hough,
Rhinebeck, NY, USA

Sustainability
Vidaris Inc.,
New York, NY, USA

Geotechnics
Langan Engineering
and Environmental,
New York, NY, USA

Hardware
Glezen Fisher Group LLC,
Campbell Hall, NY, USA

Pool
Trace Pool Design,
White Plains, NY, USA

Stone
Swenson Stone Consultants
Ltd, Hanover, NH, USA

Building Data

Site Area
1,162 sqm

Gross Floor Area
45,291 sqm

Building Footprint
990 sqm

Number of Levels
57

Number of Units
146

Building Dimensions
Length 38 m
Width 30 m
Height 253 m

Theater
TK Theaters,
Brooklyn, NY, USA

Window Washing
Entek Engineering,
Hackensack, NY, USA

Wood Floor
Janos Spitzer Flooring,
New York, NY, USA

Bibliography • Edwin Heathcote, The skyscraper architects who find inspiration in disintegration, in: Financial Times 26.02.2016 • 56 Leonard Street, in: AV Monographs 157/158, 2012 • Brigitte Hernandez, Herzog & de Meuron, les as de la déconstruction, in: Le Point 12/2011 • 56 Leonard Street, in: a+u 493, 2011 • Elie Gamburg, Pixilated Tectonics, in: 56 Leonard Street, New York 2010 • 56 Leonard Street, in: El Croquis 152/153, 2010 • Patrice Goulet, Libre, Claire et Vivante, in: L'Architecture d'Aujourd'hui 9/2009 • Andrea Schwan, 56 Leonard Street Apartments, in: eVolo 4/2009 • 56 Leonard Street by Herzog & de Meuron, in: a+u 458, 2008 • In den Himmel gestapelt, in: Häuser 11/2008 • Aaron Seward, In

Detail: 56 Leonard Street, in: The Architect's Newspaper 01.10.2008 • David Sokol, First skyscraper by Herzog & de Meuron rising in Manhattan, in: Architectural Record 10/2008 • Roman Hollenstein, Tanzender Schubladenturm, in: Neue Zürcher Zeitung 29.09.2008 • Edwin Heathcote, New Start for an Urban Form. 56 Leonard Street, in: Financial Times 17.09.2008 • Ein Stapel Luxus. A Pile of Luxury, in: Outlook Building Perspectives 10, 2008 • Una Pila de Casas de Herzog & de Meuron en Tribeca, in: Arquitectura Viva 120, 2008.

No.**306**
Pérez Art Museum Miami
Miami, Florida, USA

2006–2013

Project Phases	Project Team	Client
Concept 2006–2007	**Partners** Jacques Herzog Pierre de Meuron Christine Binswanger	Miami Art Museum, Miami, FL, USA
Schematic Design 2007–2008		
Design Development 2008–2009	**Project Team** Charles Stone (Associate)	
Construction Documents 2009–2010	Kentaro Ishida (Associate) Stefan Hoerner (Associate)	
Construction Services 2010–2013	Roman Aebi, Joana Anes, Jayne Barlow (Associate), Ida Richter Braendstrup, Jack Brough, Margarida Castro, Silja Ebert, Jason Frantzen, Yuko Himeno Dara Huang, Daekyung Jo, Sunkoo Kang, Yuichi Kodai, Hugo Moura, Adriana Mueller, Mehmet Noyan, Valentin Ott, Jeremy Purcell, Nils Sanderson, Ahmad Reza Schricker, Günter Schwob, Wei Sun, Masato Takahashi	

Planning	Specialists/Consultants	Building Data
Design Consultant Herzog & de Meuron, Basel, Switzerland	**Acoustics** Harvey Marshall Berling Associates, New York, NY, USA	**Site Area** 14,221 sqm
Executive Architect Handel Architects, New York, NY, USA	**Civil Engineering** ADA Engineer, Doral, FL, USA	**Gross Floor Area** 11,125 sqm
HVAC Engineering Arup, London, UK/ New York, NY, USA	**Facade** Front, New York, NY, USA	**Building Footprint** 8,598 sqm
Landscape Design GEO Architectonica, Miami, FL, USA	**Lighting** Arup, London, UK/ New York, NY, USA	**Gross Volume** 182,677 cubic meters
Structural Engineering Arup, London, UK/ New York, NY, USA	**Security** Lane Consultants, Greenwood Village, CO, USA	**Facade Surface** 5,176 sqm
Cost Consulting Stuart-Lynn Company, New York, NY, USA	**Sustainability** Transsolar, Stuttgart, Germany	**Number of Levels** 4
Hanging Gardens Patrick Blanc, Paris, France	**Vertical Circulation** Jenkins & Huntington Inc, New York, NY, USA	**Building Dimensions** Length 117m Width 73m Height 21m
Plumbing, Fire Protection JALRW, Doral, FL, USA	**Code** Schirmer Engineering, White Plains, NY, USA	
Structural Engineering (Local) Douglas Wood, Coral Gables, FL, USA	**Concrete** Reginald Hough, New York, NY, USA	
	Textiles Michele Rondelli, Zurich, Switzerland	
	Wood Stephen Smulski, Shutesbury, MA, USA	

Bibliography • Markus Breitschmid, Archaisch und doch spezifisch, in: Archithese 4/2015 • Ellie Stathaki, Best New Public Building Perez Art Museum Miami, US, by Herzog & de Meuron, in: Wallpaper 191, 2015 • Emily Eyestone, Stadium and Museum: Herzog & de Meuron's Architecture of Participation, in: The Miami Rail, Winter 2015 • Raymond Ryan, Herzog & de Meuron in Miami, in: Whitewall Winter 2015 • Perez Art Museum Miami, Miami USA, 2013, in: a+u 529, 2014 • Michael Webb, Miami Virtue. Miami's cultural and civic milieu is augmented by a consciously anti-iconic museum for modern art by Herzog & de Meuron, in: The Architectural Review 1408, 2014 • Pérez Art Museum Miami, in: Plot 19, 2014 • François Chaslin, Pérez Sanat Müzesi. Pérez Art Museum Miami, in: YAPI 390, 2014 • Nina Lincoff, Museum's unanticipated success triggers internal changes, in: Miami Today 10.04.2014 • Masami Kiyohara, To the new museum "PAMM" by Herzog & de Meuronl, in: Elle Decor Japan 4/2014 • Chiara Baglione, Herzog & de Meuron – Un museo a Miami,

in: Casabella 4/2014 • Pérez Art Museum Miami, in: Icon 129, 2014 • Miami on the Move, in: Frame 97, 2014 • Joann Plockova, Art under the Stars, in: Azure 30, 2014 • Lisa Zeitz, Die Verwandlung von Miami, in: Weltkunst 83, 2014 • Jörg Himmelreich, Offene Struktur, in: Architektur Technik 1/2014 • Philip Jodidio, Pérez Art Museum Miami, in: Area 132, 2014 • Pérez Art Museum Miami. Herzog & de Meuron, in: C3 361, 2014 • Gerhard Mack, Schweizer machen Stadt der Laster zur Kulturhochburg, in: Neue Zürcher Zeitung am Sonntag 08.12.2013 • Patricia Cohen, Miami Museum's Challenge: The Beach, in: The New York Times 05.12.2013 • Andres Viglucci, Miami's New Icon, in: The Miami Herald 01.12.2013 • Anne Tschida, The Dawning of a Museum, in: The Miami Herald 01.12.2013 • Alastair Gordon, Culture Club. With the new Pérez Art Museum Miami, Herzog & de Meuron have built a major artistic destination for a rapidly changing city, in: The Wall Street Journal Magazine, 12/2013 • Caroline Roux, Architect Christine Binswanger on Pérez Art Museum Miami, in: Financial

Times 30.11.2013 • Museo de Arte Pérez (PAMM), in: AV Monographs 157/158, 2012 • Herzog & de Meuron. Miami Art Museum. Miami, Florida (United States), in: Atlas. Architectures of the 21st Century. America, Bilbao 2010 • Terence Riley, Miami Art Museum, in: a+u 451, 2008 • Herzog & de Meuron: Work in Progress. Herzog & de Meuron's Miami Art Museum, Miami Art Museum, Miami 2008 • Andres Viglucci/ Daniel Chang, Art meets Park. Museum Design draws from Park, in: The Miami Herald 30.11.2007 • Herzog & de Meuron: un musée par an I, in: D'Architectures 01.2007.

No.**307**
Triangle
Paris, France

Since 2006

Project Phases
Concept Design
2006–2007, 2009
Schematic Design
2011–2012

Project Team
Partners
Jacques Herzog
Pierre de Meuron
Ascan Mergenthaler
Project Team
Raymond Jr. Gaëtan (Associate)
Stefan Goeddertz (Associate)
Michael Bär, Marta Colón de Carvajal Salis, Julien Combes, Guillaume Delemazure (Associate), Sarah Firth, Piotr Fortuna, Claire Gamet, Pauline Gaulard, Erik Gerlach, Yann Gramegna, Stefan Hörner, Shusuke Inoue, Kentaro Ishida (Associate), Anna Jach, Sara Jiménez Núñez, Daekyung Jo, Srdjan Jovanovic, Daniel Kiss, Yuichi Kodai, Pawel Krzeminski, Andrea Landell, Jaroslav Mach, Clément Mathieu, Leonardo Pérez-Alonso, Ella Ryhiner, Heeri Song, Basil Spiess, Masato Takahashi, Julie Wagner, Yves Wanger, Christian Zöllner

Client
Unibail-Rodamco, Paris, France

Planning
Architect
Herzog & de Meuron, Basel, Switzerland
Partner Architect
Valode & Pistre, Paris, France
Mechanical Engineering
Egis, Paris, France
Structural Engineering
Setec TPI, Paris, France
Climate Engineering, Environmental Engineering
Egis Concept (Elioth), Paris, France
Economist
AE75, Paris, France
Vertical Circulation
Arup, London, UK

Specialists/Consultants
Acoustics
LAMOUREUX, Paris, France
Security
SOCOTEC Construction et Immobilier, Paris, France
Fire Security / Code
CSD-FACES/APEX, Paris, France

Building Data
Site Area
7,500 sqm
Gross Floor Area
92,000 sqm
Building Footprint
5,627 sqm
Number of Levels
43
Building Dimensions
Length 200m
Width 35m
Height 180m

Bibliography • Christoph Heim, Ein pharaonischer Zacken, in: Basler Zeitung 07.07.2015 • Patrice Goulet, Conception démocratique. Democratic design, in: L'Architecture d'Aujourd'hui 12/2014 • Rudolf Balmer, Paris gegen Herzog & de Meuron, in: Basler Zeitung 21.11.2014 • Marc Zitzmann, Turmbau zu Paris. Herzog & de Meurons Tour Triangle, in: Neue Zürcher Zeitung 12.11.2014 • Bruno Monier-Vinard/Jacques Herzog, La tour Triangle, symbole d'un Paris vivant, in: Le Point 06.11.2014 • Benoît Hasse, Tour Triangle: l'expo de la dernière chance?, in: Le Parisien 31.10.2014 • Sibylle Vincendon, Tour Triangle cherche majorité, in: Libération 31.10.2014 • Bildbau. Building Images. Edited by: Hubertus Adam, Elena Kossovskaja, S AM Schweizerisches Architekturmuseum, Basel 2013 • Triángulo. Triangle, in: AV Monographs 157/158, 2012 • Herzog & de Meuron. Triangle Porte de Versailles, Paris (France), in: AV Proyectos 49, 2012 • Jean-François Chevrier, L'Objet, le Territoire, l'image, in: Le Phare 9/2011 • Stefan Ulrich, Um Himmels willen!, in: Süddeutsche Zeitung 02.04.2011 • Valérie Sasportas, Paris reprend de la Hauteur, in: Le Figaro 31.03.2011 • Triangle de Paris, in: The Tall Buildings Magazine 6/2010 • Una nuova Icona per Parigi. The Triangle, in: L'Arca 246, 2009 • Projet Triangle. Paris, France, in: L'Invention de la Tour Européenne. The Invention of the European Tower, Paris 2009 • Project Triangle in Paris by Herzog & de Meuron, in: a+u 459, 2008 • Laura Henderson, Avant-garde – at last, in: Financial Times 22.11.2008 • Aux portes de Paris, in: Le Point 20.11.2008 • Frédéric Edelmann, L'architecte Jacques Herzog's explique sur la tour qu'il doit construire à Paris, in: Le Monde 26.09.2008 • Nathalie Moutarde, Le débat sur les hauteurs est relancé, in: Le Moniteur 11.07.2008 • Martin Heller, Ein Hochhaus in Paris?, in: Modulor 1, 2008 • Una Cuña de Cristal a las Puertas de Paris, in: Arquitectura Viva 120, 2008.

No. 308
Private Residence
Los Angeles, California, USA

2006–2007

A large property up above Los Angeles, which is accessed by a picturesque road, has both woodlands and panoramic views of the city. As it stands, the existing residence is not large enough for the greater needs of the new owner. Following various volume studies with cubes and planes, Herzog & de Meuron propose a design that connects the two dominant landscape elements in a single topography. They extend the road, creating a sweeping ramp, which serves as a "roof" for the living quarters. All the various functions are arranged on the same north-south axis – from the service zone for domestic staff, to the client's private quarters, to the guest rooms and the garage. An alternative proposal envisages pitched-roof houses; another deploys simple, parallel wall panels that separate the rooms like partitions. These units can be various lengths; they allow the external windows to be placed individually and provide the means for creating extremely private verandas. More space is created under the place where the road widens out into a turning area. This contains the pool and the living area. Incisions can be used as top lights. A detached, free-floating roadway creates a protective cover over the entrance. While the external facade provides stunning views of Los Angeles, inside the curved structure there is an almost intimate garden. This design responds to the central role of the car in American life and turns apparent opposites – road and residence – into an organic combination of movement and destination, of journeying and arriving: a building block for a twenty-first-century metropolis.

Project Phases
Concept Design
2006–2007

Project Team
Partners
Jacques Herzog
Pierre de Meuron
Ascan Mergenthaler

Project Team
Charles Stone (Associate)
Jad Silvester
Edman Choy,
Chantal Reichenbach

Client
Peter Morton,
Los Angeles, CA, USA

Building Data
Site Area
13,700 sqm
Gross Floor Area
1,858 sqm
Building Footprint
2,323 sqm
Number of Levels
2
Building Dimensions
Length 107 m
Width 37 m
Height 6 m

No. 309
The Hard Field
Portsmouth, UK

2007

The city of Portsmouth, in collaboration with a private investor, wants to build a new stadium for Portsmouth Football Club, to be financed by 100,000 square meters of residential accommodation. The new location is to be a reclaimed dock near the entrance to the harbor. The city has a long history as an important naval base, always at the ready to protect the United Kingdom from French invaders, which also explains the proliferation of forts in the city. Herzog & de Meuron's concept study proposes a compact design, which lies in the former dock like a huge tanker but which also rises up – like another fort – above the carpet of terraced houses that surround the Docklands site. It also responds to the nearby, 150-meter viewing tower. Inside the stadium – as is the preference in the United Kingdom – the stands are as close to the pitch as possible. The brickwork on the outside of the stadium echoes the predominantly brick-built architecture of the rest of the city. Private apartments are integrated into the perimeter of the site – reminiscent of the architects' first football stadium, the St. Jakob stadium in Basel. The height of the complex echoes the course of the sun and increases on the waterfront side of the site. In order to ensure that the pitch receives the necessary ventilation and sunlight, the stadium takes the form of an asymmetrical ring at the harbor's edge. This also provides views of the water and of open areas that can be used for commercial enterprises. These reinstate the public character the site once had as a stretch of natural shoreline. The apartments are conceived as small units that look like individual bricks. However, the fact that two new super-size aircraft carriers will in future be based directly next to the site leads to the project being halted. A replacement project in a different location anticipates the concept of the stadium in Bordeaux. The brickwork facade – in a different, much more filigree form – is taken a stage further in the architects' design for the new stadium for Chelsea Football Club in London.

Project Phases
Concept Design
2007

Project Team
Partners
Jacques Herzog
Pierre de Meuron
Harry Gugger

Project Team
Ben Duckworth (Associate)
Tomislav Dushanov
Erik Gerlach, Daniel Kiss,
Julian Löffler, Sara
Secci, Christoph Zeller,
Christian Zöllner

Client
Sellar Property Group,
London, UK

Planning
Architect
Herzog & de Meuron,
Basel, Switzerland

Structural Engineering
Arup, London, UK

Specialists/Consultants
Visualizations
Philipp Schaerer,
Zurich, Switzerland

Building Data
Site Area
72,500 sqm
Gross Floor Area
234,005 sqm
Building Footprint
32,620 sqm
Number of Levels
25
Building Dimensions
Length 245 m
Width 167 m
Height 72 m

Bibliography · Notice Board, in: Mark. Another Architecture 9. 2007 · Stefan Reuter, Herzog & de Meurons neustes Stadion, in: Kulturmagazin, Basler Zeitung 27.04.2007 · Edwin Heathcote, Portsmouth FC signs up Top Architects, in: Financial Times 26.04.2007 · Herzog y de Meuron. Estadio de Fútbol, Portsmouth, in: AV Proyectos 23, 2007.

No.310
Project Study
London, UK

An investor thinks about an apartment building in the Borough of Southwark, which is already home to Tate Modern. Planning regulations in London list protected views that must remain unimpeded by any new buildings. Because two of these views cut right across the site, Herzog & de Meuron propose three towers of different heights, with small footprints. The shapes of the towers are entirely derived from their concrete frames: north-south wall sections determine the orientation. The protected views cut across the buildings and thus influence their overall shape and height. The space between the concrete wall sections and ceilings is filled by windows. The lift shafts lead to two apartments per floor, which, by virtue of their restricted depth, all have views to the outside in two directions. The surface of the concrete will be inset with stone, terrazzo, and glass, which will give this simple design a striking finish. With its compact, very pure architecture this project can be seen as a companion piece to the apartment block at 56 Leonard Street in New York, which was developed on the neighboring tables.

2007–2011

Project Phases
Concept Design
2007–2011

Project Team
Partners
Jacques Herzog
Pierre de Meuron
Harry Gugger
Ascan Mergenthaler

Project Team
Wim Walschap (Associate)
Jayne Barlow (Associate)
Ben Duckworth (Associate)
Jad Silvester
Peter Karl Becher, Aurélie
Blanchard, Frederik Bojesen,
Marta Brandão, Estelle
Chan, Oliver Cooke,
Simon Demeuse, Sidi
Gomes, Yann Gramegna,
Stephen Hodgson, Daniel
Kiss, Slavcho Kolevichin,
Osma Erik Lindroos, Julian
Löffler, Olivier Meystre,
Tom Powell, Ella Ryhiner,
Tilmann Schmidt, Mónica
Sedano Peralta, Fumiko
Takahama, Manuel
Villanueva, Thomas de Vries,
Jason Whiteley, Christoph
Zeller, Claudia Zipperle

Client
Sellar Property Group,
London, UK

Planning
Architect
Herzog & de Meuron,
Basel, Switzerland
Cost Consulting
Davis Langdon, London, UK
Structural Engineering,
Mechanical Engineering
Arup, London, UK
Landscape Design
Vogt Landschaftsarchitekten,
Zurich, Switzerland
Town Planning
DP9, London, UK
Chris Horn, London, UK
Ettwein Bridges, London, UK

Specialists/Consultants
Acoustics,
Civil Engineering, Facade,
Fire Protection, Traffic
Arup, London, UK

No.311
Waterfront Hotel
Helsinki, Finland

Helsinki's inner harbor reaches right into the city center. The splendid Esplanadi boulevard, with its pedestrian zone, ends here. Grand, historical buildings create an impressive skyline. The planned relocation of the freight harbor releases a number of sites directly by the water. An old terminal building for cruise ships is to be demolished and replaced with a hotel. The site is at the city end of Katajanokka, the island that forms one side of the inner harbor. Herzog & de Meuron create a design that illustrates the particular nature of this urban area. Two superimposed crosses echo the differently angled grids of the city center and the island. The ground floor – with public facilities, such as restaurant, café, and conference rooms – matches the orientation of the adjacent buildings; the diagonally placed cross shape of the upper layer with hotel accommodation is oriented toward the more distant inner city on the other side of the harbor basin. The lobby in the large, central space with its sculpturally inviting staircase, connects the private and public zones. In addition, the differently angled crosses provide covered open areas for winter and roof terraces for summer. The height of the structure as a whole takes account of the building by Alvar Aalto behind it. The facade of slightly irregular, square glass elements references the different aggregate states of water as ice and snow. A new dock will form another pearl in the string of small fishery docks dispersed around the inner harbor and connect the hotel directly with the water. A promenade extension to the Esplanadi and a new jetty connect the site to Helsinki's public spaces and open up the view back to the city center. However, the project is not approved by the Finnish Parliament, whose members vote to reject it.

2007–2008

Project Phases
Concept Design
2007–2008

Project Team
Partners
Jacques Herzog
Pierre de Meuron
Ascan Mergenthaler

Project Team
Tomislav Dushanov
(Associate)
Kivi-Mikael Keller

Client
AB Invest A/S,
Hamar, Norway

Planning
Architect
Herzog & de Meuron,
Basel, Switzerland
Construction Management
Skanska, Helsinki, Finland

Building Data
Site Area
8,500 sqm
Gross Floor Area
12,700 sqm
Building Footprint
2,450 sqm
Gross Volume
44,000 cubic meters

Eetu Arponen, Michael
Bär, Hauke Jungjohann,
Osma Lindroos, Sara
Secci, Iva Smrke

Bibliography • Marja Salmela, Eteläsatama voisi näyttää tältä. Uusi designhotelli nousee Katajanokalle, in: Helsingin Sanomat 07.03.2008 • Juha Ilonen, To Have and Have Not. Helsingin Keskeisen Rantamaiseman Uudet Tuulet. New Designs for Helsinki's Main Seafront, in: ark Arkkitehti/Finnish Architectural Review 105, 2008 • Introducing: Helsinki Waterfront Hotel, in: Nordicum 6, 2008 • Herzog y de Meuron en el frente de Helsinki, in: Arquitectura Viva 116, 2007.

Facade Surface
5,700 sqm

Number of Levels
5

Building Dimensions
Length 75 m
Width 75 m
Height 22 m

No.312
Helsinki Dreispitz
Münchenstein/Basel, Switzerland

2007–2014

Project Phases

Concept Phases
2007

Schematic Design
2008

Design Development
2008–2010

Construction Documents
2010–2011

Construction Services
2012–2014

Client
EG Basel Dreispitz,
Basel, Switzerland

Project Team

Partners
Jacques Herzog
Pierre de Meuron
Robert Hösl
Wim Walschap

Project Team
Andreas Reeg
Marc Schmidt (Associate)
Jan Ulbricht
Philip Albrecht, Liliana Filipa
Amorim Rocha, Michael Bär
(Associate), Janine Bolliger,
Luis Guzmán Grossberger,
Yuki Hamura, Carsten
Happel (Associate), Volker
Jacob, Martin Knüsel,
Slavcho Kolevichin, David
Pfister, Christian Schmitt,
Fumiko Takahama, Katharina
Thielmann, Christian Voss,
Léonie Wenz

Planning

**Project Architect,
Construction Management**
Herzog & de Meuron,
Basel, Switzerland

Electrical Engineering
Actemium,
Basel, Switzerland

HVAC Engineering
Waldhauser+Hermann,
Münchenstein, Switzerland

Plumbing Engineering
Locher Schwittay
Gebäudetechnik GmbH,
Basel, Switzerland

Structural Engineering
ZPF Ingenieure AG,
Basel, Switzerland

Client Representative
Rapp Arcoplan AG,
Basel, Switzerland

Building Ecology
Büro für Umweltchemie,
Zurich, Switzerland

Building Physics
Kopitsis Bauphysik AG,
Wohlen, Switzerland

Fire Protection
Visiotec Consulting AG,
Basel, Switzerland

Geometrician
Amman AG,
Basel, Switzerland

Consultants/Specialists

Site Management
ARGE Implenia Bau AG
and Spaini Bau AG,
Basel, Switzerland

Building Data

Site Area
1,488 sqm

Gross Floor Area
12,187 sqm

Building Footprint
991 sqm

Gross Volume
40,413 cubic meters

Facade Surface
5,582 sqm

Building Dimensions
Length 43m
Width 28m
Height 42m

Bibliography • Christophe Catsaros, L'Empilement Érigé en Symbole. Herzog & de Meuron, in: Archistorm 74, 2015 • Gerhard Mack, Kabinett der Wunder, in: Art 8/2015 • Gerhard Mack, Man muss dem Ort, an dem man lebt, Sorge tragen, in: Neue Zürcher Zeitung am Sonntag 14.06.2015 • Raphael Suter, Herzog & de Meurons Wunderkammer, in: Basler Zeitung, 10.06.2015 • Gabriele Detterer, Visionen für das Basler Dreispitzareal, in: Neue Zürcher Zeitung 07.05.2015 • Deyan Sudjic, Materia y memoria. Herzog & de Meuron's Archives in Dreispitz, in: Arquitectura Viva 174, 2015 • Deyan Sudjic, Labor und Wunderkammer. Das Archiv von Herzog & de Meuron in Basel, in: Werk 4/2015 • Rowan Moore, Two Decades of Herzog & de Meuron, in: The Architectural Review 3/2015 • Katharina Marchal, Archives and Housing, in: Mark 54, 2015 • Hubertus Adam, Kleine Schritte. Ein Basler Gewerbegebiet wird zum Kreativquartier umgebaut, in: Deutsche Bauzeitung 12/2014 • Claudia Schmid, Hohe Kunst in der Peripherie, in: SonntagsZeitung 14.09.2014 • Andres Herzog, Koloss und Quartier. Kunsthochschulen in Zürich und Basel auf neuem Campus, in: Hochparterre 9/2014 • Dominique Spirig, Der Dreispitz wird zur Edeladresse, in: Tageswoche 28.03.2014 • Daniel Wahl, Star-Architekten bauen Modelllager, in: Basler Zeitung 12.02.2014 • Axel Simon, Die Pioniertat, in: Hochparterre 10/2013.

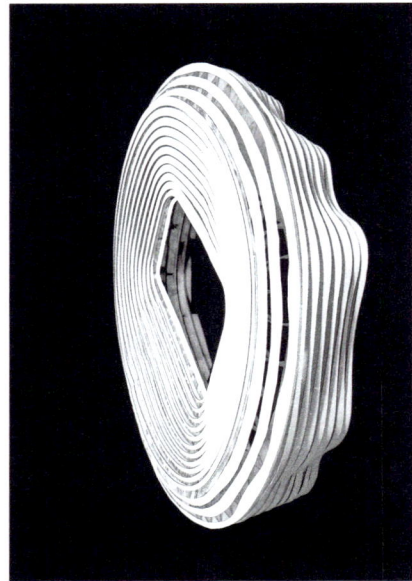

No.**313**
Nou Camp Nou Barcelona
Barcelona, Spain

2007

Barcelona Football Club decides to replace the old stadium at its ground. Herzog & de Meuron submit a competition entry that takes account of the surrounding area, so that the new stadium—in terms of its architecture and as urban landmark—will reflect and be worthy of this world-famous football club. The stadium will be encircled by a green belt containing the club's various training facilities. A new plaza can be used for parties and celebrations, for markets and other social activities on match-free days. The roads leading to the stadium will be developed as boulevards with trees and apartment blocks, thus contributing to the urban development of the neighborhood. For its part, the stadium will respond to the latter by being open to the city. The architects develop a Southern European design, which takes advan-

tage of the warm climate with its light-and-shade structure, as in the realized Nouveau Stade de Bordeaux. The open concourses turn the voluminous structure into a multiplicity of vibrant shapes containing twenty-four spiral staircases leading to the different levels in the stands. The three large dips containing the main entrances extend a welcome to the city outside. The six concourses running round the stadium look like terraces from afar and provide visitors with memorable views of Barcelona. By virtue of their very great depth they also serve as shady, sociable meeting places. The balustrades are various heights—like banners fluttering in the wind. The exterior is clad with reflective ceramic tiles. At night the light from the illuminated stadium radiates out into the city. Inside, the stadium is designed so that nothing detracts from the game. The 106,000 fans are as close to the pitch as possible in three steep tiers. The closed roof lets enough UV light through for the pitch. Additional facilities, such as a hotel, fitness center, restaurant, and small retail outlets ensure that there is still activity in the stadium when there is no football and integrate it into daily life in the surrounding area.

Project Phases	Project Team	Client	Specialists/Consultants	Building Data
Competition	**Partners**	**Client**	**Facade**	**Site Area**
2007	Jacques Herzog	FC Barcelona,	Arup, London, UK	161,900 sqm
	Pierre de Meuron	Barcelona, Spain	**Fire Protection**	**Gross Floor Area**
	Christine Binswanger		Estudi GL	200,650 sqm
			Francesc Labastida,	**Building Footprint**
	Project Team		Barcelona, Spain	54,050 sqm
	Miquel Rodríguez		**Climate Engineering**	**Gross Volume**
	(Associate)		Transsolar,	934,820 cubic meters
	Thomas de Vries		Stuttgart, Germany	**Facade Surface**
	Roman Aebi, Ida Richter		**Animation**	39,420 sqm
	Braendstrup, Alexander		Neutral, London, UK	**Number of Levels**
	Cunningham, Volker Helm,		**Visualizations**	8
	Yuko Himeno, Sara Jacinto,		Philipp Schaerer,	**Building Dimensions**
	Luis Játiva, Key Portilla		Zurich, Switzerland	Length 300m
	Kawamura, Xiaojing Lu,		Christian Zöllner,	Width 279m
	Katja Mezger, Miguel		Hamburg, Germany	Height 55m
	Ortiga, Kay Strehlke,			
	Masato Takahashi, Tobias			
	Winkelmann			

Planning
Architect
Herzog & de Meuron,
Basel, Switzerland
Cost Consulting
Integral SA,
Barcelona, Spain
Structural Engineering
Arup, London, UK
BOMA SL,
Barcelona, Spain
MEP Engineering
Arup, London, UK

Bibliography • Roberta Bosco, El Nou Camp Nou a debate, in: El País 26.09.2007 • Miquel Adrià, Nueva cara para el Barça, in: Arquine 42, 2007 • Concurso Nou Camp Nou, Barcelona. Herzog y de Meuron. Seleccionado, in: AV Proyectos 22, 2007.

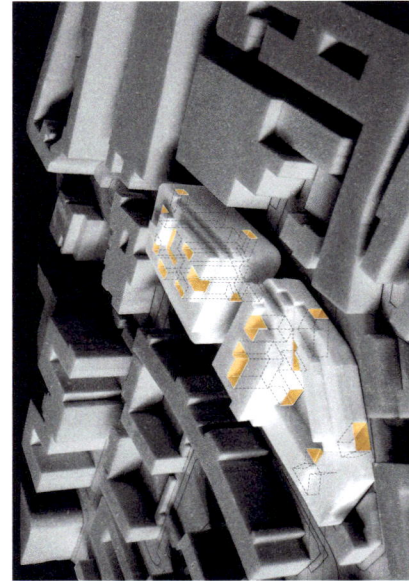

No.**314**
Project Study
London, UK

2007

The depot and office buildings, Clearings I and II, are located between Sloane Square and South Kensington Underground stations, in the heart of the Royal Borough of Kensington and Chelsea; two Underground lines cross under the site. Since the early 2000s this district has become an increasingly expensive residential area. In keeping with this trend, these two commercial properties are to be converted into apartments. Herzog & de Meuron propose retaining the 1930s building, with its concrete structure and brick facade, and extending it—in observance of

height regulations—in such a way that would take into account the two main styles of building in this area. To this end they consult the original architectural plans, which were not realized in full. Clearings I faces a large apartment block and will remain a single, solid entity. However, Herzog & de Meuron add two more stories and punctuate the building with private atriums that allow light to pour into these high-end homes. The ground floor houses a supermarket and retail outlets. Clearings II, a less compact overall shape, gains its missing parts, adjusted (by means of incisions into the building) to harmonize with the neighboring terraces. These "cuts" connect the newly added ring with the adjoining roads, providing shortcuts between the two Clearings will be turned into a green pedestrian zone, creating a closer connection between the buildings and passers-by.

Project Phases	Project Team	Client	Planning	Specialists/Consultants	Building Data
Concept Design	**Partners**	**Client**	**Architect**	**Traffic**	**Site Area**
2007	Jacques Herzog	Native Land, London, UK	Herzog & de Meuron,	Capita Symonds,	5,203 sqm
	Pierre de Meuron		Basel, Switzerland	London, UK	**Gross Floor Area**
	Harry Gugger		**Cost Consulting**		22,275 sqm
			EC Harris LLP, London, UK		**Number of Levels**
	Project Team		**Structural Engineering**		9
	Ben Duckworth (Associate)		Waterman Group,		**Building Dimensions**
	Key Portilla Kawamura		London, UK		Length 133m
	Ann Bertholdt, Yuko Himeno,		**Town Planning**		Width 45m
	Claudia da Silva		Drivers Jonas, London, UK		Height 30m

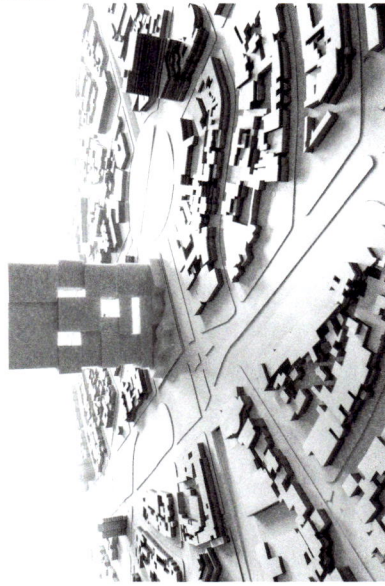

2007

The Canton of Basel-Stadt commissioned three architectural practices to prepare an experimental proposal for this area. Herzog & de Meuron's master plan refers to the study of 1991 and proposes two typologies. On the shoreline a compact development, with apartment blocks up to ten stories tall and with small public and private green spaces, lines the river in a contemporary variation on the closed, waterfront developments in the city and on the isolated modernist blocks, where the spaces between single structures are merely gaping voids. The embankments are retained as natural biotopes. Beyond this zone on the river, there are much lower, much less dense terraces and detached homes with green neighborhood roads, large, private open spaces, and a central park, reminiscent of the many versions of garden-city design that have been realized in the immediate vicinity throughout most of the twentieth century—as in the "Im Vogelsang" district, planned by Hans Bernoulli. The neighboring Hirzbrunnen district will be connected to the banks of the Rhine.

Planning

Architect
Herzog & de Meuron,
Basel, Switzerland

Specialists/Consultants

Representatives from Municipality of Riehen
Georges Tomaschett
(Head, Civil Engineering and Planning), Ivo Berweger
(Town Planning), Matthias Schmutz (Municipal Council)

Parks & Gardens Department
Susanne Brinkforth

Specialists
Marc Angélil,
Rainer Klostermann,
Urs Kohlbrenner

Building Data

Site Area
927,000 sqm

Gross Floor Area
420,000 sqm

Number of Levels
1–10

No. 315
Urban Study
Basel, Switzerland

"Basel - Eine Stadt im Werden?" (A Nascent City?), the study conducted in 1991 together with Rémy Zaugg, identifies three zones in the Basel area with outstanding potential for development. The three zones in question are the rail yards, the city on the Rhine, and the ring-shaped town, which connects zones of settlement once separated by all kinds of borders. The latter two meet in Basel Ost, a designated development area. At the point where the municipalities of Riehen and Birsfelden face each other over the Rheininsel, the redevelopment of the curved shorelines along the Rhine could add a new S-shape to the city at this "knee" in the river.

Project Phases
Concept Design
2007

Project Team

Partners
Jacques Herzog
Pierre de Meuron
Christine Binswanger

Project Team
Martin Knüsel
Soohyun Chang
Cecilia Dantas, Beatus Kopp,
Miguel Ortiga

Client
Hochbau- und Planungsamt,
Baudepartement
des Kantons Basel-Stadt,
Basel, Switzerland

Bibliography • Die Erweiterung der Stadt entlang des Rheins. Herzog & de Meuron, in: Testplanungen: Stadtrandentwicklungen Ost, Süd und Nordwest, Basel 2010.

2007–2008

Guadalajara, which is situated in an earthquake zone, consists of a mainly flat, urban landscape that has evolved from what were originally separate villages. There are few high-rise buildings here. An investor invites Herzog & de Meuron to design a high-rise building for an area that already has a number of taller buildings. The architects prepare a project study, exploring various ways of developing the city—from constructing a row of towers along the road, to clusters, to a new downtown area. Bearing in mind the unusual visibility of any new high-rise building in this area, they create an iconic shape: from one direction it looks like a thin slice, from another direction it is reminiscent of an Aztec mask. The required 75,000 square meters of floor space are arranged as a vertical town. A wide range of facilities and uses—hotel, residences, commercial units, offices, and a museum—are all accommodated in the various components of this one building. They are identifiable from outside by the clear stacking of "stone blocks." This stacking of "stone blocks" creates a connection between the relatively large scale of the building as a whole and the low structures that prevail in the city. The architects reinforce this effect by introducing open spaces—eyes, a nose, and a mouth—and planting these with gardens, which add a public use to this private investment project. However, the project is halted when the value of the land in this area vastly increases and the investor sells the site.

Building Data

Site Area
8,200 sqm

Gross Floor Area
75,510 sqm

Gross Volume
382,450 cubic meters

Facade Surface
90,000 sqm

Number of Levels
33

Building Dimensions
Length 110m
Width 25m
Height 150m

No. 316
High-rise Study
Guadalajara, Mexico

Project Phases
Concept Design
2007–2008

Project Team

Partner
Jacques Herzog
Pierre de Meuron
Stefan Marbach

Project Team
Peter Ferretto (Associate)
Andreas Fries (Associate)
Agustín Solórzano
Israel Álvarez, Joana Anes,
Andrea Landell, Maria
Ángeles Lerin Ruesca, Osma
Lindroos, Mateo Mori,
Carlos Viladoms

Client
Azul Banderas S.A. de C.V.,
Guadalajara, Mexico

No.**317**
Iglesia de la Natividad
Culiacán, Mexico

2007–2008

Project Phases

Concept Design
2007–2008

Project Team

Partners
Jacques Herzog
Pierre de Meuron
Stefan Marbach

Project Team
Peter Ferretto (Associate)
Andreas Fries (Associate)
Osma Lindroos, Agustín
Solórzano, Carlos Viladoms

Client
Enrique Coppel Luken /
Agustín Coppel Luken,
Culiacán, Mexico

Building Data

Site Area
8,200 sqm

Gross Floor Area
4,000 sqm

Gross Volume
46,000 cubic meters

Facade Surface
6,500 sqm

Number of Levels
7

Building Dimensions
Length 42 m
Width 32 m
Height 40 m

No.**318**
Actelion Research and Laboratory Building
Allschwil, Switzerland

2007–2013

Project Phases

Concept Design
2007

Schematic Design
2007–2008

Design Development
2008

Construction Documents
2008–2010

Construction Services
2009–2013

Project Team

Partners
Jacques Herzog
Pierre de Meuron
Stefan Marbach

Project Team
Martin Fröhlich (Associate)
Michael Fischer (Associate)
Martin Krapp
Christian Schmitt
Pascal Bögli, Ufuk Celik,
Christian Dehli, Carmen
Eichenberger, Catherina
Gebel, Guillaume Henry,
Roman Hutter, Hauke
Jungjohann, Hamit Kaplan,
Tanjo Klöpper, Melk Nigg,
Kevin Peter, Dulcineia Neves
dos Santos, Ralf Schwaller,
Mónica Sedano Peralta,
Hendrik Steinigeweg,
Jolanta Szybiak, Andreas
Thoma, Romy Weber

Client
Actelion Pharmaceuticals Ltd.,
Allschwil, Switzerland

Planning

Architect
Herzog & de Meuron,
Basel, Switzerland

**General Planning,
Construction Management,
Structural Engineering,
Acoustics, Building
Physics, Geometrician,
Security, Traffic,
Fire Protection**
Gruner AG, Ingenieure und
Planer, Basel, Switzerland

**HVAC Engineering,
Plumbing Engineering**
Gruneko AG, Ingenieure
für Energiewirtschaft,
Basel, Switzerland

Mechanical Engineering
Gruneko AG, Ingenieure
für Energiewirtschaft,
Basel, Switzerland
Transsolar,
Stuttgart, Germany

Electrical Engineering
Scherler AG Beratende
Ingenieure,
Basel, Switzerland

Laboratory Planning
Gruner AG, Ingenieure
und Planer,
Basel, Switzerland
Gruneko AG, Ingenieure
für Energiewirtschaft,
Basel, Switzerland

Landscape Design
Tita Giese,
Düsseldorf, Germany

Specialists/Consultants

Facade
PPEngineering,
Basel, Switzerland

Lighting
Matí AG Lichtplanung,
Adliswil, Switzerland

Building Data

Site Area
6,004 sqm

Gross Floor Area
37,200 sqm

Building Footprint
4,000 sqm

Gross Volume
137,500 cubic meters

Facade Surface
6,050 sqm

Number of Levels
6 aboveground
3 belowground

Building Dimensions
Length 135 m
Width 30 m
Height 22 m

2007–2014

No. 319
Naturbad Riehen
Riehen, Switzerland

Project Phases	Project Team	Client	Planning	Specialists/Consultants	Building Data
Concept Design 2007 **Schematic Design** 2008 **Design Development** 2008–2009 **Construction Documents** 2011–2012 **Construction Services** 2013–2014	**Partners** Jacques Herzog Pierre de Meuron **Project Team** Michael Bär (Associate) Harald Schmidt Sarah Righetti Jeanne Autran, Nathalie Birkhäuser, Nils Büchel, Judit Chapallaz-Laszlo, Tobias Josef Fritzenwenger, Benno Lincke, Miguel Palencia Olavarrieta	Gemeindeverwaltung Riehen, Riehen, Switzerland	**Architect** Herzog & de Meuron, Basel, Switzerland **Partner Architect, General Planning, Cost Consulting** Rapp Arcoplan AG, Basel, Switzerland **Electrical Engineering** Eplan, Basel, Switzerland **HVAC Engineering** Stokar + Partner AG, Basel, Switzerland **Plumbing Engineering** Locher Schwittay Gebäudetechnik GmbH, Basel, Switzerland **Structural Engineering** Ulmann & Kunz Bauingenieur AG, Basel, Switzerland Pirmin Jung, Rain, Switzerland **Timber Work** Pirmin Jung, Rain, Switzerland **Landscape Design** Fahrni und Breitenfeld, Basel, Switzerland Wasserwerkstatt Planungs- büro für Badegewässer, Bamberg, Germany **Natural Pool** Wasserwerkstatt Planungs- büro für Badegewässer, Bamberg, Germany	**Building Physics** Ehrsam und Partner, Basel, Switzerland **Civil Engineering** Gemeinde Riehen, Riehen, Switzerland **Geometrician** Jermann Ingenieure & Geometer AG, Pratteln, Switzerland **Geotechnics** Dr. von Moos AG, Zurich, Switzerland	**Site Area** 15,243 sqm **Gross Floor Area** 324 sqm **Building Footprint** 324 sqm **Gross Volume** 1,127 cubic meters **Facade Surface** 400 sqm **Number of Levels** 1

Bibliography • Piscina natural. Natural Swimming Pool, in: Arquine 73, 2015 • Natural Swimming Pool, Riehen, Switzerland, in: IW 104, 2015 • Claudia Moll, Freibäder in Oberwinterthur und Riehen von Walser Zumbrunn/Wäckerli/manoa und Herzog & de Meuron, in: Werk 6/2015 • Piscinas publicas en Riehen (Suiza). Structure and Facade in Larch Timber, in: Arquitectura Viva 174, 2015 • Finn Canonica, Man kann eine Stadt nicht einfach lassen, wie sie ist, sonst stirbt sie, in: Das Magazin 25.04.2015 • Olivier Namias, Naturbad Riehen, les bains naturels de Riehen, Suisse, in: D'Architectures 233, 2015 • Till Briegleb, Sie machen die Ausnahme zur Regel, in: Häuser 2/2015 • Tiers Paysage, in: Lotus International 157, 2015 • Alexander Hosch / Gunnar Brand, Architekturführer Schweiz. Die besten Bauwerke des 21. Jahrhunderts, München 2015 • Ulrike Kunkel, Pack die Badehose ein. Naturbad in Riehen (CH), in: Deutsche Bauzeitung 12/2014 • Priska Baechinger, Natürlich baden in Riehen.

Naturbad im Grenzbereich, in: Schweizer Bau Journal 12/2014 • Hubertus Adam, Naturbad Riehen, in: Deutsche Bauzeitung 10/2014 • Ansgar Staudt, Back to the Roots, in: Archithese 10/2014 • Teich mit Becken, in: Hochparterre 9/2014 • Ein Naturbad – natürlich mit Holz gestaltet, in: CH.Holzbau 8/2014 • Water, pure and simple. Riehen natural pool, in: sb 6/2014 • Naturbad Riehen, Natural Swimming Pool, Herzog & de Meuron, in: C3 346, 2014 • Konstanze Ziemke-Jerrentrup, Stararchitekten planen Schwimmteich bei Basel. Badi von Herzog & de Meuron, in: AB Archiv des Badewesens 11/2013 • Daniela Dietsche/Alexander Felix, Plantschen auf der Tunneldecke, in: Tec 21 01.03.2013 • Worth the Wait. The Naturbad Pool in Riehen, in: sb 3/2013 • Urs Rist, Ein dreiteiliger See für das Naturbad, in: Basler Zeitung 28.09.2011.

2008–2010

No. 320
Attila, Stage Design
The Metropolitan Opera, New York, New York, USA

Project Phases	Project Team	Client	Planning
Concept Design 2008 **Production** 2009–2010 **Premiere** 23 February 2010	**Partners** Jacques Herzog Pierre de Meuron **Project Team** Claudius Frühauf Kornelia Gysel **Collaboration (Set Design and Costume Design)** Miuccia Prada	The Metropolitan Opera, New York, NY, USA	**Stage Design, Costume Design** Herzog & de Meuron and Miuccia Prada **Conductor** Riccardo Muti **Director** Pierre Audi **Assistant Stage Directors** Gina Lapinski Paula Williams

Bibliography • Helena Matheopoulos, Miuccia Prada. Attila, in: Fashion Designers at the Opera, London 2011 • Peter Webster, From Skyscrapers to Stage Sets, in: Interior Design 9/2010 • Alexandra Lange, Attila, in: Icon 83, 2010 • Julie V. Iovine, Debut on the Rocks, in: The Architect's Newspaper 17.03.2010 • Anthony Tommasini, Dividing and Conquering,

Chorus Master
Donald Palumbo
Associate Costume Design
Robby Duiveman
Light Designer
Jean Kalman
Musical Director
James Levine
Technical Director
John Sellars
Technical Assistant
Paul Masck
General Manager
Peter Gelb

but Felled by Love, in: The New York Times 25.02.2010 • Herzog & de Meuron, Pierre Audi: Attila, in: Space 519, 2010 • Jacques Herzog/Kim Sang-ho, The Power of the Image in Architecture and the Stage, in: Space 519, 2010 • Pierre Audi/Kim Sang-ho: The Stage, Altered by Innovative Architecture, in: Space 519, 2010.

No. **321**

No. **321**
High-rise Study
New York, New York, USA

2007

During the construction boom before the real estate crisis, the historical Drake Hotel on Park Avenue in Manhattan was demolished. Together with a plot to the rear, this freed up an L-shaped site, which is now to be redeveloped with an office tower. The challenge is that the entrance has to be on Park Avenue, but the majority of the building will be located to the rear. Herzog & de Meuron create a design that envisages a small plaza on the Park Avenue side, with a public path leading diagonally toward the entrance. This path runs by a multistory department store, which the architects slightly taper toward the top like a gold bar. Above that an extremely slim building rises up like a blade into the sky above Park Avenue, partially obscuring the main building to the rear. During the planning process the client decided instead to use this site for privately owned apartments, which—according to building regulations—can be built higher than office spaces. However, the slim structure is not suitable for residential accommodation, so the architects design a single structure that is determined by the shape of the site and uses a triangulated geometry to achieve the largest possible outer shell. The rotation of the form creates an architectural design that is ultimately not approved by the client, as can be seen from the realized project.

Project Phases	Project Team	Client
Concept Design	**Partners**	Macklowe Properties,
2007	Jacques Herzog	New York, NY, USA
	Pierre de Meuron	
	Ascan Mergenthaler	
	Project Team	
	David Koch (Associate)	
	Edman Choy	
	Alexander Bürgi, Evan	
	Chakroff, Dara Huang, Yuichi	
	Kodai, Kenan Liu, James	
	Richards, Joana Simoes,	
	Christian Voss	

Planning	Specialists/Consultants	Building Data
Design Consultant	**Vertical Circulation**	**Site Area**
Herzog & de Meuron,	Jappsen Ingenieure GmbH,	39,390 sqm
Basel, Switzerland	Berlin, Germany	
Partner Architect	Arup, London, UK	
SLCE Architects,	**Zoning**	
New York, NY, USA	Development Consulting	
Moed de Armas	Services Inc,	
& Shannon Architects,	New York, NY, USA	
New York, NY, USA		
Structural Engineering		
Arup, London, UK		
Gilsanz, Murray, Steficek LLP,		
New York, NY, USA		
HVAC Engineering,		
Plumbing Engineering		
Arup, London, UK		
Cosentini Associates,		
New York, NY, USA		

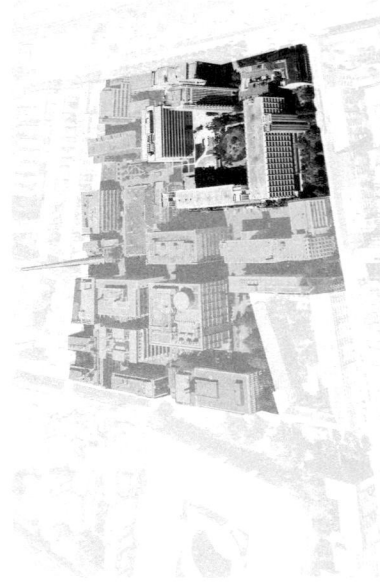

No. **322**

No. **322**
Urban Study
Basel, Switzerland

2007

The agribusiness Syngenta has relocated its research facilities and plans to restructure its global headquarters at its Rosental site in Basel. The majority of the site has been sold and the remaining 25,000 square meters directly across from the Badischer Bahnhof are to be redesigned and optimized to meet the administration requirements of a modern company. Besides a conference center, meeting rooms, and a representative entrance area, the brief also includes 1,500 work spaces, which can be used either as single offices or as office clusters. The site already has buildings from different epochs and in a range of contrasting styles and sizes. One high-rise, in very poor condition, has to be demolished. Herzog & de Meuron prepare a concept study, which makes full use of the site's business and urban poten-

tial, and develop an architectural design that reflects the company's philosophy. A concept that would largely retain the existing buildings would require the costly, full renewal of their insulation and, because of their inefficient footprints, a considerable expansion of floor space. The architects therefore propose demolishing all but one of the buildings—the historical Geigy House—and concentrating all the work spaces in a single, 110-meter high-rise block. The almond-shaped design is reminiscent of seeds, which are at the heart of Syngenta's business; its orientation at right angles to the road and the railroad tracks maximizes its visibility to all those passing by. The minimal depth of the building creates a see-through structure and prevents the tower from dominating its urban surroundings. An undulating glass facade on the city side generates complex reflections that appear to reduce the volume of the building as do the air spaces at the spindle ends. The vertical gardens, planned for these spaces, will connect with the parklands—looking out toward the city—in the reclaimed areas on the site. The design has a certain affinity with the Tour Phare in Paris, the headquarters of BBVA in Madrid, and the Roche Building 1 in Basel.

No. 323
Urban Study
Klin, Russian Federation

2007–2008

A national development program for commerce and research sees the rapid founding of new satellite towns around Moscow. They are situated at the intersections of radial routes out of Moscow and a series of concentric rings, and are to be developed by oligarchs. Herzog & de Meuron are invited to conduct an urban study for a new town, with 450,000 inhabitants, near the industrial city of Klin, ninety kilometers northwest of Moscow. Firmly sidestepping the utilitarianism and centralism of Soviet modernism, the architects propose three towns, which would more readily lend themselves to being constructed in stages and which could also be more easily adapted to changing circumstances. This area is presently made up of forests

and agricultural land; the inhabitants live in numerous villages, many of which have just one main street. The viability study draws circles around three larger settlements, which are to be developed according to different patterns, thus avoiding monotonous repetition. Particular attention is paid to the formulation of the transitions between urban areas and the open countryside; there are restrictions on development projects in forested areas. In the center of the largest circle a new university anchors the whole project. Rises in the flat landscape are used for landmark buildings. Long roads echo the prospekts that are part of traditional urban design in Russia. In the central circle the grid tends more toward a square, in the smallest circle the grid is based on a cross-shaped figure. In all three zones–in a region with many rivers–dams become a typical design feature. The name of the city–Tchaikovsky–alludes to the fact that the composer lived in Klin at the end of his life. This project is not taken further, unlike the plans for the new town of Skolkovo, designed for just 17,000 inhabitants and situated closer to Moscow.

Project Phases
Concept Design
2007

Client
Syngenta Crop Protection
AG, Basel, Switzerland

Project Team

Partners
Jacques Herzog
Pierre de Meuron
Christine Binswanger

Project Team
Christoph Röttinger
Pascal Bögli, Cecilia Dantas,
Piotr Fortuna, Jochen
Seelos, Claudia da Silva,
Fumiko Takahama

Project Phases
Concept Design
2007–2008

Client
Russian Land,
Moscow, Russian Federation

Project Team

Partners
Jacques Herzog
Pierre de Meuron

Project Team
Tomislav Dushanov
(Associate)
Anna Jach
Olga Bolshanina, Pasqual
Herrero-Vincent, Pawel
Krzeminski, Jonathan
Muecke, Karolina Slawecka

Consultant
Sustainability
Ove Arup & Partners,
Cardiff, UK/
St. Petersburg,
Russian Federation

Building Data
Site Area
53km²

Gross Floor Area
36,665,000 sqm

No. 324
New Headquarters for BBVA
Madrid, Spain

2007–2015

Project Phases
Competition
2007

Schematic Design
2008–2009

Design Development
2008–2009

Construction Documents
2009–2010

Construction Services
2009–2015

Completion Phase 1
2009–2013

Completion Phase 2
2010–2015

Client
BBVA – Banco Bilbao
Vizcaya Argentaria SA,
Madrid, Spain

Project Team

Partners
Jacques Herzog
Pierre de Meuron
Christine Binswanger
David Koch

Project Team
Nuno Ravara (Associate)
Miquel Rodríguez
(Associate)
Stefan Goeddertz
(Associate)
Benito Blanco
Alexander Franz
Mónica Ors
Thomas de Vries
Alexa Nürnberger
Xavier Molina
Enrique Peláez

Planning

**Design Consultant,
Artistic Supervision**
Herzog & de Meuron SL,
Barcelona, Spain

Joint Venture
UTE Nueva Sede BBVA
(Herzog & de Meuron SL,
Drees & Sommer,
Martínez FM Arquitectos),
Madrid, Spain

Executive Architect
Ortiz y León Arquitectos,
Madrid, Spain
CBRE FM Arquitectos,
Madrid, Spain

Specialists/Consultants

Acoustics
Estudi Acústic Higini Arau,
Barcelona, Spain

Building Physics
Transsolar,
Stuttgart, Germany
Arup, London, UK
Arup, Madrid, Spain

Catering
DIMASA, Madrid, Spain

Facade Engineering
Arup, Madrid, Spain
Enar SL, Madrid, Spain

Fire Protection
Arup, Madrid, Spain
Estudi GL
Francesc Labastida,
Barcelona, Spain

Building Data
Site Area
59,125 sqm

Gross Floor Area
251,979 sqm

Building Footprint
56,635 sqm

Gross Volume
1,004,775 cubic meters

Facade Surface
46,928 sqm

Number of Levels
3 (horizontal building)
19 (tower)

Building Dimensions
Length 290m
Width 189m
Height 93m

↑

Project Team (Continuation)
Nuria Tejerina
Manuel Villanueva
Ainoa Prats
Fernando Alonso, Joana
Anes, Edyta Augustynowicz,
Tiago Baldaque, Lucia
Bentue, Abel Blancas,
Ignacio Cabezas, Aurélien
Caetano, Soohyun Chang,
Miguel Chaves, Sergio
Cobos, Marta Colón de
Carvajal, Massimo Corradi,
Pastora Cotero, Miquel Del
Rio, Dorothée Dietz, Aurelio
Dorronsoro, Margaux
Eyssette, Salvora Feliz,
Cristina Fernández, Daniel
Fernández, Alfonso García,
Patricia García, Cristina
Génova, Silvia Gil, Jorge
Gomendio, Juan Manuel
Gómez, Juan José
González-Castellón, Ulrich
Grenz, Hendrik Gruss, Paz
Gutiérrez Plaza, Carsten
Happel, Guillaume Henry,
Pasqual Herrero, Carlos
Higinio Esteban, Dara Huang,
Esther Jiménez, Vasilis
Kalisperakis, Hyunseok
Kang, Yuichi Kodai, Isabel
Labrador, Lorenz Lachauer,
Sophia Lau, Monica Leung,
Christina Liao, Cristina
Limiñana, Jorge López,
Khaled Malas, Sara Martínez,
Natalia Miralles, Aram
Mooradian, Argel Padilla,
Svetlin Peev, Pedro Peña
Jurado, Simon Pillet, Tomas
Pineda, Pedro Polónia, Maki
Portilla-Kawamura, Jaume
Prieto, Tosca Salinas, Marc
Schmidt (Associate),
Alexandra Schmitz, Ursula
Schneider, Günter Schwob,
Mónica Sedano Peralta,
Nicola Shunter, Kai Strehlke,
Carlos Terriente, Diana-
Ionela Toader, Raúl Torres
Martin, Carlos Viladoms

Collaboration
External Supervision:
Virgilio Gutiérrez

General Planning
UTE Nueva Sede BBVA,
Madrid, Spain
Ortiz y Léon Arquitectos,
Madrid, Spain
**Electrical Engineering,
HVAC Engineering,
Mechanical Engineering,
Plumbing Engineering**
Arup, London, UK
Arup, Madrid, Spain
Grupo JG, Madrid, Spain
Estudio PVI,
Barcelona, Spain
Structural Engineering
Arup, London, UK
Arup, Madrid, Spain
BOMA SL,
Barcelona, Spain
INES, Madrid, Spain
Landscape Design
Vogt Landschaftsarchitekten,
Zurich, Switzerland
Benavidez Laperche,
Madrid, Spain
Phares, Madrid, Spain
Álvaro Aparicio,
Madrid, Spain
Urban Design
Ezquiaga SL,
Madrid, Spain
**Cost Consulting, Design
Project Management**
Drees & Sommer SL,
Barcelona, Spain
Integral SA,
Barcelona, Spain
Project Management
Hill International,
Madrid, Spain

Lighting
Arup, London, UK
Estudio PVI,
Barcelona, Spain
Artec 3, Barcelona, Spain
Security
SMDOS, Madrid, Spain
Traffic
Karajan Ingenieure GmbH,
Stuttgart, Germany

Bibliography • Pedro Blasco, El nuevo Gigante de Madrid, in: El Mundo 13.04.2015 • Laura Zamarriego, Arquitectura inteligente. Hacia la transformación urbana, in: Ethic: La van- guardia de la sostenibilidad 16, 2014 • Herzog & de Meuron. Nueva sede de BBVA. New BBVA Headquarters, Madrid (Spain), in: AV Proyectos 63, 2014 • Herzog & de Meuron. Forslag til Hovedkvarter, BBVA, Madrid 2008, in: Arkitektur Magasinet 5/2009 • Herzog & de Meuron: Nueva Sede Corporativa BBVA en Madrid. New Headquarters for the BBVA Bank in Madrid, in: Pasajes Arquitectura y Crítica 105, 2009 • Patrick Zamarián, Bankprojekt für Madrid von HdM, in: Modulor, 3/2009 • Guido Musante, Green Projects. Sette Idee di Sostenibilità. Seven Ideas for Sustainability, in: Domus 922, 2009 • The New Headquarters of BBVA, in: Architectural Creations 2/2009 • Jacques Herzog/Luis Alberto Álvarez, Queremos hacer un Oasis en un Desierto urbano, in: El Mundo 17.12.2008 • Carmen Sánchez-Silva, BBVA destinará 300 millones a 'reconstruir' su nueva sede, in: El País 07.06.2008 • El, sol de Madrid', de Dorado a Plata, in: Arquitectura Viva 122, 2008.

No. **325**
Urban Study
Basel, Switzerland

2007–2008

In their urban study "Vision Dreispitz" (2003) Herzog & de Meuron divide the approximately 125-acre, hitherto customs-free area into three zones, characterizing the development potential of each with the names Manhattan, SoHo, and Queens. For logistical reasons the central section of SoHo, with its linear, urban structure, is to be preserved; the gradual addition of apartments, lofts, studios, retail outlets, and workshops will breathe new life into this area. The anchor point is the new higher-education node, the Campus des Bildes (Campus of the Image), which the architects envisaged in their original study and which has since been realized. The Christoph Merian Foundation (which owns this site), together with the Canton of Basel-Stadt and the Canton of Basel-Landschaft, commissions Herzog & de Meuron to draw up detailed plans for the central Wien-Strasse (based on their study), which will lay the foundations for a wider urban development project. The widest street in the neighborhood–660 meters in length and just 26 meters in breadth–cuts diagonally through the new district, leading toward former marshalling yards. The architects turn the spotlight on this public thoroughfare and redesign it as a green, car-free boulevard, which will retain its status as a central Broadway when the surrounding areas have been built up. Narrow, elongated buildings are interspersed with cross-routes and green pockets. The architects also propose a sequence of detached buildings, visibly separated from one another, which line the boulevard and–with a minimum height of twelve meters–palpably enclose the space. A small park connects the boulevard with the neighboring Campus des Bildes. At its north and south ends, a high-rise building signals the special significance of this central axis. A flexible response to requirements, the cultivation of small irregularities, and a dialogue between old and new buildings can accommodate the long-term leases and measured pace of change in this district.

Project Phases

Concept
2007–2008

Project Team

Partner
Jacques Herzog
Pierre de Meuron
Christine Binswanger

Project Team
Sarah Righetti
Silja Ebert, Lisa Euler,
Judith Funke

Client

Baudepartement des
Kantons Basel-Stadt,
Hochbau- und Planungsamt,
Basel, Switzerland

Planning

**Planning Partners
Workshop**
Christoph Merian Stiftung,
Basel, Switzerland
Gemeinde Münchenstein,
Münchenstein, Switzerland
Dreispitzverwaltung,
Basel, Switzerland
Bau- und Umweltschutz-
direktion, Amt
für Raumplanung,
Liestal, Switzerland

Building Data

Site Area
35,000 sqm

Gross Floor Area
120,000 sqm

No. **326**
The Umm Lafina Island Project
Abu Dhabi, UAE

2007–2008

In the context of long-term urban development plans, to be completed in 2030, the Abu Dhabi government wants to create a new residential area for the rapidly increasing population of the largest of the emirates in the Persian Gulf. However, this new district is to retain its natural characteristics and to be constructed on a human scale. A private client commissions Herzog & de Meuron to create a master plan for the islands of Umm and Lafina. These islands are not more than ten kilometers from the center of the city and the airport, yet they still boast mangrove forests that give them a very distinct character, unlike that of the other islands selected for development, such as Saadiyat, Al Reem, and Al Nar. Initially the architects consider high-density living, but then they decide instead that the relative seclusion of these islands, combined with their proximity to the city, is better suited to a low-traffic, high-end residential area with no more than 5,000 units. The islands' natural features–water, sand, and mangroves–should all come into their own. A wide variety of dwellings is envisaged–from apartments to detached residences to luxurious palaces–interconnected by a network of walls, which accentuate the predetermined plot layout. The walls are complemented by a system of canals. Green spaces and parks form anchor points, with a number of houses arranged around them, and create a patchwork of open spaces. The sizes of the two- or three-story private dwellings all conform to the same regulations and adjoin one of the perimeter walls in order to make the best use of each building plot. Cantilevered projections into the road create shade; windows are often set far back into the walls in order to prevent the sun shining directly into the house. Two marinas on the easily navigable north side of the larger island form the urban cores. Public facilities–such as schools, hospitals, administration offices, cultural venues, restaurants, and shops–are clustered around the marinas. A mosque on the larger island and a golf course on the south island (with its greater preponderance of palaces) provide different kinds of green spaces. The entire development, even including the waste-disposal system, is solar powered and fully sustainable.

Project Phases

Concept Design
2007–2008

Project Team

Partners
Jacques Herzog
Pierre de Meuron
Harry Gugger

Project Team
Ben Duckworth (Associate)
Joris Fach
Aurélie Blanchard, Arnaldo
Hernandez, Olivier Meystre

Client

ZAYA LLC,
Dubai, UAE

Planning

Architect
Herzog & de Meuron,
Basel, Switzerland

**HVAC Engineering,
Mechanical Engineering,
Structural Engineering,
Civil Engineering, Traffic**
Arup, London, UK

Landscape Design
Vogt Landschaftsarchitekten,
Zurich, Switzerland

Building Data

Site Area
4,950,000 sqm

Gross Floor Area
1,920,000 sqm

Number of Levels
3

PROJECTS 327–447 WILL BE PRESENTED IN FUTURE VOLUMES

NO. 327 FELTRINELLI PORTA VOLTA
Milan, Italy
Project 2008–2011,
realization 2011–2016
NO. 328 FEASIBILITY STUDY
Basel, Switzerland
Project 2008
NO. 329 PORTSMOUTH HORSEA ISLAND
Portsmouth, UK
Project 2008
NO. 330 LYON, LA CONFLUENCE
Lyon, France
Project 2008
NO. 331 KOLKATA MUSEUM OF MODERN ART, KMOMA
Kolkata, India
Project 2008–
NO. 332 PROJECT STUDY
Tokyo, Japan
Project 2008
NO. 333 LORD'S MASTER PLAN
London, UK
Competition 2008,
project 2008–2009
NO. 334 PROJECT STUDY
Paris, France
Project 2008–2010
NO. 335 PRIVATE HOUSE
Napa Valley, California, USA
Project 2008–2010,
realization 2010–2012
NO. 336 PROJECT STUDY
Paris, France
Project 2008
NO. 337 HERZOG & DE MEURON AND AI WEIWEI. INSTALLATION PIECE FOR THE VENICE ARCHITECTURE BIENNALE
11. Mostra Internazionale di Architettura:
Out There: Architecture Beyond Building
Italian Pavilion, Venice, Italy
Exhibition 14 September–23 November 2008
NO. 338 PROJECT STUDY
Project 2008–2009
NO. 339 WALDORF ASTORIA
Beijing, China
Project 2008–2009
NO. 340 ATELIER IN DÜSSELDORF
Düsseldorf, Germany
Project 2008–2011,
realization 2010–2011
NO. 341 PROJECT STUDY
Monte Carlo, Monaco
Project 2009
NO. 342 QUINTA DOS
Los Cabos, Mexico
Project 2008–2009
NO. 343 SÃO PAULO CULTURAL COMPLEX LUZ
São Paulo, Brazil
Project 2009–
NO. 344 URBAN STUDY
Basel, Switzerland
Competition 2008
NO. 345 ROCHE BUILDING 1
Roche Basel Site, Basel, Switzerland
Project 2009–2015,
realization 2011–2015
NO. 346 PROJECT STUDY
Ashgabat, Turkmenistan
Competition 2009
NO. 347 BEIRUT TERRACES
Beirut, Lebanon
Project 2009–2012,
realization 2012–2016
NO. 348 GASKLOCKA, A TOWER FOR NORRA DJURGÅRDSSTADEN
Stockholm, Sweden
Project 2009–
NO. 349 PARRISH ART MUSEUM
Water Mill, New York, USA
Project 2009–2010,
realization 2010–2012
NO. 350 CASTAGNOLA 1747
Lugano, Switzerland
Project 2009–,
planned completion 2017
NO. 351 BARRANCA MUSEUM OF MODERN AND CONTEMPORARY ART
Guadalajara, Mexico
Project 2009–
NO. 352 NATIONAL ART MUSEUM OF CHINA, NAMOC
Beijing, China
Competition 2010–2011
NO. 353 SHANTOU UNIVERSITY MEDICAL COLLEGE
Shantou, China
Project 2009–2014,
realization 2014–2016
NO. 354 URBAN VISION FOR MÃE LUÍZA
Mãe Luíza, Natal, Brazil
Project 2009
NO. 354.1 ARENA DO MORRO
Mãe Luíza, Natal, Brazil
Project 2011–2012,
realization 2012–2014

NO. 355 LYON, LA CONFLUENCE, MASTER PLAN 2ND PHASE
Lyon, France
Project 2009–
NO. 356 MUSÉE UNTERLINDEN, EXTENSION
Colmar, France
Competition 2009,
project 2010–2012,
realization 2012–2015
NO. 357 URBAN STUDY
Hangzhou, China
Competition 2009–2011
NO. 358 STRUCTURE FOR THE CULIACÁN BOTANICAL GARDEN
Culiacán, Mexico
Project 2009, 2012–
NO. 359 TOUR GRAND LILLE
Lille, France
Project 2009
NO. 360 PROJECT STUDY
Switzerland
Project 2009–2010
NO. 361 DAYCARE
Allschwil, Switzerland
Project 2009–2010
NO. 362 ASKLEPIOS 8 – AN OFFICE BUILDING ON THE NOVARTIS CAMPUS
Basel, Switzerland
Project 2010–2015,
realization 2012–2015
NO. 363 BASELSTRASSE
Laufen, Switzerland
Project 2010,
realization 2013–2014
NO. 364 URBAN STUDY
Competition 2010
NO. 365 TEHUAMIXTLE MASTER PLAN
Tehuamixtle, Mexico
Project 2010
NO. 366 PROJECT STUDY
Project 2010–
NO. 367 NOUVEAU STADE DE BORDEAUX
Bordeaux, France
Competition 2010–2011,
project 2011–2012,
realization 2013–2015
NO. 368 THE BROAD MUSEUM
Los Angeles, California, USA
Competition 2010
NO. 369 RICOLA KRÄUTERZENTRUM
Laufen, Switzerland
Project 2010–2013,
realization 2013–2014
NO. 370 PAVILION AT A LAKESIDE
Project 2010,
realization 2011
NO. 371 PROJECT MONROE
Singapore
Competition 2010
NO. 372 PROJECT STUDY
Shanghai, China
Project 2010
NO. 373 PROJECT STUDY
Calvià, Majorca, Spain
Project 2010
NO. 374 CHÄSERRUGG, TOGGENBURG
Unterwasser, Switzerland
Project 2011, 2013–2014,
realization 2014–2015
NO. 374.1 TALSTATION
Unterwasser, Switzerland
Project 2014–
NO. 374.2 GONDELBAHN ESPEL– STÖFELI–CHÄSERRUGG
Toggenburg, Switzerland
Project 2014,
realization 2015
NO. 375 PROJECT STUDY
Damascus, Syria
Competition 2011
NO. 376 PROJECT STUDY
Istanbul, Turkey
Project 2011
NO. 377 KINDERSPITAL ZÜRICH
Zurich, Switzerland
Competition 2011–2012,
project 2014–,
planned completion 2021
NO. 378 PROJECT STUDY
Seoul, South Korea
Project 2011
NO. 379 VOLKSHAUS BASEL, BAR, BRASSERIE
Basel, Switzerland
Project 2011–,
realization Bar, Brasserie 2011–2012
NO. 380 HERZOG & DE MEURON WEBSITE
Basel, Switzerland
Project 2008–2011,
version 1.0 2011
NO. 381 PROJECT STUDY
Basel, Switzerland
Project 2011
NO. 382 PROJECT STUDY
Beirut, Lebanon
Project 2011–2012
NO. 383 PROJECT STUDY
São Paulo, Brazil
Competition 2011
NO. 384 OBERES KANDERGRIEN
Spiez, Switzerland
Competition 2011–2012

NO. 385 SKOLKOVO UNIVERSITY DISTRICT MASTER PLAN
Skolkovo, Russia
Project 2011–2012
NO. 386 URBAN STUDY
Basel, Switzerland
Competition 2011–2012
NO. 387 BLAVATNIK SCHOOL OF GOVERNMENT
Oxford, UK
Project 2011–2013,
realization 2013–2015
NO. 388 PRIVATE HOUSE
Mexico
Project 2011–2013,
realization 2013–2016
NO. 389 ZELLWEGERPARK USTER
Uster, Switzerland
Project 2011–2013,
realization 2013–2015
NO. 390 URBAN STUDY
Basel, Switzerland
Competition 2011–2012
NO. 391 ERNEUERUNG KLINIKUM 2
Basel, Switzerland
Competition 2012–2013
NO. 392 CITYCENTERDC
Washington, D.C., USA
Competition 2011,
project 2011–
NO. 393 URBAN STUDY
Basel, Switzerland
Competition 2012
NO. 394 SCHAULAGER SATELLITE
Messeplatz Basel/Art Basel,
Basel, Switzerland
Project and realization 2011–2012,
4–17 June 2012
NO. 395 URBAN STUDY
Project 2012–2013
NO. 396 JADE SIGNATURE
Sunny Isles Beach, Florida, USA
Project 2012–
NO. 397 PROJECT STUDY
Zurich, Switzerland
Project 2012–2014
NO. 398 ROCHE BUILDING 98
Roche Basel Site, Basel, Switzerland
Project 2012–
NO. 399 REAL MADRID STADIUM
Madrid, Spain
Competition 2012–2013
NO. 400 SERPENTINE GALLERY PAVILION, HERZOG & DE MEURON AND AI WEIWEI
Kensington Gardens, London, UK
Project and realization 2011–2012,
1 June–14 October 2012
NO. 401 THE MACALLAN NEW DISTILLERY
Easter Elchies, Craigellachie, Scotland, UK
Competition 2012
NO. 402 ERWEITERUNG DES STADT- CASINOS BASEL
Basel, Switzerland
Project 2012–,
planned completion 2019
NO. 403 FLINDERS STREET STATION
Melbourne, Australia
Competition 2012–2013
NO. 404 ONE PARK DRIVE
Canary Wharf, London, UK
Project 2012–
NO. 405 IGLESIA EN CIUDAD JUÁREZ
Ciudad Juárez, Mexico
Project 2012–
NO. 406 PROJECT STUDY
Beijing, China
Project 2012–2013
NO. 407 NEW NATIONAL STADIUM TOKYO
Tokyo, Japan
Competition 2012
NO. 408.1 SKOLKOVO INSTITUTE OF SCIENCE AND TECHNOLOGY, EAST RING
Skolkovo, Russia
Project 2012–
NO. 409 215 CHRYSTIE
New York, New York, USA
Project 2012–,
planned completion 2017
NO. 410 AREAL NAU
Laufen, Switzerland
Project 2012–2015
NO. 411 PROJECT STUDY
Seoul, South Korea
Project 2012–
NO. 412 MIU MIU AOYAMA
Tokyo, Japan
Project 2012–2014,
realization 2014–2015
NO. 413 PROJECT STUDY
Basel, Switzerland
Project 2012–2013
NO. 414 HELVETIA, EXTENSION OF HEAD OFFICE, WEST WING
St. Gallen, Switzerland
Competition 1989,
project 2013–,
planned completion 2017
NO. 415 M+
Hong Kong, China
Competition 2012–2013,
project 2013–,
planned completion 2019

NO. 416 NEW NORTH ZEALAND HOSPITAL
Hillerød, Denmark
Competition 2013–2014, project 2014–
NO. 417 VITRA SCHAUDEPOT
Vitra Campus, Weil am Rhein, Germany
Project 2013,
realization 2014–2016
NO. 418 MERET OPPENHEIM TOWER
Basel, Switzerland
Competition 2002, project 2013–
NO. 419 HELVETIA CAMPUS BASEL
Basel, Switzerland
Project 2013–
NO. 420 LEROY STREET
New York, New York, USA
Project 2013–,
planned completion 2018
NO. 421 ROCHE BUILDING 21
Roche Basel Site, Basel, Switzerland
Project 2013–
NO. 422 TESTPLANUNG PARKHAUS MESSEPLATZ
Basel, Switzerland
Project 2013–2014
NO. 423 ÎLOT A3
Lyon, France
Project 2013–
NO. 424 PRIVATE HOUSE
Switzerland
Project 2013
NO. 425 ROCHE PRED CENTER
Roche Basel Site, Basel, Switzerland
Project 2015–
NO. 426 NATIONAL LIBRARY OF ISRAEL
Jerusalem, Israel
Competition 2013, project 2013–,
planned completion 2020
NO. 427 URBAN STUDY
Basel, Switzerland
Project 2013
NO. 428 URBAN STUDY
Mexico City, Mexico
Project 2013–2014
NO. 429 STAMFORD BRIDGE
London, UK
Project 2013–
NO. 430 ASTRAZENECA'S STRATEGIC RESEARCH & DEVELOPMENT CENTRE AND GLOBAL CORPORATE HEADQUARTERS
Cambridge, UK
Competition 2013, project 2013–
NO. 431 ROCHE BUILDING 10
Roche Basel Site, Basel, Switzerland
Project 2013–,
planned completion 2017
NO. 432 URBAN STUDY
Istanbul, Turkey
Project 2013
NO. 433 MKM MUSEUM KÜPPERSMÜHLE, EXTENSION
Duisburg, Germany
Project 2013–,
planned completion 2018
NO. 434 URBAN STUDY
Monaco
Competition 2014
NO. 435 ROCHE DEVELOPMENT PLAN
Roche Basel Site, Basel, Switzerland
Project 2014
NO. 436 PROJECT STUDY
Basel, Switzerland
Project 2014
NO. 437 1111 LINCOLN ROAD EXTENSION
Miami Beach, Florida, USA
Project 2014–,
planned completion 2017
NO. 438 VANCOUVER ART GALLERY
Vancouver, Canada
Project 2014–,
planned completion 2020
NO. 439 URBAN STUDY
Berlin, Germany
Project 2014–
NO. 440 PROJECT STUDY
New York, New York, USA
Project 2014–
NO. 441 PROJECT STUDY
New York, New York, USA
Project 2014
NO. 442 URBAN STUDY
Project 2014–
NO. 443 SYDNEY MODERN
Sydney, Australia
Competition 2014
NO. 444 EXPO MILAN 2015, CONCEPTUAL MASTER PLAN
Milan, Italy
Project 2009
NO. 445 ROCHE BUILDING 2
Roche Basel Site, Basel, Switzerland
Project 2015–
NO. 446 EXPO MILAN 2015, SLOW FOOD PAVILION
Milan, Italy
Project 2014, realization 2015
Exhibition 1 May–31 October 2015
NO. 447 14 ROOMS
Hall 3, Messe Basel,
Basel, Switzerland
Exhibition 14–22 June 2014
NO. 448 BERGGRUEN INSTITUTE
Los Angeles, California, USA
Project 2015–

Appendix

p. 254

**Teaching:
The Inevitable
Specificity of Cities**

p. 256

Bibliography

p. 257

**Selected
Awards
Exhibitions**

p. 258

Partners

p. 260

Collaborators

p. 262

Illustration Credits

THE
Napoli
Nile Valley
INEVITABLE
Belgrade
Nairobi
Hong Kong
SPECIFICITY
Canary Islands
Beirut
Casablanca
OF CITIES

Edited by ETH Studio Basel

Roger Diener
Jacques Herzog
Marcel Meili
Pierre de Meuron
Manuel Herz
Christian Schmid
Milica Topalović

Lars Müller Publishers

VIEW FROM THE TOP

The volcano is dormant. Only a thin trail of smoke and faint smell of sulfur are evidence of the forces that operate underground. The gaze turns from the dark basalt rock formation and the debris fields of the crater toward the west, where a breathtaking view opens onto the bay: from the peninsula of Sorrento to the islands of Capri, Ischia, and Procida, to the Campi Flegrei (Phlegraean Fields) and finally to Naples, with its harbor, its dense, historic city center, the functionalist highrise buildings of the new center near the train station and the far-reaching chaotic zones of urban development in the plains of Campania to the north. On the other side of the volcano, the valley of the Sarno River is almost fully covered by buildings and greenhouses, and further back, the ridges of the Monti Picentini are lost in haze. Along the volcano's slopes dense settlements with narrow and irregular streets stretch until the sea. Somewhere within this clutter of buildings one can just about make out the ruins of Pompeii, explored by thousands of visitors every day. Tourists photograph one another among the ruins and the petrified remnants of ancient inhabitants, caught in a death struggle, that have been excavated from the ashes of Herculaneum. Closer to the peak lies Boscotrecase, a functionalistic settlement where hundreds of families from the region of Pozzuoli who became homeless in the earthquake of 1980 have been settled. Villas and hotels dot the area further up, giving way to forest and blossoming bushes surrounding the bleak peak of the volcano's crater. Only a short distance above the last houses, in the midst of vineyards, one can recognize a haphazardly covered deposit: a waste disposal site that triggered violent protests in Terzigno when its reopening was prepared in October 2008. For several days the local population blocked the only access to the site, resulting in growing garbage heaps on the streets and squares of Naples, as so often in recent years.

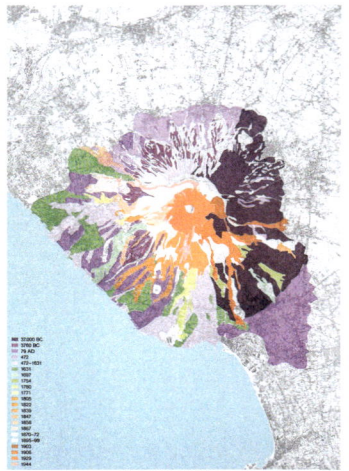

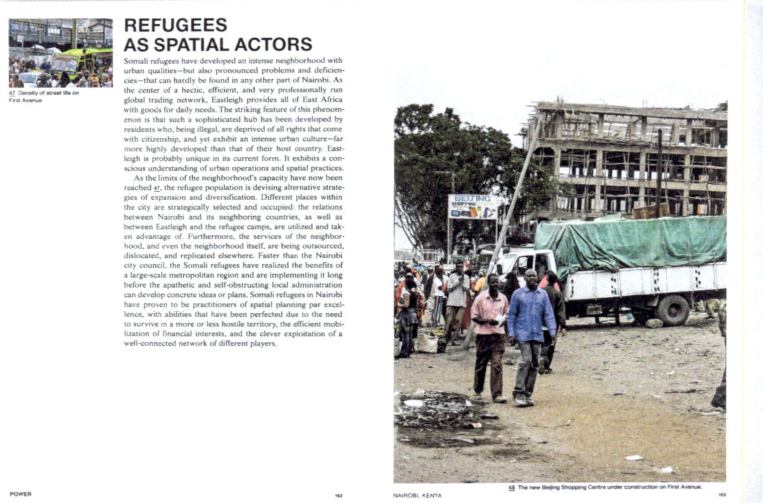

REFUGEES AS SPATIAL ACTORS

Somali refugees have developed an intense neighborhood with urban qualities—but also pronounced problems and deficiencies—that can hardly be found in any other part of Nairobi. As the center of a hectic, efficient, and very professionally run global trading network, Eastleigh provides all of East Africa with goods for daily needs. The striking feature of this phenomenon is that such a sophisticated hub has been developed by residents who, being illegal, are deprived of all rights that come with citizenship, and yet exhibit an intense urban culture—far more highly developed than that of their host country. Eastleigh is probably unique in its current form. It exhibits a conscious understanding of urban operations and spatial practices.

At the limits of the neighborhood's capacity have now been reached, the refugee population is devising alternative strategies of expansion and diversification. Different places within the city are strategically selected and occupied: the relations between Nairobi and its neighboring countries, as well as between Eastleigh and the refugee camps, are utilized and taken advantage of. Furthermore, the services of the neighborhood, and even the neighborhood itself, are being outsourced, dislocated, and replicated elsewhere. Faster than the Nairobi city council, the Somali refugees have realized the benefits of a large-scale metropolitan region and are implementing it long before the apathetic and self-obstructing local administration can develop concrete ideas or plans. Somali refugees in Nairobi have proven to be practitioners of spatial planning par excellence, with abilities that have been perfected due to the need to survive in a more or less hostile territory, the efficient mobilization of financial interests, and the clever exploitation of a well-connected network of different players.

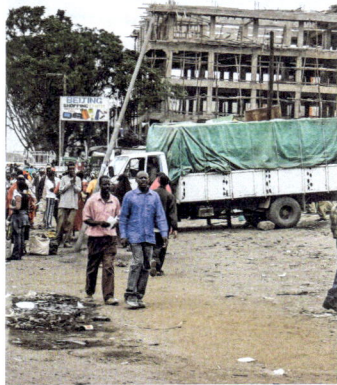

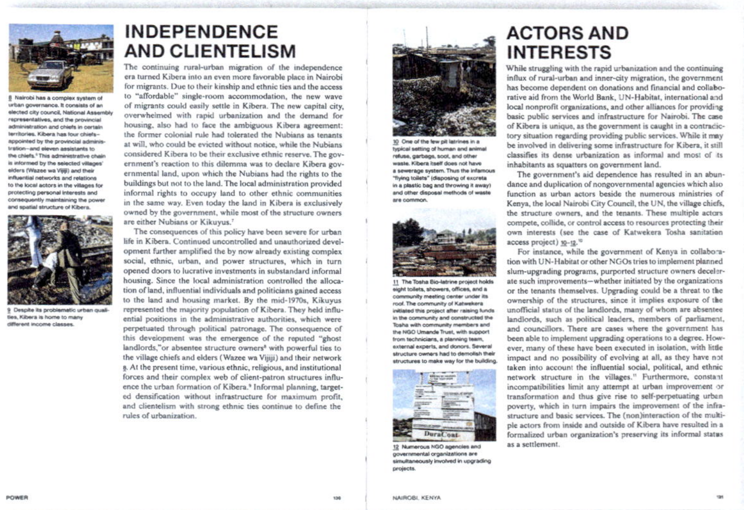

INDEPENDENCE AND CLIENTELISM

The continuing rural-urban migration of the independence era turned Kibera into an even more favorable place in Nairobi for migrants. Due to their kinship and ethnic ties and the access to "affordable" single-room accommodation, the new wave of migrants could easily settle in Kibera. The new capital city, overwhelmed with rapid urbanization and the demand for housing, also had to face the ambiguous Kibera agreement: the former colonial rule had tolerated the Nubians as tenants at will, who could be evicted without notice, while the Nubians considered Kibera to be their exclusive ethnic reserve. The government's reaction to this dilemma was to declare Kibera governmental land, upon which the Nubians had the rights to the buildings but not to the land. The local administration provided informal rights to occupy land to other ethnic communities in the same way. Even today the land in Kibera is exclusively owned by the government, while most of the structure owners are either Nubians or Kikuyus.

The consequences of this policy have been severe for urban life in Kibera. Continued uncontrolled and unauthorized development further amplified the by now already existing complex social, ethnic, urban, and power structures, which in turn opened doors to lucrative investments in substandard informal housing. Since the local administration controlled the allocation of land, influential individuals and politicians gained access to the land and housing. By the mid-1970s, Kikuyus represented the majority population of Kibera. They held influential positions in the administrative authorities, which were perpetuated through political patronage. The consequence of this development was the emergence of the reputed "ghost landlords," or absentee structure owners" with powerful ties to the village chiefs and elders (Wazee wa Vijiji) and their network. At the present time, various ethnic, religious, and institutional forces and their complex web of client-patron structures influence the urban formation of Kibera. Informal planning, targeted densification without infrastructure for maximum profit, and clientelism with strong ethnic ties continue to define the rules of urbanization.

ACTORS AND INTERESTS

While struggling with the rapid urbanization and the continuing influx of rural-urban and inner-city migration, the government has become dependent on donations and financial and collaborative aid from the World Bank, UN-Habitat, international and local nonprofit organizations, and other alliances for providing basic public services and infrastructure for Nairobi. The case of Kibera is unique, as the government is caught in a contradictory situation regarding providing public services. While it may be involved in delivering some infrastructure for Kibera, it still classifies its dense urbanization as informal and most of its inhabitants as squatters on government land.

The government's aid dependence has resulted in an abundance and duplication of nongovernmental agencies which also function as urban actors beside the numerous ministries of Kenya, the local Nairobi City Council, the UN, the village chiefs, the structure owners, and the tenants. These multiple actors compete, collide, or control access to resources protecting their own interests (see the case of Katwekera Toshi sanitation access project). While the government of Kenya in collaboration with UN-Habitat or other NGOs tries to implement planned slum-upgrading programs, purported structure owners decelerate such improvements—whether initiated by the organizations or the tenants themselves. Upgrading could be a threat to the ownership of the structures, since it implies exposure of the unofficial status of the landlords, many of whom are absentee landlords, such as political leaders, members of parliament, and councillors. There are cases where the government has been able to implement upgrading operations to a degree. However, many of these have been executed in isolation, with little impact and no possibility of evolving at all, as they have not taken into account the influential social, political, and ethnic network structure in the villages. Furthermore, constant incompatibilities limit any attempt at urban improvement or transformation and thus give rise to self-perpetuating urban poverty, which in turn impairs the improvement of the infrastructure and basic services. The (non)interaction of the multiple actors from inside and outside of Kibera have resulted in a formalized urban organization's preserving its informal status as a settlement.

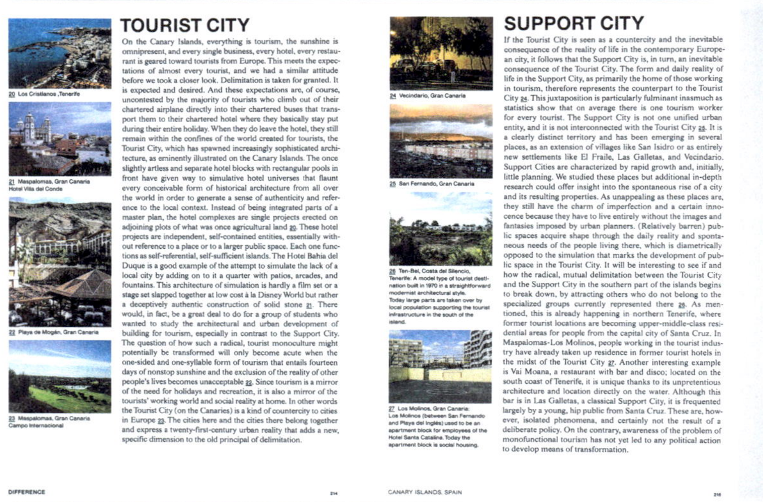

TOURIST CITY

On the Canary Islands, everything is tourism, the sunshine is omnipresent, and every single business, every hotel, every restaurant is geared toward tourists from Europe. This meets the expectations of almost every tourist, who climb out of their chartered airplane directly into their chartered buses that transport them to their chartered hotel where they basically stay put during their entire holiday. When they do leave the hotel, they still remain within the confines of the world created for tourists, the Tourist City, which has spawned increasingly sophisticated architecture, as eminently illustrated on the Canary Islands. The once slightly artless and separate hotel blocks with rectangular pools in front have given way to simulative hotel universes that flaunt every conceivable form of historical architecture from all over the world in order to generate a sense of authenticity and reference to the local context. Instead of being integrated parts of a master plan, the hotel complexes are single projects erected on adjoining plots of what was once agricultural land. These hotel projects are independent, self-contained entities, essentially without reference to a place or to a larger public space. Each one functions as self-referential, self-sufficient islands. The Hotel Bahia del Duque is a good example of the attempt to simulate the lack of a local city by adding on to it a square with patios, arcades, and fountains. This architecture of simulation is hardly a film set or a stage set slapped together at low cost à la Disney World but rather a deceptively authentic construction of solid stone. There would, in fact, be a great deal to do for a group of students who wanted to study the architectural and urban development of building for tourism, especially in contrast to the Support City. The question of how such a radical, tourist monoculture might potentially be transformed would only become more acute when the one-sided and one-syllable form of tourism that entails fourteen days of nonstop sunshine and the exclusion of the reality of other people's lives becomes unacceptable. Since tourism is a mirror of the need for holidays and recreation, it is also a mirror of the tourists' working world and social reality at home. In other words the Tourist City (on the Canary Islands) used to be as much a mirror of the cities in Europe. The cities here and the cities there belong together and express a twenty-first-century urban reality that adds a new, specific dimension to the old principal of delimitation.

SUPPORT CITY

If the Tourist City is seen as a counterpart and the inevitable consequence of the reality of life in the contemporary European city, it follows that the Support City is, in turn, an inevitable consequence of the Tourist City. The form and daily reality of life in the Support City, as primarily the home of those working in tourism, therefore represents the counterpart to the Tourist City. This juxtaposition is particularly fulminant inasmuch as statistics show that on average there is one Support City for every tourist. The Support City is not one unified urban entity, and it is not interconnected with the Tourist City. It is a clearly distinct territory and has been emerging in several places, as an extension of villages like San Isidro or as entirely new settlements like El Fraile, Las Galletas, and Vecindario. Support Cities are characterized by rapid growth and, initially, little planning. We studied these places but additional in-depth research could offer insight into the spontaneous rise of a city and its resulting properties. As unappealing as these places are, they still have the charm of imperfection and a certain innocence because they have to live entirely without the images and fantasies imposed by urban planners. (Relatively barren) public spaces acquire shape through the daily reality and spontaneous needs of the people living there, which is diametrically opposed to the simulation that marks the development of public space in the Tourist City. It will be interesting to see if and how the radical, mutual delimitation between the Tourist City and Support City in the southern part of the islands begins to break down, by attracting others who do not belong to the specialized groups currently represented there. As mentioned, this is already happening in northern Tenerife, where former tourist locations are becoming upper-middle-class residential areas for people from the capital city of Santa Cruz. In Maspalomas-Los Molinos, people working in the tourist industry have already taken up residence in former tourist hotels in the midst of the Tourist City. Another interesting example is Vai Moana, a restaurant with bar and disco; located on the south coast of Tenerife, it is unique thanks to its unpretentious architecture and location directly on the water. Although the bar is in Las Galletas, a classical Support City, it is frequented largely by a young, hip public from Santa Cruz. These are, however, isolated phenomena, and certainly not the result of a deliberate policy. On the contrary, awareness of the problem of monofunctional tourism has not yet led to any political action to develop means of transformation.

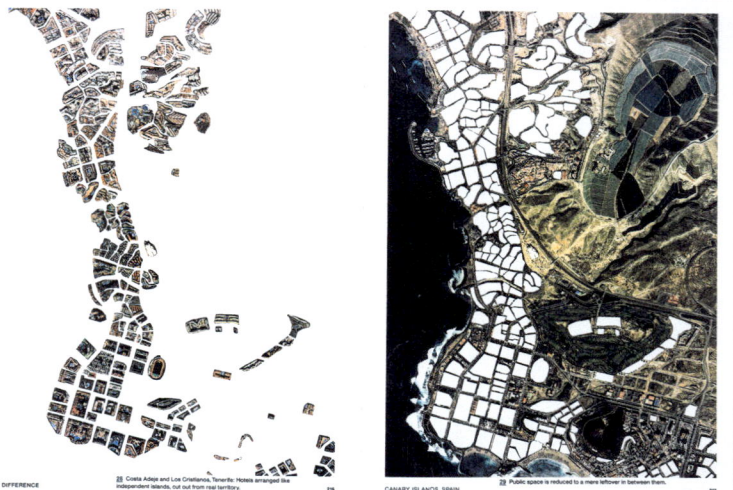

Gerhard Mack

Teaching: The Inevitable Specificity of Cities

Theories about the city are probably as old as cities themselves. The twentieth century alone spawned such iconic concepts as Le Corbusier's *The Radiant City,* Aldo Rossi's *The Architecture of the City,* Robert Venturi's *Strip* and Rem Koolhaas's *The Generic City,* presenting a wealth of different models devoted to specific aspects of contemporary urban development, though the clarity of each has diminished as cities evolve over time. ETH Studio Basel's Contemporary City Institute (CCI) has taken the opposite path ever since its inception in 1999. Instead of focusing on individual buildings, the emphasis is placed firmly on wider urban and planning contexts, while at the same time drawing upon the concrete pragmatism related to examining a specific building task. The city is, from the ground up, a field of observation of that which exists, rather than a theoretical abstraction. Insight is gleaned from the actual situation, requiring an open-minded phenomenological approach rather than one based on structural ideologies. The range of tools applied both serves and promotes awareness.

Just as Lucius Burckhardt argued in 1980 for an approach that would keep closer tabs on planners and their clients, describing the city in terms of a conceptual trio of politics, individuals, and the environment, so too do the CCI authors base their latest report on the notion of the city being defined by three vectors: power, difference, and territory. Together with the student body, they have developed a wealth of urban studies for places as diverse as Basel, Naples, Nairobi, Cairo, Hong Kong, Beirut, Casablanca, Tenerife, and Belgrade. Their approach is not based on a specific model, but first and foremost on a view of reality once posited by Ludwig Wittgenstein as "the world is all that is the case." The studies themselves reveal the many different ways in which these three factors interact. Indeed, the authors even see them as forming the basis for the specific dynamics and forms of any given city. For instance, in the case of Naples, they worked out how the confrontation with Vesuvius shaped the city and its lifestyles, which, in turn, reflected back on the territory. Beauty and danger can be seen simultaneously; the bay is the product of catastrophes, and a superimposition of catastrophes to this day. Nairobi, on the other hand, is a city that consists of not just one, but several, competing centers of power, while Belgrade saw the construction of some 200,000 illegal buildings following the collapse of Slobodan Miloševic's regime, which left a political power vacuum incapable of directing urban planning drives. And in order to understand Casablanca, it is necessary to take account of the 300 or so bidonvilles that permeate the mechanics of the city like so many ball-bearings, keeping the urban machine in motion and contributing to its vitality. It is only by acknowledging these informal zones and integrating them into the overall urban concept that ghettoization can be avoided. The key to this is the concept of "difference" in everyday life, as initially formulated by sociologist Henri Lefebvre in his architectural studies, most notably his 1968 treatise *The Right to the City,* in which difference is presented as a dynamic that should be integrated into the urban environment rather than excluded from it as had so often happened in postcolonial France.

This concept of a dynamic interaction of power, territory, and difference allows the authors of the CCI studies to extract the unique qualities of cities without treating these as a counterforce to globalization. There is no call for nostalgia. On the contrary, they underline that the dynamic of globalization actually fosters the specificity of cities. Destructive forces, in particular, reveal urban singularities. In a text formulated in 2003, in the wake of the attack on New York's World Trade Center, Jacques Herzog and Pierre de Meuron point out that each city, in its everyday existence, is vulnerable in its own way to some specific immanent threat. They see this as a sudden incursion of reality following a phase of virtual disengagement. It is this dynamic, recognizable only through the unfettered forces of globalization, that lies at the core of each city. And it is precisely those patterns to which the cities owe their successful development that are also the driving force behind their vulnerability and threats alike. It is not the strength or success of a city that makes it unique. Rather, its collective identity is shaped by the forces that have progressed and pushed it inexorably to the very edge of destruction. Paris, the city cast in stone with all its vistas and axial intersections, or Tokyo with all its perfectionism of detail, are both examples of this almost surgical view of the rise and fall of cities in the fading twilight of modernism. For it is illness and not health, weakness and not strength that reveal the singularity of a city. In much the same way, Goethe defined classicism as healthy and romanticism as sickly, paving the way for the modernist philosophical discourse of generations to come, right through to the twentieth century.

That is an approach untrammeled by the totalitarian salvationist affectations of the likes of Le Corbusier or the cynicism of smug passivity that denigrates all manner of dedication and commitment. Instead, the inversion of the avant-garde principle opens up new horizons in urbanist discourse by honing perceptions of diversity in very concrete terms and nurturing hope for potential new spheres of action, as outlined in the CCI study *Switzerland: An Urban Portrait* as well as in the study coauthored with Rémy Zaugg, "Eine Stadt im Werden?" [A Nascent City?].

One direct advantage of this approach is that the analysis of local details is not an end in itself, but can interconnect with other studies and at the same time reflect back onto Switzerland. For instance, the urbanists at CCI applied the criteria of difference to their study of Beirut. The Lebanese capital is a prime candidate for exploring the validity of this approach, given the decades of civil war that divided the city so deeply along political and religious lines. Indeed, these divisions can still be discerned today in the everyday life of the city. The Hezbollah districts are still a world unto themselves. From a Swiss point of view, this situation is almost like a test case, providing an example of the devastating consequences of ghettoization on the urban fabric of a city. But difference may also spawn a fertile dynamic by stimulating civil and cultural interactions that promote contact between diverse worlds and lifestyles within a relatively confined space. This potential can only come to fruition in Switzerland if those who do not belong to the prevailing demography—for the most part subcultures, and, increasingly today, immigrants—are neither spatially nor functionally excluded. The risk that such fundamental tenets of an open society might be permanently altered has been acutely heightened by the emergence of right-wing, nationalist polemics. Additional factors likely to exacerbate segregation in Switzerland include regional competition in matters of taxation and the gentrification of entire inner-city areas, leading to an exodus of young people and lower-income citizens. Social cohesion is undermined even by the way in which urban boundaries are drawn. Singapore demonstrates that the tables can be turned. Most of the city-state's five million residents live in publicly governed housing developments, which are subject to a quota system determining the distribution of the tenants according to their ethnicity and nationality and the respective proportion of each group within the overall population.

The concept of an "inevitable specificity of cities" is, in essence, an outstanding defense of the open city that boldly counters the rapidly increasing tendency toward narrowness, boundaries, and exclusion. The citizen, in the sense of Italo Calvino's explorer, challenges the taboo of difference as epitomized by the model of the village.

1   *The Inevitable Specificity of Cities,* ed. ETH Studio Basel: Roger Diener, Jacques Herzog, Marcel Meili, Pierre de Meuron, Manuel Herz, Christian Schmid, Milica Topalovic (Zurich, 2015).

Bibliography

SELECTED TEXTS
BY HERZOG & DE MEURON
2005–2007

OWN TEXTS

2005
• Jacques Herzog, "Tenerife, un Fenómeno arquitectónico. Tenerife, an Architectural Phenomenon," in: *Luis Cabrera*, Barcelona 2005, pp.8–11.
2006
• Jacques Herzog, "Not Knowing vs. Knowing," in: *Cities. Architecture and Society,* La Biennale di Venezia, 10. Mostra Internazionale di Architettura, vol. 1, Venice 2006, pp.70–71.

INTERVIEWS, CONVERSATIONS

2005
• François Burkhardt, Jacques Herzog, "La Reinvenzione come Processo di Ricerca continua. Re-inventing is an unceasing Research Process," in: *Rassegna* 9/2005, pp.8–13.
• Wiel Arets, Jacques Herzog, "Eberswalde Technical School, Germany (2005)," in: *Living Library*, Munich 2005, pp.181–182.
• J. Christoph Bürkle, Jacques Herzog, "Function has to be radically invisible," in: *Mark Magazine* 1, 2005, pp.78–97.
• Jacques Herzog, Robert Hösl, Frank Kaltenbach, Christian Schittich, "Unsere Stadien sind Wahrnehmungsmaschinen zwischen Zuschauer und Spielfeld. Our Stadiums are Perceptual Mechanisms between Spectators and the Playing Field," in: *Detail* 9, 2005, pp.900–906.
• Jacques Herzog, Jeffrey Kipnis, "Architects shape the new Minneapolis," in: *T/Here*, College of Architecture and Landscape Architecture, University of Minnesota, Minneapolis 2005, pp.64–67.
• Jacques Herzog, Gerhard Mack, Ralf Schlüter, Tim Sommer, "Märchenhafte Moderne", in: *Art* 11/2005, pp.24–39.
• Jacques Herzog, Hans Ulrich Obrist, "Il Museo come Amplificatore. The Museum as Amplifier," in: *Domus* 881, 2005, n.p.
• Jacques Herzog, Robin Rehm, Stefanie Wenzler, "Interview 1", in: *Stanislaus von Moos. Die Festschrift*, Zurich 2005, pp.35–41.
• Harm Tilman, "Gebouwen kunnen concreet bijdragen aan het alledaagse leven van iedereen", in: *De Architect* 3/2005, pp.24–27.
2006
• Jacques Herzog, Christoph Heim, "Fussball-stadien sind Kampfstätten", in: *Basler Zeitung* 09.06.2006, p.7.
• Jacques Herzog, Hans Ulrich Obrist, "Pékin 2008. Le Stade Olympique," in: *Paradis* 1, 2006, pp.74–97.
• Jacques Herzog, Brett Terpeluk, "Intervista a Jacques Herzog," in: *Casabella* 741, 2006, pp.24–25; pp.107–108.
• Jacques Herzog, Ulrike Zophoniasson-Baierl, "Die Stadt ist eine ewige Baustelle", in: *Kulturmagazin. Basler Zeitung* 08.08.2006, pp.4–5.
2007
• Ai Weiwei, Bice Curiger, Jacques Herzog, "Concept and Fake. Konzept und Fälschung", in: *Parkett* 81, 2007, pp.122–145.
• Jacques Herzog, Christoph Heim, "Die Messe als Stadt in der Stadt", in: *Kulturmagazin. Basler Zeitung* 07.06.2007, pp.4–7.
• Jacques Herzog, Holger Liebs, Gerhard Matzig, "Baukunst. Wenn ich das schon höre", in: *Süddeutsche Zeitung* 10.07.2007, p.13.
• Jacques Herzog, Hans Ulrich Obrist, Ezra Petronio, "On Transcending the Boundaries of Architectural Thinking," in: *Self Service* 27, 2007, pp.348–351; p.393. Reprinted in: Hans Ulrich Obrist, *Interviews, Volume 2*, Mailand 2010, pp.552–560.
• "Jacques Herzog and Pierre de Meuron. In Conversation with Tony Chapman," in: *Royal Gold Medal 2007*, London 2007, n.p.

FURTHER PUBLICATIONS
ON HERZOG & DE MEURON
2005–2007

2005
• Aric Chen, "Smells Like Team Spirit," in: *Spoon* 07/2005, pp.52–57.
• Philip Ursprung, "Toward a Critical Realism? Herzog & de Meuron and the Architecture of Spectacle," in: Colin Oglesbay (ed.), *T/Here*, College of Architecture and Landscape Architecture, University of Minnesota, Minneapolis, pp.74–81.
• Thomas Weaver, "Rumble in the Jumble," in: Cynthia Davidson (ed.), *Log 6*, New York 2005, pp.10–17.
2006
• Gerhard Mack, *Rémy Zaugg, a Monograph*, ed. by Musée d'Art Moderne Grand-Duc Jean, Luxembourg 2006, pp.232–261; pp.286–291; pp.302–329.
• Victoria Newhouse, *Towards a New Museum*, exp. ed., New York 2006, pp.272–278; pp.301–303; pp.317–320.
• Martino Stierli, "8 Punkte zum Stand der Gegenwartsarchitektur", in: *What Moves Architecture? (In the Next Five Years)*, Zurich 2006, pp.54–87.
• "Herzog & de Meuron," in: *ppaper* 31, 2006, pp.32–65.
2007
"Herzog & de Meuron," in: *Building Review* 340, Beijing 2007, pp.8–140.

SELECTED PUBLICATIONS
ON HERZOG & DE MEURON
1978–2016

1988
• *Herzog & de Meuron. Architektur Denkform*, Architekturmuseum Basel, Basel 1988.
1991
• *H&deM. Architektur im Kunstverein München*, Kunstverein München, Munich 1991.
1993–2010
• *Herzog & de Meuron, El Croquis* 60 (1983–1993), 84 (1993–1997), 109/110 (1998–2002), 129/139 (2002–2006), 152/153 (2005–2010), Madrid 1993/1997/2002/2006/2010.
1994
• *Architectures of Herzog & de Meuron. Portraits by Thomas Ruff*, New York 1994.
1995–2006
• *Herzog & de Meuron, a+u* 300, Special Issue 2/2002 (1978–2002), Special Issue 8/2006 (2002–2006), Tokyo 1995/2002/2006.
1995
• Kunsthaus Bregenz (ed.), *Herzog & de Meuron. Sammlung Goetz*, Stuttgart 1995.
1996
• Rémy Zaugg, *Herzog & de Meuron. Eine Ausstellung. An Exhibition*, Stuttgart 1996.
1996–2009
• Gerhard Mack, *Herzog & de Meuron. Das Gesamtwerk. The Complete Works*. 4 vols.; vol.1, 1978–1988; vol. 2, 1989–1991; vol.3, 1992–1996; vol.4, 1997–2001, Basel 1996/1997/2000/2009.
1997
• *Herzog & de Meuron. Zeichnungen. Drawings*, New York 1997.
1999–2012
• Herzog & de Meuron, *AV Monografías Monographs* 77 (1980–2000), 91 (Del natural), 114 (2000–2005), (1978–2007), 157/158 (2005–2013), Madrid 1999/2003/2005/2007/2012.
2000
• *Herzog & de Meuron. Eberswalde Library*, London 2000.
• Rowan Moore, Raymund Ryan (eds.), *Herzog & de Meuron. Building Tate Modern*, London 2000.
2001
• Rémy Zaugg, *Architecture by Herzog & de Meuron. Wall painting by Rémy Zaugg. A work for Roche Basel*, Basel/Berlin/Boston 2001.
2002
• Philip Ursprung (ed.), *Herzog & de Meuron. Natural History*, Montréal/Baden 2002.
2003
• *Herzog & de Meuron, Prada Aoyama Tokyo. Herzog & de Meuron*, 2nd advanced and revised edition, Milan 2003.
• *Herzog & de Meuron, Vision Dreispitz. Eine städtebauliche Studie*, Basel 2003.
2004
• Cristina Bechtler (ed.), *Pictures of Architecture – Architecture of Pictures. A Conversation between Jacques Herzog and Jeff Wall moderated by Philip Ursprung*, Vienna/New York 2004.
2005
• Andrew Blauvelt (ed.), *Expanding the Center. Walker Art Center and Herzog & de Meuron*, Minneapolis 2005.
• Roger Diener, Jacques Herzog, Marcel Meili, Pierre de Meuron, Christian Schmid, *Switzerland. An Urban Portrait*, ETH Studio Basel – Contemporary City Institute, vol.1–4, Basel 2006.
• Diana Ketcham, *The de Young in the 21st century. A new museum by Herzog & de Meuron*, London 2005.
2007
• Stephan Kunz, Gerhard Mack, Beat Wismer, *Ein Kunsthaus. Sammeln und Ausstellen im Aargauer Kunsthaus*, Baden 2007.
• Jacques Herzog, Pierre de Meuron, *The Canary Islands. Open – Closed. An urban research study on the Canary Islands*, ETH Studio Basel – Contemporary City Institute, Basel 2007.

2009
• Jacques Herzog, Pierre de Meuron, Manuel Herz, *MetroBasel. A Model of a European Metropolitan Region*, ETH Studio Basel – Contemporary City Institute, Basel 2009.
2012
• Sophie O'Brien (ed.), *Herzog & de Meuron + Ai Weiwei. Serpentine Gallery Pavilion 2012*, London 2012.
2014
• Gerhard Mack (ed.), *Herzog & de Meuron, Transforming Park Avenue Armory New York*, Basel 2014.
• Gerhard Mack, *Sieben Bauten. Seven Buildings 1983–2014. Ricola – Herzog & de Meuron*, Laufen 2014.
2015
• Roger Diener, Jacques Herzog, Marcel Meili, Pierre de Meuron, Manuel Herz, Christian Schmid, Milica Topalovic, *The Inevitable Specificity of Cities*, ETH Studio Basel – Contemporary City Institute, Zurich 2015.
2016
• Jean-François Chevrier, *From Basel – Herzog & de Meuron*, Basel 2016.
• Chris Dercon, Nicholas Serota (eds.), *Tate Modern. Building a Museum for the 21st Century*, London 2016.
• Jacques Herzog, Pierre de Meuron, *Treacherous Transparencies. Thoughts and observations triggered by a visit to the Farnsworth House*, Barcelona 2016.

Selected Awards

1987
KUNSTPREIS BERLIN 1987
Category Baukunst
• Akademie der Künste, Berlin, Germany

1994
DEUTSCHER KRITIKERPREIS 1993
Category Architektur
• Berlin and Cologne, Germany

1995
BRUNEL AWARD 1994
• Washington, D.C., USA
for Signal Box, Auf dem Wolf, Basel, Switzerland

1996
MAX-BECKMANN-PREIS 1996
• Frankfurt a. M., Germany

1999
**THE 1999 ROLF SCHOCK PRIZE
FOR THE VISUAL ARTS**
• Stockholm, Sweden

2000
PRIX MAX PETITPIERRE 2000
• Bern, Switzerland

2001
**THE PRITZKER
ARCHITECTURE PRIZE 2001**
• The Hyatt Foundation, Los Angeles, CA, USA

2003
RIBA STIRLING PRIZE 2003
• Royal Institute of British Architects, London, UK
for Laban Dance Centre, Deptford, London, UK

2004
MEDALLA DE HONOR 2004
• Universidad Internacional Menéndez Pelayo,
Santander, Spain

2005
**THE PRIZE OF THE ARCHITECTURAL
INSTITUTE OF JAPAN FOR DESIGN**
• Architectural Institute of Japan, Tokyo, Japan
for Prada Aoyama Epicenter, Tokyo, Japan

2007
RIBA ROYAL GOLD MEDAL
• Royal Institute of British Architects, London, UK

2007
PRAEMIUM IMPERIALE 2007
Category Architecture
• Japan Art Association, Tokyo, Japan

2013
EUROPEAN PRIZE FOR ARCHITECTURE
• Pro Europa, European Foundation for Culture,
Basel, Switzerland

2014
**MIES CROWN HALL AMERICAS PRIZE
(MCHAP)**
• IIT College of Architecture, Chicago, IL, USA
for 1111 Lincoln Road, Miami Beach, FL, USA

2015
RIBA JENCKS AWARD
• Royal Institute of British Architects, London, UK

Selected Exhibitions

1988
ARCHITEKTUR DENKFORM
• Architekturmuseum Basel, Switzerland

1991
**ARCHITECTURE OF HERZOG &
DE MEURON**
• 5th International Architecture Biennale, Swiss
Pavilion, La Biennale di Venezia, Venice, Italy

1994
**HERZOG & DE MEURON AND
THOMAS RUFF**
• Peter Blum Gallery, New York, NY, USA

1995
**HERZOG & DE MEURON, UNE EXPO-
SITION, CONCEIVED BY RÉMY ZAUGG**
• Centre Georges Pompidou, Paris, France

1996
**SENSING THE FUTURE –
THE ARCHITECT AS SEISMOGRAPH**
• 6th International Architecture Biennale,
International Pavilion, La Biennale di Venezia,
Venice, Italy

1996
**ARCHITECTURES
OF HERZOG & DE MEURON.
PORTRAITS BY THOMAS RUFF**
• TN Probe Exhibition Space, Tokyo, Japan

1997
**HERZOG & DE MEURON.
ZEICHNUNGEN. DRAWINGS**
• Peter Blum Gallery, New York, NY, USA

1999
THE UN-PRIVATE HOUSE
• The Museum of Modern Art, New York, NY, USA

2000
**HERZOG & DE MEURON – 11 STATIONS
AT TATE MODERN**
Curated by Theodora Vischer
In collaboration with Käthe Walser
• Tate Modern, London, UK

2000
HERZOG & DE MEURON. IN PROCESS
Curated by Philip Vergne
• Walker Art Center, Minneapolis, MN, USA

2001
**WORKS IN PROGRESS. PROJECTS
BY HERZOG & DE MEURON AND
BY REM KOOLHAAS/OMA**
• Fondazione Prada, Milan, Italy

2002
**HERZOG & DE MEURON.
ARCHÉOLOGIE DE L'IMAGINAIRE**
Curated by Philip Ursprung
• Canadian Centre for Architecture,
Montreal, Canada

2004, 2005, 2006
**HERZOG & DE MEURON. NO. 250.
AN EXHIBITION**
An Exhibition by Schaulager Basel
and Herzog & de Meuron
• Schaulager, Münchenstein/Basel, Switzerland
• Netherlands Architecture Institute,
Rotterdam, Netherlands
• Tate Modern, London, UK
• Haus der Kunst, Munich, Germany

2006
**ARTIST'S CHOICE: HERZOG &
DE MEURON, PERCEPTION RESTRAINED**
• The Museum of Modern Art, New York, NY, USA

2007
**STUDIO AS MUSE: HERZOG &
DE MEURON'S DESIGN FOR THE
NEW PARRISH**
• The Parrish Art Museum, Southampton, NY, USA

2007
**WORK IN PROGRESS: HERZOG &
DE MEURON'S MIAMI ART MUSEUM**
• Miami Art Museum, Miami, FL, USA

2008
**HERZOG & DE MEURON AND AI WEIWEI,
INSTALLATION PIECE**
• 11th International Architecture Biennale, Italian
Pavilion, La Biennale di Venezia, Venice, Italy

2012
**ELBPHILHARMONIE –
THE CONSTRUCTION SITE
AS A COMMON GROUND OF DIVERGING
INTERESTS**
• 13th International Architecture Biennale,
Arsenale Corderie, La Biennale di Venezia,
Venice, Italy

2013
**STADIUM. HERZOG & DE MEURON,
NOUVEAU STADE DE BORDEAUX**
• Arc en Rêve, Centre d'Architecture,
Bordeaux, France

2014
**TRIANGLE, PARIS.
HERZOG & DE MEURON**
• Pavillon de l'Arsenal, Paris, France

2015
**MATERIAL FUTURE: THE ARCHITECTURE
OF HERZOG & DE MEURON AND THE
VANCOUVER ART GALLERY**
• Vancouver Art Gallery, Vancouver, Canada

2016
**PRESENTATION NO. 01: SERPENTINE
GALLERY PAVILION. SELECTED WORKS
FROM THE JACQUES HERZOG UND
PIERRE DE MEURON KABINETT, BASEL**
• Helsinki Dreispitz, Münchenstein/Basel,
Switzerland

CHRISTINE BINSWANGER
1964 Born in Kreuzlingen, Switzerland
1984–1990 Degree in Architecture, ETH Zurich
1991 Collaboration with Herzog & de Meuron
1994 Partnership with Herzog & de Meuron
2001 Visiting Professor, Swiss Federal Institute of Technology, Lausanne (EPFL)
2004 Prix Meret Oppenheim

ASCAN MERGENTHALER
1969 Born in Stuttgart, Germany
1990–1997 Degree in Architecture, Stuttgart University
1993 Internship at Herzog & de Meuron
1994–1995 Studies at The Bartlett, University College London (UCL)
1995–1997 Collaboration with Konstantin Grcic Industrial Design
1998 Collaboration with Herzog & de Meuron
2001 Associate with Herzog & de Meuron
2004 Partnership with Herzog & de Meuron

STEFAN MARBACH
1970 Born in Zurich, Switzerland
1985–1986 Studies at School of Design, Basel
1986–1990 Apprenticeship as draftsman
1991–1993 Draftsman at Herzog & de Meuron
1993–1997 Degree in Architecture, Fachhochschule Nordwestschweiz (FHNW), Muttenz
1994–1995 Scholarship at the Royal Institute of Technology (KTH), Stockholm
1997 Collaboration with Herzog & de Meuron
2000 Associate with Herzog & de Meuron
2006 Partnership with Herzog & de Meuron

ROBERT HÖSL
1965 Born in Bonndorf, Germany
1984–1993 Degree in Architecture, Technical University Berlin (TU)
1992 Internship at Herzog & de Meuron
1994 Collaboration with Herzog & de Meuron
2000 Associate with Herzog & de Meuron
2004 Partnership with Herzog & de Meuron

ESTHER ZUMSTEG
1964 Born in Etzgen, Switzerland
1984–1990 Degree in Architecture, ETH Zurich
1991–1999 Collaborations with offices in Switzerland and USA
2000 Collaboration with Herzog & de Meuron
2003 Head Communications Herzog & de Meuron
2009 Partnership with Herzog & de Meuron
2015 Board Member, Jacques Herzog und Pierre de Meuron Kabinett, Basel

ANDREAS FRIES
1976 Born in Basel, Switzerland
1996–1999 Studies at ETH Zurich
1999 Internship at Herzog & de Meuron
2000 Studies at École Polytechnique Fédérale Lausanne (EPFL)
2001 Studies at the Polytechnic University of Milan
2002 Degree in Architecture, ETH Zurich
2002 Collaboration with Herzog & de Meuron
2008 Associate with Herzog & de Meuron
2011 Partnership with Herzog & de Meuron

JASON FRANTZEN
1977 Born in Laren, The Netherlands
1997–2001 Degree in Architecture, Cornell University, Ithaca, NY
2001–2002 Collaboration with Steven Holl Architects
2003–2005 Degree in Architecture, Harvard University, Cambridge, MA
2005 Collaboration with Herzog & de Meuron
2011 Associate with Herzog & de Meuron
2014 Partnership with Herzog & de Meuron

WIM WALSCHAP
1969 Born in Bornem, Belgium
1989–1993 Degree in Architecture, Sint-Lucas School of Architecture, Brussels
1993–1997 Collaboration with G. Stegen & F. Remy
1997–1999 Independent practice
1999–2007 Collaboration with Robbrecht & Deam
2007 Collaboration with Herzog & de Meuron
2010 Associate with Herzog & de Meuron
2014 Partnership with Herzog & de Meuron

MICHAEL FISCHER
1969 Born in Untersiggenthal, Switzerland
1988–1991 Apprenticeship as draftsman
1992–1996 Degree in Architecture, Fachhochschule Nordwestschweiz (FHNW), Muttenz
1996–1998 Collaboration with Burkhalter & Sumi
1998–2006 Independent practice
2003–2006 Assistant Professor, Fachhochschule beider Basel
2006 Collaboration with Herzog & de Meuron
2008 Associate with Herzog & de Meuron
2016 Partnership with Herzog & de Meuron

Partners

JACQUES HERZOG
1950 Born in Basel, Switzerland
1970–1975 Studies at the Swiss Federal Institute of
Technology Zurich (ETH) with Aldo Rossi and
Dolf Schnebli
1975 Degree in Architecture, ETH Zurich
1977 Assistant to Prof. Dolf Schnebli
1978 Partnership with Pierre de Meuron
1983 Visiting Tutor, Cornell University, Ithaca, NY
1989, 1994– Visiting Professor,
Harvard University, Cambridge, MA
1999– Professor, ETH Zurich, ETH Studio Basel
2001 Pritzker Architecture Prize
2002 Cofounder, ETH Studio Basel –
Contemporary City Institute
2007 Praemium Imperiale
2015 Cofounder, Jacques Herzog
und Pierre de Meuron Kabinett, Basel

PIERRE DE MEURON
1950 Born in Basel, Switzerland
1970–1975 Studies at the Swiss Federal Institute of
Technology Zurich (ETH) with Aldo Rossi and
Dolf Schnebli
1975 Degree in Architecture, ETH Zurich
1977 Assistant to Prof. Dolf Schnebli
1978 Partnership with Jacques Herzog
1989, 1994– Visiting Professor,
Harvard University, Cambridge, MA
1999– Professor, ETH Zurich, ETH Studio Basel
2001 Pritzker Architecture Prize
2002 Cofounder, ETH Studio Basel –
Contemporary City Institute
2007 Praemium Imperiale
2015 Cofounder, Jacques Herzog
und Pierre de Meuron Kabinett, Basel

PARTNERS AT HERZOG & DE MEURON
1991–2009 Harry Gugger
2008–2011 Wolfgang Hardt
2008–2015 David Koch
2008–2013 Markus Widmer
2012–2016 Vladimir Pajkic

ASSOCIATES 2005–2007
- Jayne Barlow
- Michael Casey
- Guillaume Delemazure
- Erich Diserens
- Ben Duckworth
- Peter Ferretto
- Martin Fröhlich
- Philippe Fürstenberger
- Carlos Gerhard
- Mia Hägg
- Wolfgang Hardt
- Jürgen Johner
- David Koch
- Mark Loughnan
- Astrid Peissard
- Miguel Rodríguez
- Stefan Segessenmann
- Charles Stone

HEADS OF DEPARTMENTS 2005–2007
- Stefan Bercx, FIN
- Doris Erzer Piffaretti, HR
- Daniel Waldmeier, FIT
- Markus Widmer, OP
- Esther Zumsteg, kitchen/COM

Collaborators

COLLABORATORS 2005–2007

- Roman Aebi
- Teresa Aguiar
- Annalisa Alge
- Israel Alvarez Matamoros
- Christiane Anding
- Joana Anes
- Thomas Arnhardt
- Renata Arpagaus
- Eetu Juho Taneli Arponen
- Enzo Augello
- Lluis Avilés
- Mark Bähr
- Michael Bär
- Jayne Barlow
- Nathan Barnhart
- Alexander Bartscher
- Ida Basic
- Lukas Baumann
- Peter Karl Becher
- Axel Beck
- Peter Becker
- Michael Bekker
- Stefan Bercx
- Patrick Berger
- Andrea Bernhard
- Rolf Berninger
- Hans von Bernuth
- José Luis Berrueta
- Ann Bertholdt
- Gabriella Bertozzi Werner
- Felix Beyreuther
- Sven Bietau
- Christine Binswanger
- Abel Blancas
- Aurélie Blanchard
- Benito Blanco Avellano
- Karl Blette
- Lukas Bögli
- Pascal Bögli
- Salomé Bolliger
- Olga Bolshanina
- Ida Braendstrup Richter
- Amélia Brandão Costa
- Evelyn Brenn
- David Brodbeck
- Christina Bronowski
- Nils Büchel
- Kord Büning-Pfaue
- Julia Katrin Buse
- Jean-Claude Cadalbert
- Marcos Carreño
- Michael Casey
- Martin Cassani
- Blanca Castañeda
- Victoria Castro
- Evan Chakroff
- Estelle Chan
- Soohyun Chang
- Judit Chapallaz-Laszlo
- Frédéric Chartier
- Miguel Ángel Chaves Gentil
- Edman Choy
- Chris Christen
- Mariano Ciccone
- Peter Ciganek
- Sergio Cobos Álvarez
- Julien Combes
- Oliver Cooke
- Massimo Corradi
- Sarah Cremin
- Yolanda Cuadrado Diaz
- Cláudia Da Silva
- Inger Damiano
- Cédric von Däniken
- Cecilia Dantas
- Guillaume Delemazure
- Simon Demeuse
- Marlies Dich
- Fabian Dieterle
- Dorothee Dietz
- Erich Diserens
- Annette Donat
- Linxi Dong
- Wenjing Dou
- Claudia Düblin
- Benjamin Duckworth
- Tomislav Dushanov
- Corina Ebeling
- Silja Kathrin Ebert
- Carmen Eichenberger
- Henrike Elsner
- Doris Erzer Piffaretti
- Lisa Kathrin Euler
- Joris Jakob Fach
- Magdalena Agata Falska
- Rodrigo Faria da Costa Lima
- Florian Felder
- Fabio Felippi
- Lucas Fernandez-Trapa Chias
- Peter Ferretto
- Enrica Ferrucci
- Katja Fiebrandt
- Simon Filler
- Julie Firkin
- Michael Fischer
- Stephan Flore
- Hans Focketyn
- Birgit Föllmer
- Bernhard Forthaus
- Piotr Fortuna
- Jason Frantzen
- Alexander Sadao Franz
- Angela Freigang
- Francisco de Freitas

- Eik Frenzel
- Andreas Fries
- Eric Frisch
- Martin Fröhlich
- Asko Fromm
- Anna Fuchs
- Philip Fung
- Philippe Fürstenberger
- Diana Garay
- Gustavo Garcia
- Mario Gasser
- Claudia Gaxiola
- Catherine Gay Menzel
- Carlos Gerhard
- Erik Gerlach
- Thomas von Girsewald
- Thomas Gluck
- Stefan Goeddertz
- Jose Gomez Mora
- Albert Gonzalez Aregall
- Marcin Grala
- Ulrich Grenz
- Jan Per Grosch
- Johann Gruber
- Patricio Guedes Barbosa
- Harry Gugger
- Franziska Gysel
- Christopher Haas
- Jeroen Hagendoorn
- Mia Hägg
- Yvonne Hahn
- Sabine Hansky
- Michael Hansmeyer
- Nikolai Happ
- Carsten Happel
- Wolfgang Hardt
- Yichun He
- Matthias Heberle
- Bernd Heidlindemann
- Guillaume Henry
- Arnaldo Hernandez
- Iela Herrling
- Jacques Herzog
- Wilhelm Heusser
- Johannes Hilfenhaus
- Yuko Himeno
- Fabienne Hoelzel
- Daniela Hofer
- Marion Hoffmann
- Philip Hogrebe
- Volker Homeier
- Ulrike Horn
- Stefan Hörner
- Robert Hösl
- Yong Huang
- Dara Huang
- Ines Huber
- Debora Hummel
- Monika Hurter-Jirasko
- Ursula Hürzeler
- Roger Huwyler
- Kentaro Ishida
- Anna Jach
- Sara Jacinto
- Kasia Jackowska
- Nina Jakob
- Luis Játiva
- Daekyung Jo
- Daniel Johansson
- Jennie Johansson
- Jürgen Johner
- Srdjan Jovanovic
- Jobst Jungclaus
- Hauke Jungjohann
- Uta Kamps
- Sunkoo Kang
- Konstantin Karagiannis
- Adrian Kast
- Edin Kasumovic
- Michel Kehl
- Thomas Keller
- Kivi-Mikael Keller
- Bettina Keller-Back
- Marie Kellermann
- Thorsten Kemper
- Angela Kennerknecht
- Yasmin Kherad
- Daniel Kiss
- Manuel Lucas Klauser
- Tanjo Klöpper
- Léonie Knecht
- Martina Knoflach
- Martin Knüsel
- David Koch
- Sebastian Koch
- Yuichi Kodai
- Alexander Kolbinger
- Bernhard König
- Gemma Koppen
- Samir Tarek El Kordy
- Benjamin Koren
- Lena Kramer
- Martin Simon Krapp
- Tomas Kraus
- Nicolai Kröger
- Pawel Krzeminski
- Andreas Künzi
- Lukas Kupfer
- Sibylle Küpfer
- Petra Kupferschmid
- Lorenz Selim Lachauer
- Hemans Lai
- Savannah Lamal
- Nicole Lambrich
- Andrea Landell

- Noémie Laviolle
- Kevin Harvey Lawson
- Gilles Le Coultre
- Young Lee
- Heike Lehmann
- Matthias Lehmann
- Anette Leins
- María Ángeles Lerín Ruesca
- Rita Maria Leuenberger
- Emily Liang
- Monika Lietz
- Jin Tack Lim
- Sebastian Lippert
- Kenan Liu
- Duarte Lobo Antunes
- Philipp Loeper
- Julian Löffler
- My Long
- Corinne Lopez
- Sara Löpfe
- Monika Losos
- Mark Loughnan
- Xiaojing Lu
- Tim Lüdtke
- Nicholas Lyons
- Donald Mak
- Matei Manaila
- Dieter Mangold
- Lush Manrecaj
- Stefan Marbach
- Klaus Marek
- Florian Marti
- Paul F. Martinez
- Josep Martínez Espinós
- Mireia Martinez Munoz
- Diego Martinez Navarro
- Jonas Marx
- Katharina Mayr
- Gabriela Mazza
- Mario Meier
- Götz Menzel
- Ascan Mergenthaler
- Dominique de Meuron
- Pierre de Meuron
- Olivier Meystre
- Katja Mezger
- Maria Monfort Leon
- Gerda Montandon
- Charlotte von Moos
- Mateo Mori Meana
- Hugo Moura
- Jonathan Muecke
- Adriana Müller
- Guy Nahum
- Marcello Nasso
- Anna-Lisa Nemeth
- Marcel Neuse
- Michael Nezis
- Betty Ng
- Monika Niggemeyer
- Tilmann Noller
- Mehmet Noyan
- Linda Nrejaj
- Alexa Nürnberger
- Severin Odermatt
- Benjamin Olschner
- Mònica Ors Romagosa
- Miguel Ortiga
- Argel Padilla Figueroa
- Kamilla Paetzold
- Vladimir Pajkic
- Miguel Pallares
- Michel Pauli
- Abigal Pearson
- Astrid Peissard
- Matthias Pektor
- Katharina Penner
- Dirk Peters
- Judith Peters
- Margot Pfefferle
- Jorge Picas de Carvalho
- Mario Piscazzi
- Maja Podvinec
- Thomas Polster
- Key Portilla Kawamura
- Maki Portilla Kawamura
- Catherine Preiswerk
- Jeremy Purcell
- Beate Quaschning
- Stefano Rabolli Pansera
- Georg Rafailidis
- Stella Rahola
- Lina Rainoni
- Pedro Ramalho
- Salome Rätz
- Nuno Ravara
- Leila Reese
- Chantal Reichenbach
- Roland Reinardy
- Sebastian Reinhardt
- Daniel Reisch
- James Richards
- Christian Riemenschneider
- Nathalie Rinne
- Miguel del Rio Sanin
- Deolinda Rodrigues
- Miguel Rodríguez Martínez
- Francisco Javier Rojo Ramirez
- Roland Rossmaier
- Luciano Rotoli
- Christoph Röttinger
- Ella Ryhiner
- Mehrdad Safa
- Nils Sanderson
- Ana Maria Santos Lima

- Philipp Schaerer
- Gabriele Schell-Steven
- Christina Scherz
- Johannes Scheutz
- Sabine Schilling
- Jennifer Schmachtenberg
- Philip Schmerbeck
- Georg Sebastian Schmid
- Chasper Schmidlin
- Marc Schmidt
- Harald Schmidt
- Tilmann Schmidt
- Michael Schmidt
- Alexandra Schmitz
- Uta Schrameyer
- Christian Schühle
- Brigitte Schulz
- Herwig Schulz
- Günter Schwob
- Sara Secci
- Mónica Sedano Peralta
- Jochen Seelos
- Stefan Segessenmann
- Gerrit Sell
- Lara Semler
- Noëlie Sénéclauze
- Jad Silvester
- Hee-Jun Sim
- Joana Simões
- Reda Slaoui
- Karolina Slawecka
- Iva Smrke Kröger
- Roman Sokalski
- Agustín Solórzano
- Heeri Song
- Henriette Spoerl
- Christine Steinemann
- Sebastian Stich
- Charles Stone
- Stephanie Stratmann
- Thomas Strebel
- Kai Strehlke
- Matthias Stücheli
- Céline Studer
- Ulf Sturm
- Wei Sun
- Fumiko Takahama
- Masato Takahashi
- Cornelia Tapparelli
- Katinka Temme
- Florian Tschacher
- Gee-Ghid Tse
- Caro van de Venne
- Pim van Wijlick
- Paul Vantieghem
- Nicolas Venzin
- Fabio Verardo
- Dag Vierfuss
- Carlos Viladoms Weber
- Lys Villalba Rubio
- Manuel Villanueva
- Christine Vischer-Rageth
- Florian Voigt
- Isabel Volkmar
- Maximilian Vomhof
- Christian Voss
- Zachary Vourlas
- Thomas de Vries
- Daniel Waldmeier
- Wim Walschap
- Yan Wang
- Xinyuan Wang
- Christof Weber
- Christin Weber
- Stephan Wedrich
- Carmen Wehmeyer
- Jason Whiteley
- Richard Wickli
- Markus Widmer
- Benjamin Wiederock
- Douwe Wieërs
- Danica Willi
- Tobias Winkelmann
- Dirk Wischnewski
- Thomasine Wolfensberger
- James Wong
- Thomas Wyssen
- Sung Goo Yang
- José Yerga
- Camia Young
- Marisa Zadotti
- Camillo Zanardini
- Iwan Zanzotti
- Monika Zecherle
- Christoph Zeller
- Christian Zerreis
- Junying Zhang
- Ying Zhou
- Daniel Zielinski
- Maximilian Zielinski
- Daniela Zimmer
- Claudia Zipperle
- Christian Zöllner
- Esther Zumsteg
- Marco Zürn

INTRODUCTION
(pp.8–17)
p.8: Katalin Deér
p.10, right column bottom: Iwan Baan
p.11, left column top:
Margherita Spiluttini
p.11, right column:
© gta Archiv ETH Zürich
p.12, left column top: Hufton+Crow
p.13, left column top: Roland Halbe
p.13, left column second from top:
key-biscayne.com
p.13, left column third from top:
© Judd Foundation / Licensed by
VAGA, New York, NY
p.13, right column: Julius Schulman,
© J. Paul Getty Trust. Getty Research
Institute, Los Angeles (2004.R.10)
p.14, left column top: © Estate
of Gordon Matta-Clark / Artists Rights
Society (ARS), New York
p.14, left column middle and bottom:
Iwan Baan
p.15, right column bottom: Iwan Baan
p.16, left column top: James Ewing

BUILDINGS AND PROJECTS
(pp.19–159)
The file codes for all illustrations are
composed of project number
followed by an abbreviation for the
illustration's category plus date,
plus serial number. The abbrevia-
tions are as follows:
• **RF**–References
• **CL**–Client Context
• **SI**–Site Context
• **SK** – Sketches
• **MO**–Models
• **MU**–Mock-ups
• **SA**–Samples
• **CI**–Composite Images
• **DR**–Standard Drawings
• **DT**–Detail Drawings
• **CO**–Construction Images
• **CP**–Completion Images

p.20: © 2017 Google / Image © 2017
DigitalGlobe / Image © 2017
TerraMetrics / Image © 2017
CNES/Airbus
p.24, • 269_RFCL_1107_701,
• 269_RFCL_1410_702:
© Beijing Film Academy
Modern Creative Media
College
• 269_SI_1701_002:
© 2017 Google / Image © 2017
DigitalGlobe / Image © 2017
TerraMetrics / Image © 2017
CNES/Airbus
p.28, • 274_RF_0506_001_TERMINA-
TOR:
James Cameron,
© TriStar Pictures
• 274_RF_0506_003_PP:
Antoine de Saint-Exupéry
• 274_RF_0507_001_FRIEDRICH:
Caspar David Friedrich,
© Alte Nationalgalerie, Berlin
• 274_RF_0507_001_RUINE:
José Carlos de Borbón,
© Museo del Prado, Madrid
• 274_RF_0511_017_CRASH,
• 274_RF_0511_015_CRASH:
David Cronenberg,
© Lions Gate Films
• 274_RFCL_0510_804_ERAS-
MUS-SAILS:
© Museo Marinaro
Tommasino-Andreatta
p.29, • 274_CP_0604_702_MR,
• 274_CP_0604_726_MR,
• 274_CP_0604_739_MR,
• 274_CP_0604_742_MR:
Monika Rittershaus
p.31, • 320_RFAR_0804_012_APO:
Francis Ford Coppola,
© Omni Zoetrope
• 320_RFAR_0809_501_DALI_
CANAUT_K:
© Gala-Salvador Dali
Foundation/DACS, London
• 320_RFNL_0608_009_FOREST:
Thomas Struth
• 320_RFNL_0805_001_QUAKE:
© Oumma
• 320_RFNL_0805_006_QUAKE:
© CCTV
• 320_RFNL_0808_503_AL_
NACHT5:
Thomas Ruff
p.32, • 320_CP_090219_701_IB,
• 320_CP_090219_702_IB,
• 320_CP_090219_711_IB,
• 320_CP_100219_704_IB:
Iwan Baan
p.34: © 2017 Google
p.37, • 276_CP_0804_717_RH,
• 276_CP_0811_714_RH,
• 276_CP_0811_744_RH:
Robert Hösl
p.38, • 276_CP_0804_734_RH,
• 276_CP_0804_741_RH,
• 276_CP_0804_742_RH,
• 276_CP_0806_701_RH,
• 276_CP_0806_703_RH,
• 276_CP_0806_705_RH,
• 276_CP_0806_714_RH,
• 276_CP_0806_718_RH,
• 276_CP_0811_706_RH,
• 276_CP_0811_721_RH,
• 276_CP_0811_732_RH,
• 276_CP_0811_733_RH,
• 276_CP_0811_741_RH,
• 276_CP_0811_742_RH:
Robert Hösl
p.40: © 2017 Google
p.43, • 279_SI_0602_501_1895,
• 279_SI_0602_502_1927,
• 279_SI_0905_503_1962:
© State Archives of Florida
p.45, • 279_CO_091129_718_IB_4213_U,
• 279_CO_091129_723_IB_4324_H,
• 279_CO_1004_954_IB_6568_U,
• 279_CO_1004_979_IB_6647_U:
Iwan Baan, © MBEACH1, LLLP
• 279_CP_1203_740_EO_40_DD_S,
• 279_CP_1203_777_EO_14_S,

• 279_CP_1203_778_EO_16_S:
Erica Overmeer / Future
Documentation
• 279_CO_0911_807_EO:
Erica Overmeer,
© MBEACH1, LLLP
• 279_CP_100904_004_ROHA_K:
Roland Halbe,
© MBEACH1, LLLP
p.46, • 279_CO_0911_819_EO:
Erica Overmeer,
© MBEACH1, LLLP
• 279_CO_1004_IB_703_
MCHAP-PRI,
• 279_CO_110212_701_IB_M_7318:
Iwan Baan
• 279_CO_091206_1013-14_IB,
• 279_CO_091206_726_IB_3677,
• 279_CO_091206_840_IB_4228,
• 279_CO_091206_881_IB_4318,
• 279_CO_1004_808_IB_6235,
• 279_CO_1004_855_IB_6371,
• 279_CP_1004_612_IB,
• 279_CP_1004_759_IB:
Iwan Baan, © MBEACH1, LLLP
• 279_CP_110111_701_JW:
Jeff Weinstein
• 279_CP_110203_709_HC,
• 279_CP_110203_720_HC,
• 279_CP_110203_725_HC,
• 279_CP_110203_730_HC:
Hufton+Crow,
© MBEACH1, LLLP
• 279_CP_1104_716_DM_0546,
• 279_CP_1104_743_DM_1191,
• 279_CP_1104_759_DM_9131:
Duccio Malagamba,
© MBEACH1, LLLP
• 279_EV_1102_503:
© UIA Management LLC
p.48: © 2017 Google
p.54: © 2017 Google / Image
© 2017 DigitalGlobe
p.57, • 282_RFSB_0611_005,
• 282_RFSB_0611_022:
© Archivo Municipal
de Zaragoza
p.58, • 282_RFSB_0608_001_RA:
Jose Gomez di Navie © Real
Academia de Bellas Artes
de San Fernando
• 282_RFSB_DEL_SORDO_1930:
Manuel Asenjo
p.62: © 2017 Google
p.66, • 284_MO_0806_004_
STRUKTUR_W:
© WGG Schnetzer Puskas
Ingenieure AG
p.67, • 284_CO_1011_821_IB_1440,
• 284_CP_110201_701_IB_U_1662,
• 284_CP_110201_742_IB_U_1045,
• 284_CP_110201_761_IB_U_1409,
• 284_CP_110201_818_IB_H_0697,
• 284_CP_110201_894_IB_H_0975,
• 284_CP_110201_943_IB_U_1298,
• 284_CP_130425_794_IB_U_1992:
Iwan Baan
p.68, • 318_CP_1309_704_IB_H,
• 318_CP_1309_705_IB_H,
• 318_CP_1309_706_IB_H,
• 318_CP_1309_722_IB_H,
• 318_CP_1309_726_IB_H,
• 318_CP_1309_729_IB_H,
• 318_CP_1309_730_IB_H:
Iwan Baan
p.70: © 2017 Google
p.74, • 293_SI_0803_EXT-HIST_026:
© Harpers Weekly
• 293_SI_0807_238_DH,
• 293_SI_0902_CO-D_1880:
Courtesy of the New-York
Historical Society
• 293_SI_070619_151_4E4_DH,
• 293_SI_0902_CO-D_EK:
Elliott Kaufman Photography
p.75, • 293_CO_110210_005_COD,
• 293_CO_1104_706_JE_H,
• 293_CO_110407_CO_D_JE_07,
• 293_CO_1105_PAA_CO_D_JE_28,
• 293_CP_110705_CO_D_JE_4592,
• 293_CP_1108_PAA_CO_D_JE_6048,
• 293_CP_110824_002_CO_D_JE,
• 293_CP_1109_718_JE_COD_H,
• 293_CP_1109_726_JE_COD_H:
James Ewing
• 293_CP_111024_739_IB_0558_H,
• 293_CP_111024_740_IB_0559_H:
Iwan Baan
p.76, • 293_SI_0603_039_DH-HIST,
• 293_SI_0804_702_1880_VT:
Courtesy of the New-York
Historical Society
• 293_SI_0603_744_HIST:
Courtesy of the Knickerbocker
Greys
• 293_SI_0603_751_HIST:
Courtesy of the Library of
Congress
• 293_SI_1107_JE_VET_01:
James Ewing
• 293_CP_160223_701_JE_H,
• 293_CP_160223_704_JE_H,
• 293_CP_160223_707_JE_H,
• 293_CP_160223_723_JE_H,

• 293_CP_160223_727_JE_H,
• 293_CP_160223_735_JE_H:
James Ewing, Courtesy of the
Park Avenue Armory
p.78: © 2017 Google
p.81, • 294_CP_130425_720_IB_5428,
• 294_CP_130425_750_IB_5524,
• 294_CP_130425_772_IB_5563:
Iwan Baan
p.84, • 294_CO_0808_004_VITRA:
Roland Briegel © Vitra
• 294_CO_0810_723_RW,
• 294_CO_0810_724_RW,
• 294_CO_0810_726_RW,
• 294_CO_0810_749_RW:
Ruedi Walti
• 294_CP_1001_745_IB_3187_K,
• 294_CP_1001_870_IB_2747_K,
• 294_CP_1001_1078_IB_3600_K:
Iwan Baan
• 294_CP_1001_702_IB_4853,
• 294_CP_1001_714_IB_5065,
• 294_CP_1001_717_IB_3660,
• 294_CP_1001_722_IB_2631,
• 294_CP_1001_724_IB_3582,
• 294_CP_1001_728_IB_2877,
• 294_CP_1001_729_IB_3700:
Iwan Baan, © Vitra
• 294_CP_1003_728_DM_028-1914,
• 294_CP_1003_732_DM_032-1846:
Duccio Malagamba
p.86: © 2017 Google / Image Landsat
/Copernicus / Image NASA /
Image © 2017 DigitalGlobe
p.88, • 266_SI_0501_011_HISTORICAL:
Georg Braun / Frans Hogenberg
• 295_CP_1206_1499_EO:
Erica Overmeer / Future
Documentation
p.90, • 295_CP_1206_0721_EO,
• 295_CP_1206_0723_EO,
• 295_CP_1206_1093_EO,
• 295_CP_1206_1295_EO,
• 295_CP_1206_1317_EO:
Erica Overmeer / Future
Documentation
p.91, • 295_RFCL_0000_059_MD_PARIS,
• 295_RFNL_0000_100,
• 295_PP_0710_074_K:
Michel Desvigne
• 295_RFAR_0000_502:
Ursula Schulz-Dornburg
• 295_CP_1206_0701_EO,
• 295_CP_1206_0738_EO,
• 295_CP_1206_0813_EO,
• 295_CP_1206_1187_EO,
• 295_CP_1206_1268_EO,
• 295_CP_1206_1314_EO,
• 295_CP_1206_1353_EO:
Erica Overmeer / Future
Documentation
p.92, • 295_CP_1206_0707_EO,
• 295_CP_1206_0725_EO,
• 295_CP_1206_0736_EO,
• 295_CP_1206_0852_EO,
• 295_CP_1206_0866_EO,
• 295_CP_1206_1070_EO:
Erica Overmeer / Future
Documentation
• 295_CP_120630_701_DM:
Duccio Malagamba
p.94: © 2017 Google / Image © 2017
DigitalGlobe
p.98, • 296_SI_1012_501:
© The National Archives UK
p.102: © 2017 Google
p.106, • 300_CP_0606_703_MP,
• 300_CP_0606_704_MP,
• 300_CP_0606_705_MP,
• 300_CP_0606_709_MP,
• 300_CP_0606_712_MP:
© The Museum of Modern
Art, New York
p.108: © 2017 Google
p.112, • 305_CO_150831_739_MG:
Miguel de Guzmán
• 305_CP_1610_0837_IB_H_2515,
• 305_CP_1610_0989_IB_H_3164,
• 305_CP_1610_1130_IB_H_3802,
• 305_CP_1610_1196_IB_H_4034,
• 305_CP_1610_1338_IB_H_4588,
• 305_CP_1610_1612_IB_H_5503:
Iwan Baan
• 305_CP_1705_501_VO_K:
Volley Studio, LLC
• 305_CP_1705_706_HC,
• 305_CP_1705_714_HC,
• 305_CP_1705_722_HC:
Hufton+Crow
p.114: © 2017 Google
p.117, • 306_RFSB_0709_016_STILTS:
key-biscayne.com
• 306_CO_1101_704:
© Smith Aerial Photos
p.118, • 306_DR_0910_501_SHADING_K:
© ARUP
p.119, • 306_CO_121113_708_DA:
Daniel Azoulay
• 306_CP_140205_726_ROHA:
Roland Halbe
p.120, • 306_CO_130824_712_DA,
• 306_CP_140806_706_DA_4:
Daniel Azoulay

• 293_CP_160223_727_JE_H,
• 306_CO_121221_720_IB_2172,
• 306_CO_121221_747_IB_1757,
• 306_CP_131203_706_IB_H,
• 306_CP_131203_719_IB,
• 306_CP_131203_720_IB,
• 306_CP_131203_729_IB_H,
• 306_CP_131205_979_IB_5065:
Iwan Baan
• 306_CP_1311_704_DIGITAL_EO:
Erica Overmeer / Future
Documentation
• 306_CP_140111_724_DM_1715_H,
• 306_CP_140111_734_DM_2277_H:
Duccio Malagamba
• 306_CP_140205_702_ROHA_H,
• 306_CP_140205_718_ROHA,
• 306_CP_140205_719_ROHA_H,
• 306_CP_140205_745_ROHA_H,
• 306_CP_140205_753_ROHA,
• 306_CP_140205_759_ROHA,
• 306_CP_140205_772_ROHA_H:
Roland Halbe
• 306_CO_120528_002:
© Smith Aerial Photos
• 306_EV_140709_708_WREYE:
© World Red Eye, Courtesy of
the Pérez Art Museum Miami
p.122: © 2017 Google
p.125, • 307_SI_0000_501_K:
© ph.guignard/air-images
p.128, • 307_CI_1502_014_PLACE:
© ph.guignard/air-images
• 307_CI_141030_004_PRI,
• 307_CI_141030_006_PRI:
© Herzog & de Meuron / SCI
Tour Triangle
p.130: © 2017 Google
p.134, • 204_SI_1924_LBS_MH01-005462:
© ETH–Bibliothek Zürich,
Bildarchiv/Stiftung Luftbild
Schweiz
• 204_SI_0200_501,
• 204_SI_0200_503:
Josef Rahm
p.135, • 312_CP_150603_740_IB_6726:
Iwan Baan
p.136, • 312_CP_1410_711_RH,
• 312_CP_1507_721_RH,
• 312_CP_1507_726_RH,
• 312_CP_1507_727_RH:
Robert Hösl
• 312_CP_141028_702_AZ_H,
• 312_CP_141028_707_AZ_H,
• 312_CP_141028_710_AZ_H,
• 312_CP_141028_715_AZ_H:
Andreas Zimmermann
• 312_CP_150604_764_IB,
• 312_CP_150604_809_IB,
• 312_CP_150604_835_IB,
• 312_CP_150618_701_IB,
• 312_CP_150618_721_IB,
• 312_CP_150618_736_IB,
• 312_CP_150618_742_IB,
• 312_CP_150619_770_IB,
• 312_CP_150619_784_IB,
• 312_CP_150619_797_IB,
• 312_CP_150619_800_IB:
Iwan Baan
• 312_CP_1602_5392_JH,
• 312_CP_1602_5398_JH:
Jacques Herzog
• 810-11_CP_150609_002:
Iwan Baan, © Jacques Herzog
und Pierre de Meuron
Kabinett, Basel
p.138: © 2017 Google / Image © 2017
DigitalGlobe
p.140, • 317_RFSB_0805_050_TECA:
© panoramio
p.144: © 2017 Google
p.148, • 319_RFcl_0000_501_K:
© Basel Tourismus
• 319_RFcl_0000_502_K:
Architeam 4, Basel
p.150, • 319_CP_140619_0706_IB_2919,
• 319_CP_140619_0727_IB_2968_H,
• 319_CP_140619_0772_IB_3069,
• 319_CP_140619_0782_IB_3087_H,
• 319_CP_140619_0795_IB_3112,
• 319_CP_140619_0817_IB_3158,
• 319_CP_140619_0824_IB_3172,
• 319_CP_140619_0848_IB_3226_H,
• 319_CP_140619_0987_IB_3579_H,
• 319_CP_140619_1023_IB_3665_H,
• 319_CP_140619_1041_IB_3710,
• 319_CP_140619_1070_IB_3772_H,
• 319_CP_140619_1070_IB_3772_H,
• 319_CP_140619_1089_IB_3799_H,
• 319_CP_140619_1123_IB_3877:
Iwan Baan
p.152: © 2017 Google / Image © 2017
CNES/Airbus / Image © 2017
DigitalGlobe
p.155, • 324_RFcl_0000_801_ARENA-
MADRID:
William Lake Price
• 324_RFsb_0810_801_SEVILLA:
Santiago Muñoz
• 324_RFsb_0000_803_DIO-
CLETIAN:
Ernest Hebrard
p.156, • 324_SI_0712_001,
• 324_CO_140428_501_K:
TAFYR

Illustration Credits

p.157, • 324_CO_140305_717_IB_0506_H,
• 324_CO_140305_724_IB_0676_H:
  Iwan Baan
• 324_CO_1309_002_K,
• 324_CO_1410_006_094057:
  TAFYR
p.158, • 324_CO_140305_703_IB_0297_H,
• 324_CO_140305_729_IB_0826_H,
• 324_CO_150527_782_IB_M_3571,
• 324_CO_150527_805_IB_M_3631,
• 324_CO_150527_921_IB_H_2382,
• 324_CO_150527_965_IB_U_2511,
• 324_CO_150527_986_IB_H_2578,
• 324_CO_150527_708_IB_H_3390,
• 324_CO_150527_1056_IB_U_2782,
• 324_CO_150527_1144_IB_M_3018,
• 324_CO_150527_1170_IB_H_3087,
• 324_CP_1601_164_IB_U_2947,
• 324_CP_1601_242_IB_U_3136,
• 324_CP_1601_763_IB_U_1646,
• 324_CP_1601_775_IB_U_1681,
• 324_CP_1601_852_IB_U_1914:
  Iwan Baan
• 324_CP_1603-04_793_DH_H,
• 324_CP_1603-04_712_DH_H,
• 324_CP_1603-04_723_DH_H,
• 324_CP_1603-04_760_DH_H:
  Dani Hunziker / MAGS AND
  MORE GmbH
• 324_CP_1608_801_RPB:
  Rubén S. Bescós

TEXTS
(pp.197–207)
p.198: James Ewing

WORK CHRONOLOGY
(pp.209–251)
p.214, No.267: Pierre de Meuron
p.217, No.274: Monika Rittershaus
p.218, No.276: Robert Hösl
p.220, No.279: Hufton+Crow
p.223, No.284: Iwan Baan
p.225, No.288: Adriano A. Biondo /
biondopictures
p.226, No.289: Robert Hösl
p.228, No.293: James Ewing
p.229, No.294: Iwan Baan
p.233, No.300: © The Museum of
Modern Art, New York
p.236, No.305: Iwan Baan
p.237, No.306: Roland Halbe
p.241, No.312: Robert Hösl
p.245, No.319: Iwan Baan
No.320: Iwan Baan
p.247, No.324: Iwan Baan

APPENDIX
(pp.253–263)
p.254: © ETH Studio Basel
p.258: Adriano A. Biondo /
biondopictures
p.259: Adriano A. Biondo /
biondopictures

IMAGES
(pp.265–320)
p.266–267: Monika Rittershaus
p.268–269: Iwan Baan
p.270–271: Iwan Baan
p.272–273: Robert Hösl
p.274–275: Robert Hösl
p.276–277: Hufton+Crow
p.278: Rasmus Hjortshøj
p.279: Rasmus Hjortshøj
p.280–281: Steven Brooke
p.282–283: Iwan Baan
p.284–285: Iwan Baan
p.286–287: Iwan Baan
p.288–289: James Ewing
p.290–291: James Ewing
p.292–293: Iwan Baan
p.294–295: Iwan Baan
p.296–297: Erica Overmeer /
Future Documentation
p.298–299: Erica Overmeer /
Future Documentation
p.300–301: Iwan Baan
p.302–303: Iwan Baan
p.304–305: Iwan Baan
p.306–307: Duccio Malagamba
p.308–309: Peter Tolkin
p.310–311: Robert Hösl
p.312–313: Robert Hösl
p.314–315: Iwan Baan
p.316–317: Iwan Baan
p.318–319: Iwan Baan
p.320: Iwan Baan
Cover inlay back: Iwan Baan,
© Jacques Herzog und Pierre
de Meuron Kabinett, Basel

Unless otherwise credited, all
sketches, model photographs,
computer–generated images
and plans are taken from the archives
of Herzog & de Meuron,
© Herzog & de Meuron, Basel.

Images